Generalizing the Regression Model

Sara Miller McCune founded SAGE Publishing in 1965 to support the dissemination of usable knowledge and educate a global community. SAGE publishes more than 1000 journals and over 800 new books each year, spanning a wide range of subject areas. Our growing selection of library products includes archives, data, case studies and video. SAGE remains majority owned by our founder and after her lifetime will become owned by a charitable trust that secures the company's continued independence.

Los Angeles | London | New Delhi | Singapore | Washington DC | Melbourne

Generalizing the Regression Model

Techniques for Longitudinal and Contextual Analysis

Blair Wheaton

University of Toronto

Marisa Young

McMaster University

Los Angeles | London | New Delhi
Singapore | Washington DC | Melbourne

FOR INFORMATION:

SAGE Publications, Inc.
2455 Teller Road
Thousand Oaks, California 91320
E-mail: order@sagepub.com

SAGE Publications Ltd.
1 Oliver's Yard
55 City Road
London, EC1Y 1SP
United Kingdom

SAGE Publications India Pvt. Ltd.
B 1/I 1 Mohan Cooperative Industrial Area
Mathura Road, New Delhi 110 044
India

SAGE Publications Asia-Pacific Pte. Ltd.
18 Cross Street #10-10/11/12
China Square Central
Singapore 048423

Printed in the United States of America

ISBN: 9781506342092

This book is printed on acid-free paper.

Acquisitions Editor: Helen Salmon
Editorial Assistant: Elizabeth Cruz
Production Editor: Gagan Mahindra
Copy Editor: Karin Rathert
Typesetter: Hurix Digital
Indexer: Integra
Cover Designer: Dally Verghese
Marketing Manager: Victoria Velasquez

SUSTAINABLE FORESTRY INITIATIVE
Certified Chain of Custody
Promoting Sustainable Forestry
www.sfiprogram.org
SFI-01028

20 21 22 23 24 10 9 8 7 6 5 4 3 2 1

BRIEF TABLE OF CONTENTS

DETAILED TABLE OF CONTENTS

REVIEWER ACKNOWLEDGMENTS

The authors would like to thank the reviewers below for their feedback in the development of this textbook.

Jennifer Hayes Clark, University of Houston

Cynthia M. Cready, University of North Texas

Lisa M. Dilks, West Virginia University

Jerald R. Herting, University of Washington

Masumi Iida, Arizona State University

Dane C. Joseph, George Fox University

Weiming Ke, University of Wisconsin–Milwaukee

David J. Maume, University of Cincinnati

Ya Mo, Boise State University

Zhidong Zhang, University of Texas RGV

Fei Zhao, The Citadel, The Military College of South Carolina

PREFACE

It's not often that you see a book published that was started over forty years earlier. I (Blair) will explain. I started teaching statistics in the late 1970s at Yale, including a graduate-level required course. Like many starting out, I used a textbook and supplemented that with lectures and presentations, in chalk, on a blackboard. A colleague in another department showed me the detailed notes he had developed in teaching his course and pointed out he had done so out of some frustration with existing texts at the time. I was impressed.

Soon, I started developing notes and copying them on a mimeograph machine: It was that long ago. In the beginning, this book was focused first on elaborating the basic regression model, beyond the linear and additive "tournament of predictors" version that seemed to take considerable space in existing references. This included an extended section on structural equation models because I was an early adopter. The goal was to impose a more analytical approach to the understanding of relationships in social data. I remember being frustrated with automatic linear thinking, with problems in findings that were left as is, and with misinterpretations caused by shortcuts in the literature.

From the beginning, I was teaching required statistics courses, the predominant situation for statistics courses in social science departments everywhere. This fact has had a continuing and evolving impact on the content and tone of this book over time. Many of you who teach statistics know this: Your classes include people with primary interests in theory or who are committed to a variant of qualitative methods. Some come with curiosity, some with an interest in learning the language, some come looking for a way to broaden their future research agenda, using the code word "mixed methods," and some come, in Hunter Thompson's famous words, with "fear and loathing."

I learned something early in teaching that has survived to this day in this book: In these courses, you are not just preaching to the choir. In fact, the constituency we should always have in mind are those who are most uncertain, those with the most misgivings. There is a subtle shift in many assumptions when you start to try to address this group explicitly. The most prominent shift is the avoidance of treating statistics as an elitist endeavor, as a special club with heavy requirements for membership. Too often, without realizing it, we do this in classrooms, creating a kind of "us" and "them" quality.

Other consequences of the shift in attention precipitated by a diverse audience involve the content and style of the course. First, make the examples interesting or relevant to actual issues rather than, for example, cute or frivolous, and do *not* make them simple. Simple examples are not what we do in research, and they clearly do not deliver the message about how these techniques are actually used in research. Second, take every opportunity to connect the specifics of a model or a technique to an important substantive perspective, even crossing boundaries where possible. Yes, the original thinking behind intersectionality is (at least) partially captured by interactions in regression models, but you really have to know how to interpret those interactions in words—carefully—before that connection is clear. Hierarchical linear models are not just a method for dealing with broken assumptions in regression due to clustering of observations—they are not just an "adjustment." In fact, they represent a theoretical model about the nesting of layers of social reality, and they force us, importantly, to make those distinctions. In doing so, we are encouraged to think about layers of inequality beyond the individual level, and we see the possibility often expressed and problematized in social theory of estimating the effects of the social contexts that we share—neighborhoods, schools, communities, states, or nations—on individual behavior, without reductionism. Third, also take every opportunity to demonstrate how changing methods can make a difference to your findings and your conclusions. Throughout the chapters here, we provide examples of essential changes in findings that result from choosing a more appropriate method. We try to emphasize the importance of these decisions. Insufficient consideration of a better approach may dot the landscape of our empirical literatures in ways that deflect the truth rather than revealing it.

We should all be suspicious when someone says "just keep it simple." That is too often the beginning of some shortcut that fundamentally infects the findings with conclusions that are not challenged. Far from it: often these shortcuts get replicated by others in research, with the logic "if it was good enough for them, it is good enough for me." Through a good portion of the chapters in this book, we beg to differ. When conducting a logistic regression, presumptively dichotomizing an ordinal outcome so it is binomial makes it easier to communicate results—so goes the reputation—but it may hide exactly *where* the real differences lie. How do we actually know whether we should designate the threshold in studying general health at "excellent" and very good," versus everything less than that (good, fair, and poor), or good to excellent versus fair or poor? We actually don't know this, but traditions grow, and too often, the citation chain dictates what is acceptable.

There are other issues in teaching statistics that inform the style and content in this book. The reader will notice and perhaps complain that we do not dwell a great deal on the assumptions built into some of the techniques we discuss. We discuss assumptions, but it is true that our approach is quite different than the predominant approach, which can be represented this way: Present every possible way in which findings can be wrong when the assumptions of an approach are broken and then modify that approach to make it work, perhaps with a new estimation method. This is laudatory in general, but the accumulated effect of this can be overwhelming for students just starting to learn these techniques. The question is, do you want to make the mountain to climb one thousand feet high, with a summit that is visible, or ten thousand feet high, therefore selecting on the truly committed at the outset? This is an issue of strategy in presentation. Our approach is to be as encouraging as possible about the potential of these methods. These techniques are not just a series of technical hurdles—which will inevitably come up anyway in practice. They are also a gateway to interesting possibilities in analysis that actually inform the way we think. That is a fundamental part of the point here: The techniques should talk to us and impose their structure and language on our thinking so that we can make the most use of them. Our starting intuition is by definition a statement of limitation; instead, the goal should be to end up feeling something is intuitive that was truly alien to begin with. To do this, I (Blair) often advise in classes to let "behavior cause attitudes": Act as if you understand, use the language, experiment with it, apply it and interpret it, and you *will* understand.

This book emphasizes interpretation more than rules. A basic motivation is to fill in this space in the presentation of statistical techniques in the existing literature. Too often, examples end with figuring out an estimation problem or with presenting the theory. Here we take time to accompany outputs with the interpretive words that accompany those findings. Throughout the book, we present *actual* output rather than derived tables. This too is part of the point: We believe that the links in the chain of understanding include running specific syntax and connecting that syntax to output. In most books in this literature, the transfer of the details of output to interpretation is mysterious. We use both SAS and STATA examples at crucial points in introducing new techniques, including the syntax we used. This is done to enable us to discuss the logic of the program that produces the results, more than to parse the syntax line by line. Our hope is that by using both SAS and STATA in essential examples, this will help promote the generality of the use of this book across disciplines.

Our book focuses on a basic theme throughout: the representation of ideas in statistical models and thus, how models and ideas interact. Though we cannot take the time to fully articulate this point in the text, quantitative methods could learn some crucial lessons from qualitative methods. One very general point is the overemphasis on parsimony as a value statement in the application of quantitative methods. I once commented that "Occam's Razor is . . . an oppression" (Wheaton, 2003, p. 545). If you take the approach that more interesting ideas deserve to reach print, even with minimal or fragile evidence, parsimony becomes the deal breaker that is often used to suppress those possibilities. This includes issues such as ruling that significance levels at $p < .10$ are out of bounds, across the board. But small data sets exist, and their specific focus may be important, and those findings at $p < .10$ could be at $p < .0001$ in larger data sets. Is the point to only publish findings from very large data sets?

The original version of this book was basically about elaborating regression in a number of directions, to make it more transparent to variation in ideas, and it included a fairly detailed discussion of structural equation models—such as unique approaches to applying identification and testing issues. There has always been an emphasis in this book—through all of its versions—on the generalized meaning and interpretation of interactions and how they find their way into the thinking of so many disciplines and perspectives. In the current version, we still emphasize a general approach to the interpretation of interactions, one that encourages a more complete understanding of the various issues we should be aware of in their interpretation. The early versions also emphasized that nonlinearity in regression should be a common expectation, as opposed to the simpler and broad assumption of linearity. A fair question to ask is this: Does anything ultimately seem plausibly linear in theory? The importance for policy and to theory of considering issues of thresholds in effects, limits to effects, specific regions for effects, and reversibility in effects points to a fundamental problem in assuming linearity too easily. But nonlinearity runs into counter-claims citing parsimony and reproducibility, when in fact it may be the complexity that is the clearest rendering of an idea or that best captures the logic of a theoretical model. The chapter here on nonlinearity represents a template of many chapters here: It has gone through multiple transformations over time, as new techniques appear, and some older approaches needed to be removed. At the same time, we do not just present a series of options and say things like "it depends on the question." In fact, we present a route through a process of considering nonlinearity, ending up with the use of piecewise linear models derived from spline regression. We argue this approach has a number of advantages, especially in trying to explain the effects of an X on a Y when that effect changes over its values. We do need a practical way to introduce the possibility that the explanation of the effect of X may be unique to and therefore change across different ranges of X.

Perhaps the essential chapter in this book is Chapter 6, on the process of transitioning to thinking in terms of models instead of equations. This is as much a chapter about interpretation as statistics. We consider the importance—always—of interpreting effects by including a distinction between control variables and mediators. Without this distinction, our interpretation of results is inherently ambiguous. In fact, many, perhaps most, articles published in sociology and related disciplines implicitly use the approach discussed in this chapter: Establish a focal association between X and Y, test whether this association "survives" various methods of controlling for prior causes, and if so, try to explain—explicate—the process by which X may affect Y through mediators.

The issue of causation is discussed in detail in this chapter: This is an issue that is usually in the background of these kinds of books. We do not take a method-specific approach to causation, arguing that causality is not a method. We argue instead that causality is a separate concept, and methods have to fulfill those separately stated criteria—or not. Once we use a method to define the terms of causality, then of course only that method can express *that* causality. This is an issue of logic and is not really about statistics per se. We propose our own view of the various criteria for *social* causality in this chapter. We also argue for a more specific—and we believe honest—approach to interpreting regression that invokes causality. We make a distinction between causal claims versus causal evidence. This is important, since generalities such as "you can't talk about causality in cross-sectional data" become automatic responses in article reviews, in statistics classes, and in general commentary—a chorus of quantitative methodologists. Yes, you can, if you allow a distinction between claims and evidence, which is fundamental to our entire discipline. Let someone publish their claims, more clearly rendered *because* of using causality, and thus make it clearer as to how the findings could be wrong—or tested more generally.

We see causality as occurring on a continuum of research designs and methods. Many research designs and some methods have *some* causal information embedded in them: We should not throw out that information just because it does not conform to the specific definitions of one specific method, even if some methods are closer to an ideal for causal inference than others. Essentially, we argue that the simple claim that "correlation is not causation" is misleading. The problem is that the word *correlation* is used as a placeholder for a vast range of methods that vary considerably in how well they control for confounding. This is not a black and white issue. We argue that relatively stable variables such as gender and race can only be causes and never consequences, and acceptance of this seemingly obvious fact would alter many literatures. For example, class would not be a "control" in analyses of race because it would have to be a mediator—a consequence of a systemically biased system that produces class as a *result* of given individual characteristics. In other words, class is part of the story of race differences, *not* an alternative interpretation. If we required a specific method to talk about causality while all others were dismissed, we would be unable to conclude that smoking causes cancer. Campbell and Stanley (1964) had the correct approach: State criteria and then see how well research designs fulfill those criteria. We advocate not throwing out the baby with the bath water and requiring one definitive study to argue we have found causation. In many epidemiological literatures, where experiments may not be ethically possible, using a time series approach is used to build evidence for and against causality. This corresponds to the approach we take: Use the causal information we can produce in all research and build a case across studies.

As I moved on to McGill University in 1985 and then to the University of Toronto in 1989, I realized that new approaches, new innovations, must be incorporated into the content of what I teach. It was in those years that the current manuscript was first committed to computer software rather than edited on a "mainframe" (look it up!). Here again, I took an approach that might be quite unusual in this field: I didn't teach my beliefs; I committed to teaching what was out there, the main techniques appearing in the major journals of social and health science disciplines. This decision proceeds from the belief that it is our responsibility to teach what people were actually using in their research, quite apart from believing in the particular method. The teaching of both structural equation models and hierarchical linear models has probably suffered because some do not believe in essential ideas at the core of these methods. Latent variables in structural equation models are a theoretical construct and "invisible," so they may seem like an unnecessary extension of the observable. And yet, my fundamental argument for these models starts with this problem: Everyone seems to believe readily in measurement error, but you have to ask: error *from what?* You can't have error without the concept of an underlying latent variable that is free of error. Again, this is an issue of logic, not statistics. One of the fundamental contributions of hierarchical linear models is the simple fact that they partition the variability in outcomes into sources at different levels of social reality—they do not blur that distinction. This should be seen as theoretically useful, but at times, people do not see neighborhoods or schools or workplaces as a different level of social unit relative to the individual level. These methods make sure you do not confuse them.

With time came the evolution of topics, and the later chapters of this book took shape: chapters on hierarchical models, growth curves, panel regression, and fixed effects, and finally event history models. Marisa became an essential partner in this long-term project at this point. Our basic criterion for adding a topic was simply the prevalence of that method in published articles. Accordingly, the chosen topics in this book should fill a fairly wide range of needs. At the same time, each topic, each method, has important claims worth considering. As an example, it is possible that many, not a few, logistic regressions published in the literature would benefit from a consideration of the timing of the target event, as in event history models. It is *not* just a matter of different questions for different methods: Some questions miss the essential implications of issues raised by other methods, and in these cases, it would be better to change methods. This perspective reflects the cornerstone of a basic philosophy expressed by this book: If a particular method does not apply because it embodies the wrong question or it ignores important distinctions, it is better to change the method to a more appropriate approach than to modify it by fixing the problem through a new estimation method.

The structure of the book—developing a more flexible and adaptable regression model, followed by an introduction to four major topics—also reflects our view of the point of required courses. Some no doubt believe it is best to do a "deep dive" on fewer topics, thus leading to a more complete understanding of each. There are problems with this, two of which should be mentioned. First, people learn these techniques in the process of their implementation and application, not by listening to the theory or checking off a list of barriers to interpretation. My statistics teacher, long ago at the University of Wisconsin, started his class, famously I think, by announcing (in retrospective paraphrase): "Let's not start by discussing all of the problems with assumptions, and putting things in the way first. Let's just go down this road and see where it takes us, and then we will have an informed discussion of the problems." That statement lives on in the way both Marisa and I approach teaching statistics: It's not about creating an impression of fragility and impossibility; it should be about opportunity. People *do* learn methods as they use them, much more efficiently than by reading or listening to lectures. Second, this book is conceived of as a survey course consciously. A survey course results in part from the belief that it is practically a professional responsibility to present as wide an array of topics in a final required course or final course in a sequence as possible. It is likely to be the last chance that some portion of the room will have to be exposed to these techniques, to the ways of thinking involved, to the possibilities for interesting applications. Part of the reason for these classes is to learn the language and be able to converse in it. If we restrict that course to only considering the general linear model, in detail, or a thorough regression course, we are also unintentionally preventing theoretically or qualitatively oriented students from having access to the substantive worlds tapped by the missing techniques or being able to make use of those techniques in their own thinking—in other words, from broadening their audiences. In other words, presenting fewer topics could be an unintentional and indirect cause of the divides in our disciplines.

At the same time, we do not want to imply that the topics discussed in this book are watered down technically or that we skip over tricky interpretive problems. Some examples are messy by nature—like real data analysis. There is also plenty of math in here. We do not believe in hiding the mathematical foundations of models because those foundations are the beginning of understanding.

Some colleagues may question whether it is even possible to teach the chapters of this book in a semester. We can report that you can: We both have done this, Blair for over twenty years, Marisa for fewer. Our hope is to walk a line and, by doing so, serve more than one purpose. A useful metaphor for the book derives from considering a horse race. There are 10 horses in the race, and all have to be taken into account. This book introduces each technique, including the necessary links in the chain to apply the technique practically, up to somewhere just around the first turn in the race. There is enough there to truly get started with each method and reach top speed, but none of the chapters here is intended to be a completed race. We have empirical evidence that there *is* enough there to allow students and colleagues to implement and learn from the analyses involved in each approach, enough to produce dissertations, presentations, and published articles in top journals. It is true that their own research is the key to completing the race, but that should be expected.

This book fits the concept of a second or even third course at the graduate level, as well as an advanced course at the undergraduate level. For example, in an advanced undergraduate course, you could use the first six chapters plus one other topic, at an elemental level, without the need for full coverage. Readers and users can select portions and still fill the topic options for their courses: Choices are intentionally built in. This is, we hope, the advantage of a single-source survey approach. At the same time, we should emphasize, because of the details involved in implementation discussed throughout the book, that this book will act as a professional reference for many. The Sage Little Green Book series is a useful example because these are sources you can actually learn from by reading. In a way, this book is pitched at a similar level but collects a series of topics in one place. In many chapters, we do develop original material that could be useful in implementing structural equation models, nonlinear regression, fixed effects, or event history models.

There are many people to thank in the process of getting here. First and foremost, my coauthor Marisa Young, who has been an integral part of the expansion of the scope of this book, both in terms of topics and expertise. Second, I am indebted to many students and teaching assistants along the way that contributed examples to this book. These include Diana Worts, Philippa Clarke, Lisa Strohschein, Lisa Kaida, Sebastien St. Arnaud, Marisa, Shirin Montazer, Sarah Reid, Patricia Louie, David Kryszajtys, and Yvonne Daoleuxay. Finally, along the way, I have been inspired by colleagues who consistently present statistical ideas with unmatched clarity and effectiveness, including Judith Singer, John Willett, Paul Allison, Scott Long, Steve Raudenbush, and Anthony Bryk. In some cases, their own presentations of material are so compelling that we have taken the unusual step of replicating those examples here in minimally altered form, with permission of course. These treatments are always friendly and, hopefully, accurate.

Finally, from a personal perspective, imagine your family putting up with this person (Blair), just after Christmas every year, spending the final days of each year and the first days of January, updating, modifying, rewriting, and revising entire sections of a statistics manuscript. So to Trish and Cameron, thank you for your patience and forbearance with this. It *is* about time.

Blair Wheaton
May, 2020

My involvement with this book did not begin over forty years ago, but it did begin thirteen years ago. While I am now an associate professor, I first met Blair in the winter of 2007 when I enrolled in his Intermediate Data Analysis graduate class at the University of Toronto. As he explains, the content of that course was based on earlier iterations of our current book. I later became the teaching assistant for this course, until I graduated from the PhD program in 2013. Throughout my time as a TA, Blair and I would discuss course notes; the rise of new methods, the evolution of examples in the book, my viewpoint on his teaching methods—what worked, what didn't—and the pedagogical contribution of the material.

I am incredibly grateful to Blair for inviting me to participate in developing what I see as an *essential textbook* for advanced statistical training at the graduate level. The lessons communicated throughout the following chapters have truly shaped me as a researcher.

In the beginning, Blair asked me to get involved because I could contribute crucially to the generality of the audience. This was most evident in our commitment to translate SAS examples into equivalent STATA examples. We wanted to present statistical programming and analyses in both software languages to offer instructors and students flexibility in their approach.

Perhaps more fundamentally, though, Blair asked me to join this project to counterbalance lessons from a *professor's* perspective with a *student's* mindset. At this point, I see our work in this book from both perspectives—from a student perspective interested in learning and applying these techniques, morphing into the demands of teaching the same material. This provides a unique viewpoint on choices in the content of our book.

I have my own view of the shared lessons we present. First is the issue of dealing with complex and "dirty" data. Too often, books address the statistical issues but not the process of producing believable results. In an ideal world, research data would be already cleaned and coded for you. Unfortunately, we do not live in an ideal world. A large portion of quantitative research includes cleaning and coding. We present examples of programming—working with missing cases or responses that must be combined and recoded to make substantive sense. Most textbooks provide examples of "clean" data, which—we believe—misrepresent the challenges students face in their own research projects. Many of our examples address these challenges and offer a more realistic approach to dealing with data. We present SAS and STATA examples using well-known publicly available data sets, including the National Study of Families and Households (Sweet & Bumpass, 2003), the National Longitudinal Survey of Youth (Bureau of Labor Statistics, U.S. Department of Labor, 2019a, 2019b), and the American National Election Survey. Our goal is to show the "messiness" of reality when it comes to research.

As social scientists, we face complexities in analyzing data that do not occur in disciplines with experimental or quasi-experimental methods. In part, this is due to our co-equal commitment to generalizability as much as causal inference. Our job is often to fit together pieces of a puzzle that defies easy logic. The social sciences present a murky reality. Depending on your argument, points are not necessarily black or white and instead fall into a grey area. As sociologists, the cloud of uncertainty is always present in the background. Yet as quantitative sociologists, we can find points of certainty: Pieces of the "statistics puzzle" fit together. For example, the variance explained in a regression relies on the covariance between the X and Y values relative to their respective means. The random variance in a hierarchical linear model or panel regression relies on the same logic. Patterns in studying deviations from an average make sense, or I should say—they can make sense. In the current book, we do our best to demonstrate that logic. We provide proof of mathematical equations without overwhelming the reader. We put together the pieces of the puzzle for all learners while providing resources guiding the instructor's approach.

Finally, we believe you should take "what you will" from this book, without the need for comprehensiveness. We do not anticipate every method in this text can be taught in the classroom. As students, it is possible to get lost in the details. As an instructor, you may not have the time nor the comfort level to teach all the topics included here. Our goal is to provide a toolbox for current and future research pursuits. We have compiled techniques and advice you might need—for both instructors—depending on course expectations—and students—depending on your research questions and data. Our book provides the resources you may revisit in the next year or the next ten years. It will become a guiding resource in your career as a quantitative scholar.

Marisa Young
June, 2020

Companion Website

A companion website at **https://edge.sagepub.com/wheaton1e** includes resources for instructors and students.

ABOUT THE AUTHORS

Blair Wheaton is currently Distinguished Professor of Sociology at the University of Toronto. He received his PhD from the University of Wisconsin in 1976 and taught at Yale University and McGill University before moving to the University of Toronto in 1989. He has taught graduate and undergraduate statistics courses for most of his career.

He was the first recipient of the Leonard I. Pearlin Award for Distinguished Contributions to the Sociology of Mental Health in 2000 and received the "Best Publication" award from the Mental Health section of the American Sociological Association in 1996. He was one of fifteen researchers selected as a member of the Consortium for Research in Stress Processes, funded by the W. T. Grant Foundation, a group that met for ten years (1984–1994) and produced three influential books on stress research over that period. He was elected to the Sociological Research Association in 2010.

His research focuses on both the life course and social contextual approaches to understanding mental health over multiple life stages. Currently, he is following up a family study that included interviews of 9- to 16-year old children from 1993 to 1996 to investigate the long-term consequences of growing up in gender-egalitarian households on work, family, and health outcomes. He is developing a method for gathering a life history residential profile of neighborhood environments, from birth to the present; he is conducting research on the long-term *positive* benefits of maternal employment histories on children into middle adulthood; and he is writing papers on the impact of 9/11 on the subjective welfare of Americans, on causality and its renderings by various methods, and on the reasons for the persistence of findings in research literatures that could be fundamentally misleading.

Marisa Young is an Associate Professor in the Department of Sociology at McMaster University, an Early Career Fellow at the Work-Family Research Network (formally the Sloan Foundation), and a Canadian Research Chair in Mental Health and Work-Life Transitions. Her research investigates the intersection between work, family, and residential contexts to bring a greater understanding to social inequalities in mental health for parents and children. Her research has been published in well-known journals, such as the *Journal of Health & Social Behavior, Journal of Marriage & Family, Family Relations, Journal of Family Issues, Society & Mental Health, Social Science Research*, and *Work & Stress*. Her contribution to work and family scholarship has also been notably recognized, receiving several nominations for the prestigious *Rosabeth Moss Kanter Award for Excellence in Work-Family Research*. Dr. Young recently received an Early Researcher Award from the Ontario Ministry of Science and Innovation to examine the impact of family-friendly community resources (FFCR) on parents' experiences of work-family conflict, health, and well-being over time.

A REVIEW OF CORRELATION AND REGRESSION

We begin by going back to the basics of the regression model in this chapter. Our goal is to build up the components of the standard multiple regression model step-by-step first, before introducing major variations of that model in the chapters ahead.

To introduce this model, we unpeel the layers of the regression framework to get down to essential core concepts that must be understood first, such as widely used but often undefined terms like "association," "independence," "controlling for," and "effect." In doing this, we also take positions on some of the foundational assumptions of the regression framework.

If this chapter is purely review, it could be skipped. But we encourage readers to start here, if only to see how we discuss these starting points.

1.1 ASSOCIATION IN A BIVARIATE TABLE

This section asks an important question: What does it mean to say that variables are "related," or associated? To investigate these terms, we look at an example from a study by Radelet (1981), assessing which individuals convicted of murder received the death penalty in Florida in 1976–1977. This is a widely used example, because it is in part so clear, and in part also sobering.

To look at the possibility of an association between the race of the victim and the likelihood of a death penalty verdict, we produce a cross-tabulation of these variables. This cross-tabulation shows the joint values of two variables: whether the victim was Black or White (variable name **victim**) and whether the death penalty (variable name **penalty**) was given in each case. We consider the race of the victim an independent variable, possibly influencing the likelihood of the death penalty—the dependent variable in this example. Notice that the column variable in the Table 1.1 is the independent variable (race of the victim), and the row variable is the dependent variable (death penalty or not).

Here are the frequencies for this two-way table:

TABLE 1.1 ● A CROSS-TABULATION OF THE RACE OF THE VICTIM AND THE USE OF THE DEATH PENALTY IN 326 HOMICIDE CASES			
		Victim	
		Black	**White**	**Total**
Penalty				
no	**Frequency**	106	184	290
yes	**Frequency**	6	30	36
Total	**Frequency**	112	214	326

There are 326 cases considered in this table. The table shows the marginal frequencies for the race of the victim (bottom row) and the marginal frequencies for the death penalty (right-hand column) overall. These are the same as the one-way frequencies. The cell frequencies show the number of cases for each possible joint value of the two variables.

Of course, all we have here are the raw frequencies. We need to make the pattern of frequencies more interpretable—to show whether there is a relationship between the two variables and what kind of relationship it is.

Table 1.1 is also hard to interpret in this form, mainly because the row and column marginal totals differ from each other. We want to see whether the tendency to receive the death penalty was related to the race of the victim. The most straightforward way to see this is to calculate the percentages in each category of the independent variable—that is, the percentages in each column. If those percentages are the same, there is no association. If they vary, there is some association.

Here is the same table with the column percentages shown:

TABLE 1.2 ● DEATH PENALTY OUTCOME BY RACE OF THE VICTIM, WITH PERCENTAGES			
		Victim	
		Black	**White**	**Total**
Penalty				
no	**Frequency**	106	184	290
	Col Pct	94.64	85.98	
yes	**Frequency**	6	30	36
	Col Pct	5.36	14.02	
Total	**Frequency**	112	214	326

It is now easy to see that there is a greater tendency to receive the death penalty when the victim is White, compared to cases when the victim is Black. It looks like the race of the victim may be **associated** with the chances of the death penalty. We can interpret the table this way: If the victim is Black, only about 5% of convicted murderers receive the death penalty, but when the victim is White, the percentage who receive the death penalty increases to about 14%.

We can refer back to probability theory to state exactly what is meant by "independence" versus "association." A relationship means that there is some form of association, or *dependence*, between the two variables. In probability theory terms, this means that the probability of Y changes with the categories of X. In this specific example, this means that the probability of the death penalty changes with the race of the victim. Notice that this probability is in fact shown in Table 1.2, since it is just the proportion in each category of victim race that receive the death penalty. So, the probability of the death penalty in cases where the victim is Black is .0536, and the probability of the death penalty in cases where the victim is White is .1402.

1.1.1 Probability Rules for Defining Independence

A formal definition of independence of variables allows us to detect departures from independence. If two "events" X and Y are independent, this means

$$Pr(Y/X) = Pr(Y)$$

In words, the probability of Y, given a level of X ($Pr\ (Y/X)$), is the same as the probability of Y overall. It would help to translate this statement into the world of variables: The probability of a given specific category of Y occurring, given a specific category of X, is the same as the overall (marginal) probability of Y. In other words, knowing the category of X tells us nothing about the probability of Y.

Notice in Table 1.2 the overall probability of the death penalty can be found from the marginal frequency in that row divided by the total number of cases—that is, 36 / 326 = .11. But the probabilities across the two categories of victim race vary around this overall probability quite a bit (.05 to .14).

Under the assumption of independence, the probability of any combination of X and Y values is

$$Pr(X_i \text{ and } Y_j) = Pr(X_i) \cdot Pr(Y_j)$$

In words, the probability of the joint occurrence of a particular value of X and a particular value of Y is equal to the **overall** probability of the ith value of X times the overall probability of the jth value of Y. What this rule says, in more specific terms, is this: If X and Y are independent, then the probability of any joint value of X and Y can be inferred from the overall probabilities of each. The probability rule above says that we can find the specific probability of any combined values of X_i and Y_j – if independent – by taking successive proportions: The proportion of people with the value Y_j as a proportion of the people with the value X_i.

But, if Y depends on X, we know that the probability of specific categories of Y will differ across categories of X. From the definition of conditional probability

$$Pr(Y_j/X_i) = \frac{Pr(X_i \text{ and } Y_j)}{Pr(X_i)},$$

we can derive $Pr(X_i \text{ and } Y_j) = Pr(X_i) \cdot Pr(Y_j/X_i)$

If this is the case, then, using the rule for independent probabilities will result in observed probabilities in the table that depart from the actual probabilities. The more that observed probabilities depart from probabilities expected under the assumption of independence, the greater the evidence of an association, or in other words, a dependence between the variables.

In Table 1.2, we can use the marginal frequencies from the table to find the overall probabilities of each category of X and Y:

$$Pr\ (Death\ Penalty = No) = 290\ /\ 326 = .89$$
$$Pr\ (Death\ Penalty = Yes) = 36\ /\ 326 = .11$$
$$Pr\ (Victim = Black) = 112\ /\ 326 = .34$$
$$Pr\ (Victim = White) = 214\ /\ 326 = .66$$

So, for example, if the race of the victim and the likelihood of the death penalty are independent, then the probability of the death penalty when the victim is Black would be the following:

$$Pr(X_1) \cdot Pr(Y_2) = .34 \times .11 = .037$$

However, the actual probability of the death penalty given a Black victim is

$$Pr(X_1\ and\ Y_2) = 6\ /\ 326 = .018$$

The actual probability is one half the probability implied by independence.

As another example: under the assumption of independence, the probability of the death penalty given a White victim is:

$$Pr(X_2) \cdot Pr(Y_2) = .66 \cdot .11 = .073$$

However the actual probability is:

$$Pr(X_2\ and\ Y_2) = 30\ /\ 326 = .092$$

which is somewhat higher.

If we set up a definition of what is implied by independence in every cell in the table, we could test the overall departure from independence to assess the existence of an association between variables. Of course, this only begins to define the many characteristics implied by the term association: There are also considerations of direction, strength, and form of the association—all issues we will eventually deal with.

We have seen how association is defined in tables, for nominal or ordinal categorized variables. Next we look at the association between variables that are interval or ratio level.

1.2 CORRELATION AS A MEASURE OF ASSOCIATION

We will use data from the United States to investigate the relationship between the mobility rate and the divorce rate in nine geographical regions. Assume that the divorce rate is measured as the number of persons per 1000 population getting a divorce or annulment. The mobility rate is the percentage of people living in a different house than five years earlier. This example is restricted to an N of 9 observations (for 9 regions), so that we can more easily see how the association works.

The data are shown in Table 1.3.

TABLE 1.3 ● MOBILITY AND DIVORCE RATES FOR NINE REGIONS OF THE UNITED STATES, 1960

Region	Mobility Rate	Divorce Rate
New England	41	4.0
Middle Atlantic	37	3.4
E. North Central	44	5.1
W. North Central	46	4.6
South Atlantic	47	5.6
East South Central	44	6.0
West South Central	50	6.5
Mountain	57	7.6
Pacific	56	5.9

FIGURE 1.1 ● SCATTERPLOT OF THE MOBILITY RATE AND DIVORCE RATE IN NINE REGIONS OF THE UNITED STATES

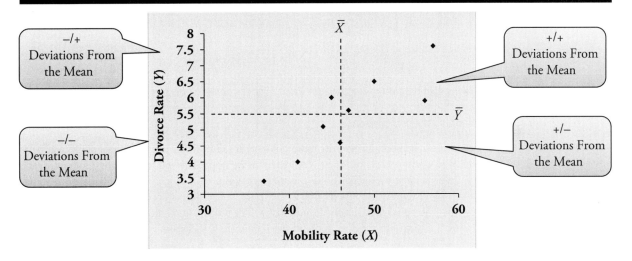

Assume you are interested in the **amount** of association between these two variables. To see visually the possibility of an association, construct a scatterplot showing the joint data points for all nine regions on values of mobility and divorce (see Figure 1.1).

The scatterplot shows the two variables are definitely "associated," or to use a synonymous term, related. Higher mobility rates are associated with higher divorce rates, *on average*. We say "on average" because there will always be exceptions, deviations from this tendency. But the issue here is to capture the pattern, not each exception.

The question is, how closely related are the mobility rate and the divorce rate? Is there a way to state the level of association on a common scale so that it can be compared across different pairs of variables or situations? How can we develop a measure of association for these data that is sensitive to the direction and strength of the association, assuming linearity? (Note: We need to assume something about form of the association at the outset.)

1.2.1 Developing a Measure of Association for Interval/Ratio Data

We have added the mean of X and Y to the scatterplot, thus dividing the plot into quadrants. From the data, we calculate that

$$\bar{X} = 46.89 \qquad\qquad \bar{Y} = 5.41$$

$$s_X = 6.56 \qquad\qquad s_Y = 1.29$$

$$s_X^2 = 43.111 \qquad\qquad s_Y^2 = 1.674$$

This shows the mean $(\bar{X}, \bar{Y})$, the standard deviation (s_X, s_Y), and the variance (s_X^2, s_Y^2) of X and Y in the scatterplot. Notice almost all of the points fall in the lower left and upper right quadrants of the scatterplot.

1.2.1.1 Developing a Measure
Version 1. The Sum of the Cross-Products

Use deviation scores on X and Y, so that *both* are positive points in the upper right quadrant, both are negative for points in lower left quadrant (with combined signs either +/+ or -/-), and the combined signs would be (+/ -) and (- /+) in the upper left and lower right quadrants. Using that information, you can sum these individual deviations from the mean, as in

$$\sum_{i=1}^{N} (X_i - \bar{X}) \cdot (Y_i - \bar{Y})$$

This is called the ***sum of the cross-products.*** The summation operator here (Σ) denotes summing across all units (i) in a sample, from 1 to N. Unless applied differently, we will drop this notation to simplify the presentation.

This measure is more positive the more points that fall in lower left and upper right quadrants (each with positive cross-products) compared to the upper left and lower right quadrants (each with negative cross-products). Thus, this measure is also more negative the more points in upper left and lower right quadrants relative to the other two. If points occur equally in all quadrants, they will cancel out when summed, since half will be positive and half will be negative. Thus, this measure is sensitive to the direction and strength of the association.

But there is a problem: The sum depends on sample size. You can increase its size just by increasing the size of the sample. This leads to the next necessary component of a useful measure of association: the covariance.

Version 2. The Covariance

Divide the sum of the cross-products by $N-1$ to get

$$\frac{\Sigma(X_i - \bar{X}) \cdot (Y_i - \bar{Y})}{N-1} = \text{the covariance, a } \textit{\textbf{very}} \text{ important associational statistic.}$$

The covariance is like the average amount of association per individual. (Note: $N-1$ is used to take into account that there are $N-1$ degrees of freedom, since the last observation on X and Y can be deduced from the other $N-1$ observations, because the sum of deviations around the mean is by definition zero.)

There is still a problem, however: X and Y have very different size units. The sum will change depending on the size of the units of each variable. If you multiply each divorce score by 10, the sum will change accordingly. This is fine if one wants the association to reflect the units of the variables, but if one wants the association to reflect how **relative** differences on one variable are related to the same relative differences on the other, or in other words, if one wants to judge the **strength** of the association, the two variables must be in the same units. This leads us to the final component defining the correlation.

Version 3. The Correlation

The correlation "equalizes" the units of the two variables by dividing each variable's deviation score by the size of its standard deviation. This puts the two variables in a standardized metric, equal to a Z score on each variable:

$$r_{xy} = \frac{\sum \left[\frac{(X_i - \bar{X})}{s_x} \cdot \frac{(Y_i - \bar{Y})}{s_y} \right]}{N-1} = \sum \frac{Z_x \cdot Z_y}{N-1}$$

In this version—the actual correlation—deviations on X and Y are measured relative to the standard deviation of each, thus removing differences in the size of the units. Scores on both variables are Z scores: They stand for the number of standard deviations above or below the mean a given X or Y score is.

Theoretically, this value varies between -1 (a perfect negative correlation) to $+1$ (a perfect positive correlation), with 0 standing for no correlation—in other words, no association. In the latter situation, you would see equally scattered points in all quadrants of the plot. As you can see in the plot, the correlation here is very high.

The formula for the correlation is often stated in an equivalent form. If you rearrange the formula above, by inverting the divisor and multiplying, you get

$$r_{xy} = \sum \left[\frac{(X_i - \bar{X})(Y_i - \bar{Y})}{s_x \cdot s_y} \cdot \frac{1}{N-1} \right] = \sum \left[\frac{(X_i - \bar{X})(Y_i - \bar{Y})}{N-1} \cdot \frac{1}{s_x \cdot s_y} \right]$$

$$= \sum \frac{\frac{(X_i - \bar{X})(Y_i - \bar{Y})}{N-1}}{s_x \cdot s_y} = \frac{s_{xy}}{s_x \cdot s_y}$$

Note the shorthand notation used for the covariance in the numerator: s_{xy}. When the correlation between mobility and the divorce rate is calculated, it is .854. (You should be able to calculate the sum of the cross-products here as 58.10.)

1.2.2 Factors Affecting the Size of *r*

1. The more dissimilar the distributions of X and Y and/or the more skewed their distributions, the lower the possible value of *r*.

2. Unreliability—random error components—in the measurement of X or Y, so that observed scores imperfectly reflect true X or Y values, will introduce noise into *r* and lower it.

3. When the range of values on X or Y is restricted, *r* will be lower (because larger deviations have a larger influence on the numerator than denominator of *r*). This is usually the result of problems in sampling: An incomplete sampling frame, a restricted population, or sample selection bias.

4. Outliers, or unusual values of X and Y, will have a major influence on r.

5. Curvilinear relationships will be underestimated by r, unless X and/or Y are transformed to reflect the nonlinearity.

1.3 BIVARIATE REGRESSION THEORY

While the correlation is a **symmetric** measure of overall linear association between X and Y, the regression coefficient is an **asymmetric** measure of the effect of X on Y—that is, how much of a change in Y results from a given change in X. There is a very important change in language that signals a change in intentions: Here we talk about X *having an effect* on Y.

Some believe this language is not appropriate because it seems to say there is a causal connection: X causally precedes Y. In our approach, we emphasize the fact that the regression model is inherently an asymmetric model and use the term "effect" to signify a causal *claim, not causal proof.* We believe this language is most consistent with the structure of the model and its intentions. Here, association is not enough because it implies simply a relationship, without regard to the direction of causation.

Consider again the scatterplot in Figure 1.1 for the relationship between the mobility rate (X) and the divorce rate (Y). The question now is, what is the line drawn through these points that maximizes our ability to predict Y from X? That is, how much do we know about the regional rate of divorce (Y) as a result of knowing the mobility rate (X)?

1.3.1 The Regression Model

The bivariate regression model expresses each observation's score on Y as a function of a combination of components:

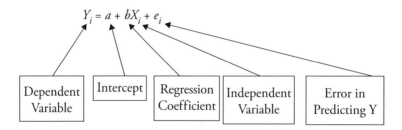

The equation says the individual score on Y is composed of:

- A constant a, called the intercept, defined as the point where the regression line crosses the Y axis and thus the predicted value of Y when $X = 0$

- The observation's score on X times b, the regression coefficient, defined as **the number of units of change in Y resulting from a one unit increase in X**

- An error term (e_i), reflecting the degree to which scores of Y are not predicted by X.

  For any case, the predicted value of Y, $\widehat{Y}$, is: $\widehat{Y}_i = a + bX_i$

  and the prediction error is: $Y_i - \widehat{Y}_i = e_i$

In other words, this is the distance on Y from the predicted point on the regression line to the actual Y_i score at a given level of X. $\widehat{Y}$ is the predicted score for anyone with the same X value.

1.3.2 The Least Squares Criterion

Perhaps the most important element of the regression framework is the development of a criterion telling us where to draw the line showing how we can maximize the prediction of Y from X and thereby minimize error in prediction. Again we develop this concept in stages (using a classic example in Wonnacott and Wonnacott, 1979):

Version 1. Minimize $\sum(Y_i - \widehat{Y}_i)$

Problem: + and - errors cancel out; so this doesn't work as a criterion. Note below that this sum is zero in both cases, but line B is a worse fit to the "sense" in the scatter of points.

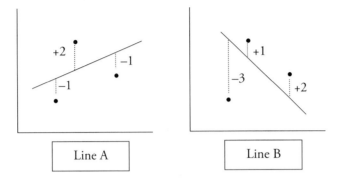

Version 2. Minimize $\sum\left|Y_i - \widehat{Y}_i\right|$ (the absolute value of the error)

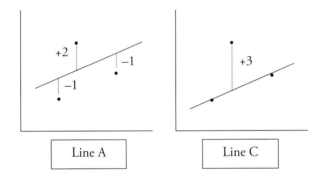

Note here that Line C is a better fit by this criterion but a less reasonable line because it ignores one data point while maximizing the fit of the other two.

Version 3. Minimize $\sum(Y_i - \widehat{Y}_i)^2$ (**The Least Squares Criterion**)

This is called the "sum of squared errors," or "sum of squares error." Note that it solves the canceling problem with Version 1 and takes all data into account by definition, unlike Version 2.

1.3.2.1 Deriving the Value of *b* That Minimizes the Sum of Squares Error

We want to find a value of b that results in the least error in the prediction of Y. This is a complicated problem, but it can be derived mathematically.

Begin with the fitted model: $\widehat{Y}_i = a + bX_i$

First, we need to express the intercept, a, in terms of the other components of the model. This will show us that the intercept depends on b, as well the means of X and Y.

First, from the complete regression model:

$$Y_i = a + bX_i + e_i$$

Divide by N:
$$\frac{Y_i}{N} = \frac{a}{N} + \frac{bX_i}{N} + \frac{e_i}{N}$$

Sum:
$$\frac{\sum Y_i}{N} = \frac{\sum a}{N} + \frac{b\sum X_i}{N} + \frac{\sum e_i}{N}$$

The sum of error is zero, by assumption, the sum of constants is N times the constant, and the sum of a constant times a variable is the constant times the sum of the variable, so . . .

$$\bar{Y} = \frac{N \cdot a}{N} + b\bar{X}$$
$$\bar{Y} = a + b\bar{X}$$
$$a = \bar{Y} - b\bar{X}$$

This shows the intercept is the mean of Y minus b times the mean of X. It is also the **bivariate formula for the intercept.**

Now substitute for a in the prediction equation:

$$\widehat{Y}_i = (\bar{Y} - b\bar{X}) + bX_i$$

Collecting terms:
$$\widehat{Y}_i = \bar{Y} + b(X_i - \bar{X})$$

Now expand the least squares criterion, substituting for $\widehat{Y}_i$ with the preceding equation:

$$\sum\left(Y_i - \widehat{Y}\right)^2 = \sum(Y_i - (\bar{Y} + b(X_i - \bar{X})))^2$$
$$= \sum((Y_i - \bar{Y}) - b(X_i - \bar{X}))^2$$

We can expand this expression using the rule for expansion of a difference squared: $(a - b)^2 = a^2 - 2ab + b^2$, applied to the equation above turns into

$$(a \quad - \quad b)^2 \quad = \quad a^2 \quad - (2 \quad a \quad \cdot \quad b) \quad + \quad b^2$$

$$\sum((Y_i - \bar{Y}) - b(X_i - \bar{X}))^2 = \sum((Y_i - \bar{Y})^2 - 2b(X_i - \bar{X}) \cdot (Y_i - \bar{Y}) + b^2(X_i - \bar{X})^2)$$
$$= \sum(Y_i - \bar{Y})^2 - 2b\sum(X_i - \bar{X}) \cdot (Y_i - \bar{Y}) + b^2 \sum(X_i - \bar{X})^2$$

This can be arranged to show it is a quadratic function of the form $a + bx + cx^2$, but you have to read the equation realizing that the b are the variables in the equation above, and the constants a, b, and c from the quadratic formula are given constants involving the sum of squared deviations in Y ($\sum(Y_i - \bar{Y})^2 = a$), twice the sum of the cross-products ($2\sum(X_i - \bar{X}) \cdot (Y_i - \bar{Y}) = b$), and the sum of squared deviations in X ($\sum(X_i - \bar{X})^2 = c$).

FIGURE 1.2 ● THE FIRST DERIVATIVE AS A FUNCTION OF VALUES OF *b*

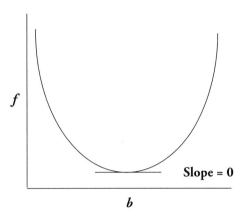

Using this, we rearrange the right-hand side of the equation as follows:

$$\sum \left(Y_i - \widehat{Y}\right)^2 = \sum (Y_i - \bar{Y})^2 - 2\sum (X_i - \bar{X}) \cdot (Y_i - \bar{Y}) \cdot b + \sum (X_i - \bar{X})^2 \cdot b^2$$

Figure 1.2 shows values of this function as we change values of *b*. To find the formula that always ensures minimizing the error in predicting *Y*, we find the *first derivative*, representing the rate of change in *Y* resulting from the smallest possible change in *b* on the right side of the equation. This rate of change is the slope of the tangent to the curve at each value of *b*. We want to take as our value of *b* the value that produces the minimum value of this function. That minimum is ensured if we choose the value that produces a first derivative of 0.

The derivative is (using rules discussed in a later chapter)

$$\frac{d(f)}{d(b)} = 0 - 2\sum (X_i - \bar{X}) \cdot (Y_i - \bar{Y}) + 2\sum (X_i - \bar{X})^2 \cdot b$$

As noted above, we want to evaluate this expression when the derivative, the slope of the function, is zero. When we do this and solve for *b*, we derive this expression:

$$-2\sum (X_i - \bar{X}) \cdot (Y_i - \bar{Y}) + 2\sum (X_i - \bar{X})^2 \cdot b = 0$$

$$2\sum (X_i - \bar{X})^2 \cdot b = 2\sum (X_i - \bar{X}) \cdot (Y_i - \bar{Y})$$

$$b = \frac{2\sum (X_i - \bar{X}) \cdot (Y_i - \bar{Y})}{2\sum (X_i - \bar{X})^2} = \frac{\sum (X_i - \bar{X}) \cdot (Y_i - \bar{Y})}{\sum (X_i - \bar{X})^2}$$

This is in fact the formula for the bivariate regression coefficient *b*.

This can written shorthand as $b = \dfrac{s_{xy}}{s_x^2} = \dfrac{\text{cov}(X, Y)}{\text{var}(X)}$

which is produced by dividing both the numerator and denominator of the derived least squares formula by $N - 1$. This formula shows that changes in *Y* associated with changes in *X* (the numerator) are measured in terms of the size of units of *X* (captured by the variance of *X*).

You can compare this formula to the previous formula for the correlation. It is very similar in the numerator, but only the variance of X occurs in the denominator here. That reflects two facts about the regression coefficient: (1) It is asymmetric, and (2) it is expressed in units change in Y *per* unit change in X.

When we calculate b using this formula, we get

$$b = \frac{58.10/8}{43.111} = .168$$

And the intercept is

$$a = 5.41 - (.168) \cdot 46.89 = -2.47$$

So the prediction equation here is

$$\widehat{Y} = -2.47 + .168X$$

Note the intercept is *negative*. How can this be? In this case, easily. This happens because the value $X = 0$ is far beyond the *observed* boundaries for values of X. In other words, a is a "meaningless" number in this case. However, it is necessary for the correct prediction of Y values.

The earlier scatterplot for mobility and divorce is reproduced in Figure 1.3, with the addition of a fitted regression line. In this case, the extension of the fitted line back to the Y axis results in the intercept as a negative number. This is not a real value of Y, but it is the correct baseline for predicting values of Y occurring in its actual range.

1.3.2.2 Interpretation of *b*

The interpretation of b follows from the definition of the first derivative, noting that in this application the smallest possible change in X is 1 unit of X. Two rules of derivatives are used here: One that states the derivative of a constant is zero, and the other that states that the derivative of a constant times a variable equals the constant:

$$\frac{dy}{dx} = \frac{d(a+bX_i)}{dX_i} = \frac{d(a)}{dX_i} + \frac{d(bX_i)}{dX_i} = 0 + b = b$$

FIGURE 1.3 ● THE FITTED REGRESSION LINE

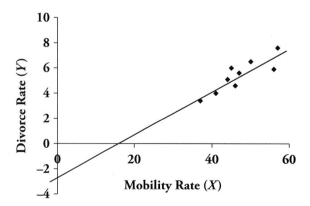

That is, *b* is the amount of change in *Y* for a one unit change in *X*—*always*! Parenthetically, the derivative can be used to figure out the effect of *X* in nonlinear and non-additive equations as well because it has a general interpretation that applies to all regression equations.

1.3.3 Unstandardized versus Standardized Coefficients

The coefficient in the preceding equation is an *unstandardized (aka metric) regression coefficient*; this means it is expressed in terms of the raw units of the *X* and *Y* variables. You can also express this coefficient in *standardized* terms—that is, where you equalize the units of the two variables by expressing the effect of *X* on *Y* in terms of the standard deviations of each variable.

Standardizing *b* involves a simple transformation:

$$\beta = b \cdot \frac{s_x}{s_y} \text{ where } \beta \text{ is the } \textbf{\textit{standardized}} \text{ regression coefficient.}$$

Note what this involves when worked out by substituting for *b*:

$$\beta = \frac{s_{xy}}{s_x^2} \cdot \frac{s_x}{s_y} = \frac{s_{xy}}{s_x \cdot s_y} \text{, which is in fact the same as } r_{xy}, \text{ the correlation.}$$

The equivalence between *r* and β holds **only in the bivariate case**.

1.3.3.1 Interpretation of β

β = the number of standard deviation unit changes in *Y* due to a one standard deviation (SD) unit increase in *X*.

To see how this works in words, suppose

$b = .92, \quad s_x = 2, \quad s_y = 3.$

> *Then, A 1 SD unit change in X = 2 raw units of X.*
> *Since b = .92, we know that a 1 raw unit increase in X leads to a .92 raw unit increase in Y.*
> *Therefore, a 1 SD—that is, 2 unit change in X, leads to a 2 × .92 = 1.84 raw unit increase in Y.*
> *Also, a 1 SD unit change in Y = 3 raw units of Y.*
> *So, in terms of SD units of Y, the 1 SD change in X leads to a 1.84/3 = .61 SD change in Y.*

$\beta = r = .61$ in this example. In words, a 1 standard deviation increase in *X* will increase *Y* by about .6 standard deviations.

1.4 PARTITIONING OF VARIANCE IN BIVARIATE REGRESSION

The regression model conceptualizes the explanation of individual *Y* values as partial, allowing for true indeterminacy. The baseline for comparison in evaluating a regression is no explanation at all, sometimes referred to as the "null model." In this case, our "best guess" about each person's *Y* score is the mean of *Y*, since that would minimize the error overall.

Partitioning of variance refers to the division of the overall variance on *Y* into two parts: (a) explained by *X* (the regression) and (b) error. The regression line in Figure 1.4 helps conceptualize how this partitioning works.

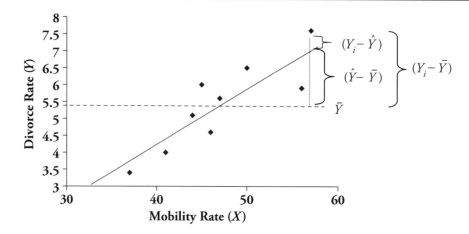

FIGURE 1.4 ● PARTITIONING OF THE TOTAL VARIANCE IN *Y*

The total variability of individual *Y* values around the mean of *Y* can be expressed as

$$\Sigma(Y_i - \bar{Y})^2 \text{ \textit{the total sum of squares.}}$$

This total sum of squares can be partitioned into two components:

(1) The sum of squared deviations of predicted *Y* values $(\hat{Y})$ around the mean $(\bar{Y})$, telling us how much the regression line helps in accounting for individual *Y* values:

$$\Sigma(\hat{Y} - \bar{Y})^2 \text{ \textit{the sum of squares regression}}$$

and (2) the sum of squared deviations of actual *Y* values around the regression line, telling us the degree to which the regression line is not predicting individual *Y* values:

$$\Sigma(Y_i - \hat{Y})^2 \text{ \textit{the sum of squares error.}}$$

So

$$\Sigma(Y_i - \bar{Y})^2 = \Sigma(Y_i - \hat{Y})^2 + \Sigma(\hat{Y} - \bar{Y})^2 \qquad \textbf{(1)}$$

SS total = SS error + SS regression.

Using the proof in the box on the next page, this equation can be shown to be equal to this:

$$\Sigma(Y_i - \bar{Y})^2 = \Sigma(Y_i - \hat{Y})^2 + \beta^2 \cdot \Sigma(Y_i - \bar{Y})^2 \qquad \textbf{(2)}$$

Divide by $\Sigma(Y_i - \bar{Y})^2$ to show this result as proportions adding to 1, where 1 is the total variance:

$$\frac{\Sigma(Y_i - \bar{Y})^2}{\Sigma(Y_i - \bar{Y})^2} = \frac{\Sigma(Y_i - \hat{Y})^2}{\Sigma(Y_i - \bar{Y})^2} + \beta^2 \cdot \frac{\Sigma(Y_i - \bar{Y})^2}{\Sigma(Y_i - \bar{Y})^2}$$

$$1 = \frac{\Sigma(Y_i - \hat{Y})^2}{\Sigma(Y_i - \bar{Y})^2} + \beta^2$$

In words:

1 = proportion of total variance due to error + proportion of variance due to regression.

This shows that β^2, which is also R^2, is the proportion of explained variance, which is also

$$\beta^2 = \frac{\sum(\widehat{Y} - \overline{Y})^2}{\sum(Y_i - \overline{Y})^2}$$

This implies that $1 - \beta^2$ is the proportion of error variance.

Proof

Looking at the last term in equation (1), we can show that:

$$\sum(\widehat{Y} - \overline{Y})^2 = b^2 \sum(X_i - \overline{X})^2$$

$$\widehat{Y}_i = (\overline{Y} - b\overline{X}) + bX_i \quad \text{(substituting for } a)$$

$$\widehat{Y}_i - \overline{Y} = -b\overline{X} + bX_i$$

$$\widehat{Y}_i - \overline{Y} = b(X_i - \overline{X})$$

$$\sum(\widehat{Y} - \overline{Y})^2 = b^2 \sum(X_i - \overline{X})^2$$

Substituting the result into (1):

$$\sum(Y_i - \overline{Y})^2 = \sum(Y_i - \widehat{Y})^2 + b^2 \sum(X_i - \overline{X})^2$$

Substituting for b^2 using: $b = \beta \dfrac{s_y}{s_x}$:

$$\sum(Y_i - \overline{Y})^2 = \sum(Y_i - \widehat{Y})^2 + \left(\beta^2 \frac{s_y^2}{s_x^2}\right)\sum(X_i - \overline{X})^2$$

Substituting for the variance of X and Y, and inverting the divisor:

$$\sum(Y_i - \overline{Y})^2 = \sum(Y_i - \widehat{Y})^2 +$$

$$\beta^2 \cdot \frac{\sum(Y_i - \overline{Y})^2}{N-1} \cdot \frac{N-1}{\sum(X_i - \overline{X})^2} \cdot \sum(X_i - \overline{X})^2$$

Canceling results in equation (2):

$$\sum(Y_i - \overline{Y})^2 = \sum(Y_i - \widehat{Y})^2 + \beta^2 \cdot \sum(Y_i - \overline{Y})^2$$

1.5 BIVARIATE REGRESSION EXAMPLE

We can run a bivariate regression example using PROC REG in SAS, a general procedure for running bivariate and multiple regressions. This program also allows you to estimate descriptive statistics and correlations as well as test specific hypotheses about the variables in the model.

In this example, we consider the impact of education on job income, separately for each parent in the Toronto Study of Intact Families. This is a study of 888 husband–wife families in Toronto, with at least one child aged 9 to 16. These are two separate bivariate regressions, but later, we specify the issue differently, by using the concept of an *interaction,* which would allow us to directly estimate the differential impact of education on income by gender of the parent in the same model.

The first results are for the mother. In Table 1.4, we show all of the requested output from PROC REG in SAS, because the different elements of the output are common to many regression programs.

TABLE 1.4 ● BIVARIATE REGRESSION OUTPUT IN SAS

Number of Observations Read	**888**
Number of Observations Used	**607**
Number of Observations with Missing Values	**281**

Descriptive Statistics						
Variable	**Sum**	**Mean**	**Uncorrected SS**	**Variance**	**Standard Deviation**	**Label**
Intercept	607.00000	1.00000	607.00000	0	0	Intercept
momeduc	8764.00000	14.43822	131290	7.84395	2.80071	mother's education in years
mjobinc	20145	33.18758	897499	377.78793	19.43677	mother's job income

Correlation				
Variable	**Label**		**momeduc**	**mjobinc**
momeduc	mother's education in years		1.0000	0.3655
mjobinc	mother's job income		0.3655	1.0000

Analysis of Variance					
Source	**DF**	**Sum of Squares**	**Mean Square**	**F Value**	**Pr > F**
Model	1	30592	30592	93.31	<.0001
Error	605	198348	327.84744		
Corrected Total	606	228939			

Root MSE	18.10656	**R-Square**	0.1336	
Dependent Mean	33.18758	**Adj R-Sq**	0.1322	
Coeff Var	54.55823			

Parameter Estimates							
Variable	**Label**	**DF**	**Parameter Estimate**	**Standard Error**	**t Value**	**Pr > |t|**	**Standardized Estimate**
Intercept	Intercept	1	−3.44034	3.86237	−0.89	0.3734	0
momeduc	mother's education in years	1	2.53687	0.26262	9.66	<.0001	0.36555

1.5.0.1 Observations Used in the Analysis

At the top of the output, you can see that 607 of the 888 observations are used in the analysis. This is because of missing values, most of which occur for job income because some mothers don't work outside of the home.

1.5.0.2 Descriptive Statistics

The descriptive statistics show that the mean level of education in this sample of mothers is 14.44 years, and the average income is $33,187.58. The value shown is income in thousands because that is the way the variable was coded. So to get to dollars, you multiple the value by 1000. This is a pretty low level of income, but there is likely to be a significant sub-sample of part-time workers here.

1.5.0.3 Correlation

Note the correlation between the variables in the analysis is .3655—moderately high, as one would expect.

1.5.0.4 Partitioning of Variance

The "Analysis of Variance" table that partitions the variance shows the sum of squares regression (explained by the model), the sum of squares error, and the "corrected" total sum of squares. This sum is corrected for the 1 degree of freedom due to the one independent variable in the model. If you divide the model by the total sum of squares, you get

$$\frac{SS_{model}}{SS_{total}} = \frac{30592}{228939} = .1336$$

Note that this is the R^2 of the model, printed below in the next table in the output. This means that mother's education explains about 13% of the total variance in mother's job incomes in this sample. Considering this is only one variable, this is not a small amount.

1.5.0.5 Regression Results

The results of the bivariate regression equation are shown in the Parameter Estimates table. The intercept is -3.44, and the regression coefficient b is 2.537. This coefficient can be interpreted this way: Each year of education increases job income by $2,537 on average among these women.

The prediction equation would look like this:

$$\widehat{Mjobinc} = -3.44 + 2.537 \cdot Momeduc$$

Notice here that the intercept value is again negative. This is caused by the fact that there are no real zero values for mother's education in this sample. In fact, the lowest year of education reported is six years. As a result, when the line is extended back to 0, it goes into the negative on the Y axis.

The Parameter Estimates table also shows the standardized estimate for the effect of mother's education on her job income. This coefficient is .3655. As discussed above, it should be exactly the same as the correlation in the bivariate case. The interpretation is that a 1 standard deviation increase in mother's education, which we see from the results is 2.8 years, increases job income by .3655 standard deviations. Given that the standard deviation in mother's job income is about 19.44, we could also say that a 2.8-year increase in mother's education leads to, on average, an increase in job income of .3655 x 19.44 = 7.1053, or just over seven thousand dollars.

The same model was run among the husbands, to compare the impact of education on job income among the husbands. The output is shown in Table 1.5.

TABLE 1.5 ● BIVARIATE RESULTS FOR THE HUSBANDS

Number of Observations Read	**888**
Number of Observations Used	**750**
Number of Observations with Missing Values	**138**

(Continued)

TABLE 1.5 ● (Continued)

Descriptive Statistics

Variable	Sum	Mean	Uncorrected SS	Variance	Standard Deviation	Label
Intercept	750.00000	1.00000	750.00000	0	0	Intercept
dadeduc	11402	15.20267	188058	19.64913	4.43273	father's education in years
fjobinc	45217	60.28979	4769362	2727.92760	52.22957	father's job income

Correlation

Variable	Label	dadeduc	fjobinc
dadeduc	father's education in years	1.0000	0.1796
fjobinc	father's job income	0.1796	1.0000

Analysis of Variance

Source	DF	Sum of Squares	Mean Square	F Value	Pr > F
Model	1	65876	65876	24.92	<.0001
Error	748	1977342	2643.50542		
Corrected Total	749	2043218			

Root MSE	51.41503	R-Square	0.0322
Dependent Mean	60.28979	Adj R-Sq	0.0309
Coeff Var	85.27983		

Parameter Estimates

Variable	Label	DF	Parameter Estimate	Standard Error	t Value	Pr > |t|	Standardized Estimate
Intercept	Intercept	1	28.12580	6.71109	4.19	<.0001	0
dadeduc	father's education in years	1	2.11568	0.42382	4.99	<.0001	0.17956

There are some notable differences in these results. The impact of education among the husbands on their income appears to be *smaller*, not larger, as you might expect. The b is 2.1157, compared to the 2.537 among the wives. This means that for every year of education the husbands' income increases on average by $2,116. Even though this is smaller, it is also misleading. Notice the differences in the average incomes of husbands and wives here. The husband's average income is $60,289, almost twice the income of the wives. Because of the fact that the husbands are starting at a higher level on average or have been working longer in the labor force, the impact of their education does not "need" to be as high. If you already have an advantage, the meritocratic impact of education may be—ironically—weaker. Following from this, note also that the R^2 and the correlation are also both much lower.

Of course, this example raises many questions, and there are many possibilities to consider in interpreting this relationship. That is why we use multiple regression: both to control for, that is, take into account, alternative explanations of the difference here and to study the role of mediating variables (intervening variables between education and income), which help to explain the effect of education.

1.5.1 Bivariate Regression Example in STATA

In Table 1.6, we present comparable results in STATA for our first regression model, predicting mother's job income from her years of education. The following model uses the *reg* procedure in STATA (note: all commands in STATA must be stated in lower case).

The first part of the output presents the Analysis of Variance table. Next to this is an overview of the model fit. Again, we see an R^2 statistic of .1322, duplicating the result in SAS.

The latter part of the output presents the relevant unstandardized coefficient (*b*, in the column labeled "Coef"), followed by its associated standard error (2.63). Dividing these two numbers, we get the *t*-statistic (9.66) and its noted significance ($P > |t|$, .000). The *beta* option in STATA produces the standardized regression coefficient. Note that one key difference in the STATA regression output relative to SAS is the placement and labeling of the *y*-intercept. You will find this value in the last row of the regression output ("_cons") rather than the first.

TABLE 1.6 ● BIVARIATE REGRESSION OUTPUT IN STATA

Source	SS	df	MS		
Model	30592	1	30592	Number of obs = 607
Residual	198348	605	327.847443	F(1, 606) = 93.31
				Prob > F = 0.0000
				R-squared = 0.1336
Total	228939	606	377.787129	Adj R-squared = 0.1322
				Root MSE = 18.1066

mjobinc	Coef.	Std. Err.	t	P>|t|	Beta
momeduc	2.53687	.26262	9.66	0.000	.3655542
_cons	-3.44034	3.86237	-.89	0.373	.

1.6 ASSUMPTIONS OF THE REGRESSION MODEL

There are a number of assumptions involved in the regression model, although some of them are not the final word on what is possible—because modifications of the model often solve the problem. We state the main assumptions here: A few of these are crucial:

- *No autocorrelation of errors:* $cov(e_i e_j) = 0$

  Y observations are independent of each other—that is, they do not have common systematic components. In other words, this means that different errors are uncorrelated. This assumption is sometimes violated when the same observations are followed through time or when sampling is clustered. Usually, however, observations are sampled independently.

- *Homoscedasticity:* $Var(e_i \mid X) = E(e_i^2) = \sigma^2$

  In words, the variance of the errors is the same at all levels of *X* and does not depend on the level on *X*. When this assumption is violated, modifications of the regression can be used to address the problem, resulting in *weighted least squares*.

- *Independence of independent variables and errors:* $E(Xe_i) = cov(Xe_i) = 0$

  Independent variables are uncorrelated with factors in the "true" error term. If this assumption is violated, the regression model is basically misspecified. This assumption amounts to saying either that all relevant explanatory variables for Y are included in the model so that what is left involves only random factors or that the excluded factors are uncorrelated with X.

- *Linearity*

  The relationship between X and Y is linear in the population. This assumption can be modified because there are many transformations of nonlinear relations which can be "fit" into a linear model.

- *No measurement error in X*

  The independent variable is measured without error. There are consequences when there is significant measurement error, but the consequences to estimates are minimal when measurement error is minimal to modest.

- *Normality of errors*

  This is a very important assumption because it is so often misunderstood. The assumption of the model is that the ***errors*** are normally distributed around the regression line. ***The assumption is not that Y is normal.*** This assumption is not necessary for unbiased estimation of b; it is necessary for correct application of significance tests. However, the central limit theorem applies, so that even when Y is skewed, suggesting errors may be skewed, an N of 100 or more will often result in a sufficiently normal sampling distribution for testing.

1.7 MULTIPLE REGRESSION

What happens when there is more than one independent variable in a regression? What does it mean to "control for" other variables or "partition" their effects or "hold constant" other variables? These are widely used synonymous terms, but one rarely sees a detailed discussion of what exactly is going on when these terms are invoked in an analysis. In general, the intention in considering more than one variable is to derive an estimate of the effect of each variable that is purged of any confounding (overlap) with the effects of all other correlated independent variables. How is this done?

Excluding the individual subscripts for variables to simplify, the general form of the multiple regression equation is

$$X_3 = a + b_{31}X_1 + b_{32}X_2 + e_i$$

Note the changes in the notation used here: The dependent variable does not have to be Y, it can be anything. Here X_3 is the dependent variable. It is helpful to distinguish the variables by using differently numbered subscripts, but you could use anything to stand for the variables: letters, acronyms, and variable names are all acceptable. Because there are now multiple independent variables, the regression coefficients also have to be distinguished. It is customary to order the subscripts for the coefficients with the dependent variable number first, then the independent variable number second.

In standardized form, where the intercept is by definition zero, the equation would look like this, using small x's to stand for the standardized variables.

$$x_3 = \beta_{31}x_1 + \beta_{32}x_2 + e_i$$

The problem in multiple regression is that X_1 and X_2 are usually correlated—that is, confounded. Therefore, the usual way of estimating b in the bivariate case would include a portion of the effect of the other independent variable. To get a better estimate of the effect of each X, the influence of the other variable must be removed.

1.7.1 Covariance Equations

The regression equation above can be used to derive ***covariance equations,*** which in turn can be used to actually solve for the coefficients, as well as form the basis of interpretation of results in causal models (in Chapter 6).

To develop covariance equations to solve the coefficients, first replace a by solving for it. This is done using a multiple regression extension of the formula for the intercept developed in the last section on bivariate regression:

$$a = \bar{X}_3 - b_{31}\bar{X}_1 - b_{32}\bar{X}_2$$

Then we have

$$X_3 = (\bar{X}_3 - b_{31}\bar{X}_1 - b_{32}\bar{X}_2) + b_{31}X_1 + b_{32}X_2 + e$$

Rearranging and factoring out the coefficients leads to an equation where the variables are expressed in deviation form:

$$X_3 - \bar{X}_3 = -b_{31}\bar{X}_1 - b_{32}\bar{X}_2 + b_{31}X_1 + b_{32}X_2 + e$$
$$X_3 - \bar{X}_3 = b_{31}(X_1 - \bar{X}_1) + b_{32}(X_2 - \bar{X}_2) + e$$

Now multiply each side of this equation by each independent variable in deviation form in turn:

$$(X_1 - \bar{X}_1)(X_3 - \bar{X}_3) = b_{31}(X_1 - \bar{X}_1)(X_1 - \bar{X}_1) + b_{32}(X_1 - \bar{X}_1)(X_2 - \bar{X}_2) + (X_1 - \bar{X}_1)e$$

$$(X_2 - \bar{X}_2)(X_3 - \bar{X}_3) = b_{31}(X_1 - \bar{X}_1)(X_2 - \bar{X}_2) + b_{32}(X_2 - \bar{X}_2)(X_2 - \bar{X}_2) + (X_2 - \bar{X}_2)e$$

Then sum and divide both sides of both equations by N - 1:

$$\sum\frac{(X_1 - \bar{X}_1)(X_3 - \bar{X}_3)}{N-1} = b_{31}\sum\frac{(X_1 - \bar{X}_1)(X_1 - \bar{X}_1)}{N-1} + b_{32}\sum\frac{(X_1 - \bar{X}_1)(X_2 - \bar{X}_2)}{N-1} + \sum\frac{(X_1 - \bar{X}_1)e}{N-1}$$

$$\sum\frac{(X_2 - \bar{X}_2)(X_3 - \bar{X}_3)}{N-1} = b_{31}\sum\frac{(X_1 - \bar{X}_1)(X_2 - \bar{X}_2)}{N-1} + b_{32}\sum\frac{(X_2 - \bar{X}_2)(X_2 - \bar{X}_2)}{N-1} + \sum\frac{(X_2 - \bar{X}_2)e}{N-1}$$

What do we have? Note the form of the term on the left-hand side of the equality—*it is the formula for the covariance between each independent variable and the dependent variable.* The covariance between the two independent variables also occurs on the right, as well as the variances of

X_1 and X_2, resulting from terms where the deviation score on an independent variable is multiplied by itself, and therefore squared.

Given that Xs do not covary with e by assumption, this produces the following covariance equations, using more efficient notation with "s" for the covariances and variances:

$$s_{13} = b_{31} \cdot s_{X_1}^2 + b_{32} \cdot s_{12}$$
$$s_{23} = b_{31} \cdot s_{12} + b_{32} \cdot s_{X_2}^2$$

Note that this is two equations in two unknowns. This means we could use these equations to solve for the two coefficients.

If you look at the covariance equations, you can see the difference between bivariate and multiple regression.

The bivariate coefficient for X_1 is

$$b_{31} = \frac{s_{13}}{s_{X_1}^2}$$

Using the first covariance equation and solving for b_{31}, the effect of X_1 in the multiple regression is now

$$s_{13} = b_{31} \cdot s_{X_1}^2 + b_{32} \cdot s_{12}$$
$$s_{13} - b_{32} \cdot s_{12} = b_{31} \cdot s_{X_1}^2$$
$$b_{31} = \frac{s_{13} - b_{32} s_{12}}{s_{X_1}^2}$$

In effect, the covariance between X_1 and X_3 needs to have the portion removed that is due to the covariance between the two independent variables X_1 and X_2 and the fact that X_2 also has an effect on the dependent variable. This amount is $b_{32} s_{12}$, which is the covariance between X_1 and X_2 times the effect of X_2 on X_3.

To provide an example, we have the following variables from the National Survey of Families and Households (NSFH), a widely used national longitudinal study of households in the United States, with three waves. Here we focus on a sample of married people at Wave 2 followed through to Wave 3:

X_3 = depression score at Wave 3 of the NSFH (Dep_3 below).

X_1 = a dummy variable for getting a divorce between Waves 2 and 3. A dummy variable (explained later) is just a 1/0 variable comparing two groups. Here it equals 1 if the person got divorced and 0 if they stayed married (Div_{23} below).

X_2 = depression score at Wave 2 of the NSFH (Dep_2 below).

We rewrite the regression equation specifically to show the variables involved:

$$Dep3_3 = a + b_{31} Div23_1 + b_{32} Dep2_2 + e$$

The subscript here gives the variable a number for reference in what follows. You could use any statistical software to derive the covariances and variances of these variables. Here we used PROC CORR in SAS to get the covariances, and PROC UNIVARIATE to get basic descriptive statistics, including the standard deviation. The results of doing this are shown in Table 1.7.

TABLE 1.7 ● BASIC DESCRIPTIVE STATISTICS FOR THE DIVORCE MODEL		
Covariances	**Standard Deviations**	**Means**
$s_{13} = .085$	$s_1 = .099$	$\bar{X}_1 = .01$
$s_{12} = .096$	$s_2 = 15.43$	$\bar{X}_2 = 13.23$
$s_{23} = 102.57$	$s_3 = 15.19$	$\bar{X}_3 = 13.06$

We ran a bivariate regression of depression at Wave 3 on getting a divorce between Waves 2 and 3, to establish a baseline. That value was

$$b_{31} = \frac{s_{13}}{s_{X_1}^2} = 8.67$$

However, in the multiple regression controlling for prior depression at Wave 2, the effect of *Dep2* (X_2) on *Dep3* (X_3) and its overlap (covariance) with *Div23* (X_1) is removed first—that is, it is "controlled." This is important because the effect of *Dep2* on *Dep3* represents the continuity in depression across waves—that is, the lack of change. Thus, in this equation, the effect of *Div23* is the effect of divorce on change in depression across waves. Also, note, previous depression could lead to a higher risk of divorce, so the causal direction could be wrong unless it is controlled here.

$$\text{Here the effect of } X_1 \text{ on } X_3 \text{ is: } b_{31} = \frac{s_{13} - b_{32} s_{12}}{s_{X_1}^2}$$

The amount to be removed from the effect of *Div23* is shown in the graphic in Figure 1.5 in paths with grey arrows, and the net effect of *Div23* after removing the overlap with *Dep2* is the Black arrow.

FIGURE 1.5 ● A MODEL FOR A TWO VARIABLE MULTIPLE REGRESSION

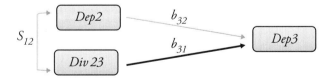

1.7.1.1 Solving the Equation

Using the given information about the variances and covariances, it is possible to solve for each unknown, because we then have two covariance equations in two unknowns. For example, we can solve for b_{31} (though we do not show the derivation of this formula):

$$b_{31} = \frac{s_{13} \cdot s_{X_2}^2 - s_{12} \cdot s_{23}}{s_{X_1}^2 s_{X_2}^2 - s_{12}^2}$$

$$b_{31} = 4.83$$

Substituting this value in the covariance equation for s_{23} leads to

$$b_{32} = .432$$

Solving for a,

$$a = \bar{X}_3 - b_{31}\bar{X}_1 - b_{32}\bar{X}_2 = 13.06 - (4.83 \cdot .01) - (.432 \cdot 13.23) = 7.23$$

The overall prediction equation is

$$\widehat{Dep3}_3 = 7.23 + 4.83\,Div23_1 + .432\,Dep2_2$$

Here we use the concept of "symptom days" to interpret results. That's because the depression questions asked how many days a week each symptom occurred. Because there are 12 symptoms, there are potentially 7 x 12 = 84 symptom days a week that could occur.

1.7.1.2 The Equation Interpreted

1. A divorce between Waves 2 and 3 leads to 4.83 more depression symptom days per week at Wave 3, over and above depression at Wave 2.

2. Each symptom day of depression at Wave 2 leads to .432 symptoms days of depression at Wave 3.

3. Note, importantly, that the effect of divorce is 4.83 / 8.67 = 56%, just over half, of its original size. This reflects the confounding and suggests that prior depression *is* also related to the risk of divorce over time.

You can calculate exactly how much the effect of divorce has been reduced by the presence of prior depression in the equation, as follows:

$$\frac{b_1 - b_2}{b_1} = \frac{8.67 - 4.83}{8.67} = .44$$

That is, controlling for prior depression explains about 44% of the original association.

The results of the regression from the SAS output are shown in Table. 1.8.

TABLE 1.8 ● RESULTS FOR THE MULTIPLE REGRESSION

Number of Observations Read	4600
Number of Observations Used	4247
Number of Observations with Missing Values	353

Analysis of Variance					
Source	DF	Sum of Squares	Mean Square	F Value	Pr > F
Model	2	189842	94921	518.58	<.0001
Error	4244	776819	183.03924		
Corrected Total	4246	966660			

Root MSE	13.52920	R-Square	0.1964
Dependent Mean	12.97078	Adj R-Sq	0.1960
Coeff Var	104.30520		

Parameter Estimates					
Variable	DF	Parameter Estimate	Standard Error	t Value	Pr > |t|
Intercept	1	7.22571	0.27373	26.40	<.0001
div23	1	4.83030	2.05421	2.35	0.0187
dep2	1	0.43160	0.01353	31.91	<.0001

You can see in the final table the regression coefficients under "Parameter Estimates." Note there is also a *t* test for each coefficient and a significance level. This significance level is "two-tailed," so if you hypothesize a direction to the effect, as for divorce, the probability here could be "one-tailed," which means you divide the printed probability by two (.0187/2 = .0094).

1.7.2 Tests for Multiple Regression

There are three basic tests used in multiple regression:

- *Significance of the whole equation*: The alternative hypothesis is that at least one of the independent variables has a significant effect on the dependent variable, against the null hypothesis that *no* independent variable has a significant effect.

$$F = \frac{R^2 / k}{\left(1 - R^2\right)/(N - k - 1)} \text{ with } k \text{ and } (N - k - 1) \text{ df}$$

Where k = number of independent variables in the equation and N = sample size.

- *Individual variables in the equation*: Tests of individual variables in the equation amount to a 1 degree of freedom test of the difference in the R^2 with the variable in the model versus the R^2 when the variable is not in the model.

The null hypothesis is that X has no effect on Y.

$$F = \frac{(R_k^2 - R_{(k-1)}^2)/1}{(1 - R_k^2)/(N - k - 1)} \text{ with } 1 \text{ and } (N - k - 1) \text{ df}$$

Where R_k^2 = the R^2 with all variables in the equation.

$R_{(k-1)}^2$ = the R^2 with the variable to be tested removed from the equation.

This test is equivalent to the test for **b** *printed by most programs.*

- *Group of variables added to an equation:* This test compares the R^2 in a model with variables added to a baseline model to the R^2 of the baseline model, to test collectively for the significance of the effect of the group of variables added.

This test is a comparison of nested models, in which Model A (the smaller model) is nested in Model B (the larger model), and thus all variables in A are contained in B, but B has additional variables.

The null hypothesis is that none of the new variables added has a significant effect on Y.

$$F = \frac{(R_B^2 - R_A^2)/(k_B - k_A)}{(1-R_B^2)/(N-k_B-1)} \quad \text{with } k_B - k_A \text{ and } N - k_B - 1 \text{ df}$$

Where R_B^2 = the R^2 from the larger model (B),

$\quad\quad R_A^2$ = the R^2 from the smaller model (A),

and k_B and k_A are the number of independent variables in B and A respectively.

1.7.3 Nested Models

One model (A) is nested in another more complex model (B) when A occurs completely as a subset of B, and B has additional variables. You could, for example, add a group of variables to the depression equation to test a single idea or hypothesis. One version of this occurs when you want to study differences across groups. Another occurs when you want to test interactions (discussed in the next chapter).

Suppose you are concerned that the effect of divorce in the previous example is confounded with ethno-racial differences in rates of divorce, and these group differences represent basic differences in status that are reflected in differences in depression. If we added groups to this equation representing race/ethnicity, we could control for this possibility as an alternative explanation.

The equations being compared here are

Model 1: $Dep3_3 = a + b_{31}Div23_1 + b_{32}Dep2_2 + e_i$

Model 2: $\quad Dep3_3 = a + b_{31}Div23_1 + b_{32}Dep2_2 + b_{33}Black + b_{34}Hispanic + b_{35}Asian + e_i$

Note that Model 1 is contained in Model 2 and thus is "nested" in Model 2. We can therefore compare the R^2 across these models. Here we added three groups—Black, Hispanic, and Asian—from the NSFH data to the equation for the effect of divorce, with the reference comparison group non-Hispanic Whites. Each group variable is coded 1 versus 0, and the reference group is the group left out of this coding. This makes that group the baseline for comparison. The relevant output is reproduced in Table 1.9.

TABLE 1.9 ● ADDING GROUP DIFFERENCES TO THE MULTIPLE REGRESSION

			Analysis of Variance		
Source	DF	Sum of Squares	Mean Square	F Value	Pr > F
Model	5	196220	39244	216.02	<.0001
Error	4241	770440	181.66465		
Corrected Total	4246	966660			

Root MSE	13.47830	R-Square	0.2030
Dependent Mean	12.97078	Adj R-Sq	0.2020
Coeff Var	103.91281		

Parameter Estimates					
Variable	DF	Parameter Estimate	Standard Error	t Value	Pr > |t|
Intercept	1	6.79018	0.28282	24.01	<.0001
div23	1	4.67567	2.04693	2.28	0.0224
dep2	1	0.42115	0.01360	30.98	<.0001
black	1	3.38370	0.60390	5.60	<.0001
hispanic	1	2.48630	1.12877	2.20	0.0277
asian	1	2.83244	2.81983	1.00	0.3152

We can see in these results that the effect of divorce is still significant and therefore independent of group differences. The net effect of divorce here (4.67) is very close to the prior model, suggesting that ethno-racial differences in divorce do *not* account for the effect of divorce in this model.

If we want to test for the effect of "race/ethnicity" here, we would need to compare the R^2 from this model to the previous model for divorce and prior depression only. This comparison isolates the effect of "race/ethnicity" and asks whether the independent partialled effect of race/ethnicity is significant over and above divorce and prior depression.

Substituting the values from the output into the *F*-test,

$$F = \frac{(.2030 - .1964)/(5-2)}{(1-.2030)/(4247-5-1)} = 11.71$$

with 3 and 4241 df. Any *F* table will verify that this is significant beyond the .0001 level. Race/ethnicity does make a difference here, but its effect is independent of the relevance of divorce.

1.8 A MULTIPLE REGRESSION EXAMPLE: THE GENDER PAY GAP

When you hear about the gender pay gap, it is often stated in bivariate terms: It is the overall difference between the average (or median) pay of men and women in the labor force. For example, you may have heard that women make something like 76 cents on the male dollar earned.

The question is how much of that pay gap is due to "natural" or expected differences in pay due to other causes. These other causes include factors that are generally rewarded with higher pay—such as education, experience, and performance—or are due to differences in economic sectors, occupations, or regional economies that have an imbalance of men and women. The concept of "equal pay for equal work" is not as easy to specify as it sounds.

This is admittedly a tricky question and thus also a good example. The entire issue is subtler than it appears, if women choose occupations that provide more "flex time," for example, which generally have lower pay, but feel constrained to choose those occupations. This possibility suggests larger causes of unequal pay are at work, limiting the sense of choice and access women have.

As an example of interpreting multiple regression, we present results from the National Survey of Families and Households, using data from Wave 2 in 1992 to1994. We would expect a substantial pay difference to exist at that point in history. To keep things as straightforward as possible, we make some simplifying assumptions, relative to the large number of alternative debates surrounding this issue.

Our dependent variable here is the wages earned per hour of work reported. This is one prevalent approach in this literature because it already takes into account gender differences in hours worked overall.

The standard approach to this issue adjusts—controls—for differences in human capital, captured by level of education and total years worked in the labor force. There may also be other confounders, if, for example, women are overrepresented in groups that are also at a pay disadvantage, but the cause is not gender per se. This happens in our example in the case of race: 19% of our employed females are Black, but only 14% of the employed males are Black.

Here is the result of a bivariate regression of wages per hour worked on gender, coded here as a two-category variable, with 1 = female, and 0 = male (see Table 1.10). This coding allows us to see the average difference in dollar income per hour directly.

TABLE 1.10 ●   BIVARIATE MODEL FOR GENDER PAY GAP

		Parameter Estimates			
Variable	DF	Parameter Estimate	Standard Error	t Value	Pr > |t|
Intercept	1	15.67842	0.36708	42.71	<.0001
female	1	−4.15118	0.49088	−8.46	<.0001

This result says that women make on average $4.15 less than men per hour worked. The results are not stated proportionally. Because of the way "female" is coded, we know that men make on average $15.68 dollars per hour worked. This is because the intercept is the value of Y when independent variables = 0. We can make the result proportional by expressing the difference in income this way:

$$female\text{-}to\text{-}male \text{ income ratio} = \frac{15.678 - 4.1511}{15.678} = .73$$

This says that in this equation, women make about 73 cents per dollar earned by a man. Given the year is around 1992 to 1994, this figure—broadly—makes sense.

This result does not control for qualifications, tenure (experience), and performance. The last is difficult to capture in most data, but the first two are represented by level of education and experience in the labor force. When you control for education and the total number of years worked in the labor force, this produces the results shown in Table 1.11.

TABLE 1.11 ●   THE GENDER PAY GAP CONTROLLING FOR EDUCATION AND SENIORITY

		Parameter Estimates			
Variable	DF	Parameter Estimate	Standard Error	t Value	Pr > |t|
Intercept	1	−9.28590	1.42357	−6.52	<.0001
female	1	−2.84527	0.48218	−5.90	<.0001
education2	1	1.50659	0.09479	15.89	<.0001
Totalworkyearswgt	1	0.26889	0.02406	11.18	<.0001

Here we see that each variable affects income controlling for the others. Each year of education (*education2*) increases average hourly income by about $1.51 per hour. The effect of labor force experience is captured by the variable "*totalworkyearswgt*." This variable is the total number of accumulated work years, weighted by whether the job was full-time or part-time. Here each weighted work year increases hourly income by about $.27, or 27 cents. In both cases, results for human capital predictors are very significant and reflect the usually observed influence of these standard predictors of pay.

You can also see here that the net effect of "female" is now -2.8453—that is, the net difference with men is now $2.85 per hour less than men. This net difference with males is considerably smaller. You cannot figure out the net female to male income ratio here, however, because now the intercept has a different interpretation. It is in fact still the predicted value of *Y* when all independent variables = 0, but now those variables include education and total years worked. This means the intercept is the predicted hourly income for men with zero years of education and zero years worked—in other words, it is not interpretable as is. The intercept is negative, mainly due to the fact that no one in the actual sample has zero years of education and reports zero years worked.

You can adjust for this problem and make the intercept interpretable again, by "centering" the control variables here. That means subtracting the *male* mean from each raw score, like a deviation score. We subtract the male mean, assuming we want to interpret the male / female difference as if female workers had the same level of education and time in the labor force as male workers.

Male (female = 0) and female (female = 1) means on the control variables are shown in Table 1.12.

TABLE 1.12 ● MALE VERSUS FEMALE MEANS ON CONTROL VARIABLES

female	N Obs	Variable	N	Mean	Std Dev	Minimum	Maximum
0	2118	education2	2118	13.5193579	2.6023414	0	20.0000000
		Totalworkyearswgt	2118	17.0931500	10.3754841	0.0833333	53.1666667
1	2687	education2	2687	13.2690733	2.4021010	0	20.0000000
		Totalworkyearswgt	2687	13.6387855	9.3584510	0.0833333	48.2500000

One thing that is very clear from this table is that women work significantly fewer years than men, despite the fact that we observe in other results that they are slightly older than the men in this sample. This is presumably due to more time in home work and childcare roles. However, it is also much less clear that there are any differences in level of education by gender.

When the education and total years worked are centered on the male mean, you get the results show in Table 1.13.

TABLE 1.13 ● RE-CENTERING THE VARIABLES FOR COMPARISON TO THE BIVARIATE DIFFERENCE

Parameter Estimates					
Variable	DF	Parameter Estimate	Standard Error	t Value	Pr > |t|
Intercept	1	15.67842	0.35447	44.23	<.0001
female	1	−2.84527	0.48218	−5.90	<.0001
educcenter	1	1.50659	0.09479	15.89	<.0001
totalyearscenter	1	0.26889	0.02406	11.18	<.0001

Note here that the intercept is essentially equal to the original intercept, and the coefficients for each variable are exactly the same—as expected. Using this result, we will compare net differences between women and men relative to that overall male mean income. Now the adjusted female to male ratio is

$$\textit{female-to-male} \text{ income ratio } = \frac{15.678 - 2.8453}{15.678} = .82$$

You can see that the net difference is smaller. Now women make 82 cents per dollar earned by men, *net of other factors representing human capital differences.*

Finally, we add race to this example, because we know that women are overrepresented among Blacks, and race is a distinct source of income discrimination. In other words, we do not want to attribute a pay difference to gender, when it is in fact due to race.

We added two variables to the equation representing race: "Black" is a comparison of Blacks] to non-Hispanic Whites (1 vs. 0), and Hispanic is a comparison of Hispanics to non-Hispanic Whites (also 1 vs. 0).

When we add these variables to the regression, using the centering approach, we get the results shown in Table 1.14.

TABLE 1.14 ● CONTROLLING FOR RACE DIFFERENCES

Parameter Estimates					
Variable	DF	Parameter Estimate	Standard Error	t Value	Pr > |t|
Intercept	1	15.67842	0.35439	44.24	<.0001
female	1	−2.78185	0.48313	−5.76	<.0001
educcenter	1	1.47579	0.09691	15.23	<.0001
totalyearscenter	1	0.27117	0.02409	11.26	<.0001
blackcenter	1	−1.30546	0.64290	−2.03	0.0424
hispcenter	1	−0.67357	0.99173	−0.68	0.4971

The net difference between women and men is now −$2.78 dollars per hour of work. Computing this as a ratio of female to male income,

$$\textit{female-to-male} \text{ income ratio } = \frac{15.678 - 2.7818}{15.678} = .82$$

The ratio is about the same: Even though Blacks receive a lower per hour income compared to Whites and there is a slight difference in proportion female among Blacks versus Whites, it does not further account for the gender pay ratio.

A caveat: There are other, more comprehensive controls we could use here, discussed widely in this literature. And of course, historical change would suggest we use more recent data as well. But the principle of accounting for the female to male difference has been demonstrated in this example, even considering this restricted set of other factors determining pay.

There is an important complication to consider in this example that will be discussed thoroughly in Chapter 6. The issue is whether standard human capital differences are really controls here, as opposed to mediators that transmit the effect of gender to pay differences—in other words, actual consequences of gender that are part of the overall gender difference in pay, not an alternative explanation.

The last model can be duplicated using the *reg* command in STATA. Again, we present results just to create a cross-walk between SAS and STATA, this time with a multiple regression example (Table 1.15).

TABLE 1.15 ● REGRESSION RESULTS FOR THE GENDER WAGE GAP IN STATA

Source	SS	df	MS		
Model	114657.249	5	22931.4499	Number of obs = 4805	F(5, 4799) = 86.21
Residual	1276521.15	4799	265.997322	Prob > F = 0.0000	R-squared = 0.0824
				Adj R-squared = 0.0815	
Total	1391178.4	4804	289.58751	Root MSE = 16.309	

wagesperhr	Coef.	Std. Err.	t	P>|t|	[95% Conf. Interval]	
female	-2.78185	.4831318	-5.76	0.000	-3.72901	-1.83469
educcenter	1.475792	.0969146	15.23	0.000	1.285795	1.665789
totalyearscenter	.2711658	.0240869	11.26	0.000	.2239445	.3183871
blackcenter	-1.305463	.6429024	-2.03	0.042	-2.565847	-.0450801
hispcenter	-.6735712	.991734	-0.68	0.497	-2.617824	1.270682
_cons	15.67842	.3543853	44.24	0.000	14.98366	16.37317

1.9 DUMMY VARIABLES

The variables in the examples in the previous section are not all "continuous" variables that vary from zero to the highest value in a sample. In those examples, divorce is a "dummy variable," equal to 1 if there was a divorce, and equal to 0 if not. "Female" is also a dummy variable, = 1 for females, and 0 for males. This kind of variable (aka an indicator variable) just stands for whether you are in a certain group or not, whether you experienced an event or not, or whether you are in a certain category or not. It is straightforward to interpret results because there are only two groups involved—divorced versus not divorced, women versus men.

A trickier case occurs when you want to assess the differences among a ***set*** of groups, considered as a set of independent variables. In this case, you have to use a set of dummy variables to represent differences among groups. This happens for variables like marital status, race, ethnicity, religion, region, and so forth. This too came up in the previous section when we added race to the model to demonstrate nested models.

There are certain rules in interpreting these variables that you need to be aware of. For one thing, there is a left-out reference group that is the comparison point. For example, to study marital status, you may have five groups in total: married, divorced or separated, widowed, never married, and cohabiting. You choose a reference group for comparison, usually a standard norm, and compare other groups to this group. In this case, you could make married the reference group.

1.9.1 How Do Dummy Variables Work in Regression?

Interpreting *b* is *always* the same in general: The amount of change in *Y* resulting from a 1-unit change in *X*. For dummy variables, that one unit represents two groups, and as a result, because of the "Least Squares Criterion" discussed in the earlier section, the *b* for a dummy variable is *also* the mean difference between the two groups on *Y*.

In this context, *a,* as usual, is the predicted value of *Y* when *X* = 0. Thus it is the mean of *Y* for the group coded 0 on the dummy variable.

1.9.1.1 Example 1: Gender—Two Categories

Imagine you are studying gender differences in starting salaries at universities at the assistant professor level. The graph in Figure 1.6 shows the difference as a regression slope comparing males (= 1) to females (= 0), based on imagined data circa 2010.

FIGURE 1.6 ● **DIFFERENCES IN STARTING SALARY OF MALE VERSUS FEMALE ASSISTANT PROFESSORS**

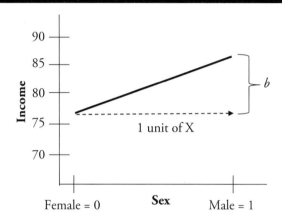

Given that there are two values of *X*, the regression line will pass **exactly** through the mean values on *Y* within each of the two groups (the conditional *Y* means).

So   *b* = the difference between the means in the two groups.

   a = the intercept, the mean of *Y* in the group coded = 0.

The equation: $\hat{Y} = 77 + 9X$

Interpreted:
When *X* = 0 (women): $\hat{Y} = 77 + 9(0) = 77$

When *X* = 1 (men): $\hat{Y} = 77 + 9(1) = 86$

The regression coefficient, *b* = 9, expresses the difference between the mean incomes in the two groups. So, the mean income for women is $77,000, and the mean income for men is $86,000.

1.9.1.2 Example 2: Divorce

In the previous section, we considered the effect of divorce on depression. Divorce is a dummy variable with two groups, coded in the previous example to be = 1 for divorced and = 0 if still married.

The output from this regression is shown in Table 1.16.
From these results, we could write out the equation as

$$\widehat{Dep3} = 12.97 + 8.57 \cdot Div23$$

TABLE 1.16 ● THE BIVARIATE EFFECT OF DIVORCE ON DEPRESSION

Analysis of Variance

Source	DF	Sum of Squares	Mean Square	F Value	Pr > F
Model	1	3344.10531	3344.10531	14.53	0.0001
Error	4589	1056268	230.17386		
Corrected Total	4590	1059612			

Root MSE	15.17148	R-Square	0.0032
Dependent Mean	13.06394	Adj R-Sq	0.0029
Coeff Var	116.13247		

Parameter Estimates

Variable	DF	Parameter Estimate	Standard Error	t Value	Pr > |t|
Intercept	1	12.97808	0.22504	57.67	<.0001
div23	1	8.56935	2.24820	3.81	<.0001

This means that those not divorced had a mean level of depression at Wave 3 of 12.97 on this scale and that the divorced had an average level 8.57 points higher than that—12.97 + 8.57 = 21.54. We note the estimate here is slightly different than the by-hand calculation, which is subject to rounding error.

1.9.2 Dummy Variables with Multiple Categories

Many categorical variables have more than two categories: *ethnicity, marital status, religion, region, employment status, family type,* to name just a few examples.

In Table 1.17, assume there are four measured marital statuses. Note in this scheme that you will see variables for divorced or separated, widowed, and never married but not for married. Each variables is coded = 1 to stand for that group and 0 for ***all other groups***. The only group with 0 on all three dummy variables is the married. Each dummy variable can be interpreted as the mean difference on Y of that group versus the reference group, in this case, the married. You cannot create a separate dummy variable for the married because they are already uniquely defined in this coding:

TABLE 1.17 ● CREATING DUMMY VARIABLES FOR THE GROUPS WITH MARRIED AS THE REFERENCE

Groups	Variable Names		
	Divsep	Widow	Nevermarr
Divorced / Separated	1	0	0
Widowed	0	1	0
Never Married	0	0	1
Married	0	0	0

If you try to create a separate dummy variable for all four groups here, you end up with one variable that is perfectly determined by the scores on three others and thus is perfectly "collinear," a term referring to the fact that the last dummy variable considered is completely determined by the values of the other three and thus is not separable from the other three.

Imagine you did create separate dummy variables for each marital status, as illustrated in Table 1.18.

TABLE 1.18 ● CREATING DUMMY VARIABLES FOR ALL GROUPS				
	Variable Names			
Groups	**Divsep**	**Widow**	**Nevermarr**	**Married**
Divorced / Separated	1	0	0	0
Widowed	0	1	0	0
Never Married	0	0	1	0
Married	0	0	0	1

In this table, ***Married*** $= 1 - Divsep - Widow - Nevermarr$.

You can do the calculation as follows:

For the divorced/separated,	Married = 1 - 1 - 0 - 0 = 0
For the widowed,	Married = 1 - 0 - 1 - 0 = 0
For the never married,	Married = 1 - 0 - 0 - 1 = 0
For the married,	Married = 1 - 0 - 0 - 0 = 1

In other words, the values on the married dummy variable are already defined by the combined information on the first three dummy variables. Basically, *you don't need the fourth dummy variable here.*

The reference group you choose is always left out of the group of dummy variables constructed. This means that each dummy variable will be the mean difference on Y between the group defined by that dummy variable and the reference group. If you want to know about mean differences *among* those groups, you can still extract that information from the regression results, since the difference in the coefficients of any two variables is equal to the difference in the means in those groups.

The ultimate lesson is this: You only need k - 1 variables to represent differences among k groups. You must choose a reference group, often a standard reference representing an extreme or what is expected, and then create dummy variables showing the differences between the other groups and this reference group.

1.9.3 Interpreting Results for Dummy Variables with Multiple Categories

This example uses the National Survey of Families and Households (NSFH) Wave 2 data to assess marital status differences in "close and trusting relations," a general scale derived from the Ryff Well-Being scales (Ryff, 1989). This scale is constructed as a 6-point scale, from 0 to 5, where 0 represents no trusting or close relations and 5 would represent strong agreement that you have close and trusting relationships with others.

Marital status at Wave 2 also considered whether the respondent was cohabiting. For all nonmarried statuses, this trumped divorce, widowhood, or never married status. Thus, everyone in the dummy variables for divorce / separation, widowhood, and never married is *not* living with a partner.

The results are shown in Table 1.19.

TABLE 1.19 ● MARITAL STATUS DIFFERENCES IN TRUSTING RELATIONSHIPS

Number of Observations Read	4600
Number of Observations Used	4242
Number of Observations with Missing Values	358

Analysis of Variance					
Source	**DF**	**Sum of Squares**	**Mean Square**	**F Value**	**Pr > F**
Model	4	179.01967	44.75492	34.62	<.0001
Error	4237	5477.06122	1.29267		
Corrected Total	4241	5656.08089			

Root MSE	1.13696	**R-Square**	0.0317
Dependent Mean	3.64785	**Adj R-Sq**	0.0307
Coeff Var	31.16793		

Parameter Estimates					
Variable	**DF**	**Parameter Estimate**	**Standard Error**	**t Value**	**Pr > |t|**
Intercept	1	3.79430	0.02179	174.10	<.0001
divsep2	1	−0.50006	0.04591	−10.89	<.0001
widow2	1	−0.26325	0.06239	−4.22	<.0001
nevermar2	1	−0.37252	0.07140	−5.22	<.0001
cohab2	1	0.08167	0.09772	0.84	0.4033

Looking at the results for the dummy variables here, you should first see that the intercept value of 3.79 *is* the mean on Y among the married, the reference group. You can also see that the divorced, widowed, and never married all experience lower levels of trusting relationships compared to the married ($p < .0001$), but cohabitors are not significantly different from the married on this outcome. The basic dividing line in the results is having a live-in partner.

You can derive the means in these groups straightforwardly, by calculating each mean as $a + b_k$. For the divorced, for example, the mean is $3.79 + (-.500) = 3.29$.

What you don't know from these results is whether the groups differ from each other. This is useful information in interpreting the results, in order to get a sense of an overall pattern and the essential differences among groups.

You can in fact run regression programs in SAS or STATA with specific options or additional statements to test the differences among the groups in the equation. The test you set up is a difference of means between two groups. You need to see first what the mean of each group is made up of and then create a test of a null hypothesis of no difference across groups.

For example, the mean among the divorced/separated in this equation is

$$a + b_1$$

The mean among the widowed in this equation is

$$a + b_2$$

So the hypothesis of no difference between these groups is

$$H_o: (a + b_1) - (a + b_2) = 0$$

When you perform the subtraction above, the intercepts cancel, resulting in

$$H_o: b_1 - b_2 = 0$$

So you can set up a difference of means test for pairs of groups by just subtracting the two coefficients. This is possible because each is a difference from the same baseline. An example of how that works is this: If the mean in the reference group is 10, the mean in Group 1 is 15, and the mean in Group 2 is 12, then the difference between Group 1 and the reference is 5, and the difference between Group 2 and the reference is 2. So the difference between has to be $15 - 12 = 5 - 2 = 3$. Results for F-tests of mean differences for all six pairs of groups here are shown in Table 1.20, using SAS output. This output names the test using a short-form of the comparison—for example, "divvwid" is divorced versus widowed.

TABLE 1.20 ● POST-HOC TESTS FOR DIFFERENCES AMONG GROUPS

1.

Test divvwid Results for Dependent Variable closetrust2				
Source	**DF**	**Mean Square**	***F* Value**	**Pr > F**
Numerator	1	14.51279	11.23	0.0008
Denominator	4237	1.29267		

2.

Test divvnmar Results for Dependent Variable closetrust2				
Source	**DF**	**Mean Square**	***F* Value**	**Pr > F**
Numerator	1	3.50184	2.71	0.0999
Denominator	4237	1.29267		

3.

Test divvcoh Results for Dependent Variable closetrust2				
Source	**DF**	**Mean Square**	***F* Value**	**Pr > F**
Numerator	1	31.76358	1.50	0.2214
Denominator	4237	1.29267		

4.

Test widvnmar Results for Dependent Variable closetrust2				
Source	**DF**	**Mean Square**	***F* Value**	**Pr > F**
Numerator	1	1.93369	1.50	0.2214
Denominator	4237	1.29267		

5.

Test widvcoh Results for Dependent Variable closetrust2				
Source	DF	Mean Square	F Value	Pr > F
Numerator	1	11.03322	8.54	0.0035
Denominator	4237	1.29267		

6.

Test nmarvcoh Results for Dependent Variable closetrust2				
Source	DF	Mean Square	F Value	Pr > F
Numerator	1	15.76829	12.20	0.0005
Denominator	4237	1.29267		

The first test shows that the divorced (−.50) are significantly lower on trusting relationships compared to the widowed (−.26). However, they are not significantly different from the never married (Test 2). As would be expected given the nonsignificant difference between cohabitors and the married, the divorced are also lower in trusting relations compared to cohabitors (Test 3). The widowed are not different from the never married (Test 4, note that the never married are between the divorced and the widowed in trusting relations) and also lower than cohabitors (Test 5), as are the never married (Test 6).

The picture that emerges is this: Groups that have no live-in partner express lower levels of trusting relationships in their life. But there is a further distinction among those without a partner, specifically when previous relationships have ended naturally or "successfully," as in the death of a spouse, relative to those who have been divorced. This puts the widowed in-between the other nonmarried groups and the partnered groups.

1.9.4 One-Way Analysis of Variance

The one-way analysis of variance refers to a simple test for any group differences in the equation. This is equivalent to the test in multiple regression for "any" effect of at least one independent variable.

The test is the significance of the R^2 in the equation: if the R^2 is significant, this could only occur because there are significant differences among the groups somewhere in the equation.

The F-test is structured as follows:

$$F = \frac{R^2 / k}{(1 - R^2) / N - k - 1}$$

testing the null hypothesis for k groups in the equation

$$H_0: b_1 = \ldots = b_k = 0$$

against an alternative that at least one group differs from one other

$$H_A: b_1 \neq \ldots \neq b_k \neq 0$$

This test is printed in the earlier regression output in the "Analysis of Variance" table. Here the F value is 34.62, with 4 degrees of freedom, significant at the .0001 level. Thus the one-way analysis of variance overall test suggests there are group differences here.

In fact, this test should be conducted first ***before*** you conduct any tests comparing specific pairs of groups. We do not take the time or space here to review the problem of cumulative Type I error, mainly because this is a large topic, also more suited to experimental data. However, we do advocate *only* comparing groups as suggested by specific hypotheses you are testing, instead of all groups.

Concluding Words

This chapter travels a considerable distance in relatively few pages. Consistent with the idea that this book is more for second courses, this chapter is intended as a review, a tune-up, more than an initial introduction. However, we did include important detail at a number of points, which will be useful as reference points for the material in the chapters ahead.

Our discussion started with a formal definition of an association between variables using probability theory. This was illustrated first using a cross-tabulation of two categorical variables. We introduced the correlation as a measure of association, in steps, to demonstrate the structure of a measure of association for more continuous variables.

The regression model was introduced in steps as well, starting with the structure of the bivariate regression model and adding to that model for the rest of the chapter. There are a number of important introductory concepts here: The Least Squares Criterion for where to fit the line through a scatter of points, unstandardized versus standardized coefficients, and the partitioning of variance. *All* of these concepts will be invoked as we move forward.

Multiple regression was introduced, initially, as a way of accounting for confounding—overlap—between different independent variables. In this demonstration, we see what it means to "control for," or " account for," or "adjust for," confounding among variables. Our example using the gender pay gap illustrates a very important feature of control variables that will come up in later chapters: For a control variable to be relevant, it must be related to *both* the focal independent variable (gender) and the outcome (pay). Usually we are trying to test the focal association at issue, so the most threatening control variables are also those whose patterns of association are consistent with the overall focal association. For example, women had fewer total years of work, and fewer years was related to lower pay. As a result, total years working partially accounted for the bivariate gender difference.

Finally, we introduced dummy variables as a special kind of variable in regression, designed to handle variables that designate membership in different groups.

At this point, all we have is the standard linear ordinary least squares regression model. The structure of it is additive—meaning that different variables push or pull *Y* up or down, but independently—and it is linear—meaning that independent variables have the *same* effect across all levels—and it is restricted to outcomes that are quasi- to completely continuous. ***All of these assumptions will be modified in the chapters ahead.*** As we will eventually see, the regression model is quite flexible, allowing a broader range of representation of the predominant ideas and styles of thinking in the social sciences than is possible using only the additive, linear model.

Generalizations of Regression: A Graphical Road Map

Here is a graphical overview of the variations of the basic multiple regression model we will consider in the chapters ahead.

The linear additive model . . . the starting point

$$Y = a + b_1X_1 + b_2X_2 + e$$

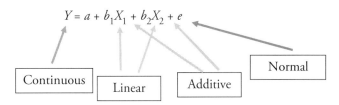

| Continuous | Linear | Additive | Normal |

Including conditional multiplicative effects . . . interactions

$$Y = a + b_1X_1 + b_2X_2 + b_3(X_1 \cdot X_2) + e$$

Not Additive

Including nonlinearity . . . multiple forms possible

$$Y = a + b_1X_1 + b_2X_2 + b_3X_1^2 + e$$

$$Y = a + b_1X_1 + b_2\ln(X_2) + e$$

Not Linear

Including categorical outcomes . . . logistic

$$\ln \text{ odds } Y = a + b_1X_1 + b_2X_2 + e$$

Categorical: 1 / 0

Where Odds $= \dfrac{\Pr(Y = 1)}{1 - \Pr(Y = 1)}$

Including nonnormal outcomes and errors (Poisson)

$$\ln Y = a + b_1X_1 + b_2X_2 + e$$

Nonnormal

Practice Questions

1. ***Bivariate Regression and Correlation***

   The output below from SAS shows the descriptive statistics and covariance for two variables from the 2015 Canadian General Social Survey (Statistics Canada, 2017):

- **overallhealth** is an index of overall physical and mental health, varying from 0 to 30.
- **hhincome** is the household's income in thousands of dollars.
  Table 1.A shows the means and standard deviations of each variable.

Table 1.A Means and Standard Deviations

Simple Statistics							
Variable	N	Mean	Std Dev	Sum	Minimum	Maximum	Label
overallhealth	22832	15.58368	2.94471	355807	0	30.00000	Overall health: Index of health, mental health, and well-being
hhincome	22832	72.91137	46.10670	1664713	0	150.00000	Household income

Table 1.B shows the variances and covariance of the two variables. The variances are in the diagonal (the cells in Row 1, Column 1, and Row 2, Column 2), and the covariance is the off-diagonal. Notice that the covariance is the same in Cells 1,2 and 2,1, as it should be.

Table 1.B Variances and Covariance

Covariance Matrix, DF = 22831		
	overallhealth	hhincome
overallhealth	8.671341	24.800833
hhincome	24.800833	2125.827490

a.   Using the information in these tables, calculate the bivariate regression equation showing the effect of household income (the independent variable) on overall health (the dependent variable), including the intercept a and the bivariate regression coefficient b.

b.   Transform the unstandardized b you have calculated to a standardized β.

2.   Dummy Variables

Results of a dummy variable regression in SAS are shown in Table 1.C. The results show differences in pride in Canada by household living arrangements (from the definition provided in Q5): "(*canadaproud*), a scale of pride in Canada that varies from 20 to 100. The living arrangements variable classified people into five categories, and these were used to develop dummy variables for four of these categories. **The reference group is living alone**.

There are four dummy variables in the regression:

- **livespouse**:   = 1 if living with spouse only; 0 otherwise
- **livenuclearfam**: = 1 if living with spouse and children; 0 otherwise
- **liveparent**:   = 1 if living with parents; 0 otherwise
- **liveother**:   = 1 if other arrangement; 0 otherwise

Table 1.C Regression Results in SAS

Analysis of Variance					
Source	DF	Sum of Squares	Mean Square	F Value	Pr > F
Model	4	44832	11208	71.87	<.0001
Error	27402	4273432	155.95330		
Corrected Total	27406	4318264			

Root MSE	12.48813	R-Square	0.0104
Dependent Mean	76.24155	Adj R-Sq	0.0102
Coeff Var	16.37969		

Parameter Estimates

Variable	Label	DF	Parameter Estimate	Standard Error	t Value	Pr > |t|
Intercept	Intercept	1	74.87337	0.15609	479.68	<.0001
livespouse	Live with Spouse Only	1	0.48689	0.21190	2.30	0.0216
livenuclearfam	Live with Spouse and Children	1	2.15710	0.20704	10.42	<.0001
liveparent	Live with one or two parents	1	3.78327	0.25753	14.69	<.0001
liveother	Live with others	1	1.22804	0.38425	3.20	0.0014

a. What is the result of the one-way analysis of variance test for any differences among these groups? (No calculations necessary; available in output).

b. What is the mean level of pride in Canada of people who live with a spouse and children?

c. Calculate the mean *difference* in pride in Canada between people who live with a spouse and children and people who live with a spouse only.

3. **Multiple Regression with Dummy Variables**

This is output from a regression of depression at Wave 2 of the National Survey of Families and Households (NSFH) on four variables: education, age, a sex dummy variable, and welfare status in childhood, also a dummy, standing for whether the respondent's parents were on welfare when they were growing up.

Table 1.D Regression of Depression on Education, Age, Sex, and Welfare Status in Childhood

Number of Observations Read	4600
Number of Observations Used	4252
Number of Observations with Missing Values	348

Analysis of Variance

Source	DF	Sum of Squares	Mean Square	F Value	Pr > F
Model	4	61418	15354	68.55	<.0001
Error	4247	951342	224.00330		
Corrected Total	4251	1012760			

Root MSE	14.96674	R-Square	0.0606
Dependent Mean	13.22474	Adj R-Sq	0.0598
Coeff Var	113.17232		

Parameter Estimates

Variable	DF	Parameter Estimate	Standard Error	t Value	Pr > |t|
Intercept	1	28.73657	1.72143	16.69	<.0001
education2	1	−0.91151	0.08780	−10.38	<.0001
age2	1	−0.12839	0.01951	−6.58	<.0001
female	1	3.92017	0.48401	8.10	<.0001
welfare	1	4.35591	0.82259	5.30	<.0001

The effect of every variable here is significant. Answer these questions:

a. What is the total difference in depression between a female who grew up in a family on welfare versus a male who did not?
b. What is the difference between a male who grew up on welfare and a female who did not?
c. Work out the difference between a person with 12 years of education who is 40 years old and someone with 16 years of education who is 60 years old.

4. Multiple Regression—with Dummy Variables

The multiple regression results below are from the National Longitudinal Survey of Youth in the United States. The dependent variable here is **level of education,** measured in **years.** In this sample, it varies from 0 to 20 years. The N (sample size) in this regression is 4,737.

The independent variables in the output below are

- **momed**: The respondent's mother's education, in years.
- **stablepov100**: A dummy variable = 1 if the person lived in a household in adolescence consistently below the poverty line; 0 otherwise.
- **unstablepov100**: A dummy variable = 1 if the person lived in a household in adolescence that was sometimes below, sometimes above the poverty line; 0 otherwise.
- **earlyMHcv**: This is an index of emotional and behavioral problems in early adolescence. It varies from 0 problems to 15 problems.
- **asvab**: This is the person's percentile rank on a national achievement test given in early high school. Here it is measured in 10% increases, so it varies from 0 to 10. The mean is 4.5, reflecting the 45th percentile on this test.
- **female**: A dummy variable = 1 if female and = 0 if male.
- **Black**: A dummy variable = 1 if the respondent identifies as African American and = 0 otherwise.
- **Hispanic**: A dummy variable = 1 if the respondent identifies as Hispanic and = 0 otherwise.

The reference group for the poverty dummy variables is "no poverty," and the reference group for the two race dummy variables is "non-Hispanic White."

Results are shown in the following table from SAS: Two models are shown: The second model adds the effects of poverty background to the first model (i.e., stablepov100 and unstablepov100).

Table 1.E Without Poverty

Root MSE	2.10799	R-Square	0.3401
Dependent Mean	12.93878	Adj R-Sq	0.3393
Coeff Var	16.29201		

Parameter Estimates					
Variable	DF	Parameter Estimate	Standard Error	t Value	Pr > |t|
Intercept	1	9.60066	0.14919	64.35	<.0001
momed	1	0.07750	0.00934	8.29	<.0001
earlyMHcv	1	−0.04787	0.01253	−3.82	0.0001
asvab	1	0.46205	0.01201	38.49	<.0001
female	1	0.58104	0.06245	9.30	<.0001
black	1	0.14741	0.08077	1.83	0.0681
Hispanic	1	−0.03119	0.08933	−0.35	0.7270

Table 1.F With Poverty

Root MSE	2.09231	R-Square	0.3501
Dependent Mean	12.93878	Adj R-Sq	0.3490
Coeff Var	16.17086		

Parameter Estimates					
Variable	DF	Parameter Estimate	Standard Error	t Value	Pr > |t|
Intercept	1	9.84612	0.15212	64.73	<.0001
momed	1	0.07136	0.00936	7.62	<.0001
stablepov100	1	−2.04608	0.41475	−4.93	<.0001
unstablepov100	1	−0.60992	0.08387	−7.27	<.0001
earlyMHcv	1	−0.04560	0.01244	−3.66	0.0003
asvab	1	0.44264	0.01214	36.47	<.0001
female	1	0.59656	0.06203	9.62	<.0001
black	1	0.22988	0.08082	2.84	0.0045
Hispanic	1	0.03816	0.08905	0.43	0.6683

a. Write out the F-test you would use to test the overall effect of childhood poverty in Model 2. Plug the relevant values into this formula, and do the calculation. Is the effect of poverty significant?

b. Using Model 2, what is the mean level of education among White males who did not grow up in poverty, had no mental health problems in adolescence, had a mother who graduated high school (12 years), and scored at the 50th percentile on the Asvab test (asvab = 5)?

c. Using Model 2 again, what is the predicted difference in education between Black females and White males? Note, you only need to state the difference, not the actual levels of each, so you can ignore other variables not involved in this comparison.

5. *Multiple Regression*

The multiple regression results in Table 1.G are from the Canadian General Social Survey in 2015 (Statistics Canada, 2017), restricted to the provinces of Quebec and Ontario.

The dependent variable here is pride in Canada *(canadaproud)*, a scale of pride in Canada that varies from 20 to 100.

The independent variables in the output are

- **educyrs**: Education in years
- **female**: A dummy variable = 1 for female and 0 for male
- **provqc**: A dummy variable = 1 if the respondent lived in Quebec and = 0 if Ontario
- **employed**: A dummy variable = 1 if working now and = 0 otherwise
- **fedvote**: A dummy variable = 1 if the person voted in the last federal election and = 0 if they did not vote
- **freqnews**: Frequency of following the news in the last week, in days
- **nrcivilgroups**: Number of civil participation groups the respondent belongs to

TABLE 1.G ● PREDICTING PRIDE IN CANADA IN A MULTIPLE REGRESSION

Parameter Estimates						
Variable	Label	DF	Parameter Estimate	Standard Error	t Value	Pr > |t|
Intercept	Intercept	1	80.86589	0.66115	122.31	<.0001
educyrs	Years of Education of Respondent	1	−0.13912	0.04740	−2.93	0.0033
female	Female =1, Male=0	1	−0.80933	0.22926	−3.53	0.0004
provqc	Province of residence: Quebec	1	−10.21617	0.23884	−42.77	<.0001
employed	Employed last week?	1	−0.57010	0.24150	−2.36	0.0183
fedvote	Voted in last federal election?	1	−0.52063	0.26723	−1.95	0.0514
freqnews	Frequency of following news and current affairs - Week	1	0.22482	0.04460	5.04	<.0001
nrcivilgroups	Civil Society Participation - Number of Groups - past 12 months	1	−0.22978	0.06828	−3.37	0.0008

a. According to the results, does education increase or decrease pride in Canada or have no effect?

b. If you follow the news every day (7 days a week), how much would this increase pride in Canada, according to the results?

c. Given a respondent who is female, lives in Quebec, and does not work, what is the total **difference** in pride in Canada compared to an employed male living in Ontario?

d. According to the results, who has the greater pride in Canada, a working person who voted in the last election or a nonworking person who did not vote?

6. *Multiple Regression*

   The multiple regression results below are from the Canadian Quality of Life Panel Survey conducted between 1977 and 1981. The variables in the output are following.

   The dependent variable is
   LQ16: life satisfaction (from 1 to 11)

The independent variables are

- **NCHILD:**   = Number of children living in the household
- **ONTARIO:**   = 1 if from Ontario, 0 otherwise (dummy)
- **FEMALE:**   = 1 if female; 0 if male (dummy)
- **HLTHPROB:** = 1 if person reports a chronic health problem, 0 otherwise (dummy)
- **Q158:**   Income, measured in $10,000 increments
- **EMPLOY77:** = 1 if working, 0 if not working (dummy)

The output is from SPSS but is essentially similar to SAS output:

- *B* = unstandardized coefficient (*b*);
- BETA = the standardized coefficient (β);
- CONSTANT = the intercept (a).
- SIG T = two-tailed significance of B.

Regression Output

```
---------------------------- VARIABLES IN THE EQUATION ----------------------------
```

VARIABLE	B	SE B	BETA	T	SIG T
NCHILD	−.099524	.036070	−.078042	−2.759	.0059
ONTARIO	−.277151	.100515	−.075744	−2.757	.0059
FEMALE	.113122	.105134	.031733	1.076	.2821
HLTHPROB	−.379606	.111195	−.094136	−3.414	.0007
Q158 *(income)*	.056744	.014720	.113645	3.855	.0001
EMPLOY77	.256317	.111073	.072146	2.308	.0212
(CONSTANT)	8.396110	.174691		48.063	.0000

a. Only one variable here does not have a significant effect on life satisfaction. What variable is that?

b. Do children in the household increase or decrease life satisfaction?

c. How much would a $20,000 increase in income increase life satisfaction, according to these results?

d. What is the *difference* in life satisfaction between an employed person in Quebec and an unemployed person in Ontario?

GENERALIZATIONS OF REGRESSION 1

Testing and Interpreting Interactions

The model of the previous chapter is **additive** in the sense that it envisions the effects of variables as *independently* and cumulatively adding to (or subtracting from) the outcome. Each variable operates independently because the effect of each X applies at all levels of other (X) variables.

The first limitation we focus on in this chapter is this issue of additivity. Imagine how often you hear someone say in response to generalizations: "Not necessarily. It depends." That hypothesis expresses the prevalence of *conditional* effects in our thinking. In other words, whether X_1 affects Y depends on the level of another variable X_2. These are called *interactions*, in regression model terms. **Interactions express the possibility that the effect of a particular X changes depending on the level of some other X in the equation**.

2.1 INTERACTIONS IN MULTIPLE REGRESSION

Interaction Defined. An interaction exists when the ***effect*** of a chosen focal variable X *changes* depending on the level (or category) of a second variable (here called Z to distinguish roles). Interactions are expressed in regression equations by forming multiplicative terms between X and Z, such as $X \cdot Z$. As shown below, this term expresses the possibility that the effect of each variable changes depending on the level of the other.

Here is an example of an equation with an interaction between X and Z:

$$Y_i = a + b_1 X_i + b_2 Z_i + b_3 (X_i \cdot Z_i) + e_i$$

Going forward, we will not show the "i" subscript for individual observations in these equations, unless the method we discuss demands a modification. In this definition, note that the effect of X now appears twice in a model—on its own and as part of a variable in which X is multiplied by Z. Now the effect of X is captured collectively by both variables—*and only by both variables*—because this effect changes depending on the level of Z. The b for the multiplicative variable here literally asks, Will the effect of X change across levels of Z (*and vice-versa if we choose to make Z the focal variable*)?

2.1.0.1 Importance of Interactions

We begin with interactions in regression because of their prevalence in our theorizing, the flexibility they introduce into regression, and the importance of avoiding the over-generalization of findings. Note these points about the ubiquity of interactions in theory, in qualitative sociology, and across a range of techniques and disciplines:

- Interactions are predicted whenever theories express historical, spatial, or cultural boundaries or social conditions that make the theory salient.

- Historical explanations commonly use interactional theorizing: Y happened only because both X and Z were present.

- Theories and qualitative perspectives, such as intersectionality, often pose the necessity of multiple conditions for an outcome to occur. If the effect of sex depends on race and class and cannot be discussed on its own, this *is* an interaction.

- Interactions take into account sources of individual identifiers as *modifiers* of the relevance of variables we study and thus help avoid overgeneralization.

- Many techniques rely on interactions for the testing of basic and important hypotheses about generalizing across societies, groups within societies, or over time.

- Interactions are the ***only*** way to test the uniqueness of specific effects in one group—for example, women, immigrants, visible minorities—relative to others. One-group studies cannot really do this.

- The study of separate subgroups (men vs. women, Black vs. White, etc.) *directly implies that an interaction exists for some variable.* You should always test an interaction ***before*** implying different effects in subgroups. In other words, you should not simply set up analyses in separate subgroups presumptively—it leads to the impression of uniqueness without testing it.

On the last point, we take the position throughout, following prevailing wisdom, that testing interactions in a full sample is preferable to splitting a sample into subgroups in order to compare coefficients across samples—for a list of reasons, see Williams (2015). There are technical issues to consider, such as statistical power to detect differences in the effect of X, but we emphasize an additional issue: Testing interactions in a single equation in a full sample encourages a theoretical focus on the combined effects of specific variables rather than the entire model while also allowing access to all of the information available in an analysis of split sub-samples. This last point may not be widely realized, and thus we focus on *completely* interpreting interactions in this chapter.

2.1.1 Two-Way Interactions Between Continuous and Categorical Variables

We begin with a classic case: The effect of a continuous variable X varies across categories of a categorical variable standing for different groups (here denoted by Z)—for example, race/ethnicity, gender, employment status, nativity, religion, occupation, marital status, etcetera.

Typically, these variables are coded originally as a single categorical variable with arbitrary numerical codes to make distinctions among groups. The ordering of the numbers means nothing. For example, in the simplified example below, race/ethnicity is assumed to be coded 1 = Black, 2 = Hispanic, and 3 = White. There is no ordering implied by these numbers.

To treat this categorical variable in an interaction, you develop a set of dummy variables standing for membership in each of the groups contained in the categorical variable—following the procedures of the previous chapter. Ordinal variables have ordering but not equal distance among categories, and as a result, they usually have to be turned into sets of dummy variables as well.

2.1.1.1 Example: The Long-Term Effects of Education on Personal Income

Suppose we are interested in predicting current personal income, coded in thousands of dollars. This is the dependent variable in this example.

We are interested in the detection of discrimination effects by racial / ethnic categories. One manifestation of discrimination may be the lower average education of minority groups, but another may be that the income *returns* to education for minority groups are lower than for the White majority. Translated, this hypothesis implies an interaction between education and racial group in predicting income, such that the largest impact of education occurs among Whites, and we see a significantly reduced impact among minorities.

To make the example more realistic, we also control for *years in the current job*, since job seniority will also predict current income.

There are three independent variables:

1. **R: race**, Black / Hispanic / White (other groups are excluded from the analysis)

2. **E: education,** in years

3. **S: job seniority,** years in current job

We need to create dummy variables to represent the racial categories. Following the discussion in Chapter 1, the most general rules for creating dummy variables here are:

1. For a categorical variable with k categories, you need to form $k - 1$ dummy variables to stand for differences among all k groups. One group is left out and is known as the reference group or category.

2. Choose a reference group that makes interpretation easier: This could be the highest or lowest group on the dependent variable or a natural comparison group (e.g., non-employed for employment status, native-born for immigration status) or a middle group standing for normal, equitable, or usual. It is up to you as the analyst.

In this case, we will create two dummy variables for race. Table 2.1 shows the coding of the original race variable and the two dummy variables derived, with B for Black, and H for Hispanic. White is the reference category.

TABLE 2.1 ● CODING RACE/ ETHNICITY INTO DUMMY VARIABLES			
		Dummy Variables	
	Race Coding	**B**	**H**
Black	1	1	0
Hispanic	2	0	1
White	3	0	0

In this coding scheme, you will actually "see" variables for Black and Hispanic, but not "White." Each variables is coded = 1 to stand for that group and 0 for all other groups. When considered as a group, each variable expresses the mean difference on Y of that group versus the reference group, in this case, Whites.

There are a number of questions that we could ask in this analysis. First we can test the predicted interaction by forming interaction terms between the continuous variable E and each of the dummy variables, specifically $E \bullet B$ and $E \bullet H$. We need to include *both* terms in the regression at once to test the *overall* interaction between education and race. This is not a small issue: It is important to test the overall interaction *first* before interpreting specific terms in the interaction involving specific groups. You cannot just search for a significant term in the overall interaction and discuss this as a "significant" interaction.

In addition, if the interaction is not significant, implying that education has the same effect on income in all three groups, we would also want to know if there are general group differences in income controlling for level of education—another form of a discrimination effect.

Note something important about interactions: We are focusing on the *impact* of X and how it changes, not the average difference in X across the groups.

2.1.2 Procedure for Testing an Interaction

1. Begin with a basic additive model for the effects of education, race, and job seniority. This includes **E, B, H,** and **S**

$$\hat{Y} = a + b_1 E + b_2 B + b_3 H + b_4 S \tag{1}$$

2. In a second model, add *both* two-way interaction terms for education and race:

$$\hat{Y} = a + b_1 E + b_2 B + b_3 H + b_4 S + b_5 (E \cdot B) + b_6 (E \cdot H) \tag{2}$$

As pointed out above, to specify the overall interaction completely, you need to multiply the continuous variable by *each* of the dummy variables in the equation representing the underlying categorical variable.

To test the current interaction, you need to assess the R^2 increase in Model 2 relative to Model 1 with an *F*-test. If the increase in R^2 is significant, retain and interpret model (2). If not, interpret Model 1. This test assesses whether unique explained variance in Y is added to the equation by the interactions, because Model 1 is "nested" in Model 2, and so the difference in R^2 can only reflect the impact of the added interaction terms.

We estimate these models in the National Survey of Families and Households. The F-test you use here is shown below, with subscripts standing for the model. The "k" in this formula refers to the number of independent variables in each model.

$$F = \frac{R^2_{(2)} - R^2_{(1)} / k_2 - k_1}{1 - R^2_{(2)} / N - k_2 - 1} \text{ with } k_2 - k_1 \text{ and } N - k_2 - 1 \text{ df}$$

The R^2 in Model 2 is .2285. The R^2 in Model 1 is .2218. k_2 is the number of independent variables in Model 2 (6). k_1 is the number of independent variables in Model 1 (4). and the sample size is 5472. The F value we calculate is

$$F = \frac{(.2285 - .2218)/2}{(1 - .2285)/5472 - 6 - 1} = 23.73 \text{ with 2 and 5465 df}$$

This is significant beyond the .0001 level; thus the interaction between education and race is significant. The following estimates are found for Model 2.

$$\hat{Y} = -26.576 + 3.142E + 14.15B + 19.67H + .615S - 1.39(E \cdot B) - 1.76(E \cdot H)$$

When there are interactions in the equation, you cannot interpret the so-called "main effects" of any of the variables involved in the interaction in the way you usually would. For example, as we shall see, education does not generally increase income by 3.142 thousand dollars per year of education, as the coefficient suggests. This effect pertains to *only one of the three racial categories—the reference group of Whites.*

To interpret interactions properly, you need to analyze the equation to derive the specific effects of education in each of the three groups. To do this, plug values into the equation standing for each of the three groups and solve for the effect of the continuous variable *E*.

Seniority is a control variable in this equation that is extraneous to the interaction and does not affect it. Thus we can set it to its mean value throughout our calculations so that it does not affect our interpretation. This mean can be found from the descriptive statistics for the regression (here it is 13.98). Note that this will adjust the intercept to a new value that will apply throughout the calculations. The mean value for **S** is substituted in each of the calculations in Table 2.2.

TABLE 2.2 ● DERIVING SUBGROUP SLOPES IN A TWO-WAY INTERACTION			
Group	**B**	**H**	**Deriving Subgroup Equations from** $\hat{Y} = a + b_1E + b_2B + b_3H + b_4S + b_5(E \cdot B) + b_6(E \cdot H)$
White	0	0	$\hat{Y} = a + b_1E + b_20 + b_30 + b_4(13.98) + b_5(E \cdot 0) + b_6(E \cdot 0)$ $\hat{y} = a + b_4(13.98) + b_1E$ Substituting coefficients and simplifying: $\hat{y} = -26.576 + .615(13.98) + 3.142E$ $\hat{y} = -17.97 + 3.142E$
Black	1	0	$\hat{Y} = a + b_1E + b_21 + b_30 + b_4(13.98) + b_5(E \cdot 1) + b_6(E \cdot 0)$ $\hat{y} = a + b_1E + b_2 + b_4(13.98) + b_5E$ $= (a + b_2 + b_4(13.98)) + (b_1 + b_5)E$ Substituting and simplifying: $\hat{y} = (-26.576 + 14.15 + .615(13.98)) + (3.142 - 1.39)E$ $\hat{y} = -3.828 + 1.752E$
Hispanic	0	1	$\hat{Y} = a + b_1E + b_20 + b_31 + b_4(13.98) + b_5(E \cdot 0) + b_6(E \cdot 1)$ $\hat{y} = a + b_1E + b_3 + b_4(13.98) + b_6E$ $= (a + b_3 + b_4(13.98)) + (b_1 + b_6)E$ Substituting and simplifying: $\hat{y} = (-26.576 + 19.67 + .615(13.98)) + (3.142 - 1.76)E$ $\hat{y} = 1.696 + 1.386E$

Follow this procedure to substitute values: (a) substitute values for each group in the interaction equation in turn and remove all terms multiplied by zero; (b) collect terms multiplying the same variable; (c) substitute actual coefficients from the results and calculate the slope for **E** in each group and the adjusted intercept in each group. Note that every term will have one of two roles: an adjustment to the slope of **E** or an adjustment to the intercept in that group.

If you just look at the coefficients for the effects of education, you can see the reduced impact of education among Blacks and Hispanics. Whites receive about $3,142 per year of education, Blacks receive just $1,752, and Hispanics receive even less, about $1,386 on average.

Each equation could be graphed to show the differences in effects, as shown in Figure 2.1.

FIGURE 2.1 ⬡ A TWO-WAY INTERACTION BETWEEN EDUCATION AND RACE

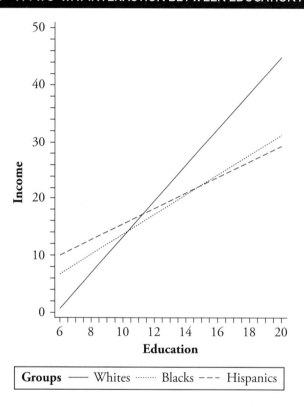

Groups —— Whites ⋯⋯ Blacks – – – Hispanics

Education has its strongest impact on eventual income among Whites, and both Blacks and Hispanics receive significantly lower returns to education. This can also be shown by the results from the regression using SAS output in Table 2.3.

TABLE 2.3 ⬡ REGRESSION RESULTS FOR THE TWO-WAY INTERACTION

Variable	Label	DF	Parameter Estimate	Standard Error	t Value	Pr > |t|
Intercept	Intercept	1	−26.57613	1.60333	−16.58	<.0001
EDUCAT	EDUCATIONAL LEVEL	1	3.14220	0.11173	28.12	<.0001
black		1	14.14565	4.24130	3.34	0.0009
hisp		1	19.67001	3.49912	5.62	<.0001
yrscurrjob		1	0.61531	0.02315	26.58	<.0001
blackxeduc		1	−1.39002	0.32659	−4.26	<.0001
hispxeduc		1	−1.75622	0.29772	−5.90	<.0001

Where

Black = a dummy variable for Black

hisp = a dummy variable for Hispanic

yrscurrjob = number of years in the current job

EDUCAT = number of years of education

blackxeduc = Black *x* educat

hispxeduc = hisp *x* educat

For those of you who are starting with this chapter rather than the review in Chapter 1, this is a typical regression output table. The column labeled "Parameter Estimate" lists the *b*'s (coefficients), with standard errors, the *t*-value, and a **two-tailed** probability under the null. *If you want a probability for a one-tailed test, divide this probability by two.*

Note that the interaction terms for "blackxeduc" and "hispxeduc," formed by multiplying each dummy variable by education, are each significant. These individual tests show the significance of the difference in the effect of education for Blacks versus Whites and Hispanics versus Whites, respectively. The equation will always show you **some** of the differences in impact among groups, but it never can show you all because you cannot see the difference between groups in the equation, in this case, Blacks versus Hispanics.

In this example, there is no overall "main effect" of education in the equation: The coefficient for the effect of education in the equation only shows the *marginal* effect among Whites, the reference group. If you interpret this as the overall effect of education, you are misled. In general, the marginal effect of *X* in an equation including interactions with other variables will always be **the effect of X when the other variables it interacts with equal zero.**

For reference going forward, following is the SAS program that was used to produce these results:

```
proc reg data=temp simple;
model rtotinc=  educat black hisp yrscurrjob;
model rtotinc=  educat black hisp yrscurrjob blackxeduc hispxeduc;
interaction:    test blackxeduc=hispxeduc=0;
blvshisp:       test blackxeduc-hispxeduc=0;
weight weight;
run;
```

There are generally two phases to a SAS program: a DATA step and a PROC step. The DATA step is used to call in variables from a data set and create new variables or alter the coding of existing variables. This step prepares the variables you use in the analysis. In the appendix to this chapter, we present both the SAS and the STATA code that can be used to generate the variables used in this analysis from the raw data. That code is broadly annotated to indicate the functions of various statements.

What you see above is the PROC step, invoked to run the SAS REG procedure. The "data" keyword states the name of the data set to analyze—here this is a temporary data set created in a previous DATA step called "temp." The "simple" keyword asks for descriptive statistics with the output (not shown). Each SAS statement ends with a semicolon.

MODEL statements specify different regression models to be estimated. The first model here is "nested" in the second model. Note the two TEST statements following the model statements. These statements can be inserted after any specific regression model to conduct many types of post-hoc tests. Here there are two: The first tests the null hypothesis that both of the interaction terms are zero—*this test is equivalent to the R^2 test mentioned above*—and the second is a specific test for the difference in the effect of education (i.e., the slopes) among Blacks versus Hispanics. You use the variable names from the model to refer to the coefficients. The logic of the first test is that if there is no interaction, then all of the interaction terms should be zero. The second test is important. As noted above, the results can only show you the difference in the slopes of groups relative to the reference group *but not with respect to each other.* Since each interaction b is the difference in the effect of education between each group in the equation and Whites, then the slope difference between those groups must be the difference between their coefficients.

In this example, the effect of education among Whites is $b = 3.142$. The effect among Blacks is 1.39 lower than that, and the effect among Hispanics is 1.76 lower than that. Thus the difference in the slopes for Blacks versus Hispanics has to be $-1.39 - (-1.76) = .37$, or $b_5 - b_6$, because their coefficients are differences from the same reference point.

This point can be more formally demonstrated as follows. You can always design tests to compare slopes in different groups once you have worked out the coefficients from the equation that contribute to each slope, as in Table 2.2.

For example, we know the following:

The effect of education among Blacks is $(b_1 + b_5)E$.

The effect of education among Hispanics is $(b_1 + b_6)E$.

The null hypothesis of "no difference" in effect between Blacks and Hispanics is

$$H_0 : b_1 + b_5 = b_1 + b_6$$

which is equal to

$$(b_1 + b_5) - (b_1 + b_6) = 0$$
$$b_1 + b_5 - b_1 - b_6 = 0$$
$$b_5 - b_6 = 0$$

This is a simple example, but in the case of three-way interactions, the specific components of the slope in each group are more complex. Table 2.4 shows the output from the "interaction" test in SAS.

An F value of 23.60, $p < .0001$ with degrees of freedom of 2 and 5568, suggests that there is a strong significant difference between the effect of education on income by racial groups.

TABLE 2.4 ● TEST OF THE INTERACTION IN PROC REG

Test interaction Results for Dependent Variable rtotinc				
Source	DF	Mean Square	F Value	Pr > F
Numerator	2	8921.78230	23.60	<.0001
Denominator	5568	378.10527		

However, the test of the differences between the slopes for Blacks versus Hispanics is not significant, as shown in the output by the test in Table 2.5.

In other words, our results imply that Blacks and Hispanics suffer a similar level of disadvantage relative to Whites in terms of returns to education.

TABLE 2.5 ● TEST OF THE DIFFERENCE IN THE EFFECT OF EDUCATION AMONG BLACKS VERSUS HISPANICS

Test blvhisp Results for Dependent Variable rtotinc				
Source	DF	Mean Square	F Value	Pr > F
Numerator	1	264.25945	0.70	0.4032
Denominator	5568	378.10527		

The regression results in Table 2.3 only show us *differences in effects,* not the actual slopes within the groups involved. Table 2.2 shows the manual way to derive the slopes in each group. But there is additional information we may still need. This is often important in specific analyses: Is the effect of X still significant in the other groups, or is the effect even significant in the opposite direction?

PROC GLM in SAS can be used to achieve what is done manually in Table 2.2 by using the "estimate" statement. We ran the same model in GLM using the syntax below to derive both an estimate of the within-group slopes and, importantly, their significance.

```
proc glm data=temp;
model rtotinc=  educat black hisp yrscurrjob blackxeduc hispxeduc;
estimate 'blacks' educat +1 blackxeduc +1 ;
estimate 'hispanics' educat +1 hispxeduc +1;
weight weight;
run;
```

You can see that GLM is set up similarly to REG, with additional *estimate* statements. The first *estimate* statement estimates and tests the significance of the slopes among Blacks by setting the b for "*educat*" to +1 and the b for "*blackxeduc*" to +1. In effect, this adds up the two effects—that is, it operationalizes $(b_1 + b_5)$. The other *estimate* statement does the same for the effect among Hispanics, using a test for $(b_1 + b_6)$. The results are shown in the output from GLM in Table 2.6.

Results show the same slopes as in Table 2.2, plus the fact that each is still significant.

TABLE 2.6 ● POST-HOC TESTS ON EDUCATION SLOPES AMONG BLACKS AND HISPANICS

Parameter	Estimate	Standard Error	t Value	Pr > |t|
blacks	1.75218596	0.30723825	5.70	<.0001
hispanics	1.38598037	0.27615313	5.02	<.0001

2.1.2.1 Syntax for a Two-Way Interaction in STATA

We can produce the same multiplicative model in STATA using the *regress* procedure. The dependent variable is listed first, followed by the independent variables. To estimate the combined impact of race and education on respondent's total income, we enter the interaction variables into the equation, along with all lower-order terms, and control for seniority. The model can be weighted using the *pweight* command followed by the designated weight variable (in this case "weight") in square brackets.

```
regress rtotinc black hisp yrscurrjob educat blackxeduc hispxeduc
[pweight=weight]
```

The *regress* command can also be shortened to *reg.* We can test the significance of the overall interaction in STATA similarly to the statement in SAS, using the following:

```
test blackxeduc=hispxeduc=0


 ( 1)   blackxeduc - hispxeduc = 0
 ( 2)   blackxeduc = 0

       F(  2,   5568) = 23.09
            Prob > F = 0.0000
```

The two-step approach to testing the interaction is noted in the first set of lines, followed by the *F*-value (with designated degrees of freedom) and the probability under the null.

We can also test for the difference in the effect of education among Blacks versus Hispanics similarly to SAS:

```
test blackxeduc-hispxeduc=0


 (1)   blackxeduc - hispxeduc = 0

       F(  1,   5568) = 1.50
            Prob > F = 0.2201
```

We note that the results of these tests are not exactly the same as in SAS, for reasons we explain later (section 2.2.1). However, the essential results are the same: The interaction is significant, and the difference between the slopes for Blacks versus Hispanics is not significant.

2.1.3 A Simpler Example

In many cases, you will want to test the difference in the effect of some X across just two groups, defined by dichotomies such as gender, work status, nativity, or any other distinction important to the issue of generalizing your results.

It is plausible to expect a two-way interaction between education and gender in the prediction of personal income. The same hypothesis applies here as in the case of race: Women may receive fewer returns to education in terms of job income relative to males.

To test this interaction, we estimate the following model:

$$\hat{Y} = a + b_1 E + b_2 F + b_3 S + b_4 (E \cdot F)$$

Where F is a dummy variable for Female (= 1 for female, = 0 for male). S is job seniority, as before, and *educxfem* in the output is the interaction between education and female. Note there is only one interaction term to be tested. This means we can test for the significance of this interaction using the t test for that term in the regression—it is equivalent to the F-test discussed earlier when only one variable is added to the model.

Estimating this model leads to the results shown in Table 2.7.

TABLE 2.7 ● A TWO-WAY INTERACTION BETWEEN EDUCATION AND GENDER

			Parameter	Standard		
Variable	**Label**	**DF**	**Estimate**	**Error**	**t Value**	**Pr > |t|**
Intercept	Intercept	1	−23.77622	1.62065	−14.67	<.0001
female		1	11.09294	2.57168	4.31	<.0001
yrscurrjob		1	0.54237	0.02274	23.85	<.0001
EDUCAT	EDUCATIONAL LEVEL	1	3.24783	0.11350	28.62	<.0001
educxfem		1	−1.50119	0.18964	−7.92	<.0001

Parameter Estimates

You can see that the interaction is significant, and the resulting estimates are

$$\hat{Y} = -23.77 + 3.25 \cdot E + 11.09 \cdot F + .542 \cdot S - 1.50 \cdot (E \cdot F)$$

What are the subgroup equations for the effect of education that apply to females versus males? To figure this out, substitute 0 for females (signifying males) in the equation and simplify, and then substitute 1 for female into the equation, and simplify.

For males ($F = 0$), the equation is

$$\hat{Y} = -23.77 + 3.25 \cdot E + 11.09 \cdot 0 + .542 \cdot 13.95 - 1.50 \cdot (E \cdot 0)$$
$$= -23.77 + (.542 \cdot 13.95) + 3.25 \cdot E$$
$$= -16.21 + 3.25 \cdot E$$

For females, the equation is

$$\hat{Y} = -23.77 + 3.25 \cdot E + 11.09 \cdot 1 + .542 \cdot 13.95 - 1.50 \cdot (E \cdot 1)$$
$$= -23.77 + 11.09 + (.542 \cdot 13.95) + 3.25 \cdot E - 1.50 \cdot E$$
$$= -5.12 + (3.25 - 1.50) \cdot E$$
$$= -5.12 + 1.75 \cdot E$$

Obviously, women receive a much smaller return for each year of education compared to males— just over half of what males receive. The question is how this combines with the issue of differential returns to race.

2.2 A THREE-WAY INTERACTION BETWEEN EDUCATION, RACE, AND GENDER

The preceding results suggest that both race and gender modify the impact of education. What happens if you consider both simultaneously—as in "race, class, gender"?

The possibility of a three-way interaction here is suggested by this reasoning: The *degree* to which race dampens the effect of education may itself depend on gender. For example, the difference in impact among White men and White women may be *larger* than the difference between minority group men and women. Some may hypothesize the opposite, as in a double jeopardy hypothesis, in which women from racialized groups are doubly disadvantaged. In either case, we have to estimate a three-way interaction to evaluate either possibility.

The three-way model is:

$$\hat{Y} = a + b_1E + b_2B + b_3H + b_4S + b_5F + b_6(E \cdot B) + b_7(E \cdot H) + b_8(E \cdot F)$$
$$+ b_9(B \cdot F) + b_{10}(H \cdot F) + b_{11}(E \cdot B \cdot F) + b_{12}(E \cdot H \cdot F)$$

where as before $F = 1$ for female and 0 for male. You must include a test for all two-way interactions first, in order to isolate—that is, partition, the three-way effect. This is an important feature of this approach: One only attributes importance to a three-way contingency after allowing for all of the combinations of two-way contingencies.

The previous two-way model would be:

$$\hat{Y} = a + b_1E + b_2B + b_3H + b_4S + b_5F + b_6(E \cdot B) + b_7(E \cdot H)$$
$$+ b_8(E \cdot F) + b_9(B \cdot F) + b_{10}(H \cdot F)$$

Note that the three-way model could only be retained if an F-test for the increase in R^2 due to adding b_{11} and b_{12} was significant compared to the model with all two-way terms. A true three-way interaction involves the idea that racial differences in the impact of education do not generalize across gender. A careful consideration of the two-way interactions suggests some alternative interpretations. If education just interacts with race and gender *separately*, this means that there are racial differences in the impact of education that apply equally to both genders *and* that there are gender differences in the effect of education that apply equally across racial groups. That is a very different interpretation than the assumption that the gender difference changes depending on the group and is specific to different groups.

2.2.1 Deriving Education Effects for Selected Groups in the Three-Way Equation

To show how you can derive subgroup slopes in a model with a three-way interaction, we provide the calculations symbolically in Table 2.8. Note now that there are six distinct groups, including every combination of race and gender, and there is a unique slope for the effect of education in each group.

In each case, you plug in the combination of values for race and gender that define a particular subgroup and simplify, as before.

You can approach this way of parsing interactions mechanically: Plug in values, remove terms including 0, collect and simplify terms multiplied by the same variable, reduce the equation to

TABLE 2.8 ● ANALYZING A THREE-WAY INTERACTION

Group	Variables			Equation for Effect of E
	B	**H**	**F**	$\widehat{Y} = a + b_1 E + b_2 B + b_3 H + b_4 S + b_5 F + b_6 (E \cdot B) + b_7 (E \cdot H) + b_8 (E \cdot F)$ $+ b_9 (B \cdot F) + b_{10} (H \cdot F) + b_{11} (E \cdot B \cdot F) + b_{12} (E \cdot H \cdot F)$
White males	0	0	0	$\widehat{Y} = a + b_1 E + b_2 (0) + b_3 (0) + b_4 (13.98) + b_5 (0) + b_6 (E \cdot 0) + b_7 (E \cdot 0) + b_8 (E \cdot 0)$ $+ b_9 (0 \cdot 0) + b_{10} (0 \cdot 0) + b_{11} (E \cdot 0 \cdot 0) + b_{12} (E \cdot 0 \cdot 0)$ $= (a + b_4 (13.98)) + (b_1) E$
White females	0	0	1	$\widehat{Y} = a + b_1 E + b_2 (0) + b_3 (0) + b_4 (13.98) + b_5 (1) + b_6 (E \cdot 0) + b_7 (E \cdot 0) + b_8 (E \cdot 1)$ $+ b_9 (0 \cdot 1) + b_{10} (0 \cdot 1) + b_{11} (E \cdot 0 \cdot 1) + b_{12} (E \cdot 0 \cdot 1)$ $= (a + b_4 (13.98) + b_5) + (b_1 + b_8) E$
Black males	1	0	0	$\widehat{Y} = a + b_1 E + b_2 (1) + b_3 (0) + b_4 (13.98) + b_5 (0) + b_6 (E \cdot 1) + b_7 (E \cdot 0) + b_8 (E \cdot 0)$ $+ b_9 (1 \cdot 0) + b_{10} (0 \cdot 0) + b_{11} (E \cdot 1 \cdot 0) + b_{12} (E \cdot 0 \cdot 0)$ $= (a + b_2 + b_4 (13.98)) + (b_1 + b_6) E$
Black females	1	0	1	$\widehat{Y} = a + b_1 E + b_2 (1) + b_3 (0) + b_4 (13.98) + b_5 (1) + b_6 (E \cdot 1) + b_7 (E \cdot 0) + b_8 (E \cdot 1)$ $+ b_9 (1 \cdot 1) + b_{10} (0 \cdot 1) + b_{11} (E \cdot 1 \cdot 1) + b_{12} (E \cdot 0 \cdot 1)$ $= (a + b_2 + b_4 (13.98) + b_5 + b_9) + (b_1 + b_6 + b_8 + b_{11}) E$
Hispanic males	0	1	0	$\widehat{Y} = a + b_1 E + b_2 (0) + b_3 (1) + b_4 (13.98) + b_5 (0) + b_6 (E \cdot 0) + b_7 (E \cdot 1) + b_8 (E \cdot 0)$ $+ b_9 (0 \cdot 0) + b_{10} (1 \cdot 0) + b_{11} (E \cdot 0 \cdot 0) + b_{12} (E \cdot 1 \cdot 0)$ $= (a + b_3 + b_4 (13.98)) + (b_1 + b_7) E$
Hispanic females	0	1	1	$\widehat{Y} = a + b_1 E + b_2 (0) + b_3 (1) + b_4 (13.98) + b_5 (1) + b_6 (E \cdot 0) + b_7 (E \cdot 1) + b_8 (E \cdot 1)$ $+ b_9 (0 \cdot 1) + b_{10} (1 \cdot 1) + b_{11} (E \cdot 0 \cdot 1) + b_{12} (E \cdot 1 \cdot 1)$ $= (a + b_3 + b_4 (13.98) + b_5 + b_{10}) + (b_1 + b_7 + b_8 + b_{12}) E$

components of the intercept and components of the effect of X, plug in coefficients to calculate. If there is one thing this calculation shows, it is the fact that it is nearly impossible to look at the results for regression equations including a three-way interaction and interpret them properly. You have to take it apart to understand it. One wonders to what degree this issue plagues hypothesizing and presenting three-way interactions.

There *are* certain things you can see in the results, such as (a) the marginal effect of education is the effect in the combined reference group of White males; (b) the difference in the effect among Blacks and Hispanics, *for males only,* is shown by the two-way interaction between education and race; and (c) the difference in the effect of education for White females is shown by the two-way interaction between education and female. After that, interpretation gets more complex.

You would need to understand these subgroup effects before you could test for differences in slopes across groups. For example, using the equation, to find the difference in effect of education between Black females and Black males:

$$H_0 : b_1 + b_6 + b_8 + b_{11} = b_1 + b_6$$
$$(b_1 + b_6 + b_8 + b_{11}) - (b_1 + b_6) = 0$$
$$b_8 + b_{11} = 0$$

The difference between Black females and Hispanic females is:

$$H_0 : b_1 + b_6 + b_8 + b_{11} = b_1 + b_7 + b_8 + b_{12}$$
$$(b_1 + b_6 + b_8 + b_{11}) - (b_1 + b_7 + b_8 + b_{12}) = 0$$
$$b_6 - b_7 + b_{11} - b_{12} = 0$$

2.2.2 Testing the Three-Way Interaction in a Sequence of Models

To test a three-way interaction, you should include tests for the simpler models first. In this example, this could include six models, from the simple additive "main effects" model to the final three-way model. One **tests** these models in reverse order: If the three-way interaction is not significant, then you consider the set of two-way interactions—education x race, education x gender, and race x gender. If one or more of these is significant, you retain and interpret that model. If not, you fall back to a main effects model.

Here is the sequence of models and what each one tests:

$$\hat{Y} = a + b_1 E + b_2 B + b_3 H + b_4 S + b_5 F \tag{1}$$

1. Model 1 tests the main effects of race, gender, seniority, and education only.

$$\hat{Y} = a + b_1 E + b_2 B + b_3 H + b_4 S + b_5 F + b_6 (E \cdot B) + b_7 (E \cdot H) \tag{2}$$

2. Model 2 adds a two-way interaction between education and race. Model 1 is nested in Model 2. Model 2 tests this interaction on its own first.

$$\hat{Y} = a + b_1 E + b_2 B + b_3 H + b_4 S + b_5 F + b_8 (E \cdot F) \tag{3}$$

3. Model 3 adds a two-way interaction between education and gender to Model 1, to test it on its own first.

$$\hat{Y} = a + b_1 E + b_2 B + b_3 H + b_4 S + b_5 F + b_9 (B \cdot F) + b_{10} (H \cdot F) \tag{4}$$

4. Model 4 adds a two-way interaction between gender and race to Model 1, to test on its own.

$$\hat{Y} = a + b_1 E + b_2 B + b_3 H + b_4 S + b_5 F + b_6 (E \cdot B) + b_7 (E \cdot H) + b_8 (E \cdot F) \tag{5}$$
$$+ b_9 (B \cdot F) + b_{10} (H \cdot F)$$

5. Model 5 adds all three two-way interaction to Model 1, to test the collective hypothesis of *any* two-way interactions involving education, race, and gender. Note that Model 1 is nested in all of the models from 2 through 5.

$$\hat{Y} = a + b_1E + b_2B + b_3H + b_4S + b_5F + b_6(E \cdot B) + b_7(E \cdot H) + b_8(E \cdot F)$$
$$+ b_9(B \cdot F) + b_{10}(H \cdot F) + b_{11}(E \cdot B \cdot F) + b_{12}(E \cdot H \cdot F) \tag{6}$$

6. Model 6 adds the two terms necessary to test the three-way interaction. Model 5 is nested in Model 6. So are the simpler models, but those comparisons are not interesting because they do not isolate specific effects.

If the three-way interaction in Model 6 is not significant and one or more of the two-way interactions in Models 2, 3, and 4 are significant, then one can use Model 5 to figure out which two-way interactions could be retained in the presence of others. However, *all* should be retained to test the three-way interaction.

We do not show results for Models 2 through 5 here, although *all* of the two-way interactions involved here were significant. But those results would be misleading if there is a three-way interaction here, and this interaction is significant. Results from the three-way model are shown in Table 2.9.

TABLE 2.9 ● A THREE-WAY INTERACTION INVOLVING EDUCATION, RACE, AND GENDER

Parameter Estimates						
Variable	**Label**	**DF**	**Parameter Estimate**	**Standard Error**	**t Value**	**Pr > |t|**
Intercept	Intercept	1	−27.81590	1.94280	−14.32	<.0001
black		1	19.26546	5.36993	3.59	0.0003
hisp		1	22.35430	4.10073	5.45	<.0001
female		1	14.33510	3.07161	4.67	<.0001
yrscurrjob		1	0.52890	0.02280	23.20	<.0001
EDUCAT	EDUCATIONAL LEVEL	1	3.59936	0.13415	26.83	<.0001
blackxeduc		1	−1.90294	0.41763	−4.56	<.0001
hispxeduc		1	−2.16029	0.34772	−6.21	<.0001
educxfem		1	−1.77564	0.22269	−7.97	<.0001
femxblack		1	−19.39456	8.19880	−2.37	0.0180
femxhisp		1	−15.11531	7.14670	−2.12	0.0345
edxfemxblack		1	1.84471	0.62959	2.93	0.0034
edxfemxhisp		1	1.56790	0.60536	2.59	0.0096

Test any3way Results for Dependent Variable Rtotinc				
Source	**DF**	**Mean Square**	**F Value**	**Pr > F**
Numerator	2	2413.99144	6.77	0.0012
Denominator	5562	356.59939		

We use the same variable naming conventions as for the earlier two-way example. For example, "edxfemxblack" is a three-way interaction term formed from multiplying these variables: *educat * female * black.*

The post-hoc tests shows that the three way interaction here is significant, and the individual terms are also significant. When you look at regression results for a three-way model, it is very difficult to "see" the results. You can refer to the calculations on page 61 to derive subgroup slopes by hand.

Looking at the equation here, however, you can see that the effect of education for White males (the reference group) is 3.599 thousand dollars of income per year of education. The net effect among Black males must be: 3.559 – 1.90 (the coefficient for blackxeduc) = 1.66 thousand dollars per year of education. The net effect among White women is 3.559 – 1.78 = 1.78—that is, *half* of the effect among White males.

Note however that the coefficients for the two three-way terms are positive. This is where things get subtle and could be misinterpreted. This result means that the effect of education is not as low as one would expect from the combined effect of being a minority and being female as suggested by the two-way interactions. In fact, being female counteracts some of the negative effect due to minority status, so that instead of a cumulative "double jeopardy" effect due to two disadvantaged statuses, we see a "ceiling effect," where either one counts, but further indicators of disadvantaged status do not add to the effects of the other. In other words, these results argue for a "one is enough" rule, which is a form of intersectionality, but it is not the form most often predicted.

As an example from the equation, the effect among Black females is 3.60 (*EDUCAT*) – 1.77 (*EDUCAT * female*) – 1.90 (*EDUCAT * Black*) + 1.84 (*EDUCAT * Black * female*) = 1.77, almost the same as the slopes for White women and Black men. These terms show what is happening in the final slope: The three-way term has to counteract the implications of the two-way disadvantages due to race and gender to get to the actual slope. It is easy to see the result in a plot, as shown in Figure 2.2.

This graph makes the nature of the three-way interaction here quite clear: *Everyone* suffers a "penalty" in the effect of education relative to White males, by a similar amount. The only advantaged group is White males. The former finding at the beginning of this section is misleading and therefore "wrong." It is not that Whites have an advantage, it is that White males specifically—and only White males—have an advantage relative to others.

If you look at the plot closely, it is clear that Black and Hispanic females do not suffer double jeopardy: Their lines are almost parallel to their male counterparts. In effect, from the point of view of gender, this also means that only White females suffer a gender disadvantage. In other groups, minority status trumps gender.

2.2.2.1 Comparing Weighted OLS Regression Results in SAS and STATA

There is one difference between OLS regression results in SAS and STATA that we must underscore. The difference results from the use of a case weight, which was included in our estimation of the previous models. Case—or sample—weights are designed to increase the generalizability of results from a sample to the broader population. Each respondent is assigned a weight that represents the proportion of the population in which their individual characteristics actually occur. These characteristics usually include basic social and demographic features, such as gender, age, marital status, education level, household income, and household size. If the combination of the respondent's characteristics are overrepresented in the sample relative to the population,

FIGURE 2.2 ● A THREE-WAY INTERACTION INVOLVING EDUCATION, RACE, AND GENDER

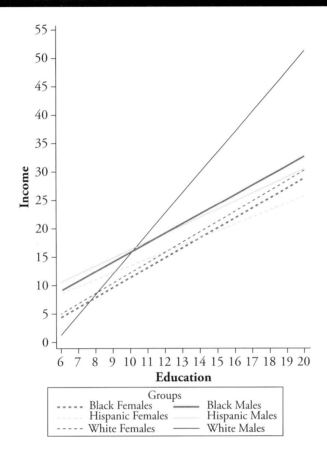

they are assigned a proportional weight less than 1. If the respondent's combined characteristics are underrepresented in the sample relative to the population, they are assigned a proportional weight greater than 1.

We discuss weights in relation to our SAS versus STATA output because in OLS regression, STATA automatically produces ***robust*** standard errors when using a sample weight in the model statement. This is not the case in SAS. Robust standard errors account for non-normal variances based on the observed data. These calculated errors are often larger than normal standard errors and make statistical significance more difficult to observe.

We present the results for the previously discussed three-way interaction model in STATA to demonstrate this difference in the reported standard errors, compared to the SAS output.

Here is the STATA code for our model:

```
reg rtotinc black hisp female yrscurrjob educat blackxeduc
hispxeduc educxfem femxblack femxhisp edxfemxblack edxfemxhisp
[pweight=weight]
```

TABLE 2.10 ● A THREE-WAY INTERACTION INVOLVING EDUCATION, RACE, AND GENDER IN STATA

```
Linear regression                              Number of obs   =    5575
                                               F( 12,  5562)   =   90.34
                                               Prob > F        =  0.0000
                                               R-squared       =  0.2723
                                               Root MSE        =  19.081
```

rtotinc	Robust Coef.	Std. Err.	t	P>|t|	[95% Conf.	Interval]
black	19.26546	5.696079	3.38	0.001	8.098921	30.432
hisp	22.3543	4.338581	5.15	0.000	13.84899	30.85962
female	14.3351	4.170218	3.44	0.001	6.159847	22.51036
yrscurrjob	.5289019	.0327844	16.13	0.000	.4646316	.5931721
educat	3.599364	.2990628	12.04	0.000	3.013084	4.185644
blackxeduc	-1.902943	.4482052	-4.25	0.000	-2.7816	-1.024285
hispxeduc	-2.160289	.3610002	-5.98	0.000	-2.86799	-1.452587
educxfem	-1.775641	.3227628	-5.50	0.000	-2.408382	-1.1429
femxblack	-19.39456	7.136857	-2.72	0.007	-33.38559	-5.403534
femxhisp	-15.11531	4.929981	-3.07	0.002	-24.77999	-5.450616
edxfemxblack	1.84471	.5527853	3.34	0.001	.761035	2.928385
edxfemxhisp	1.567895	.4145766	3.78	0.000	.7551631	2.380627
_cons	-27.8159	3.932385	-7.07	0.000	-35.52491	-20.10689

Here is the syntax to estimate the hypothesis test for the three-way interaction:

```
test edxfemxblack=edxfemxhisp=0

( 1)   edxfemxblack - edxfemxhisp = 0
( 2)   edxfemxblack = 0

       F(  2,  5562) =      8.86
           Prob > F =    0.0001
```

2.2.3 A Digression: Interactions, Intersections, Parsimony, and Complexity

There is a direct connection between what interactions test and what the intersectionality perspective claims. Intersectionality is a perspective with many variants, including anti-categorization. But a prominent version considers the essential co-presence of different sources of inequality as fundamental to understanding the total experience of inequality. The most direct translation of this idea is that there is a three-way interaction between race, class, and gender, an interaction that captures the uniqueness of occupying various configurations of multiple statuses described by those terms. If indeed there is a unique combined effect of being Black, female, and less educated, then the three-way interaction should be significant.

There are important differences under the surface between the quantitative study of interactions and the qualitative study of intersections. In testing an interaction, you are requiring that it is *necessary* to describe a given set of relationships, *over and above the cumulative impact of separate main effects, each of which is not contingent on other statuses.* This distinction is not always clearly made in discussions of intersectionality. On the other hand, some versions of intersectionality are also compatible with the notion of separate main effects of race, class, and gender, but with cumulative impacts. In a sense, the quantitative specification makes the ***theoretical*** distinction between the additive version and the interactive version a foreground issue.

The quantitative emphasis on choosing the most parsimonious model that describes the observed relationships allows for simpler cases than considering all sources of inequality at once. Basically, the claim is that not everything matters everywhere all the time. On the other hand, intersectionality draws our attention to the complexity of the combined effects of race, class, and gender and imagines unique social locations described by combinations of these statuses.

What we learn from considering higher-order interactions is that quantitative approaches can also incorporate considerable complexity. What we learn from intersectionality is that the importance of capturing complexity may at times be more important than the need for parsimony.

2.3 INTERACTIONS INVOLVING CONTINUOUS VARIABLES

You can also have interactions between continuous variables, as well as between categorical variables (next section). Sometimes these combinations of effects are seen as "different," but it is important to emphasize that ***the principles of interpretation developed in the previous section apply in the same way to all interactions.***

Those general principles involve three steps: (1) Define one variable in the interaction as focal—this is the variable whose effect you want to analyze; (2) give values to the variable(s) that define conditions under which the effect of the focal variable changes; (3) resolve the equation into subgroup equations that show the difference in the effect of the focal variable under varying conditions.

There ***are*** some specifics to dealing with interactions involving continuous variables that also have to be taken into account.

2.3.1 Interpreting an Interaction with Two Continuous Variables

Suppose you are considering an interaction between education and age, two continuous variables—for example, to study the possibility of cohort changes in the impact of education. Let us suppose that you are interested in demonstrating that the effect of education on income has declined over time. We would have to use a complicated approach to this question involving different cohorts at the same age, in different studies, but here we will take a simple approach.

The approach with continuous variables is to choose appropriately contrasting values of some variable Z, the other continuous variable in the interaction, to calculate the changing effect of the focal X, for example, at -1 and +1 standard deviations from the mean of Z. Suppose that Z = age. In the NSFH data used throughout this chapter, the mean at Wave 1 is 38, and the standard deviation is (about) 12 years. Using these values, one could calculate the effect of education at ages representing -1 SD (38 - 12 = 26) and +1 SD (38 + 12 = 50). There is nothing sacred about choosing these values: This is one convention among many. For example, some use the 25th and 75th percentiles on age. The values you use also depend on the way in which the continuous variable is coded. For example, if age was centered around its mean, the mean is then 0. In that case, you could use -12 and +12.

The overall equation with A = age and a control for seniority in current job (S) is:

$$\hat{Y} = a + b_1 E + b_2 A + b_3 S + b_4 (E \cdot A)$$

At -1 SD of age and a mean years in current job = 14,

$$\hat{Y} = a + b_1 E + b_2 (26) + b_3 (14) + b_4 (E \cdot 26) = (a + 26 b_2 + 14 b_3) + (b_1 + 26 \cdot b_4) E$$

And at +1 SD on age,

$$\hat{Y} = a + b_1 E + b_2 (50) + b_3 (14) + b_4 (E \cdot 50) = (a + 50 b_2 + 14 b_3) + (b_1 + 50 \cdot b_4) E$$

When you estimate this interaction in the NSFH data, you get this result for the overall equation:

$$\hat{Y} = 1.18 + .836 E - .535 A + .559 S + .0466 (E \cdot A)$$

The results in Table 2.11 show the interaction between age and education (*agexeduc*) is significant.

TABLE 2.11 ● AN INTERACTION BETWEEN TWO CONTINUOUS VARIABLES

Parameter Estimates						
Variable	Label	DF	Parameter Estimate	Standard Error	*t* Value	Pr > |t|
Intercept	Intercept	1	1.18109	4.18583	0.28	0.7778
age		1	−0.53503	0.09876	−5.42	<.0001
yrscurrjob		1	0.55880	0.03436	16.27	<.0001
EDUCAT	EDUCATIONAL LEVEL	1	0.83582	0.31910	2.62	0.0088
agexeduc		1	0.04661	0.00738	6.32	<.0001

If we work out the net effects of education at two ages—26 and 50—we get the following results, using the substitution of A = 26 and then A = 50 in the equation above:

$$\hat{Y} = 1.18 + .836 E - .535(26) + .559(14) + .0466(E \cdot 26)$$
$$\hat{Y} = 1.18 - .535(26) + .559(14) + (.836 + (.0466 \cdot 26)) E$$
$$= -4.904 + 2.05 E$$

That is, at 26 years old—among the young—the effect of a one-year increase in education is to increase income by just over two thousand dollars a year—given that income is coded in thousands of dollars. At age 50, the net equation for the effect of education is

$$\hat{Y} = 1.18 + .836E - .535(50) + .559(14) + .0466(E \cdot 50)$$
$$\hat{Y} = 1.18 - .535(50) + .559(14) + (.836 + (.0466 \cdot 50)E$$
$$= -17.74 + 3.17E$$

So at age 50, the effect of a one-year increase in education has increased to over three thousand dollars a year.

Whether this is the natural effect of differences in early income multiplying with age or actual cohort differences cannot be determined here. But the mechanics of figuring out the interaction are not affected by this interpretive issue.

2.4 INTERACTIONS BETWEEN CATEGORICAL VARIABLES: THE "N-WAY" ANALYSIS OF VARIANCE

In this case, we have two categorical variables. This is a more prevalent case in some disciplines, such as psychology, where experimental designs are prevalent.

You can proceed in the same way in this case as well. What *appears* to be unusual here is that all of the variables in the interaction are categorical, and thus it may seem strange to talk about the "effect" of a variable. But it is done all of the time, as long as you remember that the "effect" of a dummy variable is the mean difference on Y of two groups.

Interactions between two categorical variables are often part of what is called the "two-way analysis of variance." Basically, there is nothing unique about this term, since it is a method used to interpret the effects of two variables as either two additive "main" effects or an interaction. If there are three variables involved, we have a three-way analysis of variance.

Suppose you are interested in studying the distribution of a sense of powerlessness across two categorical variables: marital status and employment status. The hypothesis may be that the impact of unemployment on a sense of powerlessness is much higher in unpartnered marital statuses.

If there is a two-way interaction, it is your choice—depending on your analytical goals—as to which variable is the focal variable. If the point of your analysis is that the meaning of unemployment varies depending on social capital and one of your tests of that idea involves using an interaction with marital status, then you make unemployment focal.

Many people use interactions between categorical variables to derive group mean differences on Y for all groups. This is fine, but it also does not express how one variable changes the impact of the other variable succinctly. Sticking to the logic of an "effect of X" does respect the nature of the interaction.

2.4.1 An Example: A Two-Way ANOVA (Analysis of Variance)

In this case, we have two categorical independent variables, marital status and unemployment. The N is assumed to be 200. The dependent variable here is sense of powerlessness—that is, the percentage of events in your life you perceive as beyond your personal control.

The basic hypothesis to be tested is that the implications of nonemployment for sense of powerlessness will vary across marital statuses and will have a reduced effect among the married, since there is a partner available who may also work.

For simplicity, marital status here has three categories: married, single, and divorced/separated. We develop two dummy variables (**S** for single and **D** for divorced) for marital status, with married as the reference category, as follows.

	S	D
Married	0	0
Single	1	0
Divorced / separated	0	1

Unemployment has two categories; therefore there is just one dummy variable (**U**) for unemployment.

Strictly speaking, in all of the cases we explore in this chapter, you could say that the logic of the analysis is to find the most parsimonious model and yet the most effective model in predicting Y.

	U
Working	0
Unemployed	1

We predict an interaction, but if it is not significant, we should interpret the two effects of unemployment and marital status as additive and therefore independent of each other.

The general procedure follows earlier examples:

1. Estimate a model with "additive" effects (main effects) only:

$$\hat{Y} = a + b_1 S + b_2 D + b_3 U$$

$$\hat{Y} = 20 + 6S + 16D + 20U$$

$$R^2 = .20$$

2. Add all possible two-way interaction terms to test for a two-way interaction:

$$\hat{Y} = a + b_1 S + b_2 D + b_3 U + b_4 (S \cdot U) + b_5 (D \cdot U)$$

$$\hat{Y} = 20 + 6S + 12D + 16U + 2(S \cdot U) + 18(D \cdot U)$$

$$R^2 = .34$$

Results here are invented—not based on actual data.

The interaction terms stand for the possibility that mean differences for groups on one variable do *not* generalize across categories of the other group variable. To test whether there are any two-way interactions, conduct an F-test for Model (2) versus Model (1).

$$F = \frac{R^2_{(2)} - R^2_{(1)} / k_2 - k_1}{1 - R^2_{(2)} / N - k_2 - 1} \text{ with } k_2 - k_1 \text{ and } N - k_2 - 1 \text{ df}$$

$$= \frac{.34 - .20/2}{1 - .34/200 - 5 - 1} = 20.58 \ p < .0001$$

This means there *are* significant two-way interactions. So Model (2) is appropriate and should be retained. Further, this means that Model (1) is wrong and should *not* be interpreted.

2.4.2 Resolving the Equation to Show the Effect of One Variable

You can still use the method outlined in the previous sections to analyze this interaction. In fact, in psychology and in many experimental literatures, this type of interaction is what is *typically* seen as an interaction. It is helpful again to focus on the effect of one variable and show how it changes across *categories* of the other variable.

Following the logic above, assume you are discussing the effects of unemployment on sense of powerlessness. In this context, you want to show how this effect changes across marital statuses. We use the overall equation results above to substitute values for different marital status groups into the equation and then resolve the equation to show the effect of unemployment.

This process results in three equations showing the effect of unemployment within the three marital statuses. We can see immediately from the results that the effect of unemployment changes most clearly among the divorced/separated. The effect of unemployment on increasing a sense of powerlessness is much stronger among the divorced/separated, indicating the specific joint consequences of being unemployed and also divorced/separated.

TABLE 2.12 ● RESOLVING THE EFFECT OF UNEMPLOYMENT IN DIFFERENT MARITAL STATUS GROUPS				
Marital Status	**Dummy Coding**		**Equation**	**Subgroup Effect**
	S	**D**	$\hat{Y} = a + b_1 S + b_2 D + b_3 U + b_4 (S \cdot U) + b_5 (D \cdot U)$	
Married	0	0	$\hat{Y} = a + b_1 0 + b_2 0 + b_3 U + b_4 (0 \cdot U) + b_5 (0 \cdot U)$ $\hat{Y} = a + b_3 U$	$\hat{Y} = 20 + 16U$
Single	1	0	$\hat{Y} = a + b_1 1 + b_2 0 + b_3 U + b_4 (1 \cdot U) + b_5 (0 \cdot U)$ $\hat{Y} = a + b_1 + b_3 U + b_4 U$ $\hat{Y} = (a + b_1) + (b_3 + b_4)U$	$\hat{Y} = (20 + 6) + (16 + 2)U$ $= 26 + 18U$
Div/Sep	0	1	$\hat{Y} = a + b_1 0 + b_2 1 + b_3 U + b_4 (0 \cdot U) + b_5 (1 \cdot U)$ $\hat{Y} = a + b_2 + b_3 U + b_5 U$ $\hat{Y} = (a + b_2) + (b_3 + b_5)U$	$\hat{Y} = (20 + 12) + (16 + 18)U$ $= 32 + 34U$

2.4.3 Looking More Closely at the Concept of Interaction

We can go one step further in analyzing this equation to reveal exactly what is going on in this interaction, how it is expressed by the regression equation, and how an interaction indicates a specific departure from additivity of effects.

It is important to understand this because ***it is difficult to imagine how interactions are unique relative to the accumulation of multiple independent additive effects***. They *are* different, and it is very important in theoretical terms to make the distinction.

In Table 2.13, we show the predicted Y means for each of the six groups in the equation formed by the consideration of both marital status (three categories) and unemployment (two categories). Unlike before, we are plugging in values for **all** variables here, to get the predicted mean level of powerlessness for each group.

TABLE 2.13 ⬢ FIGURING OUT THE MEANS IN ALL GROUPS

Group	S	D	U	Equation: $Y = a + b_1 S + b_2 D + b_3 U + b_4 (S \cdot U) + b_5 (D \cdot U)$
Married, working	0	0	0	$Y = a + b_1(0) + b_2(0) + b_3(0) + b_4(0) + b_5(0)$ $= a = 20$
Married, unemployed	0	0	1	$Y = a + b_1(0) + b_2(0) + b_3(1) + b_4(0) + b_5(0)$ $= a + b_3 = 20 + 16 = 36$
Single, working	1	0	0	$Y = a + b_1(1) + b_2(0) + b_3(0) + b_4(0) + b_5(0)$ $= a + b_1 = 20 + 6 = 26$
Single, unemployed	1	0	1	$Y = a + b_1(1) + b_2(0) + b_3(1) + b_4(1) + b_5(0)$ $= a + b_1 + b_3 + b_4 = 20 + 6 + 16 + 2 = 44$
Divorced/separated, working	0	1	0	$Y = a + b_1(0) + b_2(1) + b_3(0) + b_4(0) + b_5(0)$ $= a + b_2 = 20 + 12 = 32$
Divorced/separated, unemployed	0	1	1	$Y = a + b_1(0) + b_2(1) + b_3(1) + b_4(0) + b_5(1)$ $= a + b_2 + b_3 + b_5 = 20 + 12 + 16 + 18 = 66$

TABLE 2.14 ⬢ TABLE OF MEANS AND COEFFICIENTS

Means	Marital Status		
Unemployment	**Married**	**Single**	**Div./Sep.**
Working	20	26	32
Unemployed	36	44	66

Coefficients Involved in Each Mean	Marital Status		
Unemployment	**Married**	**Single**	**Div./Sep.**
Working	a	$a + b_1$	$a + b_2$
Unemployed	$a + b_3$	$a + b_1 + b_3 + b_4$	$a + b_2 + b_3 + b_5$

Table 2.14 shows the so-called "cell means" for all group combinations. Note from the equation that the b's in general do *not* stand for differences between overall means across groups. You have to derive which b's are involved in the mean of each group.

2.4.3.1 Interpretation of Interaction Term Coefficients

The coefficients b_4 and b_5 show the degree to which mean differences involving the reference categories do not generalize across other levels. For example, if the mean for "div./sep., unemployed" was an additive function of being divorced / separated **plus** being unemployed, then the mean in this cell would be $a + b_2 + b_3$.

Thus, b_5 stands for the degree of departure from additivity. In this case $b_5 = 18$, which means that the actual mean in this cell (66) is 18 points higher than what is predicted by the additive model.

$$\text{That is, } a + b_2 + b_3 = 20 + 12 + 16 = 48.$$

$$b_5 = 18 \text{ is the amount you need to get to 66,}$$

$$\text{that is, } 48 + 18 = 66.$$

The interaction indicates that the specific *combination* of being divorced or separated *and* unemployed results in much higher feelings of powerlessness than would be expected from the combined increases in powerlessness for the divorced or separated when working and from unemployment when married.

2.4.4 Testing Differences Between Group Means

When the F-test for an interaction is significant, you may want to know in which groups the interaction occurs. The F-test only tells you differences do not generalize across all groups on the other variable but not which groups differ from each other.

You can use the same approach here as for interactions involving continuous variables to conduct tests. Referring to the results for the interaction model, note the equation tests for differences between the following:

- single, working versus married, working (b_1)

- div./sep., working versus married, working (b_2)

- unemployed, married versus working, married (b_3)

To test for differences between other specific groups in the equation, use the coefficients involved to construct tests for differences in effects:

- For div. / sep., unemployed versus div. / sep., working

$$\text{H}_0\text{: } (a + b_2 + b_3 + b_5) - (a + b_2) = 0$$
$$b_3 + b_5 = 0$$

- For div. / sep., unemployed versus married, unemployed

$$\text{H}_0\text{: } (a + b_2 + b_3 + b_5) - (a + b_3) = 0$$
$$b_2 + b_5 = 0$$

You can also test for *combinations* of group differences. For example,

(div./sep., unemployed − div./sep., working) − (single, unemployed − single, working) = 0

$$= ((a + b_2 + b_3 + b_5) - (a + b_2)) - ((a + b_1 + b_3 + b_4) - (a + b_1)) = 0$$
$$= (b_3 + b_5) - (b_3 + b_4) = 0$$
$$= b_3 + b_5 - b_3 - b_4 = 0$$
$$= b_5 - b_4 = 0$$

This is a test for the specific location of the interaction. If b_5 is greater than b_4, we know that the effect of unemployment among the divorced / separated is greater than among the single. If we also see that the single do not differ from the married, then we can locate exactly which group is different from the others.

You can also test specific effects of unemployment *within marital status groups* for significance. This is not a test of the difference between groups but a test of the effect of the focal variable within groups. For example, to test the significance of the effect of unemployment among the single, test

$$(b_3 + b_4) = 0$$

And to test the significance of the effect of unemployment among the divorced / separated, test

$$(b_3 + b_5) = 0$$

2.4.5 Three-Way Interactions with Categorical Variables (Three-Way ANOVA)

Studying three-way interactions in the case of categorical variables follows the same logic as with other combinations of types of variables (see section 2.2.2). It is worth emphasizing three funda-mental issues in the model-building verses model-testing logic of testing interactions:

1. Combinations of two-way interactions have to form the foundation of testing a full three-way interaction because the theoretical interpretation of these two cases is very different.

2. Model-building proceeds from the simplest additive model to the most complex three-way model, but model-testing proceeds in the reverse, starting with the most complex model.

3. The approach used in this chapter makes distinctions concerning the way in which the effects of variables combine that are not clearly articulated in theoretical models promoting the idea of joint effects.

2.5 CAUTIONS IN STUDYING INTERACTIONS

There are a number of cautions one should take into account in estimating interactions. Here we discuss four that may be important.

2.5.0.1 Multicollinearity

A basic problem in interaction models is that the product terms are made up from other variables in the model, thus introducing positive correlations among independent variables. Transforma-tions of x reduce the correlations between main effects and their interactions.

One simple way to reduce multicollinearity is to use "centered" x's—that is, subtracting means from raw x scores—that is, $x_1 = X_1 - \overline{X}_1$. In the earlier example discussing the two-way interaction between education and age, we pointed out that in that sample, the mean age was 38. Centering age here means that we subtract 38 from each individual X score. This makes the mean of age = 0, and the resulting deviation scores in age are negative values below that (e.g., –1 S.D. = –12), or positive values above that (+1 SD = +12).

2.5.0.2 The Issue of a "Main Effect" in the Presence of Interactions

In general, the safe approach is to realize that an interaction stands for the fact that there is no main effect, and thus you should interpret only the separate subgroup effects. But some do report an *averaged* main effect in the case of an interaction, standing for either an averaged effect across groups or an averaged effect across levels of a continuous variable.

Suppose you are considering an interaction between two ***continuous*** *variables*, such as

$$\hat{Y} = a + b_1 X_1 + b_2 X_2 + b_3 (X_1 \cdot X_2)$$

If you center X_1 and X_2 by subtracting their mean values, as above, thus scaling each so their mean = 0, then, by definition, the effect of X_1 is its effect at the mean of X_2, and the effect of X_2 is its effect at the mean of X_1.

A common mistake often made in models with interactions is that the marginal effect of the focal X in the equation with the interaction is still the main effect—it is not. It is only the effect of X under the condition that the variable it interacts with equals 0—which is the reference group for dummy variables or the zero point on a continuous scale.

In general, we do *not* advocate presentation of "main" effects in the presence of an interaction. The concept of an averaged main effect also denotes the fact that is hiding important variation in effects across groups or across levels of a continuous variable. We suggest this variation should be in the foreground.

2.5.0.3 Problems with Standardized Solutions

One cannot and should not interpret the standardized coefficients in a model with interactions. The model we would want to assess would be

$$\hat{Y} = a + b_1 Z_1 + b_2 Z_2 + b_3 (Z_1 \cdot Z_2)$$

where $Z_1 = X_1$ standardized

$Z_2 = X_2$ standardized

But in standard computer programs, the variables *as a whole* are standardized so that the product term is $(X_1 \cdot X_2)$ standardized, which is wrong. To get to the correct interpretation, standardize Xs ***before analysis*** and then interpret the unstandardized results, which are, in effect, standardized variables.

2.5.0.4 Number of Post-hoc Tests

You should practically limit the number of post-hoc tests you conduct to minimize the cumulative problem of committing a Type I error—assuming significance when the real value in the population is "no difference." A reasonable approach is to only test the necessary and essential contrasts for interpretation of the results. Often, the tests you should conduct are suggested by the pattern of the results. Concentrate on tests that establish whether groups differing from the reference group are equal to or different from each other and whether they form subgroups.

There are many methods available for controlling Type I error in post-hoc tests, but many of these methods apply mainly to uncorrelated independent variables in experiments. Our advice here is simple: Only investigate the specific differences in the slopes among groups *after* an overall significant *F*-test for the interaction.

2.6 PUBLISHED EXAMPLES

Interactions are ubiquitous in published research, primarily because they express a fundamental hypothesis of interest across a wide range of research questions: Is this experience shared or distinct? Does this occur in only one group rather than in all groups? Does this generalize to very different countries? Is this still true now, even if it was true then? What activates or de-activates this effect?

In this section, we consider three published examples of the use of interactions to address specific research questions. In each case, we emphasize the role of interactions and their interpretation in achieving the purposes of the research questions in the article.

2.6.1 The Gender-Specific Effect of Marriage

There is a large literature on the gender difference in the effect of marriage on well-being. This is an issue that has had prominence in public discourse for over forty years, with the standard conclusion that men benefit more from marriage than women.

Hall (1999) conducted a meta-analysis of this literature, based on 213 independent parameter estimates derived from 78 studies done from the 1930s up to the 1990s. To give some specificity to the issue being assessed in this research, Table 2.15 shows some *hypothetical* results for this issue, based on mean levels of depression in four groups: never-married males, never-married females, married males, and married females.

Hall points out that we cannot understand this effect properly by using what she calls a ***sequential contrast*** approach, represented in Table 2.15. This approach might utilize *t* test differences among never marrieds (i.e., unmarried women vs. unmarried men), *followed by t* test differences among marrieds (i.e., married women vs. married men) to build an argument for a gender-specific effect. In fact, a considerable portion of the literature in this area has taken this approach. The sequential contrast approach in Table 2.15 suggests that women are more depressed by 1 point among the never married, and that this gender difference is nonsignificant. Among the married, however, this difference increases to 2 points and is significant, suggesting that women are only more depressed than men when married. The problem with these tests is that they do not assess the hypothesis at issue directly; rather, they really only reflect the respective within-role differences and thus cannot be used to infer a gender difference in the well-being *gain* due to marriage.

The hypothesis of a gender-specific effect of marriage requires a single assessment of the female difference for the married versus never married minus the corresponding male difference, in other words, a ***differential gain*** effect requiring estimation of an interaction effect between gender and marital status. Table 2.15 represents how this assessment would work. The mental health gain for women is measured by the average reduction in depression, equal to 3 points. The reduction among men is 4 points, resulting in a differential gain among women equal to –1. That is, they have gained one less point. However, treated as a test of differences in gain—which *is* the appropriate test here—the difference in the difference may not be significant, even though significant gender differences in depression only emerged among the married. In other words, there is no evidence here of a gender-specific effect, even though the sequence of *t* test differences implies there is.

TABLE 2.15a ● THE GENDER SPECIFIC EFFECT OF MARRIAGE RE-CONSIDERED: THE "SEQUENTIAL CONTRAST" VERSUS THE "DIFFERENTIAL GAIN" APPROACH

	Rates of Depression	
	Male	**Female**
Never Married	17	18
Married	13	15

Sequential Contrast Approach

Among the never married, women have slightly higher rates: $18 - 17 = +1$ ($p > .05$).

Among the married, women have significantly higher rates: $15 - 13 = +2$ ($p < .05$).

Differential Gain Approach

TABLE 2.15b ● CALCULATIONS IN THE DIFFERENTIAL GAIN APPROACH

Gain for Women	Minus	Gain for Men	Differential Gain
$(15 - 18)$	–	$(13 - 17)$	
-3	–	-4	$= +1$ ($p > .05$)

The same problem occurs in analyses in which men and women are studied separately, even if marital gain is the focus. For example, one can study the effect of getting married among men and women separately and compare the significance versus nonsignificance of the effect of marriage in the two genders. This is still a sequential contrast approach. It studies a pattern of results, but it does not test the fundamental hypothesis.

In 2002, Robin Simon published an article in the American Journal of Sociology entitled "Revisiting the Relationships among Gender, Marital Status, and Mental Health." In that article, using the longitudinal component of the National Survey of Families and Households, she assesses (among other things) the gender-specific effects of entering marriage between Waves 1 and 2. This is studied as a test of the interaction between entry into marriage and gender. Results are shown in Table 2.16.

Simon tests the effects of entering marriage from three different nonmarried statuses: never married, divorced / separated, and widowed. Models 2 and 4 show the results of estimating interactions between gender and marital entry for all three cases. Despite the accumulated reputation of a gender-differential effect of marriage specifically applied to the transition from never married to married status, there is no evidence here of an interaction between gender and entering marriage. In fact, none of the interactions for changes in depression

TABLE 2.16 ● UNSTANDARDIZED COEFFICIENTS FROM REGRESSIONS OF DEPRESSION AND ALCOHOL ABUSE ON GENDER AND MARITAL GAIN AMONG RESPONDENTS WHO WERE UNMARRIED AT T1

	Depression		Alcohol Abuse	
	Model 1[a]	Model 2[a]	Model 3[a]	Model 4[a]
Female (0, 1)	2.10*** (.58)	2.41*** (.71)	−1.28*** (.11)	−1.42*** (1.33)
T1 depression/alcohol abuse[b]	.29*** (.01)	.29*** (.01)	2.62*** (.33)	2.61*** (.33)
Marital gain from previously never married	−3.88*** (.86)	−3.38*** (1.16)	−.24 (.16)	−.34 (.22)
Marital gain from previously separated/divorced	−2.65** (.86)	−2.08 (1.34)	−.28 (.16)	−.67** (.25)
Marital gain from previously wid- owed	−3.80 (2.38)	−3.22 (3.90)	−.22 (.45)	−1.05 (.74)
Female x marital gain from previously never married	. . .	−.98 (1.54)	. . .	.21 (.29)
Female x marital gain from previously separated/ divorced	. . .	−.92 (1.67)	. . .	.64* (.32)
Female x marital gain from previously widowed	. . .	−.87 (4.92)	. . .	1.30 (.93)
Adjusted R^2	.18	.18	.09	.09

Source: Simon, R. (2002). Revisiting the relationships among gender, marital status, and mental health. *American Journal of Sociology, 107*(4), 1082. doi:10.1086/339225

Note: Numbers in parentheses are SEs. The stably unmarried are the reference category. N = 3,407.

a. Each model controls for sociodemographic variables including age, race, education, and household income, as well as respondent's employment and parental status at T2.

b. Respondent's level of depression at T1 is included in the depression models and whether they reported alcohol problems at T1 is included in the alcohol abuse models.

* P < .05, two-tailed tests.

** P < .01.

*** P < .001.

are significant. There is one significant interaction for alcohol abuse, suggesting that men who *re*-marrry after a prior divorce do experience a greater reduction in alcohol problems. This is indicated by a significant –.67 effect among men (the group coded 0 on the gender dummy variable), counteracted by a .64 weaker effect among women, indicated by the interaction. In effect, this means the net effect among women was −.67 + .64 = −.03, in other words, no change at all. Most of the prior research on this issue centers on emotional well-being outcomes and entry into first marriage, and so the finding of no interaction for depression suggests a very different picture than what was widely assumed in the decades before this article.

This is a case where the "intuitive" approach to the issue does not actually test the hypothesis. What we learn using the interaction, applied longitudinally to the same people entering marriage over time, is that the widely assumed male advantage in first marriages does not apply.

2.6.2 Two Distinct Issues in an Interaction: Race, Gender, and Chains of Disadvantage

There is a widespread tendency in assessing interactions to present the interaction merely as a difference in the effect of some variable across groups. This leads to tables in publications where we "see" the interaction as the interaction coefficient from the estimated model expressing this difference.

But there is more one can and should extract from an interaction in many applications. The difference coefficient in the interaction only expresses a differences in slopes *but not the size of the slope within groups.* This latter issue may be fundamental to the interpretation of the interaction, beyond the issue of an effect difference. For example, imagine this general example. Suppose we find an interaction between race and sex, where each is dummy coded into two groups, Black versus White and Women versus Men. The interaction shows a baseline effect of Black on a sense of powerlessness equal to $b = .5$. The interaction with female is $-.45$. This means that there is an effect of race on a sense of powerlessness among men, but not among women. The .5 effect among men is reduced to $.5 - .45 = .05$ race difference among women, which we imagine is zero. This leads to a specific interpretation, including the fact that Black–White differences occur only among men.

If we change the baseline coefficient for race here to .2, instead of .5 but maintain the difference in effects denoted by the interaction, we get a very different interpretation. We can still imagine here that among men, Blacks have a higher sense of powerlessness. However, among women the race difference is $.2 - .45 = -.25$. In this case, the pattern suggests that Black women have a ***lower*** sense of powerlessness relative to White women, even though the interaction coefficient is the same. This obviously leads to a very different interpretation because in this case, the race difference is the opposite depending on gender and not just an issue of presence / absence. Now we should ask why White women feel more powerless than Black women.

Many, if not most, articles fail to report these within group slope differences as a regular part of the interpretation of the interaction. A significant exception occurs in a recent article by Debra Umberson and colleagues entitled "Race, Gender, and Chains of Disadvantage: Childhood Adversity, Social Relationships, and Health." This article explores, in part, the gender-specific race consequences for exposure to "chains of disadvantage" denoted first by the experience of childhood adversity and compounded by the transfer of childhood adversity into relationship strain in adulthood (Umberson et al., 2014).

In the article, Umberson et al. (2014) suggest reasoning for a race by gender interaction this way:

> This race effect is likely to be stronger among men than women because of gendered relationship processes. Gendered systems foster expressions of masculinity (e.g., self-sufficiency, independence, strength, controlled expression of emotions) that may interfere with close relationships (Connell & Messersehmidt, 2005; Courtcnay, 2000; Williams 2003). Indeed, studies show that compared with women, men are less likely to have close and confiding relationships, to share their feelings with others, and to provide and seek emotional support from others (Rosenfield, Lcnnon, and White 2005; Taylor et al. 2000; Umberson et al. 1996). Scholars suggest that these gendered processes may be more exaggerated for Black men compared with white men because many Black men lack access to other ways of practicing masculinity, such as occupational and economic success. (Connell & Messersehmidt, 2005, p. 23)

Umberson et al. (2014) show race by gender interactions for both childhood adversity and relationship strain in adulthood in Table 2.17.

TABLE 2.17 ●   HYPOTHESIS 1: ORDINARY LEAST-SQUARES MODELS ESTIMATING RACE AND GENDER DIFFERENCES IN STRESS OVER THE LIFE COURSE AND ADULT RELATIONSHIP STRAIN AND SUPPORT (N = 3,477).

Variables	Childhood Adversity		Adult Stress Burden		Relationship Strain in Adulthood		Relationship Support in Adulthood	
	Wave 1	Wave 1	Wave 1	Wave 2	Wave 1	Wave 2	Wave 1	Wave 2
	(1)	(2)	(3)	(4)	(5)	(6)	(7)	(8)
Female	.115*	.181**	.062	.060	−.001	−.042*	.120***	.098***
	(.045)	(.053)	(.037)	(.040)	(.024)	(.023)	(.024)	(.026)
Black	.061	.219**	.161***	.233***	.132***	.059**	−.025	.050
	(.046)	(.080)	(.041)	(.046)	(.035)	(.034)	(.026)	(.028)
Relationship strain in adulthood (W1)	—	—	—	—	—	.546***	—	—
						(.016)		
Relationship support in adulthood (W1)	—	—	—	—	—	—	—	.468***
								(.018)
Adult stress burden (W1)	—	—	.362***	—	—	—	—	—
			(.022)					
Female*black	—	−.237*	—	—	−.100*	—	—	—
		(.098)			(.043)			
R^2	.02	.04	.16	.22	.12	.41	.03	.32

Source: Umberson, D., Williams, K., Thomas, P. A., Liu, H., & Thomeer, M. B. (2014). Race, gender, and chains of disadvantage: Childhood adversity, social relationships, and health. *Journal of Health and Social Behavior, 55*(1), 27. doi:10.1177/0022146514521426

Note: Age controlled when predicting childhood adversity. Age, income, education, and marital status controlled for all other models. Flags for number of missing relationships are also controlled in models predicting adult relationship strain and support. W1 = Wave 1. Unstandardized coefficients. Standard errors in parentheses.

$*p < .05, **p < .01, ***p < .001$ (two-tailed test).

In both cases, Umberson et al. (2014) make the case that the race effect occurs among men but not among women, by calculating and showing the slopes among women as well. For example, in the case of childhood adversity they say this:

> This interaction term is significant and indicates that black men report significantly more childhood adversity than White men (.219); however, this difference is not significant among women (.219 − .237 = −.018).

The same point is made for the interaction predicting relationship strain, where the net race difference among women is .132 - .100 = .032. Including these within-group differences by gender is important to the overall interpretation because now we know that the race difference observed only occurs among men. We could have observed, for example, a weaker, but still significant effect among women, which leads to a more general race difference interpretation. This result, however, is very much an intersectionality interpretation: The effect only occurs in one group, and generalizations to broader considerations of race per se are misleading.

Later in the same article, Umberson et al. (2014) have the opportunity to present two two-way interactions in the same model. This often causes problems because the interpretation gets subtle. The important point is the careful language that goes with multiple two-way interactions, as opposed to a true three-way interaction. Table 2.18 shows these interactions, predicting relationship strain in adulthood. Panel C of this table has two two-way interactions, one between race and gender and the other between race and childhood adversity, in predicting relationship strain in adulthood at Wave 1 of the American's Changing Lives study.

If we concentrate on race as the focal variable, we could interpret these interactions this way: At *any* level of childhood adversity, there is a race by gender interaction in predicting relationship strain. The Black–White difference among men is nonsignificant (b = .055), but at the same time, there a significantly more negative effect among women. In fact, this effect works out to be .055 -.091 = -.036. Although it is not reported in the article, this is also likely not to be significant. So it is possible to have two within-group effects that each are not significant, but the *difference* between them can be significant—very important.

For both genders equally, there is also a two-way interaction between race and childhood adversity. This interaction says that each additional childhood adversity activates the Black–White difference further by .057. So at adversity = 2, the net effect of Black is .055 + .057*2 = .169. This enhanced impact of childhood adversity, importantly, applies to both genders because this is a two-way interaction.

This article is a good example of specific reasoning matched to interactions presented and interpreted in appropriate detail. Another possible strategy is to "take apart" the interaction, as we have in earlier examples, and show the effects within subgroups separately. This is a matter of choice, but the advantage of this approach is that you can see exactly how other variables influence an

TABLE 2.18 ● HYPOTHESIS 2: ORDINARY LEAST-SQUARES MODELS ESTIMATING THE EFFECT OF CHILDHOOD ADVERSITY AND ADULT STRESS BURDEN ON ADULT RELATIONSHIP STRAIN AND ADULT RELATIONSHIP SUPPORT, BY RACE AND GENDER (N = 3,477).

	Relationship Strain in Adulthood		Relationship Support in Adulthood	
	Wave 1 (1)	Wave 2 (2)	Wave 1 (3)	Wave 2 (4)
Panel A: Base model				
Female	−.007	−.045*	.125***	.098***
	(.024)	(.019)	(.024)	(.025)
Black	.113**	.058**	−.046	.050
	(.034)	(.019)	(.024)	(.026)
Relationship strain in adulthood (W1)	—	.547***	—	—
		(.016)		
Relationship support in adulthood (W1)	—		—	.469***
				(.018)
Female*black	−.102*	—	—	—
	(−.102)			
R^2	.14	.40	.03	.39
Panel B: Control for childhood adversity				
Female	−.014	−.048*	.131***	.101***
	(.024)	(.019)	(.024)	(.026)
Black	.104**	.057**	−.041	.050
	(.034)	(.019)	(.024)	(.026)

(Continued)

TABLE 2.18 ● Continued

	Relationship Strain in Adulthood		Relationship Support in Adulthood	
	Wave 1 (1)	Wave 2 (2)	Wave 1 (3)	Wave 2 (4)
Relationship strain in adulthood (W1)	—	.543***	—	—
		(.016)		
Relationship support in adulthood (W1)	—	—	—	.466***
				(.019)
Female*black	−.091*	—	—	—
	(.043)			
Childhood adversity	.039***	.025**	−.066***	−.024*
	(.010)	(.008)	(.012)	(.011)
R^2	.12	.39	.03	.32
Panel C: Interaction of childhood adversity with race				
Female	−.012	−.047*	.130***	.099***
	(.024)	(.019)	(.024)	(.026)
Black	.055	.023	−.030	.091**
	(.039)	(.024)	(.033)	(.033)
Relationship strain in adulthood (W1)	—	.541***	—	—
		(.016)		
Relationship support in adulthood (W1)	—	—	—	.465***
				(.018)
Female*black	−.091*	—	—	—
	(.043)			
Childhood adversity	.024	.015	−.063***	−.011
	(.011)	(.009)	(.014)	(.013)
Black*childhood adversity	.057**	.040*	−.012	−.048*
	(.022)	(.018)	(.026)	(.024)
R^2	.12	.39	.03	.32

Source: Umberson, D., Williams, K., Thomas, P. A., Liu, H., & Thomeer, M. B. (2014). Race, gender, and chains of disadvantage: Childhood adversity, social relationships, and health. *Journal of Health and Social Behavior, 55*(1), 28. doi:10.1177/0022146514521426

Note: All models control for age and number of missing relationships. Panels D and E also control for income, education, and marital status. Unstandardized coefficients. Standard errors in parentheses. W1 = Wave 1.

$+p$ = .10, *p < .05, **p < .01, ***p < .001 (two-tailed test).

effect within each subgroup. It is obvious from Table 2.18 here that the article is only explaining the effect of childhood adversity among Blacks, since the effect of adversity among Whites is not significant. Thus, tracking the effect of early adversity controlling for adult stress burden among Blacks would show the degree to which adult stress explains this effect in this group specifically.

2.6.3 A Three-Way Interaction

Everything gets interpretively more complex when you consider three-way interactions. You can see from our earlier example a basic issue in interpreting three-way interactions: It is difficult to "see" what the three-way terms actually represent because their interpretation depends on the lower-order two-way terms. As a result, presentation of three-way interactions—and the accompanying language—becomes much more difficult. The appropriate language itself is an issue: One has to avoid stating the interaction as separate additive effects, unintentionally, and it is difficult to capture the true nature of the three-way contingency.

A recent article by Jonathan Koltai and Scott Schieman includes an essential three-way interaction as part of the argument ("Job Pressure and SES-Contingent Buffering: Resource Reinforcement, Substitution, or the Stress of Higher Status?" *Journal of Health and Social Behavior*, 2015). This article (in part) studies the effect of job pressure on anxiety, using the 2008 National Study of the Changing Workforce. Usually, job pressure is considered a demand characteristic in the workplace with negative consequences. However, job-related resources may intervene to ameliorate these consequences—this is the "buffering hypothesis" of the job demands-resources model. Job resources, such as autonomy, should help to reduce the consequences of job pressure. Koltai and Schieman insert SES into this model, suggesting that the joint effect of job demands and resources has very different meanings at different levels of SES.

Their argument is that the meaning of job resources may change in higher status jobs—autonomy may not appear to be a resource because higher status jobs involve greater responsibility for workplace outcomes. Table 2 from that article (see Table 2.19) shows three-way interactions between job pressure, job autonomy, and either high education or high income, in predicting anxiety levels (Models 2 and 4). The two interactions are similar in form.

All of the components of the three-way interaction are shown in this table. Notice that none of the two-way terms in this model are significant, for either model. The three-way term, however, suggests that the effect of job pressure on anxiety is enhanced specifically

TABLE 2.19 ● ANXIETY REGRESSED ON JOB PRESSURE, JOB-RELATED RESOURCES, SOCIOECONOMIC STATUS, AND INTERACTIONS (*N* = 3,284)					
	Model 1	**Model 2**	**Model 3**	**Model 4**	**Model 5**
Job pressure					
Job pressure	.352***	.341***	.343***	.333***	.336***
Job-related resources					
Job autonomy	−.094***	−.116***	−.096***	−.113***	−.096***
Challenging work	−.126***	−.128***	−.176***	−.127***	−.128**
Socioeconomic status					
High education	−.112**	−.106**	−.118**	−.114**	−.111**
High income	−.089*	−.090*	−.088*	−.081*	−.095*
Interaction terms					
Job Pressure × Job Autonomy	—	−.050	—	−.047	—
Job Pressure × High Education	—	−.018	.007	—	—
Job Autonomy × High Education	—	−.040	—	—	—
Job Pressure × Job Autonomy× High Education	—	.105*	—	—	—
Job Pressure × Challenging Work	—	—	−.073	—	−.067
Challenging Work× High Education	—	—	.099	—	—
Job Pressure × Challenging Work × High Education	—	—	.193**	—	—
Job Pressure × High Income	—	—	—	.024	.017
Job Autonomy × High Income	—	—	—	.027	—
Job Pressure × Job Autonomy × High Income	—	—	—	.094*	—
Challenging Work × High Income	—	—	—	—	−.013
Job Pressure × Challenging Work × High Income	—	—	—	—	.173*
Constant	2.411***	2.403***	2.428***	2.398***	2.415***

Source: Koltai, J. & Schieman, S. (2015). Job pressure and SES-contingent buffering: Resource reinforcement, substitution, or the stress of higher status?" *Journal of Health and Social Behavior, 56*(2), p. 189, Table 2.

among workers with high income or high education and greater job autonomy—the "stress of higher status." But this interaction would be more difficult to interpret if some of the two-way components were also significant.

One could work out a set of subgroup slopes for the effect of job pressure, as we did earlier in the chapter, but Koltai and Schieman use another very effective method: separate graphs of the two-way interaction between job pressure and job autonomy for those without versus with a university degree. Figure 2.3 shows this graph.

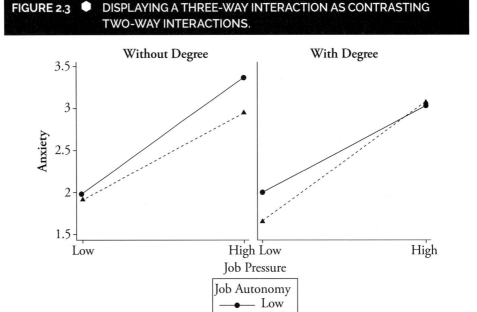

FIGURE 2.3 ● DISPLAYING A THREE-WAY INTERACTION AS CONTRASTING TWO-WAY INTERACTIONS.

Source: Koltai, J. & Schieman, S. (2015). Job pressure and SES-contingent buffering: Resource reinforcement, substitution, or the stress of higher status?" *Journal of Health and Social Behavior, 56*(2), p. 190.

The graph shows the positive effect of job pressure on anxiety, in general, but modified by levels of job autonomy. When the respondent has less than a university degree and thus a job that corresponds to this level of qualifications, job autonomy is helpful in reducing the impact of job pressure—as one would generally expect. But when the respondent has a university degree (or more), job autonomy actually increases the effect of job pressure—evidence of the stress of higher status. The graph reveals some interesting issues about the switch in the role of job autonomy: At lower levels of education, it acts as a classic resource moderator, but at higher levels, there is an initial advantage due to job autonomy at low levels of job pressure that disappears as job pressure increases. The acceleration of the effect of job pressure only makes up the difference with those low in job autonomy—it does not actually produce higher levels of anxiety at any point. It also does not produce levels of anxiety higher than the traditionally understood worse-off group here: those with high levels of job pressure, low autonomy, and less education.

What we see here is the advantage of presenting the graph of the three-way interaction: It not only communicates the three-way difference succinctly, it also shows us where the levels of anxiety are across groups, avoiding an over-interpretation of the change in direction of the role of job autonomy. The graph also efficiently illustrates the nature of a three-way interaction, by showing the difference in a two-way interaction at levels of a third variable.

Concluding Words

This chapter has considered interactions in considerably more detail than most of the discussions in the literature on this issue. It is surprising that so little space is given to the interpretation of interactions in expository statistical writing. The issue is that interactions are a natural and ubiquitous consequence of pursuing results completely, of not accepting the presumption of generalizability. We have encouraged the consideration of the intersectionality embodied by interactions for theoretical, practical, and policy reasons. Because interactions constrain our generalizations, they are an extremely important issue in a wide array of questions involving assumptions of personal, institutional, community, or national generalizability.

In this chapter, we have encouraged practices that get more out of the interactions we estimate. There is more than a difference in effects at issue: There is the issue of the existence or reversal in effects across subgroups, and there is the issue of the relative position of groups on the outcome, captured in graphs such as in Koltai and Schieman (2015). These additional pieces of information are essential to the full interpretation of interactions.

Interactions are the first form of departure from the linear additive model we see as standard in many literatures. These models introduce a multiplicative term to represent the possibility of a *condition* in the effect of *X*. In the next chapter, we consider departures from the constraint of linearity and how nonlinear relationships can be represented in these models.

Practice Questions

1. Imagine you want to study the effects of gender and a GPA above 3 on a student's grade in statistics (*Y*, measured out of 100). For gender, you define a dummy variable, *X*1, equal to 1 for females and 0 for males. For GPA, your define a dummy variable, *X*2, equal to 1 if the person has a grade-point average above 3 and 0 if they do not.

   You are interested in the possibility of an interaction between sex and grade-point average in predicting grade in statistics. So you run a regression and find the interaction is significant. The results are

   $$Y = 62 - 3X_1 + 5X_2 + 5(X_1 \cdot X_2)$$

   Interpret the interaction by calculating the effect of grade-point average for men and for women.

2. The results in Table 2.A test whether the effect of mother's education on a child's education differs among Blacks and Hispanics relative to Whites. To test this idea, interactions were tested between *momed* and *black* (*momed*black* in the results) and *momed* and *Hispanic* (*momed*Hispanic* in the results). The overall interaction test (not shown)

TABLE 2.A ● INTERACTION BETWEEN MOTHER'S EDUCATION AND RACE IN PREDICTING A CHILD'S EDUCATION

Parameter	Estimate	Standard Error	*t* Value	Pr > |t|
Intercept	8.384118921	0.19267909	43.51	<.0001
momed	0.163236396	0.01463782	11.15	<.0001
asvab	0.442150813	0.01054159	41.94	<.0001
black	1.122676462	0.29727422	3.78	0.0002
Hispanic	1.801221813	0.23440161	7.68	<.0001
momed*black	−0.068214539	0.02266732	−3.01	0.0026
momed*Hispanic	−0.147286595	0.01799430	−8.19	<.0001

was significant. Variables are defined in the same way as for question 4, chapter 1. That is:

- **momed:** The respondent's mother's education in years
- **Black, Hispanic:** dummy variables for these groups, relative to Whites.
- **Asvab:** This is the person's percentile rank on a national achievement test given in early high school. Here it is measured in 10% increases, so it varies from 0 to 10.

In the results, only **Asvab** was controlled, and its mean in this equation was 4.8.

Answer these questions:

a. What is the effect of mother's education on the child's education among Whites? No calculation is necessary here: The answer can be interpreted directly from the equation.

b. Use the results to calculate the effect of mothers' education on the child's education

among Hispanics. Show the intercept and the slope among Hispanics.

3. The results for this question assess whether the effect of education on experience of discrimination varies by whether you are a visible minority, using the 2015 Canadian General Social Survey data.

The dependent variable here is the number of institutions at which the respondent has experienced discrimination.

The independent variables are

- **educyrs**: Years of education
- **vismin**: A dummy variable = 1 if a visible minority; 0 if not

In the regression results shown in Table 2.B (using PROC GLM) in SAS, there is a significant interaction between **educyrs** and the **vismin** dummy variable (**educyrs*vismin**).

TABLE 2.B ● **AN INTERACTION BETWEEN EDUCATION AND VISIBLE MINORITY STATUS IN PREDICTING THE EXPERIENCE OF DISCRIMINATION**

Parameter	Estimate	Standard Error	t Value	Pr > |t|
Intercept	28.30707730	0.73756962	38.38	<.0001
educyrs	−0.20509793	0.05352192	−3.83	0.0001
vismin	6.13133315	0.84597840	7.25	<.0001
educyrs*vismin	−0.19211140	0.06220115	−3.09	0.0020

Answer these questions:

a. What is the effect (*the regression coefficient*) of education on reported discrimination among respondents who are in the nonvisible reference group? Just state the coefficient (the slope).

b. Use the results to calculate the effect of education on reported discrimination in visible minority groups.

c. Which group benefits more from education: visible minorities or others?

4. The results in Table 2.C focus on the relationship between child grades in school and their educational aspirations. In the regression results from SAS, there is a significant interaction between child

grades and whether the mother has had depression problems earlier in life in predicting aspirations.

The variables are:

educaspirations: The dependent variable in the regression. It is the number of years of additional education the child intends to complete.

cgrades: The child's report of their average grades in five subjects, on a scale from 1 (weak) to 5 (strong).

momdepearly: A dummy variable = 1 if the mother had depression problems earlier in life, and =0 if not

cgrades*momdepearly: the interaction between child grades and the mother's earlier depression problems.

TABLE 2.C ● THE CONDITIONAL EFFECT OF CHILD GRADES ON EDUCATION ASPIRATIONS

Parameter	Estimate	Standard Error	t Value	Pr > |t|
Intercept	3.121025443	0.11687838	26.70	<.0001
cgrades	0.183210982	0.03205754	5.72	<.0001
momdepearly	0.462464158	0.21605413	2.14	0.0326
cgrades*momdepearly	−0.126095843	0.05963589	−2.11	0.0348

Answer these questions:

a. What is the effect of child grades on aspirations for children whose mothers did not have depression problems?

b. Use the results to calculate the effect of child grades on aspirations for children whose mothers *did* have depression problems.

5. Results are shown in table 2.D from a study of 9- to 16-year old children in husband-wife families in Toronto. The dependent variable here is an index of externalizing symptoms (aggression, hostility, and anger), and the main focus is the effect of maternal caring (from the Parental Bonding scale) on externalizing symptoms. Maternal caring measures the active support and nurturance of the mother as reported by the child.

Model 1 is the additive model, Model 2 is the two-way interaction model, and Model 3 is the three-way interaction model. The independent variables in the output are

- **momcare**: Maternal caring sub-scale from Parental Bonding

- **female**: A dummy variable = 1 for female, 0 for male.
- **teen**: A dummy variable = 1 for children 13-16, 0 for children 9–12
- **femxteen**: female x teen
- **mcarexfem**: momcare x female
- **mcarexteen**: momcare x teen
- **mcarexfemxteen**: momcare x female x teen

a. Conduct a test to determine whether there is a three-way interaction between maternal care, child gender (female), and child age (teen).

b. Whether it is significant or not, calculate the subgroup slopes for the effect of maternal caring in four groups: boys 9 to 12, boys 13 to 16, girls 9 to 12, and girls 13 to 16. In which group does maternal caring have the lowest impact on externalizing symptoms? (***Note:*** *You do not have to calculate intercepts in subgroups to answer this question*).

c. Write a test statement to determine whether there is a difference in the effect of maternal caring for teenage boys versus teenage girls.

TABLE 2.D ● THREE NESTED REGRESSION MODELS USED TO ESTIMATE A THREE-WAY INTERACTION

MODEL 1

```
Number of Observations Read                    881
Number of Observations Used                    878
Number of Observations with Missing Values       3
```

Weight: famweight weight by nativity, maternal employment, income, and kids 9 to 16

Analysis of Variance

Source	DF	Sum of Squares	Mean Square	F Value	Pr > F
Model	3	94.52422	31.50807	35.26	<.0001
Error	874	780.92435	0.89351		
Corrected Total	877	875.44857			

(Continued)

TABLE 2.D ● **Continued**

Root MSE	0.94525	R-Square	0.1080
Dependent Mean	0.01780	Adj R-Sq	0.1049
Coeff Var	5309.02523		

Parameter Estimates

Variable	DF	Parameter Estimate	Standard Error	t Value	Pr > |t|
Intercept	1	1.75446	0.20776	8.44	<.0001
momcare	1	−0.08379	0.00982	−8.54	<.0001
female	1	−0.20833	0.06412	−3.25	0.0012
teen	1	0.21181	0.06559	3.23	0.0013

MODEL 2

Number of Observations Read	881
Number of Observations Used	878
Number of Observations with Missing Values	3

Weight: famweight weight by nativity, maternal employment, income, and kids 9 to 16

Analysis of Variance

Source	DF	Sum of Squares	Mean Square	F Value	Pr > F
Model	6	99.47322	16.57887	18.61	<.0001
Error	871	775.97534	0.89090		
Corrected Total	877	875.44857			

Root MSE	0.94388	R-Square	0.1136
Dependent Mean	0.01780	Adj R-Sq	0.1075
Coeff Var	5301.28200		

Parameter Estimates

Variable	DF	Parameter Estimate	Standard Error	t Value	Pr > |t|
Intercept	1	1.53797	0.33632	4.57	<.0001
momcare	1	−0.07074	0.01614	−4.38	<.0001
female	1	−0.13807	0.41760	−0.33	0.7410
teen	1	0.47442	0.40677	1.17	0.2438
femxteen	1	0.27475	0.13172	2.09	0.0373
mcarexfem	1	−0.00879	0.01965	−0.45	0.6549
mcarexteen	1	−0.01977	0.01976	−1.00	0.3174

MODEL 3

Number of Observations Read	881
Number of Observations Used	878
Number of Observations with Missing Values	3

Weight: famweight weight by nativity, maternal employment, income, and kids 9 to 16

Analysis of Variance

Source	DF	Sum of Squares	Mean Square	F Value	Pr > F
Model	7	102.92051	14.70293	16.56	<.0001
Error	870	772.52806	0.88796		
Corrected Total	877	875.44857			

Root MSE	0.94232	R-Square	0.1176	
Dependent Mean	0.01780	Adj R-Sq	0.1105	
Coeff Var	5292.53244			

Parameter Estimates

Variable	DF	Parameter Estimate	Standard Error	t Value	Pr > |t|
Intercept	1	1.20057	0.37691	3.19	0.0015
momcare	1	−0.05431	0.01814	−2.99	0.0028
female	1	0.58582	0.55569	1.05	0.2921
teen	1	1.27207	0.57341	2.22	0.0268
femxteen	1	−1.30881	0.81439	−1.61	0.1084
mcarexfem	1	−0.04354	0.02639	−1.65	0.0992
mcarexteen	1	−0.05959	0.02824	−2.11	0.0352
mcarexfemxteen	1	0.07776	0.03947	1.97	0.0491

6. The results that follow (Table 2.E) are from an analysis using data from the National Survey of Families and Households at Waves 1 and 2. This analysis considers the impact of marital problems reported at Wave 1 on the impact of divorce on depression between Waves 1 and 2 in a sample of married respondents at Wave 1.

The variables are
- **cesd2**: Depression at Wave 2
- **cesd1**: Depression at Wave 1
- **div12**: = 1 if the respondent got divorced between Waves 1 and 2
- = 0 if the respondent stayed married
- **marprob1**: An index of marital problems reported at Wave 1
- **marprobxdiv**: = div12*marprob1 (an interaction)

The displayed output includes descriptive statistics, an additive model showing the effect of divorce on depression at Wave 2 controlling for prior marital problems and depression at Wave 1, and an interactive model.

Answer these questions:

a. Conduct a test *or cite evidence in the output* concerning the significance ($p < .05$) of the interaction between divorce and prior marital problems.

b. Assuming that there is a significant interaction and using the information in the descriptive statistics about the mean and standard deviations of variables in the model, calculate (only) the effect of divorce at +1 and −1 standard deviations from the mean level of marital problems.

TABLE 2.E ● TESTING AN INTERACTION BETWEEN PRIOR MARITAL PROBLEMS AND THE EFFECT OF DIVORCE.

```
                          The REG Procedure
                           Model: MODEL1
                      Dependent Variable: cesd2
```

```
        Number of Observations Read                 5456
        Number of Observations Used                 5157
        Number of Observations with Missing Values   299
```

Descriptive Statistics

Variable	Sum	Mean	Uncorrected SS	Variance	Standard Deviation
Intercept	5853.47443	1.00000	5853.47443	0	0
div12	598.18626	0.10219	598.18626	0.10416	0.32274
marprob1	10878	1.85841	24127	0.75850	0.87092
cesd1	6003.51033	1.02563	15399	1.79241	1.33881
cesd2	6102.47533	1.04254	15303	1.73413	1.31686
marprobxdiv	1455.88158	0.24872	4264.68370	0.75690	0.87000

Weight: MUFINW93 The person weight for NSFH2 main respond

Analysis of Variance

Source	DF	Sum of Squares	Mean Square	F Value	Pr > F
Model	3	1351.23858	450.41286	305.80	<.0001
Error	5153	7589.92205	1.47291		
Corrected Total	5156	8941.16063			

Root MSE	1.21364	R-Square	0.1511
Dependent Mean	1.04254	Adj R-Sq	0.1506
Coeff Var	116.41161		

Parameter Estimates

Variable	DF	Parameter Estimate	Standard Error	t Value	Pr > |t|
Intercept	1	0.46271	0.03980	11.63	<.0001
div12	1	0.37851	0.05394	7.02	<.0001
marprob1	1	0.10501	0.02051	5.12	<.0001
cesd1	1	0.33736	0.01301	25.93	<.0001

```
                            MODEL 2
          regression ces-d on marital situation                74
                                      19:52 Monday, February 14, 2011
                          The REG Procedure
                           Model: MODEL2
                      Dependent Variable: cesd2
```

```
        Number of Observations Read                 5456
        Number of Observations Used                 5157
        Number of Observations with Missing Values   299
```

Weight: MUFINW93 The person weight for NSFH2 main respond

Analysis of Variance

Source	DF	Sum of Squares	Mean Square	F Value	Pr > F
Model	4	1358.21235	339.55309	230.70	<.0001
Error	5152	7582.94828	1.47185		
Corrected Total	5156	8941.16063			

Root MSE	1.21320	R-Square	0.1519
Dependent Mean	1.04254	Adj R-Sq	0.1512
Coeff Var	116.36940		

Parameter Estimates

Variable	DF	Parameter Estimate	Standard Error	t Value	Pr > |t|
Intercept	1	0.42442	0.04350	9.76	<.0001
div12	1	0.63165	0.12819	4.93	<.0001
marprob1	1	0.12656	0.02277	5.56	<.0001
cesd1	1	0.33700	0.01301	25.91	<.0001
marprobxdiv	1	-0.10963	0.05037	-2.18	0.0295

7. Results in this question (Table 2.F) are from a model estimating a three-way interaction between work–family conflict, gender, and perception of neighborhood disorder in predicting distress, using the 2009–2011 Toronto Study on Neighbourhood Effects on Health and Well-Being (O'Campo et al., 2015). The three-way term is significant, so you should assume there *is* a three-way interaction. There are two controls as well—education and marital status—but they are *not* relevant in this question.

The means and standard deviations for the variables that follow are part of the output. The independent variables in the output are

- **wfc**: A measure of work-family conflict
- **FEMALE**: A dummy variable = 1 for female, 0 for male
- **neighdisorder**: The respondent's perception of disorder in the neighborhoodenvironment, including the presence of trash, litter, loud noise, heavy traffic, gang activity, crime, and drug dealers
- **reduc**: Years of education

- **married**: A dummy variable for married =1 if married, 0 if not.
- **neighdisorderxwfc**: neighdisorder x wfc
- **neighdisorderxfemale**: neighdisorder x female
- **wfcxfemale**: wfc x female
- **neighdisorderxwfcxfemale**: neighdisorder x wfc x female

a. Use the output for the descriptive statistics to figure out the levels of neighborhood disorder corresponding to +1 and -1 standard deviations from the mean.

b. *ONLY* figure out the slopes in this question. Calculate the slope for the effect of work–family conflict on distress among women in neighborhoods with high disorder (+1 SD above the mean) and the slope for work–family conflict among men in neighborhoods with high disorder (+1 SD below the mean).

c. Write out a TEST statement that tests the significance of the slope for the effect of work–family conflict among women in high disorder (+1 SD) neighborhoods.

TABLE 2.F ● **A THREE-WAY INTERACTION BETWEEN NEIGHBORHOOD DISORDER, WORK-FAMILY CONFLICT, AND GENDER**

The MEANS Procedure

Variable	Label	N	Mean	Sid Dev	Minimum	Maximum
neighdisorder		1702	3.9124559	1.6565754	2.0000000	10.0000000
wfc		1702	8.9994125	3.2483885	4.0000000	16.0000000
FEMALE	Participant is female	1702	0.5329025	0.4990629	0	1.0000000
reduc		1702	7.9747356	0.3123121	1.0000000	8.0000000
married		1702	0.5564042	0.4969544	0	1.0000000

The REG Procedure
Model: MODEL1
Dependent Variable: distress

Number of Observations Read	1702
Number of Observations Used	1702

Weight: nehwweight weight by gender, nativity, hhincome, and household size

Analysis of Variance

Source	DF	Sum of Squares	Mean Square	F Value	Pr > F
Model	9	21448	2383.14004	41.60	<.0001
Error	1692	96940	57.29343		
Corrected Total	1701	118389			

Root M SE	7.56924	R-Square	0.1812
Dependent Mean	10.73710	Adj R-Sq	0.1768
Coeff Var	70.49618		

Parameter Estimates						
Variable	Label	DF	Parameter Estimate	Standard Error	t Value	Pr > Iti
Intercept	Intercept	1	7.31462	5.00171	1.46	0.1438
neighdisorder		1	−0.05368	0.45601	−0.12	0.9063
wfc		1	0.69149	0.20710	3.34	0.0009
FEMALE	Participant is female	1	5.43195	2.68617	2.02	0.0433
reduc		1	−0.34766	0.57854	−0.60	0.5480
married		1	−2.73686	0.39920	−6.86	<.0001
neighdisorderxwfc		1	0.03551	0.04952	0.72	0.4734
neighdisorderxfemale		1	−0.79922	0.62730	−1.27	0.2028
wfcxfemale		1	−0.89026	0.28612	−3.11	0.0019
neighdisorderxwfcxfemale		1	0.18287	0.06537	2.80	0.0052

8. The effect of divorce may dissipate with time—but differentially across gender. The results for this question in Table 2.G test a two-way interaction between gender and time since divorce, considered as a set of dummy variables, in predicting depression at Wave II of the NSFH. Both variables are therefore categorical in the equation, with the stably married the reference group for time since divorce.

The attached output includes only the interaction model and a post-hoc test for any interaction between time since divorce and gender. The variables are as follows:

- **divlast2**: The experience of divorce in the last two years before Wave 2.
- **div2to4**: Divorce 2 to 4 years before Wave 2
- **div4to6**: Divorce 4 to 6 years before Wave 2
- **violence**: A count of the number of violent incidents in the marriage per year at Wave 1
- **cesd2tot**: A depression scale at Wave 2

- **cesd1tot**: The same depression scale at Wave 1
- **female**: A dummy variable for female (= 1 if female, 0 if male).
- **femxdivlt2**: female x divlast2
- **femxdiv24**: female x div2to4
- **femxdiv46**: female x div4to6

a. What result in the output provides evidence that there is a two-way interaction between gender and time since divorce?

b. Calculate the slope for the effect of female on depression among those:
   1. still married
   2. divorced in the last two years
   3. divorced 4 to 6 years ago

c. Write out a TEST statement that tests the significance of the difference in the effect of divorce for women divorced 4 to 6 years ago versus 2 to 4 years ago, using the variable names in the equation.

TABLE 2.G ● GENDER SPECIFIC EFFECTS OF DIVORCE BY TIME SINCE DIVORCE

Number of Observations Read	5213
Number of Observations Used	5028
Number of Observations with Missing Values	185

Analysis of Variance

Source	DF	Sum of Squares	Mean Square	F Value	Pr > F
Model	9	207660	23073	121.76	<.0001
Error	5018	950871	189.49212		
Corrected Total	5027	1158532			

Root MSE	13.76561	R-Square	0.1792
Dependent Mean	13.05564	Adj R-Sq	0.1778
Coeff Var	105.43806		

Parameter Estimates

Variable	DF	Parameter Estimate	Standard Error	t Value	Pr > |t|
Intercept	1	6.28216	0.34066	18.44	<.0001
divlast2	1	7.12725	1.57191	4.53	<.0001
div2to4	1	3.92742	1.52619	2.57	0.0101
div4to6	1	−0.91914	1.33123	−0.69	0.4899
violence	1	1.96667	0.29385	6.69	<.0001
female	1	2.28131	0.41985	5.43	<.0001
cesd1tot	1	0.35242	0.01323	26.63	<.0001
femxdivlt2	1	1.50082	2.09839	0.72	0.4745
femxdiv24	1	2.72668	1.97904	1.38	0.1683
femxdiv46	1	4.88633	1.82143	2.68	0.0073

(Continued)

TABLE 2.G ● **Continued**

Test femxdiv Results for Dependent Variable cesd2tot				
Source	DF	Mean Square	F Value	Pr > F
Numerator	3	571.95487	3.02	0.0287
Denominator	5018	189.49212		

Appendix

We present syntax below showing how to code the two-way interaction example in this chapter in SAS and STATA. The purpose here is not to teach the basics of coding in each program but to broadly outline the differences in the organization and logic of coding.

The syntax below is annotated using comments in the coding. We encourage this in both programs. In data analysis, you have to leave a trail of evidence about what you have done in order to reproduce findings and/or make revisions to finished papers.

SAS Code to Create the Data for Running the Two-Way Interaction

```
/*1*/

/* Comments start and end with these delimiters */

/* This is a data step in SAS. This creates the new data you will eventually analyze in a
PROC step, using the raw data as input. The data step is used to create new variables for
analysis, recode variables, subset the sample, or whatever you need to do to fine tune your
variables for analysis.*/

/* Start with a DATA statement. Give a name to a temporary data set you will create for
this run only. All SAS statements end in a semi-colon */

/* The SET statement is a statement that tells SAS to read an existing data set. It has a two-
level name: the first level is a special library name which you have defined telling SAS in which
folder the data resides on your computer. After the "dot", the second level is the file name of
the data in that folder. SAS uses the parenthesis to introduce options: here "keep=" tells SAS
which variables to read in from the data set. This is mainly useful very large data sets.*/

data temp;
      set nsfhdata.nsfh1(keep=mcaseid cmint m484 m540a m540b m535--m538 m2bp01 irwage
      irearn irtot1 ihtot1 m530t01m m532t02m m532t03m m532t04m educat weight

        m532t05m m532t06m m532t07m m532t08m m532t09m m532t10m m529t01m m531t02m m531t03m
        m531t04m m531t05m m531t06m m531t07m m531t08m m531t09m m531t10m  m534t01 m534t02
        m534t03 m534t04 m534t05 m534t06 m534t07 m534t08 m534t09 m534t10);

    /* 2. This is how you subset data. Here we select people who identify as Black, White,
or Hispanic in the wave 1 NSFH data. This also excludes people missing on this variable
(codes 97 and above). The IF statement simply states a condition for reading the data. */

    if 1<=m484<=6;
```

/*3. Renaming and recoding variables.First use IF- THEN statements to recode missing values to system missing in SAS ("."). Then use "newvar= function(oldvar)" type statements to create new variables. The round function divides income in dollars by 1000 and rounds it to one decimal place. You can also use "newvar = oldvar" statements just to rename variables*/.

```
if irtot1>=999996 then irtot1=.;
if ihtot1>=99999996 then ihtot1=.;
if irwage>=999996 then irwage=.;
if irearn>=999997 then irearn=.;

if educat>=90 then educat=.;
educ=educat;

if m2bp01>95 then    m2bp01=.;
age = m2bp01;

SEI=round((m540b/100),1);
if sei>=99 then sei=.;

rtotinc=round(irtot1/1000,1);
hhinc=round(ihtot1/1000,1);
rjobinc=round(irwage/1000,1);
rearninc=round(irearn/1000,1);
```

/* 4. Using an array to figure out total years in the current job to measure seniority. Arrays are just lists of variables you can refer to with a single label, named by the ARRAY statement.

The DO loop performs the same action on each element of the array in turn.

Here we are looking for the first job in a job history that is full-time and still ongoing (endwrk(i)=9995). When this happens in the list, a new variable labeled "cmstrtjob" is created. This variable is the century month of the first month of the current job.

The IF / THEN statement tells the DO loop to leave -- to quit -- when the new   variable takes on a real value, denoted by any value greater than "."*/

```
array startwrk(10) m529t01m m531t02m m531t03m m531t04m m531t05m m531t06m m531t07m
      m531t08m m531t09m m531t10m;

array endwrk(10) m530t01m m532t02m m532t03m m532t04m m532t05m m532t06m m532t07m
      m532t08m m532t09m m532t10m;

array full(10) m534t01 m534t02 m534t03 m534t04 m534t05 m534t06 m534t07 m534t08
      m534t09 m534t10;

do i=1 to 10;
    if 0<startwrk(i)<9990 and full(i)=1 and endwrk(i)=9995 then cmstrtjob=startwrk(i);
    if cmstrtjob>. then leave;
end;
```

```
     /* 5. This creates the seniority variable "yrscurrjob" by subtracting the starting
century month of the current job from the century month of the interview ("cmint"), and
dividing by 12 to turn the result into years. Total time in the labor force is also created
here, by taking the difference between the current month and the starting century month of
the first job.*/

     yrscurrjob=(cmint-cmstrtjob)/12;
     yrslabor=(cmint-m529t01m)/12;


     /* 6. This deletes observations within a certain range of
           occupational categories on the current occupation variable.
           This was eventually deleted from the program using a single line comment (*) */

     *if 473<=m540a<=499 then delete;

     /* 7. Racial dummy variables -- white is the invisible reference
           Use IF/THEN/ELSE statements to create the dummy variables.
           The target group is coded "1", all other groups are coded "0"
           by the ELSE statement.*/

     if m484=1 then black=1; else black=0;
     if 3<=m484<=6 then hisp=1; else hisp=0;


     /* 8. Interactions created here. The "*" multiplies already created variables */

     blackxeduc=black*educat;
     hispxeduc=hisp*educat;
     agexeduc =age*educat;
run;
```

Matching STATA Code

```
*In STATA, comments start and end with asterisks only. 'Enter' serves as a delimiter for
executable statements --compared to SAS, which uses a semi-colon*

*If working in a syntax file (which is referred to as a 'do-file' in STATA) and wish to
continue a command line, use ///*

*to let STATA know you are not done with the command yet*

*Compared to SAS, STATA --by default--transforms all cases in the data after each command.*

*This is unique compared to SAS, which executes all commands used to transform data one
case at a time. The unique 'vertical*horizontal' vs. 'horizontal*vertical' treatment of the
data, and focus on one versus all cases, distinguishes the two programs*


*STATA is also unique in that you can execute line commands to make permanent changes to
the dataset. People often use the 'command' window to execute statements step by step*

*This could be done in SAS as well, but SAS usually is set up to produce a new data set
in its DATA step, much like a batch file-based program. In SAS, users are often creating
temporary data files for use in the current analysis, preserving the original data*

*This is not the case in STATA. Unless you set up the do-file in a*
```

```
*batch file-based approach and save the data as a secondary file, the commands you execute
will alter your original variables, which can become a problem*

*We therefore suggest to use such an approach when creating your do-file. See the example,
below*


*First, open the permanent dataset*


use "C:{insert path to data here}.dta", clear


*1. Keep the variables you wish to use in the analyses using the statement 'keep'*
keep mcaseid cmint m484 m540a m540b m535--m538 m2bp01 irwage irearn irtot1 ///
ihtot1 m530t01m m532t02m m532t03m m532t04m educat weight ///

m532t05m m532t06m m532t07m m532t08m m532t09m m532t10m m529t01m m531t02m m531t03m ///
m531t04m m531t05m m531t06m m531t07m m531t08m m531t09m ///

m531t10m  m534t01 m534t02 m534t03 m534t04 m534t05 m534t06 m534t07 m534t08 m534t09 ///
m534t10


*2. keep the subsample you want using a 'keep if' statment*
keep if m484==1/6



*3. renaming and recoding the individual income variables. STATA uses 'replace' 'if'
statements. Missing variables are denoted as '.'*
replace irtot1=. if irtot1>=999996

replace ihtot1=. if ihtot1>=99999996

replace irwage=. if irwage>=999996

replace irearn=. if irearn>=999997



*The following rounds the variables of interest, similar to SAS, you use a 'round' option.
Note here, the 'gen' statement - short for generate, which produces a new variable. As you
will see below, you can reduce this further to referencing 'g' only*
gen rtotinc=round((irtot1/1000),1)

gen  hhinc=round((ihtot1/1000),1)

gen rjobinc=round((irwage/1000),1)

gen rearninc=round((irearn/1000),1)


replace educat=. if educat>=90

g educ=educat


replace m2bp01=. if m2bp01>=95

g age = m2bp01

g sei=round((m540b/100),1)

replace sei=. if sei>=99
```

```
*4. using a 'loop' to generate a new set of variables for cm start job*


foreach var of varlist m529t01m m531t02m m531t03m m531t04m m531t05m m531t06m /// m531t07m
m531t08m m531t09m m531t10m {

    g cmstrtjob'var'= 'var' if foreach 'x' local endwrk

    }

    ]


*compared to SAS, three-variable based arrays are difficult to code in STATA - the
following line commands are more common for this type of variable transformation*


gen cmstrtjob=.


replace cmstrtjob=m529t01m if ((m529t01m==1/9990) & m534t01==1 & m530t01m==9995))

replace cmstrtjob=m531t02m if ((m529t02m==1/9990) & m534t02==1 & m530t02m==9995))

replace cmstrtjob=m531t03m if ((m529t03m==1/9990) & m534t03==1 & m530t03m==9995))

replace cmstrtjob=m531t04m if ((m529t04m==1/9990) & m534t04==1 & m530t04m==9995))

replace cmstrtjob=m529t05m if ((m529t05m==1/9990) & m534t05==1 & m530t05m==9995))

replace cmstrtjob=m529t06m if ((m529t06m==1/9990) & m534t06==1 & m530t06m==9995))

replace cmstrtjob=m529t07m if ((m529t07m==1/9990) & m534t07==1 & m530t07m==9995))

replace cmstrtjob=m529t08m if ((m529t08m==1/9990) & m534t08==1 & m530t08m==9995))

replace cmstrtjob=m529t09m if ((m529t09m==1/9990) & m534t09==1 & m530t09m==9995))

replace cmstrtjob=m529t10m if ((m529t10m==1/9990) & m534t10==1 & m530t10m==9995))


*5. The following creates the same variables as in the SAS program for 'yrscurrjob' and
'yrslabor'*
g yrscurrjob=(cmint-cmstrtjob)/12
g yrslabor=(cmint-m529t01m)/12


*6. We create the racial dummy variables here. Note, the unique approach to recoding and
generating new variables in the same command line*
recode m484 1=1 2/6=0, g (black)
recode m484 1/2=0 3/6=1, g (hisp)


*7. Similar to the SAS program, we generate education interactions with race by multiplying
the variables together using an asterisk*


g blackxeduc=black*educat
g hispxeduc=hisp*educat
g agexeduc =age*educat


*8. save a new dataset with the changes*
save "C:{insert path to data here}.dta", replace
```

GENERALIZATIONS OF REGRESSION 2

Nonlinear Regression

The usual approach in much quantitative research is to assume linearity: It is simple to interpret, and it is an efficient way of representing the effects of multiple variables. It is also *sometimes* an apptropriate assumption. But when you start to consider actual relationships between specific independent (X) and dependent variables (Y), it is often difficult to imagine that the effect of X is strictly linear. The reason for this is simply that it is often easy to imagine some variation of reasoning that suggests nonlinearity.

For example, if X affects Y, especially over specific ranges of change in X, but flattens out at the extremes, the relationship is nonlinear and importantly so because the linear version assumes a constant impact across all levels of X that does not apply. If there is a threshold in the effect of X, so that there is no impact up to a certain level of X, and then the effect of X accelerates quickly, then we have another kind of nonlinear effect, and it is again important, because the impact of X only occurs over higher levels of X, not all levels of X. Or as often imagined in classic forms of sociological theory, the effect of X on Y is opposite at lower versus higher levels of X, and the minimum / maximum level of Y occurs in the middle ranges of X.

In each of these cases, it is important to consider an alternative nonlinear specification of the effect of X. But be forewarned—once you use a nonlinear specification, there is no longer a constant effect of X across all levels, and so we have to interpret the effect of X specifically at a *given* level of X since the effect changes across levels of X.

There are many approaches to nonlinear regression. These approaches vary widely, between parametric approaches that fit a given functional form for the effect of X, to various "nonparametric" or semi-parametric approaches that attempt to produce a best fit without the limitations of a given functional form for the relationship (such as loess regression or quantile regression), from types of nonlinearity that allow for transcriptions that "fit" inside a linear framework to "truly" nonlinear models that do not, from smooth approaches to segmented approaches, allowing a different linear relationship at different levels of X. These options are important but beyond the scope of this book. We take a practical approach to nonlinearity in this chapter, focusing on commonly applied approaches and flexibility.

Most approaches to nonlinear regression introduce some uncertainty about the exact nature and extent of the nonlinearity. This is typical—when considering nonlinear models, the burden of responsibility often rests more on the analyst in arguing the plausibility of the chosen representation of nonlinearity. Nonlinear regression is not an automated procedure. The issue is often choosing between "too little" and "too much," and your role is to be Goldilocks.

3.1 A SIMPLE EXAMPLE OF A QUADRATIC RELATIONSHIP

If you want to study the nonlinear effect of a continuous variable, such as age, you can create a new variable, age squared, and then consider both age and age squared in a regression. Following Mirowsky and Ross (1992), for example, you can predict a nonlinear pattern in depression over the life course by adding age squared to a linear model:

$$Depression = a + b_1 age + b_2 age^2$$

This specifies a single turn in direction of the effect of age. This specification is the standard method for estimating a ***quadratic*** relationship between X and Y. In this regression, b_1 is usually the direction of the impact of age before the turn in the curve, and b_2 is the impact of age after the turn in the curve. You should see the squared term as a mathematical device in the regression that allows the direction of the effect to change.

The signs of b_1 and b_2 give you information about the shape of the curve. If b_1 is negative and b_2 is positive, the curve generally looks like this:

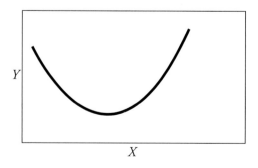

And if b_1 is positive and b_2 is negative, the curve generally looks like this:

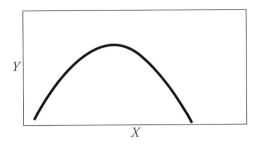

You can estimate this kind of curve in most regression programs after creating a new variable that equals age squared and then including both the linear version of age and the squared version in the same model. In SAS, we run the following simple program in PROC REG:

```
proc reg data=temp simple;
model depress=age1;
model depress=age1 age2;
output out=temp2 predicted=depression;
weight weight;
run;
```

This run of PROC REG first runs a linear model (age1 is age coded in years) and then a quadratic model including age squared (by adding age2, which is age1 squared). Notice here that we have added an "output" line after the quadratic model. This command asks SAS to output the data with one variable added: the predicted value of the dependent variable for each person in the data. Here this new variable is named "depression." Note also we give the outputted data a new name so that it does not replace the original data.

First we can look at the results for the linear model, shown in Table 3.1.

TABLE 3.1 ◆ THE LINEAR EFFECT OF AGE ON DEPRESSION

		Parameter Estimates			
Variable	DF	Parameter Estimate	Standard Error	t Value	Pr > |t|
Intercept	1	17.14265	0.47374	36.19	<.0001
age1	1	−0.01245	0.01011	−1.23	0.2182

If we had just considered the linear effect of age here, we would conclude that it has no effect. We would also be wrong—this is the problem of assuming linearity when the actual relationship is nonlinear, symmetric, and suggests X has effects in opposite directions at different levels of X. Table 3.2 shows the result from the quadratic model.

TABLE 3.2 ◆ THE QUADRATIC EFFECT OF AGE ON DEPRESSION

		Parameter Estimates			
Variable	DF	Parameter Estimate	Standard Error	t Value	Pr > |t|
Intercept	1	29.13440	1.22526	23.78	<.0001
age1	1	−0.59630	0.05597	−10.65	<.0001
age2	1	0.00607	0.00057280	10.60	<.0001

Note that the effect of "age2" is significant and positive. The significance of this term in the regression is a fairly general test of nonlinearity, at least for variables with more than 10 or so levels. Below that, this test may be less sensitive (another test is discussed later). Judging from the coefficients, it appears to be negative over earlier ages and then positive over later ages. You can graph this relationship using the outputted data, by plotting the predicted value of depression against age. This is done in SAS using a graphics program called "*SGPLOT.*"

```
proc sgplot data=temp2;
reg X=age1 Y=depression /
    legendlabel= "Quadratic Effect of Age on Depression"
    degree=2;
xaxis label="Age" min=20 max=100 values=(20 to 95 by 5);
yaxis label="Depression";
run;
```

The PROC SGPLOT line calls in the data set you outputted in PROC REG. The REG statement specifies the plot, by naming the X variable from the data—same as above—and the predicted Y variable—depression. After the slash, options are given. The "legendlabel" option is a description of what the plot is about, in double quotes, "degree" specifies the fit—here 2 refers to a second order fit for quadratic. The X axis and Y axis can be set up specifically to look the way you want. The last two statements here do this. We give a label to each axis, again using text in quotes, and then specify how we want the X axis labeled. The "min" option gives the lowest age to put on the X axis, and the "max" option puts the highest age. The "values" option defines the tick marks on the axis, going from 20 to 95, every five years.

This produces the plot shown in Figure 3.1.

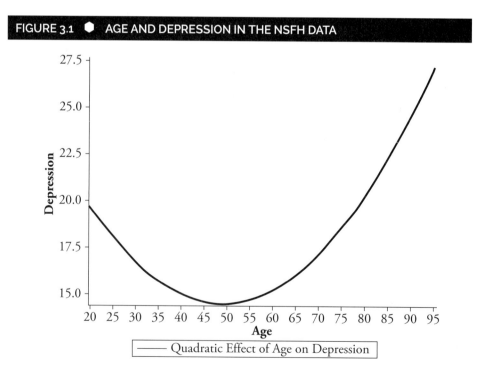

FIGURE 3.1 ● AGE AND DEPRESSION IN THE NSFH DATA

This model can be estimated in STATA using the following syntax, with outputted data including the predicted value of Y (note "pred" is simply a name we have assigned the predicted values of depression estimated from the second regression model estimating the quadratic effect of age):

```
reg depress age1 [pweight=weight]
reg depress age1 age2 [pweight=weight]
predict pred
```

Using the output from STATA the following syntax plots the curve (figure 3.2):

```
twoway qfit pred age1
```

FIGURE 3.2 ● THE AGE-DEPRESSION CURVE PLOTTED IN STATA

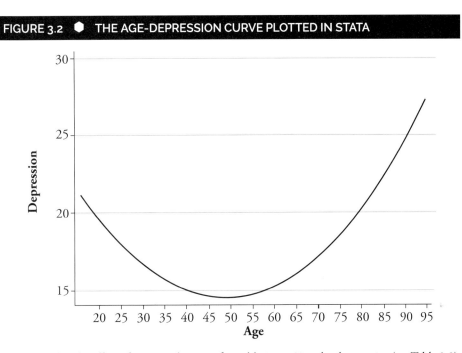

You can see that the effect of age over the ages of roughly 20 to 50 is clearly negative (see Table 3.2), meaning depression decreases over these ages. After 50, depression starts to increase again. The life course theory that suggests this relationship is well-developed in the work of John Mirowsky and Catherine Ross (Mirowsky & Ross, 1992), specifying the ebb and flow of various naturally sequenced life course issues across life stages. For example, the low depression in the middle phase of adulthood is attributed to the cumulative acquisition of statuses, power, and money from the twenties onward. The "helpful" statuses include marriage, having a steady job, promotions, having children, and increasing income—issues that co-occur over this period. But old age is the mirror process, involving loss of status, support, income, choice, and physical functioning.

It is important to remember here that the linear effect showed no relationship. This is because the linear line is flattened by fitting the rising depression at the two ends of adulthood, leaving the middle of adulthood below the line.

3.1.1 Variations in the Fit of Quadratic Curves

The quadratic specification ***generally*** suggests that as X increases, Y either first decreases and then increases or that Y actually increases and then decreases. But the data may not warrant the inference of such symmetry. Note that the quadratic will expand to fit curves ***without*** an actual

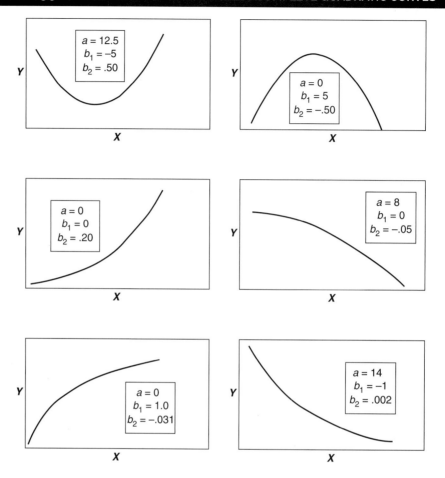

FIGURE 3.3 ● EXAMPLES OF MORE OR LESS COMPLETE QUADRATIC CURVES

bend down or up. In the examples in Figure 3.3, the size of the coefficients is a clue to the shape of the curve. The direction and balance of the b's tells us the concavity versus convexity of the curve, as well as its symmetry.

The top two curves are what is expected in a quadratic regression. There is symmetry in the curve and a clear change in direction after a middle point maximum or minimum is reached. The last four examples show how a quadratic regression can bend itself to fit the data. What you could imagine here is that the missing part of the curve that makes it symmetric is outside of the range of the data.

The b for the linear component and the b for the squared component *together* define the effect of X—you cannot consider one without the other. One intuitive way to think of these coefficients is to think of the linear b as reflecting the direction of the relationship *over the lower values of* X, while the squared b reflects the direction of the relationship *over the higher values of* X.

This feature of quadratic curve fitting makes the use of quadratic regression quite flexible, but it is not enough. This type of regression can only be sensitive to one bend in the curve. What if there are two—or more?

3.2 ESTIMATING HIGHER-ORDER RELATIONSHIPS

In the previous example, it is possible that the rise in depression in old age starts to flatten out and so the rise in depression is overestimated in older age groups. Or it is possible that there is a flat region with no change in depression in the middle of adulthood before it starts to rise in old age. This is a situation that requires two or even three bends in the curve relating age to depression. To assess the possibility of another bend in the curve, you could use a cubic model by adding x^3 to the quadratic model. If this is significant, you could also add x^4 to the cubic model. Although these terms do not have easily interpretable coefficients, they do tell us whether the curve changes direction and how much it does.

We tested both a cubic effect (labeled "age3") and then a quartic effect of age (age4) in the models that follow. A word of caution—these variables are naturally highly collinear with each other, and as a result, estimation quickly becomes unstable. The example here is for comparison to later results using a very different approach: We do not generally advocate using higher-order effects beyond the quadratic, or depending on the data, the cubic. In general, we prefer the methods we discuss later, in Section 3.6 on spline regression.

TABLE 3.3 ● HIGHER-ORDER EFFECTS OF AGE ON DEPRESSION

		Parameter Estimates			
Variable	DF	Parameter Estimate	Standard Error	t Value	Pr > |t|
Intercept	1	33.57822	3.00855	11.16	<.0001
age1	1	−0.92428	0.21038	−4.39	<.0001
age2	1	0.01328	0.00449	2.96	0.0031
age3	1	−0.00004816	0.00002578	−1.87	0.0868

		Parameter Estimates			
.000Variable	DF	Parameter Estimate	Standard Error	t Value	Pr > |t|
Intercept	1	45.60472	7.59194	6.01	<.0001
age1	1	−2.11014	0.71879	−2.94	0.0033
age2	1	0.05334	0.02365	2.26	0.0241
age3	1	−0.00060331	0.00032313	−1.86	0.0619
age4	1	0.00000270	0.00000141	1.92	0.0548

Here you can see that *age3* in the cubic model is not quite significant two tailed. If we consider the change in direction (the sign) a given, we could interpret this as a one-tailed test, since the probability is divided by 2 (.0868/2 = .0434). If you want to argue that we should maximize sensitivity to nonlinearity, you would want to pay attention to this term.

The quartic model is borderline significant two tailed and clearly significant one tailed ($\alpha = .0224$). This too is a close call. The question arising here concerns the "artistry" in knowing what to consider and interpret. If one wants to be careful about the match of trends in the curve to theoretical expectations, you may want to include higher-order terms. But if you want to be strict, you could stick with the quadratic result.

For purposes of the example, we continue with the assumption that the higher-order terms here are important. It is obvious one cannot "see" the curve in these results. Graphing the result is essential. The plot in Figure 3.4 is for the quartic (4th order) model:

FIGURE 3.4 ◆ A QUARTIC EFFECT OF AGE ON DEPRESSION

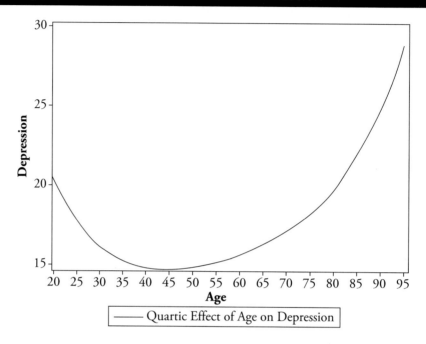

— Quartic Effect of Age on Depression

The differences between this curve and the initial quadratic fit are subtle—reflecting the fact that the higher-order terms here are barely significant and not very strong. Even though one should see three bends in this curve, only two are obvious. The third has to do with a slight adjustment to the flatness of the curve in middle age—instead of rising faster it tends to straighten out and then increase later.

The difference in interpretation of these curves is potentially important. Here we can see that the advantages of midlife occur earlier (by age 40) and basically extend until about 60, after which depression starts to increase at a faster rate. The initial curve is close but imagines a continual decline in depression until the age of 50 and also imagines an immediate and clear upswing after that rather than a flat "grace period" in life.

As a side note—you can estimate an interaction between age and different groups, to track group differences in their life trajectories. For example, we did estimate an interaction between all four components of age and gender, and there was a clear interaction. This suggests distinct trajectories that should be tracked separately. From the results (Figure 3.5), it looks as though women have a faster decline in depression than men but a higher minimum in midlife—and thus less of an upswing in later life.

Note that the male curve looks more like the original "classic" pattern, but the female curve looks quite different. Interestingly, the results suggest that the largest gender differences in depression occur in midlife. Also, women's depression starts to rise earlier in life than men's— around 40, instead of 55 for men. The plot in Figure 3.5 gives us a much more specific picture of gender differences—and leads to rather different theories about those differences.

FIGURE 3.5 ◆ GENDER DIFFERENCES IN THE EFFECT OF AGE ON DEPRESSION

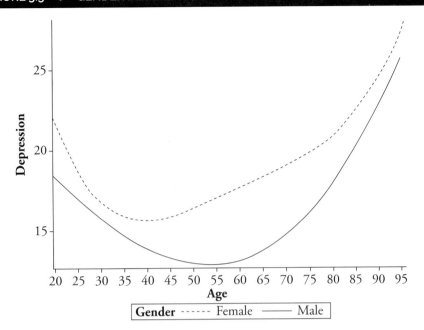

3.3 BASIC MATH FOR NONLINEAR MODELS

Interpreting the results of nonlinear models is inherently more complex than for linear models because the effect of X changes depending on the level of X considered. It is impossible to discuss nonlinear models without some reference to the way they are mathematically specified and interpreted. Rather than refer to an appendix, we want to introduce the necessary rules in the text, in part because these rules are too often mysterious. As we proceed through this chapter and the next on logistic regression, we will refer back to some of these rules.

3.3.1 First Derivatives

We need to understand the basic rules for first derivatives in order to interpret nonlinear regression. The first derivative is a very general concept.

The derivative of y with respect to x is written

$$\frac{dy}{dx} = \lim_{\Delta x \to 0} \frac{\Delta y}{\Delta x}$$

and reads as follows: The derivative of y with respect to x equals the *limit* as the change in X approaches 0 of the change in Y relative to the change in X

where

$\lim_{\Delta x \to 0}$ = the limit as the change in X approaches 0

Δx = change in x

Δy = change in y.

Given that technical definition, the derivative—for our purposes—is a statement of how Y changes with a one-unit change in X. The derivative is a slope but taken at a specific point on the curve. Formally, the derivative of a function at a point on X is ***the slope of the tangent to the curve at that point.*** In regression applications, with variables that are not truly continuous, the smallest possible change in X is always one unit.

3.3.1.1 Rules for Derivatives

Rules for Constants

1. If $y = c$ *(constant)*   then: $\dfrac{dy}{dx} = 0$

2. If $y = cx$ then: $\dfrac{dy}{dx} = c$

These rules seem self-evident. The second is the rule for interpretation of regression coefficients in a linear model.

Power Rule

3. If $y = x^n$ then: $\dfrac{dy}{dx} = \dfrac{dx^n}{dx} = nx^{n-1}$

Sum Rule

4. If w is a function of x, i.e. $w = f_1(x)$,

    and z is a different function of x, i.e. $z = f_2(x)$,

    and $y = w + z = f_1(x) + f_2(x)$ then: $\dfrac{dy}{dx} = \dfrac{dw}{dx} + \dfrac{dz}{dx}$

For example, if $y = 2 + 7x + 3x^2$, like a quadratic regression, then you can take the derivative of each component of the function separately and add them up. But there is a wrinkle here because the last term is actually two functions (using Rules 2 and 3 together), one embedded in the other. We need another rule to deal with that.

Chain Rule

This rule is like the multiplicative version of the sum rule, allowing you to separate parts of functions so you can apply other rules straightforwardly:

5. If y depends on u, and u depends on x,

    then y depends on x and $\dfrac{dy}{dx} = \dfrac{dy}{du} \cdot \dfrac{du}{dx}$

For example, using the preceding function,

$$y = 2 + 7x + 3x^2,$$

the last term on the right-hand side can be seen as two functions, one "inside" the other. Let $u = x^2$ so that we have

$y = 2 + 7x + 3u$ and $\dfrac{dy}{du} = 2x$, using Rule 3, the power rule.

Using the sum rule, the chain rule, the power rule, and the constant rule leads to

$$\frac{dy}{dx} = 0 + 7 + (3 \cdot 2x) = 7 + 6x$$

Product Rule

6. Given this kind of function,

$$y = u \cdot v$$
$$u = f_1(x)$$
$$v = f_2(x)$$

where u and v are different functions of x. Then:

$$\frac{dy}{dx} = \frac{d(uv)}{dx} = u\frac{dv}{dx} + v\frac{du}{dx}$$

An example of applying this rule is used later in this chapter.

3.3.2 Logarithms and Exponents

We include here the necessary rules that clarify the interpretation of models and methods that employ logarithms. Although exponents play a complementary role to logarithms in the methods we present, we focus on rules for logarithms, and discuss rules for exponents as necessary. In order to understand forms of nonlinear regression that use logarithms, as well as logistic regression and the general linear model to follow in the chapters ahead, you will need to have some understanding of the basic rules for exponential and logistic functions.

3.3.2.1 Exponential Functions

First, what is an exponent? Fundamentally, *exponents tell you how many times to multiply a number by itself*—for example, $4^3 = 4 \times 4 \times 4 = 64$. A *negative exponent* means divide instead of multiply, as an inverse operation. A *fractional exponent* like $1/n$ means to take the *nth root*, as in $X^{\frac{1}{n}} = \sqrt[n]{X}$.

A "natural" exponential function is of the form $y = e^x$. The variable x is part or all of the exponent; the constant e is raised to the variable's power. The constant e is a special number with properties beyond the scope of this discussion $= 2.718$.

In $y = e^x$, x is the number of times you must multiply e to get y.

3.3.2.2 Logarithms and Logarithmic Functions

In the preceding exponential function, **x** *is the logarithm of* **y** *to base* **e**—that is, $x = \ln(y)$. You can also therefore write $y = e^{\ln(y)}$. Further, also note that $\ln(e^x) = \ln(y) = x$, given the definition of the preceding exponential function.

Logarithms are exponents; they are used to define the inverse operation to raising a number to an exponent. Natural logarithms answer the following question: "To what power must e be raised to equal y?" Note the inverse operations involved:

In the exponential function, you are interested in solving for y, given x:

That is, what is y if $x = 2$ in $y = e^x$?   Answer: 7.389.

In the logarithmic function, you want to know x, given y:

That is, what is x, if $y = 7.389$ in $y = e^x$?   Answer: 2.

Interpreted: the number e must be multiplied by itself twice to equal 7.389.

Rules for exponents demonstrate that *fractional exponents* are possible and important. You can raise a number to the 1.5 power. What does that mean? It means raising a base number e to the power 3/2—that is $= e^{3/2}$. To do this calculate e^3, *then take the square root of that, using the rule for fractional exponents.* The rule that applies here is

$$x^{a/b} = x^{a \cdot \frac{1}{b}} = \left(x^a\right)^{\frac{1}{b}} = \sqrt[b]{x^a}$$

In this rule, note that the fractional exponent stands for taking the *b*th root of *x* taken to the *a* exponent. In the preceding example, we are taking the square root of *e* cubed.

3.3.2.3 Rules for Logarithms

Here we state the necessary rules for logarithms we will use throughout.

Rule	Comments
1. $e^{\ln(y)} = y$	Definitional: if $x = \ln(y)$, x is the logarithm
2. $x \cdot y = e^{\ln(x)} \cdot e^{\ln(y)} = e^{(\ln(x)+\ln(y))}$	Rule 1 with this rule of exponents: $x^a \cdot x^b = x^{a+b}$
3. $\ln(x \cdot y) = \ln x + \ln y$	Using Rules 1 and 2 and the fact of inverse operations in taking the *ln* of *e* taken to the sum of the logarithms
4. $x/y = e^{\ln(x)-\ln(y)}$	Using Rule 1 and this rule of exponents: $\dfrac{x^a}{x^b} = x^{a-b}$
5. $\ln(x/y) = \ln x - \ln y$	Using Rules 1 and 4
6. $x^n = (e^{\ln(x)})^n = e^{n \cdot \ln(x)}$	Rule 1 and this rule of exponents: $(x^a)^b = x^{ab}$
7. $\ln(x^n) = n \cdot \ln x$	From Rule 6 and Rule 1, taking logs in Rule 6 and expanding

Note the following equivalent forms of an equation:

$$\ln y = a + bx + e \qquad \text{an important form of equation}$$
$$e^{\ln(y)} = e^{(a+bx+e)} \qquad \text{takes exponential of both sides}$$
$$y = e^{(a+bx+e)} \qquad \text{uses Rule 1 above}$$
$$y = e^a \cdot e^{bx} \cdot e^e \qquad \text{uses rule of exponents for same base raised to different exponents: } x^a \cdot x^b = x^{a+b}$$

The form of model is the same as is used to show the effects of variables on the odds of *Y* in logistic regression (Chapter 4).

3.4 INTERPRETATION OF NONLINEAR FUNCTIONS

3.4.1 Interpreting Powers of *X*

3.4.1.1. Quadratic Curve

These are functions with one of two general shapes: either concave, with a minimum point, like this:

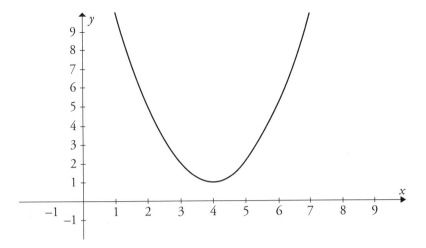

Or convex, with a maximum, like this:

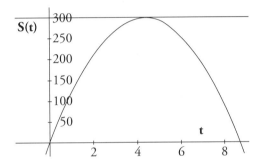

The form of the equation is

$$\widehat{Y} = a + b_1 X + b_2 X^2$$

To find an interpretation for b, take the first derivative:

$$\frac{d\widehat{Y}}{dX} = \frac{d(a + b_1 X + b_2 X^2)}{dX} \qquad \text{(using Rules 1, 2, 3, 4, and 5 for first derivatives)}$$

$$= \frac{d(a)}{dX} + \frac{d(b_1 X)}{dX} + \frac{d(b_2 X^2)}{dX}$$

$$= 0 + b_1 + 2b_2 X$$

$$= b_1 + 2b_2 X$$

This is the effect of a one-unit increase in X *at a given value of* X. We can use the results from the regression for age and depression to illustrate. Assume we want to know the effect of age on depression at ages 25 and 75. Substituting for b_1 and b_2 and $X = 25$ leads to

$$b_1 + 2b_2 X = -.59603 + 2 \cdot .00607 \cdot 25 = -.292$$

When age = 75,

$$b_1 + 2b_2 X = -.59603 + 2 \cdot .00607 \cdot 75 = .314$$

From these results, we see that the effects of age at age 25 and at age 75 are almost equal but in opposite directions.

We can also derive the minimum/maximum point on the curve: This is, by definition, the point where the slope of the tangent to the curve = 0-that is, when the first derivative is 0:

$$b_1 + 2b_2 X = 0$$
$$2b_2 X = -b_1$$
$$X = \frac{-b_1}{2b_2}$$

= value of X at minimum/maximum point on curve.

In the previous example, substituting these values produces

$$X = \frac{-b_1}{2b_2} = \frac{-(-.59603)}{2 \cdot .00607} = 49$$

That is, the minimum level of depression is achieved at 49 years old in this curve. To find the minimum value of $\widehat{Y}$, plug in this value of X and solve for Y predicted.

3.4.1.2 Cubic Curve

Generally, a cubic function allows for two changes in direction of the effect of X, not just one. These kinds of relationships are rarer than quadratics because of the complexity embodied in the substantive relationship. One area where they do occur with some frequency is in relationships with time.

Here are two typical curves produced by a cubic function:

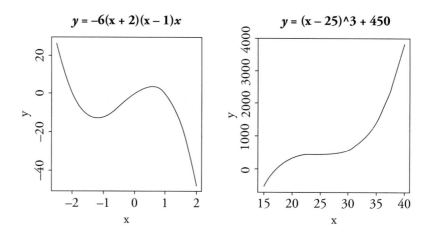

The form of the equation is

$$\widehat{Y} = a + b_1 X + b_2 X^2 + b_3 X^3$$

Interpretation of cubic effects follows the same procedure as for a quadratic, with an added term in the first derivative. Looking at the derivative above, there would be an extra term for $b_3 X^3$ from the equation. The power and chain rules for differentiation suggests that the derivative of this part is $3b_3 X^2$. This component needs to be added to the derivative for the quadratic model above, to get

$$b_1 + 2b_2 x + 3b_3 x^2$$

As before, solving for x in this equation when set to zero will reveal local maximum and minimum points (there are two). This can be done using the following formula:

$$X = \frac{-b \pm \sqrt{b^2 - 4ac}}{2a}$$

where you assume that a in the equation is $3b_3$, b in the equation is $2b_2$, and c in the equation is b_1.

3.4.2 Log Transformations

Although we have focused primarily on polynomial expansions of linear models, there are many ways to represent nonlinearity, and some are both more efficient (single parameter) and a more intuitive interpretation.

3.4.2.1 Log–Log Model
The linear form of the model is

$$\ln Y = a + b \ln X$$

This kind of curve often looks like this, with a decelerating effect as X increases:

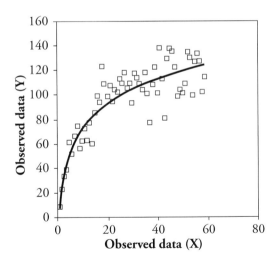

To find the actual form of this model, take the exponential of both sides:

$$e^{(\ln Y)} = e^{(a + b \ln X)}$$

$$\hat{Y} = e^a \cdot e^{b \ln X}$$

$$= e^a \cdot e^{\ln X^b}$$

$$= e^a \cdot X^b$$

The first derivative, using the product rule, is

$$\frac{d\widehat{Y}}{dX} = e^a \frac{d(X^b)}{dX} + X^b \frac{d(e^a)}{dX}$$

$$= e^a b X^{b-1} + 0$$

$$= e^a b \frac{X^b}{X} = b \frac{e^a X^b}{X}$$

$$= b \frac{\widehat{Y}}{X}$$

This shows that the effect of X depends on a chosen level of X *and* the predicted Y at that value. If you interpret the effect of b in the raw units of the variables, you need to specify a level of X, derive the predicted Y, and then adjust b by that ratio. That is the effect of a one-unit increase in X at a chosen level of X.

However, most interpretation of this model involves a further derivation of the first derivative, as follows:

$$\frac{d\widehat{Y}}{dX} \bigg/ \frac{\widehat{Y}}{X} = b$$

Dividing by the Y/X ratio on the right hand side removes it from the right hand side and inserts this division on the left hand side. When we invert *that* divisor on the left to multiply, we get this:

$$\frac{d\widehat{Y}}{dX} \frac{X}{\widehat{Y}} = b$$

Rearranging,

$$\frac{d\widehat{Y}}{\widehat{Y}} \frac{X}{dX} = b$$

Inverting the multiplier leads to

$$\frac{d\widehat{Y}}{\widehat{Y}} \bigg/ \frac{dX}{X} = b$$

This is the classic form in which log–log models are interpreted. Translated, it measures the change in predicted Y at a given level of Y, *in other words the proportional change in Y,* relative to a given change in X at a given level of X, *in other words a given proportional change in X.,* Formally, these are not percentage changes yet, but if we multiplied both of the proportional changes by 100, we would have percentage changes. But also note that we are just multiplying the left-hand side by 100/100, equal to 1, and so this is does not change the interpretation of b. The b here is called the *elasticity,* which is the b% change in Y for each 1% change in X. Thus, this model actually has a very straightforward interpretation using b.

We can illustrate what a typical (positive) log–log curve looks like using the effect of education on happiness. One of the issues with these models is the fit: Is this functional form the best representation of the nonlinearity in the relationship? The previous section suggested that at times, a quadratic regression will look very much like a power curve. However, this is a one parameter model rather than two, so it is a more efficient representation.

It is best to use this model because it expresses theoretical expectations about the relationship. Suppose we argue that education has important effects on increasing happiness *up to a point,* after which the effect flattens out. It's possible, for example, that there is a built-in ceiling effect in the consequences of education for happiness, a point beyond which awareness includes a balance of positive benefits with increasingly challenging possibilities.

Estimating this relationship using a log–log model in the National Survey of Families and Households (NSFH) data results in the following results, assuming that both education ("logeduc") and happiness ("loghappy") are logged:

TABLE 3.4 ● THE EFFECT OF LOGGED EDUCATION ON LOGGED HAPPINESS (IN NATURAL LOGS)

		Parameter Estimates			
Variable	DF	Parameter Estimate	Standard Error	t Value	Pr > |t|
Intercept	1	1.47882	0.03295	44.89	<.0001
logeduc	1	0.06337	0.01297	4.88	<.0001

The *b* coefficient here is .06337 and significant. The plot in the original metric is shown in Figure 3.6.

FIGURE 3.6 ● THE LOG–LOG EFFECT OF EDUCATION ON HAPPINESS

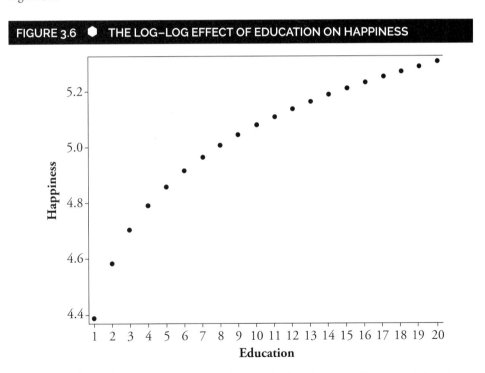

According to the result, each 1% increase in education leads only to a .06% increase in happiness. This sound small, but one should consider first what a 1% increase in education really is. If we assume that each year includes 10 months of education, then a 1% increase at 10 years of education includes one extra month (101/100 months). A 1% increase at a high school level includes slightly more than a month. If we divided education up into four year segments, as if each is a level, and then assume that each is roughly a quarter of the range in education, then we could interpret this findings as suggesting that a 25% increase in education leads to a 25 x .06337 = 1.58% increase in happiness. This is indeed quite small—so we also might conclude that, not only money, but also education doesn't really buy happiness.

3.4.2.2 The Exponential Model

The linear form of the model is in the log of Y, with the X side in original form:

$$\ln \widehat{Y} = a + bX_i$$

$$e^{\ln \widehat{Y}} = e^{(a+bX)}$$

$$\widehat{Y} = e^{(a+bX)} = e^a e^{bX}$$

This is the form the model takes in the original Y metric. This model produces curves like those that follow—one a negative effect, the other positive:

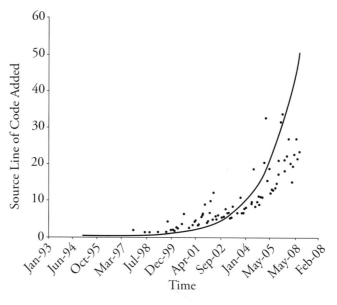

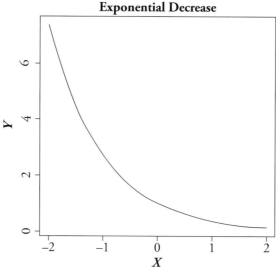

The First Derivative

Again we can use the product rule to derive the first derivative:

$$\frac{d\widehat{Y}}{dX} = e^a \frac{d(e^{bX})}{dX} + e^{bX} \frac{d(e^a)}{dX}$$

$$= e^a b e^{bX} = e^a e^{bX} b$$

$$= b\widehat{Y}$$

This uses one other rule of derivatives not shown earlier: $\frac{d(e^{bX})}{dX} = be^{bX}$

Further manipulation of this result leads to an interpretation of b:

$$\frac{d\widehat{Y}}{dX} \frac{1}{\widehat{Y}} = b$$

$$\frac{d\widehat{Y}}{\widehat{Y}} \Big/ dX = b$$

The change in Y here is still proportional, but unlike the log–log case, the changes in X and Y are not in the same metric. To turn the change in Y into a percentage change, we multiply both sides by 100, to get

$$100 \cdot \frac{d\widehat{Y}}{\widehat{Y}} \Big/ dX = 100 \cdot b$$

$$100 \cdot \frac{d\widehat{Y}}{\widehat{Y}} = 100 \cdot dX \cdot b$$

$$\% \text{ change in } Y = 100 \cdot dX \cdot b$$

The interpretation of b is that a one-unit increase in x leads to a $(b \times 1 \times 100)$ % change in y. Imagine an exponential model with log household income as the outcome and years of education as the predictor and $b = .22$. In this example, a one-year increase in education increases household income by 22%.

3.4.2.3 The Logarithmic Model

The linear form of the model is in the log of X, with Y in its original form:

$$\widehat{Y} = a + b \ln X$$

$$e^{\widehat{Y}} = e^{(a + b \ln X)}$$

$$e^{\widehat{Y}} = e^a \cdot X^b$$

A typical positive effect in a logarithmic model might look like the following graph. The negative version would look like a flipped mirror image. Note here that the decelerating effect starts earlier but takes longer and is less flat at the end than a typical power curve. The previous example using education and happiness might be better fit using this functional form, given the nature of the graph of that relationship.

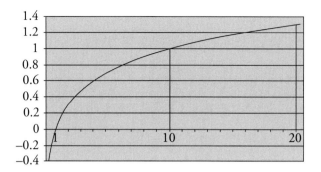

The First Derivative

In this case, we use the sum rule and then the product rule for the second term, applied to the original equation:

$$\frac{d\widehat{Y}}{dX} = \frac{d(a)}{dX} + \frac{d(b\ln X)}{dX}$$

$$= 0 + \ln X \frac{d(b)}{dX} + b\frac{d(\ln X)}{dX}$$

$$= 0 + 0 + b\frac{1}{X} \qquad\qquad (\text{using } \frac{d(\ln(x))}{dx} = \frac{1}{x})$$

$$= \frac{b}{X}$$

Here, the effect of X depends only on the chosen level of X. Going one step further to derive an interpretation of b produces:

$$\frac{d\widehat{Y}}{dX} = \frac{b}{X}$$

$$d\widehat{Y} = \frac{dX \cdot b}{X}$$

$$d\widehat{Y} = \frac{dX}{X}b$$

Multiplying both sides by 100 turns the change in X into a percentage change.

$$100 \cdot d\widehat{Y} = 100 \cdot \frac{dX}{X} \cdot b$$

The first term on the right is the percentage change in X:

$$100 \cdot d\widehat{Y} = \% \text{ change in } X \cdot b$$

$$d\widehat{Y} = \% \text{ change in } X \cdot (b/100)$$

So in this model b is interpreted this way: a 1% increase in $X \Rightarrow b/100$ unit change in y.

Results in Table 3.5 show a regression of yearly job income in dollars on the natural log of education, measured originally in years.

TABLE 3.5	● THE EFFECT OF LOGGED EDUCATION ON YEARLY EARNINGS IN DOLLARS

Parameter Estimates

Variable	DF	Parameter Estimate	Standard Error	t Value	Pr > |t|
Intercept	1	−61334	2604.79925	−23.55	<.0001
logeduc	1	32326	1026.93185	31.48	<.0001

In this case, the effect of a 1% increase in education is to produce an increase of 32326/100 = $323.26 a year in job income on average.

In each of the cases of logged equations, notice that the *raw* effect of X on Y in its original form varies depending on the chosen level of Y, or X, or both. In fact, you can interpret the raw effects of X on Y in each of these models, using the first derivative, instead of a percentage interpretation. This is usually not done, but it is possible and useful, if you want to highlight changes in the importance of X across different levels of X.

For example, using the last result and the first derivative, the effect of a one-year increase in education, when education = 12, can be found as follows:

$$\frac{d\hat{Y}}{dX} = b\frac{1}{X} = 32326 \cdot \frac{1}{12} = 2694$$

In other words, for someone with a high school education, one more year will translate into an average increase of $2694 in later job income.

3.5 AN ALTERNATIVE APPROACH USING DUMMY VARIABLES

Sometimes X has sufficiently few categories (e.g., 5 up to 10) to allow for a different test of nonlinearity. In these cases, it is possible to build in nonlinearity in the effect of X by using dummy variables *for each level of X*. This may seem inefficient, but it has the advantage of capturing all of the nonlinearity in X, no matter the form of the effect. This is because each dummy variable can independently fit changes in the direction of the effect at each level of X. This "advantage" is also a disadvantage: It's possible to be too sensitive to any nonlinearity, especially if there is no detectable pattern. There is always the danger of "overfitting" every change in direction as meaningful, when they could be temporary or random.

However, given this problem and this caution, here is an example.

3.5.1 A Dummy Variable Test for Nonlinearity

You first have to code each level of X as a separate dummy variable. To conduct a test for nonlinearity, follow these steps:

1. Run the usual linear regression of Y on X in continuous form. Note R_L^2 (L for linear).

2. Run a one-way ANOVA with the set of dummy variables for X. This is just a regression with all necessary dummy variables representing levels of X included, except for the

reference group. There should be j - 1 dummy variables, where j is the number of levels of X. **Only** dummy variables are entered—not the linear version of X as well. Note the explained variance (referred to here as R_N^2—N for nonlinear).

3. Then conduct the following F-test comparing the dummy variable model to the linear model:

$$F = \frac{(R_N^2 - R_L^2)\,/\,k-1}{(1 - R_N^2)\,/\,N-k-1} \qquad \text{with } k\text{ - 1 and } N\text{ - }k\text{ - 1 } df$$

where k = the number of dummy variables.

The results in Table 3.6 show the effect of education on depression, divided up into 14 dummy variables from *education7* (education = 7 years) to *education20* (education = 20 years).

TABLE 3.6 ● RESULTS FROM A DUMMY VARIABLE MODEL FOR THE EFFECT OF EDUCATION ON DEPRESSION

Parameter Estimates					
Variable	**DF**	**Parameter Estimate**	**Standard Error**	**t Value**	**Pr > |t|**
Intercept	1	24.15782	0.83032	29.09	<.0001
education7	1	−0.61763	1.59131	−0.39	0.6979
education8	1	−4.29403	1.19094	−3.61	0.0003
education9	1	−4.98947	1.31213	−3.80	0.0001
education10	1	−4.06050	1.21719	−3.34	0.0009
education11	1	0.51399	1.15807	0.44	0.6572
education12	1	−7.68925	0.87838	−8.75	<.0001
education13	1	−7.83673	1.00764	−7.78	<.0001
education14	1	−10.17388	1.08074	−9.41	<.0001
education15	1	−7.83822	1.11080	−7.06	<.0001
education16	1	−12.78018	1.00976	−12.66	<.0001
education17	1	−9.93018	1.34025	−7.41	<.0001
education18	1	−11.62910	1.44714	−8.04	<.0001
education19	1	−15.09200	1.42786	−10.57	<.0001
education20	1	−14.55082	1.62846	−8.94	<.0001

Each dummy variable is a contrast with six or less years of education, the reference group. Figure 3.7 shows a plot of the joined mean levels of depression at each level of education.

The results suggest a pattern of mixed influences of years and completion of levels. Education 12, 14, and 16 represent completion points—high school, college degree, and university degree. In each case, there is a significant drop in depression compared to the level before. The effect of dropping out just before completing a level is also evident: There are increases or flat points at levels just before the completion points.

Note that the nonlinear dummy variable model and the linear model *are* nested—that is, one is a restricted specification embedded in the other. The linear model is actually the dummy variable model with the restriction that there is an equal difference on Y across all adjacent levels of X. One could specify this in the model you estimate using a post-hoc test such as this:

FIGURE 3.7 ● MEAN LEVELS OF DEPRESSION AT EACH YEAR OF EDUCATION

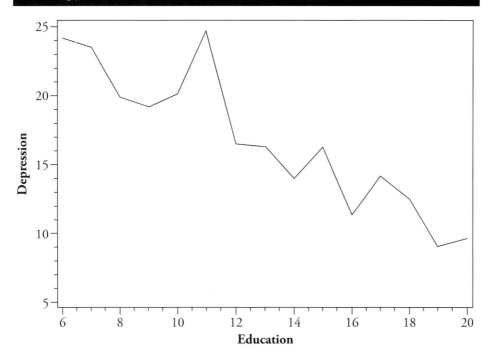

```
test education20-education19=education19-education18=education18-
education17=education17-education16=education16-education15=education15-
education14=education14-education13=education13-education12=education12-
education11=education11-education10=education10-education9=education9-
education8=education8-education7=education7;
```

This statement tests the equality of adjacent category differences across all categories, and thus imposes linearity as a constraint. The last variable is *education7*, which is already the difference between category (7) and the reference category (6 or less).

We also show the results of this test for a linear restriction, and it is very significant—meaning that there *is* nonlinearity.

TABLE 3.7 ● RESULTS FOR A TEST OF LINEARITY

Test 1 Results for Dependent Variable depress				
Source	DF	Mean Square	*F* Value	Pr > F
Numerator	12	3586.69315	8.88	<.0001
Denominator	12992	404.00403		

We do not generally advocate this approach, in part because it only gives clues to interpretation and does not produce an interpretable form of nonlinearity in many cases. But it is useful as a starting point in the exploration of nonlinearity.

3.6 SPLINE REGRESSION

This section presents an alternative approach to fitting nonlinear relationships. Spline regression is a very flexible and yet efficient technique for representing nonlinear relationships that also has some crucial attractive features relative to fitting polynomials or using dummy variables. This approach is an "in-between" case incorporating some of the sensitivity of dummy variables with the efficiency of using "smooth" functions.

Spline regression represents nonlinearity as a number of discrete segments called *splines,* one for each significant change in direction for the effect of *X.* The inflection points at which the effect changes are called *knots.* Splines are closely related to another technique called "piecewise linear regression." You can use the results of spline regression to develop a regression that shows the effect of *X* in discrete segments, using piecewise linear regression. This has the considerable advantage of allowing a separate explanation of each segment in the effect of *X.*

There are two cases to consider in applying spline regression: (1) when the knots are known or hypothesized by theory and you want to test for changes in the direction of *X* at the hypothesized knots and (2) when the knots are unknown but you want to allow for the possibility of changes in the direction of the effect of *X* at any level of *X.*

Spline regression can be used for any nonlinear relationship, but it has particularly useful features when studying the effects of time—for example, to assess social or political change and its consequences or to map changes over the life course.

3.6.1 When the Number and Locations of Knots Are Known a Priori—or Hypothesized

We introduce this approach with a hypothetical example, originally used by Marsh and Cormier (2002) and extended here. Suppose we have data every year from World War II to the year 2016 on unemployment in the United States. We want to assess the effect, if any, of Democratic versus Republican administrations on unemployment, presumably to get a net estimate of a party effect historically. Here we know the location and number of knots in the spline regression because we know which elections led to a change in government. This is a typical situation for spline regression: We know when an event happens, and we want to know whether it made a difference, so we specifically build a regression model to test this possibility. If there *was* change at the specified knot, we would expect a significant change in the slope for time as a predictor of the outcome.

To test for changes at each knot, we run a standard OLS regression using the following model:

$$\widehat{Y}_t = a_0 + b_0 t + b_1 D_1 (t - t_1) + b_2 D_2 (t - t_2) + b_3 D_3 (t - t_3) + etc.$$

where: t = time (a continuous variable);

D_k = a dummy variable equal to 0 when t is less than or equal to t_k, the year for each knot, and 1 when t is greater than t_k;

t_k = the years representing the knots, in a regression with k knots.

Notice first here that the dummy variables are "toggle switches" that turn on progressively over time. These dummy variables test the effect of the next period because while they are 0, the whole term disappears from the model, and when they turn to 1, the b then tests for a *departure* from the slope represented by the previous segment. That b is only significant when there is a significant change in direction in the slope.

When we translate this scheme into the example above, the equation would look like

$$\hat{Y} = a_0 + b_0 t + b_1 R_{52}(t-52) + b_2 D_{60}(t-60) + b_3 R_{68}(t-68) + b_4 D_{76}(t-76)$$
$$+ b_5 R_{80}(t-80) + b_6 D_{92}(t-92) + b_7 R_{00}(t-00) + b_8 D_{08}(t-08)$$

This implementation takes into account all changes in presidential party from World War II up to but not including 2016. The dummy variables here are denoted R for Republican administrations and D for Democratic administrations. The subscript is the last two digits of the knot year. Each variable in the equation multiplies this dummy variable by the difference between the current year (t) and the predicted knot (52, 60, 68, 76, 80, 92, 00, and 08—each standing for a change in administration). The dummy variable stays at 0 up until and including the knot year in question. After that point, the dummy variable changes to one, activating the relevance of that variable in the regression, and after that the variable in that time segment increases by one each year, based on the difference between the current year and the knot. This allows for shifts in the slope over time since at each knot some amount is added to or subtracted from the effect of time to that point. Here, the coefficients b_1 to b_8 each stand for *the amount of adjustment in the slope* after a given knot, not the actual slope in that time segment.

You can see how the slope changes over time by substituting into the equation for each of the segments. Up to 1952, the effect of time on unemployment is

$$\hat{Y} = a_0 + b_0 t$$

This is because all of the "toggle" dummy variables in the equation for time segments are zero in this case. But after 1952, up to 1960, when $R_{52} = 1$, this effect changes to

$$\hat{Y} = a_0 + b_0 t + b_1 R_{52}(t-52) = a_0 + b_0 t + b_1 t - b_1 52$$
$$= (a_0 - b_1 52) + (b_0 + b_1)t$$

And after 1960, given the effect up to 1960, the effect becomes

$$\hat{Y} = (a_0 - b_1 52) + (b_0 + b_1)t + b_2 D_{60}(t-60)$$
$$= (a_0 - b_1 52) + (b_0 + b_1)t + b_2 t - b_2 60$$
$$= (a_0 - b_1 52 - b_2 60) + (b_0 + b_1 + b_2)t$$

And so on . . .

Each b_k after the first linear segment tests for nonlinearity: If these were all zero, then the effect would be linear. You can test this by adding all of the knot variables to the equation at once and testing the increase in R^2. Also, you can do post hoc tests on all of the Democratic versus Republican administrations that contrast the two sets of coefficients. Essentially, the null hypothesis is that the weighted average of the slopes for Democratic years minus the weighted average of the slopes for Republican years is zero.

3.6.2 When the Number and/or Location of Knots Is Unknown

The technique of the previous section is useful for testing specific hypotheses about the effects of any known or hypothesized system input that may lead to change, including changes in government, policies, interventions, programs, social movements, life transitions, new roles, new life stages, historical periods, and so forth.

But for many types of applications, we will not know where or when knots can be specified. In these cases, we must use a technique that will also allow us to *find* the changes in direction that denote nonlinearity. Following Marsh and Cormier (2002), we discuss here the use of stepwise regression to accomplish this. ***Please note***, *we do not generally advocate the use of stepwise regression for almost any analytical situation discussed in this book since it is a technique that empirically optimizes prediction but cannot be used to assess hypotheses or explore explanations.*

Stepwise regression is a technique that "chooses" a subset of most effective predictors from a larger set of independent variables, according to some criterion. In a typical application, at each step, the variable with the largest F statistic, reflecting the variable's contribution to the model if it is included, is entered. This process continues until, for example, no more variables are significant at a specified entry level, like $\alpha = .05$. Stepwise regression also checks to make sure that prior variables entered into the model stay significant when later ones are entered; if they do not, they are removed.

This technique can be applied by specifying all *potential* knots as variables in the stepwise regression and assessing which knots are included.

3.6.2.1 Example 1: The Effect of First Child's Birth Year on the Mother's Decision to Work

Here we investigate the effect of year of birth of a first child on the mother's decision to go to or return to work in the child's first year of life, based on data from the National Survey of Families and Households. We are interested in "change points" in the effect of birth year historically, perhaps due to the social movement effects of feminism, social policy supporting work for mothers, the economy, or changing human capital among women over time. Our data covers the years 1950 to 1990.

To find out where the knots are in this relationship, we develop a variable like the knot variables in the prior section *for each year from 1950 to 1990.* To do this, follow these steps:

1. Develop one dummy variable for each year from 1950 to 1990, which will equal 1 when the current year is *greater than* the given year specified by the knot variable and 0 otherwise. These are the D_k from the earlier example.

2. Develop a variable standing for the *difference* between the current year and each year in turn from 1950 to 1990. These are the $(t - t_k)$ variables.

3. Multiply the dummy variables for each year by the time difference variable representing the difference between the current year and each hypothetical knot year. These are the knot variables from 1950 to 1990 (41 in total)—that is, the final $D_k(t - t_k)$ independent variables. The equation would then look like:

$$\widehat{Y} = a_0 + b_0 t + b_1 D_{50}(t - 50) + b_2 D_{51}(t - 51) + b_3 D_{52}(t - 52) + ... + b_{41} D_{90}(t - 90)$$

4. Run a stepwise regression where you "force" in the linear effect of year (t) as a baseline and allow the procedure to bring in significant knots.

FIGURE 3.8 ●   SPLINE REGRESSION OF THE IMPACT OF YEAR ON THE PROBABILITY OF GOING TO WORK IN THE FIRST YEAR AFTER A FIRST BIRTH

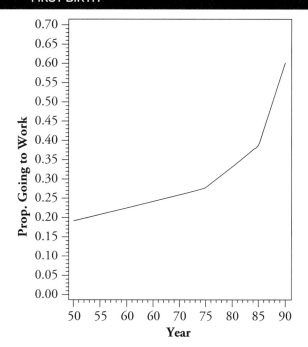

When you get the results of this kind of model, it is difficult to "see" the curve from the coefficients, so it is best to plot the resulting splines. The plot in Figure 3.8 represents the effect of year on the probability of going to work in the first year after the birth of the first child. The results reflect two knots, in 1975 and 1985. In each of those years, there was a significant acceleration in the chances of going to work for women who had a first child under one years old. Note the general increase from 1950 to 1975 increases the probability only from 19% to 26% in year one. But over the next ten years (1975–1985), the probability goes from 26% to 37%. After 1985, the probability increases very rapidly from 37% to 60%, almost the same proportion as women in the labor force overall, in just five years.

The plot shows that a smooth curve function could have been fit here, but the spline regression shows specific turning points in the chances of entering the labor force that are not clear in the smooth fit. The knots may indicate significant feminist social movement effects or government or social policy effects in the mid 80s, but further mapping of major changes in laws, policies, the economy, education of women, and so forth, would have to be conducted to develop a specific interpretation.

3.6.2.2 Example 2: The Effect of Age on Depression

The earlier example using polynomials to fit the effect of age on depression can be studied using splines—and compared to the earlier results.
To do this, we created these variables:

- A dummy variable for every age from 18 to 95

- A variable that compares the person's age to each age from 18 to 95

- The multiplication of the two—that is

$D_k(\text{age}- ageknot_k)$ where k = the (possible) age knot

There are actually 78 of these potential knots, from 18 to 95 inclusive.

You can run any standard regression to produce a stepwise regression here. In this case, we chose to use $\alpha = .05$ for inclusion. The results are then plotted, using the equation results as the basis of the plot.

There were five steps in the stepwise regression for this example. Knots were first added at ages 38, 48, 68, and 85. One knot was deleted at Step 5, however: This was the knot at age 85, which was negative, indicating a flattening of the depression curve after that age. In Step 5, however, this knot was only significant at the .1052 level and was removed.

The results from the last model are shown in Table 3.8.

TABLE 3.8 ● SPLINE REGRESSION OF AGE ON DEPRESSION

Variable	Parameter Estimate	Standard Error	Type II SS	F Value	Pr > F
Intercept	27.08658	1.16127	224639	544.05	<.0001
*age	−0.35190	0.03910	33448	81.01	<.0001
ageknot38	0.56818	0.10126	13001	31.49	<.0001
ageknot48	−0.23582	0.10677	2014.45780	4.88	0.0272
ageknot68	0.43581	0.10164	7591.33887	18.39	<.0001
* Forced into the model by the INCLUDE= option					

The form of the equation in this case is

$$\widehat{Y} = a + b_1 A + b_2 D_{38}(A-38) + b_3 D_{48}(A-48) + b_4 D_{68}(A-68)$$

where A = age, and each dummy variable = 1 after the knot age and 0 up to that age.

It is important to interpret the coefficients here properly. They are **not** the slopes within each age segment; rather, they are the *change in the slope at a given age relative to the slope up to that age.* So one has to calculate the slopes within each age segment from the model, as follows:

In general, the slope for age up to age 38 will be b_1, the slope between 38 and 48 will be $b_1 + b_2$, the slope between 48 and 68 will be $b_1 + b_2 + b_3$, and the slope above 68 will be $b_1 + b_2 + b_3 + b_4$. You can follow a procedure here similar to the method used to analyze interactions: Substitute into the equation the values that define that segment and simplify.

Substituting 0 for all dummy variables first, the model up to age 38 is therefore:

$$Y = 27.09 - .352A + .568(0)(A-38) - .236(0)(A-48) + .436(0)(A-68)$$
$$= 27.09 - .352A$$

To find the model showing the slope between 38 and 48, substitute 1 for the dummy variable for that segment:

$$Y = 27.09 - .352A + .568(1)(A-38) - .236(0)(A-48) + .436(0)(A-68)$$
$$= 27.09 - .352A + .568A + .568(-38)$$
$$= (27.09 + .568(-38)) - .352A + .568A$$
$$= 5.5 + .216A$$

To find the model showing the slope between 48 and 68, you modify this calculation by including that segment:

$$Y = 27.09 - .352A + .568(1)(A - 38) - .236(1)(A - 48) + .436(0)(A - 68)$$
$$= 27.09 - .352A + .568A + .568(-38) - .236A - .236(-48)$$
$$= (27.09 + .568(-38) - .236(-48)) - .352A + .568A - .236A$$
$$= 16.83 - .02A$$

Finally, after age 68:

$$Y = 27.09 - .352A + .568(1)(A - 38) - .236(1)(A - 48) + .436(1)(A - 68)$$
$$= 27.09 - .352A + .568A + .568(-38) - .236A - .236(-48) + .436A + .436(-68)$$
$$= (27.09 + .568(-38) - .236(-48) + .436(-68)) - .352A + .568A - .236A + .436A$$
$$= -12.81 + .416A$$

When we plot the final model (Figure 3.9), you can see these slopes in each segment clearly:

FIGURE 3.9 ● **A LINEAR SPLINE MODEL FOR AGE AND DEPRESSION**

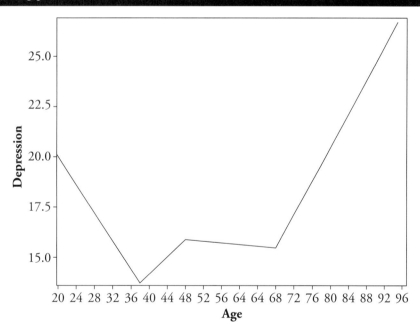

Depression drops quickly between 20 and 38, but at that age there is a slight increase until age 48. Perhaps there is a mid-life crisis effect after all. Or this is the period that maximizes stress at work and the complexity of home demands, somewhat overwhelming the benefits of that age. After 48, depression remains steady until age 68, when it starts to increase rapidly. Most studies find similar results for later life, but the spline approach suggests some variation in interpretation from the quadratic approach of Mirowsky and Ross (1992) and is closer to the earlier quartic model—because it comes closer to allowing for a flat period in mid-life. In these results, a minimum level of depression is reached earlier in life, there is a slight increase over the 40's—something not reported in this literature—and then a "grace period" of low depression until approximately retirement age, a period that appears to be a balance point in the forces acting on depression.

The issue here is the sensitivity of this approach: The knot at 48 may or may not be practically significant while introducing a complexity not usually considered.

Interpretation of the reasons for these distinct life periods is easier with the spline approach than the polynomial approach. You can design variables in a regression that stand specifically for the effect of X over specific ranges of X and then investigate what is particularly at issue in each life stage. This is called a ***piecewise linear regression.*** What this does is take the results of the spline regression and create specific variables for each segment separately, so that each stage can be studied on its own.

We present an example of a piecewise linear representation of the effect of age on depression later.

3.6.3 Nonlinear Spline Models

The examples to this point have used linear splines. Note from the plots that this kind of spline regression necessitates sudden changes in direction in the dependent variable at a certain point in time. This may be more appropriate for regressions evaluating the effects of changes in policy, interventions, or programs, or where the dependent variable responds quickly to changes than to situations where the phenomenon naturally changes more slowly.

The last example may be better rendered by a nonlinear spline that allows for more gradual changes. Depression does not change suddenly at a certain age in the population. It probably changes direction over a period of life in which life course issues are being resolved or re-defined. There is also some concern that linear splines are too sensitive to small changes and thus may overfit changes in direction.

Nonlinear splines specify higher-order polynomials for the splines. Typically, only ***quadratic*** and ***cubic*** are considered. Cubic splines are often used because they allow for smoother changes in direction and do not over emphasize the amount of change in direction. Use of a cubic spline basically means that you want to specify the knot variables to reflect ***cubed*** differences between t and the knot value, instead of linear differences. Thus the terms considered in the stepwise regression would look like this:

$$D_k(\text{age} - ageknot_k)^3$$

When we run the same regression for age and depression using cubic splines in the stepwise regression, we get a curve that looks amazingly similar to the quartic fit earlier (see Figure 3.10).

Note here that the increase between 38 and 48 in the linear spline is smoothed out. Many would find this result more believable than the linear spline, but it re-introduces the problem of interpreting the curve as a whole rather than in distinct segments.

The knots in a cubic spline are nonobvious—they represent changes in the rate at which the slope changes. The knots here are at 18, 21, and 50. Looking at the curve, however, there are three regions with distinct impacts of age: from 18 to about 38 (again), from 38 to about 70, and above 70. We could linearize these regions in a piecewise linear regression, but we would need to know where to choose the borders for each region. Eyeballing the plot may be good enough, but there is a better way.

3.6.4 Using an "Intrinsically" Nonlinear Model to Derive Critical Points on the Curve

Many statistical packages include programs that take a broader approach to fitting nonlinear relationships. Many of these programs allow you write a specific nonlinear model to estimate as part

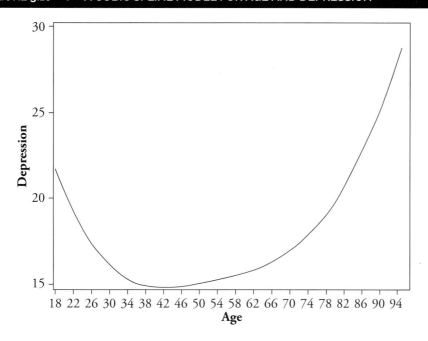

FIGURE 3.10 ● **A CUBIC SPLINE MODEL FOR AGE AND DEPRESSION**

of the program. PROC NLIN in SAS and NL in STATA will allow you to write a specific equation to be estimated and are especially relevant and useful in "nonstandard" cases of nonlinear models.

One approach you can use extracts estimates of the two critical points in the curve above or as many critical points as you define as important. The term "critical points" here is distinct from the concept of knots. *It is the implied points at which a linearization of the segments results in the least loss in fit.* Here, we provide an example of finding critical points in the age-depression curve, using NLIN. The important feature here is that you can make these critical points unknown parameters in the model you estimate, and the procedure will provide a solution for those critical points. After that, you can use the critical points to build a piecewise linear representation of the relationship.

Our goal is to provide a linearized version of the preceding cubic spline model so that we can address the effects of age in three separate segments. Thus there are five parameters to solve for here: two critical points and three slopes. We define unknown parameters c_1 and c_2 as the two critical points we want to find and parameters b_1, b_2, and b_3 as the effects in individual regression segments below c_1, between c_1 and c_2, and above c_2.

You can write a separate equation for the three segments as follows, using the two critical points on X to define the borders of each segment:

$$\widehat{Y} = a_1 + b_1 X \text{ when } X \leq c_1$$

$$\widehat{Y} = a_2 + b_2 X \text{ when } c_1 < X \leq c_2$$

$$\widehat{Y} = a_3 + b_3 X \text{ when } X > c_2$$

There is a subtlety built into these equations: The intercepts are really just extensions of the lines in each segment, so they depend directly on the slopes in that segment. But you want to impose the constraint that the lines are joined at each critical point. So you cannot estimate the three segments independently—they wouldn't join.

You have to derive one equation that expresses the overall line across the three segments. To do this, we can find equivalents for the *intercepts* in the second and third segments (a_2 and a_3) expressed in terms of the unknown critical points we want to solve for and the slopes.

Given this constraint, when $X = c_1$, the first two equations above are equal to each other since they produce the same $\hat{Y}$. So we can write

$$a_1 + b_1 c_1 = a_2 + b_2 c_1$$

If we solve for the second intercept here we get

$$a_2 = a_1 + b_1 c_1 - b_2 c_1 = a_1 + c_1(b_1 - b_2)$$

When $X = c_2$, the second and third equations are equal to each other, so we can write

$$a_2 + b_2 c_2 = a_3 + b_3 c_2$$

If we now solve for the third intercept here we get

$$a_3 = a_2 + b_2 c_2 - b_3 c_2 = a_2 + c_2(b_2 - b_3)$$

Now we can replace the intercepts in the equations above to ensure that the three equations are linked properly:

$$\text{When } X \leq c_1 : \hat{Y} = a_1 + b_1 X$$

$$\text{When } c_1 < X \leq c_2 : \hat{Y} = a_1 + c_1(b_1 - b_2) + b_2 X$$

$$\text{When } X > c_2 : \hat{Y} = a_1 + c_1(b_1 - b_2) + c_2(b_2 - b_3) + b_3 X$$

Even though this is a little involved, this example is a strong template that applies to most situations. If there is only one bend at issue, you just use the first two equations. These are the equations specified in the program and thus used to derive estimates of the parameters. The output from this procedure is shown in Table 3.9.

TABLE 3.9 ● ESTIMATES OF TWO CRITICAL POINTS AND THREE SLOPES

Parameter	Estimate	Approx Std Error	Approximate 95% Confidence Limits	
a1	25.4619	1.4409	22.6374	28.2863
b1	−0.2554	0.0497	−0.3529	−0.1579
b2	0.0299	0.0334	−0.0354	0.0953
b3	0.2812	0.0835	0.1175	0.4450
c1	37.0357	2.5321	32.0724	41.9990
c2	66.7895	4.1846	58.5871	74.9919

The first critical point is 37.04, and the second is at 66.8. We can use these estimates in building a regression in three X segments, one below 37.04 (the negative slope), one between 37.04 and 66.8, the flat part, and one above 66.8, the positive part.

We use these critical points (rounded) to build a piecewise linear model. To do this, you want to code three separate variables (*age18to37, age38to67, age68up*) to represent the three segments, as in Table 3.10.

TABLE 3.10 ● CODING OF INDIVIDUAL SEGMENTS IN A PIECEWISE LINEAR MODEL											
Variable	**Ages**										
	18	19	20 ...	... 37	38	39	40 ...	67	68	69	70 ...
age18to37	18	19	20	37	37	37	37	37	37	37	37
age38to67	38	38	38	38	38	39	40	67	67	67	67
age68up	68	68	68	68	68	68	68	68	68	69	70

Ellipses are used here to skip unnecessary repetition of the point. *Age18to37* is coded starting at age 18, the lowest age in the sample, and increasing by one year up to and including age 37. After that, note that it is held constant at 37, the highest value in this segment, for all ages above 37. *Age38to67* is held constant at its lowest value, 38, for all ages up to and including 38, when it start to increase by one for every age up to 67. Above 67, it is constant at 67. *Age68up* is held constant for all ages up to and including 68, its starting point. After that point, it increases by one until the highest age in the sample.

A standard OLS regression is used to estimate the effect of these three variables, with the results illustrated in Table 3.11.

TABLE 3.11 ● RESULTS FOR A PIECEWISE LINEAR REGRESSION					
Parameter Estimates					
Variable	**DF**	**Parameter Estimate**	**Standard Error**	**t Value**	**Pr > |t|**
Intercept	1	−0.90726	4.39317	−0.21	0.8364
age18to37	1	−0.32866	0.03648	−9.01	<.0001
age38to67	1	0.05683	0.02213	2.57	0.0102
age68up	1	0.37161	0.06727	5.52	<.0001

You can see here that the initial effect of age is negative, and significant, up to age 37. This turning point is considerably lower than is often suggested in the literature. As a result, the substantive interpretation would have to be modified to take into account the fact that improvements in depression bottom out earlier in the life course than previously expected. The middle segment reflects a very slight upward slope, so slight one might want to interpret this period of life as a flat line in terms of affective balance. This period suggests something quite different than the original quadratic curve because now there are counteracting forces at work—the playing out of benefits accumulating since early adulthood, mixed with both increasing demands and the gathering clouds of later life—holding depression at a low level but not getting better or worse. Depression

FIGURE 3.11 ● A PIECEWISE LINEAR MODEL FOR AGE AND DEPRESSION

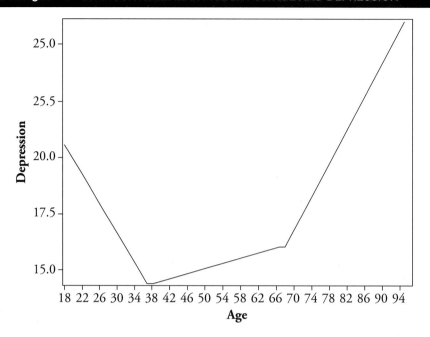

starts to rise after age 68, exactly when most lives are disengaging from major roles and there is a significant retrenchment in income.

The plot in Figure 3.11 reflects the linearized version of the cubic spline. You can see that it is quite close to that model but in simplified form.

It is clear in this example why spline regression may be an interesting alternative to the traditional application of smooth functions. In life course research, the specification of turning points is a major issue. In program/policy research, the specification of a turning point is the fundamental target of the research. The spline approach in particular allows us to focus on different stages of the effect of X, without dealing with the smooth changes in the curve inherent to polynomials. It is also very flexible—you can use cubic splines for the smooth approach and get very close to what polynomials will show you; you can use linear splines to detect changes in direction sensitively; and you can use piecewise linear regression derived from cubic splines to focus on different segments in the effect of X.

3.7 PUBLISHED EXAMPLES

In this section, we discuss three examples of regressions involving quadratic curves—and one involving splines as an alternative. A general theme emerges from these examples. Nonlinear models have the potential to have significant impacts on the major conclusions of literatures or theories that depend implicitly on linear thinking.

In these examples, there are a range of sub-themes of note: the importance of thinking in terms of single continuous variables instead of categories—and the theoretical efficiency of doing so—the generality of quadratic curves in our ideas, the ability to resolve apparently opposite theories, and the importance of fitting nonlinearity carefully, especially in terms of relevance to policy.

3.7.1 Three Quadratic Effects

3.7.1.1 Social Integration and Suicide

Durkheim's Suicide proposes (primarily) three types: altruistic, egoistic, and anomic (Durkheim, 1897). These concepts are proposed and treated categorically, as distinct social phenomena. But the first two also describe extremes of social integration. Altruistic suicide occurs when the "common conscience" of the social collective is so strong and individual goals so weak that suicide increases because the self is so deeply embedded in the group collective that the individual is more willing to sacrifice for the group. Egoistic suicide occurs in situations of the opposite extreme, where the common conscience is weak, thus the connection between the self and the collective is weak, and the self derives little meaning or purpose from the collective (Johnson, 1965). These polar opposites are sometimes treated not as categorically different types but opposite extremes of a single underlying continuum, usually labeled "social integration" (but sometimes also including corresponding differences in social regulation). Seen this way, we can imagine a concave quadratic effect predicting rates of suicide from the level of social integration (Johnson, 1965), as illustrated in Figure 3.12.

FIGURE 3.12 ● SUICIDE AS A FUNCTION OF THE LEVEL OF SOCIAL INTEGRATION

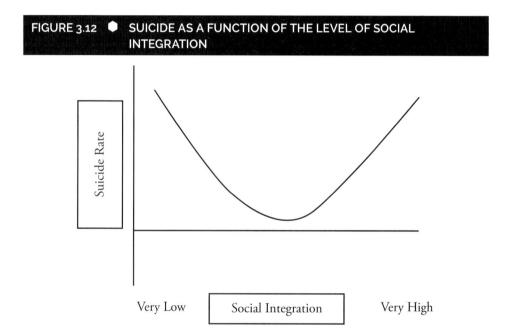

This relationship represents Durkheim's predictions—but more efficiently—and the variables one would use to address these predictions change accordingly. One would need an *overall* multi-dimensional measure of social integration in this approach rather than a group-by-group or component-by-component approach. In a sense, then, this representation is "harder" on the theory because it places extra operational demands on the concept of social integration (Gibbs & Martin, 1964).

Social science is full of theoretical reasoning that represents the extremes as dysfunctional, including most versions of structural functionalism, exchange theory, and systems theory requiring equilibrium states. The quadratic curve is especially important as an alternative to a linear model because it stands for a general hypothesis that also suggests the linear relationship may be weak to nonexistent. Further, this curve can be used to resolve what may look like contradictory theoretical reasoning.

3.7.1.2 The Psycho-Economics of Feeling Underpaid

John Mirowsky (1987) explained the association between income and the feeling of being underpaid using a nonlinear model. At first glance, one would assume that the more one makes the less you feel underpaid but not according to this article.

Mirowsky reviews two opposing theories that make opposite predictions about this relationship. The "Rainwater curve" predicts what one would expect: The sense of underpayment decreases the closer one is to the "standard package" people use as a referential baseline in judging their own situation. This standard package is determined by what seems to be true for the mainstream—that is, an average of what people get. Once people get more than the standard package, their sense of underpayment becomes negative—that is, they feel overpaid.

However, as Mirowsky points out, the "Veblen curve" predicts something quite different: People feel underpaid the more they desire and "desire more the more they are paid" (1987, p. 1410). "The tendency . . . is constantly to make the present pecuniary standard the departure for a fresh increase of wealth; and this in turn gives rise to a new standard of sufficiency . . . the normal, average person will live in chronic dissatisfaction with his present lot" (Veblen, 1899, as cited in Mirowsky, 1987, p 35). Obviously this reasoning does not sit easily next to the Rainwater expectation.

Mirowsky reasons that both can be true if each only applies across part of the income range: The Rainwater curve predominates for those below the standard package, but above that point, the Veblen curve begins to predominate. Combining the reasoning of both approaches results in a quadratic curve for the effect of income on the sense of underpayment—a creative solution to the apparent contradiction in reasoning of the two approaches (see Figure 3.13). Mirowsky does not treat the two theories as inconsistent or contradictory; instead, he reasons that both can be true but at different levels of income.

Mirowsky puts the two theories together this way:

> It is possible that the sense of underpayment is the sum of two perceived deficits, as illustrated in figure 2 [see Figure 3.13]. Analogous to the curves found by Rossi and his colleagues, there is a decelerating decrease in the Rainwater deficit as earnings go up, with the deficit becoming negative as pay increases above the level needed for the mainstream package. Analogous to a curve representing the income necessary to move up in social rank or status, there are (1) an accelerating increase in the Veblen deficit as earnings increase and (2) no negative Veblen deficits (no one feels overpaid relative to those above). (1987, p. 1412)

The predicted curve, surprisingly, suggests a quadratic relationship, including the possibility that as people make more income, their sense of underpayment *grows*. Further, no one feels overpaid in this model. Results for husbands and wives in the data are similar, to a point, but for illustration, we note the quadratic relationship for husbands in Table 3.13, controlling for spousal income.

The plot of this relationship reflects the predicted quadratic in Figure 3.13, including the increasing sense of underpayment at higher levels of income.

This article is an example of the use of a nonlinear model to resolve an apparent contradiction, making both theories plausible but within bounds. Before one thinks that theories are simply linear and unconditional, it is potentially beneficial to explore how each might apply under different conditions.

FIGURE 3.13 ● ILLUSTRATION OF HYPOTHETICAL RAINWATER AND VEBLEN CURVES RESULTING IN A U-SHAPED RELATIONSHIP BETWEEN UNDERPAYMENT AND EARNINGS

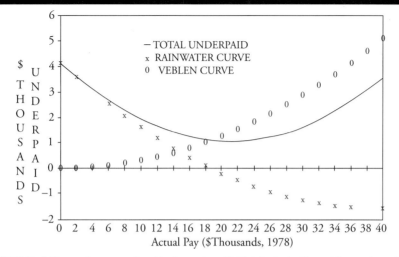

Source: Mirowsky, J. (1987, May). The psycho-economics of feeling underpaid: Distributive justice and the earnings of husbands and wives. *American Journal of Sociology, 92*(6), 1412, Figure 2.

TABLE 3.12 ● HUSBAND'S UNDERPAYMENT AND JUSTICE EVALUATION AS A FUNCTION OF HIS EARNINGS, HIS WIFE'S EARNINGS, MERIT, NEED, AND RESPONSIBILITY

	DEPENDENT VARIABLE			
	Amount Underpaid		**Justice Evaluation**	
VARIABLE	*b*	**Standard Error (b)**	*b*	**Standard Error (b)**
1. Husband's earnings	−.3313***	.1114	.0583***	.0062
2. (Husband's earnings)²	.0069***	.0027	−1.1E-3***	1.5E-4
3. Wife's earnings	−.1923*	.1299	.0151**	.0072
4. (Wife's earnings)²	.0065	.0066	−2.2E-4	3.7E-4
5. Husband's × wife's earnings	.0100**	.0052	−6.4E-4**	2.9E-4
6. Full time	1.2041	1.8531	−.0672	.1026
7. Duncan S.E.I.	.0120***	.0055	−8.3E-4***	3.1E-4
8. Race (White = 1)	−.2713	.8702	.0041	.0482
9. Age	−.0244	.0238	.0017	.0013
10. Number of children	.0359	.1472	−.0040	.0082
11. Economic strain	.3307***	.1381	−.0065	.0076
12. Traditional	.8560***	.3513	−.0276*	.0195
13. Intercept	4.4822	2.4134	−.6855***	.1337
14. R^2	.0631		.2081	

Note:—All coefficients are unstandardized. The regressions are based on 621 cases. *$P < .$ 10 (one-tailed test). ** $P < .05$ (one-tailed test). *** $P < .01$ (one-tailed test).

Source: Mirowsky, J. (1987, May). The psycho-economics of feeling underpaid: Distributive justice and the earnings of husbands and wives. *American Journal of Sociology, 92*(6), 1424, Table 2.

3.7.1.3 Spousal Alternatives and Marital Dissolution

South and Lloyd (1995) use the NLSY data to investigate the relationship between the sex ratio of unmarried males to females in the 20- to 30-age range as a predictor of the risk of divorce in marriages in that community. This is a multilevel model, as discussed later in this book. The idea is to demonstrate that contextual characteristics—apparently below the consciousness of individuals—still influence individual decisions, over and above the usual predictors of divorce at the individual level, such as age at marriage, education, number of children, and each spouse's income.

Table 3.13 shows the results in Models 1, 2, and 3. Results in Models 2 and 3 show a quadratic effect of the sex ratio—an increase in the risk of marital dissolution as the sex ratio departs from average in that age group in *either* direction. This is the importance of this finding: An excess of single males to females and an excess of single females to males both predict an increase in the

TABLE 3.13 ● COEFFICIENTS FROM PROPORTIONAL HAZARDS REGRESSION MODELS OF MARITAL DISSOLUTION: NON-HISPANIC WHITES FROM THE NLSY, 1979–1984			
Explanatory Variables	**Model 1** **b**	**Model 2** **b**	**Model 3** **b**
Individual Characteristics	.130		.084
Sex (0 = male; 1 = female)	(.097)	—	(.099)
	−.033		−.029
Age at first marriage	(.025)	—	(.025)
	−.101**		−.1 15**
Years of school	(.024)	—	(.024)
	.595**		−.552**
Home ownership (0 = no; 1 = yes)	(.115)	—	(.116)
	−.319**		−.312**
Number of children	(.063)	—	(.063)
	−.002		−.002
Wife's weeks worked	(.003)	—	(.003)
	−.005*		−.007**
Husband's weeks worked	(.002)	—	(.002)
	−.006		−.008
Wife's income	(.011)	—	(.012)
	−.037**		−.037**
Husband's income	(.007)	—	(.007)
Marriage Market Characteristics		−.034**	−.025*
Sex ratio (ratio of men to women)	—	(.012)	(.012)
		.013**	.010*
(Sex ratio)[2][a]	—	(.005)	(.005)
		.016	.028**
Percent females employed or in school	—	(.010)	(.011)
		−.008	−.009
Percent males employed or in school	—	(.008)	(.008)

Explanatory Variables	Model 1 b	Model 2 b	Model 3 b
Other Contextual Variables		−.042	.068
In MSA (0 = no; 1 = yes)	—	(.088)	(.092)
		.016**	.018**
Geographic mobility rate in county	—	(.006)	(.006)
		.027	−.103
Median monthly rent in county	—	(.140)	(.142)
−2 log likelihood	7,980.317	8,303.226	7,767.094

*$p \leq .05$ **$p \leq .01$ (two-tailed tests)

[a] Coefficient and standard error are multiplied by 100.

Note: Numbers in parentheses are standard errors. $N = 2{,}592$.

Source: South, S. J., & Lloyd, K. M. (1995). Spousal alternatives and marital dissolution. *American Sociological Review, 60*(1), 31, Table 3.

risk of marital dissolution—it is not one excess more than the other. The subtle issue that arises here is the different age of first marriage for males and females—making the average sex ratio in this age group already imbalanced (= 127). Given this fact, the alternative hypothesis here, somewhat implicit, is the idea that only a further excess of females to males will affect the risk of divorce, so the test of the quadratic effect is crucial to the larger point: Any departure from the mean sex ratio in this group affects supply and has an effect on divorce, and in this sense, gender doesn't matter.

The findings here make a nonobvious point that goes much beyond the simple application of stereotypes. First, contextual features of the community as a whole intervene in the lives of individual marriages, shifting the probability of the survival of marriages. Most of the understandings of what leads to marital dissolution start from the inside, the internal politics of the relationship. But as Levinger noted (1976), the "attraction of alternatives" is a potent force. Second, the findings make the point that the excess of *either* gender in the marriage market beyond what is usual has a similar effect.

3.7.2 Using Splines Instead of a Polynomial

A 2004 article in the *American Journal of Epidemiology* provides an important example suggesting that a quadratic fit may not be enough in important cases—in fact, the standard application of a quadratic model or any polynomial may miss crucial elements of the nonlinearity (Bagnardi, Zambon, Quatto, & Corrao, 2004). The question in this paper is the relationship between alcohol intake and the risk of mortality. The focus is on the use of splines as an alternative to a parametric "smooth function" approach.

The paper uses a meta-analysis—an analysis of all published papers on this issue from 1966 to 2000—to extract an overall model for the effect of daily alcohol intake on the risk of mortality. The authors estimate this relationship using a ladder of both integer and fractional polynomials, with the quadratic as a reference point, as well as a cubic spline fit. We concentrate here on the comparison of the quadratic fit to the cubic spline. The authors make the important point that specific functional forms implied by both polynomials and logarithmic models may miss important issues in the fit and that a more open approach may be sensitive to these issues.

Figure 3.14 compares the standard quadratic fit to the best fitting fractional polynomial and the cubic spline. The latter two are, significantly, very similar.

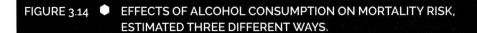

FIGURE 3.14 ● EFFECTS OF ALCOHOL CONSUMPTION ON MORTALITY RISK, ESTIMATED THREE DIFFERENT WAYS.

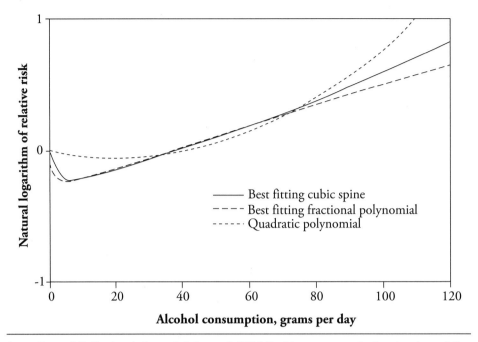

Source: Bagnardi, V., Zambon, A, Quatto, P. & Corrao, G. (2004) Flexible meta-regression functions for modeling aggregate dose-response data, with an application to alcohol and mortality. *American Journal of Epidemiology. 159*, p. 1082, Figure 2.

Alcohol intake is measured here in grams per day, given that an average alcoholic drink has about 14 grams of alcohol in it. The greatest protective effect of alcohol—the minimum—in the quadratic model occurs at 20 grams per day, equivalent roughly to 1.5 drinks, but the minimum in the cubic spline occurs at only 6 grams per day, less than half a drink per day. This is obviously a very different result, leading to very different policy recommendations. The cubic spline is able to more fully take into account the dip in risk between 0 and half a drink a day. The "last protective dose" in the quadratic model goes up to 52 grams a day, while this predicted point in the cubic spline is 46 grams a day. This is the point at which the risk exceeds zero. The figure also makes clear that the rise in risk in the cubic spline is also less than in the quadratic model at high levels of drinking.

Each of these points is potentially important to the understood impact of alcohol intake on health. As our earlier example demonstrated, the approach using splines will often suggest something not easily captured in the polynomial approach. This is one reason we advocated earlier for the use of cubic splines, followed by an identification of "critical points" in the curve and a piecewise linear representation of the overall relationship.

Concluding Words

In this chapter, we took a specific approach to the fitting of nonlinear relationships in regression. There are many other possibilities, but here, our intention was to provide something like a flexible road map. In every example used in this chapter, more careful consideration of nonlinearity fundamentally altered what we would say about the impact of X on Y. These are not subtleties. A log–log model suggests a crucial range in X over which X has most of its impact. So pretending it is linear has misleading substantive and policy implications.

Imagine you are a government official, asked to translate and apply a program intervention in the population, represented by X. The cost of your program is multiplied if you assume the effect is linear because you will not recommend targeting those at low levels of X only. If the general view is that everyone benefits, everyone is politically enfranchised. If, however, only a sub-group in the population "needs" more X, then a targeted strategy is called for—and dollars are saved.

That hypothetical highlights a practical example. Our examples also pointed to how nonlinear effects can speak to apparently conflicting theory. We advocate the careful consideration of the various possibilities embodied by nonlinear models: symmetric and opposite effects depending on the level of X, asymptotic effects of X, suggesting changes over higher levels don't matter, thresholds to the effect of X, suggesting a certain dosage is necessary to observe any effect, or the simple fact of ironic twists and turns that must be taken into account.

In the next chapter, we generalize regression one step further, by considering the form of the dependent variable. To this point, every dependent variable we have considered has been continuous, in the sense of assumed equally spaced units. In the next chapter, this changes radically so that we can consider a huge range of questions about categorical outcomes—including events, transitions, statuses, or group membership, and any outcome denoting presence/absence of some characteristic.

Practice Questions

1. The results that follow are from three models designed to assess nonlinearity in the effect of the father's controlling behavior (*dadcontrol*) on child externalizing symptoms from the Toronto Study of Intact Families in the 1990s (Wheaton, 1992).

    Model 1: is the linear effect of father's control.
    Model 2: is a dummy variable model for the effect of father's control. This variable varies from 2 to 8 in this sample; dummy variables are shown for 7 of the 8 levels of father's control (the lowest score is the excluded reference group).
    Model 3: is a model for the quadratic effect of father's control, including the linear effect (*dadcontrol*) and the effect of control squared (*dadcontrolsq*).

    a. Conduct a test to determine whether there is nonlinearity in the effect of father's control.
    b. Model 3 includes a plot of the quadratic effect of father's control. Using the results of the equation, calculate the level of control that results in the highest level of externalizing symptoms.

TABLE 3.A ● EFFECT OF PATERNAL CONTROL ON CHILD EXTERNALIZING SYMPTOMS.

The REG Procedure
Model: **MODEL 1**
Dependent Variable: externalizing

Analysis of Variance

Source	DF	Sum of Squares	Mean Square	F Value	Pr > F
Model	1	4.70210	4.70210	4.73	0.0299
Error	876	870.74646	0.99400		
Corrected Total	877	875.44857			

Root MSE	0.99700	R-Square	0.0054	
Dependent Mean	0.01780	Adj R-Sq	0.0042	
Coeff Var	5599.63643			

Parameter Estimates

Variable	DF	Parameter Estimate	Standard Error	t Value	Pr > |t|
Intercept	1	−0.21831	0.11365	−1.92	0.0551
dadcontrol	1	0.04617	0.02123	2.17	0.0299

The REG Procedure
Model: **MODEL 2**
Dependent Variable: externalizing

Number of Observations Read	881
Number of Observations Used	878
Number of Observations with Missing Values	3

Weight: famweight weight by nativity, maternal employment, income, and kids 9 to 16

Analysis of Variance

Source	DF	Sum of Squares	Mean Square	F Value	Pr > F
Model	6	18.34095	3.05683	3.11	0.0051
Error	871	857.10761	0.98405		
Corrected Total	877	875.44857			

Root MSE	0.99199	R-Square	0.0210	
Dependent Mean	0.01780	Adj R-Sq	0.0142	
Coeff Var	5571.53191			

Parameter Estimates

Variable	DF	Parameter Estimate	Standard Error	t Value	Pr > |t|
Intercept	1	-0.20961	0.15778	-1.33	0.1844
dadcontrol2	1	0.03755	0.18778	0.20	0.8416
dadcontrol3	1	0.13300	0.17218	0.77	0.4401
dadcontrol4	1	0.33769	0.17476	1.93	0.0536
dadcontrol5	1	0.42595	0.17357	2.45	0.0143
dadcontrol6	1	0.10595	0.18686	0.57	0.5709
dadcontrol7	1	0.25248	0.19406	1.30	0.1936

The REG Procedure
Model: **MODEL 3**
Dependent Variable: externalizing

Analysis of Variance

Source	DF	Sum of Squares	Mean Square	F Value	Pr > F
Model	2	10.41556	5.20778	5.27	0.0053
Error	875	865.03300	0.98861		
Corrected Total	877	875.44857			

Root MSE	0.99429	R-Square	0.0119	
Dependent Mean	0.01780	Adj R-Sq	0.0096	
Coeff Var	5584.42338			

Parameter Estimates

Variable	DF	Parameter Estimate	Standard Error	t Value	Pr > |t|
Intercept	1	-0.90788	0.30842	-2.94	0.0033
dadcontrol	1	0.34031	0.12417	2.74	0.0063
dadcontrolsq	1	-0.02842	0.01182	-2.40	0.0164

Quadratic Effect of Paternal Control on Externalizing Symptoms of Child

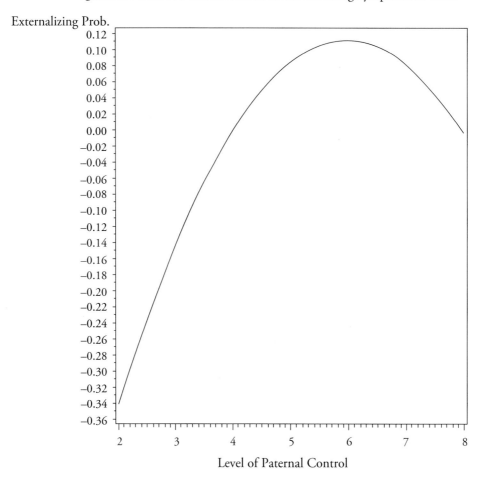

2. Results that follow in Table 3.B are from a stepwise spline regression of the effect of education on first job status. A plot of the fitted splines is also shown under the results.

The variables in the spline equation are

- **momeduc_4to22**: The linear effect of education, starting at the lowest value in the sample, which is 4 years.
- **edknot7**: There is a knot at 7 years of education. This variable is either = 0, up to and including 7 years, or it is the number of years of education greater than 7 (e.g., years of education - 7).
- **edknot18**: There is a knot at 18 years of education. This variable is either = 0, up to and including 18 years, or it is the number of years of education greater than 18 (years of education - 18).

From the results, calculate the adjusted intercept and slope *for the effect of education* at 12 years of education.

TABLE 3.B   ● A SPLINE REGRESSION FOR THE EFFECT OF EDUCATION ON FIRST JOB STATUS.

Analysis of Variance

Source	DF	Sum of Squares	Mean Square	F Value	Pr > F
Model	3	121459	40486	110.39	<.0001
Error	839	307710	366.75812		
Corrected Total	842	429169			

Variable	Parameter Estimate	Standard Error	Type II SS	F Value	Pr > F
Intercept	37.06112	24.94118	809.80941	2.21	0.1377
momeduc_4to22	-2.46847	3.63335	169.28567	0.46	0.4971
edknot7	7.17697	3.71715	1367.22932	3.73	0.0538
edknot18	-4.26792	1.59578	2623.40420	7.15	0.0076

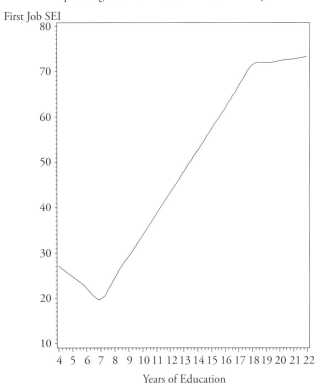

Spine Regression of Transfer of Education to Job Status

First Job SEI

Years of Education

3. The results in Table 3.C are from an analysis of the impact of years of marriage on marital satisfaction, from a study of Toronto adults between the ages of 18 and 55 (Turner & Wheaton, 1990). The model shown includes a quadratic effect of years married **but also an interaction of both components of the quadratic effect with gender.** This means that the trajectory of marital satisfaction over time is different for men and women.

The variables in the model are

- **maryears**: Years married
- **maryrsq**: Years married squared
- **female**: A dummy variable for gender = 1 for females and = 0 for males
- **yrsxsex**: Years married x female
- **yrsqxsex**: Years married squared x female

a. Derive from the results the effect of years married on marital satisfaction among men and among women. Do this by figuring out the effect of years married and years married squared separately for men and women. Note there is a graph showing the different curves for men and women that you can use as a guide.

b. Use the separate equations for men and women to figure out the number of years married that results in the minimum level of marital satisfaction among men and the maximum level of marital satisfaction among women.

c. Results are also provided for a spline regression of the same relationship but not divided by gender (Table 3.D). In these results, the final model shows knots at 8 and 29 years of marriage. Given these results, calculate the slope for the effect of years married beyond 8 and up to 29 years married.

TABLE 3.C ● QUADRATIC MODEL WITH AN INTERACTION

Number of Observations Read	671
Number of Observations Used	661
Number of Observations with Missing Values	10

Analysis of Variance

Source	DF	Sum of Squares	Mean Square	F Value	Pr > F
Model	5	4.57708	0.91542	3.01	0.0108
Error	655	199.33719	0.30433		
Corrected Total	660	203.91427			

Root MSE	0.55166	R-Square	0.0224
Dependent Mean	4.03860	Adj R-Sq	0.0150
Coeff Var	13.65975		10

Parameter Estimates

Variable	DF	Parameter Estimate	Standard Error	t Value	Pr > |t|
Intercept	1	4.12247	0.07062	58.37	<.0001
maryears	1	−0.02400	0.01137	−2.11	0.0352
maryrsq	1	0.00100	0.00036895	2.72	0.0067
female	1	−0.06209	0.09861	−0.63	0.5291
yrsxsex	1	0.02535	0.01519	1.67	0.0956
yrsqxsex	1	−0.00120	0.00047429	-2.54	0.0114

Plot of Effect of Years Married on Marital Satisfaction among Men and Women

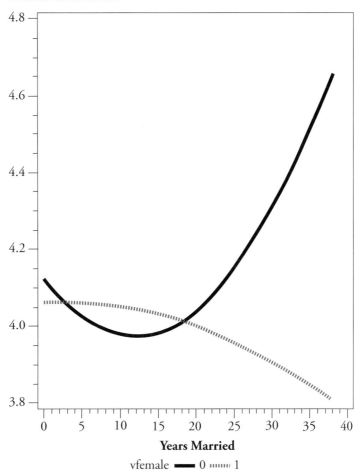

TABLE 3.D ● THE SPLINE MODEL

Analysis of Variance					
Source	DF	Sum of Squares	Mean Square	F Value	Pr > F
Model	3	2.36373	0.78791	2.75	0.0422
Error	659	189.09385	0.28694		
Corrected Total	662	191.45758			

Parameter Estimates					
Variable	Parameter Estimate	Standard Error	Type II SS	F Value	Pr > F
Intercept	4.14709	0.05970	1384.57006	4825.28	<.0001
maryears	−0.02562	0.01008	1.85466	6.46	0.0112
*marrknot8	0.03116	0.01261	1.75130	6.10	0.0137
marrknot29	−0.04420	0.02667	0.78811	2.75	0.0979
* Forced into the model by the INCLUDE= option					

4. Results in Table 3.E show a ***linear*** spline regression of the effect of age on anger. Age is coded from 20 to 80 years old; anger is the mean of a three item scale and stands for "days angry last week."

The stepwise regression kept variables that were significant at less than the .05 level. Two knots were included: one at 59 and one at 76. Variables are named by the convention *ageknotxx*, where *xx* is the age of the knot.

A plot of the resulting splines is also shown, as guidance for your answers.

   a. Use the results of the linear spline model to answer this question: Calculate the adjusted intercept and slope for the effect of age on anger for respondents between 59 and 76 years old.

   b. A cubic spline was also run, resulting in the second plot shown. After this, PROC NLIN was run to choose critical points to linearize the curve. Those critical points were 63 and 76. Those points were used to create a piecewise linear regression (Table 3.F), with three variables:

   age20to63

   age64to75

   age76up

What is the slope for the effect of age for someone who is 70 years old? For someone who is 30 years old?

TABLE 3.E ⬡ LINEAR SPLINE RESULTS—FINAL MODEL

Parameter Estimates					
Variable	Parameter Estimate	Standard Error	Type II SS	F Value	Pr > F
Intercept	1.65317	0.05043	1880.15059	1074.62	<.0001
*rage	−0.01613	0.00127	281.58816	160.94	<.0001
ageknot59	0.01799	0.00548	18.87976	10.79	0.0010
ageknot76	−0.14534	0.05146	13.95843	7.98	0.0047

Plot of Linear Splines

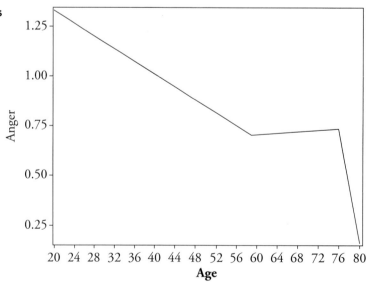

Cubic Spline Model

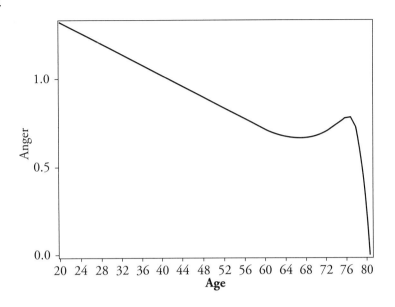

TABLE 3.F ● PIECEWISE LINEAR REGRESSION

Parameter Estimates						
Variable	**Label**	**DF**	**Parameter Estimate**	**Standard Error**	**Pr > F**	**Pr > |t|**
Intercept	Intercept	1	9.80762	2.66906	3.67	0.0002
age20to63		1	−0.01565	0.00115	−13.64	<.0001
age20to63		1	0.01179	0.00719	1.64	0.1011
age76up		1	−0.11883	0.03835	-3.10	0.0019

GENERALIZATIONS OF REGRESSION 3

Logistic Regression

The regression framework would indeed be narrow if it was limited to dependent variables that are continuous and normally distributed. Many things we want to study demand categorical distinctions. Social science is full of such questions: Why do some women choose to work? Why do some women choose to stop working? Why are some people victimized by violent crime? Which marriages include domestic violence? Why do some people vote and others don't? Why do some people go to church? Why do boys drop out of high school? Why do some people have clinical cases of depression? Why do some teenagers start smoking? What determines which workers get promoted? What leads to divorce? What influences the decision to have children? Why do some immigrants retain their native language? Why do revolutions occur? We will stop there, but the possibilities are almost limitless.

This list of questions signals the length and breadth of examples in social science in which the basic question is why someone is in one group and not another. To study these questions, we need a form of regression that allows for binary (dichotomous) outcomes—yes versus no, true versus false, in group or not, present versus absent.

The question is, how do we design a regression model suited to these types of outcomes?

4.1 A FIRST TAKE: THE LINEAR PROBABILITY MODEL

Suppose we first try one apparently minor modification of the usual OLS regression model: Use a dichotomous dependent variable rather than a more continuous variable. We could code this variable like a dummy variable, = 1 to stand for the event we want to predict, and = 0 for the reference group. A ***linear probability model*** is any standard OLS regression applied to a two-value (1/0) categorical dependent variable.

4.1.1 Development of the Linear Probability Model

The OLS model assumes Y is on at least an interval scale and that there are no theoretical restrictions on values of Xs and therefore on Ys.

If $y = 1$ and 0:

$$E(Y_i) = a + b_1 X_1 + \ldots + b_k X_k$$

where we use $E(Y_i)$ to stand for the predicted value of Y given the model. The expected value of Y is the sum, in the population, of each possible value of Y multiplied by its probability. That is

$$E(Y_i) = \sum (Y_i \cdot Pr(Y_i))$$

Applying this definition to a Y with two values, 0 and 1, results in

$$\begin{aligned} E(Y_i) &= (0 \cdot Pr(Y_i = 0)) + (1 \cdot Pr(Y_i = 1)) \\ &= Pr(Y_i = 1) \\ \therefore E(Y_i) &= Pr(Y_i = 1) = a + b_1 X_1 + \ldots + b_k X_k \end{aligned}$$

Therefore, the effects of Xs in this case can be interpreted as affecting the $Pr(Y = 1)$—that is, a 1 unit change in X produces a b unit change in $Pr(Y)$. This means changes in the probability are a *linear* function of changes in Xs, thus the term "linear probability model."

This is a simple model to implement: Run an OLS regression, interpret b as above. Notice here, as in all of the interpretive approaches used for categorical outcomes that follow, the working concept for interpretation involves some transformation of the outcome dichotomy or polytomy into a continuous variable that allows (1) an exact statement of the effect of X and (2) comparison of the size of the effect of different independent variables.

4.1.2 Violated Assumptions of OLS

While this model is very straightforward, it violates one of the fundamental assumptions of the OLS model. In this model, the errors, designated e_i, can only take on two values:

Given:	$e_i = Y_i - a - bX_i$,
when $Y = 1$:	$e_i = 1 - a - bX_i$,
and when $Y = 0$:	$e_i = -a - bX_i$

The estimation of b itself is not biased here; the issue is that the error variances depend on the level of X—that is, change with the level of X, as shown by this result for the error variance in this situation:

$$\mathrm{Var}(e_i) = Pr(Y_i = 1) \cdot (1 - Pr(Y_i = 1)) = \widehat{Y}_i \cdot (1 - \widehat{Y}_i)$$

This definition shows that the variance of the errors in the linear probability model depends on the predicted Y in the model. This variance will therefore change depending on the level of X, resulting in *heteroscedastic errors* and thus violating one of the assumptions of OLS estimation.

There *is* another problem to consider. Values of $\widehat{Y}$ in this model can fall outside the theoretical range of the probability. That is, you can get predicted values above 1 and below 0. If too many predicted values fall outside this range, this suggests the model is misspecified and that the basic linear form of the model distorts reality too much. In other words, X does not—cannot, in fact—have a *linear* relationship with the Pr (Y) over its entire range.

There are various corrections to and generalizations of this model that have been applied (e.g., Goldberger, 1964). We return to the linear probability model below—because it may still be useful for certain purposes and under certain conditions.

4.2 THE LOGISTIC REGRESSION MODEL

If we use a probability model, it should recognize that the concept of probability is bounded by 0 and 1, first. In addition, these bounds suggest that the effect of X on the probability has to be nonlinear—that is, it is less relevant when the probability is very low and very high than for ranges of probability in the middle—the range where X has most of its effect.

The logistic model is such a model. It includes the idea that the effect of changes in X on Pr(Y) are small at first, but there is a critical region over which X has a stronger and substantial effect on the probability. Once this probability is already high, further changes in X must be substantial for discernible effects on the Pr(Y).

For example, consider the effect of family wealth on Pr (home ownership):

- If family has $0 in savings, an increase of $25,000 may not be enough to shift the probability significantly.

- However, an increase from $25,000 to $50,000 might reach a threshold beyond which the probability increases rapidly.

- Increases in wealth up to $100,000 continue to have a strong impact, but at that point, the probability of owning a home is already high.

- If a family already has $100,000, adding $25,000 more may make little difference.

Following through this example, the form of the model is shown in Figure 4.1:

FIGURE 4.1 ● THE LOGISTIC MODEL

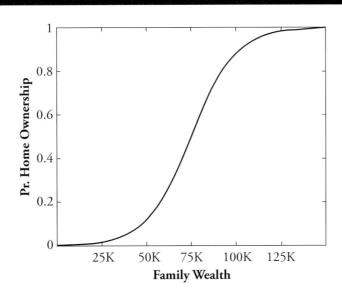

Using "$a + bX$" as a short form for whatever is included in the regression equation (as independent variables), the general form of the logistic model is

$$P = Pr(Y) = \frac{1}{1 + e^{-(a+bX)}} = \frac{e^{(a+bX)}}{1 + e^{(a+bX)}}$$

These are different but equivalent forms of the model: Some disciplines use the first version; some use the second. Here is a proof that they are the same:

$$\frac{1}{1 + e^{-(a+bX)}} = \frac{1}{1 + \frac{1}{e^{(a+bX)}}} = \frac{1}{\frac{e^{(a+bX)}+1}{e^{(a+bX)}}} = 1 \cdot \frac{e^{(a+bX)}}{1 + e^{(a+bX)}}$$

Notice the logistic model has the constant e in it (= 2.7818). We saw the use of this constant when discussing the rules of logarithms in the previous chapter (section 3.3.2). The regression equation is the exponent of e in this model. We can guess from seeing this that the form of the effect of X on the $Pr(Y)$ is inherently nonlinear. But it can be transformed to a form that is linear and can be estimated quite straightforwardly.

4.2.1 Transforming the Probability Function for the Logistic Model

This derivation is important to understanding logistic model: It is a good idea not to bypass it. It is a clue to much of how this model works.

$$Pr(Y) = P = \frac{1}{1 + e^{-(a+bX)}}$$

$$P(1 + e^{-(a+bX)}) = 1 \qquad \text{Multiplying both sides by the denominator}$$

$$P + Pe^{-(a+bX)} = 1 \qquad \text{Multiplying through by } P \text{ on the left}$$

$$Pe^{-(a+bX)} = 1 - P \qquad \text{Subtracting } P \text{ from both sides}$$

$$P \cdot \frac{1}{e^{(a+bX)}} = (1 - P) \qquad \text{Negative exponent is the inverse}$$

$$P = (1 - P) \cdot e^{(a+bX)} \qquad \text{Multiply both sides by denominator}$$

$$\frac{P}{1 - P} = e^{(a+bX)} \qquad \text{Divide both sides by } (1 - P)$$

The left hand side here is very important: It is the ***odds*** that Y occurs. The right-hand side is in the form of some of the nonlinear models of the last chapter where the equation is an exponent of the constant e.

4.2.1.1 The Odds

The odds of an "event" happening is the probability of the event happening divided by the probability the event does not happen.

If the probability of an event is .5, then the odds that the event will happen are .5/.5 and therefore 1. If the probability of the event is .666, then the odds the event will happen are 2/1—that is, .6666 / .3333. Table 4.1 converts various probabilities to the corresponding odds.

Note some characteristics of the odds ratios in this table. First, a zero association, reflecting a situation in which the event is no more likely to happen than not happen, produces a value of 1, not 0. Second, values ***above*** 1 reflect positive association, and values ***below*** 1 reflect negative association. Third, the odds ratio appears to increase / decrease more quickly as you get to probability extremes.

TABLE 4.1 ● THE RELATIONSHIP BETWEEN PROBABILITIES AND ODDS		
Probability of Event	**1 – Pr of Event**	**Odds = P/(1 - P)**
No Association		
.5	.5	1
Positive Association		
.6	.4	1.5
.6666	.3333	2
.75	.25	3
.80	.20	4
.90	.10	9
Negative Association		
.40	.60	.6666
.3333	.6666	.50
.25	.75	.3333
.20	.80	.25

This is an example of the fact that the odds are a multiplicative number, not an additive number—the *relative* sizes of odds are the same for equal differences in probabilities on either side of .5. For example, a probability of .666 produces an odds of 2, and a probability of .8 produces an odds of 4—twice as much. On the negative side, the mirror image differences work the same way: A probability of .333 produces an odds of .5, and a probability of .20 produces an odds of .25—half as much.

4.2.1.2 The Linear Form of the Model

Taking the natural logarithm (*ln*) of both sides of the model for the odds, we get

$$\ln \frac{P}{1-P} = \ln(e^{(a+bX)}) = a + bX$$

This is the estimation form of the logistic model. On the left is the **log** of the odds of Y. The right-hand side looks like any other regression: a series of independent variables considered additively. This model is linear in the log of the odds—but only in the log of the odds. The $\ln \frac{P}{1-P}$ is sometimes called a logit, as a shorthand reference.

There are many ways to interpret this model. We will discuss four different approaches before providing a more extended example:

1. Effects on the log odds of Y

2. Exact effects on the probability of Y for given values of X

3. Effects on the odds of Y

4. The first derivative of the probability function, including the average marginal effect

4.3 INTERPRETING LOGISTIC MODELS

4.3.1 Effects on the Log Odds of Y

This approach involves simply interpreting the derived coefficients as effects of 1 unit increases in X on the "log odds of Y." This is not an intuitive concept and is not used often. There are other approaches to interpretation that bypass this problem and also have other useful features.

4.3.2 Effects on the Probability of Y

Here we use an example derived from the DeMaris (1992) presentation in the Sage Little Green Book series but updated to the 2012 election. The equation that follows predicts the log odds of voting for Obama in the 2012 election versus Romney, using the 2012 American National Election Survey (2016).

There are four independent variables in this equation:

- **RvsDPartyID**: A seven-point scale measuring party identification, from 1 = strong Democrat to 7 = strong Republican
- **ConvsLib**: Also a 7-point scale, from 1= very liberal to 7 = very conservative
- **Black**: A dummy variable = 1 if self-reported Black, = 0 if self-reported non-Hispanic White
- **educinyears**: Years of education

The results are as follows:

$$\widehat{Logodds}\ (\text{vote Obama}) = 1.05 - .742(RvsDPartyID) - .362(ConvsLib) + 1.01(\text{Black}) + .169(educinyears)$$

You can always calculate effects of changes in X variables on the probability of Y, using the logistic function. One common way of doing this is to set all variables at their mean level, except the one whose effect you want to interpret, and then plug contrasting values of that X into the function to derive predicted probabilities in each case. The effect is the difference in the probability.

Suppose you want to estimate the effect of Black versus White, a dummy variable. You could set the other three variables at their mean level, then substitute 0 for *Black* into the equation and calculate a predicted log odds in that case:

$$\widehat{Logodds}\ (\text{vote Obama}) = 1.05 - .742(3.65) - .362(4.23) + 1.01(0) + .169(13.9) = -.84046$$

This is the value of the equation in the exponent of the probability function. Substitute this value into the logistic probability function to get

$$P = \frac{1}{1 + e^{-(-.84046)}} = .301$$

Now substitute *Black* =1 into this equation, to derive the log odds:

$$\widehat{Logodds}\ (\text{vote Obama}) = 1.05 - .742(3.65) - .362(4.23) + 1.01(1) + .169(13.9) = .1695$$

The corresponding probability is

$$P = \frac{1}{1 + e^{-(.1695)}} = .542$$

So the effect of Black versus White on the probability of voting for Obama, at the mean of other variables, is .542 - .301 = .241—that is, being Black increases the probability by about .24—a substantial difference. Of course, setting other variables at their mean here does not mean you are comparing the average White to the average Black in this calculation since they will differ on the other variables as well.

4.3.2.1 A Closer Look

You can set the other variables to any set of values of interest in your calculations. This could be done, for example, to show differential effects at either the low end or the high end of the probability function. Or you could do this to contrast the effect of a particular variable under very different conditions described by other variables.

Does being Black matter as much when someone is also a conservative Republican? We substitute values into the equation that represent a conservative Republican first and then calculate the effect of Black in that case, assuming education is still at its mean. We set variables for party identification and conservative views to 7 in both cases, to specify a (very) conservative Republican. Then we substitute *Black* = 0 and *Black* = 1 in succession, as before, to calculate the effect of being Black:

Substituting for Whites first:

$$\widehat{Logodds} \text{ (vote Obama)} = 1.05 - .742(7) - .362(7) + 1.01(0) + .169(13.9) = -4.329$$

The probability of voting for Obama in this case is only

$$P = \frac{1}{1 + e^{-(-4.329)}} = .013$$

For Blacks, the log odds and probability now are

$$\widehat{Logodds} \text{ (vote Obama)} = 1.05 - .742(7) - .362(7) + 1.01(1) + .169(13.9) = -3.319$$

$$P = \frac{1}{1 + e^{-(-3.319)}} = .035$$

In this extreme situation, when the probability of voting for Obama is already very low, the Black versus White voter distinction makes little difference. The actual effect on the probability here is .035 - .013 = .022. This is typical of changes in the probability of the outcome at the extremes.

A second question we could ask is this: What is the effect of conservative views when someone is a Democrat? To do this, we could set the mean of both education (13.9) and the race dummy variable (.224) to their means, set party identification to 1, and then vary the value of political views.

For the liberal Democrat we have

$$\widehat{Logodds} \text{ (vote Obama)} = 1.05 - .742(1) - .362(1) + 1.01(.224) + .169(13.9) = 2.521$$

$$P = \frac{1}{1 + e^{-(2.521)}} = .925$$

For the conservative Democrat we have

$$\widehat{Logodds} \text{ (vote Obama)} = 1.05 - .742(1) - .362(7) + 1.01(.224) + .169(13.9) = .3493$$

$$P = \frac{1}{1 + e^{-(.3493)}} = .586$$

When someone identifies as a strong Democrat, the effect of very conservative versus very liberal views is to decrease the probability of voting for Obama .586 - .925 = -.339. This is a substantial impact. The same effect calculated among strong Republicans is only -.11. This shows a very important characteristic of the logistic model: It is nonlinear, and the effect of variables depends on the levels of other variables considered.

4.3.3 Effects on the Odds

Let R = *RvsDPartyID,* C = *Convslib,* B = *Black,* and E = *educinyears.* From the original model for the log odds we re-write it more efficiently this way:

$$\ln\frac{P}{1-P} = a + b_1 R + b_2 C + b_3 B + b_4 E$$

Exponentiate both sides and use Rules 1 and 2 for logarithms to get a model for the odds:

$$e^{\left(\ln\frac{P}{1-P}\right)} = e^{a+b_1 R+b_2 C+b_3 B+b_4 E}$$

$$\frac{P}{1-P} = e^a e^{b_1 R} e^{b_2 C} e^{b_3 B} e^{b_4 E}$$

Each e^{b_i} is the impact of a 1-unit increase in X on the **odds** of Y. This is a multiplicative effect, and so the change in X **multiplies** the odds.

Using the log odds voting equation above and taking the exponential of each coefficient leads to

$$\frac{P}{1-P} = 2.86 \cdot 476^R \cdot 696^C \cdot 2.74^B \cdot 1.18^E$$

One of the most important characteristics of the model for the odds is that odds multipliers are the same across values of the other variables. So in this case, simple and general interpretive statements are possible.

For example, Blacks had about 2.74 times the odds of voting for Obama compared to Whites. And each year of education increases the odds of voting for Obama by 1.18 or about 18%. This may seem like a modest effect, but it is the impact of a one-year increase in education. If you wanted to interpret an effect over a bigger difference in education, for example, 4 years, you can raise the 1.18 multiplier to the 4th power, resulting in a proportionate increase in odds equal to 1.94 or about 94%.

Note that effects here below 1 are like a negative relationship in the additive model. For example, each unit of conservative views *reduces* the odds of voting for Obama by a factor of .696. This means that each unit increase in this variable leads to about .70 of the odds of voting for Obama, or put still another way, it reduces the odds by about 30%.

4.3.4 Using the First Derivative

We would like to know how P changes *in general* as X changes. Therefore, find $\frac{dP}{dx}$ where P equals the logistic function above. Taking this derivative shows that the probability of Y changes with a simple transformation of b, the regression coefficient in the logistic regression:

$$\frac{dP}{dx} = b \cdot P \cdot (1-P)$$

Where: b = the regression coefficient and P is a chosen baseline probability to evaluate the effect. Often the average probability is used here, but other values can be chosen. It is important to note that this approach only applies to binary logistic regression.

Using the same example, we could use the average probability of voting for Obama to substitute for P in this model. That "average probability" is just the proportion of the sample voting for Obama. In this sample, $\overline{P} = .43$.

TABLE 4.2 ● CALCULATING THE FIRST DERIVATIVE AT THE MEAN PROBABILITY			
	(1)	**(2)**	**(3)**
So	b	$P(1-P)$	**Effect on Pr**
R (Republicanism)	−.742		−.182
C (Conservatism)	−.362	$.43 \cdot (1-.43) = .2452$	−.089
B (Black)	1.01		.248
E (Education)	.169		.041

Effects are calculated in Table 4.2 as Column 1 x Column 2 = Column 3. These are effects of *unit* changes in each X. Setting $P = \overline{P}$, in effect, assumes other Xs are at mean values. In words, each point increase in Republicanism decreases the probability of voting for Obama by .182. Given this is a 7-point scale, this variable is of key importance in determining voting. Each unit increase in conservatism decreases the probability by .09, about half of the effect. Blacks have a .25 higher probability of voting for Obama than Whites, on average (note how close this is to the earlier calculation). Each year of education increases the probability of voting for Obama by .04, so a 4-year increase would result in an increase in the probability equal to .16 (4 x .04 = .16).

This approach is straightforward, but there are important cautions using this approach, and it only provides limited information about how variables affect the probability in combination. One important problem is highlighted by the effect of "Black" here: Holding other variables at their mean leads to comparison of people across groups who are not equally representative of those groups.

4.3.4.1 The Average Marginal Effect

A related approach using the first derivative calculates the "average marginal effect" of each variable. The average marginal effect of each variable is the average across the sample of the impact on the predicted probability of changing one X by one unit, given the *actual* values that person has on other independent variables.

Although SAS and STATA calculate average marginal effects for you, we review the logic of producing them manually, for the purpose of better understanding the difference with the previous application of the first derivative:

1. Run a logistic regression as usual, and output the predicted log odds and predicted probability for each observation as added variable(s) in your input data. This is usually an option in most software.

2. Make up new variables for each person, using the formula for the first derivative. For example: Marginal Effect $= b \cdot \widehat{P} \cdot (1 - \widehat{P})$ where $\widehat{P}$ is the predicted probability of Y variable for each observation.

3. If one of your variables is a dummy variable, you should take a different approach. In these cases, calculate two new variables: a predicted log odds when the dummy variable = 0, and a predicted log odds when the dummy variable = 1. Convert both of these log odds to predicted probabilities and take the difference, also as a new variable.

4. Average the estimated marginal effects across the entire sample, using a descriptive statistics or data summary procedure.

The resulting number is an average of the estimated marginal effects per observation. It is the average impact on the probability of Y of a 1 unit change in that variable. We report results using this approach applied to the following example using the voting model.

4.3.5 The Linear Probability Model Revisited

A string of articles in the late 1970's addressed the problems of using the linear probability model (Goodman, 1976). These articles all made a similar point: If the average probability of the outcome studied is between .10 and .90, results using the linear probability model will usually come close to the predicted results using the logistic model.

We re-estimated the voting example using a standard OLS regression. Results are reported in Table 4.3 and compared to estimates from the average marginal effects approach.

TABLE 4.3 ⬢ AVERAGE MARGINAL EFFECTS VERSUS LINEAR PROBABILITY ESTIMATES		
Variable	**Linear Probability Estimate**	**Average Marginal Effect**
R (**Republicanism**)	−.107	−.093
C (**Conservatism**)	−.046	−.045
B (**Black**)	.157	.137
E (**Education**)	.017	.021

Although the average marginal effects are often close to the linear probability estimates, they are not as close for the dummy variable in the model—a result that may reflect the general problem of using a discrete variable to predict a linearly restricted probability. Note the effect of "Black" is larger in the linear probability model: This could be caused by the unbounded nature of the predicted probability in this approach, allowing effects at the extreme that are equal to effects in the middle range of Y.

Average marginal effects can be estimated in both STATA and SAS, including the estimation of standard errors. As noted by Allison (1999), Mood (2010), and others, effects of specific independent variables **cannot** be compared across models when you add new variables progressively to the model. The problem is that the estimated b for the log odds in each model depends on the unobserved heterogeneity, which changes across models, making comparison of coefficients as you add variables problematic.

Two common solutions involve using the linear probability model in this situation or average marginal effects (Wooldridge, 2002; Mood, 2010).

4.3.6 Interaction Effects in Logistic Regression

In this chapter, we do not go into detail about interaction effects in logistic regression, but we should underscore a key point: The interpretation of these modelled effects is not the same as in standard OLS regression, mainly due to differences in estimation methods. In the latter, the conditional effect of X on Y was best interpreted across values of Z by manipulating the coefficients for the interaction and lower-order terms. The interpretation of interactions in logistic regression also requires post-estimation steps, but they are quite different than what we did in Chapter 2 (Long & Mustillo, 2018; Mize, 2019).

To best determine the size and significance of the underlying interaction effect, we must calculate predicted probabilities and the average marginal effects. Next, we have to see whether these average marginal effects vary across values of a third (or conditioning variable) Z. Wald tests corresponding to these differences are then estimated to determine statistically significant variations across values of Z, which is essentially the "interaction" between X and Z predicting $P(Y = 1)$ (see Mize, 2019). A later example in this chapter uses this approach.

4.3.7 Choosing an Interpretive Method

Odds ratios are popular because they have intuitive appeal, but they also have the important characteristic that ***they are constant effects*** and so do not depend on the current level of X or other levels of Xs in the equation. In a sense, they are an analog to the usual approach to interpretation in the linear additive model.

There are other approaches to consider. Many researchers like to report probabilities, in part because they also have direct intuitive meaning but also because the logistic model is fundamentally a nonlinear model for the probability, and this approach recognizes that fact. Interpretation in terms of effects on the probability "respects" the basic way in which X presumably affects the probability of an event, and thus some consider this approach closer to the true nature of the model.

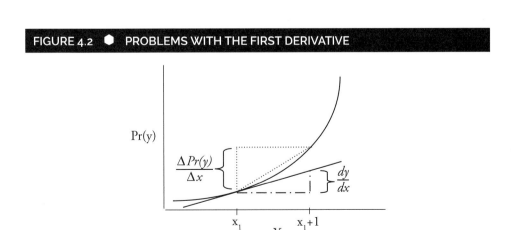

FIGURE 4.2 ⬢ PROBLEMS WITH THE FIRST DERIVATIVE

Caution should be used when using $b \cdot P \cdot (1 - P)$, the marginal change in the probability. The approximation used in this method applies less well to very discrete variables with few categories. The problem is illustrated in Figure 4.2.

For dummy variables in particular, note that the actual change in the $\Pr(Y)$ is greater than the estimated change according to dy/dx, at this point on the curve. In this example, we are observing the lower end of the curve: The opposite could be true at the higher end.

This happens because the 1 unit change in X is the total possible change in X, and thus the derivative gives a poorer approximation, compared to variables with many levels, where the notion of the derivative is better approximated. The conclusion is that it is safer to use computed probabilities for discrete changes in X (the first method) for dummy variables especially.

If one is interested in general statements about effects on the probability, using the average marginal effects approach seems to be the safest. This approach respects the actual configuration of values on variables for each observation in calculating the net effect on the probability. The linear probability model generally will work as an approximation, but our example using both approaches suggests the average marginal effects approach may be more generally preferable.

4.4 RUNNING A LOGISTIC REGRESSION IN STATISTICAL SOFTWARE

Most statistical packages have extensive commands / procedures to estimate logistic models. SAS uses a program called PROC LOGISTIC to estimate logistic regressions; STATA uses a command called *logistic*. Each package has multiple options for running these kinds of models.

4.4.1 The Voting Example

The running example of voting in the 2012 election was estimated by PROC LOGISTIC in SAS, with results shown in Tables 4.4 through 4.8.

TABLE 4.4 ⬥ RESPONSE PROFILES FOR THE VOTING EXAMPLE		
Response Profile		
Ordered Value	**vote_Obama**	**Total Frequency**
1	1	1853
2	0	2450

Many programs first print a response profile, showing the number of cases in each category of the outcome variable.

You can calculate the average probability from this information. Here the average probability of voting for Obama—in this sample—is 1853 / (1853 + 2450) = .43.

Descriptive statistics can be requested in most programs. In Table 4.5, we see the means, standard deviations, and minimum / maximum values within categories of the outcome, as well as overall.

TABLE 4.5 ● DESCRIPTIVE STATISTICS IN THE VOTING EXAMPLE

Descriptive Statistics for Continuous Variables					
Variable	vote_Obama	Mean	Standard Deviation	Minimum	Maximum
RvsDPartyID	1	2.008095	1.297713	1.000000	7.000000
	0	4.882857	1.862722	1.000000	7.000000
	Total	3.644899	2.174159	1.000000	7.000000
Convslib	1	3.384781	1.310501	1.000000	7.000000
	0	4.877143	1.286615	1.000000	7.000000
	Total	4.234488	1.492613	1.000000	7.000000
Black	1	0.405828	0.491184	0	1.000000
	0	0.086531	0.281203	0	1.000000
	Total	0.224030	0.416990	0	1.000000
educinyears	1	14.189962	2.643417	8.000000	18.000000
	0	13.791020	2.593849	8.000000	18.000000
	Total	13.962817	2.622457	8.000000	18.000000

We used these values earlier when substituting mean values for variables in calculating effects on the probability. In Table 4.6, we have the actual estimates of effects on the log of the odds of voting for Obama:

TABLE 4.6 ● PARAMETER ESTIMATES IN THE VOTING EXAMPLE

Analysis of Maximum Likelihood Estimates					
Parameter	DF	Estimate	Standard Error	Wald Chi-Square	Pr > ChiSq
Intercept	1	1.0460	0.2759	14.3693	0.0002
RvsDPartyID	1	−0.7419	0.0304	596.5805	<.0001
Convslib	1	−0.3623	0.0362	100.2376	<.0001
Black	1	1.0083	0.1090	85.4936	<.0001
educinyears	1	0.1693	0.0171	98.4241	<.0001

The Wald chi-square test for each variable is highly significant. Most programs also output many other kinds of optional output—for example, odds ratios and the percentage of cases correctly classified by the model. The latter compares predicted probabilities above (predicted 1) and below (predicted 0) the average to actual 1/0 values on voting, classifies correct and incorrect cases, and calculates the sensitivity—the percentage of correctly identified cases equal to 1—the specificity—the percentage of cases correctly identified as 0—as well as false positives (predicted 1s that are 0) and false negatives (predicted 0s that are 1). This kind of information is useful in judging the predictive success of the model and where there are problems. When we use the average probability of .43 as a cut point to decide on predicting a vote for Obama, we get the classification shown in Table 4.7.

TABLE 4.7 ● CLASSIFICATION TABLE FOR THE VOTING MODEL

Classification Table									
Prob Level	Correct		Incorrect		Percentages				
	Event	Non-Event	Event	Non-Event	Correct	Sensi-tivity	Speci-ficity	False POS	False NEG
0.430	1599	1954	496	254	82.6	86.3	79.8	23.7	11.5

The model is quite successful, with sensitivity and specificity rates at or over 80%. False positives, however, are too high, at 24%. Considering further predictors here would help convert some of these errors into successful predictions.

The odds ratios produced by SAS are shown in Table 4.8.

TABLE 4.8 ● ODDS RATIOS FOR THE VOTING MODEL

Odds Ratio Estimates			
Effect	Point Estimate	95% Wald Confidence Limits	
RvsDPartyID	0.476	0.449	0.505
Convslib	0.696	0.648	0.747
Black	2.741	2.213	3.394
educinyears	1.184	1.146	1.225

Of course, these values are just the exponential of the b coefficients in the model.

4.4.1.1 The Voting Example in STATA

We include here the syntax and output in STATA that replicates the voting example. First we use a *logit* command to estimate the log odds model: We show the maximum likelihood iterations explicitly (we discuss this method later) to make the point that there *is* a fitting process going on (these iterations also occur in SAS but are not included in the output).

```
logit vote _ obama rvsdpartyid convslib black educinyears

Iteration 0:   log likelihood = -2941.0644
Iteration 1:   log likelihood = -1729.5413
Iteration 2:   log likelihood = -1697.6966
Iteration 3:   log likelihood = -1697.4688
Iteration 4:   log likelihood = -1697.4688

Logistic regression                             Number of obs   =     4303
                                                LR chi2(4)      =  2487.19
                                                Prob > chi2     =   0.0000
Log likelihood = -1697.4688                     Pseudo R2       =   0.4228

-----------------------------------------------------------------------------
   vote _ obama |      Coef.  Std. Err.       z   P>|z|  [95% Conf. Interval]
----------------+------------------------------------------------------------
    rvsdpartyid |  -.7419259  .0303757  -24.42   0.000  -.8014611   -.6823907
       convslib |  -.3622568  .0361827  -10.01   0.000  -.4331737     -.29134
          black |   1.008261  .1090451    9.25   0.000   .7945364    1.221985
     educinyears |   .1692973  .0170647    9.92   0.000   .1358511    .2027436
          _cons |   1.046019  .2759446    3.79   0.000   .5051772     1.58686
-----------------------------------------------------------------------------
```

STATA uses a Z test instead of the Wald chi-square used in SAS. The two are a simple function of each other: One is the square of the other.

The *logistic* command produces the odds ratios for this model. Unlike SAS, the log odds and odds ratios are produced through two different commands.

```
logistic vote _ obama rvsdpartyid  convslib black educinyears
```

Logistic regression				Number of obs	=	4303
				LR chi2(4)	=	2487.19
				Prob > chi2	=	0.0000
Log likelihood = -1697.4688				Pseudo R2	=	0.4228

vote _ obama	Odds Ratio	Std. Err.	z	P>|z|	[95% Conf.	Interval]
rvsdpartyid	.4761959	.0144648	-24.42	0.000	.4486729	.5054073
convslib	.6961036	.0251869	-10.01	0.000	.6484479	.7472616
black	2.74083	.2988742	9.25	0.000	2.213415	3.39392
ducinyears	1.184472	.0202127	9.92	0.000	1.145511	1.224758
_cons	2.846297	.7854204	3.79	0.000	1.657279	4.888377

The classification table produced by STATA arranges the outcome classified by the model versus the true value in a row x column table—which is easier to read.

estat classification

```
Logistic model for vote _ obama
```

	------------ True ------------			
Classified	D	~D		Total
+	1534	418		1952
-	319	2032		2351
Total	2.1853	2450		4303

```
Classified + if predicted Pr(D) >= .5

True D defined as vote _ obama != 0
```

Sensitivity	Pr(+| D)	82.78%
Specificity	Pr(-|~D)	82.94%
Positive predictive value	Pr(D| +)	78.59%
Negative predictive value	Pr(~D| -)	86.43%
False + rate for true ~D	Pr(+|~D)	17.06%
False - rate for true D	Pr(-| D)	17.22%
False + rate for classified +	Pr(~D| +)	21.41%
False - rate for classified -	Pr(D| -)	13.57%
Correctly classified		82.87%

You can see that the numbers in the classification table here are not the same as in SAS. STATA and SAS use different defaults for the threshold probability to distinguish categories: SAS uses the actual probability in the sample (here .43), while STATA uses .5. This default can be modified in both programs, but here we show the difference in the classification table caused by the different thresholds. In other words, the chosen threshold should be considered carefully.

4.4.2 Domestic Violence in Married Couples

The example below considers the occurrence of domestic violence among married couples in the National Survey of Families and Households data. The outcome here is whether there have been *any* physical arguments between the spouses in the last year.

This example predicts reported violence using the respondent's gender (*female*), the respondent's age in years (*rage*), the respondent's education in years (*reduc*), whether the respondent at age 16 lived with one or both biological parents (*rbhome*)—here coded so that living with one or no parents =1 versus living with both parents = 0—whether the spouse was living with one or both parents at age 16 (*sbhome*), and both respondent and spousal self-esteem (*resteem* and *sesteem*, each are scales).

Two sets of results are shown in this example: The second adds an interaction between the one-parent background of the respondent and spouse. We begin with the simpler model shown in Table 4.9.

TABLE 4.9 ● RESULTS FOR THE MARITAL VIOLENCE MODEL

Model Information		
Data Set	WORK.TEMP	
Response Variable	marviol	
Number of Response Levels	2	
Weight Variable	WEIGHT	USED WHEN INDIVIDUALS UNIT OF ANALYSIS
Model	binary logit	
Optimization Technique	Fisher's scoring	

Number of Observations Read	6780
Number of Observations Used	4578
Sum of Weights Read	7878.496
Sum of Weights Used	5306.14

Response Profile			
Ordered Value	marviol	Total Frequency	Total Weight
1	1	330	327.1553
2	2	4248	4978.9847

Descriptive Statistics for Continuous Variables					
Variable	marviol	Mean	Standard Deviation	Minimum	Maximum
female	1	0.549880	0.496109	0	1.000000
	2	0.466696	0.540174	0	1.000000
	Total	0.471825	0.537500	0	1.000000
rage	1	38.513859	13.845871	17.000000	75.000000
	2	45.459385	16.705433	16.000000	90.000000
	Total	45.031152	16.612232	16.000000	90.000000
reduc	1	12.520523	2.551177	3.000000	20.000000
	2	12.898424	3.449698	0	20.000000
	Total	12.875124	3.394086	0	20.000000
rbhome	1	0.277503	0.446510	0	1.000000
	2	0.210115	0.441103	0	1.000000
	Total	0.214270	0.441790	0	1.000000
sbhome	1	0.245164	0.428976	0	1.000000
	2	0.175442	0.411819	0	1.000000
	Total	0.179741	0.413426	0	1.000000

Descriptive Statistics for Continuous Variables					
Variable	marviol	Mean	Standard Deviation	Minimum	Maximum
rsesteem	1	4.013648	0.599058	2.000000	5.000000
	2	4.143871	0.607325	1.000000	5.000000
	Total	4.135842	0.607605	1.000000	5.000000
ssesteem	1	3.937764	0.665810	1.000000	5.000000
	2	4.096908	0.626576	1.000000	5.000000
	Total	4.087096	0.630757	1.000000	5.000000

> The likelihood ratio (chi-square) for the model is shown for each model. This is a test of the significance of the overall model. This value is just the difference between the -2 log likelihood for an intercept only model and one with "covariates" (independent variables) added.

Model Fit Statistics		
Criterion	Intercept Only	Intercept and Covariates
AIC	2458.742	2349.089
SC	2465.171	2400.521
-2 Log L	2456.742	2333.089

Testing Global Null Hypothesis: BETA=0			
Test	Chi-Square	DF	Pr > ChiSq
Likelihood Ratio	123.6534	7	<.0001
Score	120.7489	7	<.0001
Wald	115.2858	7	<.0001

Analysis of Maximum Likelihood Estimates					
Parameter	DF	Estimate	Standard Error	Wald Chi-Square	Pr > ChiSq
Intercept	1	2.0112	0.6096	10.8836	0.0010
female	1	0.2264	0.1167	3.7600	0.0525
rage	1	-0.0342	0.00440	60.4097	<.0001
reduc	1	-0.0540	0.0208	6.7580	0.0093
rbhome	1	0.2143	0.1331	2.5931	0.1073
sbhome	1	0.2857	0.1368	4.3599	0.0368
rsesteem	1	-0.3312	0.1022	10.5089	0.0012
ssesteem	1	-0.3715	0.0948	15.3695	<.0001

Odds Ratio Estimates		
Effect	Point Estimate	95% Wald Confidence Limits
female	1.254	0.998 1.576
rage	0.966	0.958 0.975
reduc	0.947	0.910 0.987
rbhome	1.239	0.955 1.608
sbhome	1.331	1.018 1.740
rsesteem	0.718	0.588 0.877
ssesteem	0.690	0.573 0.830

In the column under "Estimate," you see the b's for the effect of each variable on the log odds of violence. The variable "female" is borderline significant here. If we interpret this as an effect on the odds, we would say that females are about $e^{.2264} = 1.25$ times more likely than males to report domestic violence (about 25% more). Since the gender of the respondent is chosen randomly—all are married couples and all are presumably reporting on the same events, and so gender should not be *theoretically* significant—we can consider this finding as indicating a reporting effect in one of two senses: Either females have a lower perceived threshold for violence, or males are under-reporting violence (e.g., if they are disproportionately perpetrators).

Age, education, and self-esteem all reduce the log odds of violence. One must be careful in interpreting the effects of continuous variables. For example, the coefficient for education is -.054, and the computed effect on the odds is .947 (all effects on odds are shown in the output). This effect would be interpreted in words this way: Each year of education reduces the odds of violence by a factor of .947. This seems small, but education has 20 levels, so a 1-unit increase is very small relative to its range. To interpret the effect of an 8-year difference (pre-high school to university), first multiply the b by 8: -.054 x 8 = -.432. Exponentiating this effect leads to an effect on the odds of $e^{.432}$ = .649. This suggests that an 8-year difference reduces the odds of violence by just over one third.

The marginal effect on the probability can be calculated using the average P in the sample as a reference point. This can be calculated from the "Response Profile" information in the output. This shows that the average P, which is just the proportion of couples reporting domestic violence, is 330 / (330+4248) = 330 / 4578 = .072. The denominator is the total sample size, and the numerator is the number of cases = 1 on the outcome. Applying the formula to the effect of respondent self-esteem, which is measured on a 5-point scale, we get

$$b \cdot P \cdot (1-P) = -.3312 \cdot .072 \cdot (1-.072) = -.022$$

This says that each level of self-esteem reduces the probability of the occurrence of violence by .022, at the average probability. This is not a small effect either. Remember that the phenomenon we are modeling is quite rare in this sample and reportedly occurs in under 10% of couples. Given that this effect is one unit on a 5-unit scale of self-esteem, we can see that the effect—all things considered—is important.

The relative rarity of the event here also will affect the average marginal effects. For example, the calculated marginal effect of female is .016, and the average marginal effect of having a spouse from a one-parent home is .018. This should be expected for either rare or highly prevalent events.

Here are the results when adding an interaction between *rbhome* and *sbhome* (Table 4.10). The original idea for doing this involved "double jeopardy" reasoning: The effect of coming from a one-parent home may be magnified when the spouse is also from the same background.

TABLE 4.10 ⬢ ADDING AN INTERACTION BETWEEN FAMILY BACKGROUNDS TO THE ADDITIVE MODEL

Model Information		
Data Set	WORK.TEMP	
Response Variable	marviol	
Number of Response Levels	2	
Weight Variable	WEIGHT	USED WHEN INDIVIDUALS UNIT OF ANALYSIS
Model	binary logit	
Optimization Technique	Fisher's scoring	

Number of Observations Read	6780
Number of Observations Used	4578
Sum of Weights Read	7878.496
Sum of Weights Used	5306.14

Response Profile			
Ordered Value	marviol	Total Frequency	Total Weight
1	1	330	327.1553
2	2	4248	4978.9847

Descriptive Statistics for Continuous Variables					
Variable	marviol	Mean	Standard Deviation	Minimum	Maximum
female	1	0.549880	0.496109	0	1.000000
	2	0.466696	0.540174	0	1.000000
	Total	0.471825	0.537500	0	1.000000
rage	1	38.513859	13.845871	17.000000	75.000000
	2	45.459385	16.705433	16.000000	90.000000
	Total	45.031152	16.612232	16.000000	90.000000
reduc	1	12.520523	2.551177	3.000000	20.000000
	2	12.898424	3.449698	0	20.000000
	Total	12.875124	3.394086	0	20.000000
rbhome	1	0.277503	0.446510	0	1.000000
	2	0.210115	0.441103	0	1.000000
	Total	0.214270	0.441790	0	1.000000
sbhome	1	0.245164	0.428976	0	1.000000
	2	0.175442	0.411819	0	1.000000
	Total	0.179741	0.413426	0	1.000000
rsesteem	1	4.013648	0.599058	2.000000	5.000000
	2	4.143871	0.607325	1.000000	5.000000
	Total	4.135842	0.607605	1.000000	5.000000
ssesteem	1	3.937764	0.665810	1.000000	5.000000
	2	4.096908	0.626576	1.000000	5.000000
	Total	4.087096	0.630757	1.000000	5.000000

Model Fit Statistics		
Criterion	Intercept Only	Intercept and Covariates
AIC	2458.742	2347.014
SC	2465.171	2404.875
-2 Log L	2456.742	2329.014

R-Square	0.0275	Max-rescaled R-Square	0.0663

Testing Global Null Hypothesis: BETA=0			
Test	Chi-Square	DF	Pr > ChiSq
Likelihood Ratio	127.7278	8	<.0001
Score	124.3371	8	<.0001
Wald	118.6004	8	<.0001

Analysis of Maximum Likelihood Estimates					
Parameter	DF	Estimate	Standard Error	Wald Chi-Square	Pr > ChiSq
Intercept	1	1.9691	0.6098	10.4277	0.0012
female	1	0.2302	0.1168	3.8837	0.0488
rage	1	−0.0342	0.00439	60.5277	<.0001
reduc	1	−0.0529	0.0208	6.4817	0.0109
rbhome	1	0.3709	0.1513	6.0067	0.0143
sbhome	1	0.4626	0.1589	8.4802	0.0036
rsesteem	1	−0.3284	0.1019	10.3888	0.0013
ssesteem	1	−0.3776	0.0950	15.8114	<.0001
rbhome*sbhome	1	−0.6085	0.3067	3.9366	0.0472

Odds Ratio Estimates			
Effect	Point Estimate	95% Wald Confidence Limits	
female	1.259	1.001	1.583
rage	0.966	0.958	0.975
reduc	0.948	0.911	0.988
rsesteem	0.720	0.590	0.879
ssesteem	0.686	0.569	0.826

This model adds an interaction between the respondent's and the spouse's childhood parental status. Given the earlier discussion about interactions in logistic regression, we proceed with caution, but we do not fully estimate here a difference of differences in predicted probabilities using averaged marginal effects (Mize, 2019). However, in Tables 4.11 and 4.12, we do calculate the predicted probabilities derived from the averaged marginal effects and compare them to the predicted probabilities from this model. In this case, results show the same pattern.

Taken at face value, the finding is interesting and points to the importance of not taking the linear effects on the log of the odds at face value. There is a significant *negative* interaction here, which suggests that when **both** spouses are from one-parent backgrounds, the effect is to **reduce** the odds of violence relative to when only one comes from a one-parent background. In other words, matching on this background characteristic **suppresses** the rate of domestic violence—not a finding usually reported.

We calculated the predicted probability of violence for all combinations here, setting other variables to fixed mean values. Using this approach, we find this the results reported in Table 4.11.

TABLE 4.11 ⬦ PREDICTED PROBABILITIES FROM THE MODEL WITH AN INTERACTION

Obs	sbhome	rbhome	predprob
1	0	0	0.045405
2	0	1	0.064476
3	1	0	0.070236
4	1	1	0.056215

We might be skeptical of these results because we used mean values for other variables. When we use averaged marginal effects, thus taking into account each person's actual X values, the predicted probabilities look like those in Table 4.12.

TABLE 4.12 ◆ PROBABILITIES BASED ON AVERAGED MARGINAL EFFECTS

Variable	N	mean
prob_both0	4999	0.0589833
prob_rbonly	4999	0.0826140
prob_sbonly	4999	0.0896292
prob_bothbhome	4999	0.0724871

This pattern in the predicted probabilities is replicated in both tables, so that in this case, the probabilities from the model would not mislead us. However, importantly, they are lower than the averaged marginal effects in the second table. Using that second table, we see that the net predicted probability of violence when both spouses come from a one-parent background (prob_bothbhome) is not accentuated by that fact; instead, it is slightly suppressed. The highest risk situation is when one of the spouses comes from a one-parent background (prob_rbonly, prob_sbonly), and the lowest is when neither does (prob_both0). Of course, we do not know whether a further test for differences in these differences would be significant.

This result may at first seem counter-intuitive, but on further consideration, it may not be. In the circumstance where both spouses some from a one-parent background, both may benefit from the fact that there is a lower probability of significant or prolonged exposure to parental violence. In other words, the absence of one parent reduces the chances of witnessing domestic violence growing up, which could disrupt any intergenerational transmission.

4.5 MULTINOMIAL LOGISTIC REGRESSION

Not all categorical outcomes involve only a binary distinction. What do we do in this case?

Suppose we expand the original voting example to include a third group: "non-voters." Then we have a three-category dependent variable. Note that in the dichotomous case, we define the odds as

$$\frac{P_i}{1 - P_i} = e^{(a + bX)}$$

A more general statement of the odds would replace $1 - P$ with P_j, the probability of the "excluded" reference category of the dependent variable. *Only* in the dichotomous dependent variable case does $1 - P_i = P_j$. When the dependent variable has three or more categories, we cannot use $\frac{P}{1 - P}$ as the odds of interest, since $1 - P$ gives us the *total* probability of **all** other categories rather than the probability of a reference category.

Given three categories, we choose a reference category and then form two equations, each expressing the log odds of responses in each of the other two categories versus the reference category. For example:

$$\ln\left(\frac{P_1}{P_3}\right) = a_1 + b_1 X$$

and:

$$\ln\left(\frac{P_2}{P_3}\right) = a_2 + b_2 X$$

Note then that (***very important***)

$$\ln\left(\frac{P_2}{P_1}\right) = \ln\left(\frac{P_2}{P_1} \cdot \frac{P_3}{P_3}\right) = \ln\left(\frac{P_2}{P_3} \cdot \frac{P_3}{P_1}\right) = \ln\left(\frac{P_2/P_3}{P_1/P_3}\right) = \ln\left(\frac{P_2}{P_3}\right) - \ln\left(\frac{P_1}{P_3}\right)$$

$$= (a_2 + b_2 X) - (a_1 + b_1 X) = (a_2 - a_1) + (b_2 - b_1) X$$

In other words, coefficients for the third log odds for Group 2 versus Group 1 are just the difference between the coefficients for the first two log odds. This is an important result because it means we can recover the effects of independent variables on the log odds of different categories represented in the equation.

Given that $P_1 + P_2 + P_3 = 1$, by definition, we can derive

$$\frac{P_1}{P_3} = e^{(a_1 + b_1 X)} \Rightarrow P_1 = e^{(a_1 + b_1 X)} \cdot P_3$$

and:

$$\frac{P_2}{P_3} = e^{(a_2 + b_2 X)} \Rightarrow P_2 = e^{(a_2 + b_2 X)} \cdot P_3$$

Substituting for P_1 and P_2 allows us to define P_3 in this case:

$$1 = e^{(a_1 + b_1 X)} P_3 + e^{(a_2 + b_2 X)} P_3 + P_3$$

$$1 = P_3 (e^{(a_1 + b_1 X)} + e^{(a_2 + b_2 X)} + 1)$$

$$P_3 = \frac{1}{1 + e^{(a_1 + b_1 X)} + e^{(a_2 + b_2 X)}}$$

In general, where J = the reference category in a J category variable,

$$P(Y = J) = \frac{1}{1 + \sum_{j=1}^{J-1} e^{(a_j + b_j X)}}$$

Based on the examples for each category above, the probability for the other categories can be written

$$P(Y = j) = e^{(a_j + b_j X)} \cdot P_J = e^{(a_j + b_j X)} \cdot \frac{1}{1 + \sum_{j=1}^{J-1} e^{(a_j + b_j X)}} = \frac{e^{(a_j + b_j X)}}{1 + \sum_{j=1}^{J-1} e^{(a_j + b_j X)}}$$

This is the multinomial logistic model. Remember that in the J category case, the odds refer to a reference category, so each log odds, individually, is relative to this chosen category. In this sense, each log odds is very much like the binomial case. What is new here is that one must remember that there is a log odds for the difference between the categories *in the equation.* As the derivation above shows, this can be studied by taking the difference between the coefficients for each category.

4.5.1 Interpreting Effects in a Multinomial Model

This example is taken from a multinomial logistic regression of attitudes toward gender roles, as indicated by agreeing that parents should encourage as much independence in their daughters as their sons. The focus here is on the effect of schooling (education) within two groups, Blacks versus all other groups in the United States but predominantly Whites. There are controls in the equation for age (M2BP01) and marital status (dummy variables *sep_or_div, widow, and single,* with married as the reference group). The outcome (*genderroleagree*) here has four categories indicating levels of agreement (1) to disagreement (4). Note that in this case (PROC LOGISTIC in SAS), the procedure will model each of categories 1, 2, and 3, versus 4 as the reference group.

The main results from the model are shown in Table 4.13.

TABLE 4.13 ● STUDYING GENDER ATTITUDES IN THE MULTINOMIAL MODEL

Analysis of Maximum Likelihood Estimates							
Parameter	genderroleagree	DF	Estimate	Standard Error	Wald Chi-Square	Pr > ChiSq	Standardized Estimate
Intercept	1	1	−0.6727	0.6286	1.1454	0.2845	
Intercept	2	1	1.5290	0.6200	6.0819	0.0137	
Intercept	3	1	1.6121	0.7433	4.7045	0.0301	
schooling	1	1	0.2788	0.0322	74.9117	<.0001	0.3864
schooling	2	1	0.1112	0.0312	12.7198	0.0004	0.1542
schooling	3	1	0.0107	0.0375	0.0818	0.7749	0.0149
black	1	1	−0.5947	0.1981	9.0147	0.0027	−0.1318
black	2	1	−0.2212	0.1952	1.2836	0.2572	−0.0490
black	3	1	0.0635	0.2344	0.0733	0.7865	0.0141
M2BP01	1	1	−0.0179	0.0158	1.2746	0.2589	−0.0540
M2BP01	2	1	−0.0197	0.0157	1.5700	0.2102	−0.0595
M2BP01	3	1	−0.0411	0.0190	4.6746	0.0306	−0.1242
sep_or_div	1	1	0.0678	0.1978	0.1175	0.7318	0.0158
sep_or_div	2	1	−0.0948	0.1964	0.2328	0.6294	−0.0221
sep_or_div	3	1	−0.3189	0.2467	1.6706	0.1962	−0.0745
widow	1	1	0.2311	0.7653	0.0912	0.7627	0.0148
widow	2	1	0.3908	0.7489	0.2724	0.6017	0.0250
widow	3	1	0.8566	0.8180	1.0968	0.2950	0.0549
single	1	1	0.1987	0.2254	0.7772	0.3780	0.0470
single	2	1	−0.0776	0.2248	0.1193	0.7298	−0.0184
single	3	1	−0.0380	0.2664	0.0204	0.8865	−0.00899

Odds Ratio Estimates				
Effect	**genderroleagree**	**Point Estimate**	**95% Wald Confidence Limits**	
schooling	1	1.322	1.241	1.408
schooling	2	1.118	1.051	1.188
schooling	3	1.011	0.939	1.088
black	1	0.552	0.374	0.813
black	2	0.802	0.547	1.175
black	3	1.066	0.673	1.687
M2BP01	1	0.982	0.952	1.013
M2BP01	2	0.981	0.951	1.011
M2BP01	3	0.960	0.925	0.996
sep_or_div	1	1.070	0.726	1.577
sep_or_div	2	0.910	0.619	1.337
sep_or_div	3	0.727	0.448	1.179
widow	1	1.260	0.281	5.647
widow	2	1.478	0.341	6.415
widow	3	2.355	0.474	11.702
single	1	1.220	0.784	1.897
single	2	0.925	0.596	1.438
single	3	0.963	0.571	1.623

One thing to note is that there are different coefficients for each comparison: 1 versus 4, 2 versus 4, and 3 versus 4. For example, education increases the log odds of agreeing strongly versus disagreeing strongly by .2788, which turns into an effect on the odds equal to 1.322. This means that every year of schooling increases the odds of agreeing **strongly** by 1.322 but relative specifically to disagreeing. The effect on level 2 versus 4 for education refers to an impact on the log odds of .1112, which is an effect of $e^{1112} = 1.12$. In other words, each year of education multiples the odds of **agreeing** by 1.12 relative to disagreeing. According to the derivation earlier, we also know from this that the effect of education on the log odds of agreeing strongly versus just agreeing is .2788 - .1112 = .1676, which, when exponentiated, is $e^{1676} = 1.18$.

The same model estimated using the STATA *mlogit* command produces the same output but arranged differently: In STATA, effects on log odds for each level are grouped together. Note in the model syntax, we use the option "baseoutcome" and specify the comparison category of the dependent variable preferred in brackets. Without this option, STATA will choose the most frequent outcome as the comparison.

```
mlogit genderroleagree schooling black m2bp01 sep _ or _ div widow
single, baseoutcome(4)

Multinomial logistic regression           Number of obs    =       3656
                                           LR chi2(18)      =     252.51
                                           Prob > chi2      =     0.0000
Log likelihood = -3746.2157                Pseudo R2        =     0.0326

------------------------------------------------------------------------------
   genderrole~e |      Coef.   Std. Err.      z    P>|z|     [95% Conf. Interval]
----------------+-------------------------------------------------------------
1               |
      schooling |   .2788306   .0322154     8.66   0.000     .2156895     .3419716
          black |  -.5947535   .1980885    -3.00   0.003    -.9829998    -.2065071
```

m2bp01	-.0178589	.0158189	-1.13	0.259	-.0488634	.0131457
sep _ or _ div	.0678124	.1978372	0.34	0.732	-.3199413	.4555661
widow	.2311212	.7652955	0.30	0.763	-1.26883	1.731073
single	.198716	.2253986	0.88	0.378	-.243057	.6404891
_ cons	-.6727394	.6285558	-1.07	0.284	-1.904686	.5592072
2						
schooling	.111248	.0311924	3.57	0.000	.0501121	.1723838
black	-.2211892	.1952293	-1.13	0.257	-.6038317	.1614533
m2bp01	-.0196807	.0157075	-1.25	0.210	-.0504668	.0111054
sep _ or _ div	-.0947666	.1963984	-0.48	0.629	-.4797004	.2901672
widow	.3908531	.7488487	0.52	0.602	-1.076863	1.85857
single	-.0776423	.2247932	-0.35	0.730	-.5182289	.3629442
_ cons	1.528995	.620002	2.47	0.014	.3138136	2.744177
3						
schooling	.0107323	.0375278	0.29	0.775	-.0628209	.0842855
black	.0634838	.234415	0.27	0.787	-.3959611	.5229287
m2bp01	-.0410576	.0189899	-2.16	0.031	-.0782771	-.003838
sep _ or _ div	-.3188678	.2467033	-1.29	0.196	-.8023973	.1646618
widow	.8564951	.8179636	1.05	0.295	-.7466841	2.459674
single	-.038032	.2664199	-0.14	0.886	-.5602053	.4841414
_ cons	1.612114	.7432564	2.17	0.030	.1553578	3.068869
4	(base outcome)					

In STATA, you ask for relative risk ratios ('rrr') in the output, rather than odds ratios, because in the multinomial case, they are the same:

mlogit genderroleagree schooling black m2bp01 sep_or_div widow single, baseoutcome(4) rrr

```
Multinomial logistic regression          Number of obs   =      3656
                                          LR chi2(18)     =    252.51
                                          Prob > chi2     =    0.0000
Log likelihood = -3746.2157               Pseudo R2       =    0.0326
```

genderrole~e	RRR	Std. Err.	z	P>|z|	[95% Conf. Interval]	
1						
schooling	1.321583	.0425754	8.66	0.000	1.240717	1.40772
black	.5516986	.1092851	-3.00	0.003	.3741869	.8134205
m2bp01	.9822996	.0155389	-1.13	0.259	.9523112	1.013232
sep _ or _ div	1.070164	.2117183	0.34	0.732	.7261916	1.577066
widow	1.260012	.9642815	0.30	0.763	.2811603	5.646708
single	1.219836	.2749492	0.88	0.378	.7842268	1.897409
_ cons	.5103087	.3207575	-1.07	0.284	.1488694	1.749285
2						
schooling	1.117672	.0348628	3.57	0.000	1.051389	1.188134
black	.801565	.156489	-1.13	0.257	.5467128	1.175218
m2bp01	.9805117	.0154014	-1.25	0.210	.9507855	1.011167
sep _ or _ div	.9095852	.1786411	-0.48	0.629	.6189688	1.336651
widow	1.478241	1.106979	0.52	0.602	.3406624	6.414555
single	.9252953	.2080001	-0.35	0.730	.5955745	1.437556
_ cons	4.613538	2.860403	2.47	0.014	1.368635	15.5518

3

schooling	1.01079	.0379328	0.29	0.775	.9391117	1.087939
black	1.065542	.249779	0.27	0.787	.6730329	1.686961
m2bp01	.9597739	.018226	-2.16	0.031	.9247081	.9961693
sep _ or _ div	.7269717	.1793463	-1.29	0.196	.4482531	1.178994
widow	2.354893	1.926216	1.05	0.295	.4739355	11.701
single	.9626822	.2564777	-0.14	0.886	.5710918	1.622781
_cons	5.013396	3.726239	2.17	0.030	1.168076	21.51756

4 (base outcome)

You can interpret results in terms of probabilities as well, either using exact predicted probabilities and taking the difference in these predicted probabilities, given fixed values of other X variables, as in the first binomial example; or by using the first derivative; or by using averaged marginal effects. The first derivative here, however, is somewhat more complicated (see section 4.5.1.1 below)

Software can be used to generate predicted probabilities in various ways. For example, you can write the equation as variables, successively insert different values of a target variable, and then subtract the two predicted probabilities. This is just an automation of what was done by hand in our first example.

As a specific example, we estimated the predicted probabilities for Blacks versus others, separately for cases where education = 8 versus education = 16 (years), using the results from Table 4.13. Other variables were set to their mean values in the coding. This produces the results shown in Table 4.14.

TABLE 4.14 ● PREDICTED PROBABILITIES IN THE MULTINOMIAL MODEL									
Obs	black	edu	eq_1	predprob1	eq_2	predprob2	eq_3	predprob3	predprob4
1	0	8	1.09228	0.25923	1.79606	0.52400	0.40071	0.12982	0.08696
2	0	16	3.32291	0.61590	2.68603	0.32578	0.48658	0.03612	0.02220
3	1	8	0.49753	0.18142	1.57487	0.53280	0.46419	0.17547	0.11031
4	1	16	2.72816	0.51358	2.46485	0.39469	0.55006	0.05817	0.03356

"Predprob1" shows the effect of agreeing strongly versus disagreeing; "Predprob2" shows the effect of agreeing versus disagreeing, and "Predprob3" shows the effect of being neutral versus disagreeing. It helps to remember this is a categorical outcome, and the *direction* of the effects does not have to be the same across categories.

At 8 years of education, the effect of Black versus other on the probability of agreeing strongly is .181 - .259 = -.078; in others words, Blacks in this situation have on average a .078 lower probability of agreeing strongly. Comparing this to the result for just agreeing, we see the effect of Black versus other has basically disappeared: .533 - .524 = .009. It is possible this result is a consequence of the simple fact that Blacks tend to "just" agree more often than agree strongly. When education = 16—that is, standing for a university degree, results are quite different. The Black–other difference for agreeing strongly is .513 - .616 = -.103, but the same difference for just agreeing is .395 - .326 = .069. In this case, it appears the Black versus other difference is somewhat reversed for "agreeing" relative to "agreeing strongly."

4.5.1.1 The First Derivative in the Multinomial Model

One can interpret multinomial results using the average marginal effect approach discussed for the binomial case, but here the first derivative is different, due to the presence of extra categories of the dependent variable. We will not review the marginal effect approach here again, but it is important to point out that the first derivative for the Pr $(Y = j)$, where j is any of the non-reference categories of the outcome, with respect to any X_k in the equation is

$$\frac{dP_j}{X_k} = P_j(b_{jk} - \Sigma \sum_{j=1}^{j-1} P_j b_{jk})$$

This first derivative measures the change in P in a particular category j due to a 1-unit change in a specific X_k in the equation and is equal to the P for that category times a quantity that is the b for that X in the equation for j, minus the sum of values resulting from P times the b for that variable added across other categories in the equation. Using this value instead of the binomial version will allow interpretation in terms of averaged marginal effects or on the probability at selected levels of P_j.

4.5.2 The Voting Example Expanded

In the first example in this chapter, we considered a model to predict voting for Obama versus Romney. But this equation only considers those who voted. We could add "not voted" as a third category and then use a multinomial approach to predict voting for Obama or voting for Romney versus not voting.

In the example below, we add "not voted" as a reference category = 3, with voting for Obama = 1, and voting for Romney = 2 (Table 4.15).

TABLE 4.15 ● A MULTINOMIAL VOTING MODEL INCLUDING NON-VOTERS

	Analysis of Maximum Likelihood Estimates					
Parameter	**vote_combined**	**DF**	**Estimate**	**Standard Error**	**Wald Chi-Square**	**Pr > ChiSq**
Intercept	1_obama	1	0.0626	0.2882	0.0472	0.8280
Intercept	2_romney	1	−4.9788	0.3300	227.6574	<.0001
RvsDPartyID	1_obama	1	−0.5663	0.0325	304.4749	<.0001
RvsDPartyID	2_romney	1	0.3999	0.0321	155.2701	<.0001
convslib	1_obama	1	−0.2171	0.0382	32.3878	<.0001
convslib	2_romney	1	0.4243	0.0446	90.6370	<.0001
black	1_obama	1	0.6901	0.1118	38.1267	<.0001
black	2_romney	1	−1.6289	0.2228	53.4434	<.0001
educinyears	1_obama	1	0.2041	0.0178	131.8771	<.0001
educinyears	2_romney	1	0.1165	0.0189	38.1606	<.0001

It is important to note that the coefficients in this model only compare voting for each candidate to not voting. For example, the -.5663 b for the effect of Republican party identification shows that Republicans were less likely to vote for Obama than not vote at all. On the other hand, Republicans clearly were also more likely to vote for Romney than not vote (b = .3999). Because the reference point for these coefficients is common to both, and as shown earlier, the net effect of Republican party identification on voting for Romney versus Obama here is .3999 − (−.5663) = .9662. This means that Republican party identifiers have $e^{.9662}$ = 2.63 the odds of voting for Romney relative to Obama. Using post-hoc tests, one can construct a complete "shadow" equation for the odds of Obama versus Romney from the results of this model *and* test the significance of those differences.

4.6 THE ORDINAL LOGIT MODEL

Some dependent variables are ordinal, as in the example above focusing on gender attitudes. There is a temptation to do one of two things with these variables when they appear as dependent: Dichotomize them presumptively or just pretend an OLS regression will work. We advocate neither position. The collapsing of the ordinal variable into two categories may result in missing important differences at specific categories that are combined. This problem applies to dichotomizing multinomial outcomes as well. And pretending that an ordinal variable works in OLS regression is basically just whistling past the graveyard.

Instead, we advocate taking full advantage of the ordered properties of the categories in the way we model this dependent variable. There are many different kinds of ordinal logistic models. The most common approach and the one we focus on here is called the "cumulative odds," or "proportional odds" model. There are a number of advantages of the proportional odds model. One notable advantage is that it is efficient, resulting in interpretations that are close to the binomial case—that is, there is one effect for each variable.

The proportional odds logit model considers the *cumulative* odds of being in the first *j* categories of a dependent variable relative to all categories above. The restriction in this model is that shifts in the comparison threshold on the ordinal scale do not affect the estimates—that is, each additional category considered in the target group has the same effect, relative to the categories "up" the scale. If this assumption holds, we can use *one* coefficient to study shifts between any categories on the dependent variable.

Table 4.16 shows the differences in interpretation of three related models where the analytical questions differ, for a hypothetical four-category outcome variable. The proportional odds models makes three implicit comparisons, using three splits, with the restriction that one coefficient describes these comparisons in general. The continuation ratio model produces a unique set of coefficients for each comparison. In that model, effects are calculated for the log odds of Category 1 versus 2 through 4, then leaving Category 1 out, Category 2 versus 3 and 4, then leaving 1 and 2 out, Category 3 versus 4. The purpose is to compare the specific effect of being in each lower category relative to all categories above that category. Changes in the coefficients suggest differences in the effects of variables at crucial points on the ordinal outcome. Finally, the adjacent categories model is actually a type of multinomial model where every category is treated as potentially unique and only compared to the next adjacent category in the ordinal outcome.

TABLE 4.16 ● DIFFERENT MODELS FOR ORDERED CATEGORIES

Cumulative Odds	Continuation Ratio	Adjacent Categories
Category 1 vs. 2–4	Categories 1 vs. 2–4	Category 1 vs. 2
Categories 1 and 2 vs. 3–4	Categories 2 vs. 3–4	Category 2 vs. 3
Categories 1 thru 3–4	Category 3 vs. 4	Category 3 vs. 4

Our approach here is to present the most commonly used proportional odds model, followed by a significant modification called the partial proportional odds model. If the partial proportional odds model reveals unique effects at each level of the outcome, it may be best to apply a multinomial logistic approach.

Under the assumption of proportional odds, given a dependent variable with J ordered categories, the jth *cumulative* odds is the probability of a response in the first j categories relative to the probability of a response in category $(j + 1)$ or higher.

The odds implied are

$$O_{\leq j} = \frac{P_1 + P_2 + ...P_j}{P_{j+1} + ...P_J}$$

Thus, a total of $j - 1$ cumulative logits can be formed from a J category variable. If these odds *increase* by the same amount each time j increases, we have a "proportional odds" model. In this model, the effect of X is the same in each comparison, but the intercept differs.

For example, imagine a four-category ordinal outcome. If the proportional odds model holds, then the individual logistic regression of cumulative logits would look like Figure 4.3.

FIGURE 4.3 ━ THE PROPORTIONAL ODDS MODEL

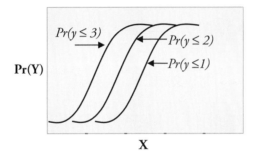

Note that the slopes for the effect of X are the same, but the inflection point for this effect shifts due to the intercepts.

In a four-category cumulative logit equation, there are three intercepts:

$$\ln\left(\frac{Pr(Y \leq j)}{Pr(Y > j)}\right) = \alpha_1 + \alpha_2 + \alpha_3 + bX$$

Each intercept applies to its corresponding cumulative logit. For example, α_2 refers to the log odds of $Y \leq 2$.

Note that the ordinal cumulative logit model is, in a sense, like the binary model in its attempt to set up a single contrast between two categories. However, it achieves this by making an assumption, which *can* be tested.

4.6.0.1 Example: Effects of Premarital Cohabitation on Marital Instability

We use a well-known example (Demaris, 1992) looking at the effect of premarital cohabitation (single-instance, serial, and none) on predicted marital instability (3 categories): very unstable (1), somewhat unstable (2), and stable (3). The dependent variable here is a subjective prediction made by the respondent.

There are two cumulative odds:

$$O_{\leq 1} = \text{odds of being very unstable versus somewhat unstable or stable}$$

$$O_{\leq 2} = \text{odds of being very or somewhat unstable versus stable}$$

Table 4.17 shows a cross-tabulation of 2,023 married respondents in the National Survey of Families and Households (NSFH) adapted from Demaris (1992).

TABLE 4.17 ● CROSS-TABULATION OF COHABITATION HISTORY AND PREDICTED MARITAL INSTABILITY				
	Marital Instability			
Cohabitation	**Very Unstable**	**Somewhat Unstable**	**Stable**	**Total**
Single	107	48	204	359
Serial	50	25	67	142
None	327	218	977	1522
Total	***484***	***291***	***1248***	***2023***

Note, for example, that the ratio of the odds of being ***very*** unstable versus more stable, for single instance versus non-cohabitors is

$$\frac{107}{(48+204)} \Big/ \frac{327}{(218+977)} = 1.55$$

These odds are the same as one gets from fully calculating $P/(1-P)$ because in this odds ratio the denominator is the collapsed upper categories in the comparison, resulting in two groups being compared. That is, for the numerator here, P is $f_{11}/f_{1.}$ (where $f_{1.}$ is the total of the first row) and $(1-P)$ is $(f_{12}+f_{13})/f_{1.}$.

And the ratio of the odds of being ***very or somewhat*** unstable versus stable, for single-instance versus non-cohabitors is

$$\frac{(107+48)}{204} \Big/ \frac{(327+218)}{977} = 1.36$$

Imagine one starts with *separate* equations for these odds rather than the constrained ordered logit model:

$$\ln O_{\leq 1} = a_1^1 + b_1^1 (\text{single}) + b_2^1 (\text{serial})$$

$$\ln O_{\leq 2} = a_1^2 + b_1^2 (\text{single}) + b_2^2 (\text{serial})$$

assuming non-cohabitation is the reference group.

To estimate, you could use binomial logistic regression for each contrast separately, by constructing two versions of the dependent variable:

- $O_{\leq 1} = 1$ if couple very unstable; 2 otherwise

- $O_{\leq 2} = 1$ if couple very or somewhat unstable; 2 otherwise

Here are the results:

$$\ln O_{\leq 1} = -1.296 + .439(\text{single}) + .686(\text{serial})$$

$$\ln O_{\leq 2} = -.583 + .309(\text{single}) + .696(\text{serial})$$

Note that the coefficients here are quite similar. Here are the transformed odds from these coefficients:

$e^{.439} = 1.55$ is the increase in odds of very unstable due to single instance versus none

$e^{.309} = 1.36$ is the increase in odds of very or somewhat unstable due to single instance versus none

$e^{.686} = 1.99$ is the increase in odds of very unstable due to serial versus none

$e^{.696} = 2.00$ is the increase in odds of very or somewhat unstable due to serial versus none

If the b's are similar across models, it implies the effects for each step in the contrasts are similar. A test called the proportional odds test will evaluate the equality of these b's. If it is ***non-significant***, one can estimate a more efficient single ordinal logit model, with two intercepts, one for the "very unstable" group and one for the "very or somewhat unstable" group. Other effects (b's) are estimated as single parameters for contrasting *any* more unstable versus more stable category. So, if the proportional odds test is *not* rejected, we can represent results with the single logistic equation:

$$\ln O_{\leq j} = a_1 + a_2 + b_1(\text{single}) + b_2(\text{serial})$$

4.6.0.2 When the Proportional Odds Test Fails

It is important to realize that this test often results in rejection of the proportional odds assumption: This test is "anticonservative" because it is so sensitive to small variations in effects at cumulative splits of the outcome variable. You do not want to jump to a full J category analysis without further attempts to keep the results as simple as possible. This could include, for example, sensitivity analyses of more complex models to ensure results in the proportional odds model are not misleading.

Formally, if this test is significant, it means that the b's for successive comparisons are *not* equal at some point. You can try two things to simplify interpretation: (1) You can conduct tests to see if some categories of the dependent variable can be collapsed, or (2) you can use a "partial proportional odds" model. We demonstrate each of these in Sections 4.6.1 and 4.6.2.

4.6.1 An Example Using Ordinal and Multinomial Logistic Regression

As an example, consider "General Health" as an outcome estimated in 3 levels: 1 = excellent; 2 = good; 3 = fair to poor, as a function of generalized chronic stress (in work, family, financial, parental, residential, social, and health life domains), sex, and number of roles occupied (worker, married, parent). These variables are labeled *cstot, female,* and *rolecocc* in the output.

The SAS code runs PROC LOGISTIC to test for the proportional odds assumption in the cumulative logit model (SAS assumes the ordinal model for multiple category outcomes).

```
proc logistic data=temp simple;
model genhth=cstot female roleocc /  stb rsquare;
run;
```

The (partial) output in Table 4.18 shows

- The number of responses in each category of the outcome.

- The proportional odds test is not significant, so the proportional odds model *is* reasonable.

- Results for this model with two intercepts, where Intercept 1 is for Category 1 versus Categories 2 and 3, and Intercept 2 is for Categories 1 and 2 versus Category 3.

TABLE 4.18 ● RESULTS FOR A PROPORTIONAL ODDS MODEL FOR GENERAL HEALTH

Response Profile		
Ordered Value	GENHTH	Total Frequency
1	1	157
2	2	307
3	3	66

Proportional odds test not significant; proportional odds assumption holds.

Score Test for the Proportional Odds Assumption		
Chi-Square	DF	Pr > ChiSq
4.5927	3	0.2042

Model Fit Statistics		
Criterion	Intercept Only	Intercept and Covariates
AIC	996.270	979.014
SC	1004.815	1000.378
-2 Log L	992.270	969.014

Analysis of Maximum Likelihood Estimates						
Parameter		DF	Estimate	Standard Error	Wald Chi-Square	Pr > ChiSq	Standardized Estimate
Intercept	1	1	−0.4780	0.2288	4.3657	0.0367	
Intercept	2	1	2.4396	0.2597	88.2766	<.0001	
cstot		1	−0.0501	0.0128	15.4218	<.0001	−0.1917
female		1	−0.3771	0.1745	4.6692	0.0307	−0.1040
roleocc		1	0.1263	0.0912	1.9195	0.1659	0.0667

The language that goes with this model is more general than the usual specific comparisons used for multinomial logistic models. For example, females have a $e^{.3771} = .68$ the odds of ***better*** health relative to males. The term "better health" means *any* category of better health relative to any category representing poorer health. The odds of .68 indicates that females have significantly lower odds of better health in general.

Since the proportional odds test is not significant, normally we would retain this model. However, in order to show what to do when the proportional odds test is significant, we proceed as if it is, after showing the same results in STATA.

STATA uses an *ologit* command for ordinal logistic regression and outputs the log odds. The results for this model are as follows:

`ologit genhth  cstot female roleocc`

```
Ordered logistic regression                      Number of obs   =       530
                                                  LR chi2(3)      =     23.26
                                                  Prob > chi2     =    0.0000
Log likelihood = -484.50698                       Pseudo R2       =    0.0234
```

genhth	Coef.	Std. Err.	z	P>|z|	[95% Conf. Interval]	
cstot	.0501344	.0127576	3.93	0.000	.02513	.0751389
female	.3770457	.1744151	2.16	0.031	.0351983	.7188931
roleocc	-.1263487	.0895294	-1.41	0.158	-.3018231	.0491258
/cut1	-.4779946	.2239811			-.9169895	-.0389997
/cut2	2.439616	.2555024			1.93884	2.940391

Note the coefficients are the same value as in SAS but in the opposite direction. This again is a function of the default approach in the two programs. SAS targets the "1" code as the target to be predicted, making "3," in effect, the lowest value. STATA, on the other hand, targets the highest value as the direction of the coded variable so that "3" is highest and "1" is lowest. These defaults can be manipulated in both programs, but the simplest solution is to follow one of the fundamental rules of data analysis: Code higher values to represent the way you want to interpret the results. If you want to talk about better health, default SAS would be the choice; if you want to talk about worse health, STATA would naturally present results that way.

4.6.1.1 Collapsing Categories in a Multinomial Model

You can run a multinomial logit in PROC LOGISTIC. This is done using a "link=glogit" option after the model statement. The code to run the model this way is as follows:

```
proc logistic data=temp simple;
model genhth= cstot female roleocc / link=glogit;

all1vs2:  test cstot_1-cstot_2=0,female_1-female_2=0,roleocc_1-roleocc_2=0;
stress1vs2:  test cstot_1-cstot_2=0;
female1vs2:  test female_1-female_2=0;
role1vs2:  test roleocc_1-roleocc_2=0;
all2vs3:  test cstot_2=0, female_2=0, roleocc_2=0;
```

Note the TEST statements after the model statement. It is the logic of these statements that is important. These tests can be used to assess the non-significance of *differences* in coefficients across adjacent categories. The first test is a global test for any effects on Category 1 versus Category 2, labeled "all1vs2." Note the way in which you refer to the levels in these tests: The effect of stress on Level 1 versus 3 is labeled "cstot_1," while the effect of stress on Level 2 versus 3 is labeled "cstot_2." This collective test of no differences in effects on Category 1 versus 2 lists three contrasts (which under the null of no difference should be zero), with commas between each individual hypothesis. Essentially, if the difference between 1 and 3 is the same as the difference between 2 and 3, then 1 versus 2 will be non-significant, and you could collapse Categories 1 and 2 of the outcome. The global test is followed by the three individual tests for each variable, in case the global test is significant, so you can pinpoint which variables have effects on Category 1 versus 2.

You can also test for any differences for Level 2 versus 3 with a global test for any effects on 2 versus 3. Things look different here because the individual tests in the equation *are* the effects on 2 versus 3. Selected results for this model are shown in Table 4.19.

TABLE 4.19 ● MULTINOMIAL MODEL FOR GENERAL HEALTH

Parameter	GENHTH	DF	Estimate	Standard Error	Wald Chi-Square	Pr > ChiSq
Intercept	1	1	1.7376	0.4228	16.8899	<.0001
Intercept	2	1	2.1800	0.3863	31.8455	<.0001
cstot	1	1	−0.0746	0.0221	11.4346	0.0007
cstot	2	1	−0.0155	0.0182	0.7293	0.3931
female	1	1	−0.7857	0.3102	6.4159	0.0113
female	2	1	−0.6325	0.2853	4.9137	0.0266
roleocc	1	1	0.1204	0.1641	0.5387	0.4630
roleocc	2	1	−0.0681	0.1506	0.2044	0.6512

Analysis of Maximum Likelihood Estimates

Odds Ratio Estimates

Effect	GENHTH	Point Estimate	95% Wald Confidence Limits	
cstot	1	0.928	0.889	0.969
cstot	2	0.985	0.950	1.020
female	1	0.456	0.248	0.837
female	2	0.531	0.304	0.929
roleocc	1	1.128	0.818	1.556
roleocc	2	0.934	0.695	1.255

Linear Hypotheses Testing Results

Label	Wald Chi-Square	DF	Pr > ChiSq
all1vs2	15.9016	3	0.0012
stress1vs2	12.6850	1	0.0004
female1vs2	0.5732	1	0.4490
role1vs2	3.1689	1	0.0751
all2vs3	6.0693	3	0.1083

Looking at the parameter estimates first, note the interpretation of the coefficients. The parameter for female at level 1 is -.7857. This stands for the effect of being female (versus male) on the log odds of excellent versus poor health (1 versus 3). The parameter for female at Level 2 is -.6325. This is the effect of being female on the log odds of good versus poor health (2 versus 3). Note that -.7857-(-.6325) = -.1532 is the log odds difference of excellent versus good health (1 versus 2).

4.6.1.2 Post-hoc Tests

The tests are listed in the output by their label. First, we see that the overall test for any differences for Level 1 versus 2 is significant, suggesting that these categories cannot be collapsed. The effect of stress on excellent versus good health is significant, but there is no gender effect or role occupancy effect at this level. Thus, stress distinguishes excellent from good health. However, the test for Level 2 versus 3 differences is not significant, although it is close. In this case, you could consider collapsing Levels 2 and 3 of health. The problem here with doing that is the significant effect of female on good versus poor health in the equation, standing for the fact that females have lower chances of good versus poor health.

In this example, you would probably retain the ordered logit model overall, since the proportional odds test did not fail. However, if the post-hoc results here followed a significant test and there are only three outcome categories, you might consider keeping all three categories, especially if gender effects were the focus of the analysis, since the results indicate an important female disadvantage in even achieving good versus poor health. This suggests importantly that gender differences in health extend to the more serious end of the health spectrum.

4.6.2 The Partial Proportional Odds Model

In the case that the proportional odds assumption is not met, according to the test, you do not have to immediately resort to a multinomial model. The *partial proportional odds model* allows you to test for the possibility that specific variables in the model do not meet the proportional odds assumption, while others do. If one variable has different effects at different thresholds of the cumulative odds, you can use this model to both derive the general effects of some variables and the level-specific effects of others. In that sense, this model is an ideal combination of information and efficiency.

The previous example is not ideal for this model because the proportional odds test holds. However, we can add age to the model as a predictor and re-assess the fit of the proportional odds assumption in that model. When the proportional odds model is run with age added, it produces the results shown in Table 4.20.

TABLE 4.20 ● PROPORTIONAL ODDS MODEL WITH AGE ADDED

Score Test for the Proportional Odds Assumption		
Chi-Square	DF	Pr > ChiSq
11.9108	4	0.0180

Analysis of Maximum Likelihood Estimates						
Parameter		DF	Estimate	Standard Error	Wald Chi-Square	Pr > ChiSq
Intercept	1	1	0.6430	0.3090	4.3286	0.0375
Intercept	2	1	3.6982	0.3597	105.7096	<.0001
cstot		1	−0.0682	0.0135	25.5736	<.0001
female		1	−0.3394	0.1762	3.7131	0.0540
roleocc		1	0.2810	0.0965	8.4817	0.0036
ageinyrs		1	−0.0342	0.00629	29.6180	<.0001

Now the proportional odds test produces a significant result. This may be expected if at later ages the odds of poor health are increasing more rapidly than merely "good" health. Most software will allow you to modify the general proportional odds models to take into account variables that do *not* meet the general assumption of the model while retaining the more general effects of variables for which the proportional odds assumption holds.

For example, in SAS, you can use PROC LOGISTIC to estimate this kind of model, using an "unequalslopes" option in the MODEL statement, followed by TEST statements for the equality of effects for each variable, as follows:

```
proc logistic data=temp simple;
model genhth= cstot female roleocc ageinyrs / link=clogit unequalslopes;

cs: test  cstot_1=cstot_2;
fem: test  female_1=female_2;
roles: test roleocc_1=roleocc_2;
age: test ageinyrs_1=ageinyrs_2;
run;
```

This approach runs the cumulative logit model allowing for distinct effects for each variable on each cumulative logit. The TEST statements assess the equality of slopes for each variable, one at a time. Only one of these tests is significant, showing age has unique effects at different levels of general health (results not shown).

With this information, we run a partial proportional odds model by specifying "unequalslopes=ageinyrs":

```
proc logistic data=temp simple;
model genhth= cstot female roleocc ageinyrs / link=clogit
unequalslopes=ageinyrs;
run;
```

This yields the results in Table 4.21, showing unique effects only for age.

TABLE 4.21 ● THE PARTIAL PROPORTIONAL ODDS MODEL

Parameter	GENHTH	DF	Estimate	Standard Error	Wald Chi-Square	Pr > ChiSq
Intercept	1	1	0.2967	0.3271	0.8227	0.3644
Intercept	2	1	4.5466	0.4798	89.7991	<.0001
cstot		1	−0.0700	0.0136	26.3762	<.0001
female		1	−0.3368	0.1764	3.6454	0.0562
roleocc		1	0.2493	0.0954	6.8243	0.0090
ageinyrs	1	1	−0.0225	0.00704	10.2448	0.0014
ageinyrs	2	1	−0.0515	0.00857	36.1393	<.0001

Analysis of Maximum Likelihood Estimates

The effect of age in predicting excellent (1) versus poor health (b = -.0225) is less than half the effect of age in predicting excellent to good (2) versus poor health (b= -.0515). Interpreting these effects in five-year segments, the effect on the odds of excellent versus poor health due to age is $e^{5 \cdot (-.0225)}$ = .89, while the effect on the odds of good versus poor health is $e^{5 \cdot (-.0515)}$= .77—a finding that suggests age affects those with only good health more than those with excellent health.

One other finding of note here is the emergence of a general protective effect of role occupancy, sometimes interpreted as a sign of "social competence" or social integration. The difference in its effect here compared to earlier suggests that role occupancy is patterned by age and may increase with age, up to a point. The data have only 23 respondents above 70, after which some of these roles may disappear, resulting in an overall positive correlation between age and role occupancy. When age is brought into the model, this "removes" a net negative component from the effect of role occupancy since it is positively correlated with age but age is negatively correlated with health. As a result, a positive effect of role occupancy emerges. As we will note in a later chapter, this is an example of a *suppression* effect.

4.6.3 Probability Interpretation of Ordinal Logit Models

The first derivative for the proportional odds model can be used to interpret results in terms of average marginal effects, as in the previous cases considered here. In fact, interpretation of the first derivative reduces to one equivalent with the binary case because the constructed logit in this model is also a binary comparison.

Remember the logit in the cumulative ordinal logit model looks like this:

$$\ln\left(\frac{\Pr(Y \le j)}{\Pr(Y > j)}\right) \text{ for an outcome with } J \text{ categories.}$$

So for any chosen split you want to study, you can assume that the first derivative is essentially the same as the binary case. That is

$$\frac{dP}{dx} = b \cdot P_{Y \le j} \cdot (1 - P_{Y \le j})$$

The last term above is by definition also $P_{Y>j}$. As a result, one can proceed in the construction of averaged marginal effects in the same way as for the binary case.

4.7 ESTIMATION OF LOGISTIC MODELS

Our only discussion to this point of the *estimation* of regression models occurred in Chapter 1, when we introduced the least squares criterion for fitting regression equations. This criterion is the basis for "ordinary least squares" regression. However, it turns out that ordinary least squares (OLS) is inappropriate in the logistic model. OLS methods lose their ***desirable properties as estimators*** when applied to this kind of model: They are *not* as efficient as other estimation methods. What does this mean?

4.7.1 Desirable Properties of Estimators

Ways of estimating parameters in a regression model vary, depending on the situation. There are criteria available for picking the "best" estimator in any given estimation situation. The basic qualities that are important are (a) ***unbiasedness***—the mean of an estimator in its sampling distribution equals the true population value, (b) ***consistency***—the variance of the sampling distribution and any bias both decrease as sample size increases, and (c) ***efficiency***—the variance of its sampling distribution is smaller than competing estimation methods. Of course, the less the variance of the sampling distribution, the higher the chance of estimating a value close to the true value in any sample.

To give some detail to these statements, we review these properties in general, using the symbol $\hat{\theta}$ to stand for any sample estimator, $E\left(\hat{\theta}\right)$ to stand for the mean of the estimator in its sampling distribution, and θ to stand for the true population parameter.

4.7.1.1 Consistency

A ***minimal*** criterion for an estimator is that it is consistent—that is, the variance of its sampling distribution and any tendency not to center on the true population value approach zero *as N increases*. This is considered a "weak" property of estimators since (a) it refers to a limiting characteristic but not how fast the estimator approaches that limit and (b) because many estimators have consistency built into them, given the standard error of the sampling distribution is known and it depends on N.

Figure 4.4 shows the sampling distribution for a single sample estimator, at three different sample sizes, $N = 5$, $N = 50$, and $N = 500$.

In this figure, the estimator is consistent because both the variance of the distribution and its bias decrease with increases in sample size.

FIGURE 4.4 ● CHARACTERISTIC SAMPLING DISTRIBUTIONS FOR A CONSISTENT ESTIMATOR AS SAMPLE SIZE INCREASES

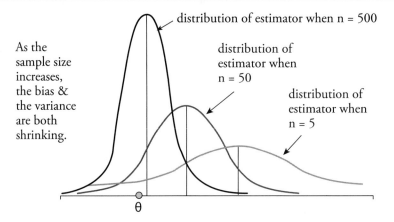

4.7.1.2 Unbiasedness

An estimator is unbiased if its expected value equals the true population parameter, in other words, the mean of its sampling distribution centers on the true value (see Figure 4.5).

Note, bias is not a matter of sample size, simply where the sampling distribution is centered.

FIGURE 4.5 ◆ AN UNBIASED VERSUS BIASED ESTIMATOR

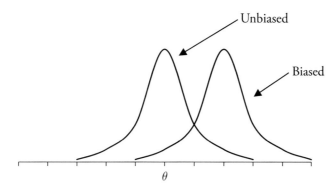

4.7.1.3 Relative Efficiency

Given a certain sample size, N, we would choose the estimator with less variance in its sampling distribution, other things being equal. This means that the most efficient estimator is one that has the least chance of being "significantly" wrong in a particular sample. In Figure 4.6, the sampling distributions of two estimators at $N = 100$ are shown. $\hat{\theta}_1$ is more efficient.

FIGURE 4.6 ◆ A MORE VERSUS LESS EFFICIENT ESTIMATOR

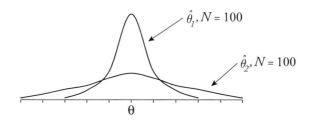

Estimation theory is in fact a series of value statements about the properties of "best" estimators in a given situation. In the case of logistic regression, we introduce maximum likelihood as a very general and very powerful method of estimation that will be used for many of the analytical models used in the remainder of this book. Because of this, we take some time to introduce maximum likelihood here.

4.7.2 Introduction to Maximum Likelihood

When we estimate a population parameter in a given sample, our treatment of OLS demonstrated that specific formulas for these parameters could be derived from the application of the least squares criterion. We may be used to thinking that we estimate statistics using a formula for it.

Thinking about the approach to estimation embodied by the maximum likelihood approach requires a very different perspective. This approach may seem "upside down" relative to the traditional view of how estimates of parameters are derived. In this section, we take a very simple approach to the logic behind maximum likelihood (ML), in part to communicate how unique this approach is relative to OLS.

Suppose you want to estimate the mean of a population. To do this using an ML estimate, follow these steps:

1. Gather a random sample of observations, $x_1 ... x_N$.

2. Assume different possible population values for the mean (and their implied sampling distributions), and calculate the joint probability of obtaining the observed sample values given each distribution.

3. The maximum likelihood estimate is the value implied by a population distribution that maximizes the probability (likelihood) of obtaining the observed sample.

A, B, and C in Figure 4.7 are different population distributions with different means.

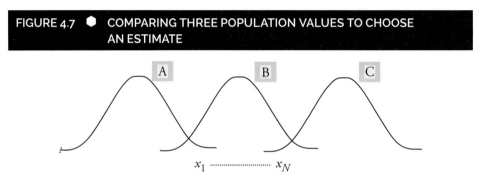

FIGURE 4.7 ● COMPARING THREE POPULATION VALUES TO CHOOSE AN ESTIMATE

The question is to which population does the sample $(x_1 ... x_N)$ most likely belong? Note the $Pr(x_1$ and x_2 and....and $x_N)$ for A and C is less than B. So we choose B as the ML estimate of the mean.

4.7.2.1 ML Estimate of a Probability

Moving a step closer to the issue of estimating parameters in a probability model for a dichotomous outcome, let's consider a case where $Y = 1$ or $Y = 0$, and we want to estimate the proportion—that is, the probability that $Y = 1$, in a population. The probability $(Y = 1)$ is P and the probability $(Y = 0)$ is $(1 - P)$.

Suppose you now take a random sample of three observations of Y from a population. The observed values of Y in this sample are 1,1, and 0. Which population value of P is most likely to generate this sample?

This is an *iterative* method: Try various values, and calculate the likelihood of each, as in Table 4.22. Of course, we could use a much more fine-grained approach to be more precise, but it is the principle we are interested in, so we simplify the choices.

For each possible population value of P and assuming .10 increments in the possibilities considered, we see a calculated probability of the {1,1,0} sample, using the rule for independent probabilities because the observations are assumed to be independent. This list of probabilities for various population values is called the likelihood function. The ML estimate here is .70 since it is that value that produces the maximum probability for the sample (= .147).

Figure 4.8 plots observed values from the iterative calculations (and smooths them). What should be obvious from this diagram is that the estimated probabilities of the sample will rise and then fall. Because of this, one can use the point at which the slope of the tangent to the function curve is zero to derive the maximum likelihood estimate. This is the point at which the first derivative of the function value with respect to the probability is zero.

TABLE 4.22 ● ITERATIVE APPROACH TO CHOOSING AN ML ESTIMATE OF A PROPORTION				
IF	$P =$	Then: $\Pr(1, 1, 0) =$	$\Pr(Y = 1)$ *and* $\Pr(Y = 1)$ *and* $\Pr(Y = 0)$	$= f$
IF	$P = 0$	Then: $\Pr(1, 1, 0) =$	$0 \times 0 \times 1$	$= 0$
IF	$P = .10$	Then: $\Pr(1, 1, 0) =$	$.10 \times .10 \times .90$	$= .009$
IF	$P = .20$	Then: $\Pr(1, 1, 0) =$	$.20 \times .20 \times .80$	$= .032$
IF	$P = .30$	Then: $\Pr(1, 1, 0) =$	$.30 \times .30 \times .70$	$= .063$
IF	$P = .40$	Then: $\Pr(1, 1, 0) =$	$.40 \times .40 \times .60$	$= .096$
IF	$P = .50$	Then: $\Pr(1, 1, 0) =$	$.50 \times .50 \times .50$	$= .125$
IF	$P = .60$	Then: $\Pr(1, 1, 0) =$	$.60 \times .60 \times .40$	$= .144$
IF	$P = .70$	Then: $\Pr(1, 1, 0) =$	$.70 \times .70 \times .30$	$= .147$
IF	$P = .80$	Then: $\Pr(1, 1, 0) =$	$.80 \times .80 \times .20$	$= .128$
IF	$P = .90$	Then: $\Pr(1, 1, 0) =$	$.90 \times .90 \times .10$	$= .081$
IF	$P = 1$	Then: $\Pr(1, 1, 0) =$	$1 \times 1 \times 0$	$= .000$

FIGURE 4.8 ● A PLOT OF THE LIKELIHOODS FOR VARYING VALUES OF THE PROPORTION

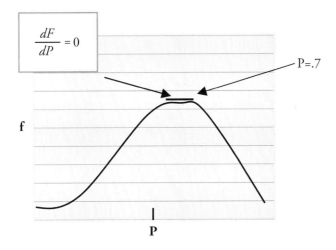

4.7.3 ML Estimate of Logistic Regression Parameters

The logic of ML applied to logistic regression is the same. We want to choose the values for a and b in the equation that maximize the likelihood of the observed pattern of 1s and 0s on the dependent variable in the sample. That is,

$$L = \Pr(Y_1, \ldots Y_N) = \prod_{i=1}^{N} P^{Y_i}(1 - P)^{1-Y_i} \text{ where } L = \text{the likelihood function.}$$

This likelihood function calculates an overall probability of the sample of N observations of Y, conditional on X. Note that P is raised to the power Y_i, the value of Y for individual i, and $(1 - P)$ is raised to the power $(1 - Y_i)$. So when $Y = 1$, the contribution of the ith observation to the likelihood function is P, and when $Y = 0$, the contribution of the ith observation is $(1 - P)$. These values are multiplied across N observations.

Using this approach, we want to find the point on the likelihood function that is its maximum. This maximum occurs at the point where, by taking the derivative of L with respect to the parameters of the model (a, b) that determine P, we find a derivative as close to zero as possible. The ML method is "experimental": It searches by noting successive plus and minus changes in the likelihood it finds by trying different parameter values.

In practice, it is easier to evaluate the $\ln(L)$ since that turns the evaluation process into a sum that can be maximized. It is basically easier to locate how changes in parameters affect the likelihood.

$\ln L = \sum_{i=1}^{N} [Y_i \cdot \ln P + (1 - Y_i)\ln(1 - P)]$ is used, by taking the logarithm of the previous expression. Often $-\ln(L)$ is used in computations, so the sum is actually minimized. We add this here because you will often see negative log likelihood values in statistical output, and this could be confusing.

What is not obvious from this approach is what is behind the scenes. Algorithms to implement maximum likelihood—search algorithms—are trying out a myriad of combinations of values for all of the parameters in the equation at once, and assessing the fit at each iteration. That is the way maximum likelihood works: All parameters are "solved" at once. When maximum likelihood is applied to very complex models—as with structural equation models—the problem can become sufficiently complex that a clear solution cannot be reached, leading to the classic and unfortunate feedback: "The model did not converge." With logistic regression, however, this is rarely the case.

4.7.3.1 Properties of ML Estimates

We state three properties of maximum likelihood as an estimator:

1. Its properties as an estimator are *not* well defined in small samples. Some suggest samples smaller than 100 are problematic while samples over 500 should be adequate. The zone in-between is a matter of other issues in the analysis, like the number of variables, their distribution, and the number of parameters estimated.

2. However, one *can* state asymptotic properties of ML (i.e., in larger samples and/or as sample size increases).

3. ML estimators are asymptotically *unbiased, efficient,* and *consistent* in large samples.

4.8 TESTS FOR LOGISTIC REGRESSION

We review the main tests used in logistic regression, paralleling the logic of the tests discussed for multiple regression in the first chapter.

1. Individual coefficients are assessed with appropriate versions of t or χ^2 ($t = {}^{b_k}\!/_{\sigma_{bk}}$ (with $N - k$ df).

2. The test of "significance" of the whole equation is analogous to the F-test in OLS regression, but in this case, the test is a is a "likelihood" ratio test that is distributed as a χ^2:

$$L.R. = -2\left(\frac{L0}{L1}\right)$$
$$= -2(\ln L0 - \ln L1) \qquad \text{(because the } \ln(x/y = \ln x - \ln y)$$
$$= -2\ln L0 - (-2\ln L1)$$

where $L0$ = value of likelihood if all coefficients are zero (i.e., "null model") and $L1$ = value of L for observed model. The last line above contrasts two values, each being $-2\,x$ the log of the likelihood. The null model is referred to in various ways, as the "intercept only" model or the "empty model," or the "no covariates" model. This is printed in most programs. The test has k - 1 df (k = # of independent variables).

3. The test of significance of variables added to a model also follows the logic of the F-test in multiple regression and is in fact a special case of the previous test. So for two models, A nested in B (the larger model, B, containing A plus "new variables"):

$$L.R. = -2\ln L_A - (-2\ln L_B)$$

df = number of variables added in model B.

While this test has been used traditionally to test interactions or groups of variables added to a base model, current approaches discussed earlier suggest this test could be misleading. The recent approaches suggested by Long et al. (2018) and Mize (2019) may be more appropriate. A later example discusses these approaches. A still different approach is to develop statistics that compare the prediction performance of two nested models (Pepe, Kerr, Longton, & Wang, 2013).

4.9 PUBLISHED EXAMPLES

Logistic regression is widely used because categorical outcomes are so prevalent. Here are some examples: Studying the probability of revolution based on income inequality and political organization; the probability of voting for Obama in the 2008 election based on party; the probability of giving birth to a low birthweight child based on the poverty level of a neighborhood and the distribution of public health resources; the probability of women going back to work after their first child, based on historical decade and changes in social policy about maternal leaves; the probability of adult onset of a major depression episode based on cumulative exposure to traumatic experience in childhood; the probability of losing a job based on the intersection of race, gender, and education; and so on, and so on.

Because logistic regression is regularly applied to a wide array of issues, it is difficult to capture the rich possibilities of this model in a few examples. Given this caveat, we review four examples that represent some of the variation in how logistic regression is used in the literature, both in terms of interpretation and type of logistic model chosen.

4.9.1 The Presidential Vote in 2008

Logistic regression is often used to study voting behavior—as the initial example of this chapter demonstrates. An article by Michael Lewis-Beck and others on whether and how racism affected the 2008 vote for Obama is an appropriate example. The emphasis is on the effect of racism, over and above, and together with, the usual study of party and political ideology (left-right). The title and abstract follows:

Obama's Missed Landslide:
A Racial Cost?

Michael S. Lewis-Beck, *University of Iowa*
Charles Tien, *Hunter Goliege and the Graduate Center, CUNY*
Richard Nadeau, *University c Montreal*

ABSTRACT Barack Obama was denied a landslide victory in the 2008 presidential election. In the face of economic and political woe without precedent in the post-World War II period, the expectation of an overwhelming win was not unreasonable. He did win, but with just a 52.9 percentage point share of the total popular vote. We argue a landslide was taken from Obama because of race prejudice. In our article, we first quantify the extent of the actual Obama margin. Then we make a case for why it should have been larger. After reviewing evidence of racial bias in voter attitudes and behavior, we conclude that, in a racially blind society, Obama would likely have achieved a landslide.

The table from the article showing a logistic regression is reproduced in Table 4.23.

TABLE 4.23 ● LOGISTIC REGRESSION OF THE 2008 PRESIDENTIAL VOTE			
	β	S.E.	Sig.
Age	−1.35	(.20)	**
Gender (Female)	.13	(.09)	
Education	.16	(.15)	
Income	−.25	(.17)	
Race (Black)	1.98	(.20)	**
Party ID	3.47	(.12)	**
Ideology	5.44	(.24)	**
Economy	3.37	(.25)	**
Favor blacks	−.96	(.25)	**
Favor blacks - Economy	−1.46	(.30)	**
Racism	1.26	(.28)	**
Racism - Economy	.27	(.34)	
Correct predictions	91%		
Pseudo R_2	.69		
N	8.829		

**p ≤ .01, two-tailed tests.

Note: Dependent variable equals 1 if voting intention for Obama. 0 otherwise. Party ID equals 0 for Republicans, .5 for Independents, and 1 for Democrats. Economy equals 0 for much better, better, and the same; .5 for worse; and 1 for much worse. Favor Blacks equals 1 if respondents think the election of Obama will favor Blacks and 0 otherwise. Racism equals 1 if respondents agree (strongly or somewhat) that "generations of slavery and discrimination have created conditions that make it difficult for African Americans to work their way out of the lower class." Control variables: Age (in years), Gender (Female), Education (seven categories), Income (14 categories), Race (black), Ideology (Scale ranging from 0 (very conservative) to 1 (very liberal); DKs = .5), The pseudo R_2 is McFadden.

Source: Lewis-Beck, M. S., Tien, C. & , Nadea, R. (2010). Obama's missed landslide: A racial cost? PS: Political Science and Politics, 43(1) 69–76. www.jstor.org/stable/25699295.

The coefficients presented are the linear b in the model for the log odds of voting for Obama. The variables in this regression are described under the table. Party ID is like a dummy variable for Democrat versus Republican, except it includes a .5 value in-between for independents. Economy indicates how bad the respondent thinks things are, from 0 = much better, better or the same now compared to a past reference point, to 1 = much worse now, "favors Blacks" is 1 (vs. 0) for those that think Obama will favor Blacks—interpreted in the article as a relatively nonobtrusive indicator of racial prejudice, and "racism" actually stands for racial esteem interpretively because it indicates agreement that historical racism and discrimination "have created conditions that make it difficult for African Americans to work their way out of the lower class" (Lewis-Beck, Tien, Nadeau, 2010, p 24.) Thus this variable is actually the opposite of what the name implies. On this issue, we always advocate naming variables in the direction of their coding, and here higher values mean *less* racism. Controls include age, gender, education, income, race, and an ideology scale going from 0 = very conservative to 1 = very liberal.

The basic argument of the paper is that racism deprived Obama of a landslide that would have occurred if racism was not an issue in voting. Here is what Lewis-Beck et al. say (see Table 4.23) (2010, 74–75):

> In table 4, a multivariate equation of the 2008 vote is estimated in a logistic regression. The model specification holds vote as a function of socio-demographics, party identification, ideology, and retrospective sociotropic economic evaluation (E). To this standard political behavior frame is added the above variable on "favoring Blacks" (F), and the interaction term, ($E·F$). Also added is the above variable on racism (R) and its interaction term, ($E·R$).
>
> One observes that the model fits the data well, and demonstrates the usual pattern of significance and sign, on the sociodemographic, party, ideology, and economic variables. What captures our attention are the racial-sentiment variables, and their interactions. Note, first, that the above reported relations ... on racial prejudice, economics, and Obama support continue to stand. That is, those who believe Obama favors Blacks are significantly less likely to vote for him, even in the face of these extensive control variables. As well, the interaction term is strongly significant, suggesting that voters who believe Obama shows Black favoritism are much less likely to convert their economic dissatisfaction into a vote for Obama.
>
> Is this negative racial charge canceled out by a positive one, coming from a sympathetic attitude toward Blacks? Those who believe that Blacks are worse off because of the continuing effects of racism are more likely to vote for Obama, thus directly offsetting those who would vote against him because he favors Blacks. However, the negative interaction effect the economic vote receives is not balanced by a positive one. That is, those who are more sympathetic toward Blacks are no more likely to convert their economic discontent into an Obama vote. Thus, racial esteem does not cancel out racial prejudice, at least according to this evidence.

Lewis-Beck et al. use these results to calculate a net loss in vote percentage of 5% in the 2008 election. It is interesting to see how these authors work with the results in the table. To estimate the loss in percentage vote due to racism, they first assume that the operative value of "favor Blacks" should be 0. This removes the negative influence of favoring Blacks on the positive effect of a bad economy, setting its effect = 3.37. But when "favor Blacks" = 1, the effect of a bad economy is reduced to 1.91.

These values can be derived in the usual way using the approach in Chapter 2. You need to substitute the extreme values of the dummy variable for favor Blacks into the model and calculate the differences in the effect of "economy" on the log odds of voting for Obama. To do this, notice that you only have to substitute for terms in the equation involving the effect of "economy."

When favor Blacks = 0, the ***effect*** of economic dissatisfaction on the log odds is:

$$\ln \widehat{\text{odds}} \ (Obama) = 3.37 \cdot Economy -1.46 \cdot (0 * Economy) = 3.37 \cdot Economy$$

When favor Blacks =1, the effect of economic dissatisfaction on the log odds is:

$$\ln \widehat{\text{odds}} \ (Obama) = 3.37 \cdot Economy -1.46 \cdot (1 * Economy) = 1.91 \cdot Economy$$

Using these values, the authors then calculate the probability difference in voting for Obama due to a bad economy among those who think Obama does not favor Blacks (= 0) versus those who do and find that the difference is 46% versus 37%, a difference of 9%. This estimate of the change in probability is at the mean of other variables. Since about 56% of the sample felt that Obama favored Blacks, the reduction in the net vote for Obama would be .56 x .09 = .0504 or about 5%.

You could also use the coefficients in the model to derive effects on the odds. For example, the effect of party ID (Democrat) is 3.47 on the log odds of voting for Obama. When you exponentiate that coefficient, it becomes: $e^{3.47} = 32.14$. Technically, you would report this as follows: The odds of voting for Obama are 32 times greater among Democrats compared to Republicans.

4.9.2 Support for Market Reform in Russia

Gerber (2000) reports research on attitudes toward market reform in the post-Soviet Russia of the 1990s and the implications of these attitudes for voting in the 1995 election, in which a multitude of parties were involved, from the Communist group of parties to reformist to centrist to nationalist right parties. The clearest opposition here was between the Communist parties and the reformist parties—the latter representing arguments for privatization and free market reform. Here we emphasize the results predicting classification as a "statist" (implying state control of the market), "uncertain," or "marketizer" (implying moderate belief in a free market system), treated as a multinomial set of categories.

Table 4.24 from the article reports results for the multinomial logistic regression. The coefficients are effects on the log odds of belonging to a certain category versus the reference group "uncertain," the middle position.

As the authors predict, age, education, income, and urban residence in Moscow or St. Petersburg (the Russian "capitals") each predict attitudes toward market reform. The pattern for age suggests that older Russian support a statist-controlled market ($b = .031**$), relative to uncertainty, while younger Russians support a freer market ($b = -.022**$), relative to uncertainty. As in any multinomial model, the full difference between statist versus marketizer has to be derived from the equation. Here that difference is $.031 - (-.022) = .053$. The effect on the odds of being a statist versus marketizer is $e^{.053} = 1.054$. This seems like a small effect because it is per year of age. Over a decade, the effect on the odds is $e^{10 \times .053} = 1.70$—that is, every decade of age increases the odds of endorsing state control by 70%.

The effect of female here is interesting: Females are both less likely to endorse a statist position and a free market position, relative to uncertainty. The article offers various interpretations of this finding, one of which is that women in Russia are less political in general because of the double burden of employment and housework in a high proportion of households. The effect of living in the two main urban centers is not to decrease support for statism but to increase support for the free market, relative to uncertainty. This effect is net of education: With a post-secondary education as the reference group, we see that less education lowers support for the free market, as predicted, but this variable also has little effect on support of statism. Even being a former member of the Communist party (KPSS) does not predict a statist position, and it also does not predict support for a free market.

TABLE 4.24 ●	A MULTINOMIAL LOGISTIC REGRESSION PREDICTING ECONOMIC IDEOLOGIES IN RUSSIA

A. Views on Market Reform ("Reform" Classes)

Variable	Statist vs. Uncertain B	S.E.	Marketizer vs. Uncertain B	S.E.
Age (minus 19)	.031**	.00	−.022**	.06
Female	−.582**	.12	−.688**	.11
Education[a]				
Less than secondary degree	.135	.22	−1.822**	.19
Secondary degree	−.185	.22	−.778**	.15
Moscow/St. Petersburg resident	−.340	.25	.616**	.18
Former KPSS member	.270	.18	.208	.17
Household income (logged)[b]	−.221**	.09	.618**	.08
Constant	−1.326**	.23	1.158**	.18

Baseline log-likelihood = −2290.52
Model log-likelihood = −1973.16
Model χ^2 (14 df) = 634.69
Weighted N = 2,168[c]
Model BIC = −527

Source: Gerber, T. P. (2000). Market, state, or don't know? Education, economic ideology, and voting in contemporary Russia. *Social Forces, 79*(2), 477–521. doi:10.2307/2675507.

Gerber summarizes these findings this way:

> Russian's economic idelogies may be diverse and complex, yet their complexity is hardly "formless"(Alexander 1997). Instead, Russians' view on market institutions are predictably shaped by background factors, including age, sex, education, residence, and income. Each of these variables independently affects the likelihood that an individual Russian will support market institutions, reject them, or feel too uncertain to take a position either way. Former membership in the KPSS, however, does not influence Russians' current economic views. Taken together, these finding depict an ideological tableau of *structured* complexity.

> *(Gerber, 2000, p. 497)*

As in all cases of multinomial models, the third comparison, often of interest, is not the direct focus of the discussion. Results here are quite clear about the statist versus marketizer difference because in many cases there are significant effects in the opposite direction relative to the middle position. Carrying through these findings, Gerber does report that marketizers were more likely to vote in the 1995 election than either of the other two groups. Among those who voted, in another multinomial logistic regression, they also find that marketizers are more likely to vote for any other party relative to the Communist option, including the nationalist parties.

4.9.3 Predicting the Sexual Perpetrator

Most research on sexual assault understandably focuses on the issue of who is victimized and in what circumstances. But a recent article by Thompson, Swartout, and Koss (2013) moves the focus to the perpetrator of sexual assaults and asks what predicts sexual aggression. The data come from a survey of a sample of 800 males enrolled at a "large southeastern university" in the United States. This sample was followed across the full four years of university. The first phase of this research was to track trajectories of sexual assault over the four years of university, using latent class analysis. This technique allows a depiction of the most common trajectories in the sample as distinct groups. In this case, four were extracted from the data: stable low/none, increasing, decreasing, and persistent high. It is these classes that provide the four outcome categories for a multinomial logistic regression.

Predictors over time include two measures of "hostile masculinity," one a measure of beliefs that support rape, and the second a measure of hostile attitudes toward women; the number of previous sexual partners, prior to the first wave and also during university; alcohol misuse, basically a measure of the number of occasions in which alcohol was overused; and peer norms regarding approval / disapproval and pressure for engaging in sexual coercion with women.

Table 4.25 shows separate panels for three categories: increasing, decreasing, and high, each relative to none. It also shows something somewhat unusual in the presentation of logistic regression findings: the effect on the probability of class membership due to a 1 standard deviation increase in the explanatory variable, when other variables are held at their mean.

Estimates can be compared for Year 1 and Year 4 to get a sense of changes in the effects of predictors. For example, hostile masculinity (HM) does not predict membership in the "increasing" category at

TABLE 4.25 ● PREDICTING SEXUAL PERPETRATORS

Logistic Regressions predicting latent trajectory membership

Latent trajectory	Wave	Variable	*b*	SE	Odds ratio	OR 95% CI	Change in probability of membership[a]
Increasing		Intercept	–2.14***	.18			
	1	HM	.03	.21	1.03	.68, 1.55	3%
		Alcohol misuse	.16	.18	1.18	.83, 1.68	16%
		Peer norms	.19	.20	1.21	.82, 1.80	19%
		Sex partners	–.08	.24	.92	.58, 1.49	–7%
	4	HM	.54**	.20	1.72	1.16, 2.55	60%
		Alcohol misuse	.07	.18	1.08	.76, 1.53	7%
		Peer norms	61***	.17	1.84	1.32, 2.55	69%
		Sex partners	.12	.14	1.13	.86, 1.47	11%
Decreasing		Intercept	–1.79***	.15			
	1	HM	.60**	.19	1.82	1.26, 2.63	63%
		Alcohol misuse	.18	.16	1.20	.88, 1.64	17%
		Peer norms	72***	.15	2.06	1.53, 2.78	79%
		Sex partners	.13	.15	1.14	.86, 1.53	12%
	4	HM	–.08	.17	.92	.66, 1.29	–7%
		Alcohol misuse	.34*	.15	1.40	1.05, 1.89	33%
		Peer norms	.12	.15	1.13	.81, 1.58	11%
		Sex partners	–.16	.14	.85	.64, 1.13	–13%

Latent trajectory	Wave	Variable	*b*	SE	Odds ratio	OR 95% CI	Change in probability of membership[a]
High		Intercept	–3.02***	.29			
	1	HM	.64*	.26	1.89	1.14, 3.15	82%
		Alcohol misuse	.31	.17	1.36	.97, 1.92	34%
		Peer norms	.52**	.19	1.69	1.16, 2.45	63%
		Sex partners	.32*	.15	1.37	1.03, 1.83	35%
	4	HM	72**	.24	2.05	1.27, 3.32	96%
		Alcohol misuse	.21	.20	1.24	.84, 1.83	22%
		Peer norms	.81***	.18	2.25	1.58, 3.20	112%
		Sex partners	–.09	.17	.92	.65, 1.28	–8%

Source: Thompson, M. P., Swartout, K. M., & Koss, M. P. (2013, July 1). Trajectories and predictors of sexually aggressive behaviors during emerging adulthood. *Psychology of violence, 3*(3), 19–20. doi:10.1037/a0030624

Wave 1 but does predict this category at Wave 4—reflecting the pattern of change in this category. The same can be said of peer norms, but neither alcohol misuse or number of partners is related.

The decreasing pattern works as a mirror image in the results: Both HM and peer norms predict Year 1 sexual aggression but not Year 4. By using this approach, the article links *changes* in sexually aggressive behavior to these two predictors. The "high" category shows a consistent tendency for both HM and peer norms to predict consistently high sexual aggression. The only place that alcohol appears to predict a trend is for the decreasing group, where it predicts membership in Year 4, but not in Year 1. This finding seems to suggest that alcohol, as measured here, tends to dampen the chances of sexual aggression specifically among those who have committed aggression in the past.

This research suggests that peer influences and individual gender attitudes have more of an effect in this age group than some factors widely studied in this literature, including alcohol abuse and sexual history.

Note that the changes in the probability of membership are not actual probability changes but percentage changes in the probability. This accounts for the high numbers, including estimates that exceed 100%.

4.9.4 Job Insecurity, Labor Markets, and Fertility Decisions

This example considers an important question regarding the status and interpretation of interactions in a logistic model, based on a paper by Glavin, Young, and Schieman (2020) entitled "Labour Market Influences on Women's Fertility Decisions: Longitudinal Evidence from Canada."

Most literature focusing on the reasons for declining fertility rates reference broader economic downturns and depressed labor market opportunities. However, Glavin et al. introduce an alternate line of inquiry and examine the impact of *perceptions of job insecurity* on fertility decisions. The authors theorize that when women feel insecure in their job, they are less likely to start a family or—if already a mother—less likely to have more children, not knowing if they will have financial resources to support their family in the near future. The authors compare mothers and nonmothers, on the assumption that job insecure women who have yet to have children might be even more likely to postpone parenthood until they find secure employment. Further, Glavin et al. (2019) argue that fertility decisions for both mothers and nonmothers will be influenced by women's labor market opportunities, based in part on the local labor market unemployment rate—fewer labor market opportunities might make job insecure women more concerned about having a child for fear their job and financial situation will continue to be precarious.

The previous reasoning implies a series of interactions between job insecurity (categorical), parenthood status (binary), and labor market measures (education and the local unemployment rate). The latter contingency is tested by a three-way interaction involving the two former measures.

Given the need to test interactions in a logistic model context, the authors cannot simply rely on the interaction coefficient's size, direction, and significance to understand where the differences lie. As discussed earlier in this chapter, here it is best to estimate the *average marginal effects* of the focal independent variable (in this case, job insecurity) across categories of the second (and, in this case, third) independent variable. We show an example of this from their paper.

The original regression models indicated that there were significant three-way interaction effects, specifically highlighting nonmothers who felt they were very likely to lose their jobs residing in low unemployment regions compared to otherwise. The authors present the necessary calculations and contrasts in the Table 4.26.

TABLE 4.26 ● PROBABILITY OF BIRTH FOR NONMOTHERS AND MOTHERS BY PERCEIVED JOB INSECURITY AND UNEMPLOYMENT

	Nonmothers			Mothers			Third Difference (Nonmothers - Mothers)[c]
	Pr (Birth)	First difference[a] (AMEs)	Second difference[b]	Pr (Birth)	First difference[a] (AMEs)	Second difference[b]	
Low Unemployment (−1 SD)[d]							
Not at all likely to lose job	.149 (.039)			.068 (.021)			
Very likely to lose job	.010 (.011)	.010 − .149 = −.139*** (.038)		.044 (.031)	.044 − .068 = −.024 (.033)		
High unemployment (+1 SD)[d]			−.139 − .050 = −.189* (.075)			−.024 − (−.019) = −.005 (.032)	
Not at all likely to lose job	.105 (.035)	.155 − .105 = .050 (.068)		.057 (.019)	.038 − .057 = −.019 (.033)		−.189 − .005 = −.184* (.084)
Very likely to lose job	.155 (.064)			.038 (.030)			

Source: Glavin, P., Young, M., & Schieman, S. (2020, May–July). Labour market influences on women's fertility decisions: Longitudinal evidence from Canada. *Social Science Research, 88–89,* 102417.

[a] First differences represent the average marginal effects (AMEs) of job insecurity. A negative sign within a first difference means a lower probability of a birth for women reporting the respective level of job insecurity compared to the reference category.

[b] Second differences are the difference in the marginal effect of job insecurity between those in low and high unemployment regions (i.e. the first difference for job insecure women in low unemployment regions minus the first difference for job insecure women in high unemployment regions). A positive sign across the second difference means that the marginal effect of job insecurity is larger for women in low unemployment).

[c] The third difference represents a test of whether the 2 second differences are equal for nonmothers and mothers.

[d] Low and high unemployment represent −1 and +1 standard deviations from the mean unemployment rate for the year preceding a risk period.

In the first column for both mothers and nonmothers, the authors present the predicted probability for women in job insecurity categories (not at all and very likely to lose job in next two years) living in high versus low unemployment regions. The second column presents the differences between these probabilities: These are the "first differences."

The third column then presents what is referred to as the "second difference"—meaning the difference of the first differences—which exactly expresses the concept of an interaction. The second difference is significant among nonmothers, indicating the probability of birth changes among nonmothers *differentially* due to perceived job insecurity, depending on the unemployment rate. One can see in the results that job insecurity matters more in the context of low unemployment—this is in fact tested by the second difference.

But this second difference is not mirrored among mothers, suggesting a three-way interaction. The final column of the table presents the significant differences reflecting the three-way interaction term. This column is titled "third differences," essentially testing the *difference* between the second differences across nonmothers and mothers. The three-way interaction here is essentially this: Job insecurity makes more of a difference in fertility decisions among nonmothers in a low unemployment setting than among mothers, while differences between nonmothers and mothers in a high unemployment setting are less evident. The third difference tests for the unique relevance of the combined effect of parental status and the unemployment rate on the impact of job insecurity on fertility.

The results provide an ideal example of how to decompose significant differences between groups given a logistic model (or in this case, multiple groups, as specified by the three-way interaction). In Figure 4.9, we show a novel approach to presenting these significant differences for nonmothers using STATA's graphing options. The graph includes confidence bands, thus allowing a view of regions for significant difference on fertility due to differences in job insecurity. Essentially, the effect of job insecurity occurs in this group when unemployment is below 7%.

FIGURE 4.9

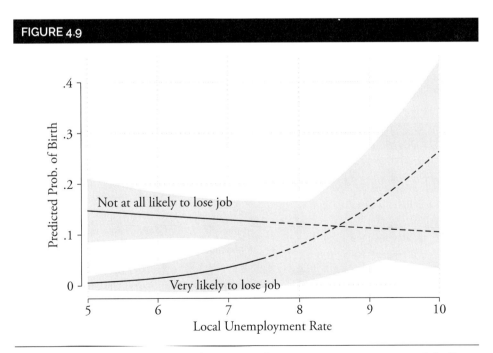

Source: Glavin, P., Young, M., & Schieman, S. (2019, May–July). Labour market influences on women's fertility decisions: Longitudinal evidence from Canada. *Social Science Research, 88–89*, Figure 3.

Concluding Words

In this chapter, we consider a number of variants of the logistic regression model. We discussed models for binomial, ordinal, and multinomial outcomes, and partial variants that allowed a hybrid of both ordinal and multinomial features, depending on the variable in the model. The point was to introduce as much generality and flexibility as possible, but it is important to also add that there are a number of other variants of logistic models we did not address. Still, the options discussed include the most widely used variants. Since this is not a book on logistic regression per se, enough is enough.

We also spent some time discussing interpretation in more detail than many other sources. We believe this is important. One of the frustrations of statistical sources is that they stop short, too often, of demonstrating how methods are applied in real research; they do not demonstrate how to work with results, and they do not attach words to actual findings.

The four articles used here allow us to attach real-case implementations to the kinds of language and thinking authors use to address their findings. You can see that often the approach is quite compressed, as necessitated by journal space requirements. Spending some time with the original articles will be useful, in order to get a sense of the match of an analysis to the ideas under discussion more fully.

Logistic regression is a remarkably flexible technique that naturally fits the way a large number of social science questions are posed. But we should point out one feature of this kind of model we only commented on briefly early in this chapter. No matter what, we never directly study a categorical outcome as a categorical outcome per se. Metaphysically, not statistically, there is no way to do this without further help because we are always thinking about the possibility of multiple causes. How do we apportion the role of multiple causes if all we discuss is explicit membership in categories? Notice that what is done in this model is that the categorical distinctions among categories are transformed, always, into some continuous concept for interpretation: an odds, a probability, even a log of the odds. It is only when using these concepts that we can compare the roles of different variables. Thus, all approaches to studying categorical outcomes use some transformation to get back to a continuous concept for the purposes of interpretation.

In the next chapter, we complete our elaboration of the basic regression model by considering the "general linear model," a collection of similar models that includes some kinds of regression we have not yet considered.

Practice Questions

1. Results below show three logistic regressions shown for child academic performance using data from the National Survey of Families and Households. The first is an ordinal logistic model; the second is a multinomial model; and the third is a binomial model. In all models, the dependent variable is derived from a question asked of mothers about their focal child's academic performance, with ratings from (1) top student, (2) above the middle, (3) at the middle, (4) below the middle, (5) near the bottom.

Variables in the output are

*   **acadper**: An ordinal coding of student performance, from 1 = top student to 4 = below or near the bottom (collapsing 4 and 5 above)
*   **highschool**: Mother's education high school = 1; otherwise = 0
*   **somepost**: Mother's education some post high school = 1; otherwise = 0
*   **univ**: Mother's education university or higher = 1; otherwise = 0

- **matage**: Mother's age, in years
- **finalbehprob**: A seven-item child behavior problems scale
- **nonwhite**: A dummy variable for visible minority = 1; otherwise = 0

Note that there are three dummy variables for mother's education in the equations, with "less than high school" the excluded reference group.

Answer these questions:

a. According to the results from the ordinal model, (Table 4.A), do the assumptions of the proportional odds model hold? Cite the evidence in the output you use to reach this decision.

b. Use the multinomial results (Table 4.B) to derive the effects of having a mother with a university education on the **odds** of being a top student

(vs. below or near the bottom) and interpret in words. **Also,** use these results to derive the effect of child behavior problems on the odds of being a top student (Category 1) versus a *middle* student (Category 3).

c. According to the multinomial results for post-hoc tests designed to assess whether any adjacent categories can be collapsed, would you collapse any of the outcome categories, and if so, which ones?

d. In the binomial model (Table 4.C), the outcome is a dichotomized version of student performance, with 1 = above average and 2 = at or below average. Using these results, calculate the impact of behavior problems on the probability of being an above average student *at the average probability, using the first derivative approach.*

TABLE 4.A ⬢ LOGISTIC REGRESSION OF CHILD ACADEMIC PERFORMANCE: ORDINAL MODEL

Score Test for the Proportional Odds Assumption		
Chi-Square	DF	Pr > ChiSq
20.3366	12	0.0610

Model Fit Statistics		
Criterion	Intercept Only	Intercept and Covariates
AIC	2920.258	2825.391
SC	2935.406	2870.834
-2 Log L	2914.258	2807.391

Testing Global Null Hypothesis: BETA=0			
Test	Chi-Square	DF	Pr > ChiSq
Likelihood Ratio	106.8669	6	<.0001
Score	101.8723	6	<.0001
Wald	101.1523	6	<.0001

Analysis of Maximum Likelihood Estimates						
Parameter		DF	Estimate	Standard Error	Wald Chi-Square	Pr > ChiSq
Intercept	1_top	1	1.2139	0.4350	7.7888	0.0053
Intercept	2_abovemid	1	2.4469	0.4395	30.9959	<.0001
Intercept	3_mid	1	4.6763	0.4588	103.8999	<.0001
finalbehprob		1	−0.1877	0.0242	59.9981	<.0001
matage		1	−0.00838	0.00933	0.8072	0.3690
highschool		1	0.4715	0.1507	9.7925	0.0018
somepost		1	0.5322	0.1685	9.9717	0.0016
univ		1	1.1606	0.2079	31.1480	<.0001
nonwhite		1	-0.2051	0.1149	3.1847	0.0743

TABLE 4.B ● LOGISTIC REGRESSION OF CHILD ACADEMIC PERFORMANCE: MULTINOMIAL MODEL

Analysis of Maximum Likelihood Estimates						
Parameter	acadper	DF	Estimate	Standard Error	Wald Chi-Square	Pr > ChiSq
Intercept	1_top	1	6.6099	1.0292	41.2469	<.0001
Intercept	2_abovemid	1	5.2537	1.0362	25.7080	<.0001
Intercept	3_mid	1	4.8464	1.0008	23.4519	<.0001
finalbehprob	1_top	1	−0.4050	0.0544	55.4087	<.0001
finalbehprob	2_abovemid	1	−0.3213	0.0543	35.0362	<.0001
finalbehprob	3_mid	1	−0.2256	0.0519	18.8814	<.0001
highschool	1_top	1	0.6852	0.3311	4.2815	0.0385
highschool	2_abovemid	1	0.6326	0.3353	3.5597	0.0592
highschool	3_mid	1	0.1249	0.3146	0.1577	0.6912
somepost	1_top	1	0.5984	0.3719	2.5888	0.1076
somepost	2_abovemid	1	0.5780	0.3761	2.3617	0.1243
somepost	3_mid	1	−0.1080	0.3599	0.0901	0.7640
univ	1_top	1	2.4085	0.7749	9.6604	0.0019
univ	2_abovemid	1	2.3069	0.7781	8.7903	0.0030
univ	3_mid	1	0.8119	0.7880	1.0615	0.3029
matage	1_top	1	−0.0280	0.0207	1.8254	0.1767
matage	2_abovemid	1	−0.0196	0.0209	0.8830	0.3474
matage	3_mid	1	−0.0224	0.0201	1.2528	0.2630
nonwhite	1_top	1	−0.2443	0.2757	0.7849	0.3757
nonwhite	2_abovemid	1	−0.1799	0.2786	0.4170	0.5184
nonwhite	3_mid	1	0.0447	0.2713	0.0272	0.8690

Linear Hypotheses Testing Results			
Label	Wald Chi-Square	DF	Pr > ChiSq
aca1vs2	0.1720	3	0.9820
aca2vs3	22.5775	3	<.0001
aca3vs4	1.6064	3	0.6579
finalbp1vs2	5.6745	1	0.0172
finalbp2vs3	7.4941	1	0.0062
finalbp3vs4	18.8814	1	<.0001
age1vs2	0.3966	1	0.5288
age2vs3	0.0446	1	0.8327
age3vs4	1.2528	1	0.2630
min1vs2	0.1608	1	0.6884
min2vs3	1.8438	1	0.1745
min3vs4	0.0272	1	0.8690
all1vs2	6.2361	6	0.3973
all2vs3	36.1131	6	<.0001
all3vs4	22.2958	6	0.0011

TABLE 4.C ● LOGISTIC REGRESSION OF CHILD ACADEMIC PERFORMANCE: BINOMIAL MODEL

Response Profile		
Ordered Value	student	Total Frequency
1	1_above	729
2	2_below	423

Analysis of Maximum Likelihood Estimates					
Parameter	DF	Estimate	Standard Error	Wald Chi-Square	Pr > ChiSq
Intercept	1	2.1992	0.5062	18.8743	<.0001
finalbehprob	1	−0.1809	0.0281	41.5525	<.0001
highschool	1	0.5584	0.1696	10.8355	0.0010
somepost	1	0.6810	0.1918	12.6119	0.0004
univ	1	1.6576	0.2733	36.7820	<.0001
matage	1	−0.00557	0.0108	0.2650	0.6067
nonwhite	1	−0.2514	0.1340	3.5216	0.0606

2. Results from the Toronto Study of Intact Families (Wheaton, 1992) are copied following the question. The dependent variable here is an ordinal measure of the child's estimated closeness to the mother in these families, in three categories: "very," "somewhat," and "not close." There are two logistic regressions shown: The first is an ordinal logistic model (Table 4.D), and the second is a multinomial logistic model (Table 4.E).

TABLE 4.D ● ORDINAL LOGISTIC REGRESSION OF CHILD CLOSENESS TO THEIR MOTHER

Response Profile			
Ordered Value	kidclosetomom	Total Frequency	Total Weight
1	1_very	534	530.91333
2	2_some	258	253.18929
3	3_not	67	66.80462

Score Test for the Proportional Odds Assumption		
Chi-Square	DF	Pr > ChiSq
29.5546	5	<.0001

Analysis of Maximum Likelihood Estimates						
Parameter		DF	Estimate	Standard Error	Wald Chi-Square	Pr > ChiSq
Intercept	1_very	1	1.0810	1.0214	1.1201	0.2899
Intercept	2_some	1	3.2048	1.0289	9.7015	0.0018
femchld		1	0.3172	0.1458	4.7289	0.0297
kidage		1	−0.2623	0.0368	50.8912	<.0001
cgrades		1	0.0567	0.0117	23.5995	<.0001
momage		1	−0.0407	0.0157	6.6901	0.0097
mcesd		1	−0.0219	0.00976	5.0490	0.0246

Odds Ratio Estimates			
Effect	Point Estimate	95% Wald Confidence Limits	
femchld	1.373	1.032	1.828
kidage	0.769	0.716	0.827
cgrades	1.058	1.034	1.083
momage	0.960	0.931	0.990
mcesd	0.978	0.960	0.997

TABLE 4.E ● MULTINOMIAL LOGISTIC REGRESSION OF CHILD CLOSENESS TO THEIR MOTHER

Response Profile			
Ordered Value	kidclosetomom	Total Frequency	Total Weight
1	1_very	534	530.91333
2	2_some	258	253.18929
3	3_not	67	66.80462

Logits modeled use kidclosetomom='3_not' as the reference category.

Analysis of Maximum Likelihood Estimates						
Parameter	kidclosetomom	DF	Estimate	Standard Error	Wald Chi-Square	Pr > ChiSq
Intercept	1_very	1	2.1436	2.0079	1.1397	0.2857
Intercept	2_some	1	0.1112	2.0689	0.0029	0.9572
femchld	1_very	1	0.0737	0.2859	0.0664	0.7966
femchld	2_some	1	−0.4161	0.2928	2.0203	0.1552
kidage	1_very	1	−0.4783	0.0763	39.2585	<.0001
kidage	2_some	1	−0.2896	0.0778	13.8589	0.0002
cgrades	1_very	1	0.1282	0.0238	28.9146	<.0001
cgrades	2_some	1	0.1033	0.0243	18.0165	<.0001
momage	1_very	1	−0.0775	0.0311	6.2092	0.0127
momage	2_some	1	−0.0519	0.0318	2.6531	0.1033
mcesd	1_very	1	−0.0360	0.0175	4.2416	0.0394
mcesd	2_some	1	−0.0235	0.0179	1.7213	0.1895

Odds Ratio Estimates				
Effect	kidclosetomom	Point Estimate	95% Wald Confidence Limits	
femchld	1_very	1.076	0.615	1.885
femchld	2_some	0.660	0.372	1.171
kidage	1_very	0.620	0.534	0.720
kidage	2_some	0.749	0.643	0.872
cgrades	1_very	1.137	1.085	1.191
cgrades	2_some	1.109	1.057	1.163
momage	1_very	0.925	0.871	0.984
momage	2_some	0.949	0.892	1.011
mcesd	1_very	0.965	0.932	0.998
mcesd	2_some	0.977	0.943	1.012

Linear Hypotheses Testing Results			
Label	Wald Chi-Square	DF	Pr > ChiSq
all1vs2	42.6856	5	<.0001
kidsex1vs2	9.5285	1	0.0020
kidage1vs2	22.3617	1	<.0001
grades1vs2	3.9171	1	0.0478
momage1vs2	2.2668	1	0.1322
cesd1vs2	1.3209	1	0.2504
all2vs3	38.9798	5	<.0001

Independent variables in the output are
- **femchld**: A dummy variable = 1 for female child, 0 for male child
- **kidage**: The child's age, from 9 to 16
- **cgrades**: The child's average grade in school, in percentages
- **momage**: The mother's age in years
- **mcesd**: The mother's depression score, measured as the number of days per week with symptoms

Answer these questions:

a. Cite a test shown in the results to decide whether you would interpret the ordinal or the multinomial model.

b. Assuming that you should interpret the multinomial model, answer these questions:

1. What is the effect of each year of the child's age on the odds of being very versus not close to the mother?

2. What is the effect of each day per week of maternal depression on the odds of being very versus not close?

c. According to the results of post-hoc tests designed to assess whether any adjacent categories can be collapsed, would you collapse any of the outcome categories, and if so, which ones?

d. According to the post-hoc tests and using the results in the multinomial model, calculate the effect of a female child on the **log odds** of being *very versus somewhat* close to the mother and then exponentiate this effect to show the effect on the odds. What test can you use to assess the significance of this effect?

3. The results below are from an ordinal logistic regression of perceived job discrimination among women, in a study of married women. The dependent variable is a four-level ordinal response to a question asking whether discrimination had ever played a part in "getting a promotion or raise on a job," with 1 = definitely yes, 2 = probably yes, 3 = probably no, and 4 = definitely no, the four possible responses. This means that in the ordinal logistic regression results, we are predicting greater versus less discrimination.

The independent variables are

- **momdepearly**: A dummy variable = 1 if the mother had experienced a depression episode before or during her twenties

- **mparcare**: Parental bonding scale for closeness of mother to her parents (range is 4 lowest to 20 highest)

- **momeduc**: The woman's education in years

- **timelfyears**: Time in labor force in years, from first job to present

- **mparrole**: Maternal commitment to parenting, from 1 = lowest to 4 = highest

After the results for the ordinal model, there are results for a multinomial model as well. Answer these questions:

a. According to the results of the test for proportional odds in the output for the ordinal model, would you conclude that the ordinal model is justified, or would you interpret the multinomial results instead?

b. Assume for this question that you must use the multinomial model. What is the effect of early depression (momdepearly) on *the odds* of definitely yes versus definitely no?

c. Using the results for mother's education, calculate the effect on the odds of each year increase in mother's education on *the odds* of definitely yes versus probably no.

TABLE 4.F ● LOGISTIC REGRESSION OF PERCEIVED JOB DISCRIMINATION AMONG WOMEN

```
                The LOGISTIC Procedure
        Number of Observations Read      869
        Number of Observations Used      852

                    Response Profile

        Ordered      discrim_          Total
        Value        promote       Frequency
          1             1               85
          2             2              111
          3             3              120
          4             4              536
Ordinal: Probabilities modeled are cumulated over the lower Ordered Values.
```

Score Test for the Proportional Odds Assumption

Chi-Square	DF	Pr > ChiSq
23.0677	10	0.0105

Analysis of Maximum Likelihood Estimates

Parameter	DF	Estimate	Standard Error	Wald Chi-Square	Pr > ChiSq
Intercept 1	1	−4.0197	0.7770	26.7643	<.0001
Intercept 2	1	−3.0042	0.7709	15.1874	<.0001
Intercept 3	1	−2.3060	0.7679	9.0168	0.0027
momdepearly	1	0.3270	0.1559	4.3977	0.0360
mparcare	1	−0.0741	0.0225	10.8645	0.0010
momeduc	1	0.0886	0.0258	11.7502	0.0006
timelfyears	1	0.0203	0.0144	1.9740	0.1600
mparrole	1	0.3500	0.1210	8.3724	0.0038

Odds Ratio Estimates

Effect	Point Estimate	95% Wald Confidence Limits	
momdepearly	1.387	1.022	1.883
mparcare	0.929	0.889	0.970
momeduc	1.093	1.039	1.149
timelfyears	1.020	0.992	1.050
mparrole	1.419	1.120	1.799

The LOGISTIC Procedure

Response Profile

Ordered Value	discrim_ promote	Total Frequency
1	1	85
2	2	111
3	3	120
4	4	536

Multinomial: **Logits modeled use discrim_promote=4 as the reference category.**

The LOGISTIC Procedure

Analysis of Maximum Likelihood Estimates

Parameter	discrim_ promote	DF	Estimate	Standard Error	Chi-Square	Wald Pr > ChiSq
Intercept	1	1	−4.1111	1.3170	9.7443	0.0018
Intercept	2	1	−3.5707	1.1735	9.2587	0.0023

(Continued)

TABLE 4.F	Continued					
Intercept	3	1	−2.5220	1.1228	5.0457	0.0247
momdepearly	1	1	0.8546	0.2475	11.9211	0.0006
momdepearly	2	1	0.0846	0.2418	0.1225	0.7263
momdepearly	3	1	−0.3409	0.2569	1.7602	0.1846
mparcare	1	1	−0.0878	0.0373	5.5371	0.0186
mparcare	2	1	−0.0743	0.0339	4.7998	0.0285
mparcare	3	1	−0.0631	0.0334	3.5788	0.0585
momeduc	1	1	0.1344	0.0441	9.2977	0.0023
momeduc	2	1	0.0992	0.0389	6.5204	0.0107
momeduc	3	1	0.0141	0.0379	0.1391	0.7092
timelfyears	1	1	0.0205	0.0248	0.6783	0.4102
timelfyears	2	1	0.0143	0.0221	0.4165	0.5187
timelfyears	3	1	0.0304	0.0209	2.1309	0.1444
mparrole	1	1	0.2823	0.2067	1.8661	0.1719
mparrole	2	1	0.4292	0.1855	5.3544	0.0207
mparrole	3	1	0.3788	0.1791	4.4747	0.0344

4. The table attached for Question 4 is from an article by Welsh, Dawson, and Nierobisz (2002) on the settlement of sexual harassment cases brought to the Canadian Human Rights Commission. The table shows results of a binomial logistic regression of the settlement versus dismissal of sexual harassment cases—where settlement refers to sufficient evidence to result in some form of settlement between the parties involved. *Fifty-nine percent of the cases sampled were settled.*

The effect of experienced psychological distress by the complainant is a dummy variable. Interpret this effect in two ways, focusing on Model 1.

a. Interpret this effect as an effect on the odds of settling the case versus dismissal.

b. Interpret this effect as a marginal effect on the probability of settlement at the average probability in this sample.

c. Model 2 adds an interaction to Model 1 between *quid pro quo* harassment—the clearest and most serious form—and the time period of the complaint, to detect change over time. When this article was published, this way of estimating the interaction was the standard approach. Use the discussion in this chapter to outline in a number of steps how you would test this interaction using averaged marginal effects.

TABLE 4.G ● LOGIT ESTIMATES OF THE EFFECTS OF LEGAL, EXTRA-LEGAL, CASE-PROCESSING VARIABLES, AND INTERACTION TERM ON SEXUAL HARASSMENT CASE OUTCOMES, CANADIAN HUMAN RIGHTS COMMISSION (CORPORATE RESPONDENTS, FEMALE COMPLAINANTS, N = 267)

variable	Model 1			Model 2		
	B	S.E.	Odds	B	S.E.	Odds
Legal variables						
Quid pro quo sexual harassment	.802*	.314	2.229	.482	.353	1.619
Psychological distress experienced	.712*	.337	2.039	.770*	.342	2.161
Complainant no longer in job	−.057	.342	.943	−.006	.346	.994
Number of prior complaints	−.002	.050	.998	−.004	.051	.996
More than one harasser	−.486	.418	.615	−.567	.426	.567
More than one complainant	.089	.343	1.093	.035	.347	1.036
Extra-legal variables						
Harasser in position of authority	.047	.412	1.093	.093	.414	1.036
Complainant temporary/on probation	.488	.361	1.629	.520	.363	1.682
Non-federal respondent	.146	.328	1.157	.151	.329	1.175
Size of organization (logged)	−.181*	.087	.835	−.186*	.088	.830
Case-processing variables						
Case occurred between 1984–1989	1.606***	.453	4.983	.904	.577	2.469
Case occurred between 1990–1993	1.798***	.512	6.040	1.816***	.514	6.149
Case went to conciliation	2.836***	.505	17.040	2.855***	.504	17.378
Harassment and time period interaction						
*Quid pro quo** 1984-1989				1.4091[a]	.744	4.091
Constant	−.287			−.129		
−2 Log Likelihood	278.875			275.148		

*p < .05   **p < .01   ***p < .001

[a]One-tailed significance test. Significant at .058 for two-tailed.

GENERALIZATIONS OF REGRESSION 4

The Generalized Linear Model

In previous chapters, we progressively added options and flexibility to the basic additive regression model. In this chapter, we fill in some of the remaining gaps in this model, by invoking the *generalized linear model* concept introduced by McCullagh and Nelder (1989). We do not attempt here to cover fully the implications of this model; instead, we use the model to introduce three other variants of regression: Poisson regression, a closely related form known as negative binomial regression, and complementary log-log regression. Each of these has a role to play in our choices in analyzing data because each introduces flexibility in specific situations that arise quite often.

5.1 OVERVIEW OF THE GENERALIZED LINEAR MODEL

The generalized linear model is a single framework for viewing the various extensions of the basic linear regression model. The basic framework is to express the regression model in terms of three components:

1. *A linear predictor set (Xβ)* on which a transformed version of *Y*, denoted by *y*, depends: $y = a + b_1 X_1 + \ ... \ b_k X_k$.

2. *A random component* of *Y*, standing for the error in the model, having one of the following response probability distributions: normal, Poisson, binomial, negative binomial, multinomial, gamma, and inverse-Gaussian.

3. *A link function* $L(y_i)$, a transformation that linearizes the dependence of *Y* on *X*. The link functions include the following:

   - *The identity link:* $L(y_i) = Y_i = 1$ for normal linear regression

   - *The log link:* $L(y_i) = \ln Y_i$ for an exponential fit

- *The inverse link:* $L(y_i) = 1/Y_i$
- *The square-root link:* $L(y_i) = \sqrt{Y_i}$
- *The logit link:* $L(y_i) = \ln\left(\dfrac{Pr(Y)}{1 - Pr(Y)}\right)$
- *The probit link:* $L(y_i) = \Phi(Pr(Y))$ where Φ is the cumulative normal distribution function
- *The complementary log-log link:* $L(y) = \ln(-\ln(1 - P(Y)))$

As we will see in later chapters, the last model is useful in survival and event history models. Actual models are formed by combining specifications of the distribution of the errors with link functions, as illustrated in Table 5.1.

TABLE 5.1 ● VARIATIONS OF THE GENERALIZED LINEAR MODEL

Error Distribution	Link Function	Model
normal	identity	linear regression
binomial	logit	binary logistic regression
multinomial	cumulative logit	ordinal logistic regression
Poisson	log	regression with count data
negative binomial	log	regression with count data

5.2 THE POISSON REGRESSION MODEL

Poisson regression is designed to study the rate of rare events happening over a given time frame—for example, the number of doctor visits in a year, the number of traumatic events over childhood, crime victimizations per year, days absent from work per month, or the number of awards and honors in a career. Essentially, this distribution is most useful for events that occur only rarely to most people and, when they do, their frequency declines as the number of events increases, tapping into increasingly rare experiences in a population. As the overall rate of events increases, this distribution becomes increasingly "normal" looking and less skewed.

The form of the model can be stated in probability terms as follows:

$$Pr(Y = y) = \frac{e^{-\mu}\mu^{y}}{y!}$$

This is the probability that the number of events over a given time period is y. The mean number of events over a time period (μ) is the only parameter in the Poisson distribution, and

$$E(Y) = \text{var}(Y) = \mu$$

That is, the mean of this distribution equals its variance. This requirement comes under close scrutiny in many applications because often the variance exceeds the mean, resulting in a situation called *overdispersion*. The *negative binomial model* is one way to take overdispersion into account: This model has the same mean structure as the Poisson model but does not assume equidispersion.

Of course, we are interested in specifying why or how individuals experience different numbers of events around the mean value. The Poisson model is from the exponential family of models, and thus, broadly, we can state

$$\widehat{Y} = e^{(a+bX)}$$

$$\ln(\widehat{Y}) = a + bX$$

The Poisson distribution describes the probability distribution for the occurrence of events; the regression model predicts varying number of events using a log link function. Note that the time period is assumed to be constant across observations here, though this is not necessary in the most general application of the model, where time appears as a variable.

The Poisson model assumes that event occurrence over time is independent. As noted by Long (1997), this means that when an event occurs, it does not alter the probability of a future event. This is often a difficult assumption to meet, primarily because many events stand for the increasing or decreasing probability of the next event occurrence. This assumption is often not addressed directly in research and is kept in the background of many published articles using Poisson regression. For example, the number of doctor visits does not seem to describe a sequence of unrelated events. The number of articles published by a scholar in five years also does not seem to describe independence since reputation and recent history can help sway editorial decisions.

The Poisson model is not appropriate for non-integer data: Events either occur or they don't, so the only values the dependent variable can take on start at 0 and increase by increments of 1 (1, 2, 3, 4, etc.).

5.2.0.1 Negative Binomial Model

The negative binomial modification of the Poisson model includes a less restrictive definition of the variance of the distribution. Instead of simply equaling the mean count of some event over time, the variance here includes a "dispersion" parameter that adds a constant amount to the mean.

The option of considering the negative binomial model arises from the problem of overdispersion. There are actually two approaches to adjusting for overdispersion. One is to adjust the standard errors and test statistics within the Poisson model to take into account the overdispersion. In an overdispersed model, the variance may still be proportional to the mean, and as a result, we could adjust the mean by a *scale parameter* to get to the actual variance, as follows:

$$\text{Var}(Y) = \varphi\mu$$

where φ, the scale parameter is

$$\varphi = \chi^2 / (N - p)$$

and is thus estimated from the χ^2 goodness of fit of the model, the sample size N, and $p =$ the number of parameters (independent variables) in the model. When this value is considerably greater than 1, we have to consider adjusting for the overdispersion.

A second approach is to use negative binomial regression, which accounts for overdispersion differently but does add a component to the definition of the variance:

$$\text{Var}(Y) = \mu + D\mu^2$$

Where D is the dispersion parameter.

Given these various issues, questions, and options, we proceed to show how the Poisson and negative binomial model can be applied to data.

5.2.1 The Number of Physical Arguments per Year in Married Couples

Poisson regression is most useful for dependent variables that are counts of relatively rare phenomena and are therefore highly skewed. The plot in Figure 5.1, for number of domestic physical attacks on the respondent per year taken from National Survey of Families and Households (NSFH) data, illustrates the highly skewed distribution typical of a variable that would be considered for a Poisson regression. Note that this variable is a *rate* of something—number of events over a given time period.

Although count data are sometimes treated as continuous (i.e., modeled using ordinary least squares regression), this can result in inefficient, inconsistent, and biased estimates, particularly with uncommon events. The Poisson regression model is designed to deal explicitly with the characteristics of count data and incorporates a maximum likelihood approach to estimation.

5.2.1.1 An Example of Poisson Regression

The first wave of the NSFH asked married and cohabiting couples about the occurrence of domestic violence in the past year. Here we focus on one question: "During the past year, how many fights with your husband/wife resulted in him/her hitting, shoving, or throwing things at you?" with answers 0 for none, 1 for one, 2 for two, 3 for three, and 4 for four or more. For the purposes of this example, the variable is coded to represent the prevalence of physical arguments, *among those who reported arguing at all.* Zero means no serious physical arguments (not the absence of any arguments), and the remainder of the distribution indicates the number of physical arguments with the respondent as the victim (not the perpetrator—that is a separate

FIGURE 5.1 ● NUMBER OF PHYSICAL ARGUMENTS PER YEAR WITH RESPONDENT AS VICTIM

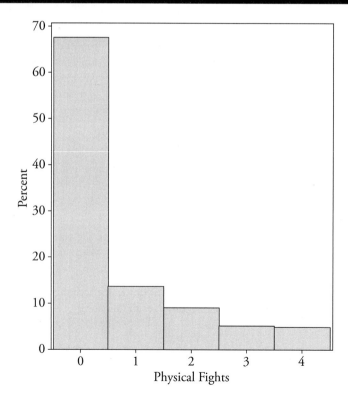

question). Note that in the plot, we see that almost 70% of all arguments are non-physical and that the distribution has marked positive skewness.

We model the expected number of attacks on the respondent first using Poisson regression. In SAS, the procedure is called PROC GENMOD. In STATA, we use the *Poisson* command. Both procedures fit a generalized linear model to the data with maximum likelihood estimates of the parameters using a Poisson error distribution. In SAS, the code looks like this:

```
proc genmod data=temp;
class race(param=ref ref=first);
model fightcountvictim=female race rage reduc rdrinks sdrinks rsesteem
ssesteem / link=log dist=poisson type3 scale=0;
title 'Poisson of Victim of Marital Violence with scale parameter';
weight weight;
run;
```

This program has many of the same elements as SAS programs already discussed but also includes a CLASS statement to specify categorical variables as a set of dummy variables. The main distinctions occur as options in the MODEL statement. To run the Poisson model, specify the link function as LINK=LOG and the distribution as DIST=POISSON. To change this to the negative binomial model, you simply change the distribution to DIST=NEGBIN (but leave the link function as LINK=LOG). Note there is a SCALE option, set to 0 initially, so we can compare to results that do adjust for overdispersion. This scale parameter can be re-specified in later estimations (e.g., scale=D), to take into account the level of departure from the 1 to 1 correspondence of the variance and the mean. The scale parameter is useful because, when specified, SAS adjusts the standard errors to take into account the effect of not meeting the assumptions of the model by multiplying standard errors by this factor. This will often reduce the significance of variables in the model.

The independent variables here include "race," coded as Black versus White, and other versus White, age, education, whether the respondent has a drinking problem (*rdrinks*), whether the spouse has a drinking problem (*sdrinks*), and both respondent (*resteem*) and spousal (*sesteem*) measures of self-esteem (on a scale from 1 to 5).

The output from GENMOD looks like Table 5.2.

TABLE 5.2 ● POISSON RESULTS FOR THE DOMESTIC VIOLENCE MODEL

Class Level Information			
Class	Value	Design	Variables
race	1 White	0	0
	2 Black	1	0
	3 Other	0	1

(Continued)

TABLE 5.2 ● Continued

Criteria for Assessing Goodness of Fit			
Criterion	DF	Value	Value/DF
Deviance	429	637.8318	1.4868
Scaled Deviance	429	637.8318	1.4868
Pearson Chi-Square	429	816.9272	1.9043
Scaled Pearson X2	429	816.9272	1.9043
Log Likelihood		−355.6009	
Full Log Likelihood		−479.7170	
AIC (smaller is better)		979.4340	
AICC (smaller is better)		979.9481	
BIC (smaller is better)		1020.2790	

Analysis of Maximum Likelihood Parameter Estimates					Wald 95% Confidence Limits		Wald Chi-Square	Pr > ChiSq
Parameter		DF	Estimate	Standard Error				
Intercept		1	3.3647	0.6325	2.1250	4.6045	28.30	<.0001
female		1	−0.1036	0.1339	−0.3660	0.1589	0.60	0.4394
race	2 Black	1	0.1952	0.1872	−0.1718	0.5622	1.09	0.2972
race	3 Other	1	0.2178	0.2116	−0.1969	0.6326	1.06	0.3033
rage		1	−0.0464	0.0060	−0.0582	−0.0346	59.25	<.0001
reduc		1	−0.0176	0.0279	−0.0724	0.0372	0.40	0.5288
rdrinks		1	0.1600	0.2065	−0.2448	0.5648	0.60	0.4386
sdrinks		1	0.4316	0.2016	0.0365	0.8268	4.58	0.0323
rsesteem		1	−0.5010	0.0976	−0.6923	−0.3097	26.35	<.0001
ssesteem		1	−0.0334	0.0963	−0.2222	0.1554	0.12	0.7292
Scale		0	1.0000	0.0000	1.0000	1.0000		

We see three significant effects here: age (negative), whether the spouse drinks (positive), and respondent self-esteem (negative). However, we also note that the Scaled Pearson χ^2 / DF ratio is about 1.9, considerably beyond 1.

Running the same Poisson model in STATA uses the *poisson* command. Compared to the previous STATA commands introduced so far, this line includes the *xi:* preface. This preface allows us to elaborate categorical variables (which begin with *i.* in the model, for example, **i.race**). STATA creates new dummy variables for each respective category. These generated variables are then modeled in comparison to the default reference category and given unique names.

Finally, to make the output equivalent to the SAS output, we use the *vce(oim)* option in this command, resulting in the same standard errors.

```
xi: poisson fightcountvictim female i.race rage reduc rdrinks
sdrinks rsesteem ssesteem [pweight=weight], vce(oim)

Iteration 0:   log likelihood = -479.75773
Iteration 1:   log likelihood = -479.71704
Iteration 2:   log likelihood = -479.71702
```

```
Poisson regression                                    Number of obs  =      439
                                                      Wald chi2(9)   =  102.41
Log likelihood = -479.71702                           Prob > chi2    =  0.0000
```

fightcountvictim	Coef.	Std. Err.	z	P>|z|	[95% Conf.	Interval]
female	-.103553	.1339265	-0.77	0.439	-.3660442	.1589382
_Irace_2	.1951803	.187249	1.04	0.297	-.171821	.5621815
_Irace_3	.2178481	.2116271	1.03	0.303	-.1969334	.6326296
rage	-.0463789	.0060254	-7.70	0.000	-.0581884	-.0345695
reduc	-.0175997	.0279419	-0.63	0.529	-.0723649	.0371655
rdrinks	.1599757	.206533	0.77	0.439	-.2448217	.564773
sdrinks	.4316246	.2016002	2.14	0.032	.0364954	.8267539
rsesteem	-.5010036	.0975967	-5.13	0.000	-.6922897	-.3097176
ssesteem	-.0333525	.0963271	-0.35	0.729	-.2221502	.1554453
_cons	3.36474	.6325326	5.32	0.000	2.124999	4.604481

There is no test of the significance of this scale parameter in the Poisson output. In SAS, we must run the negative binomial version of the model and include "noscale" among the options, as follows:

```
proc genmod data=temp;
class race(param=ref ref=first);
model fightcountvictim=female race rage reduc rdrinks sdrinks rsesteem
ssesteem / link=log dist=negbin type3 noscale scale=0;
title 'Negative Binomial of Victim of Marital Violence with scale=0';
weight weight;
run;
```

This produces the output shown in Table 5.3.

TABLE 5.3 ● NEGATIVE BINOMIAL TEST OF OVERDISPERSION

Parameter		DF	Estimate	Standard Error	Wald 95% Confidence Limits		Wald Chi-Square	Pr > ChiSq
Intercept		1	2.5127	0.6126	1.3120	3.7134	16.82	<.0001
female		1	−0.1005	0.1305	−0.3563	0.1553	0.59	0.4414
race	2 Black	1	0.1855	0.1603	−0.1287	0.4997	1.34	0.2472
race	3 Other	1	0.1919	0.2046	−0.2091	0.5928	0.88	0.3483
rage		1	−0.0362	0.0060	−0.0480	−0.0244	36.12	<.0001
reduc		1	−0.0076	0.0261	−0.0588	0.0435	0.09	0.7705
rdrinks		1	0.1783	0.2012	−0.2159	0.5726	0.79	0.3753
sdrinks		1	0.3669	0.1891	−0.0037	0.7375	3.77	0.0523
rsesteem		1	−0.4077	0.1891	−0.5936	−0.2219	18.48	<.0001
ssesteem		1	−0.0168	0.0912	−0.1955	0.1619	0.03	0.8537
Dispersion		0	0.0000	0.0000				

Table header spanning: Analysis of Maximum Likelihood Parameter Estimates

(Continued)

TABLE 5.3 ● Continued

Lagrange Multiplier Statistics		
Parameter	**Chi-Square**	**Pr > ChiSq**
Dispersion	32.2050	<.0001 *

* One-sided p-value

We do not yet focus on the results here because this model has no scale parameter. However, the test of the dispersion parameter is very significant, beyond the .0001 level. So we return to the Poisson model first and incorporate an adjustment for the scale parameter, by changing the *scale=0* option to *scale=d,* for the calculated dispersion parameter.

At least one crucial finding does change: Now spousal drinking has no significant effect (See Table 5.4). The difference in the probability of the null is small but crosses an important threshold and thus could affect overall conclusions about the causes of domestic violence, especially if this was the only model run as part of an analysis.

TABLE 5.4 ● POISSON RESULTS WITH A SCALE PARAMETER

Analysis of Maximum Likelihood Parameter Estimates								
Parameter		**DF**	**Estimate**	**Standard Error**	**Wald 95% Confidence Limits**		**Wald Chi-Square**	**Pr > ChiSq**
Intercept		1	3.3647	0.7713	1.8531	4.8764	19.03	<.0001
female		1	−0.1036	0.1633	−0.4236	0.2165	0.40	0.5260
race	2 Black	1	0.1952	0.2283	−0.2523	0.6427	0.73	0.3926
race	3 Other	1	0.2178	0.2580	−0.2879	0.7236	0.71	0.3985
rage		1	−0.0464	0.2580	−0.0608	−0.0320	39.85	<.0001
reduc		1	−0.0176	0.0341	−0.0844	0.0492	0.27	0.6055
rdrinks		1	0.1600	0.2518	−0.3336	0.6536	0.40	0.5253
sdrinks		1	0.4316	0.2458	−0.0502	0.9134	3.080	0.0791
rsesteem		1	−0.5010	0.1190	−0.7342	−0.2678	17.72	<.0001
ssesteem		1	−0.0334	0.1175	−0.2636	0.1969	0.080	0.7764
Scale		0	1.2193	0.0000	1.2193	1.2193		

Instead of just adjusting for the overdispersion, however, we can change the model to the negative binomial and include a scale parameter in that model as well. This involves running the following code:

```
proc genmod data=temp;
class race(param=ref ref=first);
model fightcountvictim=female race rage reduc rdrinks sdrinks rsesteem
ssesteem / link=log dist=negbin type3 scale=d;
title 'Negative Binomial of Victim of Marital Violence with scale=d';
weight weight;
run;
```

Results do suggest a different result (all things considered) for the effect of spousal drinking, which is now significant exactly at the .05 level, as shown in Table 5.5.

TABLE 5.5 ● NEGATIVE BINOMIAL RESULTS WITH A SCALE PARAMETER

Criteria For Assessing Goodness of Fit			
Criterion	DF	Value	Value/DF
Dispersion		345.9997	0.8065
Scaled Deviance	429	429.0000	1.0000
Pearson Chi-Square	429	415.7642	0.9691
Scaled Pearson X2	429	515.5000	1.2016
Log Likelihood		−398.2496	
Full Log Likelihood		−453.9838	
AIC (smaller is better)		929.9677	
AICC (smaller is better)		930.5860	
BIC (smaller is better)		974.8972	

Analysis of Maximum Likelihood Parameter Estimates					Wald 95% Confidence Limits		Wald Chi-Square	Pr > ChiSq
Parameter		DF	Estimate	Standard Error				
Intercept		1	3.2276	0.8381	1.5850	4.8703	14.83	0.0001
female		1	−0.1522	0.1691	−0.4837	0.1793	0.81	0.3681
race	2 Black	1	0.3403	0.2361	−0.1223	0.8030	2.08	0.1494
race	3 Other	1	0.2794	0.2897	−0.2884	0.8471	0.93	0.3348
rage		1	−0.0440	0.0075	−0.0587	−0.0294	34.70	<.0001
reduc		1	−0.0093	0.0337	−0.0753	0.0567	0.08	0.7823
rdrinks		1	0.2219	0.2763	−0.3197	0.7635	0.64	0.4219
sdrinks		1	0.5427	0.2776	−0.0015	1.0869	3.82	0.0506
rsesteem		1	−0.4961	0.1340	−0.7587	−0.2335	13.71	0.0002
ssesteem		1	−0.0436	0.1306	−0.2996	0.2123	0.11	0.7383
Dispersion		1	1.3462	0.2382	0.9517	1.9044		

Of course, in reality, we would expect some important interactions in this model involving gender multiplied by the risk factors. Thus we caution the reader to refrain from interpreting these results as "final."

We compare the results using Poisson without a scale adjustment, with a scale adjustment, and the negative binomial to a regular OLS regression in Table 5.6. We consider the OLS regression in two naïve forms: the usual OLS results, ignoring the skewness of the outcome, and a less naïve version, modeling the *log(Y)*. This latter version may be considered to be an adjustment for the skewness of *Y*, for example. In this latter model, of course, the error structure is still wrong since it is assumed to be normal.

The different approaches here are not comparable in metric terms, but at least we can see which predictors are significant under the varying conditions expressed by each model.

TABLE 5.6 ● NUMBER OF TIMES *R* WAS VICTIM IN A PHYSICAL FIGHT WITH PARTNER IN PAST YEAR					
	OLS Regression	OLS Regression with *log(Y)*	Poisson Regression (no scale)	Poisson Regression (with scale)	Negative Binomial Regression
Constant	2.628***	1.017*	3.365	3.365***	3.227***
Female	−.046	−.581***	−.104	−.104	−.152
Black vs. White	.165	1.022***	.195	.195	.340
Other race/ethnicity vs. White	.224	1.437***	.218	.218	.279
Age	−.018***	−.072***	−.046***	−.046***	−.044***
Education	−.004	−.036*	−.018	−.018	−.009
Respondent has a problem with alcohol	.082	−.053	.160	.160	.222
Spouse/partner has a problem with alcohol	.272	1.498***	.432*	.432	.543*
Self-esteem	−.297***	−.887***	−.501***	−.501***	−.496***
Self-esteem of spouse/partner	−.033	−.169*	−.033	−.033	−.044

$* = p < .05$

$** = p < .001$

$*** = p < .0001$

5.2.1.2 Differences in Results across Models

First we consider which model to interpret in this situation. Normally you would not use OLS here, unless you can demonstrate that the errors are normally distributed. Tests of normality here will reveal significant skewness, so we know the OLS model is in fact not applicable. Note that the results in the first column are not comparable to results in later columns because the dependent variable is just the count, not the log count—so the coefficients look very different.

Results in the table show important differences across the models estimated. A normal OLS run using the count variable reveals only two significant predictors: age and respondent self-esteem (first column). If we used this model, we would report a number of effects as nonsignificant that are often thought to be involved in domestic violence. One way to account for the skewness of the outcome is to use the log of the dependent variable in OLS. Results here are *very* different (Column 2). Now results suggest that most of the variables we consider as predictors have a significant effect on the risk of victimization: being female (but negatively, suggesting lower risk!), any racial-ethnic category other than White, younger age, lower education, having a partner with a drinking problem, and lower self-esteem for both the respondent and the partner. Only one variable considered—respondent has a drinking problem—has no effect. We present these results because it is quite common practice to adjust for skewness simply by taking the *log* of the dependent variable.

Results from the Poisson model *without a scale adjustment* (third column) are again quite different, compared to the logged OLS model. Interestingly, they are more similar to the raw count model using OLS. But there is an important difference: In the Poisson model, the effect of spousal drinking is significant. Obviously, getting the best possible evidence for this predictor is important. When we compare results here to the logged OLS model, we also see widespread and striking differences, leading to very different potential conclusions about the sources of domestic violence. The coefficients in this model are consistently smaller than in the logged OLS model, and as a result, gender, race, and education are now not significant. Three effects survive: age, respondent self-esteem, and a spousal drinking problem.

The Poisson results with the adjustment for overdispersion produce exactly the same coefficients; only the standard errors differ. As a result of this, the effect of spousal drinking is no longer significant in this model. However, given the test for overdispersion, we also have the alternative of switching to a negative binomial regression. The last column show these results. Overall, the important difference with the scale-adjusted Poisson is the fact that spousal drinking again has a significant effect.

How do we decide which approach is best here? Our advice is the same as our advice throughout this book: Rather than modify a model to make it work, when assumptions are broken, change the model to one which comes closer to meeting its assumptions.

In this case, the difference in results comes down to an important issue: whether a research publication reporting the causes and predictors of domestic violence includes evidence for the effect of spousal drinking or not. We favor results suggesting it does because the model is more appropriate. Rather than stretch the applicability of the Poisson model, we would choose the negative binomial in this case.

5.2.2 Interpreting the Results of the Poisson/Negative Binomial Model—Three Ways

There are several ways to interpret results from the Poisson / negative binomial models. As shown earlier, these models are exponential models, so that if you take the exponential of both sides of the equation for *ln Y* you get *Y* in original form as dependent, as follows:

$$\ln Y = a + bX_i$$
$$e^{\ln Y} = e^{(a+bX)}$$
$$Y = e^{(a+bX)} = e^a e^{bX}$$

In this form, we interpret the coefficients by taking the antilog (i.e., exponentiation) of the parameter estimates. We can do this in two different ways. Note that in this case, you are discussing the effect of an independent variable on *multiplying* the rate of *Y*—that is, changing it by a factor.

First, by simply exponentiating the parameter estimates $\left(e^{bX}\right)$, we can calculate the effect of a one-unit change in an independent variable multiplicatively on the expected number of attacks over the year. For example, the results indicate that if the spouse/partner has a drinking problem, the expected number of attacks on the respondent increases by a factor of 1.72 ($= e^{.543}$), holding all other variables constant.

Or you can also calculate the *percentage* change in the expected number of attacks by using the exponentiated regression coefficients in the following formula: $100(e^{bX} - 1)$. Thus, we can conclude that each 1-point increase on the 5-point self-esteem reduces the rate of attacks by 39% ($= 100(e^{-.496} - 1)$).

We can also interpret the coefficients directly from the **_additive_** form of the model, using the first derivative, which is the effect of a one-unit change in X at a given level of predicted $Y = \beta \cdot \hat{Y}$. This is *not* the same as in the exponentiated case because now you are considering additive changes to the predicted number of attacks per year. This approach takes advantage of the first derivative, thus asking "at what rate does the expected value of Y change with small changes in X?"

For example, the effect of a five-year increase in age at an expected value of $Y = 2$ is

$$(-.044 \times 5) \times 2 = -.44$$

Thus, at the point on the curve where $Y = 2$, or in other words, when there are two attacks per year, a five-year increase in the age of the respondent reduces the expected number of attacks by .44 attacks on average. It is more common to use this approach to evaluate an effect at the mean level of Y (here = .70). At this level, the effect would be smaller:

$$(-.044 \times 5) \times .70 = -.154$$

This leads to a much smaller change in the number of expected attacks on the respondent. Note that, as in all nonlinear models, the effect of X depends on the level of Y.

5.3 THE COMPLEMENTARY LOG-LOG MODEL

Like the logit and probit models, the complementary log-log model is used for binomial outcomes. But unlike the logit and probit models, the complementary log-log model is an *asymmetric* nonlinear probability model for Y. This means this model has added flexibility in the way X affects the probability of Y. The asymmetric nature of this function means that, as X increases, the probability of Y increases slowly over lower values of X and much more rapidly at higher values of X. The log-log model models the opposite kind of asymmetry to the complementary log-log model: $Pr(Y)$ increases rapidly over lower values of X and more slowly over higher values of X.

Here we emphasize the *complementary* log-log model because it will be useful in discussing event history (aka survival) models in later chapters.
The basic probability model here is

$$P(Y) = 1 - e^{-e^{bX}}$$

The linearized version of this model—linear in the predictors—looks like this:

$$\ln(-\ln(1 - P(Y))) = bX$$

The log-log model is defined as

$$-\ln(-\ln(1 - P(Y))) = bX$$

Some phenomena may fit these models better than the standard logistic model. In the graph in Figure 5.2 we see typical differences between the log-log, complementary log-log, probit, and logistic functions.

The probit function closely approximates the logit function. The complementary log-log function approximates the logistic function at lower values of X, increasing in $Pr(Y)$ slowly. But as

FIGURE 5.2 ● SYMMETRIC AND ASYMMETRIC PROBABILITY MODELS

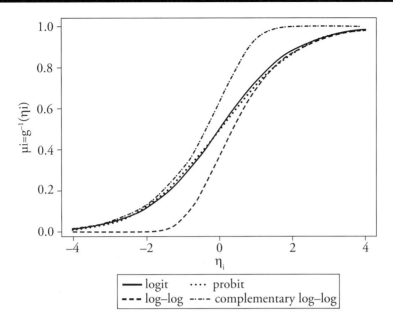

X increases, the probability curve accelerates more quickly than in the logistic case, and the asymptotic approach to 1 occurs more sharply. The log-log model has the opposite tendencies: It accelerates slowly at first and then converges to the logistic at higher levels of *X*.

What types of phenomena might fit these curves? Our earlier example using savings to predict home ownership may be better fit by a complementary log-log function because once the probability starts to increase, it should increase quickly and more definitively. The log-log function may be most useful for "threshold" cases where qualification is more restrictive. Note that the rate of acceleration is similar to the complementary log-log but delayed. Another case might be modeling the probability of acceptance for citizenship or permanent residence: A number of criteria are required before one even qualifies, but once they are satisfied, the probability should increase quickly.

The probability functions above look complicated, but they can be taken apart and parsed using the following graphs. Looking at the complementary log-log function, note first that it uses $1 - P$. $1 - P$ runs in the opposite direction from P: as P increases, $1 - P$ gets smaller:

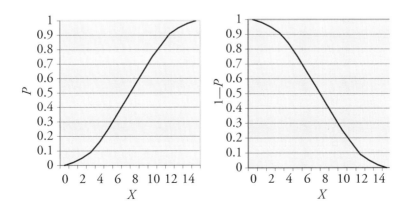

Thus, we take $-\ln$ of $1-P$, not $\ln(1-P)$. This ensures effects in the same direction as X.

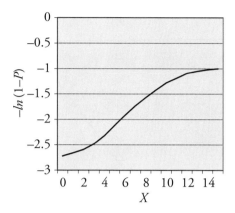

Taking the log of the minus log results in the asymmetric behavior of this function:

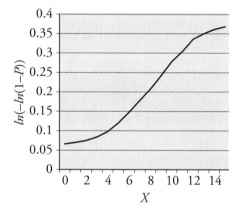

5.3.1 An Example of the Complementary Log-Log Model: Being a Victim of Domestic Violence

We illustrate the complementary log-log model by returning to the domestic violence data in the National Survey of Families and Households (NSFH). This time, however, we model the *probability* of being a victim of violence overall rather than the *count* of the number of attacks on the victim as we did for the Poisson / negative binomial regression example.

Again, we can use the GENMOD procedure in SAS to run a generalized linear model, but here we specify the complementary log-log link function and a binomial error distribution:

```
proc genmod data=temp descending;
class racec;
model victim = female racec sdrinks / link=cloglog dist=binomial type1 type3;
weight weight;
run;
```

The comparable command in STATA is the *xi:* command followed by a *cloglog* specification. The output from the GENMOD procedure is printed in Table 5.7.

TABLE 5.7 ● COMPLEMENTARY LOG-LOG MODEL FOR VIOLENT VICTIMIZATION

Response Profile			
Ordered Value	victim	Total Frequency	Total Weight
1	1	258	238.5915
2	0	6499	7609.253

Criteria For Assessing Goodness Of Fit			
Criterion	DF	Value	Value/DF
Log Likelihood		−1030	.4409
Full Log Likelihood		−1030	.4409
AIC (smaller is better)		2070	.8818
AICC (smaller is better)		2070	.8907
BIC (smaller is better)		2104	.9734

Analysis of Maximum Likelihood Parameter Estimates								
Parameter		DF	Estimate	Standard Error	Wald 95% Confidence Limits		Wald Chi-Square	Pr > ChiSq
Intercept		1	−3.6928	0.1019	−3.8926	−3.4930	1.0000	<.0001
female		1	−0.0539	0.1338	−0.3162	0.2084	0.16	0.6872
racec	1_other	1	0.3696	0.2244	−0.0701	0.8093	2.71	0.0995
racec	2_black	1	0.8226	0.1887	0.4527	1.1925	19.00	<.0001
racec	3_white	0	0.0000	0.0000	0.0000	0.0000	.	.
sdrinks		1	1.8204	0.1935	1.4411	2.1998	88.47	<.0001
Scale		0	1.0000	0.0000	1.0000	1.0000		

Interpreting these results requires new concepts not yet discussed but introduced in Section 5.3.2.

5.3.2 Interpreting the Results of the Complementary Log-Log Model

We can transform and interpret the coefficients as effects on the probability of being a victim of domestic violence. Remembering that each link function linearizes the dependence of Y on X, we can see how the complementary log-log probability function is linearized:

$$P(Y) = 1 - e^{-e^{bX}}$$

$-P(Y) = -1 + e^{-e^{bX}}$ (multiplying both sides of the equation by minus one)

$1 - P(Y) = e^{-e^{bX}}$ (adding one to both sides)

$\ln(1 - P(Y)) = -e^{bX}$ (taking the natural log of both sides)

$-\ln(1 - P(Y)) = e^{bX}$ (multiplying both sides by minus one)

$\ln(-\ln(1 - P(Y))) = bX$ (taking the natural log of both sides)

Thus, we can use the probability function $[P(Y) = 1 - e^{-e^{bX}}]$ to express the probability of violence in the past year as a function of the b's from the complementary log-log model. For example, the probability of being a victim of domestic violence among Black females whose spouse/partner does NOT have a drinking problem is

$$1 - e^{-e^{-3.69-.05(female)+.8226(2\_black)+1.82(sdrink}}$$

$$= 1 - e^{-e^{-3.69-.05(1)+.8226(1)+1.82(0)}}$$

$$= 1 - e^{-e^{-2.92}} = .05$$

Similarly, the predicted probability of being a victim of domestic violence in the past year among Black females whose spouse/partner DOES have a drinking problem is

$$= 1 - e^{-e^{-1.1}} = .28$$

Thus, living with a spouse/partner who has a problem with alcohol increases the probability of domestic violence in the past year among Black females from 5% to 28%—a 23 percentage point increase in the probability.

5.3.2.1 The Relative Risk versus the Odds Ratio

Another way to interpret complementary log-log results is to use the concept of relative risk, which is closely related to the odds. Consider the results in Table 5.8 from a study of the risk of coronary heart disease (CHD).

TABLE 5.8 ⬡ BLOOD CATECHOLAMINE AND CHD				
	Blood Catecholamines (1960)			
		High	**Low**	**Total**
CHD	Present	27	44	71
(1967)	Absent	95	443	538
Total		122	487	609

Label the cells as follows, using row-column subscripts in that order and totals across rows or columns using ".":

$$f_{11} \quad f_{12} \quad f_{1\bullet}$$

$$f_{21} \quad f_{22} \quad f_{2\bullet}$$

$$f_{\bullet 1} \quad f_{\bullet 2} \quad f_{\bullet\bullet}$$

The relative risk is the ratio of the probability of being a case (having CHD) for people high on the risk factor versus the probability of being a case for people low on the risk factor.

That is $RR = \dfrac{P_1}{P_2} = \dfrac{f_{11}/f_{\bullet 1}}{f_{12}/f_{\bullet 2}}$

$$= \frac{27/122}{44/487} = \frac{.221}{.090}$$

$$= 2.45$$

In other words, men with high CAT in the blood have 2.45 times the **risk** of CHD compared to men with low CAT.

The odds ratio here is
$$\text{OR:} \frac{\dfrac{P_1}{1-P_1}}{\dfrac{P_2}{1-P_2}} = \frac{\dfrac{.221}{.779}}{\dfrac{.090}{.910}} = \frac{.2837}{.099} = 2.87$$

That is, men with high CAT have 2.87 times the **odds** of CHD relative to men with low CAT.

The concepts of relative risk and the odds ratio are especially closely related for rare outcomes. Note that when an outcome is rare, that is, P_1 and P_2 are small, this means that $1-P_1$, and $1-P_2$ in the denominator of the odds approach 1. In this case,

$$OR \approx RR$$

In general, if $p < .2$ overall, results start to be approximately equal. If $p < .1$, they get quite close, and if $p < .05$, they are *very* close.

In the complementary log-log model, when you take e^{bX}, you produce effects on the **relative risk** of the outcome, not the odds. For rare outcomes, you could interpret the results as approximate effects on the odds. But, on the other hand, the concept of relative risk is straightforwardly interpretable, as well as a more precise interpretation of results. In the earlier results, when we exponentiate the effect of spousal drinking ($e^{1.82} = 6.17$), we can say that spousal drinking multiples the risk of violence over six times.

5.4 PUBLISHED EXAMPLES

5.4.1 Protest Behavior

Sebastian Valenzuela and colleagues have published a series of articles modeling protest behavior using Poisson regression. The fundamental question in these articles is whether (and how) social media use promotes political participation. A recent article in *American Behavioral Scientist* is an example (Valenzuela, 2013).

The article uses a survey in Chile of political behavior ($N = 1{,}737$) to investigate the link between social media use and participation in protests in Chile in 2011. Three mechanisms for this effect are discussed: (1) seeking and awareness of news through online sources; (2) expression of political opinion online; and (3) joining and participating in online political and social causes. Social media use is measured in terms of frequency of use of key online sites; protest behavior is an index measuring the number of distinct modalities of protest activities in the last 12 months, including attendance at demonstrations, public debates, signing petitions, sending letters, and meetings with authorities to express dissent. Other variables enter as controls in this analysis as well: grievances about the current government, left–right political values, membership in voluntary groups, education, and gender.

The discussion in the article about modeling protest behavior is interesting: Results are presented for *both* OLS and Poisson regressions because, in part "OLS is the most common type of regression used by previous research on interactive technologies and political participation" (Valenzuela, 2013, p. 930). It may be the case that reviewers suggested this approach, but it allows us to compare results—as we did earlier—using "traditional" versus more appropriate approaches.

Table 5.9 shows results for both Poisson and OLS in predicting an overall protest behavior index. Of course, the OLS results and the Poisson results are not in the same metric, so coefficients are not directly comparable: OLS is predicting the number of protest events while Poisson is predicting the log of the number of protest events.

As can be seen in Table 5.9, results show that social media use predicts protest behavior using both approaches. Social media use is scaled from 0 (none) to 1 (the highest usage). Thus coefficients must be interpreted as a contrast between no activity and the highest level of activity—the full range, which is unusual for a scale. According to OLS, this contrast produces on average .91 more protest activities in the last year. In the Poisson model, we exponentiate the b of 1.17 to get 3.22 $(= e^{1.17})$, suggesting that the highest versus lowest levels of media use multiply the risk of protest involvements by 3.22—over three times. Note the difference in the metric of the interpretation. We note also that there are cases where results differ: For economic outlook, government responsiveness, and watching TV news, results in OLS are significant but are not significant in the Poisson model. Age has different signs in the two models! These are not trivial differences. A simple principle suggests using the Poisson model: Given a choice, choose results for the model that has a greater chance of being the correct model.

TABLE 5.9 ● POISSON VERSUS OLS RESULTS FOR PREDICTING PROTEST BEHAVIOR

	Protest behaviour index	
	Pssn *b*	OLS *b*
Social media use	1.17***(0.18)	0.91***(0.12)
Anger	0.67(0.51)	0.41(0.24)
Economic outlook	−0.21(0.13)	−0.20**(0.08)
Government job approval	0.08(0.15)	−0.05(0.06)
Government job responsiveness	−0.02(0.14)	0.19**(0.07)
Postmaterialism	0.69***(0.19)	0.32***(0.10)
Left-wing ideology	0.45***(0.09)	0.23***(0.05)
Female	−0.13(0.08)	−0.07(0.04)
Education	1.06***(0.22)	0.38***(0.10)
Civic group member	1.15***(0.15)	0.98***(0.09)
Age	−0.26(0.21)	0.20*(0.09)
TV news	−0.55(0.33)	−0.35*(0.16)
Radio news	0.02(0.23)	−0.06(0.11)
Newspaper	−0.39(0.36)	−0.14(0.15)
Online news	1.94***(0.37)	1.82***(0.26)
Offline political discussion	0.68***(0.18)	0.18*(0.07)
Total R^2	.48	.38
Weighted *N*	1,464	1,464

5.4.2 School Violence

A paper by Huang and Cornell (2012) compares the results of OLS, Poisson, Poisson adjusted for overdispersion, and negative binomial regression in studying school violence—specifically, the number of reported bullying events at the school in the last year. The data come from a study of public high schools in Virginia in 2008 (Klein & Cornell, 2010). Figure 5.3 shows the distribution of bullying incidents across schools and clearly suggests this situation is a strong candidate for a Poisson or negative binomial model.

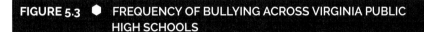

FIGURE 5.3 ● FREQUENCY OF BULLYING ACROSS VIRGINIA PUBLIC HIGH SCHOOLS

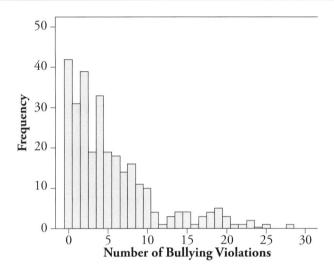

Predictors of school bullying include a proxy measure of school-level poverty (% students eligible for free / reduced-priced meals), percentage non-White students, a diversity index, urbanicity measured by number of people per square mile in the school zone, and school size. Results for all four approaches are shown in Table 5.10.

TABLE 5.10 ● COMPARISON OF RESULTS FROM OLS, POISSON, ADJUSTED POISSON, AND NEGATIVE BINOMIAL

	OLS (1)			PR (2)			
	b	**SE**	**P**	**b**	**SE**	**P**	**exp(b)**
Intercept	−1.00	1.11	.37	0.46**	0.11	<.01	1.58
FRPM	1.19	2.39	.62	−0.26	0.25	.30	0.77
Diversity index	5.48*	2.06	.01	1.09**	0.22	<.01	2.97
Proportion non-White	−2.07	1.85	.26	−0.09	0.20	.66	0.91
Urbanicity	0.00	0.26	.99	−0.01	0.02	.61	0.99
School size	3.93**	0.56	<.01	0.64**	0.05	<.01	1.90

(Continued)

TABLE 5.10 ● Continued							
	Overdispersed PR (3)			NBR (4)			
	b	**SE**	**P**	**b**	**SE**	**P**	**exp(b)**
Intercept	0.46*	0.21	.03	0.45*	0.21	.03	1.57
FRPM	−0.26	0.47	.58	−0.42	0.46	.37	0.66
Diversity index	1.09**	0.41	<.01	0.90*	0.38	.02	2.46
Proportion non-White	−0.09	0.38	.81	0.01	0.36	.97	1.01
Urbanicity	−0.01	0.04	.79	−0.02	0.05	.69	0.98
School size	0.64**	0.10	<.01	0.72**	0.11	<.01	2.05

Model 1 is OLS; Model 2 is unadjusted Poisson; Model 3 is Poisson with standard errors adjusted by the scale parameter; and Model 4 is the negative binomial model. The estimated scale parameter here is 3.51, suggesting strong overdispersion. In terms of significance, results are remarkably consistent across all approaches, but there are important differences in the implied size of the effects for key variables as well. If we focus on school size, for example, we see that the OLS model says that each 1,000 students predicts 3.93 more bullying incidents per year. The *b* of .64 in the Poisson model, interpreted as a first derivative when the number of incidents per year = 1, implies an increase of .64 x 1 = .64 incidents per year, obviously a much smaller effect. But we could also say that all of the nonlinear models here suggest that each additional 1,000 students basically doubles the *rate* of bullying incidents.

Whether one uses the additive or multiplicative approach to interpretation considerably affects the overall impression left by the results. This is an issue in all research that uses odds ratios, relative risks, or exponentiated multiplicative interpretations for relatively rare events—a situation common in research in the social sciences and epidemiology. Doubling a rate sounds impressive, but the absolute *number* of events affected may be quite small.

Concluding Words

As in the case of many of the techniques discussed so far in this book, it is often difficult to push people beyond linear and additive OLS. There has been much effort spent to show that OLS sometimes produces the same results as other techniques—and it does have some interpretive advantages. However, in many cases, using OLS amounts to producing biased estimates of the parameters we wish to estimate. The word "biased" is technical; a better synonym is "more likely to be wrong than the alternative."

We advocate using a variant of the Poisson / negative binomial models for rare events that are counted through time. We have not discussed all of these variants, including also zero-inflated Poisson models and hurdle models. However, these alternatives need to be explored in order to fit cases outside of the boundaries discussed here. Here is an example: Physician visits are often a two-step process. The first visit determines the need for further visits. As a result, visits are not independent of each other. The more complex, uncertain, or serious the initial presenting complaint, the more likely there will be further visits. The hurdle model divides the overall visit distribution into two questions: the determinants of any positive versus zero visits (a binary) and the determinants of the number of visits, given at least one. The "hurdle" is getting by the first step to the subsample addressed in the second step.

This chapter completes our discussion of generalizations of regression. Starting with a linear additive model, we first added interactions, which indicate a conditional effect of one variable depending on values of others, we added nonlinearity to accommodate what is likely to be widespread (but unexplored) violations of linearity, taking a flexible approach using splines, we then generalized the kind of dependent variables we can consider to include categorical and ordinal outcomes, allowing us to use regression to study any kind of outcome we can measure, and finally, in this chapter, we further generalized our specification of the dependent variable to include highly skewed outcomes and our specification of probability models to allow for asymmetric models for the effect of X on the probability of Y.

The cumulative flexibility—and thus analytical power—allowed by these additions should be considered in totality because the prevalent impression of regression is simply a competition among predictors in a constrained, inexorable, linear model. As we are about to see in the next chapter, this is far from the case when we start to consider how the independent variables are related to each other—when equations become "models." Our argument is that we cannot interpret regression results clearly without having a model to interpret them with, as guidance and for clarity. If we just study equations and make all predictors co-equal players, we quickly run into a myriad of ambiguities in trying to see what the results say.

Practice Questions

1. Results for this question are from a Poisson regression and a negative binomial regression of the rate of delinquent acts over the last year in a sample of 9-16 year old children in Toronto. The main focus in the analysis is the effect of the family environment, parent-child relationships, and parental statuses.

The variables in the attached output are:

- **totaldelinquency**: The dependent variable is a scale of delinquent acts, with scores from 0 to 28.
- **closectof**: The child's assessment of closeness to the father, from 1 to 4.
- **closectom**: The child's assessment of closeness to the mother, from 1 to 4.
- **parmaxeduc**: Total years of education of the parent with the maximum education.
- **pconflictfam**: A scale measuring levels of conflict in the family environment (range 7–21)
- **grades**: The child's grade performance in school, measured on a 5-point scale relative to other students.
- **parpunish**: Scale measuring extent of parental use of punishment (from 10 to 30).
- **mworkpart, mworkfull**: Dummy variables for maternal employment status, part-time and full-time, with "not working" as the reference group.

The first model is a Poisson regression with a scale parameter (Table 5.A); the second is a negative binomial regression with a test for overdispersion (Table 5.B); and the third is a negative binomial regression with a scale parameter (Table 5.C).

Answer these questions:

a. Use the test for overdispersion to decide which model to interpret.
b. Using the results from the appropriate model, interpret the effect of closeness to mother on *multiplying* the rate of delinquent acts.
c. Using the results from the appropriate model, interpret the effect of a 1-point increase in

grade level on the ***number*** of delinquent acts per year, when the number of delinquent acts is at 2.

d. There is some controversy about the effect of maternal employment on delinquency, implying that mothers who work raise the risk of delinquency in their children. What conclusion would you reach about that hypothesis in these findings?

TABLE 5.A ◆ POISSON REGRESSION WITH A SCALE PARAMETER

Model Information		
Data Set	WORK.TEMP2	
Distribution	Poisson	
Link Function	Log	
Dependent Variable	totaldelinquency	
Scale Weight Variable	famweight	weight by nativity, maternal employment, income, and kids 9 to 16

Criteria For Assessing Goodness Of Fit			
Criterion	DF	Value	Value/DF
Deviance	862	3347.1339	3.8830
Scaled Deviance	862	862.0000	1.0000
Pearson Chi-Square	862	3442.7104	3.9939
Scaled Pearson X2	862	886.6142	1.0286
Log Likelihood		507.6239	
Full Log Likelihood		−2785.5152	
AIC (smaller is better)		5589.0303	
AICC (smaller is better)		5589.2394	
BIC (smaller is better)		5631.9571	

Analysis of Maximum Likelihood Parameter Estimates				Wald 95%		Wald Chi-	
Parameter	DF	Estimate	Standard Error	Confidence Limits		Square	Pr > ChiSq
Intercept	1	2.3500	0.3777	1.6097	3.0903	38.71	<.0001
closectof	1	−0.1841	0.0471	−0.2764	−0.0919	15.30	<.0001
closectom	1	−0.2301	0.0515	−0.3310	−0.1293	19.99	<.0001
parmaxeduc	1	−0.0293	0.0107	−0.0502	−0.0083	7.47	0.0063
pconflictfam	1	0.0475	0.0120	0.0241	0.0709	15.78	<.0001
grades	1	−0.1248	0.0577	−0.2378	−0.0118	4.68	0.0304
parpunish	1	0.0410	0.0085	0.0244	0.0576	23.51	<.0001
mworkpart	1	0.2181	0.1040	0.0142	0.4219	4.40	0.0360
mworkfull	1	0.1091	0.0870	−0.0613	0.2796	1.58	0.2094
Scale	0	1.9705	0.0000	1.9705	1.9705		

TABLE 5.B ● NEGATIVE BINOMIAL REGRESSION WITH TEST FOR OVERDISPERSION

Model Information

Data Set	WORK.TEMP2
Distribution	Poisson
Link Function	Log
Dependent Variable	totaldelinquency
Scale Weight Variable	famweight weight by nativity, maternal employment, income, and kids 9 to 16

Analysis of Maximum Likelihood Parameter Estimates

Parameter	DF	Estimate	Standard Error	Wald 95% Confidence Limits		Wald Chi-Square	Pr > ChiSq
Intercept	1	2.3365	0.1947	1.9549	2.7181	144.02	<.0001
closectof	1	−0.1632	0.0242	−0.2106	−0.1158	45.53	<.0001
closectom	1	−0.1980	0.0273	−0.2516	−0.1445	52.52	<.0001
parmaxeduc	1	−0.0246	0.0056	−0.0355	−0.0137	19.59	<.0001
pconflictfam	1	0.0396	0.0063	0.0272	0.0520	39.38	<.0001
grades	1	−0.1806	0.0298	−0.2391	−0.1221	36.62	<.0001
parpunish	1	0.0427	0.0043	0.0342	0.0511	96.84	<.0001
mworkpart	1	0.1453	0.0532	0.0410	0.2497	7.46	0.0063
mworkfull	1	0.0975	0.0458	0.0079	0.1872	4.54	0.0330
Dispersion	0	0.0000	0.0000				

Lagrange Multiplier Statistics

Parameter	Chi-Square	Pr > ChiSq	
Dispersion	291.8137	<.0001	*

* One-sided p-value

TABLE 5.C ● NEGATIVE BINOMIAL REGRESSION WITH A SCALE PARAMETER

Model Information

Data Set	WORK.TEMP2
Distribution	Poisson
Link Function	Log
Dependent Variable	totaldelinquency
Scale Weight Variable	famweight weight by nativity, maternal employment, income, and kids 9 to 16

Analysis of Maximum Likelihood Parameter Estimates

Parameter	DF	Estimate	Standard Error	Wald 95% Confidence Limits		Wald Chi-Square	Pr > ChiSq
Intercept	1	2.4485	0.4500	1.5665	3.3304	29.61	<.0001
closectof	1	−0.1938	0.0599	−0.3112	−0.0763	10.45	0.0012
closectom	1	−0.2279	0.0669	−0.3590	−0.0968	11.60	0.0007
parmaxeduc	1	−0.0319	0.0124	−0.0562	−0.0077	6.69	0.0097

(Continued)

TABLE 5.C ● Continued

Parameter	DF	Estimate	Standard Error	Wald 95% Confidence Limits		Wald Chi-Square	Pr > ChiSq
pconflictfam	1	0.0472	0.0147	0.0183	0.0760	10.29	0.0013
grades	1	−0.1510	0.0681	−0.2846	−0.0175	4.91	0.0267
parpunish	1	0.0443	0.0097	0.0253	0.0634	20.75	<.0001
mworkpart	1	0.1870	0.1193	−0.0468	0.4208	2.46	0.1170
mworkfull	1	0.1079	0.0993	−0.0867	0.3025	1.18	0.2771
Dispersion	1	0.6863	0.0547	0.5871	0.8022		

Analysis of Maximum Likelihood Parameter Estimates

2. Results for this question are from the same data as Question 1, using the same dependent variable (rate of delinquent acts) and the same sample of children. Again, comparisons are made between a Poisson regression and a negative binomial regression. In this model, however, the main focus in the analysis is the child's generational status in Canada, with controls for gender, age, parental education, and maternal employment status.

The generation dummy variables are

- **firstgen**: First generation: Child foreign born and immigrated after the beginning of school
- **onepfivegen**: 1.5 generation: Child foreign born but immigrated before the beginning of school
- **secondgen**: Second generation: Child native-born, but parents foreign-born
- **twopfivegen**: 2.5 generation: Child native-born, with one parent foreign-born, and one parent native-born

The reference group for the generation dummy variables is third or later generation Canadian-born children.

The control variables are

- **female**: A dummy variable for female child (= 1 if female, = 0 if male)

- **teen**: A dummy variable for child age 13 to 16 (= 1) versus 9 to 12 (= 0)
- **parmaxeduc**: Total years of education of the parent with the maximum education
- **mworkpart, mworkfull:** Dummy variables for maternal employment status, part-time and full-time, with "not working" as the reference group

The first model is a Poisson regression with a scale a parameter (Table 5.D); the second is a negative binomial regression with a test for overdispersion (Table 5.E); and the third is a negative binomial regression with a scale parameter (Table 5.F).

Answer these questions

a. Use the test for overdispersion to decide which model to interpret.
b. Using the results from the appropriate model, interpret the effect of being a teenager on *multiplying* the rate of delinquent acts.
c. Using the results from the appropriate model, interpret the effect of being in the "twopointfive" group on the number of delinquent acts per year, when the number of delinquent acts is previously at 1.

TABLE 5.D ● POISSON REGRESSION WITH A SCALE PARAMETER

Criterion	DF	Value	Value/ DF
Deviance	836	3314.3980	3.8830
Scaled Deviance	836	836.0000	1.0000
Pearson Chi-Square	836	3441.0578	4.1161

Criteria For Assessing Goodness Of Fit

Criteria For Assessing Goodness Of Fit

Criterion	DF	Value	Value/DF
Scaled Pearson X2	836	867.9477	1.0382
Log Likelihood		464.9671	
Full Log Likelihood		−2721.7373	
AIC (smaller is better)		5463.4745	
AICC (smaller is better)		5463.7380	
BIC (smaller is better)		5510.8797	

Analysis of Maximum Likelihood Parameter Estimates

Parameter	DF	Estimate	Standard Error	Wald 95% Confidence Limits		Wald Chi-Square	Pr > ChiSq
Intercept	1	1.9931	0.1945	1.6119	2.3744	105.00	<.0001
firstgen	1	0.2332	0.1163	0.0053	0.4611	4.02	0.0449
onepfivegen	1	−0.0909	0.1300	−0.3457	0.1639	0.49	0.4843
secondgen	1	0.0480	0.0815	−0.1118	0.2077	0.35	0.5562
twopfivegen	1	0.3961	0.1143	0.1720	0.6201	12.01	0.5562
female	1	−0.5948	0.0705	−0.7329	−0.4566	71.17	<.0001
teen	1	0.5085	0.0685	0.3744	0.6427	55.19	<.0001
parmaxeduc	1	−0.0401	0.0110	−0.0617	−0.0185	13.23	0.0003
mworkpart	1	0.0920	0.1081	−0.1199	0.3039	0.72	0.3947
mworkfull		−0.0047	0.0916	−0.1843	0.1749	0.00	0.9593
Scale	0	1.9911	0.0000	1.9911	1.9911		

TABLE 5.E ● NEGATIVE BINOMIAL REGRESSION WITH TEST FOR OVERDISPERSION

Criteria For Assessing Goodness Of Fit

Criterion	DF	Value	Value/DF
Deviance	836	3178.9161	3.8025
Scaled Deviance	836	3178.9161	3.8025
Pearson Chi-Square	836	3352.1874	4.0098
Scaled Pearson X2	836	3352.1874	4.0098
Log Likelihood		1578.3184	
Full Log Likelihood		−2652.4725	
AIC (smaller is better)		5324.9450	
AICC (smaller is better)		5325.2085	
BIC (smaller is better)		5372.3502	

Analysis of Maximum Likelihood Parameter Estimates

Parameter	DF	Estimate	Standard Error	Wald 95% Confidence Limits		Wald Chi-Square	Pr > ChiSq
Intercept	1	1.8469	0.0992	1.6524	2.0413	346.58	<.0001
firstgen	1	0.1853	0.0638	0.0603	0.3103	8.45	0.0037
onepfivegen	1	−0.0514	0.0710	−0.1906	0.0878	0.52	0.4693
secondgen	1	0.0581	0.0416	−0.0235	0.1397	1.95	0.1626
twopfivegen	1	0.3562	0.0606	0.2374	0.4749	34.56	<.0001

(Continued)

TABLE 5.E ● Continued

Analysis of Maximum Likelihood Parameter Estimates							
Parameter	DF	Estimate	Standard Error	Wald 95% Confidence Limits		Wald Chi-Square	Pr > ChiSq
female	1	−0.5208	0.0359	−0.5911	-0.4504	210.36	<.0001
teen	1	0.5458	0.0352	0.4768	0.6147	240.90	<.0001
parmaxeduc	1	−0.0367	0.0056	−0.0476	-0.0258	43.46	<.0001
mworkpart	1	0.0977	0.0546	−0.0093	0.2046	3.21	0.0734
mworkfull	1	0.0208	0.0475	−0.0722	0.1138	0.19	0.6618
Dispersion	0	0.0000	0.0000				

Lagrange Multiplier Statistics			
Parameter	Chi-Square	Pr > ChiSq	
Dispersion	291.8137	<.0001	*

* One-sided p-value

TABLE 5.F ● NEGATIVE BINOMIAL REGRESSION WITH SCALE PARAMETER

Criteria For Assessing Goodness Of Fit			
Criterion	DF	Value	Value/DF
Deviance	836	1012.2257	1.2108
Scaled Deviance	836	836.0000	1.0000
Pearson Chi-Square	836	876.5552	1.0485
Scaled Pearson X2	836	723.9494	0.8660
Log Likelihood		1771.6345	
Full Log Likelihood		−2085.7023	
AIC (smaller is better)		4193.4047	
AICC (smaller is better)		4193.7212	
BIC (smaller is better)		4245.5504	

Analysis of Maximum Likelihood Parameter Estimates							
Parameter	DF	Estimate	Standard Error	Wald 95% Confidence Limits		Wald Chi-Square	Pr > ChiSq
Intercept	1	1.9596	0.2213	1.5259	2.3933	78.42	<.0001
firstgen	1	0.1821	0.1445	−0.1011	0.4654	1.59	0.2076
onepfivegen	1	−0.0022	0.1444	−0.2853	0.2809	0.00	0.9878
secondgen	1	0.0575	0.0922	−0.1232	0.2381	0.39	0.5329
twopfivegen	1	0.3757	0.1405	0.1002	0.6512	7.15	0.0075
female	1	−0.5727	0.0782	−0.7260	-0.4194	53.61	<.0001
teen	1	0.5620	0.0797	0.4057	0.7182	49.69	<.0001
parmaxeduc	1	−0.0408	0.0124	−0.0652	-0.0165	10.78	0.0010
mworkpart	1	0.0520	0.1241	−0.1911	0.2952	0.18	0.6750
mworkfull	1	0.0014	0.1044	−0.2031	0.2060	0.00	0.9890
Dispersion	1	0.7017	0.0570	0.5984	0.8229		

3. In Table 5.G Montazer and Wheaton (2011) show the results of a Poisson regression (pre-publication version) of the combined effects of the generational status of children and the gross national product (GNP, in three groups) of the parental country of origin, on the log rate of their externalizing and internalizing symptoms. These symptom counts are totals over the last six months.

In the table, generation is categorized as first (foreign-born children), second (parents are foreign-born, child is Canadian born), and 2.5 (one foreign-born parent, one Canadian-born, child is Canadian born). GNP is categorized as upper, middle, and lower. Nine groups are formed from these combinations, with the reference group being Canadian-born third or later generation.

Answer these questions:

a. Using results in Model 4 for externalizing symptoms, calculate the effect of being a first generation child from a lower GNP background on multiplying the rate of expected symptoms, and interpret in words.

b. Using Model 4 for internalizing symptoms, calculate the effect of being a 2.5 generation child from a lower GNP background on multiplying the rate of expected symptoms, and interpret in words.

c. Using Model 4 for externalizing symptoms, calculate the effect of mother's education on the **number** of externalizing symptoms for a person with one symptom, and interpret in words.

TABLE 5.G ● POISSON REGRESSION OF EXTERNALIZING AND INTERNALIZING SYMPTOMS BY GENERATIONAL STATUS AND COUNTRY OF ORIGIN

Effects:	Externalizing Symptoms				Internalizing Symptoms			
	(1)	(2)	(3)	(4)	(1)	(2)	(3)	(4)
1. Generation only [a]								
First	−.043				−.032			
Second	.112				−.044			
Two point five (2.5)	.129				.052			
2. Generation/ GNP [a]								
First Upper		.177	.071	.063		.085	.037	.040
First Middle		.147	.019	−.052		−.082	−.272	−.367**
First *Lower*		−.177*	−.315***	−.414***		−.046	−.216*	−.331***
Second Upper		.161	.122	.086		−.138	−.093	−.141
Second Middle		.127	.041	−.084		.050	−.033	−.158
Second Lower		.072	.034	−.046		−.064	−.074	−.163
2.5 Upper		.117	.078	.067		−.039	−.033	−.056
2.5 Middle		.008	.012	−.066		.107	.053	−.018
2.5 Lower		.284*	.312**	.248*		.320**	.323**	.288*

(Continued)

TABLE 5.G ● Continued

Effects:	Externalizing Symptoms				Internalizing Symptoms			
	(1)	(2)	(3)	(4)	(1)	(2)	(3)	(4)
Plus:								
3. Controls								
Female			−.172***	−.165***			.140**	.142**
Child 12 to 13 years old[b]			.141*	.145**			−.320***	−.304***
Child 14 to 16 years old[b]			.260***	.272***			−.203***	−.198***
Foreign-born mother had affect prob. before Canada			.249**	.258**			.363***	.355***
Canadian born mother had affect prob. before 24			.255	.264*			.305*	.318*
Mother's Education			−.028***	−.026**			−.015	−.013
Household Income			−.001	−.001			−.003***	−.003***
4. Ethnic/Racial Groups								.291**
Black				.300**				.158*
Mediterranean				.150*				.521***
Middle East				.218				.285*
East Asian Pacific Rim				.344**				.087
Mixed				.176*				
Deviance	2934.16	2893.32	2681.16	2627.53	2701.25	2669.75	2421.12	2358.42
DF	834	828	821	816	833	827	820	815
N	838	838	838	838	837	837	837	837

Source: Montazer, S., & Wheaton, B. (2011). The impact of generation and country of origin on the mental health of children of immigrants. *Journal of Health and Social Behavior, 52(1) 23–42.*

4. (4 points) Results are attached for a Poisson regression and a negative binomial regression of frequency of smoking in the last week among 9- to 16-year old children in Toronto (Table 5.H). The four predictors are:
   - **femchild**: A dummy variable = 1 for female child, 0 for male
   - **kidage**: The child's age in years
   - **grades**: The quintile of the child's grades in his or her class (1 = lowest to 5 = highest)
   - **parclose**: Closeness to parents (varies from 1 to 8)

The confidence limits for the dispersion parameter test whether there would be overdispersion in the Poisson model and are printed in the results for the negative binomial model. If confidence limits include the value 0, then the null hypothesis of equidispersion cannot be rejected, but if they do not, the alternative of overdispersion can be "accepted."

Answer these questions:

a. From the results for the dispersion parameter, decide which model is preferable in this situation.

b. Interpret the effect of grades on smoking in the last week by (a) transforming the coefficient to allow an interpretation of the effect of each quintile in grades on the expected frequency of smoking and (b) interpreting the effect of a 1-quintile increase in grades at the third quintile (= 3) in terms of percentage change in expected frequency of smoking.

TABLE 5.H ● POISSON AND NEGATIVE BINOMIAL REGRESSIONS OF THE FREQUENCY OF SMOKING

Poisson Regression

The GENMOD Procedure

Model Information

Data Set	WORK.TEMP
Distribution	Poisson
Link Function	Log
Dependent Variable	smoking

Criteria for Assessing Goodness of Fit

Criterion	DF	Value	Value/DF
Deviance	835	529.8272	0.6345
Scaled Deviance	835	529.8272	0.6345
Pearson Chi-Square	835	1022.4170	1.2245
Scaled Pearson X2	835	1022.4170	1.2245
Log Likelihood		−281.3475	

Analysis Of Parameter Estimates

Parameter	DF	Estimate	Standard Error	Wald 95% Confidence Limits		Chi-Square	Pr > ChiSq
Intercept	1	−7.3889	−0.9390	9.2293	−5.5485	61.92	<.0001
femchild	1	0.3575	0.1636	0.0368	0.6782	4.77	0.0289
kidage	1	0.6146	0.0532	0.5103	0.7190	133.29	<.0001
grades	1	−0.5144	0.0972	−0.7049	−0.3239	28.01	<.0001
parclose	1	−0.2801	0.1085	−0.4928	−0.0675	6.67	0.0098
Scale	0	1.0000	0.0000	1.0000	1.0000		

NOTE: The scale parameter was held fixed.

(Continued)

TABLE 5.H ● Continued

Negative Binomial Regression

The GENMOD Procedure

Model Information

Data Set	WORK.TEMP
Distribution	Negative Binomial
Link Function	Log
Dependent Variable	smoking

Number of Observations Read	888
Number of Observations Used	840
Missing Values	48

Criteria for Assessing Goodness of Fit

Criterion	DF	Value	Value/DF
Deviance	835	231.4189	0.2771
Scaled Deviance	835	231.4189	0.2771
Pearson Chi-Square	835	564.3509	0.6759
Scaled Pearson X2	835	564.3509	0.6759
Log Likelihood		−226.1792	

Algorithm converged.

Analysis of Parameter Estimates

Parameter	DF	Estimate	Standard Error	Wald 95% Confidence Limits		Chi-Square	Pr > ChiSq
Intercept	1	−8.0648	1.4390	−10.8852	−5.2443	31.41	<.0001
femchild	1	0.4573	0.2666	−0.0653	0.9799	2.94	0.0863
kidage	1	0.6830	0.0809	0.5245	0.8416	71.29	<.0001
grades	1	−0.4582	0.1672	−0.7859	−0.1305	7.51	0.0061
parclose	1	−0.4431	0.1954	−0.8261	−0.0602	5.14	0.0233
Dispersion	1	3.7348	0.8242	2.1195	5.3502		

NOTE: The negative binomial dispersion parameter was estimated by maximum likelihood

FROM EQUATIONS TO MODELS

The Process of Explanation

This chapter is not about statistical models per se—in fact, it is more of a "theory" chapter. It is also an essential chapter that speaks to *all* of the previous chapters on regression. Accepting what we have discussed so far, there is a basic problem. In many to most regression applications, the independent variables are related to each other so that some are in fact dependent variables with respect to other independent variables. As a result, the effects of *some* independent variables are more "hidden" than others, mainly because part of their effect is transmitted through other variables in the equation. Pretending this is not the case simply obscures the relative roles of different independent variables in explaining a dependent variable, and it renders ambiguous the meaning of the regression coefficients.

What do we do? The entire focus in this chapter is on the interpretation of results from regression equations, using a widely adopted logic for understanding the "process of explanation." But we take this perspective further in this chapter than is usually discussed in books about statistics. We take a very specific position on the role of causality in understanding regression results. We will not consider all of the recent variations in the implementation of methods to assess causality (Morgan & Winship, 2007; Pearl, 2009b); instead, we stick to more generic **conceptual requirements** of causality. This means that we try to avoid defining causality specifically with reference to a particular methodological framework or technique—in other words, causality is not a method. Our definition overlaps with many existing definitions, but it does have some unique elements that are important to the application of causality in the social and behavioral sciences.

This chapter has three fundamental premises: (1) Regression equations and structural equation models raise the issue of causality, by definition; (2) the study of individual outcomes—that is, single equations—necessarily results in interpretive ambiguity; and

(3) it is **always** better to think in terms of models than equations. A *model* is any multi-equation representation of process, in which at least one variable appears both as an independent and a dependent variable.

Of course, our claim is that most researchers *do* think in terms of models by arraying their results in a specific sequence of issues, sometimes referred to as the "progressive adjustment" model (Mirowsky, 2013). Here we advocate that we make this causal thinking explicit in our work, in order to be clear about our claims in research.

6.1 WHAT IS WRONG WITH EQUATIONS?

We start with the assumption that studying equations in terms of a competition of predictors is inherently misleading. This statement means, in effect, that research in which the goal is to explain a single dependent variable in terms of "free-for-all" group of independent predictors is fundamentally ambiguous in interpretation.

The problem derives from the fact that not all independent variables are created equal. The fact that some may be dependent on other independent variables in the equation implies an unspecified process leading to the dependent variable in question. The study of *process* is inherent in the interpretation of the results of estimating any equation. But we often have no guidelines about the steps in a process from thinking in terms of a single equation.

Instead, we need to think in terms of models that embody process. Without an appropriate distinction between mediating variables and control (i.e., confounding), variables—defined later—research is doomed to ambiguities that promote confusion.

6.1.1 Regression as a Competition among Predictors

The model in Figure 6.1 represents the strict "all variables are created equal" approach to regression. We recognize this is a "straw man," and yet many presentations of regression implicitly presume this model. In this approach, each variable is interpreted as having an equal chance to affect the outcome; they are confounded to a degree, but we conceive of this as a correlation whose effects we want to remove—no more and no less. As a result, the estimated coefficient in

FIGURE 6.1 ⬤ REGRESSION AS A COMPETITION AMONG PREDICTORS

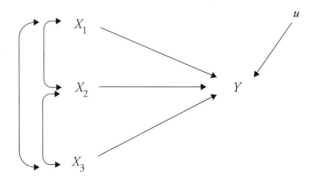

the regression is simply the net *direct effect* of the variable on the outcome, controlling for confounding of any and all types. Part of its **actual** effect may be hidden in correlations with other independent variables, if a particular variable first impacts these other variables, and in turn those variables also affect the outcome.

In this diagram, single-headed arrows represent causal effects, and double-headed arrows represent correlation only. The *X*s are three independent variables; *Y* is dependent;. "*u*" is an error term in the equation for *Y*.

6.2 EQUATIONS VERSUS MODELS: SOME EXAMPLES

6.2.1 The Difference Between Direct Effects and Total Effects

From the literature on social support as a "buffer" of stress, consider this hypothetical example derived from an actual published example—but with specific coefficients altered to make our point clearly and with names withheld to protect the "guilty." The example begins with a regression showing that stress affects levels of depression with a standardized coefficient of .24. The authors hypothesize that social support reduces the impact of stress and that stress activates social support from others.

They control for social support in a regression, with the results shown in Table 6.1.

TABLE 6.1 ⬣ AN ADDITIVE MODEL FOR STRESS AND SOCIAL SUPPORT	
	Coefficient
Stress	0.08
Social Support	−0.40

They conclude that support has reduced the impact of stress because the effect of stress is now .08. Why is this wrong? The answer is this: Because it fails to see that the total impact of stress has **not** been changed if social support is an intervening variable activated by the presence of stress.

We can see this in the form of a causal model, embodying the argument in the article (Figure 6.2).

Note the effect of stress on support equals −.40. This is hidden by the single equation approach. We could estimate another equation with support as the dependent variable, but then we would have a model. This effect here is plausible but is the opposite of what is often predicted—that is, stress is thought to activate support, not deplete it.

FIGURE 6.2 ⬣ PARSING THE TOTAL EFFECT OF STRESS

The results overall show that stress affects distress in two ways—that is, by two pathways, each ending in changes to distress.

So when stress increases by 1 unit, the results are as follows:

It has a "direct effect" on distress	= .08
It has an "indirect effect" on distress, due to the −.40 reduction in support leading to a (−.40*−.40) effect on distress	= .16
Thus, the actual "total effect" is	= .24

In fact, the effect of stress has not changed at all. Part of it has been "re-routed" by including an intervening variable that expresses part of the *reason* stress affects distress. This indirect effect was buried in the total effect originally estimated (*b* = .24). In this model, this total effect is divided between a direct effect and an indirect effect.

The crucial element of this model is the indirect effect of stress through support. To understand the logic of the indirect effect, we can interpret it this way:

1. A 1-unit increase in support reduces distress by .4 units.

2. Stress reduces support by .4 units.

3. As a result, we observe a proportion of the usual effect of support on distress—in fact, −.4 of its usual −.4 effect resulting from a full 1-unit change, resulting in a −.4 * −.4 = .16 change in distress.

6.2.2 When a "Control" Variable Is Not a Control Variable

In an article in the epidemiological literature on the effect of family structure on conduct disorder in children (again we alter the actual coefficients to make a point and withhold the names of the authors), the authors "control for" the effect of household income.

What is the logic of doing this? Presumably, we want to make sure that we do not attribute an effect to single parent status when it is due to household income. In other words, in the perspective taken in the article, the effect of single parent status may in part be due to a more fundamental causal process starting with lower household income, which may both affect the risk of disorder and the risk of single parent status (inversely). Using the logic of this argument, the implied model is shown in Figures 6.3A and 6.3B: Figure 6.3A represents the generic argument about confounding; Figure 6.3B represents the explicit argument about income as a control.

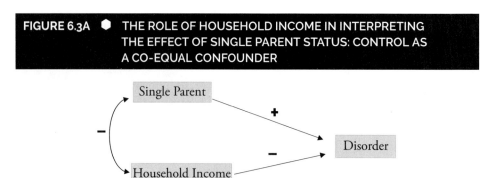

FIGURE 6.3A ● THE ROLE OF HOUSEHOLD INCOME IN INTERPRETING THE EFFECT OF SINGLE PARENT STATUS: CONTROL AS A CO-EQUAL CONFOUNDER

FIGURE 6.3B ⬡ THE ROLE OF HOUSEHOLD INCOME IN INTERPRETING THE EFFECT OF SINGLE PARENT STATUS: CONTROL AS A BACKGROUND COMMON CAUSE

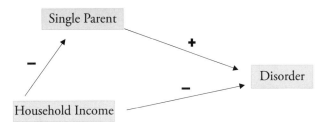

Household income only works as a re-interpretation of the relationship between being a single parent and disorder *if* it acts as a common cause of both (as in Figure 6.3B). Then it clearly plays the role of the "real" cause, suggesting ***spuriousness*** in the relationship between single parent status and disorder. In fact, it could be even more misleading to control for household income because the first version above (Figure 6.3A) includes the possibility that single-parent status is a cause of household income. To the degree that single-parent status reflects the onset of divorce, we know this is a very real possibility.

As a result, this model may be seriously misspecified if household income is as much or more affected *by* single parent status than it affects the risk of single parent status in the first place. In the re-specified model, household income appears as a mediator of the relationship between single parent status and conduct disorder in children, as shown in Figure 6.4.

FIGURE 6.4 ⬡ HOUSEHOLD INCOME AS A MEDIATOR

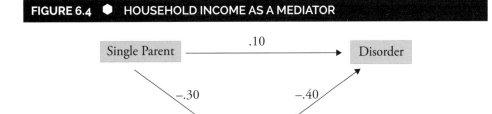

If this model is correct, then the interpretation that the effect of single parent status, controlling for household income, is only .10 is simply wrong. In fact, using the calculation from the previous example, its effect is what we see in Table 6.2.

TABLE 6.2 ⬡ THE DIRECT AND INDIRECT EFFECT OF SINGLE-PARENT STATUS

Direct	= .10
Indirect: −.30 * −.40	= .12
Total effect	= .22

You will not see this from the regression equation, where the coefficient for single parent status is .10 and you will not see it if you assume a variable operates as a "confounder" (control) for the relationship rather than as a mediating explanatory factor. In both models, the relevant effect we must understand is the ***total effect*** of a variable, not just its direct effect. Household income acts to help understand how the effect occurs, but it does not challenge the causal role of single parent status.

In both examples, the regression coefficient is misleading. In the first example, it goes from .24 to .08 when support is controlled, but its total effect has not changed. In the second example, the assumed model may be misspecified, and so the direct effect of .10 may not be the total effect.

Of course, the likelihood is that both examples are too simple. For example, it is likely that income both affects the risk of single-parent status and is affected in turn by it. This kind of dynamic requires, at the minimum, a longitudinal model. If income plays both roles, then it is likely that the effect of single-parent status is partially explained by the common dependence of this status and conduct disorder in children on this prior cause, but it is also likely that the loss of income resulting from transitions to single parent status may in part explain the connection between single-parent status and conduct problems. The two possibilities are not mutually exclusive.

In general, we can only fully understand the roles of a set of variables if we posit how they are interrelated *in a process*. Otherwise, we are stuck with the ambiguity caused by attempting to interpret one or a series of regression equations but without a clear model as a starting point. In the approach adopted in this chapter, *it is more important to be clear than it is to be correct!*

6.3 WHY CAUSALITY?

In 1965, a conference on the concept of causality (Lerner, 1965) included presentations on the nature of causality from prominent representatives of a wide range of disciplines. The discussant was the philosopher of science, Ernest Nagel. Without reviewing the substance of the debates involved, the tone of the various presentations was striking: Causality was a difficult, even ephemeral, concept to capture in research, and thus many disclaimed the use of causal language. Nagel's response was just as striking. His comments, in so many words, basically said this: Although the word "cause" may not be used explicitly, much, if not most, of the work he reviewed across disciplines used ***causal thinking*** regularly. As a result, there is a disjunction between the causal thinking driving much of what is claimed theoretically and the pre-causal and therefore "careful" interpretation of results. In this disjunction, "careful" turns into unclear.

6.3.1 Causal Claims and Causal Evidence

In this chapter and throughout this book, we make a distinction between *causal claims* and *causal evidence*. The two are often confused. Causal claims are misinterpreted as claims on evidence, when in fact they are just consistent with the logic and/or structure of the analytical techniques used or what is predicted by a theoretical perspective. For example, it is often claimed that you cannot refer to causality in cross-sectional data because there is no way to decide causation. But you can because the point is to make causal claims that clarify what you are and *are not* saying.

We encourage the use of causal claims, even in cross-sectional data, primarily because the grounds for proving findings wrong are only defined in the context of causal language. Saying a variable is a confounder, thus leading to control of that variable, does not fully tell us what kind of confounding role it plays. Being explicit about that role can be revealing. For example, many articles state a list of controls, citing prior evidence for their effect on the dependent variable. But this is not enough, since the role of confounding also implies this variable affects X in the equation as well.

There is widespread misunderstanding about what is being claimed when interpreting regression results causally. These are usually not statements of evidence—simply what is implied by the implicit model you have in mind. It is a matter of being explicit and consistent with the inherent *structure* of that model.

On the other hand, we believe that many designs, not just statistics, include varying degrees of causal information. We do not take the position that there is only one model for studying causation, simply because that position dismisses the information in models or designs with uncertain or multiple interpretations. It is possible, for example, that over time, across measures and designs and samples, evidence for causal inference is accumulating when results are consistent. Following the famous work of Campbell and Stanley (1964), it is possible to see that some designs contain more causal information than others, just by virtue of their structure and logic.

6.3.2 Causality versus Association

Much of the debate around use of the term causality revolves around a distinction between causal and associational analysis. For example, Pearl (2009a), as well as others, argues that regression is strictly a statistical technique and thus is restricted on its own to the study of association while causal analysis "goes one step further" (2009a, p. 99) because it is specifically concerned with change under changing conditions, such as with experimental treatments. Of course, regression is not restricted to studying static conditions—far from it. Most of the techniques we discuss in this book use some kind of regression framework to study or take analytical advantage of change. It is helpful to distinguish in this debate between the statistical model used and the design of the research and its accompanying structural characteristics: Regression is not restricted to cross-sectional surveys, obviously.

Some argue that regression is basically and only about describing the "conditional distribution" of Y, given X. This would be the case if our sole intention was to predict Y. Our starting assumption, however, is that regression is conceived and applied primarily as a kind of structural model rather than simply describing associations between X and Y. In the regression model, we interpret b as the ***effect*** of a 1-unit increase in X on changes in Y. The notion that the b in a regression model is not a structural coefficient is a fine semantic point while ignoring key basic analytical features of the regression model. The widely heard and repeated dictum that "correlation is not causation" ignores a substantial range of differences in causal information resulting from differences in design, measures, and samples.

We take the position that regression naturally expresses *some* of the basic definitional components of what is supposed to be involved in causality, and thus, regression is one form of expressing the possibility of causality. First and foremost, the regression model captures one of the starting requirements of causality: The relationship between X and Y is asymmetric; Y *depends* on X. Let us not mistake reciprocal asymmetry as symmetry: Reciprocal causation describes two asymmetrical relationships. Given this, it is actually difficult to understand "symmetry" as anything other than a synonym for association, signifying no particular precedence in the relationship between X and Y. To equate the notion of association with regression, therefore, removes one of its defining characteristics. Second, in practice, researchers usually attempt to be careful about ensuring that the independent variables are causally prior to the dependent variable. This is done in a variety of ways—including establishing temporality through use of longitudinal data, citing previous findings, arguing from theory, or even relying on differences in the nature of the variables involved. This attention to causal priority signals the fact that researchers are using regression as a tool to promote causal reasoning. Third, some forms of regression take specific advantage of features of research design to address some of the fundamental issues in causality—for example, alternative explanations of the relationship between X and Y. Unless the design is a "true" experiment, what is achieved in these cases is partial, but we should understand that the glass is half (somewhat?) full, not empty. Our concern is that we keep looking for definitive cases for studying causality without reasoning that there is already partial causal information in existing data. In the approach taken in this book, we assume that longitudinal methods take us on the road to causality because they induce temporal order and allow for tests of reciprocity while not delivering us at that destination. Causality needs to be considered as a probabilistic continuum rather than a categorical truth.

6.4 CRITERIA FOR CAUSALITY

The history of the discussion of causality in the social sciences often invokes a particular method as an ideal representation of causality. This may be the randomized experiment (Campbell & Stanley, 1964) or the counterfactual model (Morgan & Winship, 2015). While both methods may be efficient at testing causality, we must remember that causality is a *concept* and cannot be reduced to the particulars of any one method. This in turn implies that the terms of defining causality must exist apart from the framework of any one method. All methods are different potential routes to uncovering causality; some are much more efficient than others.

Here we review what we see as the basic and necessary components of a concept of causality "in use" in the social and behavioral sciences. We attempt to make these criteria as generic as possible—that is, not tied to the requirements of a single method but applicable across methods and types of analysis. Even though some of the words we use sound like they are specifically about statistical models (e.g., spuriousness), in fact, their meaning in the process of discovering causality applies across a range of methods. We rely on an amalgamation of criteria from Duncan's (1975) book on causal models, Bollen's (1989) book on structural equation models, discussions of causality in the philosophy of science (Bunge, 1959) and in sociology (Marini & Singer, 1988), and Hill's criteria for causality in epidemiology (1965). We avoid, however, criteria that apply only to a specific subject area. Most of the criteria we use are well-known, a few are unique.

Why bother with a detailed account of the criteria for causality? The answer to this question informs most of the interpretive language of this book: Because the social sciences need to have a general and usable concept of causality *that takes into account the realities of causation in the social world.* This means a concept of causality that does not require experimentation for its legitimacy, thus enfranchising many to most of the concepts in social science that cannot be manipulated; does not rely on specifics of a single method such as the potential outcome model (Morgan & Winship, 2015) where the concept of causality is defined in terms of the conceptual framework of the method; and does not use logic to define the terms of causal inference.

6.4.1 Criteria for the Social Sciences

1. *Asymmetry*

    Causality starts from the idea of an asymmetric relationship between X and Y where "asymmetric" implies one takes precedence over the other—one produces change in the other. As noted above, association implies the absence of causation by making X and Y functionally equal partners in the relationship.

2. ***Substantive Plausibility***

An argument must be available that provides a rationale, a mechanism, for the effect of X on Y and therefore makes the relationship at least plausible or understandable. Often this argument can be seen as positing an intervening (mediating) variable, which represents the middle stage of a process linking X to Y. Obviously, invocation of this criterion is simply a way of discounting the myriad possible examples of nonsense correlations that surface in empirical work. But this criterion raises a difficult issue at the same time: How can we argue the plausibility of a truly unknown cause? The answer to that question is that suggesting a cause entails an imagined process linking that cause to the effect: It is not a random cognition. Articulation of this process should be possible, even if only imagined.

3. ***A (Meaningful) Significant Total Effect of* X *on* Y***

An often cited criterion for causality is observed covariance between X and Y. But this criterion is stated in general terms and can be misinterpreted in two ways. One problem is that piece-by-piece requirements of covariance in a causal chain make possible an infinite regress—in other words, a trivialized definition of causation. If A covaries with B, B covaries with C, and C covaries with D, one can build a causal argument that A is a cause of D. But endless indirect links, each individually meaningful, do not automatically describe a "causal chain."

This requirement states that A must have an observable "total effect" on D—that is, an overall effect on changing D—or else we admit trivial cases to the realm of causation. If the original change in A has no effect on D at the end of the chain, A cannot be a cause of D. Note that this requirement says nothing about the intervening processes involved.

This criterion is more specific in another way than the general requirement of covariance. We could have stated the requirement in terms of a significant overall covariance between A and D, but this version retains the language of association. We prefer to state the requirement implying the causal precedence of X. However, it is true that the total effect and the covariance amount to the same thing—before there are controls in the model.

Note that the "significant total effect" criterion can be tested by purposely leaving out all intervening variables (in a causal chain) in a regression equation.

4. ***Causal Priority***

Causal priority can be established in various ways and not just by the temporal ordering of X and Y. Although this criterion is often reduced to the issue of temporal order, temporal order is not the only way in which causal priority occurs, and it is often misunderstood in actual use.

The most common way in which temporal order is misunderstood derives from the misunderstanding that the measured states of X and Y in the present—as in a cross-sectional survey—do not reflect when each variable last changed. Thus, cross-sectional one-time-only surveys may be interpreted as noncausal in part because X and Y are only measured in the present. However, the important issue is which variable changed first and which last. Some variables reach a final value early in the life course; others change throughout adulthood. This fact can be incorporated into our understanding of causal priority.

We cite four ways of establishing causal priority:

a. ***Temporal ordering:*** Clear time ordering of X and Y. This is most easily achieved in longitudinal panel surveys where the same variables are measured over time. But the issue is trickier than it seems. Simply using a past measure of X to predict the current state of Y does establish temporal order, but it does not take into account the effects of past states of Y that could affect both the past state of X and the current value of Y. This could allow for the past effect of Y on X to be manifest as the effect of past X on current Y. As a result, it is generally preferable to also control for past (lagged) states of Y.

b. ***Logical causal precedence:*** Even without time-ordering, sometimes causal priority can be determined by the nature of the variables—that is, X usually or predominantly does not change, but Y can (e.g., gender and job income, ethnicity and political behavior, race and job discrimination, etc.). Basically, this criterion states that (essentially) stable variables must be causally prior to time-varying variables. Some will find this criterion controversial, but it is necessary in order to allow fixed or stable variables as causal sources of outcomes.

   This is important in many important cases in the social sciences. Gender cannot be the source of job discrimination unless we allow gender to be causal. A less obvious example involves race and social class. Many investigators treat these two variables as implicitly co-equal, but they are not. Controlling for social class in an equation attempting to isolate the effects of race on life outcomes actually underestimates the impact of race because *race is a cause of social class*, due to systemic and multi-generational discrimination.

c. ***Life course timing of events:*** Many events in the life course are quite strictly scheduled, even though there are also exceptions. Causal assumptions can take advantage of this fact. The causal ordering of a *main* or *initial* educational period early in life and job income later in life is clear. The ordering of childhood neighborhood and adult functioning is clear. The effect of first job characteristics after education on later job characteristics follows a clear sequence. The effect of parental drinking while growing up on one's own later drinking, of parental divorce during childhood on the risk of one's own divorce, follow a clear temporal order.

   It is important to realize in making these statements that we do not refer to the difficulties in reporting past events, which is a measurement issue. If measurement is valid, the causal ordering expressed in these examples is self-evident.

d. ***Valid separation of reciprocal causal effects:*** Even in cross-sectional data and when the effect of X on Y is short-term or "instantaneous," methods exist that claim to separate the effect of X on Y from the effect of Y on X. These "simultaneous equation models" are a type of structural equation model. If assumptions about the unique causation of X and Y from past variables holds, then the causal direction of X on Y can be distinguished from the opposite case.

   Note that a simple OLS regression using Y to predict X does nothing to inform this problem because that second regression makes assumptions that contradict the regression for the effect of X on Y.

5. ***Lack of spuriousness (i.e., no explanation by prior causes)***

   This criterion is the *sine qua non* of establishing causality. All past and current methods do something to address this problem, some better than others.

   The issue of spuriousness arises because both X and Y may depend on prior causes, and if these relationships are strong enough, we may find that there is no inherent causal connection between X and Y. Literally, in this case, some individual or set of related past variables Z combine to explain the covariance between X and Y entirely. How does this happen? One obvious example is that Z increase levels of both X and Y, thus precipitating a covariance between them. Formally, this criterion can be stated this way: There exists no individual or set of related prior causes of X and Y that give rise to the covariance between X and Y.

The reason this is such a difficult criterion to fulfill is the fact that it is difficult to conceive of all of the possible common prior causes, and most designs only successfully account for some of these common causes.

6. *Generalizability*

Generalizability does not refer simply to inferences to a larger population. Instead, this criterion refers to the need to have reproducible findings in other samples, other populations, using other designs, and possibly different but equivalent measures. Generalizability occurs cumulatively over studies and requires *consistency* of the basic finding. Any broadening of the sample studied or replication over time suggests greater generalizability.

The fact that this criterion is necessary is exemplified by the argument that smoking causes cancer. Original findings suggesting this link had to cumulate over time, designs, and samples before the notion of causation was accepted. But there is no clear threshold of reproducibility and consistency that defines the inference that a relationship is causal. Importantly, however, the counter-argument that the relationship is noncausal eventually becomes practically impossible to maintain, and thus we know that threshold has been reached.

7. *Indirect causation*

Indirect causation is defined by the fact that X causes Y through intermediate processes. Most of social causation is likely to be indirect. We assert that indirect causation is consistent with the overall concept of causality.

This claim may be controversial in some fields. In medicine, for example, it is often the last cause in the chain that is seen as "the" cause. However, causal starting points in multi-step processes are no less causal—simply more difficult to detect.

We note that there is an argument in the philosophy of science that all causation beyond the physical world is by necessity indirect (Bunge, 1959; Marini & Singer, 1988). This criterion therefore draws our attention to causal origins and less to the most proximal precipitating cause, which only appears because of the original cause.

6.4.2 Excluded Criteria

Referring back to the more general concept of causality fashioned around the physical sciences (Bunge, 1959), we must also exclude some criteria that make causality by definition incompatible with the probabilistic and multivariate notion of causation in the social sciences:

- *Uniqueness of the cause to the effect or of the effect to the cause:* These requirements imagine that each effect may have a unique cause or that each cause has one and only one effect. These requirements make probabilistic causation inherently ambiguous. Fundamentally, these requirements are antithetical to the proper understanding of how social causes work: Social causes can have many consequences, and each outcome can have many causes. The principle of the *disjunctive plurality of causes* says that one of many different cause may be sufficient to precipitate Y, under different circumstances, and the principle of *conjunctive plurality of causes* says that a set of multiple causes of Y must be present before Y occurs.

- **Complete determinism**: Ultimate determinism is unnecessary to the concept of causality as practiced; in fact, error is explicitly acknowledged and always occupies a place in all of the techniques we use. This is interpreted here as *not* a passing fact but instead an inherent statement about the social world.

  This is a widely misunderstood issue: Methods that are sometimes rendered as "deterministic" actually leave a (large) space for unknowable causes that do not replicate across situations—the error term. In fact, our results often remind us how incomplete our best deterministic models are, achieving maybe 30% of the explained variance in Y.

6.5 THE ANALYTICAL ROLES OF VARIABLES IN CAUSAL MODELS

As defined earlier, a model is defined by the fact that it embodies a process, in which a dependent variable at one stage of the process is an independent variable at a later stage of the process. A model almost always revolves around a particular focal association, which defines a relationship of interest between X and Y. The roles of other variables in the model derive from their relationships to both X and Y in the model and their influence on this focal association.

6.5.1 Focal Association

A model often starts with the desire to understand a focal association between an X and a Y, most commonly measured as a correlation or a covariance between them or a significant bivariate effect of X on Y in a regression. We want to know, what accounts for this relationship?

In this case, we define

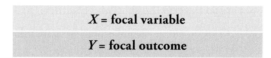

X = **focal variable**

Y = **focal outcome**

To understand the X–Y relationship, we define the possible roles of other variables with respect to this association. We refer to the link between X and Y as an association at this point because we don't yet know whether it is causal. The total association could arise from many forces at work, including prior common causes giving rise to the association.

This discussion below assumes the relationship between X and Y is positive, to simplify the distinctions. But every distinction used here applies to inverse relationships as well.

6.5.2 Roles of Other Variables

1. **Mediating variables** (M) are intervening variables that help to explicate (explain) the nature of the effect of X on Y. Their role is to express part or all of the transmission of the effect of X on Y. Sometimes these variables are also called *mechanisms* for the causal effect, or explanatory variables. Rationales in theories posit mediating variables.

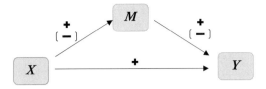

In this diagram, X affects Y through two pathways: directly and indirectly through resulting changes in M due to the change in X. The plus signs denote positive relationships; the minus signs denote negative relationships.

The diagram shows that the mediator must have relationships with both X and Y that together operate in the same direction as the overall focal association. In this case, where the X–Y association is positive, either X must affect M positively and M must affect Y positively, or both relationships are negative (amounting to a positive indirect effect). To convince yourself of the latter, use this reasoning: X causes M to decrease, and then because M and Y are inversely related, the decrease in M causes Y to increase. The net result is that the increase in X results in an increase in Y. In the earlier example, the effect of stress on distress was mediated by social support. This was actually due to the fact that stress caused a decrease in support and that loss of support from others then led to an increase in distress.

If the X – Y association is negative, then there are two possibilities for mediation: Either X affects M positively while M affects Y negatively, or X affects M negatively while M affects Y positively—both amounting to a negative indirect effect consistent with the overall association.

It is important to understand that variables whose impact operates in a direction opposite to the X–Y association cannot be mediators. They are more commonly known as suppressors and are discussed separately later.

2. ***Control variables*** (C) are prior common causes of both X and Y that may render the relationship between X and Y as wholly or partially spurious. C must be causally prior to both X and Y.

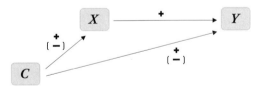

This model says that a variable C precedes both X and Y and affects X and Y in such a way to give rise to part or all of the association between X and Y, a condition suggesting that the relationship between X and Y is "spurious." What does this mean interpretively? The diagram shows that C may either increase both X and Y or decrease both X and Y. In both cases, C is causing X and Y to change *in the same direction*, giving rise to a positive association between them. In this case, X is not the "real" cause of Y, and our attention should shift to C, a more basic (fundamental) cause of Y.

As we discuss below in an extended example, many (to most) analyses published in journals consider control variables as the first issue of importance. The reason is as follows: If there is no evidence of even a potentially causal effect of X on Y, then we should not be trying to explain that effect by testing the role of mediators.

Note again that a control variable should operate in the same direction as the overall association. If it does not, it suppresses the association, and its effect needs to be removed before we consider whether there is a net overall association in the opposite direction. The same general sign rules apply for controls as for mediators: If the association is negative, C must either positively affect X while negatively affecting Y or negatively affect X while positively affecting Y.

3. **Modifier variables** (Mo) define a condition or range of conditions under which the effect of X occurs. These variables are those that interact with X. Modifiers act to change the actual total effect of X on Y.

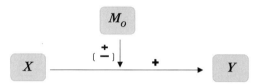

In this diagram, the effect of M_O is shown as directly impacting the effect of X on Y. This impact may be positive or negative. These variables are often referred to as "moderators" in the research literature. This is a misleading term, however, since it implies that this variable only dampens the relationship between X and Y—that is, the interaction is negative. Though this is a seemingly small semantic point, it is important in actual practice because the term "moderator" leads to the search for—or seems to only include—variables that reduce the impact of X on Y. But some variables—as they are naturally stated—*amplify* the effect of X on Y—that is, the interaction is positive. The term "modifier" is more general and allows for both roles.

It is important to note—unfortunately—that some of the roles here are logically mutually exclusive (controls vs. mediators) but others are not (modifiers vs. mediators). There is a mistaken impression that once a variable is a modifier, that is all it does. This is incorrect: As we note in the following discussion, a variable can be *both* a mediator and a modifier.

4. **Independent causes** (I): variables that cause Y but are uncorrelated with X. They do not affect the interpretation of the effect of X on Y because they are uncorrelated with X.

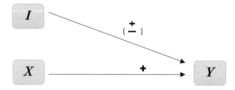

Although I is shown as concurrent with X, it actually doesn't matter where it occurs in a temporal sequence with respect to X. Independent causes may be important for some purposes, but they do not inform the focal association between X and Y.

Independent causes are important in part because they are often (mistakenly) treated as control variables. The literature is full of examples in which the reasoning about controlling for a variable proceeds from its relationship with Y *but not necessarily with* X. As a result, some controls included in analyses have no impact because they are in fact independent of X.

5. **Associated causes** (A) are variables represented as correlated with X that are also causes of Y. The model does not specify whether these variables are causally prior or intervening.

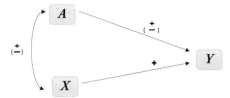

The rules for confounding in this model are the same as for the model for controls. If there is a variable A that is positively (negatively) correlated with X and also positively (negatively) affects Y, then part of the focal association may be due to this associated causation.

This model states an uncertainty about causation: We are not willing to commit to X affecting A or A affecting X. The first role would make A a mediator, the second a control. The uncertainty reflects care in ambiguous situations, but it also preserves that ambiguity.

The issue could be crucial to the overall interpretation of the effect of X on Y. If A is primarily a mediator but we use this model to interpret results, we are treating A as equivalent to a control—that is, removing the portion of the X–Y association that is due to an overlapping cause of Y. In this case, we underestimate the causal effect of X.

Because of this, we could consider this model as specified as unfortunate. Wherever possible, it would clarify the interpretive meaning of results if we committed to a causal order for A and X. If the causal direction is reciprocal, then we have parts of both roles as a mediator and a control involved.

6.5.3 Assigning Roles to Variables in an Analysis

The purpose of the distinctions in the previous section is twofold: First, making these distinctions will promote a focus on the essential issues both in estimating a *series* of regression models and in interpreting results, and second, these distinctions represent a predominant perspective across a wide array of research areas.

The pictures used to represent the different roles variables play also imply a set of regressions that can be used to assess the model. For example, in the mediational model, two equations are implied: One predicting the mediator as dependent with the focal X as independent, and the other predicting Y with both the focal X and the mediator M. The model for controls implies something different: First an equation predicting the focal X as dependent on the control variable as independent, and then a second equation predicting Y with both the focal X and the control variable C. Of course, in the context of structural equation models (next chapter), these equations can be estimated in one step.

Distinguishing Controls from Mediators

A common question is how to distinguish controls as a class of variables from mediators. This distinction is fundamental in many pieces of research, as the earlier examples suggest. Here are some guidelines:

1. Whether a variable is a control or a mediator depends on its causal status with respect to X. If it is temporally or logically prior to X, it is a possible control. If it is theoretically a consequence of X but also a cause of Y, then it is a mediator. One way to decide this is to ask whether X *could* cause this variable: Can unemployment cause gender or ethnicity or age? Of course not, so these can only be controls with respect to unemployment.

2. For a variable to qualify as an important control, the diagrams above require that it is not only related to Y, *but* X *as well.*

3. Fixed variables are likely to be controls in considering the effect of time-varying Xs. If the focal variable is fixed, then other fixed variables act as associated causes.

4. The goal of putting controls in an equation is to see if the effect of X survives—that is, is "real." If it is, the goal of putting mediators in the equation is the opposite: To make the effect of X go away—that is, it is "re-routed" through other pathways expressed by mediators in the model.

Most articles set up tables to respect and communicate the logic of this process—whether or not you see diagrams in the paper. If the paper organizes the analysis by first establishing an overall association between X and Y, then adds controls to test the putative causal status of the effect of X, and then adds mediators to explain this effect, they are thinking in terms of a model, not just a series of equations.

6.6 INTERPRETATING AN ASSOCIATION USING CONTROLS AND MEDIATORS

This section presents a more detailed example of parsing an association using the interpretive logic of the previous section. The focal association involved is the relationship between household income and well-being using the National Survey of Families and Households (Sweet & Bumpass, 2002).This association has been studied widely and in cross-national perspective. Here we study the effect of household income at Wave 2 (1992–1994) on life satisfaction at Wave 3 (2001–2003). Life satisfaction is an index of satisfaction in a range of life areas, including neighborhood, city or town, financial situation, leisure time, health, friendships, family life, and present job. Items were pre-screened for internal coherence: The correlations between each item and the total of the rest is typically between .4 and .55, and the overall alpha reliability is .83.

In this initial simplified model, we look at the effect of household income on life satisfaction controlling for overall happiness at Wave 1. There is no comparable measure of life satisfaction at Wave 1, but overall happiness at Wave 1 will serve as a proxy. We control for prior levels of happiness to take into account the possibility that prior happiness has some impact on income accumulation over time—a proxy for the opposite causal effect. The accompanying argument is that happiness promotes commitment to goals, consistency in performance, coping with passing difficulties, positive reactions from others, including co-workers, and the attribution of responsibility for successful outcomes.

In the model we propose, we assess the mediating role of the "sense of control," a psychosocial resource measuring the degree to which you *believe* your life outcomes are under your control. Essentially, this concept proposes that individuals differ in their tendency to make internal attributions for life outcomes (e.g., do to their effort or ability) versus external attributions (e.g., due to luck or task difficulty). Formally, this is the same as a sense of mastery (Pearlin, Menaghan, Lieberman, & Mullan 1981). Instrumentalism (Wheaton, 1980), self-efficacy (Bandura, 1977), or locus of control (Rotter, 1966), Mirowsky and Ross (2003) have found a sense of internal (as opposed to external) control to be a key element of success in adult life, and studies in Britain of 7500 adults followed since birth report that early life sense of control is associated with a lower risk of overweight, poor health, or distress later in adulthood. We propose that higher income "trains" for higher sense of control, allowing a generalized sense of efficacy in life outcomes, and this in turn promotes life satisfaction.

A model that represent the reasoning is shown in Figure 6.5.

FIGURE 6.5 ● A BASIC MODEL FOR INCOME AND LIFE SATISFACTION

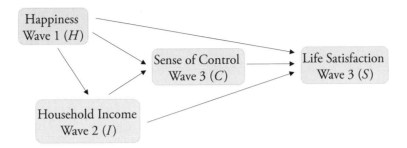

In Chapter 1, we showed how using the method of covariance equations allowed us to solve for coefficients in a multiple regression equation. Here we show how to use a modified version of that method to derive the estimates of the model above, but also, to demonstrate exactly what is involved in estimating the effects of controls and mediators on the focal association.

As we shall see, only this algebra makes explicit the underlying "structure" giving rise to the associations among variables. This is perhaps the most important consequence of taking the time to demonstrate the components of each association here, and it clarifies a point that has recently been left behind in many discussions of regression.

We begin here by writing the structural equations which correspond to this model, using letters to represent variables: As in Figure 6.5, H = happiness, I = household income, C = sense of control, and S = life satisfaction:

$$I = a_I + b_{IH} H$$

$$C = a_C + b_{CI} I + b_{CH} H$$

$$S = a_S + b_{SC} C + b_{SI} I + b_{SH} H$$

To simplify the presentation, we use the standardized version of the model—which in effect removes the intercept in these equations and sets all variances to 1.

6.6.1 The Structural Equations in Standardized Form

The transformed standardized versions of the preceding structural equations allow us to concentrate on the structure of the model. The equations for this model can now be written this way, given that the intercept is by definition = 0 in a standardized model:

$$I = \beta_{IH} H \tag{1}$$

$$C = \beta_{CI} I + \beta_{CH} H \tag{2}$$

$$S = \beta_{SC} C + \beta_{SI} I + \beta_{SH} H \tag{3}$$

Our goal is to produce "normal equations" from these structural equations that form the basis of interpreting the model. There is a standard set of steps to uncovering the underlying structure of the model. For *each* structural equation, we can derive as many normal equations as there are independent variables in that equation, where each equation shows the structure of the overall correlation between that independent variable and the dependent variable.

To do this, follow these steps, either manually or mentally:

1. Multiply through the structural equation by each independent variable in turn:

   For equation 1, this would be

   $$HI = \beta_{IH} HH$$

2. Sum both sides of the equation, divide by $N - 1$ and bring constants outside the summation:

   $$\sum \frac{HI}{N-1} = \beta_{IH} \sum \frac{HH}{N-1}$$

3. It is important to see what these summations represent. In Chapter 1, the correlation is defined this way:

   $$r_{xy} = \frac{\sum \left(\frac{(X_i - \bar{X})}{s_x} \cdot \frac{(Y_i - \bar{Y})}{s_y} \right)}{N-1} = \sum \frac{Z_x \cdot Z_y}{N-1}$$

   Remembering that variables here are standardized, this means we can re-write the equation above as

   $$r_{HI} = \beta_{IH} r_{HH}$$

   But the correlation of something with itself is 1, so this can be simplified further:

   $$r_{HI} = \beta_{IH}$$

This is the only normal equation for Equation 1. It does show that the standardized coefficient in a bivariate regression equals the correlation.

Doing the same for Equation 2 proceeds as follows:

The structural equation is

$$C = \beta_{CI} I + \beta_{CH} H$$

Multiplying through by each independent variable results in

$$IC = \beta_{CI} II + \beta_{CH} IH$$

$$HC = \beta_{CI} IH + \beta_{CH} HH$$

Summing and dividing by $N - 1$ on both sides results in

$$r_{IC} = \beta_{CI} + \beta_{CH} r_{HI}$$

$$r_{HC} = \beta_{CI} r_{HI} + \beta_{CH}$$

Because the correlation on the right hand side here has a causal interpretation in the normal equation for the first equation, we replace that correlation here to show explicitly this interpretation:

$$r_{IC} = \beta_{CI} + \beta_{CH}\beta_{IH}$$

$$r_{HC} = \beta_{CI}\beta_{IH} + \beta_{CH}$$

These are the normal equations for Equation 2, predicting sense of control. The first normal equation shows that the overall correlation between income and sense of control, in this model, has two components: a direct effect of income on sense of control (β_{CI}), and a second component resulting from the common dependence of sense of control and income on prior happiness ($\beta_{CH}\beta_{IH}$). This component is *a source of spuriousness in the relationship between income and sense of control.* As a result, this component cannot be interpreted as part of the causal effect of income and needs to be removed from the correlation in order to interpret the causal portion of the effect.

Without the details, we also write out the normal equations for the essential third equation. The rules used above can be used to derive these equations, but with some practice you can also reason through what will happen as a result of multiplying through by independent variables, summing and dividing by N - 1, and simplifying.

Starting with this equation for life satisfaction:

$$S = \beta_{SC}C + \beta_{SI}I + \beta_{SH}H,$$

we end up with three initial normal equations:

$$r_{SC} = \beta_{SC} + \beta_{SI}r_{IC} + \beta_{SH}r_{CH}$$

$$r_{SI} = \beta_{SC}r_{IC} + \beta_{SI} + \beta_{SH}r_{IH}$$

$$r_{SH} = \beta_{SC}r_{HC} + \beta_{SI}r_{IH} + \beta_{SH}$$

What you should notice here is that the correlations on the right hand side each have a structure in the model and need to be replaced for a completely explicit resolution of components of each correlation. The second normal equation here represents the focal association of interest, between income and life satisfaction. In that equation, we replace both r_{IC} and r_{IH} with their equivalent already derived expressions in terms of the model to get the following:

$$r_{SI} = \beta_{SC}(\beta_{CI} + \beta_{CH}\beta_{IH}) + \beta_{SI} + \beta_{SH}\beta_{IH}$$

$$= \beta_{SC}\beta_{CI} + \beta_{SC}\beta_{CH}\beta_{IH} + \beta_{SI} + \beta_{SH}\beta_{IH}$$

| Total association | Indirect effect | spurious | direct effect | spurious |

This expression traces all of the linkages between income and life satisfaction and labels their interpretation. Generalizing this example, we propose below an exhaustive scheme for interpreting all of the components of an association. But note first that this normal equation also shows us that correlations / covariances are *produced* by the parameters of an underlying structural model, suggesting that the notion of an association and a structural *effect* should be kept distinct.

6.6.2 A Scheme for Decomposing Correlations into Parts

We define these concepts (see Figure 6.6):

- *Total association*: The total correlation (or covariance) available to be analyzed.

- *Total causal effect*: The direct effect plus all indirect causal effects through mediators.

- *Total noncausal association*: All components that link the focal X and Y due to links with prior *or associated* causes in the model, in two versions, spuriousness and simple noncausal association.

- *Simple noncausal association*: Due to associated causes of Y. This only happens for starting points in the model when there are multiple independent variables but no causal priority among them. These variables are shown as simply correlated.

- *Spuriousness*: Any part of the association due to the co-dependence of X and Y on common or correlated prior causes in the model.

- *Direct effect*: The net regression coefficient in the regression for Y, thus only standing for part of the total causal effect in a models with mediators.

- *Indirect effect*: The effects of X on Y via pathways through mediating variables. This is an inherent part of the causal effect of X, so the total effect = direct + indirect.

FIGURE 6.6 ● REGRESSION AS A COMPETITION AMONG PREDICTORS

Total Association

Total Noncausal Association

Total Causal Effect

Simple Noncausal Association

Spuriousness

Direct Effect

Indirect Effect

There are two things to notice in the analysis of this focal association. First, there are two spuriousness components: $\beta_{SC}\beta_{CH}\beta_{IH}$ and $\beta_{SH}\beta_{IH}$.

These components are extracted from the complete model in the following:

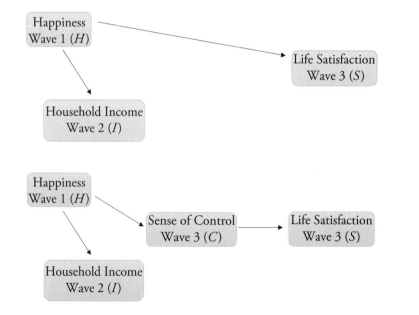

Second, there are two components to the total causal effect, one direct (β_{SI}) and one indirect ($\beta_{SC}\beta_{CI}$), shown in the following image.

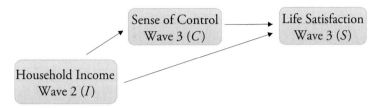

The issue going forward is the mix of these two components: How much of the association is noncausal, and how much is causal? How much of the total causal effect is mediated? You can use the derived normal equation earlier to answer these questions—and you can also just run the appropriate regressions to estimate the coefficients.

6.6.2.1 Types of Direct and Indirect Effects

There is in fact an ambiguity in the interpretation of direct and indirect effects as defined here, pointed out by Pearl (2005). The model for mediation says that X affects both M and Y as a consequence of a 1 unit increase in X. But the coefficient we use for the direct effect formally holds M constant. This leads to a distinction between the *controlled* direct effect, where M is constant, versus the *natural* direct effect, where M can change as expected due to a hypothetical change in the value of X. We do not distinguish between these concepts here, in part because we stick to linear effects. But in nonlinear and interactive models, these distinctions become important, and the two values differ.

6.6.3 Estimating the Model

When you run a series of regressions to analyze the focal association, you first consider the bivariate effect of income on life satisfaction—to establish the causal criterion requiring a significant total effect of X on Y. As a second step, you would add control variables, consistent with the logic of accounting for spuriousness. If a significant total effect remains, then, and only then, do we investigate the possible mediation of that effect. Although we use a series of equations here in a regression framework, this entire model can be estimated directly using a structural equations model (next chapter).

Here is a run using PROC REG in SAS testing the pieces of this model sequentially:

```
proc reg data=tempfullmiss plots=none corr simple;
/* Model 1 X-Y Bivariate*/      model lifesat3 = hhinctot2;
/* Model 2 X on C*/             model hhinctot2 = happy1;
/* Model 3 Y on X and C */      model lifesat3 = hhinctot2 happy1;
/* Model 4 M on X */            model sensecontrol3 = hhinctot2;
/* Model 5 M on X and C */      model sensecontrol3 = hhinctot2 happy1;
/* Model 6 Full Y Model */      model lifesat3 = hhinctot2 happy1
   sensecontrol3;
run;
```

The first model (1) estimates the bivariate effect of household income at Wave 2 on life satisfaction at Wave 3 to establish the total focal association to be explained. Model 2 assesses the plausibility of the control for prior happiness by estimating a regression with income dependent on prior happiness at Wave 1. If this coefficient is not significant, then prior happiness will have little effect as a control. If there is an effect in this model, it only establishes a necessary condition for the importance of this control variable since it also must affect life satisfaction. Model 3 adds happiness to Model 1, to assess its overall impact on the effect of income and to test for spuriousness. If the coefficient for income in this model is no longer significant, the association is spurious. If it is diminished but significant, we know from Model 2 and 3 combined that it has accounted for part of the association. If the coefficient is essentially the same, this means that prior happiness either did not affect income or life satisfaction or both over time.

Given a persistent effect at that point, we add sense of control as a mediator. We do this in two stages. First, we estimate a model (4) in which sense of control is dependent on income, to establish the effect of income on a sense of control, required by the first step in the mediating process. Second, we add happiness as a control in Model 5 because the effect of income on sense of control could be spurious if happiness also predicts a greater sense of control in general. Finally, in Model 6, we add sense of control as a mediator to Model 3 to assess its overall mediating role. To the extent that sense of control does mediate this relationship, we expect to see a large decline in the net remaining effect of income on satisfaction in this model, compared to Model 3. In effect, our hope is that the remaining effect of income is nonsignificant.

Note that here we will present the unstandardized coefficients, in part to show that the same logic applies. The results from running all of these models are shown starting in Table 6.3.

Reviewing the main findings, model by model:

TABLE 6.3 ● ESTIMATING THE INCOME AND LIFE SATISFACTION MODEL

The REG Procedure
Model: MODEL1
Dependent Variable: lifesat3

Number of Observations Read	4234
Number of Observations Used	4108
Number of Observations with Missing Values	126

Analysis of Variance

Source	DF	Sum of Squares	Mean Square	F Value	Pr > F
Model	1	3056.92105	3056.92105	33.02	< .0001
Error	4106	380077	92.56622		
Corrected Total	4107	383134			

Root MSE	9.62113	R-Square	0.0080
Dependent Mean	61.25216	Adj R-Sq	0.0077
Coeff Var	15.70742		

Parameter Estimates

Variable	DF	Parameter Estimate	Standard Error	t Value	Pr > |t|
Intercept	1	60.29189	0.22462	268.41	< .0001
hhinctot2	1	0.17887	0.03113	5.75	< .0001

The REG Procedure
Model: MODEL2
Dependent Variable: hhinctot2

Number of Observations Read	4234
Number of Observations Used	4108
Number of Observations with Missing Values	126

Analysis of Variance

Source	DF	Sum of Squares	Mean Square	F Value	Pr > F
Model	1	587.80472	587.80472	25.42	<.0001
Error	4106	94961	23.12743		
Corrected Total	4107	95549			

Root MSE	4.80910	R-Square	0.0062
Dependent Mean	5.36863	Adj R-Sq	0.0059
Coeff Var	89.57779		

Parameter Estimates

Variable	DF	Parameter Estimate	Standard Error	t Value	Pr > |t|
Intercept	1	3.74303	0.33106	11.31	<.0001
Happy1	1	0.30068	0.05964	5.04	<.0001

The REG Procedure
Model: MODEL3
Dependent Variable: lifesat3

Number of Observations Read	4234
Number of Observations Used	4108
Number of Observations with Missing Values	126

Analysis of Variance

Source	DF	Sum of Squares	Mean Square	F Value	Pr > F
Model	2	26643	13322	153.40	<.0001
Error	4105	356491	86.84303		
Corrected Total	4107	383134			

Root MSE	9.31896	R-Square	0.0695
Dependent Mean	61.25216	Adj R-Sq	0.0691
Coeff Var	15.21409		

Parameter Estimates

Variable	DF	Parameter Estimate	Standard Error	t Value	Pr > |t|
Intercept	1	50.17256	0.65144	77.02	<.0001
hhinctot2	1	0.13978	0.03024	4.62	<.0001
Happy1	1	1.91057	0.11593	16.48	<.0001

(Continued)

TABLE 6.3 ● Continued

The REG Procedure
Model: MODEL4
Dependent Variable: sensecontrol3

Number of Observations Read	4234
Number of Observations Used	4108
Number of Observations with Missing Values	126

Analysis of Variance					
Source	DF	Sum of Squares	Mean Square	F Value	Pr > F
Model	1	927.54641	927.54641	139.04	<.0001
Error	4106	27392	6.67118		
Corrected Total	4107	28319			

Root MSE	2.58286	R-Square	0.0328
Dependent Mean	14.63951	Adj R-Sq	0.0325
Coeff Var	17.64310		

Parameter Estimates					
Variable	DF	Parameter Estimate	Standard Error	t Value	Pr > |t|
Intercept	1	14.11055	0.06030	234.00	<.0001
hhinctot2	1	0.09853	0.00836	11.79	<.0001

The REG Procedure
Model: MODEL5
Dependent Variable: sensecontrol3

Number of Observations Read	4234
Number of Observations Used	4108
Number of Observations with Missing Values	126

Analysis of Variance					
Source	DF	Sum of Squares	Mean Square	F Value	Pr > F
Model	2	1597.24176	798.62088	122.68	<.0001
Error	4105	26722	6.50967		
Corrected Total	4107	28319			

Root MSE	2.55140	R-Square	0.0564
Dependent Mean	14.63951	Adj R-Sq	0.0559
Coeff Var	17.42821		

Parameter Estimates					
Variable	DF	Parameter Estimate	Standard Error	t Value	Pr > |t|
Intercept	1	12.40541	0.17835	69.55	<.0001
hhinctot2	1	0.09194	0.00828	11.10	<.0001
Happy1	1	0.32194	0.03174	10.14	<.0001

The REG Procedure
Model: MODEL6
Dependent Variable: lifesat3

Number of Observations Read	4234
Number of Observations Used	4108
Number of Observations with Missing Values	126

Analysis of Variance					
Source	DF	Sum of Squares	Mean Square	F Value	Pr > F
Model	3	59185	19728	249.93	<.0001
Error	4104	323949	78.93486		
Corrected Total	4107	383134			

Root MSE	8.88453	R-Square	0.1545
Dependent Mean	61.25216	Adj R-Sq	0.1539
Coeff Var	14.50484		

Parameter Estimates					
Variable	DF	Parameter Estimate	Standard Error	t Value	Pr > |t|
Intercept	1	36.48276	0.91669	39.80	<.0001
hhinctot2	1	0.03832	0.02926	1.31	0.1904
Happy1	1	1.55530	0.11190	13.90	<.0001
sensecontrol3	1	1.10353	0.05435	20.30	<.0001

- Model 1 shows that income has a significant total effect on later life satisfaction (up to 10 years later). The **b** is .179 ($p < .0001$).

- Model 2 shows that indeed prior happiness does positively affect income over time: The **b** is .301 ($p < .0001$). This suggests that happiness does translate into higher income over time and that happiness *may* be an important control.

- Controlling for prior happiness at Wave 1 does reduce the net causal part of the impact of income on life satisfaction to some degree, from .179 in Model 1 to .140 in Model 3. In fact, we can say that the opposite causal direction here—well-being to income—accounts for (.179 − .140) / .179 = 22% of the focal association, less than one quarter. But, importantly, the remaining effect of income is still positive and significant. Thus, we can proceed assuming there is a total causal effect to be interpreted.

- Model 4 establishes that indeed income is linked to sense of control, verifying the first step in the mediation process.

- Model 5 verifies that the impact of income on sense of control is not due to the prior effect of happiness. The coefficient for income only changes from .098 in Model 4 to .092 in Model 5. But note that happiness *does* predict higher sense of control.

- Adding sense of control in Model 6 to the equation for life satisfaction in Model 3 has a substantial impact on the net effect of income. The effect changes from .140 to just .038 in the final model. This is a 73% reduction in the net effect ((.140 − .038) / .140)). Remember that the ***total*** causal effect here is still .140. But you can now say that sense of control basically explains most of the causal effect and that the remaining effect of income is also nonsignificant. This is an example where the causal effect exists, but we have explained it.

You can calculate the indirect effect of income here at least two different ways, but there is an added wrinkle due to the fact that the variables are not standardized. This means that the variances of variables become potentially relevant in the calculation. For example, if we just analyze the total effect of income in the life satisfaction equation, ignoring the background effect of happiness, we have

$$S = a_S + b_{SC}C + b_{SI}I$$

Assuming the variables are at least centered (to remove the intercept) and multiplying through by I to get the covariance between income and satisfaction results in

$$\text{cov}(IS) = b_{SC}\,\text{cov}(CI) + b_{SI}\,\text{cov}(II)$$

We need to replace the covariance between control and income (CI) with its equivalent in this simplified model. Because only income is independent in the simpler model, we can deduce that

$$\text{cov}(CI) = b_{CI}\,\text{cov}(II) = b_{CI}V(I)$$

We replace this covariance in the covariance equation for satisfaction with its equivalent value to get

$$\text{cov}(IS) = b_{SC}b_{CI}V(I) + b_{SI}V(I) = V(I) \cdot (b_{SC}b_{CI} + b_{SI})$$

This result shows that the total effect here is multiplied by a scalar—the variance of income. But notice that the decomposition of the total effect into direct and indirect components will work *proportionately* even when ignoring the role of the variance of income. If you want to analyze the *absolute* sizes of these components properly, you need to use the variance of income as well.

Using the absolute values and the fact that the variance of income is 23.36 results in these calculations for the indirect and direct effects:

$$\text{cov}(IS) = (1.10 \cdot .092 \cdot 23.26) + (.038 \cdot 23.26)$$
$$= 2.35 + .884$$
$$= 3.24$$

The indirect effect here is 2.35 / 3.24 = 73% of the total effect, as before, and so proportionately the remaining direct effect is the same as well. You can also just use the coefficients to calculate these proportions: Either total - direct = .140 − .038 = .102, the indirect effect proportionate to a total effect of .140, or you can multiply the relevant coefficients directly: .092 x 1.10 = .1012 (with rounding error). If all you are interested in is the relative success of the mediator, you can just use the coefficients. If you want to know the size of the total effect and its components, the full version using the variance is necessary. Here, each $10,000 of income increases life satisfaction by 3.24 points on average—not by only .140 points.

These calculations tells us something rarely appreciated or understood: You do NOT need to conduct a regression to figure out what the effect of income on sense of control is. You only need Models 3 and 6 here focusing on life satisfaction because that effect is directly implied by the results from those models, as follows:

1. You know in Model 3 that the total effect is .140.

2. You know in Model 6 that the effect of sense of control is 1.10 and the remaining effect of income is now .038.

3. According to the decomposition of the total effect above, we therefore know

$$.140 = b_{SC}b_{CI} + b_{SI} = 1.10b_{CI} + .038$$

We can solve for the missing piece using this equation as follows:

$$b_{CI} = \frac{.140 - .038}{1.10} = .092$$

In other words, we do not really need to run a regression for the mediator to derive the effect at the first stage of mediation.

6.6.4 An Expanded Model

The preceding example is purposely simplistic. We could make the example more like the examples in published papers by considering more controls and more mediators, in part to better account for spuriousness—although *any* set of controls will usually fall short of entirely accounting for the possibility of spuriousness—and in part to test different theories about the mechanisms by which income affects well-being.

First, we add three more controls to the model: (1) gender, a dummy variable for female, assuming that women have lower household incomes on the whole and due to greater cumulative demands in social roles, lower satisfaction as well; (2) the current highest occupational status in the household, based on occupational status scores of household members, assuming that occupation is a major determinant of income and an input to life satisfaction on its own; and (3) childhood stress, a count of stressful life events occurring before the age of 18, including parental deaths or divorce, exposure to household conflict, and family substance abuse. Stress is assumed to negatively affect educational attainment and thus income indirectly and also lower life satisfaction in the long run.

We consider three sets of mediators in this model. First, we expand the psychosocial resources argument to include two other resources: trusting relationships with others and self-esteem. We enter these variables as a group to generally test a broad argument for the importance of psychosocial resources. Second, we consider the effects of work strain—demanding and draining work leaving one exhausted much of the time. We theorize that this will be a mediator *if* the benefits of higher income include greater control over work, better scheduling, and less physical work. Third, we consider the effects of domestic situation, with three variables: number of domestic task hours worked per week, overall assessment of inequitable distribution of work in the household, and arguments with a partner. Each of these problems is assumed to be—reduced—by higher income and, in turn, when reduced will predict great life satisfaction. In each case, we consider these variables as a set to test the arguments generally. The one thing we do not do here explicitly is break down each class of mediators into the effects of individual variables, but we will be able to tell which variable(s) are most important from patterns in the findings.

The run of PROC REG which will produce the needed results is organized this way:

```
proc reg data=tempfullmiss plots=none corr simple;
/*Model 1*/    model lifesat3 = hhinctot2;
/*Model 2*/    model lifesat3 = hhinctot2 happy1 female hhsei stressto18;
/*Model 3*/    model lifesat3 = hhinctot2 happy1 female hhsei stressto18
               workstrain3;
/*Model 4*/    model lifesat3 = hhinctot2 happy1 female hhsei stressto18
               rtaskhrs3 overallunfairme3 argue3;
```

```
/*Model 5*/     model lifesat3 = hhinctot2 happy1 female hhsei stressto18
                sensecontrol3 closetrust3 selfesteem3;
/*Model 6*/     model lifesat3 = hhinctot2 happy1 female hhsei stressto18
                workstrain3 rtaskhrs3 overallunfairme3 argue3 sensecontrol3
                closetrust3 selfesteem3;
run;
```

Notice the order of these models:

- Model 1 estimates the overall association.

- Model 2 adds all controls

- Models 3 through 5 add each type of mediator in turn, so that there is some evidence of the contributions of different arguments to explaining the effect of income.

- Model 6 estimates the collective effect of the mediators in explaining the effect of income and can be compared to Model 2.

It is helpful to see how these results might look in a table in a paper rather than present the results in SAS. We have just transferred the results to a table (Table 6.4). The usual approach is to set up the table with the models as the columns and the variables as the rows, so the design of this table maps to what is commonly presented in journals.

TABLE 6.4 ● Analyzing the Effect of Household Income on Life Satisfaction over Time

Variables	Model 1: Bivariate	Model 2: w/ Controls	Model 3: +Work Strain	Model 4: +Domestic Burden	Model 5: +Psychosocial Resources	Model 6: Full
Household Income	.188***	.157***	.155***	.139***	.038	.034
Controls						
Prior Happiness		1.88***	1.79***	1.78***	1.35***	1.26***
Female		1.09**	1.38***	1.29***	1.14***	1.50***
HH SEI		–.085	–.116	–.097	–.445	–.432
Stress to 18		–.834***	–.799***	–.745***	–.601**	–.541**
Mediators						
Work Strain			–2.27***			–1.157***
Domestic Burden						
Task Hours				.051		.091
Unfair to Me				–1.525***		–1.654***
Arguments				–.273***		–.194***
Resources						
Sense of control					.562***	.526***
Trust					2.076***	1.694***
Self-esteem					1.086***	1.072***

*** = $p < .0001$

** = $p < .01$

* = $p < .05$

Model 1 reports the basic bivariate effect of household income at Wave 2 on life satisfaction at Wave 3 ($b = .188$, $p < .0001$). This is the effect to be explained. Model 2 adds all controls together, though they can be added one at a time as well—to show which ones matter most in accounting for the association in Model 1. There is some reduction in the effect of income in Model 2, but it is minor: The remaining total effect is .157 / .188 = 84% of the original association. Thus there is an imputed causal effect to explain.

Sets of mediators are added one at a time in Models 3 through 5. This is done to allow some assessment of the individual role of each set of mediators in explaining the effect of income. Although both work strain and domestic burden clearly have the predicted effect on life satisfaction, they do little to explain the effect of income. There is a small decrease in the net effect of income in the model with domestic burdens, from .157 in Model 2 to .139 in Model 4, but this is too small a change to claim there is much of a mediational effect there. We note that only sense of unfairness and arguments with a partner predict lower life satisfaction: Domestic tasks hours do not. This is telling because only domestic task hours is negatively correlated with income, so the links in the mediational argument are broken either at the first stage or at the second stage.

Results in Model 5 make very clear that the greater availability of psychosocial resources that are useful and necessary in dealing with life difficulties, challenges, and threats at higher income levels is the primary transmitter of the effects of income on life satisfaction. These resources are very effective in and of themselves, since all three have separate and strong effects on life satisfaction. But in results not shown, we also observe that each is strongly related to higher income. The net result is that the effect of income is completely explained in Model 5.

Model 6 combines all mediators, but there is little more to be achieved here; the net effect is a very low .034, but it is no lower than a model with only resources as the mediator. Interestingly, the effects of other mediators remain significant in the presence of the three resource variables. In the final model, we can claim that the model as specified has explained .188 - .034/.188 = 82% of the original association, and .157-.034 / .157 = 78% of the causal effect. This example is clearer—and more successful overall—than many in the literature, mainly because so much of the effect is explained; the control variables do not account for a large portion of the association, and the role of one mediator predominates.

6.7 SPECIAL CASES

6.7.1 Suppressor Variables

A suppressor variable is either *a control variable or an intervening variable* that affects the overall association between X and Y in a direction **opposite** to the main association between X and Y. The following model shows a case of a *prior suppressor* variable.

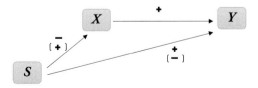

In this model, S *either* reduces X while increasing Y, *or* S increases X while reducing Y. In both cases, this creates a negative component in the positive correlation between X and Y, which, when removed by controlling for S, leaves a **larger** estimated positive causal effect of X on Y.

A basic and important question is how to interpret suppressors as part of an overall association. We recommend *removing* the impact of the suppressor and then analyzing the components consistent with the direction of the overall association. This is a hypothetical analysis because the suppressor has a real impact on the association. The language involved often involves references like "were it not for the suppressor." An important question in these cases is whether the remaining opposite association would be significant if the suppressor did not exist.

6.7.2 Two Examples

6.7.2.1 Time Series of Suicide Rates

The model in Figure 6.7 represents a case with an *intervening suppressor*, using time series data from Canada from 1920 through 1982.

The model imagines that increases in unemployment at the macro level have two very different (and counteracting) consequences: The divorce rate increases, but so do mental hospital admissions. The total causal effect of unemployment on suicides is

$$0.12 + (.30 \cdot .22) + (.20 \cdot -.25)$$

$$= .12 + .066 - .05 = .136$$

Note the effect of mental hospital admissions in this model. In effect, mental hospital admissions reduce the otherwise positive causal effect of unemployment (by -.05). This is because the increase in mental hospital admissions partly counteracts the increase in the suicide rate due to increases in divorce because mental hospital admissions have a negative effect on suicides.

Mental hospital admissions is acting in the role of a suppressor variable that dampens the size of a relationship operating in the opposite direction. This role can apply to common causes as well, thus operating as the opposite of spuriousness problems. In this case, the total causal effect can be *larger* than the total association.

What to do: Remove the suppressor effect and analyze the rest of the components acting in the same direction. Here the ***positive*** causal effect amounts to .12 + .066 = .186. So the indirect effect is .066/.186 = 35% of the positive causal effect.

FIGURE 6.7 ● A TIME SERIES MODEL OF UNEMPLOYMENT AND SUICIDE RATES

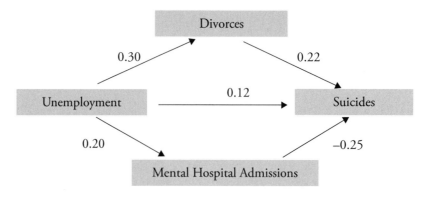

6.7.2.2 The Black-White Paradox in Mental Disorder

A paper by Louie and Wheaton (2019) provides another example, using the National Co-morbidity Survey of Adolescents. The fact that Blacks in the United States do not have higher rates of some psychiatric disorders—given the higher levels of stress, poverty, and discrimination experienced in this group—compared to Whites is sometimes referred to as the "Black–White" paradox. In this paper, they analyze the countervailing effects of higher stress exposures among Blacks versus higher levels of helpful personal resources, such as self-esteem.

Results using linear probability estimates are shown in Table 6.5.

TABLE 6.5 ● LINEAR PROBABILITY MODELS FOR MOOD DISORDER				
	(1) +Race	**(2)** +Self-Esteem	**(3)** +Traumatic Stressors	**(4)** +Race, Self-Esteem, Traumatic Stressors
	b (SE)	*b* (SE)	*b* (SE)	*b* (SE)
Race				
Black	.006 (.009)	.018* (.009)	−.021* (.010)	−.004 (.010)
Coping resource				
Self-Esteem		−.033*** (.003)		−.031*** (.002)
Stress measure				
Traumatic Stressors			.023** (.002)	.017*** (.002)

† *p* < .10, **p* < .05, ***p* < .01, ****p* < .001

Note: All models adjusted for gender, parent's education, household income, and age.

The analysis of suppression here can be taken directly from the article (noting that the probability estimates are small because the overall prevalence is .10):

> Results in [*this table*] assess the association between race and 12-month DSM-IV mood disorders. Model 1 reveals a null association between race and mood disorders (*b* = .006, *p* > .05), with all controls entered in the model. However, in Model 2, the association between race and mood disorders becomes positive and statistically significant with the inclusion of self-esteem (*b* = .018, *p* < .05). Blacks have a higher probability of mood disorders than whites net of race differences in self-esteem. This positive effect occurs because (1) blacks have higher levels of self-esteem than whites ([*earlier table*], *b* = .331, *p* < .01) and (2) self-esteem is associated with lower levels of mood disorders ([*this table*], *b* = −.033, *p* < .001). Thus, the indirect effect of race through self-esteem in Model 2 is negative (.331 × −.033 = −.011). . . . Because the negative component of the association between race and mood disorder is removed in . . . Model 2, the net effect of black versus white is positive and significant—a classic example of suppression. (Louie & Wheaton, 2019, p. 175–176)

Model 3 controls for traumatic stressors where Blacks have a higher rate than Whites. As a result of the net positive indirect effect through traumatic stress, the resulting Black–White difference

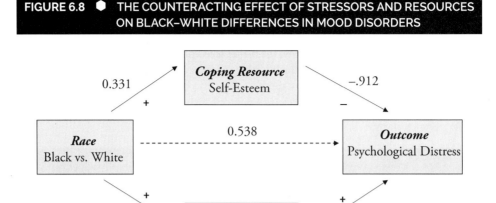

FIGURE 6.8 ● THE COUNTERACTING EFFECT OF STRESSORS AND RESOURCES ON BLACK–WHITE DIFFERENCES IN MOOD DISORDERS

Source: Adapted from Louie, P., & Wheaton, B. (2019, May 9). The Black-White paradox revisited: Understanding the role of counterbalancing mechanisms during adolescence. *Journal of Health and Social Behavior, 60 (2), 169–187*

is now *negative* and significant—consistent with the Black–White paradox finding. When both self-esteem and stressors are considered in Model 4, the counteracting indirect effects are fully realized, producing the null direct effect on mood disorder.

Figure 6.8 from the paper shows the way in which suppression acts to reduce an overall black-white difference in distress (not disorder, a different outcome).

The figure shows a net null effect of race on distress, once both stress exposure and differences in self-esteem are taken into account. While there is higher risk implied by greater stress exposure among Blacks, in fact, Black adolescents also have higher self-esteem, and this counteracts the higher risk due to traumatic life events.

6.7.3 Mediating/"Moderating"

This section introduces the complexities that can result when variables in a model play multiple roles at once. I use the term "moderating" because of its prevalence, but it is not the most general term, as the following example will demonstrate. This section is meant to convey the message that variables do not need to be in a single role so that they are somehow naturally a "mediator" or a "moderator" by nature. Questions abound in literatures across disciplines about whether a specific variable is one or the other. This is the wrong question. The general answer is that variables can be both, and we have to deal with it.

There is excellent recent work on the multiple roles of variables in models. Ross and Mirowsky (2001) developed a "structural amplification model," which reflects the dual roles discussed here. The recent book by Vanderweele (2015) is in part dedicated to these multiple roles. We cannot consider all of the complexities of these models, but we can walk through an example of what happens in a model because a variable is *both* a mediator and a moderator (here termed "modifier").

The type of model at issue here is shown in Figure 6.9: It is a combination of the mediator and modifier models.

FIGURE 6.9 ● A MEDIATOR / MODIFIER MODEL

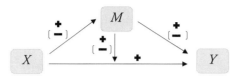

Carrying through with an earlier example, we will assume that X = exposure to stress, M = social support, and Y = some measure of depression. There are three different models to consider: (1) as a baseline, an independence model in which X has no effect on M; (2) a ***depletion*** model in which X decreases the level of M; and (3) an ***activation*** model in which X increases M.

Even if X and M are not connected, we note that the "total effect" of X on Y is affected by the interaction with M. In effect the first derivative dy/dx is

$$b_{yx} + b_{y \cdot mx} M$$

where the first b is the baseline effect of X when $M = 0$, and the second b is the interaction between X and M. The overall effect of X changes depending on the level of M; thus the "total effect" to be explained is not static. What does one do? A simple approach would be to set M at alternative high and low values and assess the model overall at each level. This would be appropriate if there are other mediators, for example.

X may deplete M or activate it, and M in turn may moderate the effect of X or amplify it. Here we discuss only two possibilities, varying the effect of X on M but holding constant the nature of the interaction. Following the literature, we expect that support would moderate the impact of stress, and thus the interaction is negative. In the scenarios that follow, we assume that support starts at a level of 10 on a scale.

As a baseline, we assume the following two equations for the independence model:

$$Support = 10 - 0(stress)$$
$$Depression = 16 + 3(stress) - .1(support) - .2(stress \text{ x } support)$$

The zero coefficient for stress on support reflects the independence assumption. As a result of this, assessing the impact of changes in stress on depression requires considering only the second equation for depression. Substituting stress = 0 and stress = 1 in turn in this equation results in the following change in depression:

$$Depression = 16 + 3(0) - .1(10) - .2(0) = 16 - 1 = 15$$
$$Depression = 16 + 3(1) - .1(10) - .2(1 \cdot 10) = 16 + 3 - 1 - 2 = 16$$

That is, depression increases by 1 symptom in this case, from 15 to 16. Without the interaction, depression would have increased more.

The ***depletion*** model assumes that stress undermines the level of support. The equations for this model are

$$Support = 10 - 2(stress)$$
$$Depression = 16 + 3(stress) - .1(support) - .2(stress \text{ x } support)$$

What happens now when stress goes from 0 to 1? When stress = 0, predicted depression is still 15:

$$Support = 10 - 2(0) = 10$$
$$Depression = 16 + 3(0) - .1(10) - .2(0 \cdot 10) = 16 - 1 = 15$$

When stress = 1, depression in this model is

$$Support = 10 - 2(1) = 8$$
$$Depression = 16 + 3(1) - .1(8) - .2(1 \cdot 8) = 16 + 3 - .8 - 1.6 = 16.6$$

Note what happens: In the depletion model, depression increases by 1.6 symptoms due to the 1 unit increase in stress. The stress "buffering" properties of support are partially hampered by the fact that stress has reduced the level of support available to reduce stress in the first place.

The ***activation*** model assumes that stress increases the level of support. The equations for this model would be

$$Support = 10 + 2(stress)$$
$$Depression = 16 + 3(stress) - .1(support) - .2(stress \text{ x } support)$$

In this case, when stress increases from 0 to 1, we get a very different view of the total effect of stress. When stress = 0, as before, depression will equal 15. When stress = 1, depression will be

$$Support = 10 + 2(1) = 12$$
$$Depression = 16 + 3(1) - .1(12) - .2(1 \cdot 12) = 16 + 3 - 1.2 - 2.4 = 15.4$$

Obviously, the net impact on depression is smaller in this case. Stress helps to activate the resource that reduces its ultimate impact.

This example helps illustrate that one must consider mediators and modifiers in their joint role simultaneously rather than separately or cumulatively. One can work out relevant scenarios from hypothetical "what ifs" in these models to figure out the ultimate impact of these joint roles. Note in these examples two things are happening: The effect of stress on support is carried through as a mediator or suppressor, and the new level of support is what is available to reduce the direct impact of stress.

6.8 FROM RECURSIVE TO NON-RECURSIVE MODELS: WHAT TO DO ABOUT RECIPROCAL CAUSATION

Up to this point, we have only considered models that represent unidirectional causation. But reciprocal causation exists and is often assumed to be an important possibility. Consider these possibilities taken from research: job complexity and cognitive flexibility, physician visits and health, grades and educational aspirations, candidate preference and party identification, crime rates and arrest rates, job performance and job satisfaction, deviant behavior and labeling, friend's values and personal values, and childbearing and labor force participation.

What happens when we start to consider reciprocal causation as a general possibility? In examples to this point, we use longitudinal data to help estimate the possibility of reciprocal causation.

This is in fact a prevalent approach, and we will invoke this approach again in the next chapter. But there are other approaches as well.

The "recursive" models we have presented so far have two defining features: (1) one-way causation between variables and (2) error terms for different dependent variables in the model that are uncorrelated with each other. Not only may unidirectional causation be an unreasonable assumption in many cases, the assumption of uncorrelated error terms for different dependent variables is also sometimes difficult to fulfill: The more similar the dependent variables, the more likely they share in common excluded causes.

The *non-recursive* model allows for reciprocal causation between variables and/or correlated error across disturbances of equations. We begin to use the term "structural equation model" here, but in fact, *all* of the structural causal models discussed in this chapter are a type of structural equation model. In their most general form, these types of models also draw our attention to the fundamental issue of *identification,* a concept that is one of the cornerstones of estimating even simple regression equations, as we shall see.

6.8.0.1 Terminology for Structural Equation Models

Distinguish the following variable "types" in causal models:

- *Exogenous* variables appear only in an independent variable role. They have no represented causes in the model.

- *Endogenous* variables have explicitly represented causes in the model and thus appear as dependent variables somewhere in the model.

6.8.0.2 Notation for Structural Equation Models

The general non-recursive structural equation model can be written symbolically as

$$Y_1 = \alpha_1 + b_{11}Y_1 + b_{12}Y_2 + \ldots + b_{1M}Y_M + \gamma_{11}X_1 + \gamma_{12}X_2 + \ldots + \gamma_{1N}X_N + d_1$$

$$Y_2 = \alpha_2 + b_{21}Y_1 + b_{22}Y_2 + \ldots + b_{2M}Y_M + \gamma_{21}X_1 + \gamma_{22}X_2 + \ldots + \gamma_{2N}X_N + d_2$$

$$\vdots \qquad\qquad\qquad \vdots \qquad\qquad\qquad \vdots$$

$$Y_M = \alpha_M + b_{M1}Y_1 + b_{M2}Y_2 + \ldots + b_{MM}Y_M + \gamma_{M1}X_1 + \gamma_{M2}X_2 + \ldots + \gamma_{MN}X_N + d_M$$

where

$Y_1 \ldots Y_M$ = M endogenous variables

$X_1 \ldots X_N$ = N exogenous variables

$d_1 \ldots d_M$ = M disturbances (error) terms

b = effects of endogenous variables on each other

γ = effects of exogenous variables on endogenous variables

and all $b_{m_i m_i}$ are 0 by definition. Note here, unlike earlier, b is used for the unstandardized coefficients among endogenous variables only, as a contrast to the γ coefficients used for exogenous variables. This could be confusing, but the fact is that different statistical traditions use the same symbols for unique meanings, and we choose to respect those traditions here, mainly to allow transference to other presentations from the same tradition.

6.8.0.3 The Consequences of Reciprocal Causation

The general version of structural equation models allows for the possibility of reciprocal causation among endogenous variables. As a result, however, there are two major consequences: (1) OLS is no longer appropriate as an estimator—in fact, it is a biased estimator in this situation; and (2) we can no longer derive unique estimates of the parameters, without further assumptions. That is, the model may not be ***identified***.

This is a new term, so we will take some time to provide an example of the problem.

6.8.1 The Identification Problem

Consider Figure 6.10.

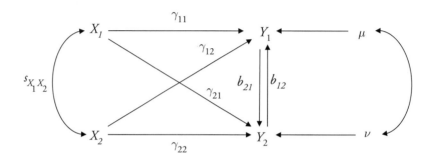

This is a model in which we want to consider the possibility that Y_1 and Y_2 cause each other. The model allows for common causation by two exogenous variables, X_1 and X_2. Note the curved arrow representing correlated error for the Y_1 and Y_2 equations. It stands for missing *common* components in determining each of the Y endogenous variables. Where does this correlation come from? Note that v, the error for Y_2, indirectly affects Y_1 in this model, through Y_2. Note also that u indirectly affects Y_2 in this model through Y_1. This is caused by the presence of the reciprocal causation. Two things result from this: (1) each Y is now correlated with the error for the other endogenous variable, breaking one of the fundamental assumptions of OLS; (2) u and v become necessarily correlated with each other because, for example, v is related to Y_1 and so is its error u, and u is related to Y_2 and so is its error v. So we cannot simply remove that parameter from the model or pretend it does not exist without biasing the estimation of the connection between Y_1 and Y_2. Of course, if we try to ignore this issue and just use successive OLS regressions to estimate the reciprocal effect here, we will get biased estimates because we are ignoring the underlying actual structure of the model.

The following assumes we could derive equations for each covariance between each independent variable and each dependent variable in the model, showing the parameters contributing to that covariance—much like the parsing of the correlations in the earlier simplified path model. According to the diagram, there are six structural (causal) parameters, two error variances, and the covariance between the errors to be estimated (nine parameters in total). The information we have to derive these nine parameters is the set of given variances and covariances among the four variables. There are $((n + m)(n + m + 1))/2$ covariances and variances in a model with $(n+m)$ variables. In this case, we have $(2 + 2)(2 + 2 + 1)/2 = (4 \cdot 5)/2 = 10$ variances/covariances. However, some of these variances and covariances are not "useful" in estimating the unknown parameters of the model.

The variances and covariances involving exogenous variables do not help in identification since they only provide information about the given variances and covariances among exogenous variables. Discounting these three variances/covariances, we have seven variances/covariances available to distinguish among the nine unknown parameters. We cannot solve for nine unknowns using only seven (independent) equations—we need at least nine variance/covariance equations in nine unknowns to solve the model. In other words, ***this model cannot be estimated in this form—it is "underidentified."***

What is identification? In a model, you are using "known" or "given" information to solve unknown parameters. Usually, the given information is the set of covariances and variances among the variables of the model, or in a standardized model, the correlations. ***Identification of a model, or equation, is demonstrated by showing that the unknown parameters are functions only of given information and that these functions produce unique solutions of these parameters in the population.*** To do this, we must have, at a minimum, at least as many independent variance/covariance equations as there are unknowns to solve.

6.8.1.1 *t*-rule for a Model (a necessary condition)

In the general case, the number of parameters to be estimated (t) must be less than or equal to

$$t \leq \frac{(n+m)\cdot(n+m+1)}{2} - \frac{(n)\cdot(n+1)}{2}$$

where m = # of endogenous variables, and n = # of exogenous variables.

The value $((n + m)(n + m + 1))/2$ refers to the total number of available covariances/variances among all variables in the model (or alternatively, the number of correlations plus number of variables), discounted by the number of covariances and variances among exogenous variables $(((n)(n+1))/2)$. This rule ensures nothing specifically about the identification of specific parameters, only that there is a chance the model is identified. If this rule fails, the model is not identified *somewhere*.

6.8.1.2 A Rule of Thumb for Identification

How could we identify the model in Figure 6.10? If we could assume, based on theory, that X_1 was only a *direct* cause of Y_1 and X_2 was only a direct cause of Y_2, we could remove two paths from the model at the outset. The model would then look like Figure 6.11.

FIGURE 6.11 ● A SIMPLIFIED TWO-WAVE PANEL MODEL FOR RECIPROCAL EFFECTS

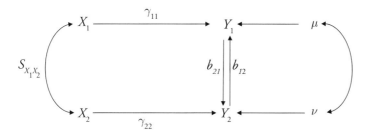

The ***rule of thumb*** is this: There must be at least one predetermined (exogenous) variable in the system for each endogenous Y involved in a reciprocal relationship that directly causes that Y but ***not*** the other Y in that reciprocal relationship.

Note that this is now a model with seven unknowns to estimate and seven usable variance/covariance equations. The model is identified—although formal proofs of this require an examination of each variance/covariance equation to ensure each parameter has a unique solution.

The issue in this kind of model is the set of assumptions that makes identification possible: Now the exogenous variables are "instrumental variables" that help with identification, but you have to be able to argue plausibly that there is no direct effect of each X on the other endogenous Y. This is often difficult, unless the study data involved are designed to include these kinds of variables. It also helps if there are multiple instruments for each Y and if the relationships between each X and its Y are quite strong. But notice, following our discussion of causal criteria, that a successful set of assumptions here formally allows estimation of reciprocal effects. The problem is that finding persuasive instrumental variables in these cases is often a delicate, if not difficult, task.

6.8.2 Identification of Recursive Models

We are used to proceeding in regression models without thinking about identification. The issue simply never comes up. That is because a standard regression (which by definition is recursive) usually invokes a number of "invisible" restrictions that make the underlying model identified. Consider the simple recursive model in Figure 6.12, which shows a model for a simple two-variable regression, with X_2 a mediator of the effect of the other independent variable X_1 on X_3.

With three variables in the model, the counting rule above implies there are $6 - 1 = 5$ available covariances and variances to estimate parameters. But in the full model, there are 11 unknown parameters. Due to the assumptions of no reciprocal effects and no correlations across error terms, there are in fact five parameters to estimate in the recursive model. Recursive models are thus "just-identified." However, note the number of "invisible" assumptions that are regularly invoked but *cannot* be tested. At times, these invisible and untested assumptions could and should make us quite uncomfortable.

FIGURE 6.12 ● THE INVISIBLE ASSUMPTIONS IN A RECURSIVE MODEL

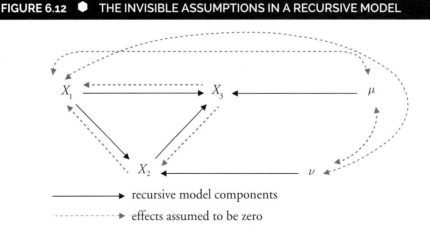

——————▶ recursive model components

------------▶ effects assumed to be zero

6.9 PUBLISHED EXAMPLES

In this section, we consider three other examples of applying the thinking of models to data analysis, based on published sources.

6.9.1 Using a Model to Decide Theory: The Miller-Stokes Model of Democratic Representation

This example is taken from the discussion in the Sage Little Green Book series on causal modeling (Asher, 1983), because it provides an excellent application of using models to test theory. Figure 6.13 is a simplified version of the classic Miller-Stokes model of democratic representation. This model can be used to test two alternative theories about how democracy works, using two different mediating variables.

The main issue in this model is how (and to what degree) voters' attitudes affect the voting behavior of their elected representatives. Do voters control their representatives by electing those who share their own views, and then in following his or her own convictions, the representative does the constituent's will? Or is it that the effect on the representative's behavior occurs as a result of the representative's *perception* of district attitudes—and thus vote in accordance with that perception? If the first argument applies, then democracy works by election of officials with similar positions to voters. If the second argument applies, then democracy works through an informal social control system in which representatives are expected to vote in accordance with voters' positions, regardless of their own—or they won't be reelected. The second model assumes either that voters express opinions to representatives regularly or that representatives regularly canvass their districts to discover voter positions.

The model addresses two important alternative interpretations of how democracy works. Although this model was first applied in the United States, it is important to note that democracy may work through different mechanism in different societies. A crucial assumption in this model is the one-way arrow from perceptions of district attitudes to the representative's own attitudes. As is noted in Asher (1983), this relationship could easily be bi-directional.

The issue posed by this model basically involves an analysis of indirect effects of X_1 on X_4. The direct effect will be zero if the causal effect is entirely explained by some combination of the indirect effects. Looking at the model, we can derive the structure of the overall association between X_1 and X_4 directly:

$$r_{14} = b_{41} + b_{42}b_{21} + b_{43}b_{31} + b_{43}b_{32}b_{21}$$

FIGURE 6.13 ● THE MILLER-STOKES DEMOCRATIC REPRESENTATION MODEL

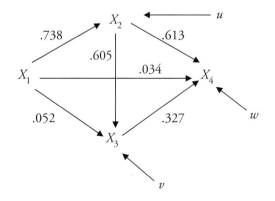

X_1 = district attitudes

X_2 = representative's perceptions of district attitudes

X_3 = representative's attitudes

X_4 = representative's voting behavior in Congress

Parsing the components of this association into indirect and direct effects produces the following results:

Indirect Effects:		
Election of similar representative:	$b_{43}b_{31} = 0.052 \cdot 0.327$	$= 0.017$
Representative's belief in following perceived will of constituency:	$b_{42}b_{21} = 0.613 \cdot 0.738$	$= 0.452$
Effect of perceived attitudes on representative's own attitudes:	$b_{43}b_{32}b_{21} = 0.327 \cdot 0.605 \cdot 0.738$	$= 0.146$
Direct Effect:	b_{41}	$= 0.034$
Total:		$= 0.649$

The model *is* successful in explaining the direct effect, estimated to be only 5% of the total association (.034/.649). The coefficient .034 is not significant.

The question, then, is which indirect route from district attitudes to representatives behavior accounts most for the causal effect. There are actually three hypotheses—explanations—that can be evaluated here—the third one formed by the double indirect path involving both mediators.

The indirect effect $b_{42}b_{21}$, which expresses the effect district attitudes has on the perceived attitudes *reported* by the representative and, subsequently, the effect of those perceived attitudes on the representative's behavior, is the primary main indirect effect (.452). This is 70% (.452/.649) of the total causal effect and 73% of all indirect effects (.452/(.649 − .034).

This means that voters control their representatives—in this case— because (a) representatives correctly perceive their district's attitudes (b_{21}), and (b) representatives believe in basing their voting on these perceived attitudes (b_{42}). As a mechanism, this indirect effect points to the invisible influence of channels of communication between constituents and representatives: Without this communication, the representative gets the attitudes wrong, potentially, and is at immediate risk of losing the next election. Results here do not confirm the notion that voters vote for candidates with similar positions, possibly because they are hard to find, and in the United States, there are only two parties.

6.9.2 The Progressive Adjustment Model

Mirowsky (2013) has produced a template example of the logic of many published data analyses, using the "progressive adjustment" model. It is closely related to the approach used in this chapter, but our approach here is a bit more general. In his model, each mediator is causally arrayed with respect to other mediators, and for applications with clear causal ordering, this is the preferred method. In many cases, however, the causal arrangements among mediators are uncertain, or mediators are entered in groups to stand for an overall hypothesis. In these cases, our "one-by-one then all" approach may be all that is practically achievable with the data.

The accompanying figure (6.14) is taken from Mirowsky (2013) and shows the flow involved in his overall causal argument. The focal association studied here involves the relationship between parental divorce in childhood and adult depression. Relationships involving confounding variables, aka control variables in our approach, are in unbolded arrows, and relationships involving mediators are in bolded arrows.

FIGURE 6.14 ● THE PROGRESSIVE ADJUSTMENT MODEL

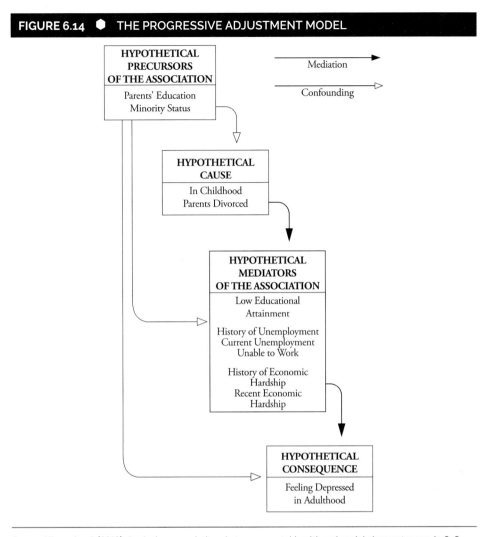

Source: Mirowsky, J. (2013). Analyzing associations between mental health and social circumstances. In C. S. Aneshensel, J. C. Phelan, & A. Bierman (Eds.), *Handbook of the sociology of mental health* (p. 143–165). Springer Science + Business Media.

There are two control variables: parents' education and minority status. The argument for each is that minority status and lower education each potentially predict adult depression but also increase the risk of divorce.

The figure shows three mediators, actually arrayed in a sequence themselves. Childhood parental divorce is thought, first, to increase the risk of poor school performance and thus dropping out of school earlier. Lower educational attainment, in turn, increases the risk of unstable employment histories, and thus higher rates of unemployment in the past and present. Finally, this history cumulates over time into higher levels of economic hardship as a result. Together, these mediators increase the risk of depression in turn.

The results from the paper are shown in the Table 6.6; this table basically follows the same template as in our earlier example. Model 1 shows an initial effect of parental divorce equal to .236, significant beyond the .001 level. After controls are added in Model 2, this effect is essentially the same (b =.244***). The first mediator, the person's own education, is added in Model 3, and the net effect of divorce drops to .17 and is now significant at the .05 level only. Educational attainment accounts for about $((.244 - .17)/.244) = 30\%$ of the total effect. Adding current and historical unemployment further reduces the effect to .149. Here the role of unemployment must be judged relative to the previous model, so we would say that unemployment explains $((.17-.149) / .17)$, just 12% of the *remaining* direct effect. Finally, when economic hardship is added, the effect is entirely explained, and the net direct effect is a low .066 (over half of the remaining direct effect). As results show clearly, the effect of divorce is progressively explained by the three mediators, but problems with educational attainment and later economic hardship explain more than unemployment problems per se.

TABLE 6.6 ● **PROGRESSIVE ADJUSTMENT: DIFFERENCE IS DEPRESSION[a] BETWEEN PERSONS WHO EXPERIENCED PARENTAL DIVORCE OR SEPARATION IN CHILDHOOD AND OTHERS, ADJUSTING PROGRESSIVELY FOR SOCIOECONOMIC ORIGINS AND SOCIOECONOMIC ORIGNIS AND CONSEQUENCES OF THE BREAKUP[b]**

Row	Independent	Model 1	Model 2	Model 3a	Model 3b	Model 3c
1	Parents divorced (/no)	0.236*** (3.398)	0.244*** (3.496)	0.170* (2.455)	0.149* (2.274)	0.066 (1.039)
2	Minority (/other)		0.156* (2.262)	0.157* (2.318)	0.050 (.774)	−0.025 (−.405)
3	Mother's education − 12[c]		−0.012 (−1.152)	0.003 (0.277)	0.007 (0.661)	0.003 (0.297)
4	Father's education − 12[c]		−0.021* (−2.278)	−.008 (−0.832)	−0.007. (−0.811)	−0.009 (−1.036)
5	Person's education — 12[c]			−0.090*** (−8.768)	−0.069*** (−7.055)	−0.047*** (−4.871)
6	Unable to work				1.921*** (13.907)	1.657*** (12.283)
7	History of long[d] unemployment				0.557*** (8.202)	0.374*** (5.570)
8	Current unemployment				0.569*** (3.802)	0.392** (2.702)
9	Economic hardship ever[e]					0.105* (12.017)
10	Recent economic hardship[e]					0.470*** (12.017)
11	Intercept	0.889***	0.837***	0.995***	0.827***	0.611***

*$p<0.050$, **$p<0.010$; *** $p<0.001$, one-tailed t test

[a] Depression is the weekly number of days per symptom, for seven symptoms

[b] Unstandardized coefficients with t-values in parentheses. Data are from a 1995 US survey of 2,539 adults ages 18 through 95 (National Institute on Aging, 1R01-AG1 2393; John Mirowsky P.I., Catherine E. Ross Co-P.I.).

[c] Education is scored as the person's actual years of formal education minus 12 years

[d] Any period of 6 months or more during adulthood

[e] Ever contrasts people with at least one period in adulthood of difficulty paying bills or buying food, etc., with those who have not. Recent ranges from 0 = no difficulties in the past 12 months, to 1 = not very often, 2 = fairly often, and 3 = very often

Source: Mirowsky, J. (2013). Analyzing associations between mental health and social circumstances. In C. S. Aneshensel, J. C. Phelan, & A. Bierman (Eds.), *Handbook of the sociology of mental health* (p. 143–165). Springer Science + Business Media.

This example provides a useful "ideal" of what we would want to see as results supporting an overall causal claim, at least theoretically. The fact is that most of the variables have a natural causal order as well. Of course, given that finite sets of measured control variables are used, there are always questions about further sources of spuriousness at the same time.

6.9.3 Impact of Spousal Work-Family Conflict

Young, Schieman and Milkie (2013) provide another template example of the tables so often presented in the literature. This article studies the effects of *spousal* work-to-family conflict in dual-earner couples, mediated by family stressors and the respondent's own family-to-work conflict. The model used to analyze and interpret the data is shown in Figure 6.15.

The main focal association here involves the effect of spousal work-family conflict (SPWFC) on the respondent's mental health problems. The figure shows just one of many controls considered: the respondent's own work-family conflict. Leaving out controls in the figure when there are many is a prevalent practice, but the results in the table show all of them. The model proposes two stages of mediators: family stressors resulting from the work-family conflict, including spousal arguments, children's problems (school, peers, health), and marital dissatisfaction, which together in turn increase the respondent's *family-to-work* conflict. Note the figure includes another layer, denoting the possibility that the whole process differs for men and women. This is shown using multiple paths intervening at various stages of the model and includes (initially) gender as a control.

We will not discuss the results of the implied interaction here, but results for the model above are shown in Table 6.7.

FIGURE 6.15 ● A MODEL FOR THE EFFECTS OF SPOUSAL WORK-FAMILY CONFLICT

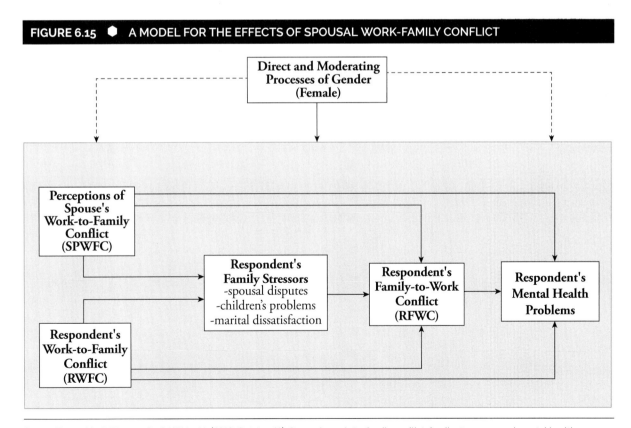

Source: Young, M., Schieman, S., & Milkie, M. (2013, October 11). Spouse's work-to-family conflict, family stressors, and mental health among dual-earner mothers and fathers. *Society and Mental Health 4*, 1–20. https://doi.org/10.1177/2156869313504931

TABLE 6.7 ● REGRESSION OF DISTRESS ON SPOUSAL WORK-FAMILY CONFLICT, RESPONDENT FAMILY-WORK CONFLICT, AND MEDIATORS

Variable	Psychological Distress							
	Model 1		Model 2		Model 3		Model 4	
	b SE		b SE		b SE		b SE	
SPWFC	.098***	(.018)	.062***	(.018)	.041*	(.017)	.027	(.017)
RWFC	—		.238***	(.022)	.215***	(.022)	.192***	(.024)
Family stressors								
Spousal disputes	—		—		.097***	(.019)[a]	.083***	(.019)
Children's problems	—		—		.078***	(.029)[a]	.054*	(.029)
Marital dissatisfaction	—		—		.071*	(.039)	.060	(.038)
RFWC	—		—		—		.116***	(.028)*
Focal controls								
Gender (female)	.134**	(.051)	.105**	(.049)	.117*	(.048)	.112*	(.047)
Age	−.007	(.003)	−.007*	(.003)	−.006*	(.003)	−.006*	(.003)
White	−.063	(.053)	−.04I	(.052)	−.023	(.051)	−.020	(.051)
High school[b]	−.067	(.115)	−.046	(.III)	−.054	(.109)	−.050	(.106)
Associate's degree"	−.082	(.117)	−.078	(.112)	−.082	(.109)	−.087	(.106)
Some college"	−.148	(.113)	−.113	(.110)	−.103	(.107)	−.105	(.104)
College[b]	−.062	(.109)	−.073	(.107)	−.074	(.104)	−.085	(.100)
Postgraduate degree[b]	−.030	(.116)	−.049	(.113)	−.043	(.110)	−.056	(.106)
Personal income[c]	.001	(.005)	.001	(.005)	.001	(.005)	.002	(.004)
Work hours	.005***	(.002)	−.001	(.002)	.001	(.002)	.001	(.002)
Spouse's work hours	−.003	(.002)	−.00I	(.002)	.001	(.002)	.001	(.002)
Previous mental health	.530***	(.055)	.393***	(.050)	.351***	(.049)	.350***	(.049)
Spouse's general health	−.121***	(.019)	−.105***	(.018)	−.077***	(.018)	−.073***	(.018)
Children under 6	.011	(.031)	−.012	(.029)	−.015	(.028)	−.020	(.028)
Children 6 to 11	−.010	(.024)	−.025	(.023)	−.032	(.023)	−.027	(.023)
Children 12 to 18	.017	(.028)	.006	(.027)	−.006	(.026)	−.002	(.026)
Domestic tasks	−.005	(.036)	−.010	(.034)	−.025	(.033)	−.025	(.033)
Constant	2.509***	(.232)	2.162***	(.225)	1.634***	(.228)	1.564***	(.226)
R^2	.168		.275		.308		.321	

Note: SPWFC = respondent's perceptions of their spouse's work-to-family conflict, RWFC = respondent's work-to-family conflict, RFWC = respondent's family-to-work conflict.

Source: Young, M., Schieman, S., & Milkie, M. (2013, October 11). Spouse's work-to-family conflict, family stressors, and mental health among dual-earner mothers and fathers. *Society and Mental Health 4*, 1–20. https://doi.org/10.1177/2156869313504931

The main association here is significant (b = .098***). Adding the respondent's work-family conflict as a control reduces the net effect to .062, but this effect is still significant. Notice that previous mental health is controlled, allowing some control for the opposite causal effect of mental health on the level of work-family conflict. Adding family stressors as a group reduces the net effect of SPWFC to .041 (p < .05). This group of mediators explains just over one third (.062 - .041 / .062) of the total effect. In the last model, the respondent's family-work conflict explains another (.041 - .027 / .041) one third of the remaining direct effect, resulting in an entirely explained effect by the last model. Family stressors and RFWC together explain (.062 - .027 / .062) = 56% of the causal portion of the association and result in a successful "full" explanation of the effect because the remaining effect is nonsignificant.

Concluding Words

We have taken some time in this chapter to develop a specific analytical and interpretive framework for multiple regression techniques. The issue here is the thinking behind the regression more than the statistical issues that arise. There are two general points. First, we contend that in most applications of regression, researchers are thinking in terms of a model anyway, and so we promote explicit representation of the model in research, for the sake of clarity, but also to make clear the grounds for falsification. Second, where researchers in fact apply regression as a tournament competition among predictors, which does happen in some sciences and professions focusing purely on prediction issues, we argue that this approach hides inherent ambiguities that can only obscure the real roles of variables in predicting outcomes. Thus, in this approach, the effects of some variables will regularly be underestimated relative to others.

We encourage an explicit linkage between the issue of causality and our interpretation of results, using a modeling perspective. X *affects, influences, shifts, changes* Y, because that is the way the regression model is structured, and saying X *is associated with* Y simply obscures what is being claimed. If it is just an association, we say, then don't use a method that requires asymmetry in the relationship. Of course, we advocate as well the clear distinction between *causal claims* and *causal evidence*, essentially paralleling the distinction between theory and evidence.

We introduced the more general version of a structural equation model later in the chapter, as a bridge to where we are going in the next chapter. This allowed us to introduce the concept of identification, which becomes very important in the general discussion of structural equation models in the chapters ahead. However, we should note that all of the models in this chapter are a type of structural equation model—involving only observed variables. In the next chapter, we introduce the "full" structural equation model, which adds another layer to the models of this chapter by specifying a role for "latent variables," conceptualized as the underlying true constructs that act as the source of what we observe in measurement but with error. One of the primary functions of the full model is to take into account and adjust for the effect of this measurement error.

Practice Questions

1. Below is a model showing the effect of community disorder (at the neighborhood level) on psychological distress (Turner, Shattuck, Hamby, & Finkelhor, 2013). Community disorder is a measure of the prevalence of social and physical signs of disorder in neighborhoods—including drug sales on the street, presence of gangs, seeing a police raid, extensive graffiti, deteriorated housing, and violence in the local school.

The model shows three indirect effects of community disorder on distress, through three mediators: (1) the rate of adverse life events in the past year; (2) family social support; and (3) the number of personal victimizations in the past year. The remaining direct effect after taking mediators into account is .05 and not significant.

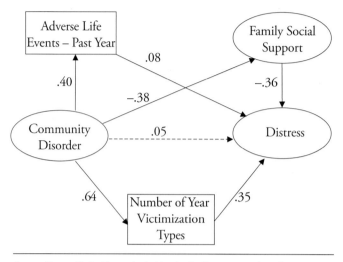

Source: Turner, H. A., Shattuck, A., Hamby, S., Finkelhor, D. (2013). Community disorder, victimization exposure, and mental health in a national sample of youth. Journal of Health and Social Behavior, 54(2), 268, Figure 2.

a. Calculate the indirect effect of disorder on distress *through the number of victimizations in the past year.*

b. One of the three indirect effects is much less important than the other two in explaining the effect of disorder. Which indirect effect is this?

c. Calculate the total effect of community disorder using the results in the model.

d. Calculate the percentage of the total effect explained in this model overall by the three mediating variables.

2. Consider the causal model that follows, showing the effects of parent's education and child intelligence on the child's educational achievement. Parental income and the child's achievement motivation both mediate the effect of parent's education.

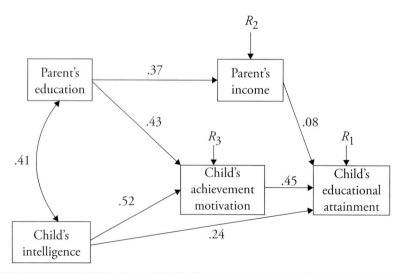

Answer these questions:

a. What is the indirect effect of parent's education on the child's education (a) through parent's income as a mediator, and (b) through the child's achievement motivation as a mediator?

b. Which indirect effect is more important in explaining the effect of parent's education?

c. Looking at the effect of a child's intelligence on child education, what is the total effect?

3. A few years ago in an undergraduate class on the sociology of mental health, a survey was conducted to explain grades on the term test. The following variables were measured (shown in the following model).

X_1: Overall **GPA** in university, measured in percentages

X_2: **Previous Class**, a dummy variable = 1 if the student had been in a previous class from the same professor and = 0 if not

X_3: **Classes Missed** = the number of classes **not** attended up to the first test

X_4: **Readings Not Read** = the number of readings the student had **not** read on the reading list at the time of the test

X_5: **Test Grade** = the term test grade in percentages

The model below shows the standardized coefficients estimated in a causal model in which **GPA** and **Previous Class** are exogenous, **Classes Missed** and **Readings Not Read** are intervening in a sequence, and the outcome is **Test Grade.**

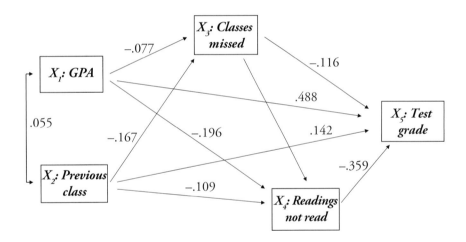

a. Write out the structural equation for X_5 only and derive (completely) the normal equation for r_{15}, using the following normal equations for prior variables:

$$r_{13} = \beta_{31} + \beta_{32}\, r_{12}$$
$$r_{23} = \beta_{32} + \beta_{31}\, r_{12}$$
$$r_{14} = \beta_{41} + \beta_{42}\, r_{12} + \beta_{43}\, \beta_{31} + \beta_{43}\, \beta_{32}\, r_{12}$$
$$r_{24} = \beta_{42} + \beta_{41}\, r_{12} + \beta_{43}\, \beta_{32} + \beta_{43}\, \beta_{31}\, r_{12}$$
$$r_{34} = \beta_{43} + \beta_{42}\, r_{12}\, \beta_{31} + \beta_{42}\, \beta_{32} + \beta_{41}\, \beta_{31} + \beta_{41}\, \beta_{32}\, r_{12}$$

b. Label each of the components of r_{15}, showing whether it is a direct effect, an indirect effect, a spuriousness component, or noncausal association.

c. From the results, show the four components of the *total causal effect* of **GPA** on **Test Grade.** Substitute coefficients and calculate the proportion of the total causal effect that is indirect.

4. There is a partially drawn causal model following this question, followed by a series of regression outputs. You will finish the drawing of the model in answering this question.

The results use data from Wave 1 of the National Survey of Families and Households. The issue addressed is the effect of women's job earnings on her hours of domestic work, in a sample of married or cohabiting women. The variables involved in this model and the attached results are as follows:

- **Rtaskhrs1:** The number of hours of domestic work reported by the woman.
- **Irearn1:** The woman's current earnings from employment
- **nkidathome:** The number of children in the household
- **momeduc:** The woman's mother's education
- **sideology1:** The gender attitudes of her partner, scored so that higher scores reflect more liberal gender attitudes

a. The next paragraph describes the structure of this model. Use this description to label each box in the model with the appropriate variable. All of the necessary paths in the model are already included.

The focal association in this model is between the woman's job earnings and her hours of domestic work—the ultimate dependent variable in this model. There are two control variables considered in this model in analyzing this association and thus there are two exogenous variables in the model: her mother's education and the number of children at home. Each may have an effect on both her earnings and the hours of domestic work. The causal part of the effect of her earnings on domestic work may be mediated by her partner's gender attitudes: The argument for this is that her earnings may liberalize her partner's attitudes, which may in turn reduce her domestic work. Because partner gender attitudes is a mediator, earlier controls in this model may also affect this variable directly as well.

b. The attached results show the standardized coefficients necessary to analyze the paths in this model. Use the results to put the appropriate coefficients on the appropriate paths in the model, using standardized coefficients only. Each output from PROC REG shows which dependent variable is involved in each model and the independent variables.

There are five models in Tables 6.A through 6.E:

Model 1: The effect of number of kids at home and mother's education on the woman's employment earnings

Model 2: The effect of number of kids at home, mother's education, and the woman's employment earnings on her partner's gender attitudes

Model 3: The bivariate effect of her earnings on her domestic task hours

Model 4: The effect of her earnings on domestic task hours controlling for number of kids at home and her mother's education

Model 5: Model 4 plus the mediating effect of her partner's gender attitudes.

c. Use the coefficients you have put on the paths in the model to calculate (without having to use normal equations):

c1. The total causal effect of her earnings on domestic work.

c2. The indirect causal effect of earnings on domestic work mediated by her partner's gender attitudes. What percentage of the total causal effect is explained by the partner's gender attitudes?

c3. *Given* that the total correlation between her earnings and her domestic work is shown by the standardized coefficient in Model 3, what percentage of the association is actually causal?

d. Use either the paths from the model or a normal equation you either derive or write out from the model to specify two components of spuriousness in the relationship between earnings and domestic work (there are more than two of this type of component in the focal association). Use whatever information necessary from answers to this or previous questions to calculate the percentage of the total association that is spurious.

Question 1 – The Form of the Causal Model

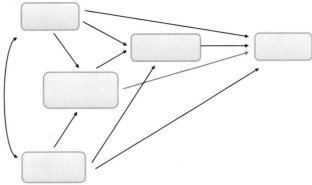

TABLE 6.A ● MODEL 1 FROM PROC REG; DEPENDENT VARIABLE: IREARN1

		Parameter Estimates				
Variable	DF	Parameter Estimate	Standard Error	t Value	Pr > |t|	Standardized Estimate
Intercept	1	3.54232	1.22919	2.88	0.0040	0
nkidathome1	1	−1.42145	0.25845	−5.50	<.0001	−0.16201
momeduc	1	0.77167	0.11097	6.95	<.0001	0.20484

TABLE 6.B ● MODEL 2 FROM PROC REG; DEPENDENT VARIABLE: SIDEOLOGY 1

		Parameter Estimates				
Variable	DF	Parameter Estimate	Standard Error	t Value	Pr > |t|	Standardized Estimate
Intercept	1	1.88194	0.10161	18.52	<.0001	0
nkidathome1	1	0.03684	0.02157	1.71	0.0880	0.04858
momeduc	1	0.03304	0.00933	3.54	0.0004	0.10147
irearn1	1	0.03004	0.00245	12.24	<.0001	0.34762

TABLE 6.C ● MODEL 3 FROM PROC REG; DEPENDENT VARIABLE: RTASKHRS1

		Parameter Estimates				
Variable	DF	Parameter Estimate	Standard Error	t Value	Pr > |t|	Standardized Estimate
Intercept	1	5.42457	0.11786	46.03	<.0001	0
irearn1	1	−0.07127	0.00774	−9.21	<.0001	−0.26451

TABLE 6.D ● MODEL 4 FROM PROC REG; DEPENDENT VARIABLE: RTASKHRS1

			Parameter Estimates			
Variable	DF	Parameter Estimate	Standard Error	t Value	Pr > |t|	Standardized Estimate
Intercept	1	5.78106	0.31957	18.09	<.0001	0
irearn1	1	−0.05794	0.00772	−7.51	<.0001	−0.21505
nkidathome1	1	0.57120	0.06784	8.42	<.0001	0.24162
momeduc	1	−0.11262	0.02936	−3.84	0.0001	-0.11095

TABLE 6.E ● MODEL 5 FROM PROC REG; DEPENDENT VARIABLE: RTASKHRS1

			Parameter Estimates			
Variable	DF	Parameter Estimate	Standard Error	t Value	Pr > |t|	Standardized Estimate
Intercept	1	6.49130	0.36258	17.90	<.0001	0
irearn1	1	−0.04661	0.00816	−5.71	<.0001	−0.17297
sideology1	1	−0.37740	0.09313	−4.05	<.0001	−0.12105
nkidathome1	1	0.58510	0.06747	8.67	<.0001	0.24750
momeduc	1	−0.10015	0.02932	−3.42	0.0007	−0.09867

AN INTRODUCTION TO STRUCTURAL EQUATION MODELS

In this chapter, we present the essential ingredients necessary for understanding and applying structural equation models. Compared to the last chapter, this chapter considers the "full" structural equation model, thus incorporating latent variables into these models.

We fully concur with the Bollen and Pearl (2013) caution that SEM (structural equation modeling) is not a magical technique for discovering causality. This is a misunderstanding of both SEM and the issue of causal inference in general. As pointed out in the previous chapter, causal inference is as much a matter of design and measurement as analytical technique. But SEM models do add analytical power to cases using only measured variables, and it is true that some of the techniques we consider in the chapters ahead address *some* of the problems facing causal inference.

There are two important issues incorporated into the full SEM model that help address core issues in causal inference. One is the adjustment for measurement error made possible in this model, thus putting variables on the same ground when concerned about the possibility of reciprocal causation. The other contribution is the use of an explicit measurement model for each underlying latent variable, thus separating conceptually the issue of measurement from the issue of substantive effects of X on Y or of Y on X, while also allowing the identification of certain noise parameters that can interfere with the estimation of causal effects. These "noise" parameters are typically sources of *nonrandom* (systematic) measurement error.

In this chapter, we consider the consequences, the many consequences, of adding latent variables to the observed variable models of the previous chapter.

7.1 LATENT VARIABLES

Latent variables are a type of unobserved variable in structural equation models. In general terms, they are the underlying "true" constructs that constitute the predominant systematic content portion of our observed measures, with random error as the rest of the content. Simply put, they stand for what we *want* to measure.

In general, *random error* refers to small, unsystematic, and volatile forces that are no more likely to affect observed scores on measures positively as negatively—in other words, the term is a general referent for the usually unnoticed and passing environmental and personal states that are **not** replicated over time.

The concept of measurement error logically implies that a "true score" exists that would be observed if measurement were perfect. This fact can be represented by the diagram in Figure 7.1.

FIGURE 7.1 ● OBSERVED MEASURES AS A FUNCTION OF A TRUE SCORE PLUS ERROR

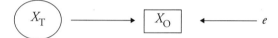

where

X_T = the "true score" on X,

X_O = the observed score on X,

e = measurement error in X.

The true score for X is a latent variable. The idea that the "true" variable is one we cannot observe directly can be a difficult idea to accept.

Latent variables are also sometimes defined like factors in a factor analysis—that is, the substantive core of what is shared in common among a number of measures, each imperfect, but sharing a common theme. Be aware of synonymous terms for latent variables, such as *unobserved variable*, *construct*, or *factor*.

If you are not convinced that a latent "true variable" exists, consider the concept of error. It is easy to accept the notion of measurement error; the question is *error from what?* In effect, the concept of measurement error **implies by definition** the presence of an unobserved true variable we are trying to measure.

7.1.0.1 Reliability

The model above can be expressed in equation form as follows:

$$X_{observed} = X_{true} + error$$

$$X_o = X_t + e$$

This is the basic equation of classical measurement theory. Using this equation, we can define reliability. In words, *the reliability of a measure is the amount of variance explained in the observed score by the true score.*

We use this equation to derive the definition of reliability. First, take the variances of both sides of the preceding equation:

$$V(X_O) = V(X_T) + V(e)$$

If we divide both sides of the equation by $V(X_O)$, we get

$$\frac{V(X_O)}{V(X_O)} = \frac{V(X_T)}{V(X_O)} + \frac{V(e)}{V(X_O)}$$

$$\text{Or}\quad 1 = \frac{V(X_T)}{V(X_O)} + \frac{V(e)}{V(X_O)}$$

This equation represents each component of the variance of X_O as a proportion of the total variance in X_O. On the left side, this equals 1. On the right side, $\frac{V(X_T)}{V(X_O)}$ is the proportion of the total variance due to variance in the true score—that is, the ***reliability***. The other component is thus the proportion of error variance, the unreliability of the measure.

We could look at the measurement equation as a bivariate regression with an independent and a dependent variable. There is no "b" for the regression coefficient shown explicitly because in this model it is 1 by assumption (unstandardized). Transforming the b to its standardized equivalent simplifies to

$$\beta = 1 \cdot \left(\frac{s_t}{s_0}\right) = \frac{s_t}{s_0}$$

which when squared (β^2) is the reliability of the observed measure, since

$$\beta^2 = \frac{s_t^2}{s_0^2} = \frac{V(X_T)}{V(X_O)}$$

This is a direct estimate of the reliability—not using the assumptions necessary in classical theory to support the concept of internal consistency (α). The main purpose of this demonstration, however, is to show that the true score on X is "free" of the effects of the random measurement error still contained in the observed score on X.

7.1.1 Why Latent Variables?

A fundamental issue is the point of using latent variables. There are four basic answers to this question. Latent variables

- Reduce the effects of measurement error on findings
- Identify models that would not be otherwise identified
- Estimate change in longitudinal data
- Estimate nonrandom error in variables

7.1.1.1 Reduce the Effects of Measurement Error on Findings

By specifying latent variables in structural equation models as separate from observed measures, as above, we achieve the ability to adjust for measurement error in observed variables. As a result,

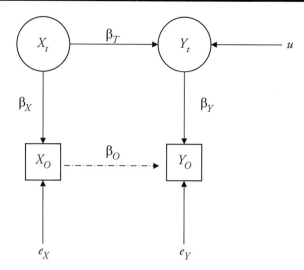

FIGURE 7.2 ● A MODEL FOR THE EFFECT OF "TRUE" X ON "TRUE" Y

latent variables are formally free of measurement error. The main consequence of this is that we avoid the underestimation or overestimation of effects resulting from measurement error in variables.

Use the model in Figure 7.2 as an example. Here we have two observed variables, X_O and Y_O, and the true score on X is assumed to be a cause of the true score of Y.

β_X is the (standardized) effect of the true score X_t on X observed, β_Y is the (standardized) effect of the true score Y_t on Y observed, β_O is the observed (standardized) regression coefficient for the effect of observed X on Y, and β_T is the true (standardized) effect of X_t on Y_t.

First we note that if X has random error (usually), then its unstandardized effect on Y will be underestimated: The lower its reliability, the higher the underestimation. The relationship between observed and true b can be written as follows:

$$b_o = b_t \cdot r^2_{X_O X_T}$$

$$b_o = b_t \cdot (\text{reliability of } X)$$

This means that the observed coefficient will *always* be less than true coefficient in this situation. Also, the unreliability of X will indirectly lead to the *overestimation* of the effects of other independent variables in the model. This has consequences in models where the other variables are controls or mediators since we then underestimate the direct effect and overestimate the associated effects. Or if the other variables have higher levels of measurement error, then we underestimate their role and overestimate the direct effect.

If we look at the model in terms of *standardized* effects of X, we can see that the effect we normally estimate in a regression is composed of three effects in the model. Using the standard rules of decomposing the association between observed variables (paths joining X_O to Y_O):

$$\beta_O = \beta_X \cdot \beta_T \cdot \beta_Y$$

Since the effects of each true score on each observed score will by definition be less than 1, we see again that the observed coefficient is attenuated relative to the true coefficient. In fact, the greater the unreliability, the more the true effect is being proportionalized in the observed coefficient. This problem is quite common in most research.

In general, it would be helpful to take measurement error into account where it exists. Models that incorporate latent variables explicitly are a way of dealing with these problems in order to get "better" estimates of relationships between variables—that is, estimates of effects that are formally free of random measurement error. If we believe measurement error exists, then we should be representing and estimating it in our models.

7.1.1.2 Identify Models That Would Not Be Otherwise Identified

When we use latent variables *that have multiple indicators (measures)* or we use latent variables *with single indicators at three or more points in time*, we will be able to identify parameters in models that we otherwise could not estimate. Specifically, by using what is called "restricted" factor models, which assume that the effects of some latent variables on some measures can be assumed to be zero, we can derive estimates of underlying ***unobserved*** covariances and variances of latent variables. Given these covariances and variances, we can then proceed to estimate structural equations for latent variables—in other words, estimate regressions involving variables we do not even observe!

7.1.1.3 Estimate Change in Longitudinal Data

If latent variables are free of measurement error, then estimating change in latent variables over time is not affected by that type of measurement problem (although others are possible). This means that we can improve our estimates of factors that do influence change in that latent variable and also adjust for *differential measurement error* in variables in the assessment of reciprocal effects of variables over time. It also means that we can estimate the proper level of stability versus change in variables through time because that stability is not underestimated due to measurement error.

7.1.1.4 Estimate Nonrandom Error in Variables

Under some conditions, we can also estimate levels of ***nonrandom*** error in variables and thus take into account the effects of this type of error on results. Nonrandom error results from stable or systematic sources of error in measures. These types of error may result from missing variables, response biases in measures, or shared methods variance over time. SEM is not entirely unique in its ability to incorporate nonrandom error, but it often allows for less restricted estimation of nonrandom error than some other approaches.

7.2 Identifying the Factor Analysis Model

The distinction between observed and latent variables introduces a new level to structural equation models. Now there is a "measurement" level, expressing the relations between underlying latent variables and their measured indicators, and a "structural" level, where we specify and estimate the effects of (latent) variables on each other, using structural equations that function in exactly the same way as for observed variable models.

A fundamental issue in all models with latent variables is how we identify parameters expressing relationships among variables that are not observed. If we look at the formula for a correlation, the working parts of it involve the actual scores on X and Y. How do we estimate a correlation when those parts are not observable? The answer to this question is to realize that correlations among latent variables as well as regression coefficients among latent variables are just parameters in an overall structural model that can be identified and, if so, estimated. This identification is possible via restrictions of the "usual" exploratory factor model.

7.2.1 The Exploratory Factor Analysis Model

To provide contrast, we begin with the traditional exploratory factor model, shown in Figure 7.3. The usual idea was to search for concepts underlying sets of measures. Given some restriction on the number of factors (concepts) involved, one had to allow for the possibility that any factor could affect scores on any measure, in order to "discover" which measures coalesced as factors. In the model expressed in the following equations, there are two factors (F), and five X measures. Error terms are denoted here by d.

The equations that express the accompanying model are:

$$X_1 = b_{11}F_1 + b_{12}F_2 + d_1$$
$$X_2 = b_{21}F_1 + b_{22}F_2 + d_2$$
$$X_3 = b_{31}F_1 + b_{32}F_2 + d_3$$
$$X_4 = b_{41}F_1 + b_{42}F_2 + d_4$$
$$X_5 = b_{51}F_1 + b_{52}F_2 + d_5$$

FIGURE 7.3 ● AN EXPLORATORY FACTOR MODEL

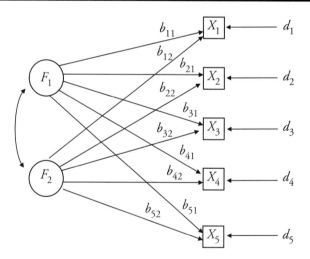

These equations are just like regression equations, with the assumption that variables are pre-centered so that there is no intercept. The so-called factor loadings here are just regression coefficients showing the effect of unobserved factors on the observed scores on the Xs. In effect, the factors are the "invisible hand" guiding the actual observed measures—but imperfectly.

The issue would be where the b's were high or low in these equations. Where they were high, measurement of that factor would be indicated. The question is whether the b parameters can be solved uniquely given the information available—the identification issue again.

7.2.1.1 Generalized *t*-Rule for Identification

We apply ***a generalized version of the* t-*rule*** to this model, where t is the number of unknown parameters again, but now we count the total number of covariances and variances among measured variables in the model available for the estimation of parameters. This assumes that we need to estimate not only the structural parameters but the error variances of the Xs as well. The *general form of the* t-*rule for structural equation models with both latent and measured variables is*:

$$t \le \frac{(p+q)(p+q+1)}{2}$$

where in general p = # of measures of endogenous latent variables,

q = # of measures of exogenous latent variables.

In the factor analysis model, only exogenous latent variables exist, so here

$\frac{(p+q)(p+q+1)}{2} = \frac{(0+5)(0+5+1)}{2} = \frac{(5 \cdot 6)}{2} = 15$ variances/covariances. There are, however, a total of 18 parameters to be estimated, including (a) 10 factor loadings, (b) 5 error variances for Xs, (c) the variances of the two factors, and (d) the correlation between F_1 and F_2.

Thus, there are 15 independent sources of information available to solve 18 parameters: the model is therefore ***underidentified***.

This problem was handled traditionally by superimposing guiding algorithms to arrive at a "solution" of the model. In an underidentified model, the problem is that an infinite number of solutions will reproduce the variances and covariances among the variables equally well, and thus algorithms for a solution are necessary.

7.2.2 The Confirmatory Factor Model

Now we consider another model that is a simplified version of the first. The word "simplified" here means that some paths are now missing, indicating that there is no effect of a particular factor on a particular measure—in other words, measures only measure certain things. Another word for simplified here is *restricted.* This is an important term because it implies that the investigator can make decisions a priori about what measures are influenced by what factors and specify his or her model to reflect this fact. In most cases, we have a good idea what measures are supposed to measure but also *not measure,* and here we take advantage of that fact. This leads to restricting certain paths to be zero.

The result of this is that we go from an underidentified to an overidentified model, one in which we (apparently) have excess information with which to distinguish between parameters (Figure 7.4). In the restricted factor model, the number of parameters to be solved is now 13, and so this model passes the counting rule. However, this rule is only a necessary condition, and further restrictions (assumptions) are necessary to identify this model (discussed later).

The idea is to impose restrictions judiciously where you strongly believe such restrictions are justified (usually meaning where there should be zero effects), and then test your ideas by estimating the restricted model and seeing whether the restricted model comes close to predicting the same covariances among variables as the observed covariances you start with. This is why this approach is called ***confirmatory*** factor analysis, although in reality some erosion of a pure confirmatory stance is usually necessary.

FIGURE 7.4 ● A CONFIRMATORY FACTOR MODEL

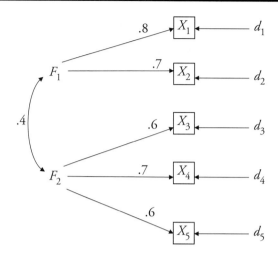

The difficult thing to realize is that, by imposing restrictions, you can identify all of the covariances and variances of the latent (unobserved) variables and thereby gain access to estimating structural relations among the latent variables as well. Once you have the covariances and variances of factors identified as parameters, you have the working materials necessary to estimate the structural equations among factors.

7.2.3 Identification Example for a Confirmatory Factor Model

Every model you estimate has to be identified—or the results are meaningless. The possibly new element of thinking here is that parameters are estimated as unknowns that can be solved for but not by algebraic formulas. Eventually, we will develop some guidelines to help you to decide whether a specific model is identified (in the next chapter). The "ultimate" proof of the identification of a model is to demonstrate algebraically how each parameter can be solved in terms of given information—that is, a set of covariances and variances among variables.

To give an example of how an SEM model can be solved for the parameters, we draw on an example in Scott Long's book on *Confirmatory Factor Analysis* (1983). Figure 7.5 shows the model we are concerned with. In this model, there are two factors, and each has two observed measures. One of the measures (X_2) shares nonrandom error with another (X_4).

The equations for the model are

$$X_1 = b_{11}F_1 + d_1$$

$$X_2 = b_{21}F_1 + d_2$$

$$X_3 = b_{32}F_2 + d_3$$

$$X_4 = b_{42}F_2 + d_4$$

To find out whether this model can be identified, we use the method of **_covariance algebra_** introduced by example in the previous chapter. We can use covariance algebra here to derive

FIGURE 7.5 ● A TWO FACTOR; TWO-INDICATOR MODEL

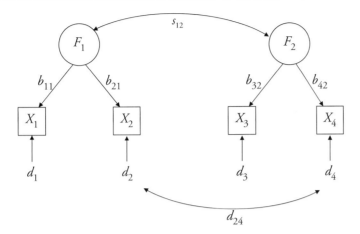

equations showing the structure of all covariances and variances of the measures in a model, as a function of the parameters of the model. We utilize the three general rules of covariance algebra:

1. $\mathbf{cov\ (c, X_1) = 0}$

The covariance between a constant and variable must be zero.

2. $\mathbf{cov\ (cX_1, X_2) = c \cdot cov\ (X_1, X_2)}$

The covariance between a constant times a variable and another variable is the constant times the covariance of the variables.

3. $\mathbf{cov\ ((X_1 + X_2), X_3) = cov\ (X_1, X_3) + cov\ (X_2, X_3)}$

The covariance between the sum of two variables and a third variable is the covariance of each variable in the sum with the third variable, added up.

We should first apply the t-rule to this model. Note there are four observed Xs in this model, and a total of 12 parameters to be estimated (four factor loadings (b); two factor variances for F_1 and F_2, their covariance; four error variances (d); and one covariance of errors (d_{24}).

Thus $t = 12$.

$$\text{But } \frac{(p+q)(p+q+1)}{2} = 10$$

Note the "10" reflects four variance equations and six covariance equations available to solve for parameters.

Thus this model is not identified as is. What can be done? ***In all models with latent variables, we need to impose restrictions to identify the variances of the latent factors. Usually this is done by fixing one loading for each factor to 1.*** This allows the variances of factors to be identified, since now there will be 10 parameters to solve, not 12. Another way to do this is to directly fix the variance of each factor to 1, which can be done only for factors that are exogenous.

To proceed, we set $b_{11} = 1$ and $b_{32} = 1$. It does not matter which factor loading you choose to set to 1 for each factor.

Now the structural equations are

$$X_1 = F_1 + d_1$$

$$X_2 = b_{21}F_1 + d_2$$

$$X_3 = F_2 + d_3$$

$$X_4 = b_{42}F_2 + d_4$$

because $b_{11} = b_{32} = 1$.

7.2.3.1 Deriving Variance/Covariance Equations

Assuming we are solving the parameters of the model in a given sample, first form a covariance of each endogenous variable with itself—in other words, its variance. For example,

$$\text{cov}(X_1X_1) = \text{cov}((F_1 + d_1),(F_1 + d_1))$$

$$= \text{cov}(F_1^2 + F_1d_1 + F_1d_1 + d_1^2)$$

$$s_{X_1}^2 = s_{F_1}^2 + s_{d_1}^2$$

For X_2,

$$\text{cov}(X_2,X_2) = \text{cov}((b_{21}F_1 + d_2),(b_{21}F_1 + d_2))$$

$$= \text{cov}(b_{21}^2 F_1^2 + d_2^2)$$

$$s_{X_2}^2 = b_{21}^2 s_{F_1}^2 + s_{d_2}^2$$

These results can be used to infer the structure of the other X variances here:

$$s_{X_3}^2 = s_{F_2}^2 + s_{d_3}^2$$

$$s_{X_4}^2 = b_{42}^2 s_{F_2}^2 + s_{d_4}^2$$

There are six covariances among the four observed variables to derive. For example, to get s_{13},

$$\text{cov}(X_1X_3) = \text{cov}((F_1 + d_1),(F_2 + d_3))$$

$$= \text{cov}(F_1F_2 + F_1d_3 + d_1F_2 + d_1d_3)$$

$$s_{13} = s_{F_1F_2} = s_{12}$$

For s_{14},

$$\text{cov}(X_1, X_4) = \text{cov}((F_1 + d_1), (b_{42} F_2 + d_4)),$$

$$= \text{cov}(F_1 \, b_{42} F_2)$$

$$s_{14} = b_{42} s_{F_1 F_2} = b_{42} s_{12}$$

Following this for other covariances produces

$$s_{23} = b_{21} s_{12}$$

$$s_{24} = b_{21} s_{12} b_{42} + d_{24}$$

$$s_{12} = b_{21} s_{F_1}^2$$

$$s_{34} = b_{42} s_{F_2}^2$$

Note the difference for s_{24}, caused by the correlated error.

Parameters can now be solved as follows:

$$s_{12} = s_{13}$$

$$b_{42} = {s_{14}} \big/ {s_{12}}$$

$$b_{21} = {s_{23}} \big/ {s_{12}}$$

$$s_{F_1}^2 = {s_{12}} \big/ {b_{21}}$$

$$s_{F_2}^2 = {s_{34}} \big/ {b_{42}}$$

The error variances are usually identified after the other parameters are solved. For example, look at the variance equation for X_2 and isolate the variance of the error in that equation:

$$s_{d_2}^2 = s_{X_2}^2 - b_{21}^2 s_{F_1}^2$$

Note also

$$d_{24} = s_{24} - b_{21} s_{12} b_{42}$$

This proves we can in fact identify a correlated error term between X_2 and X_4. Of course, we do not prove the identification of each model individually. Instead, we can use developed proofs as guidelines to the models we can assume are identified (in the next chapter). However, this derivation of parameters demonstrates specifically what is meant by solving for parameters, and it shows that unobserved variances and covariances can be solved, even though we never have direct observation of the latent variables in a model.

7.2.4 Back to the Causal Model for Observed Variables

The literature on causal models began by using observed variables and necessarily assuming perfect measurement. One point needs to be made here: Models with observed variables, as in the previous chapter and in much of the literature, can be seen as a particular sub-case of more general models involving unobserved variables and explicit representation of relationships between latent and observed variables. One can imagine the classic observed variable model as one in which, for every variable, a full specification would show complete determination by true scores of observed scores and all measurement errors would be zero (see Figure 7.6). In many cases, this implicit specification may be fatally unrealistic.

FIGURE 7.6 ●   THE MEASUREMENT ASSUMPTIONS IN A MODEL WITH OBSERVED VARIABLES

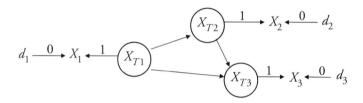

7.3 THE FULL SEM MODEL

The full structural equation model represents an integration of factor analysis and structural equation models for observed variables. By restricting the factor model, one gains the ability to estimate structural equation models for ***factors***—that is, latent variables. In this version, we estimate the structural equation model among the latent variables, instead of the observed variables.

Each SEM (structural equation model) involves

- *A <u>measurement</u> model showing how a set of hypothesized latent variables are measured by a set of observed indicators*

- *A <u>structural</u> model that takes the covariance and variances of the latent variables and estimates a causal system of relationships among them*

7.3.1 A Brief Note on Estimation

SEM models are usually ***overidentified***. In these models, one has, in effect, multiple estimates of each parameter. The question is how to use the multiple sources of information most efficiently.

In overidentified models, ordinary least squares estimators will usually be less desirable than any one of a range of alternative estimators. Maximum likelihood (ML) has optimal properties under these conditions:

- In sufficiently large samples, it is *asymptotically* unbiased and efficient.

- Formally these properties hold only under conditions of multivariate normality.

7.3.1.1 Maximum Likelihood (ML) Fitting Function

The ML fitting function generally has the following form:

$$F_{ML} = (tr(S\widehat{\Sigma}^{-1}) - (p+q)) + (\log\left|\widehat{\Sigma}\right| - \log|S|)$$

where

tr = the *trace* matrix function, described below,

S = the sample covariance matrix for all measured variables,

$\widehat{\Sigma}$ = the covariance matrix among measured variables produced by a particular set of parameter estimates,

$p + q$ = the total number of measured variables, and

$|...|$ = notation for the determinant of a matrix.

The idea is to find a version of $\widehat{\Sigma}$ that is as close as possible to S. It is difficult to see how this function works, but it helps to look at it in two parts. Looking at the first set of parenthesized relations, we see that the inverse of sigma is taken. This can be seen as dividing by that number, in this case, matrix. As S and sigma become more similar (desirable), the value $S\Sigma^{-1}$ will approach an identity matrix with 1's in the diagonal and 0's off the diagonal. The trace (tr) of a matrix is the sum of the diagonal elements, so as the fit improves this sum approaches ($p + q$). Thus, ($p + q$) is subtracted from this value so that the value approaches 0 as fit improves.

The second set of terms involves the difference in the log of the determinants of Σ and S. Obviously, as they become more similar, so do their determinants, and this value will also approach zero.

7.3.1.2 Goodness of Fit

All SEM software produces a χ^2 (chi-square) test of fit for overidentified models that equals $N - 1$ times the minimum value of the fitting function (i.e., $\chi^2 = (N - 1)F_{ML}$). It is essential that this "test" is understood from two perspectives:

1. The null hypothesis is one of "perfect fit" of the model. Thus, one wants ***not*** to reject the null. Here rejecting the null means the model may not fit very well. The probability level under the null is printed; values ***greater*** than .01 or .05 are welcome.

2. However, the formula for χ^2 shows it depends directly on sample size. Therefore, very trivial departures from good fit can cause χ^2 to be significant in large samples. Thus it is often not very useful. In the next chapter we will propose other measures of fit.

7.3.2 Example 1: A Confirmatory Factor Model

We begin with an example testing a specific factor structure for the structure of well-being, based on seven items taken from Ryff's general measure of well-being and included in Wave 2 of the National Survey of Families and Households. In this and the later examples, we *will* show how PROC CALIS in SAS can be used to specify each model, but we will also duplicate certain models here with matching STATA code. We do not show the coding of variables here, but in general, you want to do two things: (1) recode any missing data codes to a system missing value; and (2) reverse code variables that are coded in the opposite direction to the factor as stated in the model. For example, if the statement is, "I have not experienced many warm and trusting relationships," but the underlying factor is Positive Relations, we suggest reverse coding this item before you run the program.

The results we show in this chapter are not the final results in general because we defer the issue of fitting these models until the next chapter. This means, basically, that results here generally suggest there are fit problems between the imputed covariance matrix implied by the model and the actual observed covariances. Thus we should not "believe" these estimates until we consider better fitted models. In a later chapter, we also change the way in which this model is estimated.

The example fits a three-factor model for these items, based on the original assumptions of this measurement model. The hypothesized factors and their measures (shown by variable name) are shown in Table 7.1.

TABLE 7.1 ● COMPONENTS OF A SIMPLIFIED RYFF MEASUREMENT MODEL OF WELL-BEING	
Factor	**Items**
SELF-ACCEPTANCE (SA)	*personal*: "I like most parts of my personality."
	turnout: "When I look at the story of my life, I am pleased about how things have turned out."
	disapp: "I feel disappointed about my achievements . . ." (reversed)
POSITIVE RELATIONS (PR)	*close*: "Maintaining close relationships has been difficult." (reversed)
	trust: "I have not experienced many warm and trusting relationships . . ." (reversed)
AUTONOMY (AUT)	*opinions*: "I have confidence in my own opinions, even if they are different from the way most other people think."
	judge: "I judge myself by what I think is important, not by the values of others . . ."

To specify this exact factor structure, you implicitly set factor loadings on *other* factors to zero. In our approach, we allow covariances (correlations) among the factors since these parameters are identified.

Here is the PROC CALIS run that estimates this model, followed by a discussion of what each statement does:

```
ods graphics on;
proc calis data=temp pestim cov method=ml mod simple;
var personal_sa turnout_sa disapp_sa close_pr trust_pr opinions_aut
judge_aut;

lineqs

personal_sa =SA_1 f_sa + d1,
turnout_sa  =SA_2 f_sa + d2,
disapp_sa   =SA_3 f_sa + d3,
close_pr    =PR_1 f_pr + d4,
```

```
trust_pr     =PR_2 f_pr + d5,
opinions_aut =AUT_1 f_aut + d6,
judge_aut    =AUT_2 f_aut + d7;

std
        d1-d7=errord1-errord7,
        f_sa f_pr f_aut = 1 1 1;

cov
                f_sa f_pr  = cov21,
                f_sa f_aut = cov31,
                f_pr f_aut = cov32;

pathdiagram diagram=all exogcov;
weight mufinw93;
run;
```

- **ods graphics:** This line turns on the ODS graphics system that allows output of a graphical version of the model and its results.

- **proc calis:** This statement specifies *temp* as the data to use, uses the *pestim* keyword to ask for essential output for the estimates, tells PROC CALIS to analyze a covariance matrix (*cov*), specifies the use of maximum likelihood (*method=ml*), asks for modification indices (*mod*) for model-fitting—showing areas of bad fit in the model—and asks for simple statistics *(simple)*. Many of these are standard choices.

- **lineqs:** This single statement takes a number of lines in the program. This is where you write the equations for the model. Each line ends with a comma until the final equation, which ends with a semicolon. Each equation names a dependent variable on the left side of the equal sign and independent variables on the right. On the right side, you need to give names to the factors starting with an "f," so SAS knows what it is. You also have to give names to the parameters you want SAS to estimate, here the "SA_1," "SA_2," and so forth. These are parameter names for the factor loadings. You also give names to the error terms, here d1 to d7.

- **std:** This statement is an acronym for "standard deviations," as a proxy for variances. Here you give names for the estimated error variances in the equation: "errord1-errord7," using the dash convention to allow listing of variable names ending in consecutive numbers. This statement also sets all of the variances of the factors to 1, a choice possible because all of the factors in the model are exogenous. This is done by listing the variable names before an equal sign and then the same number of 1's after. This is a way of fixing a set of parameters to a given value.

- **cov:** This is where you specify covariances among the factors. This statement gives names to the covariances to be estimated among factors, considered as free parameters in this model.

- **pathdiagram:** This asks for a path diagram of the results. We ask for all types of solutions and to include covariances among exogenous factors.

- **weight:** This assigns a case weight for the analysis, using the variable "mufinw93."

Selected parts of the output are shown in Table 7.2:

TABLE 7.2 ● RESULTS FOR THE CONFIRMATORY FACTOR MODEL

Simple Statistics		
Variable	Mean	Std Dev
personal_sa	1.85990	0.83383
turnout_sa	2.34424	1.32459
disapp_sa	2.90745	1.52304
close_pr	2.72915	1.59328
trust_pr	2.58393	1.64113
opinions_aut	1.88529	1.05468
judge_aut	1.74893	1.00549

This table shows simple statistics.

Iteration	Restarts	Function Calls	Active Constraints	Objective Function	Objective Function Change	Max Abs Gradient Element	Lambda	Ratio Between Actual and Predicted Change
1	0	4	0	0.09166	0.0166	0.0434	0	1.201
2	0	6	0	0.08907	0.00259	0.0126	0	1.270
3	0	8	0	0.08865	0.000426	0.00583	0	1.369
4	0	10	0	0.08857	0.000077	0.00244	0	1.406
5	0	12	0	0.08855	0.000014	0.00108	0	1.424
6	0	14	0	0.08855	2.679E-6	0.000466	0	1.430
7	0	16	0	0.08855	5.048E-7	0.000200	0	1.432
8	0	18	0	0.08855	9.528E-8	0.000088	0	1.433
9	0	20	0	0.08855	1.799E-8	0.000037	0	1.434
10	0	22	0	0.08855	3.398E-9	0.000016	0	1.434
11	0	24	0	0.08855	6.42E-10	6.978E-6	0	1.434

This table shows the iteration process arriving at a solution, where the function meets a criterion for finding a near zero slope of the function value, indicating a minimum.

Fit Summary		
Modeling Info	Number of Observations	9514
	Number of Variables	7
	Number of Moments	28
	Number of Parameters	17
	Number of Active Constraints	0
	Baseline Model Function Value	1.0692
	Baseline Model Chi-Square	10171.3054
	Baseline Model Chi-Square DF	21
	Pr > Baseline Model Chi-Square	<.0001
Absolute Index	Fit Function	0.0886
	Chi-Square	842.3836
	Chi-Square DF	11
	Pr > Chi-Square	<.0001
	Z-Test of Wilson & Hilferty	22.9838
	Hoelter Critical N	223
	Root Mean Square Residual (RMR)	0.0821
	Standardized RMR (SRMR)	0.0510
	Goodness of Fit Index (GFI)	0.9747

This is a table of fit statistics we will deal with more explicitly in the next chapter. For the moment, notice that there are many, and the information here can be used in various ways. You can see that the chi-square test of the model is significant, and in general, the model does not fit sufficiently.

Fit Summary		
Parsimony Index	Adjusted GFI (AGFI)	0.9356
	Parsimonious GFI	0.5106
	RMSEA Estimate	0.0891
	RMSEA Lower 90% Confidence Limit	0.0841
	RMSEA Upper 90% Confidence Limit	0.0943
	Probability of Close Fit	<.0001
	ECVI Estimate	0.0921
	ECVI Lower 90% Confidence Limit	0.0825
	ECVI Upper 90% Confidence Limit	0.1025
	Akaike Information Criterion	876.3836
	Bozdogan CAIC	1015.1125
	Schwarz Bayesian Criterion	998.1125
	McDonald Centrality	0.9572
Incremental Index	Bentler Comparative Fit Index	0.9181
	Bentler-Bonett NFI	0.9172
	Bentler-Bonett Non-normed Index	0.8436
	Bollen Normed Index Rho1	0.8419
	Bollen Non-normed Index Delta2	0.9182
	James et al. Parsimonious NFI	0.4804

This is the solution for the measurement part of the model in unstandardized terms. In these kinds of models, usually the standardized solution is more useful.

Linear Equations						
personal_sa	=	0.4546 (**)	f_sa	+	1.0000	d1
turnout_sa	=	0.7437 (**)	f_sa	+	1.0000	d2
disapp_sa	=	0.8041 (**)	f_sa	+	1.0000	d3
close_pr	=	1.2179 (**)	f_pr	+	1.0000	d4
trust_pr	=	1.0850 (**)	f_pr	+	1.0000	d5
opinions_aut	=	0.5792 (**)	f_aut	+	1.0000	d6
judge_aut	=	0.5675 (**)	f_aut	+	1.0000	d7

This is the standardized solution. The factor loadings look acceptable for all three factors, varying from about .54 to .76. What these results do not tell us is whether there are missing loadings not estimated in this model.

Standardized Results for Linear Equations						
personal_sa	=	0.5452 (**)	f_sa	+	1.0000	d1
turnout_sa	=	0.5615 (**)	f_sa	+	1.0000	d2
disapp_sa	=	0.5280 (**)	f_sa	+	1.0000	d3
close_pr	=	0.7644 (**)	f_pr	+	1.0000	d4
trust_pr	=	0.6611 (**)	f_pr	+	1.0000	d5
opinions_aut	=	0.5492 (**)	f_aut	+	1.0000	d6
judge_aut	=	0.5644 (**)	f_aut	+	1.0000	d7

Covariances Among Exogenous Variables						
Var1	Var2	Parameter	Estimate	Standard Error	t Value	Pr > |t|
f_sa	f_pr	cov21	0.68969	0.01326	51.9962	<.0001
f_sa	f_aut	cov31	0.70692	0.01755	40.2764	<.0001
f_pr	f_aut	cov32	0.19500	0.01778	10.9703	<.0001

Because we standardized the factors, the covariances among them are in fact correlations. These correlations are quite high, in two of three cases, raising a question as to whether the factors involved are in fact necessarily or functionally distinct.

FIGURE 7.7 ● THE CONFIRMATORY MODEL PARAMETERS

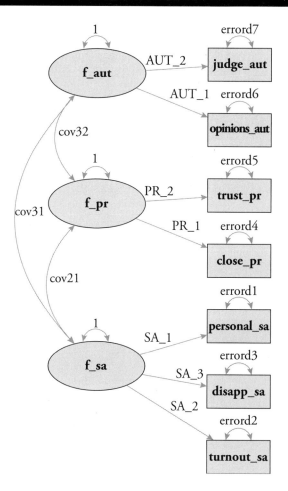

Two path diagrams for this model are shown: (1) a model showing where the parameters estimated occur in the model (Figure 7.7) and (2) a model with the standardized results (Figure 7.8).

This diagram in Figure 7.7 allows you to check that your model is specified as you intended. Note that variances are represented as curved arrows pointing at the same variable.

Figure 7.8 shows the simplest way to assess the results overall, including the standardized factor loadings and the fit. The self-acceptance factor (**f_sa**) seems to overlap considerably with the other two factors.

We argue that this is the preferable way to conduct factor analyses, for a number of reasons. First, you have to posit a model first, which means you have to know what measures what before you begin. This is a good thing, and in most cases is not a problem. Second, this approach produces a test of the fit of the model and thus gives you direct information about the assumptions in your measurement model. This model doesn't yet fit, so something is missing. The next step here would be to modify the model to achieve acceptable fit, since this may change the pattern of findings significantly. Third, you can test simpler versus more complex models directly using a test to assess the change in fit across models, to be discussed in the next chapter.

FIGURE 7.8 ● THE STANDARDIZED RESULTS FROM THE CONFIRMATORY FACTOR MODEL

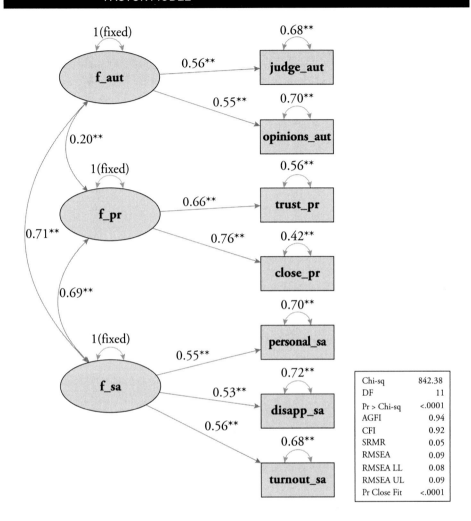

Chi-sq	842.38
DF	11
Pr > Chi-sq	<.0001
AGFI	0.94
CFI	0.92
SRMR	0.05
RMSEA	0.09
RMSEA LL	0.08
RMSEA UL	0.09
Pr Close Fit	<.0001

7.3.2.1 Confirmatory Factor Analysis in STATA

We present the code in STATA and the standardized output for the same model. Some comments are embedded in the code, but we explain running SEM in STATA with a more complete example later. Note again that defaults in SAS and STATA differ in ways that will slightly affect the findings. The coefficients in the standardized output are the same, but the robust standard errors in STATA mean the standard errors will not match.

NOTE make sure that the factors are in capital letters to tell STATA that they are latent variables

```
*names of variables: mufinw93 personal _ sa turnout _ sa disapp _ sa close
_ pr trust _ pr opinions _ aut judge _ aut*
```

```
*use this command to run the standardized model for interpretation*

sem (F_AUT -> opinions_aut judge_aut) (F_PR -> close_pr trust_pr)
(F_SA -> personal_sa turnout_sa disapp_sa)
[pweight=mufinw93], stand
(491 observations with missing values excluded;
 specify option 'method(mlmv)' to use all observations)


Endogenous variables

Measurement: opinions_aut judge_aut close_pr trust_pr
personal_sa turnout_sa disapp_sa


Exogenous variables

Latent:    F_AUT F_PR F_SA


Fitting target model:

Iteration 0:  log pseudolikelihood = -104712.43
Iteration 1:  log pseudolikelihood = -104615.65
Iteration 2:  log pseudolikelihood = -104561.04
Iteration 3:  log pseudolikelihood = -104557.8
Iteration 4:  log pseudolikelihood = -104557.69
Iteration 5:  log pseudolikelihood = -104557.69


Structural equation model          Number of obs   =   9514
Estimation method = ml
Log pseudolikelihood= -104557.69


    (1) [opinions_aut]F_AUT = 1
    (2) [close_pr]F_PR = 1
    (3) [personal_sa]F_SA = 1
```

Standardized	Coef	Robust StdErr	z	P>|z|	[95% ConfInterval]	
Measurement opinions_aut <-						
F_AUT	.5491536	.0214509	25.60	0.000	.5071106	.5911967
_cons	1.78859	.0187442	95.42	0.000	1.751852	1.825328

judge _ aut <-						
F_AUT	.5644312	.0220275	25.62	0.000	.5212582	.6076043
_cons	1.74039	.0196633	88.51	0.000	1.70185	1.778929
close _ pr <-						
F_PR	.7643915	.0148534	51.46	0.000	.7352794	.7935035
_cons	1.713917	.0115675	148.17	0.000	1.691245	1.736589
trust _ pr <-						
F_PR	.6611054	.0143949	45.93	0.000	.6328919	.6893189
_cons	1.575405	.0100114	157.36	0.000	1.555783	1.595027
personal_sa <-						
F_SA	.5452312	.0184999	29.47	0.000	.5089721	.5814903
_cons	2.23185	.029441	75.81	0.000	2.174147	2.289553
turnout _ sa <-						
F_SA	.5614783	.0152837	36.74	0.000	.5315228	.5914338
_cons	1.770817	.012963	136.61	0.000	1.74541	1.796224
disapp _ sa <-						
F_SA	.5279444	.0168854	31.27	0.000	.4948496	.5610392
_cons	1.910096	.0143968	132.67	0.000	1.881879	1.938313
Variance						
e.opinions_aut	.6984303	.0235597			.6537475	.7461671
e.judge_aut	.6814174	.024866			.634383	.731939
e.close_pr	.4157057	.0227076			.3734993	.4626814
e.trust_pr	.5629397	.0190331			.5268446	.6015077
e.personal_sa	.7027229	.0201734			.6642755	.7433956
e.turnout_sa	.6847421	.0171629			.6519163	.7192208
e.disapp_sa	.7212747	.0178291			.6871632	.7570794
F_AUT	1				.	
F_PR	1				.	
F_SA	1				.	
Covariance						
F_AUT						
F_PR	.1950037	.0224628	8.68	0.000	.1509774	.2390301
F_SA	.7069331	.0308035	22.95	0.000	.6465594	.7673069
F_PR						
F_SA	.6896861	.0202488	34.06	0.000	.6499992	.7293729

7.3.3 Example 2: Social Class, Mastery, and Depression

Here we consider a typical application of the full structural equation model, an example that includes longitudinal data and the specification of a baseline measure of depression at the first time point in the NSFH, so we can estimate the effect of social class net of baseline depression. That means that any effect of social class is on *changes* in depression over the six-year lag between Waves I and II. This example follows the logic of examples in the previous chapter by also asking whether mastery mediates the effect of social class on depression.

Figure 7.9 represents the model we want to estimate. There are four latent variables in this model: depression in 1988 (exogenous), SES in 1988 (exogenous), mastery in 1994 (endogenous), and depression in 1994 (endogenous). Each of these latent variables has multiple indicators (observed measures), although this is not necessary. If you only have one indicator for a latent variable, however, you must *fix its error term to zero and its factor loading in the program to 1*—or the model will not be identified.

The gray arrows in the diagram go from the latent variables to the observed indicators. The multiple indicators of each latent variable must be intended to be "equivalent" measures of the

---

FIGURE 7.9 ● THE FULL SEM MODEL FOR SES, MASTERY, AND DEPRESSION

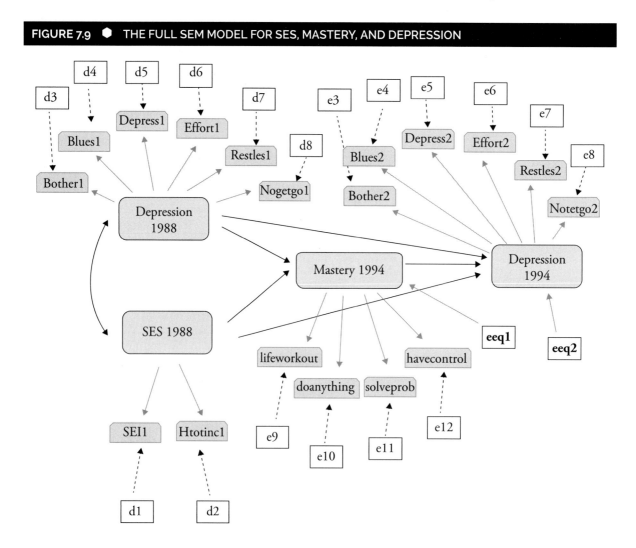

underlying concept represented by the latent variable. This is not a technique for measures that do not overlap enough—that is, are not sufficiently correlated—to assume they do measure the same underlying concept. Basically, if the pool of measures for each factor is not sufficiently cohesive, this will result in a model that fits the set of input covariances poorly. Usually, this means that multiple factors are being measured, not one. We emphasize this because a common error in the early application of these models is an overly broad assumption about the nature of latent variables.

Each measure (indicator) has an error term—the measurement error that is independent of the underlying latent variable. The assumption is that this error is random, but this can be modified. The errors for exogenous measures are labeled starting with "d," and the errors for endogenous measures are labeled starting with "e."

The structural part of the model is represented by the Black arrows between latent variables. This part is interpretively the same as the models of the last chapter, but these relationships are estimated formally free of measurement error. Finally, there are equation error terms (**eeq1** and **eeq2**) at the structural level of the model as well.

The measures here are

- *For SES*
  - ○ SEI1 : the occupational status score for the respondent
  - ○ Htotinc1: Total household income

- **For Depression** (in days per week)**:**
  - ○ Botherx: "Feeling bothered by things that usually don't bother you"
  - ○ Bluesx: "Feeling that you could not shake off the blues"
  - ○ Depressx: "Feeling depressed"
  - ○ Effortx: "Feeling that everything you did was an effort"
  - ○ Restlesx: "Sleeping restlessly"
  - ○ Nogetgox: "Feeling that you could not get going"

- **For Mastery** (the belief that you have control over life outcomes)
  - ○ lifeworkout: "I have always felt pretty sure my life would work out the way I wanted it to."
  - ○ doanything: "I can do just about anything I really set my mind to do."
  - ○ solveprob: "There is really no way I can solve some of the problems I have" (**reverse-coded**).
  - ○ havecontrol: "I have little control over the things that happen to me" (**reverse-coded**).

The basic point of the model is to first estimate the effects of social class on depression, over time, controlling for baseline depression, so that we observe the effect of social class on the changes in depression, over a six-year period, and then second, to test the role of mastery in explaining the effect of social class. The basic hypothesis is that social class bestows, through access to opportunity and essential resources, learned mastery, and in turn, mastery is a fundamental key to avoiding depression.

You do not have to estimate this model in two stages, as in the last chapter, using a regression approach. Output from this model includes estimates of the total effect of SES – the same that you would get if mastery was removed from this model – as well as the direct and indirect effects. The total association is also available, so that the reduction in the causal portion of the effect due to controls can be calculated as well.

7.3.3.1 Estimating the Model in SAS

As before, you prepare variables for use in the model by ensuring missing data is coded as missing and by reverse-coding selected variables as necessary. Note that you are ***not*** adding up items into overall scores in any way—that misses the point. The variables fed to the model are the individual measures for the latent variables in the model.

The run of PROC CALIS for this model is shown following. We comment on new statements and options in this program relative to the example for confirmatory factor models.

```
ods graphics on;

proc calis data=sesmh cov pcorr maxiter=500 maxfunc=1000 pshort stderr /
*effpart*/ simple mod method=ml;
lineqs

/* measurement model equations */

          htotinc1 = 1. fSES88 + d1,
          bestSEI1 = SES12 fSES88 + d2,

          bother1 = dep11 fdep88 + d3,
          blues1 = dep12 fdep88 + d4,
          depress1 = 1. fdep88 + d5,
          effort1 = dep14 fdep88 + d6,
          restles1 = dep15 fdep88 + d7,
          nogetgo1 = dep16 fdep88 + d8,

          bother2= dep21 fdep94 + e3,
          blues2=  dep22 fdep94 + e4,
          depress2= 1. fdep94 + e5,
          effort2= dep24 fdep94 + e6,
          restles2= dep25 fdep94 + e7,
          nogetgo2= dep26 fdep94 + e8,

      lifeworkout = control1 fmastery + e9,
      doanything = control2 fmastery + e10,
      solveprob = control3 fmastery + e11,
      havecontrol = 1. fmastery + e12,

/* latent variable structural equations */

          fmastery = bSESC fses88 + bdepc fdep88 + eeq1,
          fdep94 = bSESd fses88 + bdepd fdep88 + bcontrol fmastery + eeq2;

/* variances */
          std
```

```
            e3-e12 = errore3-errore12,
            d1-d8 = errord1-errord8,
            fSES88 = varSES88, fdep88 = vardep88,
            eeq1 = erroreqc, eeq2 = erroreqd;

/* covariances */

cov
            fSES88 fdep88 = cov88;
    /* This section not relevant in the initial model. Used later to fit the
    model. Commented out here.*/
    *e9 e10 = errorcov1,
            e6 e8 = errorcov2,
            d4 d5 = errorcov3;
            *e7 d7 = errorcov4;
            /*eeq1 eeq2 = coveq*/

pathdiagram diagram=all exogcov;
weight mufinw93;

run;
```

Here is an annotated overview of setting up this program:

- **PROC CALIS:** The options used here together run a standard model. Note there are many other options possible. New options include the following:
  ○ **pcorr**: Print the computed input matrix as part of the output.
  ○ **maxiter**: This is the allowed number of iterations of the maximum likelihood algorithm.
  ○ **maxfunc**: Total number of allowed function calls during iterations. You can increase these numbers.
  ○ **pshort**: Ask for the shorter version of the output.
  ○ **stderr:** Asks for standard errors. You will get t tests anyway.

- *The lineqs statement*: Here the equations include both measurement and structural model equations, using these conventions:
  ○ Remember there must be one factor loading for each latent factor set to 1, in order to identify the variance of the latent factor.
  ○ The made-up names for the free factor loadings are "SES12" for the loading on SES, "depxx" for the depression loadings, where "xx" is the factor number then the variable number, and "controlx" for the mastery loadings.
  ○ Errors for exogenous latent variables start with "d," errors for endogenous latent variables start with "e."
  ○ The program includes two structural equations: one predicting mastery as a mediating variable and one predicting depression at Wave 2 (fdep94). These equations are written out, without intercept, using names for the b coefficients to be estimated times each independent variable in that equation. For example, the effect of SES in 1988 on depression in 1994 is "bSESd," and the effect of mastery in this equation is "bcontrol."

- **std**: This statement gives names to the error variance parameters for the measures. These are free parameters to be estimated. Two other variances are referenced here as free parameters to be estimated: (1) the variances of the two **exogenous** factors (varSES88 vardep88)—not the endogenous factors because they are estimated automatically as a function of other estimated parameters in the program; and (2) the error variances for the structural equations (erroreqc, erroreqd).

- **cov**: There is just one covariance between the two exogenous factors named here.

7.3.4 Selected Output

We do not show all of the output from this run, just the essential parts.

7.3.4.1 Descriptive Statistics

This output (Table 7.3) lists the mean and standard deviation of every measured variable in the model.

TABLE 7.3   ● MEANS AND STANDARD DEVIATIONS OF THE MEASURED VARIABLES

Simple Statistics		
Variable	**Mean**	**Std Dev**
bother1	1.35972	1.65508
bother2	1.34540	1.60635
blues1	0.81470	1.57943
blues2	0.83345	1.49679
depress1	1.12867	1.68148
depress2	1.10529	1.61586
effort1	1.37630	1.89289
effort2	1.16266	1.72457
restles1	1.49344	1.87856
restles2	1.58365	1.87532
nogetgo1	1.31435	1.74140
nogetgo2	1.15527	1.59273
htotinc1	40.21352	42.26012
bestSEI1	38.38017	20.20039
lifeworkout	3.71015	0.89881
doanything	4.08593	0.82815
solveprob	3.43004	1.11205
havecontrol	3.65246	1.04259

7.3.4.2 Covariances

The output prints out the covariances among all variables (shown in Table 7.4). This is the input covariance matrix (referred to as the S matrix) that is used to estimate the entire model. We compare imputed covariances derived from the model estimates to this covariance matrix to assess the fit of the model.

TABLE 7.4 ● THE SAMPLE COVARIANCE MATRIX

Covariance Matrix (DF = 6782)

	bother1	bother2	blues1	blues2	depress1	depress2	effort1	effort2	restles1	restles2	nogetgo1	nogetgo2	htotinc1	bestSEI1	lifeworkout	doanything	solveprob	havecontrol
bother1	2.73928	0.55922	1.40029	0.49767	1.49833	0.52091	1.31297	0.48773	1.18538	0.45772	1.22927	0.49699	-6.36029	-2.14033	-0.12823	-0.09651	-0.23679	-0.20633
bother2	0.55922	2.58035	0.47902	1.29830	0.55545	1.29073	0.53268	1.18860	0.49471	1.11541	0.55052	0.97655	-5.00221	-2.69333	-0.19872	-0.15202	-0.29027	-0.24069
blues1	1.40029	0.47902	2.49460	0.65149	2.00230	0.70606	1.60916	0.56192	1.33967	0.56477	1.48515	0.58577	-6.60485	-2.97221	-0.17077	-0.09988	-0.22698	-0.17797
blues2	0.49767	1.29830	0.65149	2.24039	0.73479	1.85212	0.66537	1.44433	0.58216	1.25485	0.64764	1.30300	-5.46853	-2.83775	-0.29545	-0.23132	-0.36568	-0.31490
depress1	1.49833	0.55545	2.00230	0.73479	2.82737	0.88192	1.84031	0.70262	1.58640	0.61876	1.70981	0.68587	-7.03427	-2.81659	-0.22489	-0.15892	-0.27163	-0.21227
depress2	0.52091	1.29073	0.70606	1.85212	0.88192	2.61099	0.73038	1.65094	0.66517	1.47763	0.72918	1.46050	-5.39839	-2.62637	-0.36642	-0.29265	-0.43718	-0.36571
effort1	1.31297	0.53268	1.60916	0.66537	1.84031	0.73038	3.58302	0.88894	1.63096	0.69473	1.97116	0.74699	-9.07334	-4.34606	-0.22022	-0.14936	-0.30208	-0.23742
effort2	0.48773	1.18860	0.56192	1.44433	0.70262	1.65094	0.88894	2.97414	0.55599	1.42175	0.71703	1.66993	-8.29438	-4.10266	-0.29470	-0.31156	-0.44271	-0.41640
restles1	1.18538	0.49471	1.33967	0.58216	1.58640	0.66517	1.63096	0.55599	3.52900	1.08682	1.63252	0.63760	-5.04947	-2.70050	-0.15715	-0.12739	-0.26699	-0.19351
restles2	0.45772	1.11541	0.56477	1.25485	0.61876	1.47763	0.69473	1.42175	1.08682	3.51681	0.66496	1.37088	-5.51987	-3.24453	-0.30520	-0.26422	-0.36253	-0.28880
nogetgo1	1.22927	0.55052	1.48515	0.64764	1.70981	0.72918	1.97116	0.71703	1.63252	0.66496	3.03249	0.90634	-8.75423	-3.37758	-0.23373	-0.16357	-0.27970	-0.19625
nogetgo2	0.49699	0.97655	0.58577	1.30300	0.68587	1.46050	0.74699	1.66993	0.63760	1.37088	0.90634	2.53679	-6.58537	-3.24695	-0.31995	-0.26626	-0.38084	-0.31670
htotinc1	-6.36029	-5.00221	-6.60485	-5.46853	-7.03427	-5.39839	-9.07334	-8.29438	-5.04947	-5.51987	-8.75423	-6.58537	1785.9177	192.04808	2.20212	1.77670	3.25157	5.35541
bestSEI1	-2.14033	-2.69333	-2.97221	-2.83775	-2.81659	-2.62637	-4.34606	-4.10266	-2.70050	-3.24453	-3.37758	-3.24695	192.04808	408.05581	0.59957	0.62553	2.76521	3.45252
lifeworkout	-0.12823	-0.19872	-0.17077	-0.29545	-0.22489	-0.36642	-0.22022	-0.29470	-0.15715	-0.30520	-0.23373	-0.31995	2.20212	0.59957	0.80786	0.33235	0.18673	0.13308
doanything	-0.09651	-0.15202	-0.09988	-0.23132	-0.15892	-0.29265	-0.14936	-0.31156	-0.12739	-0.26422	-0.16357	-0.26626	1.77670	0.62553	0.33235	0.68584	0.19250	0.19348
solveprob	-0.23679	-0.29027	-0.22698	-0.36568	-0.27163	-0.43718	-0.30208	-0.44271	-0.26699	-0.36253	-0.27970	-0.38084	3.25157	2.76521	0.18673	0.19250	1.23666	0.53075
havecontrol	-0.20633	-0.24069	-0.17797	-0.31490	-0.21227	-0.36571	-0.23742	-0.41640	-0.19351	-0.28880	-0.19625	-0.31670	5.35541	3.45252	0.13308	0.19348	0.53075	1.08699

7.3.4.3 Fit Statistics

Table 7.5 shows the various fit statistics calculated by the program. Certain ones printed here are discussed in the next chapter.

TABLE 7.5 ●	TABLE OF FIT STATISTICS	
Fit Summary		
Modeling Info	Number of Observations	6783
	Number of Variables	18
	Number of Moments	171
	Number of Parameters	42
	Number of Active Constraints	0
	Baseline Model Function Value	6.5524
	Baseline Model Chi-Square	44438.4808
	Baseline Model Chi-Square DF	153
	Pr > Baseline Model Chi-Square	<.0001
Absolute Index	Fit Function	0.5931
	Chi-Square	4022.7239
	Chi-Square DF	129
	Pr > Chi-Square	<.0001
	Z-Test of Wilson & Hilferty	51.7844
	Hoelter Critical N	264
	Root Mean Square Residual (RMR)	0.4846
	Standardized RMR (SRMR)	0.0396
	Goodness of Fit Index (GFI)	0.9327
Parsimony Index	Adjusted GFI (AGFI)	0.9108
	Parsimonious GFI	0.7864
	RMSEA Estimate	0.0667
	RMSEA Lower 90% Confidence Limit	0.0649
	RMSEA Upper 90% Confidence Limit	0.0685
	Probability of Close Fit	<.0001
	ECVI Estimate	0.6056
	ECVI Lower 90% Confidence Limit	0.5756
	ECVI Upper 90% Confidence Limit	0.6367
	Akaike Information Criterion	4106.7239
	Bozdogan CAIC	4435.2553
	Schwarz Bayesian Criterion	4393.2553
	McDonald Centrality	0.7505
Incremental Index	Bentler Comparative Fit Index	0.9121
	Bentler-Bonett NFI	0.9095
	Bentler-Bonett Non-normed Index	0.8957
	Bollen Normed Index Rho1	0.8926
	Bollen Non-normed Index Delta2	0.9121
	James et al. Parsimonious NFI	0.7668

7.3.4.4 Unstandardized Output

CALIS will first print out the unstandardized solution for the estimated parameters. Table 7.6 shows both the measurement model and structural model results. Generally, the standardized output is used, but there are some applications that require the unstandardized output—like when you compare models across groups. We will comment on interpreting the standardized output since the structure of the table is the same.

TABLE 7.6 ● UNSTANDARDIZED EQUATIONS IN THE MODEL

			Effects in Linear Equations			
Variable	**Predictor**	**Parameter**	**Estimate**	**Standard Error**	**_t_ Value**	**Pr > |t|**
htotinc1	fSES88		1.00000			
bestSEI1	fSES88	SES12	0.51928	0.04854	10.6981	<.0001
bother1	fdep88	dep11	0.70918	0.01284	55.2514	<.0001
blues1	fdep88	dep12	0.89196	0.01106	80.6782	<.0001
depress1	fdep88		1.00000			
effort1	fdep88	dep14	0.90462	0.01417	63.8214	<.0001
restles1	fdep88	dep15	0.77396	0.01472	52.5672	<.0001
nogetgo1	fdep88	dep16	0.84539	0.01296	65.2068	<.0001
bother2	fdep94	dep21	0.68932	0.01313	52.5063	<.0001
blues2	fdep94	dep22	0.90303	0.01079	83.6563	<.0001
depress2	fdep94		1.00000			
effort2	fdep94	dep24	0.87964	0.01334	65.9310	<.0001
restles2	fdep94	dep25	0.77619	0.01546	50.1956	<.0001
nogetgo2	fdep94	dep26	0.78990	0.01245	63.4356	<.0001
lifeworkout	fmastery	control1	0.67732	0.02703	25.0539	<.0001
doanything	fmastery	control2	0.67732	0.02569	26.3651	<.0001
solveprob	fmastery	control3	1.09867	0.03818	28.7784	<.0001
havecontrol	fmastery		1.00000			
fmastery	fSES88	bSESC	0.00915	0.00100	9.1025	<.0001
fmastery	fdep88	bdepc	−0.08871	0.00765	−11.5972	<.0001
fdep94	fSES88	bSESd	−0.00197	0.00160	−1.2319	0.2180
fdep94	fdep88	bdepd	0.27880	0.01330	20.9667	<.0001
fdep94	fmastery	bcontrol	−0.95153	0.04731	−20.1129	<.0001

7.3.4.5 Standardized Output

The standardized output is annotated to guide you to different parts of the output. The measurement model in Table 7.7 is shaded in lighter gray; the structural model is shaded in darker gray.

TABLE 7.7 ● STANDARDIZED EQUATIONS IN THE MODEL

			Standardized Effects in Linear Equations			
Variable	**Predictor**	**Parameter**	**Estimate**	**Standard Error**	**_t_ Value**	**Pr > |t|**
htotinc1	fSES88		0.45507	0.02414	18.8535	<.0001
bestSEI1	fSES88	SES12	0.49436	0.02574	19.2091	<.0001
bother1	fdep88	dep11	0.62472	0.00818	76.3573	<.0001
blues1	fdep88	dep12	0.82337	0.00497	165.7	<.0001
depress1	fdep88		0.86708	0.00428	202.6	<.0001
effort1	fdep88	dep14	0.69677	0.00707	98.5299	<.0001
restles1	fdep88	dep15	0.60068	0.00853	70.4323	<.0001
nogetgo1	fdep88	dep16	0.70779	0.00689	102.7	<.0001
bother2	fdep94	dep21	0.59929	0.00852	70.3166	<.0001
blues2	fdep94	dep22	0.84255	0.00461	182.8	<.0001
depress2	fdep94		0.86428	0.00427	202.6	<.0001
effort2	fdep94	dep24	0.71233	0.00679	104.9	<.0001
restles2	fdep94	dep25	0.57803	0.00882	65.5422	<.0001
nogetgo2	fdep94	dep26	0.69261	0.00711	97.4265	<.0001

(Continued)

TABLE 7.7 ● Continued						

Variable	Predictor	Parameter	Estimate	Standard Error	*t* Value	Pr > |t|
lifeworkout	fmastery	control1	0.45058	0.01307	34.4820	<.0001
doanything	fmastery	control2	0.48901	0.01280	38.2110	<.0001
solveprob	fmastery	control3	0.59072	0.01221	48.3806	<.0001
havecontrol	fmastery		0.57349	0.01229	46.6657	<.0001
fmastery	fSES88	bSESC	0.29415	0.02635	11.1628	<.0001
fmastery	fdep88	bdepc	−0.21631	0.01782	−12.1386	<.0001
fdep94	fSES88	bSESd	−0.02710	0.02194	−1.2353	0.2167
fdep94	fdep88	bdepd	0.29106	0.01326	21.9510	<.0001
fdep94	fmastery	bcontrol	−0.40739	0.01654	−24.6336	<.0001

The factor loadings for depression at both time points are very strong—all are above .75. This reflects a set of items that are pretty strongly correlated—that is, internally cohesive. The factor loadings for mastery are lower but still high enough, ranging from .45 to .59. One of the things that makes them acceptable is that the loadings do not differ from each other by much. If they did, it might indicate two rather than one underlying concept. The loadings for SES are lower, from .45 to .49. This is also acceptable because they are close in value. These loadings are like adjustment coefficients telling us how much measurement error has to be adjusted to derive the underlying latent factor.

In output not included here, we see that the total effect of SES on depression six years later was -.165, significant at the .0001 level. Thus there was a negative effect to explain.

Essentially this model argues that the effect of low SES is due to the resulting lower mastery in low SES environments, caused by cumulative blocked access to opportunities, lower quality or less access to resources, and the stresses accompanying economic hardship. In this model, we see that mastery completely explains the effect of SES: The net coefficient is now just -.027; in other words, this one mediator explains the effect entirely (Wheaton, 1980). In addition, we can see the two-step process involved in this mediational effect. SES in 1988 has a strong effect on mastery in 1994 (β = .294), and mastery in turn has a strong negative effect on depression in 1994 (β = -.4073). These two links show us how SES produces lower depression over time. And it is important to note, we are controlling for the effect of depression on SES in the original correlation between the two and the estimated stability of depression through time.

The graphic output for the standardized solution of the model produced by PROC CALIS is shown in Figure 7.10. In general, this output collects important parts of the output and allows direct interpretation of the results.

However, we do not yet interpret this model because the fit is not sufficient according to standards we discuss in the next chapter.

7.3.5 The SES and Mental Health SEM Model in STATA

We present the same standardized results for the previous example in STATA. Defining the latent constructs, parameters, variances, and covariances in STATA is straightforward. In the following code, we demonstrate the use of the *sem* command to reproduce the SES and mental health example.

```
sem (FSES88 -> htotinc1 bestsei1) (FDEP88 -> depress1 bother1 blues1
effort1 restles1 nogetgo1) (FDEP94 -> depress2 nogetgo2 bother2
blues2 effort2 restles2 )(FMASTERY -> havecontrol lifeworkout
doanything solveprob ) (FSES88 FDEP88 -> FMASTERY)(FMASTERY FSES88
FDEP88->FDEP94) [pweight=mufinw93], stand
```

FIGURE 7.10 ● THE STANDARDIZED MODEL FOR SES, MASTERY, AND DEPRESSION

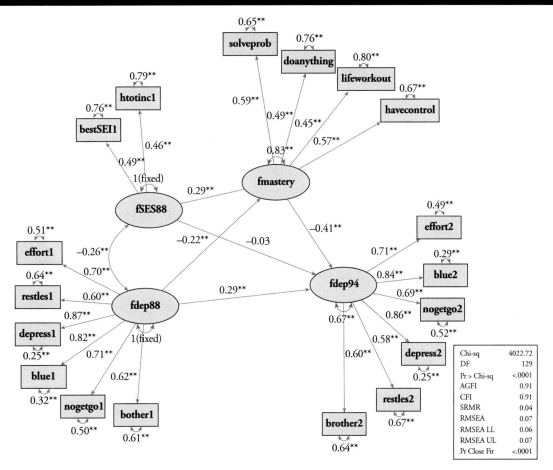

In the brackets, we first identify variables defining our latent constructs, **FSES88**, **FDEP88**, **FDEP94**, and **FMASTERY**, respectively. Note all latent variables must be in capital letters for STATA to register them as such. STATA uses ML estimation by default. It also does not require specification of covariances. It does this automatically. The parameter of the first variable noted in the defined factor is fixed to 1 automatically. Compared to SAS, it is not necessary to specify this in the syntax.

The final parts of the code define the structural components of the model; predicting **FMASTERY** from **FSES88 FDEP88**, for example. We then specify the person weight. The option *stand* following the comma asks for standardized solutions. If you exclude this, STATA will only estimate the unstandardized results.

To generate fit statistics for the model, use the following code:

```
estat gof, stats(all)
```

7.3.5.1 STATA Output for SES and Mental Health Example

As you will note in the following output, the structural components of the model are first presented, followed by the measurement of the latent constructs. The latter part of the output includes the corresponding variances and relevant covariances. The fit statistics are presented after the SEM output, following.

```
Endogenous variables


Measurement: htotinc1 bestsei1 depress1 bother1 blues1 effort1
restles1 nogetgo1 depress2 nogetgo2 bother2 blues2 effort2 restles2
havecontrol lifeworkout doanything solveprob
Latent:    FDEP94 FMASTERY


Exogenous variables


Latent:    FSES88 FDEP88


Fitting target model:


Iteration 0:  log pseudolikelihood = -227551.94
Iteration 1:  log pseudolikelihood = -227484.76
Iteration 2:  log pseudolikelihood = -227481.97
Iteration 3:  log pseudolikelihood = -227481.94
Iteration 4:  log pseudolikelihood = -227481.94


Structural equation model          Number of obs   =    6783
Estimation method = ml
Log pseudolikelihood= -227481.94


 (1) [depress2]FDEP94 = 1
 (2) [havecontrol]FMASTERY = 1
 (3) [htotinc1]FSES88 = 1
 (4) [depress1]FDEP88 = 1
```

Standardized	Coef.	Robust Std. Err.	z	P>|z|	[95% Conf. Interval]	
Structural						
FDEP94 <-						
FMASTERY	-.4074032	.0234715	-17.36	0.000	-.4534065	-.3613999
FSES88	-.0271051	.0236844	-1.14	0.252	-.0735257	.0193156
FDEP88	.2910544	.0189835	15.33	0.000	.2538473	.3282614
FMASTERY <-						
FSES88	.2941159	.0354502	8.30	0.000	.2246347	.3635971
FDEP88	-.2163199	.0252037	-8.58	0.000	-.2657182	-.1669217
Measurement						
htotinc1 <-						
FSES88	.4550795	.034519	13.18	0.000	.3874235	.5227355
_cons	.916813	.0545036	16.82	0.000	.809988	1.023638
bestsei1 <-						
FSES88	.4943473	.0296442	16.68	0.000	.4362459	.5524488
_cons	1.830571	.0172091	106.37	0.000	1.796842	1.8643

depress1 <-						
FDEP88	.8670766	.0077483	111.91	0.000	.8518903	.882263
_cons	.6467171	.0078859	82.01	0.000	.631261	.6621732
bother1 <-						
FDEP88	.6247202	.014182	44.05	0.000	.596924	.6525163
_cons	.7915376	.0093918	84.28	0.000	.77313	.8099453
blues1 <-						
FDEP88	.8233663	.0099479	82.77	0.000	.8038688	.8428638
_cons	.4969745	.0072703	68.36	0.000	.4827249	.5112241
effort1 <-						
FDEP88	.6967709	.0133928	52.03	0.000	.6705215	.7230204
_cons	.7005326	.0083402	83.99	0.000	.6841862	.7168791
restles1 <-						
FDEP88	.6006807	.0140518	42.75	0.000	.5731396	.6282217
_cons	.7659506	.0090247	84.87	0.000	.7482625	.7836388
nogetgo1 <-						
FDEP88	.7077884	.0127762	55.40	0.000	.6827475	.7328293
_cons	.7271944	.0087556	83.05	0.000	.7100337	.744355
depress2 <-						
FDEP94	.8642776	.0092644	93.29	0.000	.8461196	.8824355
_cons	.6590394	.0081315	81.05	0.000	.643102	.6749767
nogetgo2 <-						
FDEP94	.6926057	.0133001	52.08	0.000	.6665381	.7186733
_cons	.6988447	.0085333	81.90	0.000	.6821197	.7155698
bother2 <-						
FDEP94	.5992894	.0141181	42.45	0.000	.5716183	.6269605
_cons	.80696	.0095828	84.21	0.000	.788178	.825742
blues2 <-						
FDEP94	.8425543	.008976	93.87	0.000	.8249616	.860147
_cons	.5364842	.0075534	71.03	0.000	.5216799	.5512885
effort2 <-						
FDEP94	.7123275	.0133967	53.17	0.000	.6860706	.7385845
_cons	.6495499	.0079759	81.44	0.000	.6339174	.6651823
restles2 <-						
FDEP94	.5780273	.0139213	41.52	0.000	.550742	.6053125
_cons	.8136261	.0093932	86.62	0.000	.7952157	.8320364
havecontrol <-						
FMASTERY	.5734356	.0341185	16.81	0.000	.5065646	.6403067
_cons	3.375295	.0409259	82.47	0.000	3.295082	3.455509
lifeworkout <-						
FMASTERY	.4506418	.039739	11.34	0.000	.3727547	.5285288
_cons	3.977073	.048078	82.72	0.000	3.882842	4.071304

doanything <-						
FMASTERY	.4890726	.0358261	13.65	0.000	.4188547	.5592905
_cons	4.753576	.0755547	62.92	0.000	4.605492	4.901661
solveprob <-						
FMASTERY	.5906642	.0330041	17.90	0.000	.5259772	.6553511
_cons	2.971751	.0331405	89.67	0.000	2.906797	3.036705
Variance						
e.htotinc1	.7929027	.0314178			.7336553	.8569346
e.bestsei1	.7556207	.029309			.7003054	.8153053
e.depress1	.2481781	.0134367			.2231918	.2759616
e.bother1	.6097247	.0177195			.5759657	.6454625
e.blues1	.322068	.0163815			.2915094	.3558301
e.effort1	.5145103	.0186634			.4792007	.5524216
e.restles1	.6391827	.0168813			.6069377	.6731408
e.nogetgo1	.4990356	.0180857			.4648179	.5357722
e.depress2	.2530243	.016014			.223506	.2864411
e.nogetgo2	.5202973	.0184234			.4854127	.557689
e.bother2	.6408522	.0169217			.6085299	.6748914
e.blues2	.2901022	.0151256			.2619211	.3213155
e.effort2	.4925895	.0190856			.4565675	.5314536
e.restles2	.6658845	.0160938			.6350767	.6981868
e.havecontrol	.6711716	.0391295			.5986986	.7524175
e.lifeworkout	.796922	.0358161			.7297266	.8703049
e.doanything	.760808	.0350431			.6951338	.832687
e.solveprob	.6511158	.0389887			.5790132	.7321972
e.FDEP94	.6676949	.0182262			.632911	.7043904
e.FMASTERY	.834175	.0208431			.7943074	.8760437
FSES88	1	.			.	.
FDEP88	1	.			.	.
Covariance FSES88						
FDEP88	-.2556184	.0220664	-11.58	0.000	-.2988677	-.212369

Fit statistic	Value	Description
Size of residuals		
SRMR	0.038	Standardized root mean squared residual
CD	0.936	Coefficient of determination

Note: model was fit with vce (robust); only stats (residuals)

7.3.6 Example 3: Income and Depression

The previous example specified a general latent variable for SES (socioeconomic status), but in some cases, you may want to track a more specific relationship between each indicator of SES and depression. Here we estimate a classic two-wave panel model for income and depression using the same data, in part to explicitly represent the possibility of reciprocal effects over time.

To simplify the presentation of the model, we exclude the measurement components. Essentially, depression is measured using the same items as the previous example. The initial specification of the model, however, contains some assumptions necessitated by the fact that income is a single-item measure. Here we must set its loading to 1 (fixed) in the program *and also* fix its measurement error to 0. This is necessary to identify the model when there is only one or two cases of the same single-item variable in the model. As noted earlier, this amounts to assuming perfect measurement for those variables.

Both household income and the CESD depression items are measured in 1988 and 1994 (Waves I and II) while sex and age are added here as fixed controls that are measured in 1988 at the beginning of the study. Both sex and age also only have one indicator, and as a result, their loadings must be fixed at 1 and their errors at 0 as well.

This model therefore has four exogenous factors, all measured in 1988, and two endogenous factors measured in 1994. Note the structure of the model (see Figure 7.11): The effect of depression on income is specified as occurring over time rather than instantaneously (because it would take time for depression to lower income) while the effect of income on depression is immediate (because current income reflects current socioeconomic advantage vs. disadvantage and thus is

FIGURE 7.11 ● THE INCOME AND DEPRESSION TWO-WAVE MODEL

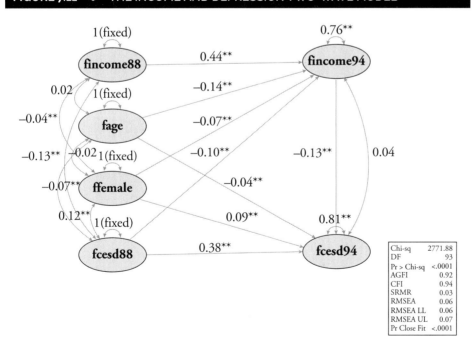

expected to have immediate relevance for mental health). Female and age are allowed to have effects on both income and depression in 1994, net of each in 1988.

In a panel model such as this, you should recognize that the effect of each of the two main focal variables on each other takes into account baseline states of the other variable—that is, effects are on changes in the other variable after the measured baseline state. This is why panel models are often associated with the assessment of causal issues: The causal direction assumption is "protected" in each case by the structure of the model.

The model also includes estimates of the stability of both income and depression over time. The stability reflects each variable's natural resistance to change and gives us a clue about the inherent difficulty in producing changes in the variable over time. Put another way, stabilities tell us how persistent inequalities are in the population or how impervious variables are to outside influence, including associated social changes or policy interventions. The estimated stability is important to understanding the inherent inertia of social phenomena.

The run of PROC CALIS that estimates this model is:

```
ods graphics on;

proc calis data=incdep cov pcorr maxiter=500 maxfunc=1000 pshort stderr simple
mod method=ml;
        lineqs
fincome94 = g11 fincome88 + g12 ffemale + g13 fage + g14 fcesd88 + e11,
fcesd94 = b21 fincome94 + g22 ffemale + g23 fage + g24 fcesd88 + e22,

               htotinc2= 1. fincome94 + e1,
               bother2= dep21 fcesd94 + e2,
               blues2=  dep22 fcesd94 + e3,
               depress2= 1. fcesd94 + e4,
               effort2= dep24 fcesd94 + e5,
               restles2= dep25 fcesd94 + e6,
               nogetgo2= dep26 fcesd94 + e7,

               htotinc1 = 1. fincome88 + d1,
               female = 1. ffemale + d2,
               age = 1. fage + d3,
               bother1 = dep11 fcesd88 + d4,
               blues1 = dep12 fcesd88 + d5,
               depress1 = 1. fcesd88 + d6,
               effort1 = dep14 fcesd88 + d7,
               restles1 = dep15 fcesd88 + d8,
               nogetgo1 = dep16 fcesd88 + d9;
        std
               e1 d1 d2 d3 0 0 0 0,
               e2-e7 = errore2-errore7,
               d4-d9 = errord4-errord9,
               fincome88 = varinc88, ffemale = varfem, fage = varage, fcesd88
= vardep88,
               e11 = erroreq11, e22 = erroreq22;
        cov
               fincome88 ffemale  = covincfem,
               fincome88 fage     = covincage,
               fincome88 fcesd88 = covincdep,
```

```
              ffemale fage      = covfemage,
              ffemale fcesd88   = covfemdep,
              fage fcesd88      = covagedep,
              e11 e22 = coveq;

pathdiagram diagram=all exogcov arrange=flow structural(only)
                  noerrorvariance /*noerrorcovariance nocov novariance*/
                  destroyer=(fcesd88==>fcesd94, ffemale==>fcesd94,
fage==>fcesd94);
weight mufinw93;
run;
```

There are two structural equations in this model: one for depression in 1994 and one for income in 1994. There is a lagged effect of depression in 1988 on income in 1994 (g14), and a reciprocal short-term effect of income in 1994 on depression in 1994 (b21). The STD statement sets the necessary error terms to 0 (e1 d1 d2 d3).

The path diagram statement reflects the complexity of the total model. Initial versions of this model were difficult to interpret visually, and so simplifications were used to focus on the essential findings The "structural(only)" option removes the measurement components. Destroyer paths are paths that do not fit the usual assumptions in the layout and so can be specified to be added *after* the initial layout. This usually straightens out crooked paths in the diagram.

The output table (Table 7.8) shows the main results, but the graphic output is much more useful.

TABLE 7.8 ● STANDARDIZED SOLUTION FOR THE INCOME—DEPRESSION MODEL

Variable	Predictor	Parameter	Estimate	Standard Error	t Value	Pr > |t|
fincome94	fincome88	g11	0.44368	0.00960	46.2249	<.0001
fincome94	ffemale	g12	−0.06978	0.01060	−6.5801	<.0001
fincome94	fage	g13	−0.13849	0.01049	−13.2062	<.0001
fincome94	fcesd88	g14	−0.09547	0.01132	−8.4358	<.0001
fcesd94	fincome94	b21	−0.12951	0.02674	−4.8427	<.0001
fcesd94	ffemale	g22	0.08760	0.01205	7.2725	<.0001
fcesd94	fage	g23	−0.03761	0.01233	−3.0495	0.0023
fcesd94	fcesd88	g24	0.37996	0.01245	30.5128	<.0001
htotinc2	fincome94		1.00000			
bother2	fcesd94	dep21	0.60845	0.00837	72.6894	<.0001
blues2	fcesd94	dep22	0.84146	0.00466	180.5	<.0001
depress2	fcesd94		0.85940	0.00439	196.0	<.0001
effort2	fcesd94	dep24	0.71118	0.00680	104.6	<.0001
restles2	fcesd94	dep25	0.56975	0.00891	63.9761	<.0001
nogetgo2	fcesd94	dep26	0.68431	0.00723	94.6350	<.0001
htotinc1	fincome88		1.00000			
female	ffemale		1.00000			
age	fage		1.00000			
bother1	fcesd88	dep11	0.63157	0.00802	78.7968	<.0001
blues1	fcesd88	dep12	0.82729	0.00485	170.6	<.0001
depress1	fcesd88		0.86841	0.00420	206.7	<.0001
effort1	fcesd88	dep14	0.69617	0.00702	99.1617	<.0001
restles1	fcesd88	dep15	0.59907	0.00848	70.6155	<.0001
nogetgo1	fcesd88	dep16	0.71302	0.00675	105.7	<.0001

Table header spanning: **Standardized Effects in Linear Equations**

Income in 1994 has a net negative effect on depression in 1994, controlling for baseline depression in 1988 (β = -.13**). But in addition, depression in 1988 reduces income in 1994 (β = -.10**), so we observe here a dynamic form of reciprocal causation over time.

7.3.7 Example 4: The Reciprocal Effects of Public and Private Life Satisfaction

This example is based on The Canadian Quality of Life data from 1981 (Atkinson, Blishen, Ornstein, & Stevenson). We show this example here to support the later discussion of fit issues in these models but also to provide a contrasting example, in which there is an attempt to estimate a reciprocal effect of two variables using cross-sectional data.

The basic purpose of the model is to estimate the reciprocal dependence of satisfaction with public life versus satisfaction with private life. One theory is that the public environment limits the achievable well-being in private life; another is that private life shapes and informs our perception of the state of public life. The model to be estimated is shown in the Figure 7.12.

FIGURE 7.12 ● A MODEL FOR PUBLIC AND PRIVATE LIFE SATISFACTION AS RECIPROCAL CAUSES

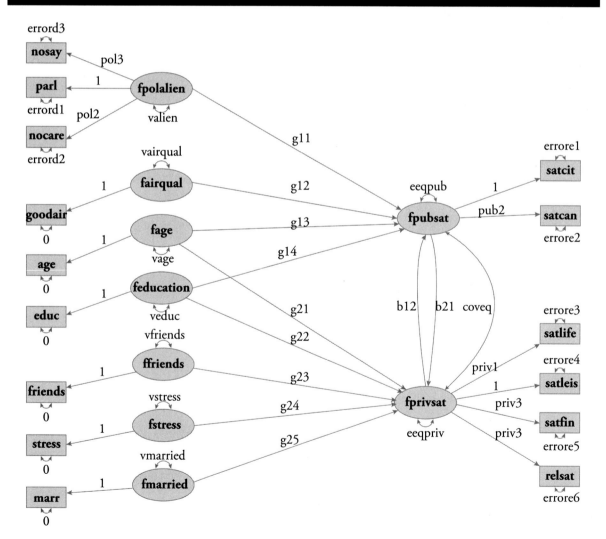

The variables in this model are defined in Table 7.9 with the exogenous *X* measures numbered in order and the endogenous *Y* measures numbered in order.

TABLE 7.9 ◆ MEASURES IN THE PUBLIC VERSUS PRIVATE LIFE SATISFACTION MODEL		
Measures	**Name**	**Meaning**
X_1	parl	Citizens have no control over Parliament
X_2	nocare	Elected officials don't care
X_3	nosay	Individuals have no say in what politicians do
X_4	goodair	Estimate of clean air in local area
X_5	age	Age in years
X_6	educ	Education in years
X_7	friends	Number of close friends
X_8	stress	Number of stressful events this year
X_9	marr	Married
Y_1	satcit	Satisfaction with city or town of residence
Y_2	satcan	Satisfaction with life in Canada
Y_3	satlife	Overall life satisfaction
Y_4	satleis	Satisfaction with leisure time
Y_5	satfin	Satisfaction with finances
Y_6	satrel	Satisfaction with relationship

The specification of the structural model includes sets of instrumental variables for public and private life satisfaction, *in order to identify the reciprocal effects*. The main assumptions are that political alienation and the quality of air affect public life satisfaction directly but not private life satisfaction. And the number of close friends, stressful events, and marital status affect private life satisfaction directly but not public life satisfaction. In addition, age and education may affect both. As noted in the previous chapter, one must restrict at least one effect from an exogenous variable to each endogenous variable to zero when the endogenous variables are reciprocally related, in order to identify the model.

The measurement model assumes that satisfaction with local area and Canada in general together measure public life satisfaction and that satisfaction with one's relationship, finances, leisure time, and life overall reflect satisfaction with private life. However, it is possible that both life satisfaction and satisfaction with finances may measure public life satisfaction as well. This is a unique possibility in SEM models: Measures can be confounded, measuring two concepts, and this still does not compromise the estimates of the effects of the latent variables.

The standardized results are shown in Table 7.10, from the output and in a graphic version in Figure 7.13.

If we just focus on the reciprocal effects here, we see that satisfaction with public life appears to have a stronger effect on satisfaction with private life, than vice-versa. In fact, the standardized effect of public on private is almost twice the size. We emphasize "appears" because we would have to conduct a test of the equality of these parameters in the program to actually demonstrate this is a significant difference. But we present these estimates for comparison with results *after* we achieve a better fit in this model. Currently, the chi-square of the model is 939.47 with 64 degrees of freedom, which is obviously very significant.

FIGURE 7.13 ● RESULTS FOR THE PUBLIC VERSUS PRIVATE LIFE SATISFACTION MODEL

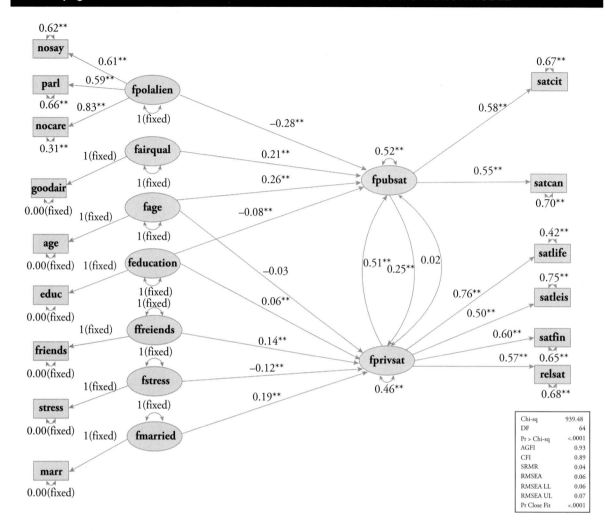

TABLE 7.10 ● THE RECIPROCAL EFFECTS OF PUBLIC VERSUS PRIVATE LIFE SATISFACTION

Standardized Effects in Linear Equations						
Variable	Predictor	Parameter	Estimate	Standard Error	t Value	Pr > |t|
fpubsat	fprivsat	b12	0.24812	0.06623	3.7465	0.0002
fpubsat	fpolalien	g11	−0.27791	0.02742	−10.1370	<.0001
fpubsat	fairqual	g12	0.20508	0.02322	8.8337	<.0001
fpubsat	fage	g13	0.26292	0.02578	10.1978	<.0001
fpubsat	feducation	g14	−0.07763	0.02408	−3.2240	0.0013
fprivsat	fpubsat	b21	0.50564	0.04849	10.4275	<.0001
fprivsat	fage	g21	−0.02657	0.02380	−1.1162	0.2644
fprivsat	feducation	g22	0.06405	0.01895	3.3801	0.0007
fprivsat	ffriends	g23	0.14337	0.01681	8.5299	<.0001
fprivsat	fstress	g24	−0.12493	0.01729	−7.2256	<.0001

Variable	Predictor	Parameter	Estimate	Standard Error	t Value	Pr > |t|
fprivsat	fmarried	g25	0.19182	0.01747	10.9813	<.0001
parl	fpolalien		0.58566	0.01496	39.1578	<.0001
nocare	fpolalien	pol2	0.82985	0.01431	58.0072	<.0001
nosay	fpolalien	pol3	0.61383	0.01476	41.5987	<.0001
goodair	fairqual		1.00000			
age	fage		1.00000			
educ	feducation		1.00000			
friends	ffriends		1.00000			
stress	fstress		1.00000			
marr	fmarried		1.00000			
satcit	fpubsat		0.57675	0.01881	30.6609	<.0001
satcan	fpubsat	pub2	0.54681	0.01856	29.4594	<.0001
satlife	fprivsat	priv1	0.76077	0.01217	62.5003	<.0001
satleis	fprivsat		0.49861	0.01567	31.8129	<.0001
satfin	fprivsat	priv3	0.59546	0.01137	52.3755	<.0001
relsat	fprivsat	priv3	0.56764	0.01116	50.8591	<.0001

7.4 PUBLISHED EXAMPLES

Since this chapter is already a series of examples, we will present examples from the literature that simply illustrate two more specific examples of the ways SEM models are applied. There could be many more examples, including how SEM models are used to express and test some of the models we present later in this book, but at this stage, we present two classic examples. Typically, articles simplify the model as presented in order to communicate the main messages of the model without needing to be sidetracked by all of the details. There is an important lesson here: If you try to be too detailed in what you present, you could distract the reader away from the main issues you want to focus on.

7.4.1 Gender Role Attitudes and Marital Quality

Amato and Booth (1995) analyzed a two-wave panel model to study the reciprocal effects of gender role attitudes and perceived marital quality. The data are from a national study of marital instability, with an N = 2033 married persons at Wave 1. These are not couples: Husbands and wives are studied separately. Perceived marital quality is measured by two positive indicators—reported marital happiness and frequency of marital interaction across five activities—and three negative indicators—disagreements, marital problems, and divorce proneness. Gender role attitudes is a 7-item scale scored to indicate more egalitarian, less traditional gender attitudes.

The model to be tested uses the panel nature of the data to identify the possible reciprocal effects at Wave 2 (eight years after Wave 1).

The structural model is restricted so that there is no direct effect of marital quality in 1980 on gender attitudes in 1988 and no direct effect of gender attitudes in 1980 on marital quality in 1988. Panel data over extended periods are suited to this kind of assumption, and in this case, the assumptions seem reasonable. All that is required is that there is no *direct effect*: Each variable can still affect the other through its indirect effect over time, consisting of the stability of the variable over time and the effect of that variable on the other at Wave 2.

The model also allows for covariances across the errors for the same measures over time. These parameters typically reflect nonrandom error in the measures that is present at both waves, thus causing a nonzero covariance. This could be due to common causes not included in the model, to the effects of similar wording, or to more specific associations between some items over time.

Each latent variable in the marital quality measurement model has two indicators. The two indicators for gender attitudes were formed by creating two sub-scales from the overall measure: one the even items and the other the odd items.

Table 7.11 reports the main findings separately for husbands and wives. Whether the results actually differ between husbands and wives is a question. Amato and Booth address this important question by estimating a "cross-group" constrained model, in which parameters can be first set equal across groups and then allowed to vary. The difference in the fit comparing the constrained

TABLE 7.11 ● STANDARDIZED MAXIMUM LIKELIHOOD COEFFICIENTS FOR THE RECIPROCAL RELATIONSHIP BETWEEN CHANGES IN MARITAL QUALITY AND CHANGES IN GENDER ROLE ATTITUDES: U.S. HUSBANDS AND WIVES, 1980 AND 1988

Variable			
Independent	**Dependent**	**Wives**	**Husbands**
POSITIVE MARTIAL QUALITY		.551[+++]	.822[+++]
(1) Martial Quality 1980 →	Martial Quality 1988	.686[+++]	.720[+++]
(2) Gender Role Attitudes 1980 →	Gender Role Attitudes 1988	.061	−.145
(3) Martial Quality 1988 →	Gender Role Attitudes 1988	−.150[+]	.218[+]
(4) Gender Role Attitudes 1988 →	Martial Quality 1988		
Measures of Fit:			
Degrees of freedom		41	41
Chi square		51.00	45.40
Probability		.136	.294
Goodness of fit		.990	.987
Adjusted goodness of fit		.968	.955
NEGATIVE MARTIAL QUALITY			
(5) Martial Quality 1980 →	Martial Quality 1988	.670[+++]	.619[+++]
(6) Gender Role Attitudes 1980 →	Gender Role Attitudes 1988	.710[+++]	.672[+++]
(7) Martial Quality 1988 →	Gender Role Attitudes 1988	−.073	.019
(8) Gender Role Attitudes 1988 →	Martial Quality 1988	.153[++]	−.151[+]
Measures of Fit:			
Degrees of freedom		69	69
Chi square		83.84	71.83
Probability		.108	.384
Goodness of fit		.986	.981
Adjusted goodness of fit		.965	.952

Source: Amato, P. R., & Booth, A. (1995). Changes in gender role attitudes and perceived marital quality. *American Sociological Review, 60,* (1), 58–66. www.jstor.org/stable/2096345

FIGURE 7.14 ●   ESTIMATING THE RECIPROCAL EFFECT OF MARITAL QUALITY AND GENDER ROLE ATTITUDES

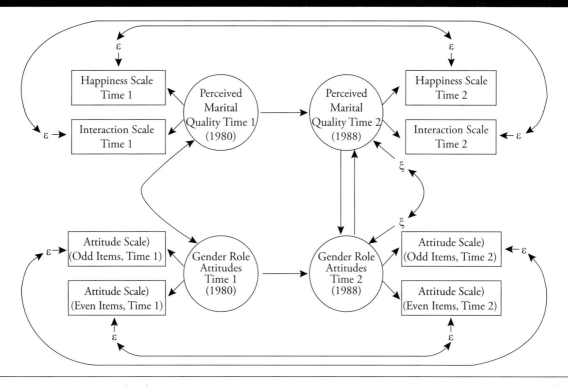

Source: Amato, P. R., & Booth, A. (1995). Changes in gender role attitudes and perceived marital quality. *American Sociological Review, 60,* (1), 58–66. www.jstor.org/stable/2096345

model to the "free" model tells us whether the findings for husbands and wives are equivalent. In this case, they are not. The fit improves significantly when parameters are allowed to be unique in each group. This finding amounts to evidence of an interaction of model parameters with gender. We discuss these methods in a later chapter.

Results are reported separately for positive and negative indicators of marital quality. What is striking in the results is that for both husbands and wives, marital quality does not affect gender role attitudes, but the opposite effect is significant. In other words, gender role attitudes do affect marital quality but not vice-versa. However, the effects of gender role attitudes have opposite sign effects on marital quality for wives versus husbands. When wives report more support for gender equality over time, this results in a decline in marital quality, including both a loss of positive features (Row 4), and an increase of negative features (Row 8). When husbands report more support, this actually increases their view of the positive features of the marriage and lowers their views of the negative features. Ironically, then, increasingly progressive gender attitudes in the household result in more *divergent* views of the marriage rather than greater consensus.

7.4.2 Community Disorder, Victimization, and Mental Health among Youth

A recent article by Turner, Shattuck, Hamby, and Finkelhor (2013) provides an example of the application of structural equation models that takes advantage of some of its strongest features. The data are from the National Survey of Children's Exposure to Violence, a cross-sectional study of 4,549 children in the United States between 10 and 17 years old. The article estimates the effect of neighborhood disorder—called community disorder—on the mental health of youth, through three potential mediators: the rate of exposure to stressful life events, the level of family support, and the rate of six types of victimization (property, peer, maltreatment, sexual, witnessing family violence, and witnessing community violence). Community disorder refers to a series of indicators of the loss of social control and trust in the neighborhood context.

Figure 7.15 is a fairly complete structural equation model, including the measurement model.

Community disorder has eight indicators. There are indirect effects at the factor level of disorder through adverse life events—essentially a one-item measure—as well as family social support (four indicators) and six different types of victimization. There are also nine controls in the model. Results are shown for individual types of victimization first, which allows us to see that peer victimization has the greatest role in transmitting the effect of community disorder. This can be seen by the combined facts that disorder has its second largest impact on peer victimization, which in turn has the largest effect on distress. Importantly, note that the effect of community disorder is completely explained here: The dotted path signifies a non-significant effect.

FIGURE 7.15 ● STRUCTURAL EQUATION MODEL OF COMMUNITY DISORDER AND DISTRESS: MEDIATING EFFECTS OF ADVERSE LIFE EVENTS, FAMILY SUPPORT, AND SIX AGGREGATE VICTIMIZATION TYPES

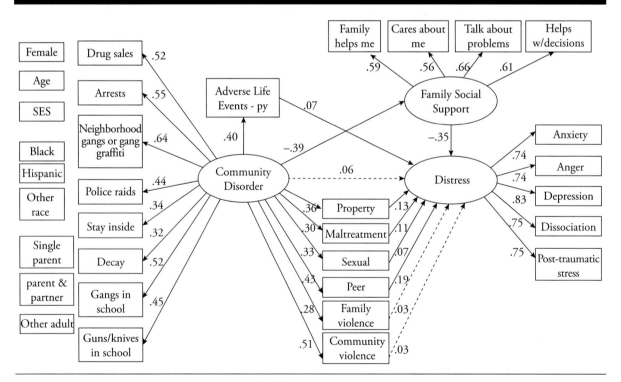

Source: Turner, H. A., Shattuck, A., Hamby, S., Finkelhor, D. (2013). Community disorder, victimization exposure, and mental health in a national sample of youth. *Journal of Health and Social Behavior, 54*(2), 258–75.

But this model makes it hard to judge the overall role of victimization, so they present a simplified version, simply counting the number of victimizations (Figure 7.16). It is clear from these results that victimization is the main mediator in this model. The indirect effect through victimization is .64 x .35 = .224, while the indirect effect through family support is -.38 x -.36 = .137. Both are important, resulting in no net effect of disorder, but the role of victimization is dominant in the overall explanation. We also should note that community disorder undermines family support, and as a result, the loss of family support becomes part of the problem in difficult circumstances rather than a resource that counteracts the effect of contextual threat.

FIGURE 7.16 ● A SIMPLIFIED MEDIATION MODEL

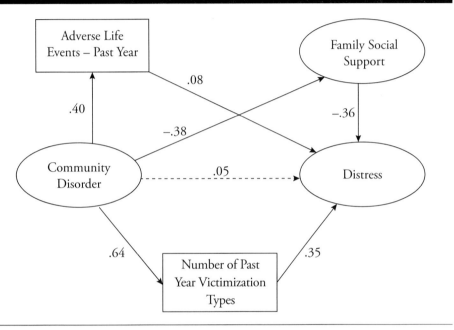

Source: Turner, H. A., Shattuck, A., Hamby, S., Finkelhor, D. (2013). Community disorder, victimization exposure, and mental health in a national sample of youth. *Journal of Health and Social Behavior, 54*(2), 258–75.

Concluding Words

In this chapter, we presented four diverse but representative examples of how structural equation models are applied. But even with the considerable detail included in this chapter, we are only part of the way there. We cannot really use the model results as presented here without further testing of these models, which we turn to in the next chapter. Our goals are to provide a useful approach to modifying the fit of the initial models presented here to achieve acceptable fit—a concept we have to define—and also present a comprehensive list of rules that must be used to ensure the identification of models.

Practice Question

1. A structural equation model and accompanying results are shown following this question, derived from PROC CALIS in SAS, using the National Survey of Families and Households (NSFH) data. The model focuses on the over time effect of gender on depression, between Waves 2 and 3 of the NSFH and the possible explanation of this effect through mediating variables.

    The latent variables in the model each have multiple measures, except for female. These latent variables are:

    *   **fdep2**:   Depression at Wave 2
        *   o   Measures include five standard symptoms of depression, labeled bother2, blues2, depress2, effort2, and sad2 in the output.
    *   **frelfund2**:   Religious fundamentalism at Wave 2
        *   o   Measures include two items measuring fundamentalist beliefs, labeled wordofgod2 and bibleanswer2 in the output.

    *   **ftrust3**:   Trust in others Wave 3
        *   o   Measures include close3 and trust3, taken from the Ryff scale used earlier.

    *   **fdep3**:   Depression at Wave 3
        *   o   Measures include the same five depression items at wave 3, labeled bother3, blues3, depress3, effort3, and sad3 in the output.

*   **ffemale**:   A single-indicator latent variable for female

    The model shown only includes the part involving the structural relations among latent variables; the measurement relations (factor model) are left out but are included in the output. The error terms for the equations in the model are also left out to simplify the model diagram further.

    The initial model includes all of the paths among the latent variables shown plus the paths not shown for the effect of all factors on their measures and all error terms. The effect of gender on depression at Wave 3 in this model could be mediated in part by a preexisting difference in depression at Wave 2, differences in religious fundamentalist beliefs, or differences in trust in others.

    The results shown are from the final model, including the standardized solution for the structural effects and the factor loadings. The results are arranged by equation, first for latent variables, showing the effects among latent factors, and then for measured variables, showing equations for the measurement model.

    Answer these questions:

    a.   Use the results shown to fill in the missing parts of the model diagram, including the structural effects and the factor loadings. Also draw in the measurement errors and equation errors—constrained to 1 in this standardized solution.
    b.   Calculate the indirect effect of female on depression at Wave 3 through (a) depression at Wave 2 and (b) trust at Wave 3, using the results from the model. Using these calculations, answer this question: Are gender differences in depression at Wave 3 explained more by preexisting and continuing differences in depression or by differences in trust?

FIGURE 7.A ⬢   A MODEL FOR THE EFFECT OF GENDER ON DEPRESSION

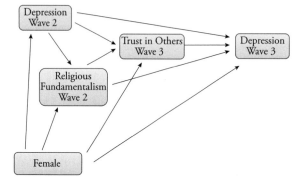

TABLE 7.A ● STANDARDIZED RESULTS FOR THE MEDIATION OF GENDER DIFFERENCES IN DEPRESSION

Standardized Results for Linear Equations

fdep2 =0.1447 *female +1.0000 d1
Std Err 0.0162 bd2fem
t Value 8.9298

frelfund2 =0.0660 *fdep2 +0.1249 *female +1.0000 d2
Std Err 0.0178 bRD2 0.0170 brelfem
t Value 3.7116 7.3535

ftrust3 =-0.0539 *frelfund2 +-0.3320 *fdep2 +0.1029 *female +1.0000 d3
Std Err 0.0213 bTR 0.0203 bTD2 0.0200 btrustfem
t Value -2.5288 -16.3492 5.1563

fdep3 =0.3100 *fdep2 +-0.3602 *ftrust3 +0.00864 *frelfund2 +0.0649 *female +1.0000 d4
Std Err 0.0177 bD3D2 0.0210 bD3T 0.0167 bD3R 0.0158 bD3fem
t Value 17.5587 -17.1237 0.5185 4.1185

female =1.0000 ffemale +1.0000 e1

bother2 =0.5943 *fdep2 +1.0000 e11
Std Err 0.0112 bdep21
t Value 53.1869

blues2 =0.8424 *fdep2 +1.0000 e12
Std Err 0.00568 bdep22
t Value 148.3

depress2 =0.9194 fdep2 +1.0000 e13
Std Err 0.00414
t Value 222.1

effort2 =0.6927 *fdep2 +1.0000 e14
Std Err 0.00894 bdep24
t Value 77.5227

sad2 =0.8275 *fdep2 +1.0000 e15
Std Err 0.00598 bdep25
t Value 138.4

bother3 =0.6022 *fdep3 +1.0000 e21
Std Err 0.0113 bdep31
t Value 53.1824

blues3 =0.8213 *fdep3 +1.0000 e22
Std Err 0.00731 bdep32
t Value 112.4

depress3 =0.8685 fdep3 +1.0000 e23
Std Err 0.00680
t Value 127.6

effort3 = 0.6074 *fdep3 +1.0000 e24
Std Err 0.0111 bdep34
t Value 54.7357

sad3 = 0.7633 *fdep3 +1.0000 e25
Std Err 0.00915 bdep35
t Value 83.3801

wordof god2 = 0.8436 frelfund2 +1.0000 e3
Std Err 0.0347
t Value 24.2847

bible answer2 = 0.8934 *frelfund2 +1.0000 e4
Std Err 0.0366 brel22
t Value 24.4037

close3 = 0.7265 *ftrust3 +1.0000 e5
Std Err 0.0220 btrust11
t Value 33.0443

trust3 = 0.5616 ftrust3 1.0000 e6
Std Err 0.0193
t Value 29.0752

IDENTIFICATION AND TESTING OF MODELS

In this chapter, we consider some basic criteria for specifying and modifying models to a point of "acceptable fit." The problem of fit arises because SEM models are typically *overidentified*. This means, essentially, that there are more variance/covariance equations available using the observed variables in the model than parameters to estimate, resulting in the fact that the model does not fit perfectly. This means, in turn, that the estimated covariances among measures implied by the restricted model you estimate are not exactly the same as the input covariances you start with. This sounds bad, but ultimately, this is a good thing because the idea is to be as efficient as possible—that is, use the fewest number of parameters you can in reproducing the data as closely as possible. Reproducing the data closely implies that the left out parameters are mostly zero, and so can be left out without contributing to poor fit.

However, before we get to the problem of fitting a model, we must ensure first that the model we are trying to estimate is in fact identified. This amounts to checking the specification of the model to make sure that there are no parameters that cannot be identified first.

8.1 IDENTIFICATION

Every model has to be identified to be interpretable. This concept may be foreign to those who are used to dealing with equations one by one, but in fact, assumptions allow the identification of every equation and every model we estimate.

Many people have worked on the identifiability of SEM models, and over time, some guidelines have developed. There is no one place in the literature that collects all of these rules into a set of guidelines—thus motivating the list of criteria we present here. We do not prove the identification of the models we present because other sources have already demonstrated the identification of each case. We recommend aggregating the rules used here to assess the identification of the complete model.

8.1.1 A Three-Stage Strategy

The most prevalent advice about identifying SEM models is to use a multi-stage strategy to ensuring identification:

- First, apply the ***t*-rule** to the model, as discussed in the last chapter. If the model fails this rule, we know the model is underidentified somewhere.

- If the model passes the *t*-rule, you should ensure the identification of the measurement model, including the covariances (or correlations) among factors.

- Once the measurement model is identified, you can approach the identification of the structural model in the same way as you would for observed variables.

To implement this approach, we present general rules for identifying the measurement model without elaboration.

8.1.2 The General *t*-rule

The *t*-rule discussed earlier is repeated here so that you can proceed through the assessment of identification using this section only:

$$t \le \frac{(p+q)(p+q+1)}{2}$$

where in general p = # of measures of endogenous variables (Y)

q = # of measures of exogenous variables (X)

t = number of parameters to be estimated

In words, the number of parameters to be estimated (t) must be less than or equal to the number of covariances and variances among measured variables in the model. You simply count p, q, *and* t, and apply the rule.

8.1.3 Identification of Measurement Models

1. **The Scaling Rule for Latent Variables**

   Every latent variable in the model must have a fixed unit of measurement, achieved by doing one of the following:

   a. Fixing one loading to 1
   b. Fixing the factor variance (usually to 1)
   c. Fixing the factor's error term variance to 1

   Usually, we set one loading to 1 for all variables. In confirmatory factor analysis, option (b) is often used.

2. **Rules for One-Indicator Variables**

   a. ***Variable measured once or twice over time:*** Fix the error variance to 0. Together with the loading fixed to 1, this will identify the factor variance and allow identification of covariances with other factors.

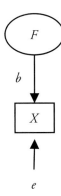

b. **Same variable measured three times:** Assuming that the error variances are the same over time—that is, $V(e_1) = V(e_2) = V(e_3)$, the rest of the model is just-identified, allowing for estimation of the error variance and identification of factor variances and covariances.

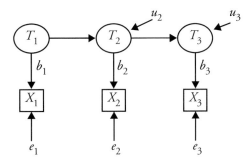

c. **Same variables measured four or more times:** All "inner" error variances and loadings are individually identified. The first/last error variances and loadings are not, without further assumptions, such as equality with the adjacent error variance.

3. **Rules for two-indicator variables**

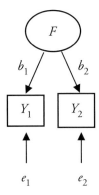

a. **One two-indicator variable:** If there is only one latent variable in the model with two indicators, and the rest are single indicator latent variables, the loadings (*b*) are not identified unless they are set equal.

b. ***Two or more two-indicator variables:*** With at least two latent variables with two indicators each, all loadings are identified, as well as factor variances and covariances, and error variances.

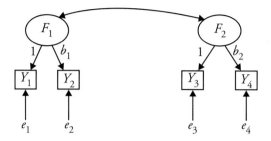

4. **Rules for Three-Indicator Variables**

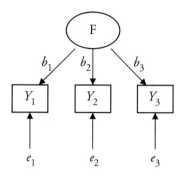

A single three-indicator latent variable is sufficient to identify the loadings, the error variances, and the factor variance for that latent variable. This allows identification of covariances with other latent variables.

5. **Rules for Four or More Indicator Variables**

A single four or more indicator latent variable is overidentified for the loadings, the variance, and the error variances, and thus its measurement structure can be tested.

6. **Double Loadings Rule**

If an indicator loads on two underlying factors (factor complexity = 2), there must be at least one other indicator *for each* factor that loads exclusively on that factor and does not share any correlated error with the double loading indicator.

7. **Constraints Rule**

If a model is proven to be identified, then *adding* a constraint to that model will result in an identified model as well.

NOTE: Some models may be identified *by* constraints, as for one-indicator variables over time.

8. **Rules for Models with Correlated Errors**

a. ***FC1 rule*** *(Davis, 1993):* The factor loadings are identified if, for every loading, its error is uncorrelated with the error of at least one other variable that is also uncorrelated with the error of the scaling indicator (fixed to 1) for that factor.

b. ***Rule for factor variances and covariances:*** If all factor loading parameters for factors are identified, then factor variances and covariances are identified if at least one error variance for each pair of factors is uncorrelated.

c. ***Identification of error variances/covariances:*** If both factor loadings and their covariances are identified, then these parameters can be used to identify the variances and covariances of errors.

8.1.3.1 Applying the FC1 Rule

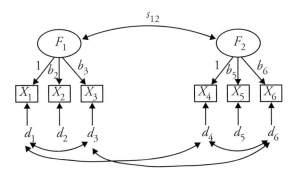

Is this model identified? Yes, it is. See the following:

- b_2 is identified because both X_1 and X_2 are uncorrelated with the error for X_6.

- b_3 is identified because both X_1 and X_3 are uncorrelated with the error for X_5.

- b_5 is identified because both X_4 and X_5 are uncorrelated with the error for X_3.

- b_6 is identified because both X_4 and X_6 are uncorrelated with the error for X_5.

To generalize the rule, looking at the model, there are multiple measurement errors that are *not* correlated across factors. Thus, the factor variances and their covariance are identified. Then because the rest of the measurement model is identified, error variances and covariances are identified.

8.1.4 Identification of Structural Models

8.1.4.1 The Distinction Between Recursive and Nonrecursive Models—Again

Identification proceeds differently in recursive versus nonrecursive models, and so we need to review the features that distinguish these types of models. ***Recursive models*** have causal flow exclusively in one direction and no correlated errors across endogenous variables. As a class, ***nonrecursive models*** represent *any* departure from these conditions. That is, they become "nonrecursive" due to any one of three conditions occurring:

- Reciprocal effects for any pair of endogenous variables

- Feedback loops, in which the indirect effect of an endogenous variable on another endogenous variable is accompanied by a direct or indirect effect in return

- Correlated errors across equations in the model

We state the identification rules uniquely for the two classes of models.

8.1.4.2 Recursive Models

If a model is completely recursive, then the *recursive rule* says that the model is identified. This is possible only if there are no correlated errors in the model and unidirectional causal flow. This is a simple rule that has been applied (often by assumption) to many models.

8.1.4.3 Nonrecursive Models

If a model is nonrecursive, things get more complicated. There are many variations of nonrecursive models and some proven shortcuts, but here we stick to the universal requirements for the identification of the structural model.

8.1.4.4 Nonrecursive Model with Reciprocal Effects and/or Correlated Error

Given identification of all factor variances and covariances using the rules for measurement models, a set of known necessary and sufficient condition rules for identification of structural equations apply. There are two conditions—the *order condition* and the *rank condition*. We review first a generalized version of the order condition.

8.1.4.5 Order Condition

The *order* condition is a necessary condition. For each equation in the model, define all causally *prior* variables not involved in a reciprocal relationship with the endogenous dependent variable as "predetermined." Given that there are m endogenous variables in each equation, *at least m - 1 predetermined variables must be excluded as independent variables from that equation.*

Consider the following model:

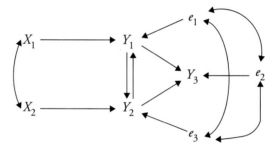

This model has reciprocal causes (between Y_1 and Y_2) and error across the equations of all 3 Y variables, so we need to apply the order and rank conditions. For this model, the number of endogenous variables in the equation for Y_1 (m) is 2. So you have to exclude at least m - 1 = 1 predetermined variable from that equation. X_2 is excluded, and so the equation for Y_1 qualifies. The equation for Y_2 leaves out X_1, so it also qualifies. The equation for Y_3 leaves out X_1 and X_2, and m - 1 = 2 in this case. So the order condition is satisfied in this model.

Now consider the following model:

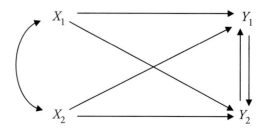

Is the equation for Y_1 possibly identified? No, because $m - 1 = 1$, but the number of predetermined variables excluded = 0.

These results suggest a modification of the model may help. Suppose we know that X_2 does *not* cause Y_1, at least directly:

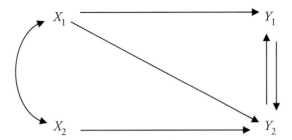

Now in the equation for Y_1, the number of excluded variables is 1, and so the order condition is fulfilled. If X_1 also does not cause Y_2 directly, we have the following:

Then in the equation for Y_2, we have 1 excluded variable as well, and the order condition is fulfilled for both endogenous variables. There is a ***general rule of thumb*** suggested in this discussion. For an equation to qualify for identification that involves an endogenous causal variable (that is also caused in return), at least one predetermined variable must be found that does not cause the dependent variable in the equation directly but does cause the other endogenous causal variable.

So consider the following:

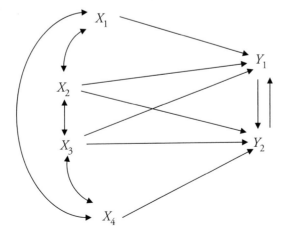

This model is identified, since X_1 does not cause Y_2, and X_4 does not cause Y_1.

8.1.4.6 The Rank Condition

The rank condition is a necessary *and* sufficient condition for the identification of an *equation* in the structural part of the model when there are reciprocal effects or correlated errors. It can be stated as follows:

> ⇒ *An equation in a model of* M *equations is identified if and only if at least one nonzero determinant of a matrix of* M - 1 *rows and columns (order = M - 1) exists in the matrix of coefficients of the structural equations remaining after omitting all columns of nonzero coefficients in the equation and omitting the row of coefficients for that equation.*

This is obviously difficult to understand in this form, so we demonstrate the rank condition by example. We will use the Miller and Stokes democratic representation model, in nonrecursive form, assuming that perception of district attitudes and the representative's actual attitudes may be reciprocally related. Here we add X_5 and X_6 as separate causes of X_2 and X_3 respectively:

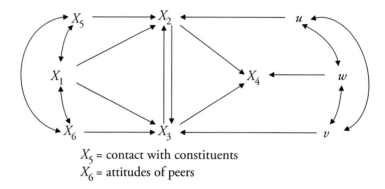

X_5 = contact with constituents
X_6 = attitudes of peers

Begin by working out the equations and then isolating the error terms on the right hand side (using nonrecursive model notation introduced earlier):

$$X_2 = \gamma_{21}X_1 + \gamma_{25}X_5 + b_{23}X_3 + u$$

$$X_3 = \gamma_{31}X_1 + \gamma_{36}X_6 + b_{32}X_2 + v$$

$$X_4 = b_{42}X_2 + b_{43}X_3 + w$$

then

$$X_2 - \gamma_{21}X_1 - \gamma_{25}X_5 - b_{23}X_3 = u$$

$$X_3 - \gamma_{31}X_1 - \gamma_{36}X_6 - b_{32}X_2 = v$$

$$X_4 - b_{42}X_2 - b_{43}X_3 = w$$

Form a matrix, called *c*, of coefficients arranged with order endogenous | exogenous:

$C=$		X_2	X_3	X_4	X_5	X_1	X_6
	X_2	1	$-b_{23}$	0	$-\gamma_{25}$	$-\gamma_{21}$	0
	X_3	$-b_{32}$	1	0	0	$-\gamma_{31}$	$-\gamma_{36}$
	X_4	$-b_{42}$	$-b_{43}$	1	0	0	0

This is the "matrix of coefficients" referred to by the rank condition. To see if the equation for X_2 is identified:

- Cross out row 1 of C
- Cross out all columns in which a nonzero coefficient in row 1 of C appears
- Form a sub-matrix of C from the remaining rows and columns

That is, $C_1 = \begin{bmatrix} 0 & -\gamma_{36} \\ 1 & 0 \end{bmatrix}$

The determinant of a 2 x 2 matrix

$$\det \begin{vmatrix} a & b \\ c & d \end{vmatrix} = ad - bc$$

here is $0 \cdot 0 - (1 \cdot -\gamma_{36}) = \gamma_{36}$

Therefore the determinant is nonzero and the X_2 equation is identified.
The equation for X_3 is identified, based on the submatrix:

$$\det \begin{bmatrix} 0 & -\gamma_{25} \\ 1 & 0 \end{bmatrix} = 0 \cdot 0 - (1 \cdot -\gamma_{25}) = \gamma_{25}$$

For X_4, cross out the last row and the first three columns. This leaves

$$C_3 = \begin{bmatrix} -\gamma_{25} & -\gamma_{21} & 0 \\ 0 & -\gamma_{31} & -\gamma_{36} \end{bmatrix}$$

Note this is not a square matrix. But you can construct three 2 x 2 matrices from this matrix, and if the determinant of any *one* of these matrices is nonzero, the equation is identified.
The three 2x2 matrices are

$$\begin{bmatrix} -\gamma_{25} & -\gamma_{21} \\ 0 & -\gamma_{31} \end{bmatrix} \begin{bmatrix} -\gamma_{25} & 0 \\ 0 & -\gamma_{36} \end{bmatrix} \begin{bmatrix} -\gamma_{21} & 0 \\ -\gamma_{31} & -\gamma_{36} \end{bmatrix}$$

The determinant of all three of these matrices is nonzero, so the X_4 equation is identified.

The submatrix you are evaluating may be a 3 x 3 or higher order matrix. To calculate the determinant in this situation, use *proc iml* in SAS or any language allowing calculation of determinants. For example, suppose the submatrix is

$$\begin{bmatrix} -\gamma_{25} & -\gamma_{21} & -\gamma_{26} \\ 0 & -\gamma_{31} & -\gamma_{36} \\ 0 & 0 & 0 \end{bmatrix}$$

To calculate the determinant, assign arbitrary (small) numbers to the coefficients and run the program that follows in SAS:

```
proc iml;

sub={-.05    -.10    -.02,
        0    -.2     -.08,
        0     0       0 };

det_sub=det(sub);

print sub det_sub;

quit;
run;
```

This program starts iml, the SAS matrix language, sets up a matrix in three rows called "sub" (note the use of braces), creates a variable called "det_sub," which is the determinant of *sub*, and then prints the result. In this case, the determinant is in fact zero, and the equation in question would not be identified.

8.1.4.7 Distinguishing Between Just-Identified and Over-Identified Equations

If the equation is identified and the number of excluded variables = $m - 1$, then the equation is just-identified. If the equation is identified and the number of excluded variables > $m - 1$, then the equation is over–identified.

8.2 TESTING AND FITTING MODELS

The concept of fit requires that you have some understanding of what is going on in the estimation of this model. First, the model is overidentified, due to the restrictions we make—the parameters we leave out are assumed to be zero. Sometimes, occasionally, they may be fixed to known values. If you look just at the measurement part of the model, there are many such parameters. These "left-out" parameters can also exist at the structural level, but the tendency there is to initially include either most or all possible pathways. We have also left out possible covariances across the errors of different measures: These stand for shared specificities in measurement, such as the style of the response format or the content of the item that is not captured by the underlying factor, or they stand for more specific or separate factors not taken into account. These specificities can persist over time, creating covariances between specific repeated error terms.

The paths left out are due to our theories of what measures what, what affects what, and what is independent. The program produces a solution to the restricted model as specified and then uses those parameter estimates to try to reproduce the input covariance matrix. But if the parameters included in the model leave out significant relationships, the fit between the reproduced covariance matrix (called $\hat{\Sigma}$) and the actual covariance matrix (S) will be affected.

What we want to have is a model that comes close to reproducing the original covariances closely. Criteria for sufficient fit are variable and debatable in the SEM world: Unfortunately, there is no one universal standard. But one thing that is clear is that, usually, initial models fail to fit sufficiently under most criteria.

Here we follow the recent trend to use multiple criteria for fit, but we also propose our own blend of measures. We also present a specific strategy for testing and fitting models in this section. Remember that $\chi^2 = (N-1)F$ for a given model, where F = the minimum value of the fitting function. The structure of the χ^2 shows it is closely related to sample size, so it becomes increasingly easy to reject the null of "good fit" in larger samples. In effect, a good-fitting model produces smaller values of χ^2, converging to 1 for each degree of freedom in the model. Thus, one wants to retain the null hypothesis, expressing a "minimal" departure of the model from perfect fit. However, very trivial departures in fit cause large χ^2 values in large samples, so *all* models appear not to fit. This problem has spawned a cottage industry of alternative fit measures—none of which are perfect or entirely solve the problem. Because of this, recent advice tends to emphasize the use of multiple fit measures and require that standards of fit are met for all, *given* that it is possible to do so in view of the data.

There are two kinds of measures to be considered. **Absolute** fit measures assess how well a model reproduces the sample data (covariances). The point of comparison in an absolute fit measure is to the saturated model with 0 degrees of freedom, a model that fits perfectly. **Incremental** measures assess the proportional improvement in fit of a model relative to a *more* restricted baseline. For some measures of incremental fit, this baseline is the so-called "null model," a model that assumes no relationships among any variables. These incremental fit indices thus measure the improvement in fit due to observed relations among variables relative to the assumption that there are no relationships among variables. These indices can be interpreted as overall measures of fit and generally vary between 0 and 1. Other incremental indices measure the change in fit from model to model where additional parameters are considered in a second model relative to a more restricted first model.

We advocate the use of four fit measures with distinct qualities to assess overall fit and three fit measures to assess incremental *gains* in fit across models. Both issues must be assessed at each step of fitting a model. The fundamental rule is to require that the standards of *all* fit measures be satisfied.

In choosing fit measures from the available simulations of their behavior, we invoke three criteria: (1) independence of sample size; (2) penalty for model complexity (adjustment for degrees of freedom); and (3) reliability of estimation (smaller variation due to sampling).

8.2.1 Four Measures of Overall Fit Status

1. *The χ^2 Test*

   Despite its problems, it is important to report the χ^2 test of the null hypothesis of acceptable fit. This statistic is

$$\chi^2 = (N-1) \cdot F$$

where F = the minimum value of the fitting function. This measure is reported automatically in most programs; it is a measure of absolute fit.

2. **RMSEA (Root Mean Square Error of Approximation)**

$$\varepsilon = \sqrt{F_0 / df}$$

where

$$F_0 = \text{Max} \left\{ \left(F - \frac{df}{n} \right), 0 \right\}$$

F = value of fit function,

df = degrees of freedom,

$n = N - 1$

Since F_0 is a function of the fit of the imputed covariance matrix to an observed input covariance, ε becomes a measure of discrepancy in fit *per* degree of freedom used in the model.

Note that since

$$\chi^2 = (N - 1) \cdot F$$

$$\therefore F = \frac{\chi^2}{N-1} = \frac{\chi^2}{n}$$

Thus the value F_0 is:

$$F_0 = F - \frac{df}{n} = \frac{\chi^2}{n} - \frac{df}{n} = \frac{\chi^2 - df}{n}$$

This value is so called the "noncentrality" parameter of the χ^2 distribution. It is a measure of "fit per person," given that χ^2 converges to the degrees of freedom in a good-fitting model.

The RMSEA divides this value by df, so that it takes into account the fit *per* degree of freedom as well. In this way, both sample size and degrees of freedom (model complexity) are accounted for. The square root is like a square root of "unexplained variance" for the model.

This statistic is printed in most programs, with an estimated percentage confidence interval. Browne and Cudeck (1993) suggest that the value of RMSEA should be .05 or less, and the p value for a test of $\varepsilon < .05$ should be greater than .05. When this hypothesis cannot be rejected, this is one piece of information suggesting an acceptable fit. This is also an absolute fit measure.

3. **The Non-normed Fit Index (NNFI)**

This index was developed by Bentler and Bonett (1980) and takes the following form, where the "o" subscript stands for the null model, and "h" stands for the hypothesized model:

$$NNFI = \rho_{HO} = \frac{\left(\chi_o^2 / df_O \right) - \left(\chi_h^2 / df_h \right)}{\left(\left(\chi_o^2 / df_O \right) - 1 \right)}$$

Note that in a correctly specified model, $\chi^2 = df$ of the model, so the χ^2/df ratio converges to 1 as fit improves. This is why 1 is subtracted in the denominator.

The structure of the index suggests NNFI measures improvement in fit relative to a null baseline model assuming no relationship among variables (thus, it is an incremental fit measure). This measure is relatively insensitive to sample size, but it also contains a penalty for model complexity. This can be seen by realizing that fit improves not only due to a lower χ^2 in the hypothesized model but also due to *more* degrees of freedom in the hypothesized model. Thus, for a given χ^2, a simpler model will produce a higher fit value.

4. ***Relative Noncentrality Index (RNI)***

   This index from McDonald and Marsh (1990) is based on the noncentrality parameter as an indicator of poor fit.

   The noncentrality parameter $\delta = \dfrac{\chi^2 - df}{N-1}$ was introduced earlier as a measure of discrepancy in fit per person.

   The RNI is

   $$RNI = 1 - \left(\frac{\chi_h^2 - df_h}{\chi_O^2 - df_O} \right)$$

This measures the improvement in fit relative to a null model (thus, it is also an incremental measure) where the numerator of the ratio converges to 0 for a perfect fit. As fit improves, the ratio gets smaller and smaller, and thus smaller values are subtracted from 1. For example, when the numerator is .10 of the denominator, the baseline amount of poor fit, we have specified .90 of the discrepancy in fit. The RNI actually depends on δ because $N - 1$ cancels in the numerator and denominator of the ratio.

The RNI has been recommended based on the results of multiple simulation studies (Gerbing & Anderson, 1992). It has the important property of independence of sample size, but it also has the specifically desirable characteristic of a lower standard error and therefore more precision than the NNFI. On the other hand, it has no penalty for lack of parsimony. Therefore, we suggest using both.

This statistic is *not* printed by many programs and must be calculated by hand. However, it is a simple calculation, understanding that the χ^2 and *df* for the "independence model" or "null model" in the output is the information needed.

The frequently suggested criterion for "acceptable fit" for both the NNFI and the RNI is .90, but this level of fit, in our experience, is often insufficient, given other indicators. *Many models fit more satisfactorily when these statistics get closer to .95.* (Hu and Bentler, 1999).

8.2.2 Measuring the Incremental Change in Fit

1. ***Modification Indices***

   Sorbom (1989) showed that the first derivative of the likelihood function with respect to fixed parameters in the model indicates the expected improvement in fit resulting from freeing these parameters. Of course, such parameters must be identified and interpretable. These first-order derivatives are the basis for a computed modification index for each fixed parameter, equal to the expected decrease in χ^2 for the model resulting from freeing the parameter. Thus, one wants to free the largest interpretable modification index in each model. This procedure should be done a parameter at a time, until fit is satisfactory. This test is usually called the Lagrange multiplier test (LM test) in the literature.

2. **The χ^2 Difference across Models**

   Given models *H1* and *H2*, in which *H1* is a more restricted model nested in *H2*, the χ^2 difference between *H1* and *H2* is itself a χ^2, with $df_1 - df_2$ degrees of freedom.

   $$\text{So } \chi^2_{12} = \chi^2_{H1} - \chi^2_{H2}$$

   with $df_1 - df_2$ degrees of freedom. This test is used to assess the significance (or non-significance) of parameters added to a model or of constraints added to a model.

   However, the sample size problem of the χ^2 test in each model also affects this test:

   $$\chi^2_{12} = (N-1)F_1 - (N-1)F_2$$

   $$= (N-1)(F_1 - F_2)$$

   Again, we should supplement this test with other information.

3. **The BIC Statistic (Bayesian Information Criterion)**

   The *BIC* (as discussed by Raftery (1995)) is based on Bayesian reasoning used to derive estimates of the relative posterior probability of two models, given the observed data, which can be interpreted as approximately equal to the relative probability of the observed data given one model relative to the probability of the observed data given a second model. That is

   $$\frac{\Pr(M_2/D)}{\Pr(M_1/D)} \approx \frac{\Pr(D/M_2)}{\Pr(D/M_1)}$$

   where D = the data
   M_2 = Model 2
   M_1 = Model 1

Raftery defines the term on the right as a "Bayes factor," the ratio of the marginal likelihoods of two models. The Bayes factor for M_2 versus M_1 is symbolized B_{21}.

Raftery defines the *BIC* as

$$BIC_{HS} = -2\ln B_{HS} = L^2_H - df_H \ln(N(p+q))$$

where

H = the hypothesized model

S = the saturated (just-identified) model

L^2 = the likelihood ratio χ^2 for Model H

df_H = the degrees of freedom for Model H

N = the sample size

$(p + q)$ = the number of observed variables

Because every model is compared to a saturated model, we can directly compare the fit of models.

$$BIC_{12} = BIC_{1S} - BIC_{2S}$$

Note that the saturated model here produces a fit value of 0. Note also that there is a built in accounting for model complexity and for sample size. In fact, one of the basic reasons for using the BIC to compare models is that it is independent of sample size.

According to Raftery, $BIC_{HS} > 0$ reflect models that do not fit sufficiently, while $BIC_{HS} < 0$ reflect models that fit better than the saturated model—a good thing. However, how much better a model should fit than the saturated model is not clear.

The BIC statistic has one feature that makes it more straightforwardly applied than some of the other descriptive measures here. Raftery has derived standards for "strong" and "very strong" evidence for a difference (effect). When the probability of a model, given the data, exceeds .95 but is not more than .99, BIC will be in the range of 6 - 10. When the probability of a model given the data exceeds .99, BIC will be greater than 10. Thus, 6 and 10 function as analogs to a .05 and .01 level of significance respectively. Use of criteria allows us to apply *some* standard to changes in model fit across models.

There is another advantage to the use of these criteria. We can adjust critical values for χ^2 for individual parameters in the model, such as for the modification indices or for tests with multiple degrees of freedom as well. For example, at an N of 1000 and with 8 observed variables, we can require χ^2 for a 1 *df* test to be at least

$$6 = L^2 - \ln(1000 \cdot 8)$$

$$6 = L^2 - 8.99$$

$$L^2 = 6 + 8.99 = 14.99$$

instead of the usual 3.84.

8.2.2.1 The "One Step Beyond" Rule

We advocate the general wisdom of going one step beyond given criteria. The reason for this is to see whether essential results of the model are affected and to recognize the inherent uncertainty of using general criteria to accept a model. Another issue in going "one step beyond" is the possible importance of the parameter that would be freed according to the modification index.

8.3 EXAMPLES OF FITTING MODELS

8.3.1 The Mastery Model

Our second example of the previous chapter, the first one using the full SEM model, considered the effect of SES on depression, as mediated by mastery, and controlling for prior depression. Table 8.1 is the table of fit measures from that model:

TABLE 8.1 ● FIT MEASURES FROM THE INITIAL MODEL FOR SES, MASTERY, AND DEPRESSION

Fit Summary		
Modeling Info	**Number of Observations**	6783
	Number of Variables	18
	Number of Moments	171
	Number of Parameters	42
	Number of Active Constraints	0
	Baseline Model Function Value	6.5524

(Continued)

TABLE 8.1 ● Continued

	Fit Summary	
	Baseline Model Chi-Square	44438.4808
	Baseline Model Chi-Square DF	153
Absolute Index	**Pr > Baseline Model Chi-Square**	<.0001
	Fit Function	0.5931
	Chi-Square	4022.7239
	Chi-Square DF	129
	Pr > Chi-Square	<.0001
	Z-Test of Wilson & Hilferty	51.7844
	Hoelter Critical N	264
	Root Mean Square Residual (RMR)	0.4846
	Standardized RMR (SRMR)	0.0396
	Goodness of Fit Index (GFI)	0.9327
Parsimony Index	**Adjusted GFI (AGFI)**	0.9108
	Parsimonious GFI	0.7864
	RMSEA Estimate	0.0667
	RMSEA Lower 90% Confidence Limit	0.0649
	RMSEA Upper 90% Confidence Limit	0.0685
	Probability of Close Fit	<.0001
	ECVI Estimate	0.6056
	ECVI Lower 90% Confidence Limit	0.5756
	ECVI Upper 90% Confidence Limit	0.6367
	Akaike Information Criterion	4106.7239
	Bozdogan CAIC	4435.2553
	Schwarz Bayesian Criterion	4393.2553
	McDonald Centrality	0.7505
Incremental Index	**Bentler Comparative Fit Index**	0.9121
	Bentler-Bonett NFI	0.9095
	Bentler-Bonett Non-normed Index	0.8957
	Bollen Normed Index Rho1	0.8926
	Bollen Non-normed Index Delta2	0.9121
	James et al. Parsimonious NFI	0.7668

We have highlighted the overall measures of fit discussed in the previous section. The χ^2 is 4022.724, and the model has 129 degrees of freedom. Obviously, the test of the null of perfect fit fails here, at < .0001 probability.

The RMSEA is .0667, close to .05, but not quite there. The probability of close fit—that is, having an RMSEA under .05, is also less than .0001. We want this probability to get above .05. The Bentler-Bonett Non-normed Index is .8957. We calculate the RNI using the baseline fit as the null model, as follows:

$$RNI = 1 - \left(\frac{4022.7239 - 129}{44438.4808 - 153} \right) = .912$$

Again this value could be higher.

How do we decide where areas of poor fit exist in this model? We use the modification indices printed at the end of the CALIS printout. There are many printed there, but it is best to concentrate on two tables (see Table 8.2).

In the first table, areas of bad fit indicating possible correlated error terms are listed by size of the LM statistic. The size of the LM statistics matters, since it indicates the possible improvement in

TABLE 8.2 ● MODIFICATION (LM) INDICES FOR THE INITIAL MODEL

Rank Order of the 10 Largest LM Stat for Error Variances and Covariances				
Var1	Var2	LM Stat	Pr > ChiSq	Parm Change
e9	e10	885.32851	<.0001	0.26054
e11	e12	678.00979	<.0001	0.42554
e5	e4	558.48822	<.0001	0.38902
d5	d4	546.08865	<.0001	0.42708
e8	e6	469.89617	<.0001	0.42562
d8	d6	397.62775	<.0001	0.47336
e7	d7	354.44401	<.0001	0.55631
e9	e12	326.97547	<.0001	-0.20761
e8	d8	210.52268	<.0001	0.27679
e11	e10	195.18330	<.0001	-0.16443

Rank Order of the 10 Largest LM Stat for Paths from Exogenous Variables				
To	From	LM Stat	Pr > ChiSq	Parm Change
havecontrol	fSES88	51.59481	<.0001	0.00874
effort2	fSES88	36.66328	<.0001	−0.00831
doanything	fSES88	29.82482	<.0001	−0.00517
depress2	fSES88	27.84947	<.0001	0.00568
effort1	fSES88	24.64613	<.0001	−0.00764
nogetgo2	fdep88	20.19071	<.0001	0.05444
nogetgo2	fSES88	18.18045	<.0001	−0.00551
nogetgo1	fSES88	17.30331	<.0001	−0.00582
depress1	fSES88	16.73323	<.0001	0.00461
lifeworkout	fdep88	15.09449	0.0001	−0.03264

fit resulting from estimating that parameter as a part of the model (aka, "freeing" the parameter). You should note that there is sometimes another table showing sources of bad fit between actual measures in the model. Usually, these indices simply reflect the corresponding missing correlations between their error terms, so we concentrate on this table first. The missing covariance with the largest modification index is a covariance between two measures of mastery (e_9 and e_{10} in the original model). What would this stand for? Note that these two items on the Mastery factor are stated positively, and the other two are stated negatively. Just the direction of the wording could create a higher association than is captured by the underlying Mastery construct. This is a standard methods effect.

You want to free one parameter at a time, because the LM values are not independent of each other—others could change when you free one. You free this parameter by adding one statement to the COV statement as follows and rerunning the model:

```
e9 e10 = errorcov1;
```

When you rerun the model, this parameter turns up in the table for covariances among exogenous variables (Table 8.3).

The correlation here is a substantial .342. The new fit table shows the resulting improvement in fit (Table 8.4).

TABLE 8.3 ●	THE CORRELATED ERROR BETWEEN TWO INDICATORS OF MASTERY

Standardized Results for Covariances Among Exogenous Variables						
Var1	Var2	Parameter	Estimate	Standard Error	*t* Value	Pr > |t|
fSES88	fdep88	cov88	−0.25231	0.02097	−12.0296	<.0001
e9	e10	errorcov1	0.34214	0.01080	31.6730	<.0001

TABLE 8.4 ●	FIT STATISTICS FROM THE SECOND MODEL

	Fit Summary	
Modeling Info	Number of Observations	6783
	Number of Variables	18
	Number of Moments	171
	Number of Parameters	43
	Number of Active Constraints	0
	Baseline Model Function Value	6.5524
	Baseline Model Chi-Square	44438.4808
	Baseline Model Chi-Square DF	153
	Pr > Baseline Model Chi-Square	<.0001
Absolute Index	Fit Function	0.4611
	Chi-Square	3127.1116
	Chi-Square DF	128
	Pr > Chi-Square	<.0001
	Z-Test of Wilson & Hilferty	45.6812
	Hoelter Critical N	338
	Root Mean Square Residual (RMR)	0.5068
	Standardized RMR (SRMR)	0.0410
	Goodness of Fit Index (GFI)	0.9472
Parsimony Index	Adjusted GFI (AGFI)	0.9295
	Parsimonious GFI	0.7924
	RMSEA Estimate	0.0588
	RMSEA Lower 90% Confidence Limit	0.0570
	RMSEA Upper 90% Confidence Limit	0.0606
	Probability of Close Fit	<.0001
	ECVI Estimate	0.4738
	ECVI Lower 90% Confidence Limit	0.4475
	ECVI Upper 90% Confidence Limit	0.5012
	Akaike Information Criterion	3213.1116
	Bozdogan CAIC	3549.4651
	Schwarz Bayesian Criterion	3506.4651
	McDonald Centrality	0.8017
Incremental Index	Bentler Comparative Fit Index	0.9323
	Bentler-Bonett NFI	0.9296
	Bentler-Bonett Non-normed Index	0.9191
	Bollen Normed Index Rho1	0.9159
	Bollen Non-normed Index Delta2	0.9323
	James et al. Parsimonious NFI	0.7777

We can see that the NNFI is now .9191—better but not up to .95. Also, the RMSEA is now lower and equal to .0588, closer to the .05 standard. But the probability of close fit is still at .0001. The calculated RNI is now .932.

Calculating the improvement in fit relative to the first model proceeds as follows:

1. The χ^2 difference across models 1 and 2 is : $\chi^2_{12} = 4022.72 - 3127.11 = 895.61$. Because this is a 1 df test, this is highly significant beyond the .0001 level.

2. The BIC in model 1 is $BIC_{1S} = 4022.72 - 129 \cdot ln(6783(18)) = 2511.80$. The BIC in Model 2 is (calculations not shown) 1627.90. The improvement is 2511.80 - 1627.90 = 883.9, again way beyond strict significance guidelines.

We can construct a table to track the improvements in fit (Table 8.5).

TABLE 8.5 ● FIT ASSESSMENT OF THE SECOND MODEL FOR SES, MASTERY, AND DEPRESSION

MODEL /ADDED PARAMETER	χ^2	df	$\Delta\chi^2$	RMSEA	Pr RMSEA < .05	NNFI	RNI	BIC	Δ BIC
1. Initial Model	4022.72	129	—	.0667	.0001	.896	.912	2511.80	—
2. corr. Error (e_9, e_{10})	3127.11	128	895.61	.0588	.0001	.919	.932	1627.90	884

The modification indices from this model suggest the need to free another correlated error between blues2 and depress2 (e_4 and e_5). The LM statistic is 555.13. This parameter is added to the covariance statement:

```
e4 e5 = errorcov2;
```

And the model is rerun. The fit table (Table 8.6) produced by this model again shows improvement.

TABLE 8.6 ● FIT STATISTICS FROM THE THIRD MODEL

Fit Summary		
Modeling Info	Number of Observations	6783
	Number of Variables	18
	Number of Moments	171
	Number of Parameters	44
	Number of Active Constraints	0
	Baseline Model Function Value	6.5524
	Baseline Model Chi-Square	44438.4808
	Baseline Model Chi-Square DF	153
	Pr > Baseline Model Chi-Square	<.0001
Absolute Index	Fit Function	0.3855
	Chi-Square	2614.4656
	Chi-Square DF	127
	Pr > Chi-Square	<.0001
	Z-Test of Wilson & Hilferty	41.6549
	Hoelter Critical N	401
	Root Mean Square Residual (RMR)	0.4494
	Standardized RMR (SRMR)	0.0387
	Goodness of Fit Index (GFI)	0.9565
Parsimony Index	Adjusted GFI (AGFI)	0.9414

(Continued)

TABLE 8.6 ⬤ Continued

Fit Summary		
	Parsimonious GFI	0.7939
	RMSEA Estimate	0.0537
	RMSEA Lower 90% Confidence Limit	0.0520
	RMSEA Upper 90% Confidence Limit	0.0555
	Probability of Close Fit	0.0003
	ECVI Estimate	0.3985
	ECVI Lower 90% Confidence Limit	0.3745
	ECVI Upper 90% Confidence Limit	0.4236
	Akaike Information Criterion	2702.4656
	Bozdogan CAIC	3046.6413
	Schwarz Bayesian Criterion	3002.6413
	McDonald Centrality	0.8325
Incremental Index	Bentler Comparative Fit Index	0.9438
	Bentler-Bonett NFI	0.9412
	Bentler-Bonett Non-normed Index	0.9323
	Bollen Normed Index Rho1	0.9291
	Bollen Non-normed Index Delta2	0.9439
	James et al. Parsimonious NFI	0.7812

The RMSEA is now .0537, and that value produces a nonzero probability under the null of .0003. The NNFI is now .932, and the RNI is .944, close to the suggested threshold. Adding Model 3 results to the previous table of fit measures does show improvement in fit again (Table 8.7).

TABLE 8.7 ⬤ FIT ASSESSMENT OF THE THIRD MODEL FOR SES, MASTERY, AND DEPRESSION

MODEL /ADDED PARAMETER	χ^2	df	$\Delta\chi^2$	RMSEA	Pr RMSEA < .05	NNFI	RNI	BIC	Δ BIC
1. Initial Model	4022.72	129	—	.0667	.0001	.896	.912	2511.80	—
2. Corr. Error (e_9, e_{10})	3127.11	128	895.61	.0588	.0001	.919	.932	1627.90	884
3. Corr. Error (e_4, e_5)	2614.46	127	512.65	.0537	.0003	.932	.944	1126.97	501

The *BIC* shows substantial improvement again, but the absolute fit measures are not quite there. The LM statistics for this model show the need to free the same correlated error at Wave 1 for the two most specific measures of depression, between d_4 and d_5 (LM = 579.15). All of the correlated errors estimated in these models are substantial in size, as shown by the results in Table 8.8.

TABLE 8.8 ⬤ CORRELATED ERRORS IN THE FOURTH MODEL

Covariances Among Exogenous Variables						
Var1	Var2	Parameter	Estimate	Standard Error	t Value	Pr > |t|
fSES88	fdep88	cov88	−6.75233	0.64861	−10.4105	<.0001
e9	e10	errorcov1	0.25414	0.00934	27.2035	<.0001
e4	e5	errorcov2	0.39623	0.01886	21.0101	<.0001
d4	d5	errorcov3	0.43530	0.02085	20.8827	<.0001

This model produces the following measures of fit, calculated from the results (not shown) (Table 8.9).

TABLE 8.9 ⬢ FIT ASSESSMENT OF THE FOURTH MODEL FOR SES, MASTERY, AND DEPRESSION									
MODEL /ADDED PARAMETER	χ^2	df	$\Delta\chi^2$	**RMSEA**	**Pr RMSEA < .05**	**NNFI**	**RNI**	**BIC**	**Δ BIC**
1. Initial Model	4022.72	129	—	.0667	.0001	.896	.912	2511.80	—
2. Corr. Error (e_9, e_{10})	3127.11	128	895.61	.0588	.0001	.919	.932	1627.90	884
3. Corr. Error (e_4, e_5)	2614.46	127	512.65	.0537	.0003	.932	.944	1126.97	501
4. Corr. Error (d_4, d_5)	2080.99	126	533.47	.0478	.9752	.947	.956	605.21	522

This model essentially fits by all criteria. The RMSEA is below .05, its probability now much higher than .05, and the RNI is .956. We invoke the "one step beyond rule" and estimate one more parameter. The highest modification index occurs for a correlated error between restlessness at Waves I and II (e_7 and d_7). This parameter was freed in the next model. The fit statistics table including this model is shown in Table 8.10.

TABLE 8.10 ⬢ FIT ASSESSMENT OF THE FINAL MODEL FOR SES, MASTERY, AND DEPRESSION									
MODEL /ADDED PARAMETER	χ^2	df	$\Delta\chi^2$	**RMSEA**	**Pr RMSEA < .05**	**NNFI**	**RNI**	**BIC**	**Δ BIC**
1. Initial Model	4022.72	129	—	.0667	.0001	.896	.912	2511.80	—
2. Corr. Error (e_9, e_{10})	3127.11	128	895.61	.0588	.0001	.919	.932	1627.90	884
3. Corr. Error (e_4, e_5)	2614.46	127	512.65	.0537	.0003	.932	.944	1126.97	501
4. Corr. Error (d_4, d_5)	2080.99	126	533.47	.0478	.9752	.947	.956	605.21	522
5. Corr. Error (e_7, d_7)	1727.82	125	353.17	.0435	1.000	.956	.963	269.75	335

According to our criteria, this model fits. The results of this model do not differ substantially from the original results, but since we also can have more faith in results in a model that fits strictly according to criteria we would usually report this final model (Figure 8.1).

8.3.2 The Relationship Between Public and Private Life Satisfaction

First we reproduce the initial results here from the previous chapter (Figure 8.2).

The highest modification index was used in three successive modifications to arrive at a final model, summarized in Table 8.11. The first modification allowed for a direct and specific effect of marital status on relationship satisfaction, suggesting that the general factor for private life satisfaction did not capture this connection sufficiently. The next modification index suggested freeing an effect of age directly on financial satisfaction—*but this parameter is not identified in the model.* However, the next modification index suggested a loading for financial satisfaction directly on satisfaction with public life. This kind of model can accommodate the issue of "confounded" measures by allowing a specific measure to be determined by different latent factors

FIGURE 8.1 ● STANDARDIZED SOLUTION FOR THE FINAL MODEL

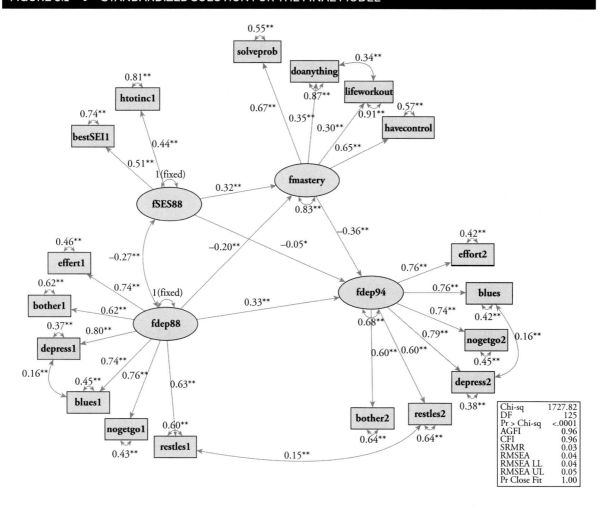

that are related to each other at the structural level. The final model also included a correlated error between two of the measures of political alienation in the model.

Model 4 fits by most criteria, but the NNFI is an anomaly. This is part of the point of using multiple measures. Because every other measure qualifies and the changes in the *BIC* are getting notably smaller with successive changes in the model, we may stop at this point.

The final results are quite different in the balance of the reciprocal effects. The estimates from the final model are reproduced in Figure 8.3.

One obvious important difference is the balance of the reciprocal effects in the final model. Unlike the original model, in this model public and private life satisfaction affect each other almost equally. The conclusion you would reach about these reciprocal effects may be quite different: Rather than public life dominating in the exchange, each supports the other equally, and in this case, we can point out the interesting implications of the fact that private life satisfaction helps shape our view of the state of public life.

TABLE 8.11 ⬡ FIT ASSESSMENT OF THE FINAL MODEL FOR PUBLIC AND PRIVATE LIFE SATISFACTION

MODEL /ADDED PARAMETER	χ^2	df	$\Delta\chi^2$	RMSEA	Pr RMSEA < .05	NNFI	RNI	BIC	Δ BIC
1. Initial Model	939.48	64	—	.063	.0001	.820	.891	244.98	—
2. MARRIED → RELSAT	619.40	63	320.08	.051	.373	.884	.930	−64.24	309.2
3. PUBSAT → SATFIN	500.21	62	119.2	.045	.981	.907	.945	−172.6	108.3
4. corr. error (PARL, NOCARE)	440.10	61	60.11	.042	.999	.93	.952	−221.8	49.2

FIGURE 8.2 ⬡ THE INITIAL MODEL FOR PUBLIC VERSUS PRIVATE LIFE SATISFACTION

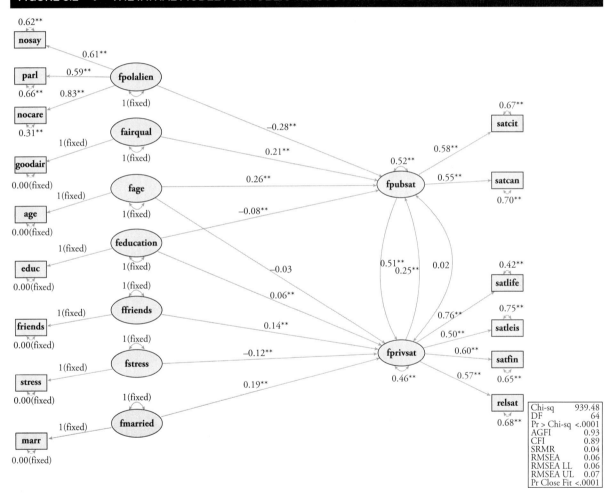

This is a model in which one indicator—satisfaction with finances—is allowed to be "confounded"—a measure of two concepts—and yet it doesn't matter because the model is able to separate the measurement model from the structural effects.

FIGURE 8.3 ● THE FINAL MODEL FOR PUBLIC VERSUS PRIVATE LIFE SATISFACTION

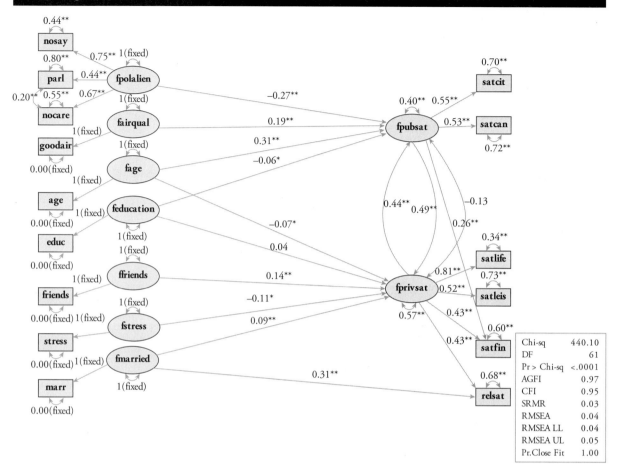

Concluding Words

This chapter gives specific guidelines for two important issues in evaluating structural equation models: their identification and their fit to the observed data. Rather than just review fit measures, we propose a specific set of measures and criteria to use in fitting models. There will no doubt be other approaches, but we need to also point out that the issue of fit will not produce one magic solution in the form of an all-knowing, perfectly behaving fit measure. The main point of multiple measures is to allow the advantages of one to fill in the gaps in others and then require meeting criteria on all measures. Our examples here are "typical," but they are not exhaustive. When it comes to achieving better fit, there are no simple templates.

Our guide to identification gathers together rules from a large number of sources and thus becomes a single source practical guide to considering identification problems. But our list does not speak to all cases. For example, we do not consider many cases where equality constraints may identify the model. Each of those cases needs to be considered on a one-by-one basis, since every model can include a unique configuration of parameters.

Just as in the case of our early chapters on regression, we can generalize the structural equation model further in the next chapter. Three issues will be considered: the estimation of models in which the measured variables are mainly ordinal in nature—as opposed to the interval measures assumed in this and the previous chapter—cross-group comparative structural equation models, and the incorporation of nonlinearity into these models.

Practice Questions

1. This question refers to the same model as was used for the practice question in the last chapter. Refer to that question for details about the model. Here we focus on fitting information and identification issues in this model.

Answer these questions:

a. Table 8.A shows *some* of the results of fitting four models: the initial model plus three models that free specific covariances among the errors for measures of depression.

TABLE 8.A ⬡ FIT MEASURES FOR FOUR NESTED SEM MODELS

	Model 1 Initial	Model 2 freed cov e14 and e24	Model 3 freed cov e11 and e12	Model 4 freed cov for d25 and d26
Model Chi-square	887.68	709.31	594.67	531.40
Model df	81	80	79	78
N	3984	3984	3984	3984
$(p + q)$	39	40	41	42
Null model chi-square	26888.13	26888.13	26888.13	26888.13
Null model df	105	105	105	105
Chi-square diff	—	—	—	—
Change in BIC	—			
NNFI	0.961	0.969	0.974	0.977
RNI				
RMSEA	0.050	0.044	0.040	0.038
$Pr <.05$ of RMSEA	0.047	0.998	0.999	0.999

First, fill in the necessary calculations for *two* of the missing statistics in this table: the change in the *BIC* for Models 2, 3, and 4, and the RNI for all models. (Forget the difference in chi-square: It is very significant across all models).

Then, using the results in this table, decide which model should be used for interpretation. Use both the absolute and incremental change in fit measures to arrive at a decision.

b. Using the fitted model, assess whether the measurement model for depression at Waves 2 and 3 is identified using the FC1 rule. If it is, then assess the identification of the structural part of the model.

2. The table and figure following this question (Table 8.B and Figure 8.A) are from output generated by LISREL 8.72. The structure of the model is important to this question more than the specific results. The model assesses the reciprocal effects of income (**INCOME1, INCOME2, INCOME3**) and depression (**CESD1, CESD2, CESD3**) at three points in time in the National Survey of Families and Households. Income is measured by a single indicator at each point in time, in this case the respondent's total income in each year of the survey. Depression has the same six indicators at each point in time.

At Wave 1 (1987–1988), there are four exogenous latent variables in the model: **INCOME1, CESD1,**

and **AGE,** and **FEMALE**, the last two measured by a single indicator. The order of the exogenous latent variables in the program is: **INCOME1, CESD1, FEMALE,** and **AGE**. The order of the endogenous latent variables is: **INCOME2, CESD2, INCOME3,** and **CESD3**.

An important feature of this model is that there are three waves of measured income. Thus, you do not have to assume that income is perfectly measured here. The results are from the standardized solution.

Note that certain parts of the model are not shown: The covariances among the four exogenous latent variables are not shown in the diagram, but they exist in the model; the error terms for the equations at Waves 2 and 3 are not shown but exist, and there are also covariances across equation errors at the same point in time.

The model shown reflects the initial specification of the model. Modification indices were used to fit the model beyond this point. Parameter names in the table reflect LISREL conventions for correlated errors. The fit statistics and parameters freed for each model are shown in Table 8.B.

a. Given these results, just using the fit statistics shown (not the *BIC* or the RNI), which model would you choose to interpret based on criteria for sufficient fit? Give reasons for our choice.

TABLE 8.B ● FIT MEASURES FOR A THREE-WAVE MODEL FOR INCOME AND DEPRESSION

Model and Added Parameter	χ^2	df	χ^2 change	Pr. (χ^2 change)	RMSEA	Pr. (RMSEA <.05)	NNFI
1. original	4308.89	210	---	---	.065	.000	.96
2. + TE 7, 5	3787.96	209	520.93	<.0001	.061	.000	.96
3. + TE 11,10	3390.55	208	397.41	<.0001	.058	.000	.96
4. + TH 6, 6	3005.24	207	385.31	<.0001	.054	.000	.97
5. + TD 7, 5	2708.13	206	297.11	<.0001	.051	.09	.97
6. + TE 13, 6	2486.29	205	221.84	<.0001	.049	.77	.97
7. + TE 12, 5	2326.21	204	160.08	<.0001	.048	.99	.98

b. The effects of income on depression appear to be different at Waves 2 and 3. This hypothesis was tested by imposing an equality constraint on these parameters in a further run of the model. The chi-square change for the constrained model with these effects equal is 7.32, with 1 degree of freedom. Although this is technically significant, the *BIC* is -4.2. Given this result, would you conclude the null hypothesis of equal effects hold? Explain your answer.

c. Concentrating on the latent variables for depression at Wave 2 and Wave 3 only, use the FC1 rule to show that the factor loadings and error terms are all identified and thus that the correlated errors are identified.

FIGURE 8.A ● A THREE-WAVE INCOME AND DEPRESSION MODEL

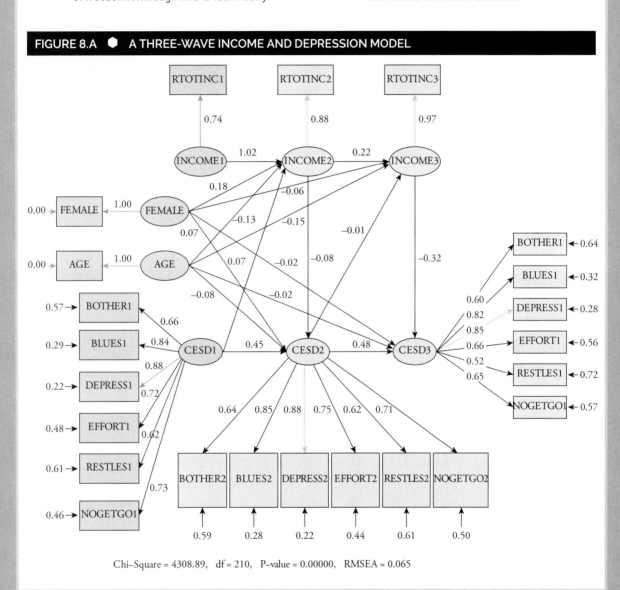

Chi–Square = 4308.89, df = 210, P–value = 0.00000, RMSEA = 0.065

VARIATIONS AND EXTENSIONS OF SEM

In the first five chapters, we discussed a variety of ways of generalizing the basic linear, additive regression model. In this chapter, we do the same for SEM—up to a point. We will focus on three issues that create more analytical flexibility and also allow for a broader range of types of data.

First, we focus on the application of structural equation models to the analysis of models across groups—therefore including countries, neighborhoods, cities, or any geo-political unit in data that allows you to distinguish cases by that unit, as well as all groups defined by sociodemographic categories—like gender, race, religion, or marital status. The goal of these analyses is to assess the comparability of both the measurement and structural model across groups. This allows the researcher to assess, separately, the issue of measurement invariance across groups versus the structural effects of variables. Of course, the hypothesis of measurement inequality looms large in comparative research of all types.

Second, we extend the SEM model to include ordinal variables. To this point, we have assumed interval-level measurement. But in many cases, our variables will be measured by ordinal responses. We want to be able to include and model these types of variables as part of an overall SEM model, possibly including mixed variable types. This is important because restricting our variables to interval measurement means that many concepts will just not be included in this framework.

Third, what do we do about nonlinear relations in the SEM framework? We do not discuss here the *many* recent approaches to the estimation of nonlinear and interactive SEM models—mainly because this area is very much "in development" and includes multiple competing approaches, each with its own advantages and disadvantages. Moreover, some of these recent approaches are not implemented yet in existing software. But we will discuss one recent approach based on a marginal maximum likelihood approach discussed recently by Codd (2011) and Harring, Weiss, and Hsu (2012). Our goal here is straightforward: to demonstrate that SEM models *can* accommodate nonlinear effects.

9.1 THE COMPARATIVE SEM FRAMEWORK

One of the most important applications of structural equation models (SEM) is the comparison of models across groups. This approach allows the direct test of the equality of the measurement and structural model, as separate issues in the model, but in most applications, it is understood that the measurement model must be equal before we can compare structural coefficients.

The ability to separate measurement issues from the effects of variables on each other means that core problematic issues of comparative research can be assessed via tests of equality of measurement parameters, independent of tests of the equality of effects of variables across groups. This is important because these two issues are confounded in standard approaches to comparative research, and thus there is uncertainty about whether differences in observed results are due to differences in measurement or differences in the structural effects of variables on each other.

The fact that this issue is in the background of much comparative research seems obvious. The approach used here puts this issue in the foreground. One of the most common interpretations in comparative research—across gender, race, citizenship, countries, and so forth—is that the measures do not "mean" the same thing in different contexts, and so the effects of variables seem to differ but only due to unequal measurement. The SEM approach clarifies this problem by explicitly testing the equality of parameters in the measurement model first. The assumption in this test is that equality reflects a common pattern of meaning among the indicators—or the correlations among them would not be equal.

"Groups" can be defined broadly: You can compare results across gender—to test hypothesis about gender inequality—for example, marital status groups, ethnicities, cultures, countries, cities, social classes, foreign versus native born, or *any* variable that is amenable to classification.

The important feature in most software for SEM is that you can impose equality restrictions on the same parameter or set of parameters in different groups and thus test whether the parameter(s) are equal or different across groups. This is done by comparing the fit of models where the parameters are defined as equal versus one in which they are allowed to vary.

When you compare models across groups in this way, you should realize that you are also testing an interaction that corresponds to a continuous *x* categorical interaction in regression: If the parameters are equal, there is no interaction; if the parameters are not equal, there is an interaction.

9.1.1 Implementing Multiple-Group Models

The extension of the usual SEM syntax to include multiple groups, with features for testing for equality, is now commonly included in most software. What do we need? First, we want to estimate the same basic model in multiple groups in the same run—not successively. Second, we want to have a way to constrain parameters across groups to be equal, or more broadly, a function of each other. Third, we want to assess differences in fit across models, comparing models where a set of parameters are allowed to vary to one where the same set is constrained to be equal. A "significant" difference in fit implies the parameters are not equal.

The χ^2 difference between free versus restricted models can be used to assess the plausibility of the equality restriction. In this context, one is looking for a non-significant difference across models. The *BIC* can also be used here. If the χ^2 or *BIC* difference is significant, this indicates a difference in effect across groups, in other words, an interaction.

9.1.1.1 Comparisons of Parameters across Groups

It is important to realize that within-group standardized solutions *cannot* be compared across groups. This is because standardized coefficients can vary purely due to the fact that the variances of variables vary across groups.

Remember that the structure of a standardized coefficient is

$$\beta = b \cdot \frac{s_X}{s_Y}$$

Thus, if $b = .4$ in two groups but the variance of Y is .7 in one group and 1 in another while $V(X) = 1$ in both, then

$$\beta_1 = b_1 \cdot \frac{s_{X_1}}{s_{Y_1}} = .4 \cdot \frac{1}{1} = .4$$

$$\beta_2 = b_2 \cdot \frac{s_{X_2}}{s_{Y_2}} = .4 \cdot \frac{1}{.7} = .57$$

The apparently larger effect in Group 2 is not a larger effect per se but really a reflection of less variance in Group 2. The standard advice about cross-groups comparisons is to use *unstandardized* coefficients for comparison of parameters across groups.

9.2 A MULTIPLE GROUP EXAMPLE

9.2.1 The SES-Depression Model among Black and White Americans

In both of the last two chapters, we have estimated a model designed to understand the effects of SES on depression, as mediated by mastery. Here we ask this question: Does this model apply equally to both Black and White subsamples in the National Survey of Families and Households (NSFH) data?

A repeated concern in testing for equality in the usual regression model—for example, by testing an interaction between some X and the group variable—is that the test confounds differences due to structural effects with differences due to unequal measurement of the underlying concepts. To repeat an important point, a common criticism of comparative work estimating the same model in different cultural contexts is that the "meaning" of the measures and/or concepts differ.

In an SEM framework, we can specify what the equivalent meaning of measures should look like: an equivalent factor pattern across groups. If measures differ in meaning across groups, then some indicators should be more or less closely associated with other indicators. For example, if "crying" as a measure of depression occurs more generically and frequently in one group for cultural reasons, then its correlation with other measures of depression will be disrupted. In turn, its factor loading should look different in that group.

In order to test equivalent structural effects, we first have to establish whether the factor pattern in the measurement model is equivalent because if it is not, it is not clear how the structural effects can be compared at all. This is because the latent variables will not have the same "definition" in groups if the factor pattern varies. The situation is actually more complex than that and is often not discussed in the literature on measurement models. Showing that the measurement models are not formally equivalent, according to these rules, is not prima facie evidence of *functionally* nonequivalent measurement. The discussion of comparative measurement is actually more involved because for some concepts, some groups *may have partially or completely different indicators for the same concept.* This possibility suggests we must be very careful to conclude nonequivalent measurement if, for example, indicators in one group are at least functionally equivalent to indicators in another group, in the sense of construct validity. Gendered channeling of emotional expression is sometimes cited to suggest that indicators of depression among men and women may differ naturally. Thus, the theory of measurement that applies to a specific group must be considered, even when measurement models are not "equal."

Here we follow the formal definition of equivalent measurement. If measurement models are equal, then we can ask whether the structural model as a whole is equivalent, or we can ask about equivalence of key parameters in an underlying structural model. In our example, we do both. Our hypothesis is that the linkage between SES and depression will be differentially mediated by mastery among Blacks compared to Whites. It is possible, for example, that the linkage between SES and mastery is weaker among Blacks and that the implications of mastery in lowering depression are also weaker. Some have predicted the opposite: When a minority group does have upward mobility, then the benefits of recently acquired status seem particularly acute, thus strengthening the link between SES and mastery. If mastery is in fact scarce in one group, it could mean its value when present may be *greater.*

9.2.2 Estimating the Model

We showed the syntax for PROC CALIS in SAS that estimated the original model in Chapter 7. Here we extend that syntax to show how the multiple group model works.

The first thing you need to do is to subdivide the original data you use into two subsamples representing each group. To do this, read in the data set for the whole sample, with all measured variables included, and then select on the variable representing the groups you want to compare. For example, you could select Blacks in one run, save the data under a new name, then select Whites in another run and save the data under another new name. At that point, you have two data sets to read into PROC CALIS.

The following syntax will estimate the model across groups, with equal factor loadings embedded as a constraint. This is the model you estimate to test for equality of measurement:

```
proc calis /*data=sesmh*/ cov pcorr maxiter=500 maxfunc=1000 pshort stderr
/*effpart*/ simple mod method=ml;

title 1 'Comparing African-Americans and Whites in the SES-Mental Health model';
title 2 'Equal measurement model—loadings only';

group 1 / data=sesmhblacks label="African-Americans" nobs=950;
group 2 / data=sesmhwhites label="Whites" nobs=5345;
```

```
model 1 / groups = 1;
        lineqs

/* measurement model equations */

                htotinc1 = 1. fSES88 + d1,
                bestSEI1 = SES12 fSES88 + d2,


                bother1 = dep11 fdep88 + d3,
                blues1 = dep12 fdep88 + d4,
                depress1 = 1. fdep88 + d5,
                effort1 = dep14 fdep88 + d6,
                restles1 = dep15 fdep88 + d7,
                nogetgo1 = dep16 fdep88 + d8,


                bother2= dep21 fdep94 + e3,
                blues2=  dep22 fdep94 + e4,
                depress2= 1. fdep94 + e5,
                effort2= dep24 fdep94 + e6,
                restles2= dep25 fdep94 + e7,
                nogetgo2= dep26 fdep94 + e8,

        lifeworkout = control1 fmastery + e9,
        doanything = control2 fmastery + e10,
        solveprob = control3 fmastery + e11,
        havecontrol = 1. fmastery + e12,

/* latent variable structural equations */

        fmastery = bbSESC fses88 + bbdepc fdep88 + eeq1,
        fdep94 = bbSESd fses88 + bbdepd fdep88 + bbcontrol fmastery + eeq2;

/* variances */
        variances
                e3-e12 = berrore3-berrore12,
                d1-d8 = berrord1-berrord8,
                fSES88 = bvarSES88, fdep88 = bvardep88,
                eeq1 = berroreqc, eeq2 = berroreqd;

/* covariances */
cov
                fSES88 fdep88 = bbcov88,
                e9 e10 = berrorcov1,
                e6 e8 = berrorcov2,
                d4 d5 = berrorcov3,
                e7 d7 = berrorcov4;
                /*e4 e5 = errorcov2,
                d4 d5 = errorcov3,
                e7 d7 = errorcov4
                eeq1 eeq2 = coveq*/
```

```
model 2 / groups = 2;
            lineqs

/* measurement model equations */

            htotinc1 = 1. fSES88 + d1,
            bestSEI1 = SES12 fSES88 + d2,

            bother1 = dep11 fdep88 + d3,
            blues1 = dep12 fdep88 + d4,
            depress1 = 1. fdep88 + d5,
            effort1 = dep14 fdep88 + d6,
            restles1 = dep15 fdep88 + d7,
            nogetgo1 = dep16 fdep88 + d8,

            bother2= dep21 fdep94 + e3,
            blues2= dep22 fdep94 + e4,
            depress2= 1. fdep94 + e5,
            effort2= dep24 fdep94 + e6,
            restles2= dep25 fdep94 + e7,
            nogetgo2= dep26 fdep94 + e8,

        lifeworkout = control1 fmastery + e9,
        doanything = control2 fmastery + e10,
        solveprob = control3 fmastery + e11,
        havecontrol = 1. fmastery + e12,

/* latent variable structural equations */

        fmastery = wbSESC fses88 + wbdepc fdep88 + eeq1,
        fdep94 = wbSESd fses88 + wbdepd fdep88 + wbcontrol fmastery + eeq2;

/* variances */
        variances
            e3-e12 = werrore3-werrore12,
            d1-d8 = werrord1-werrord8,
            fSES88 = wvarSES88, fdep88 = wvardep88,
            eeq1 = werroreqc, eeq2 = werroreqd;

/* covariances */
cov
            fSES88 fdep88 = wcov88,
            e9 e10 = werrorcov1,
            e6 e8 = werrorcov2,
            d4 d5 = werrorcov3,
            e7 d7 = werrorcov4;

pathdiagram diagram=all exogcov;
weight mufinw93;
run;
```

This syntax includes two group definition statements, designating Group 1 as the Black subsample and Group 2 as the White subsample. These statements label the groups and specify the sample size in each group. Following these statements are two whole blocks of statements for each group, specifying the model in each group. These statements follow the same rules as for a single-sample analysis. Each block of statements begins with a model statement, which specifies which group is being modeled by the statements below. For example, the statement

```
model 1 / groups = 1;
```

says that this is Model 1 using Group 1, which in this case are Blacks. The *lineqs, variances,* and *cov* statements following work the same way as for a general sample. This is followed by the model for Group 2, which is Whites. What is unique here is that the parameter names for factor loadings in the two groups *are the same*—telling SAS to assume these parameters have the same value. These parameters are highlighted in the code. Other parameter names—for the structural coefficients, for variances, and for errors, have unique names in the two groups, signaling that these parameters should be unique in each group.

This model is the second in a sequence of models estimated to test equivalence overall. The first model, the "free" model, allows all parameters to vary across groups. The second—this model—constrains the measurement model to be equal. We do not go further and set the error variances equal because these variances may vary while not affecting the equality of the factor pattern overall. In the third model, we add further constraints by setting all structural coefficients equal for latent variables. We do this by giving the same names to these parameters across models. This tests for the equality of the structural model, over and above the measurement model.

9.2.2.1 Fitting the Model First

In order to test for the equality of parameters, we first fit a model in both groups, using the criteria of the last chapter. That is why there are statements in both groups freeing certain correlated errors. Our approach here is to free the *same* parameters in both groups, even if the fit problem really only occurs in one. By doing this, we start with a model with the same free parameters before we test for equality across groups.

Table 9.1 shows the results of a number of progressive tests to assess the equivalence of the model among Blacks and Whites. Model 1 is the fitted model, as a starting point, with all parameters free to vary in both groups. Model 2 is the equal measurement model, as above, with factor loadings constrained equal. Model 3 is a test of an equal structural model. Because of our specific interest in the inequality of the role of mastery, we also show results for a model in which only two structural parameters were set equal—the effect of SES on mastery and the effect of mastery on depression, together representing the indirect effect of SES on depression.

Sample size issues enter into the interpretation of these tests, giving more weight to the BIC statistic. We know that the χ^2 difference test is sensitive to large sample sizes, and so small changes in model conditions will often produce a significant difference, especially when the N is 6,295. Because of this, in our tests, we also use the adjusted critical chi-square to judge changes in fit, as discussed in the previous chapter.

The test for the equivalence of the measurement model looks significant under the usual chi-square difference test, but the change in the BIC is 127.40 more negative, suggesting both a better model and one that far exceeds the BIC criterion for "strong" evidence (10).

TABLE 9.1 ● SES, MASTERY AND DEPRESSION MODEL

	L2	df	Δ Chi-sq p value	Adjusted Critical Chi-sq	BIC	Δ BIC
1. Fitted model	1901.04	250			−1008.43	
2. Equal measurement model	1936.07	264	35.03	168.93	−1136.33	127.40
			0.001			
3. Equal structural model (all parts)	1942.68	269	6.61	64.19	−1187.91	50.98
			0.251			
3a. Equal indirect effect through mastery	1939.91	266	3.84	29.27	−1155.77	19.44
			0.147			
3b. Equal total effect of SES	1939.92	267	0.540	40.91	−1167.39	31.06
			0.462			

The adjusted χ^2 also shows that the change in chi-square falls far short of the adjusted critical value. Both this result and the BIC result (and of course, they are a different representation of the same information) suggest that the hypothesis of equivalent measurement holds here—despite widespread belief that the meaning of the depression and/or mastery indicators may be unique among Blacks versus Whites. We find no evidence for that in this model.

Because this hypothesis holds, we can proceed to test the equivalence of the structural model, by setting equal the five coefficients in the structural model. Applying the test criteria in the same way suggests that the hypothesis of equivalent effects cannot be rejected either. In other words, this model *is* equivalent in essential respects across race. In fact, not even the usual chi-square difference test is significant here, comparing Model 3 to Model 2. The change in the BIC is 50.98. In effect, there is really no evidence here for the differential effects of SES on depression overall or through mastery, controlling for earlier depression.

We also show results for individual tests of differences in structural parameters across groups in Models 3a and 3b. We do this because often researchers will focus on specific differences in the model, based on their theoretical interest. In this case, we examine the equality of the indirect effect through mastery, setting equal two parameters: the effect of SES in 1988 on mastery in 1994 and the effect of mastery in 1994 on depression in 1994. This model should be compared to Model 2 to detect changes in fit. Again, there is no evidence here of any difference in the indirect effect across groups. The usual chi-square difference test is again not significant. In Model 3b, we expand the test to include the total effect of SES, both direct and indirect. Again, we do not find any evidence for differences: SES has as much of an effect but no more of an effect among Black compared to Whites.

Despite widespread concerns about differences in the measurement of depression and/or mastery across these groups, our tests do not suggest differences. And further, despite very plausible reasoning that SES may have enhanced or dampened effects among Blacks compared to Whites, we find no evidence for this in this model.

The results of the best fitted and constrained model, with all structural parameters involved in the total effect of SES set equal, are shown below in ***unstandardized*** form. These parameters are the ones that are directly comparable across groups, but you have to remember that the sizes of the units of variables here are very different—for example, units of SES (income) versus units of mastery (5 points).

FIGURE 9.1 ● THE SES—MENTAL HEALTH MODEL AMONG BLACKS

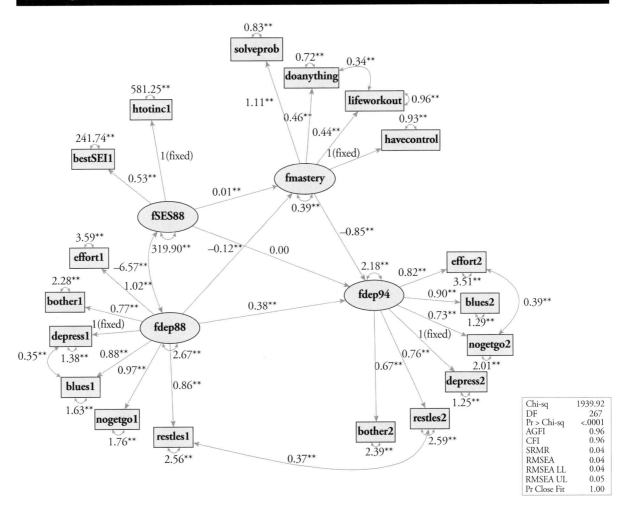

FIGURE 9.2 ● **THE SES—MENTAL HEALTH MODEL AMONG WHITES**

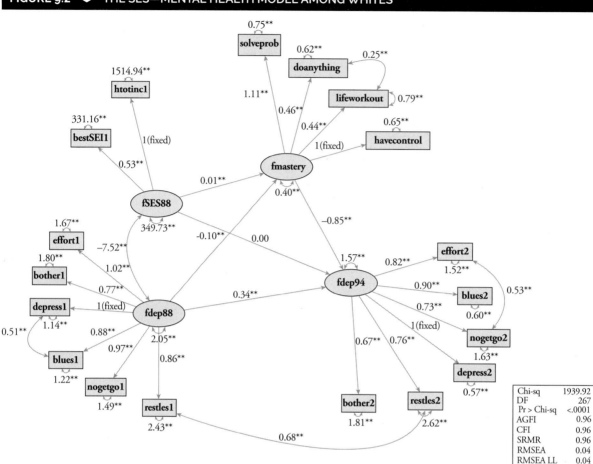

Chi-sq	1939.92
DF	267
Pr > Chi-sq	<.0001
AGFI	0.96
CFI	0.96
SRMR	0.96
RMSEA	0.04
RMSEA LL	0.04
RMSEA UL	0.05
Pr Close Fit	1.00

9.3 SEM FOR NONNORMAL AND ORDINAL DATA

Throughout the discussion to this point, we have assumed that measures are interval or quasi-interval. But we know that in survey data, *many* variables are measured ordinally. We have also assumed that the data conform to an assumption of multivariate normality. Again, we would prefer the flexibility of not having to consider this sometimes restrictive assumption.

9.3.1 Nonnormality

The problems that result from using variables with nonnormal distributions include the following:

1. *Theoretically*: Inaccurate standard errors and χ^2 goodness of fit values. ML estimators are consistent and unbiased but are no longer efficient, especially when kurtosis ("fatter" or "thinner" tails) occurs.

2. *Empirically (via simulations)*: (a) ML estimators produce χ^2 values that are too large as nonnormality increases. Thus the fit of the model looks worse than it really is; (b) simulations suggest moderate to severe under-estimation of standard errors of parameter estimates. This means that many parameters will "appear" to be significant when they are not; and (c) other model fit indices may be somewhat underestimated.

9.3.1.1 Detection of Nonnormality

Measures of skewness (departure from symmetry of a distribution) and kurtosis (peakness vs. flatness) indicate departures from normality. Moments around the mean of a distribution can be defined generally by

$$\mu_r = \frac{\sum (X_i - \mu_1)^r}{N} \text{ for r > 1}$$

Note that the variance is defined by $r = 2$, the skewness when $r = 3$, and the kurtosis when $r = 4$. Because it is possible to have univariate normal variables but not multivariate normality of the distribution of all variables and ML depends on the assumption of *multivariate normality*, it is advisable to assess multivariate normality directly.

Mardia (1970; 1980) has developed tests of multivariate skewness and multivariate kurtosis, each following a Z normal distribution, and an omnibus test of normality based on

$$K^2 = \left(b_3\right)_z^2 + \left(b_4\right)_z^2$$

where b_3 is a multivariate measure of skewness, b_4 is a multivariate measure of kurtosis, and the z subscript denotes the fact that these measures are transformed first to have standardized normal distributions for testing. K^2 has a χ^2 distribution with 2 degrees of freedom.

Although we do not demonstrate this test here, most SEM software includes options to test multivariate normality.

9.3.1.2 Possible Solutions

1. **Normal scores**

Most software allows you to produce normalized scores for each variable. Once the variables have been transformed, one can re-test for multivariate normality.

2. **Transformations**

One can also use explicit transformations of the raw variables before using them in an SEM model. For example, log transformations may help achieve univariate normality and thus indirectly multivariate normality. But one can also use any transformation that would help, including square roots, raising the variable to powers, and so forth.

3. **Estimation under different assumptions**

The purpose of the two prior approaches is to preserve the ML approach to estimating the model. In fact, this is not necessary. Browne (1984) developed a new class of estimators that do not require multivariate normality, generally referred to as **"*distribution free" weighted least squares* (WLS)**. This approach to estimation produces a weight matrix from the estimated covariances and variances—referred to in software as the asymptotic covariance matrix.

This estimator, theoretically, has some important desirable characteristics: (a) It does not require multivariate normality; in fact, the distribution of the variables does not matter; (b) the estimator is an asymptotically efficient estimator in the situation of nonnormality of the data; and (c) a χ^2 test based on the WLS fitting function can be derived that does not depend on the distribution of variables for its appropriateness.

At the same time, the WLS approach can have some important practical limitations, as well: (a) The properties of the estimator obtain only in large samples, some say only in samples above 1000; and (b) the derivation of the weight matrix places considerable demands on computation, and when there are many variables in the model, this approach may have trouble reaching convergence and thus final estimates. Because of these problems, it is not always possible to use WLS, and attempts to transform the variables may be more successful.

9.3.2 Ordinal Variables

Bengt Muthén (1984) pioneered the development of SEM models for variables with various levels of measurement. Essentially, there is an extra step in this model, described by a set of rules that relate the observed categorical measures to underlying latent variables that are in fact continuous and normally distributed. In other words, ordinal variables are treated as coarse measures of underlying normal, continuous latent concepts. *Note that the approach discussed here does not include models with categorical indicators of underlying **categorical** latent variables, such as "latent class" variables, although extensions of the estimator used here do allow for this generalization as well.*

This model proposes an unobserved latent measure for each ordinal variable, denoted by y^*, which does conform to the assumptions of the usual model. Observed y's in this case are categorized versions of the underlying true y^*, which in some ways distorts the distribution of y^*. Some nonlinear function is needed to adjust for the categorization in measured y. One such function is a "threshold model," which sees the different response categories in y as reflecting the person's position in an underlying normal distribution on y^*.

For example, in a model with four thresholds for five ordinal categories

$$y = \begin{cases} 1, & \text{if } y^* \le a_1 \\ 2, & \text{if } a_1 < y^* \le a_2 \\ 3, & \text{if } a_2 < y^* \le a_3 \\ 4, & \text{if } a_3 < y^* \le a_4 \\ 5, & \text{if } y^* > a_4 \end{cases}$$

Note that given c categories of y, there are $c - 1$ thresholds in the underlying distribution. These thresholds have to be determined. Assuming y^* is multivariate normal suggests the thresholds can be estimated by

$$a_i = \Phi^{-1}\left(\sum_{k=1}^{c} \frac{N_k}{N}\right)$$

where Φ^{-1} is the inverse of the normal distribution function, N_k is the number of cases in the kth category, and N is the total number of cases. Thresholds are calculated from the normal distribution. The example in Table 9.2 shows how thresholds are calculated:

TABLE 9.2 ● CALCULATING THRESHOLDS FROM AN ORDINAL VARIABLE							
Category	1	2	3	4	5	6	7	8
Frequency	8	13	5	13	5	22	4	5
Proportion	.107	.173	.067	.173	.067	.293	.053	.067
Cumulative	.107	.280	.347	.520	.587	.880	.933	1.00
Threshold	−1.24	−.58	−.39	.05	.22	1.17	1.50	

These thresholds are used to "place" the observed scores in terms of an underlying normal distribution. We can see this by plotting the preceding thresholds (see Figure 9.3).

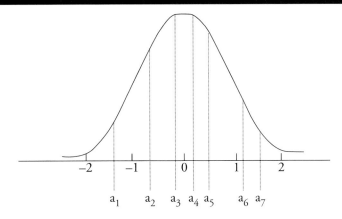

FIGURE 9.3 ● ORDINAL THRESHOLDS FOR AN UNDERLYING CONTINUOUS LATENT VARIABLE

In this situation, standard ML estimation is formally inappropriate. The assumptions involved in estimating the covariance matrix among observed variables do not hold for ordinal variables. Thus the input matrix is a biased estimate of the actual covariances.

Browne's distribution–free weighted least squares estimator (1984) is the most efficient approach to estimation in this situation. In this case, one has to estimate covariances or correlations in raw data appropriate to the level of measurement as follows:

TABLE 9.3 ● TYPES OF CORRELATIONS APPROPRIATE FOR VARIABLES WITH VARYING MEASUREMENT CHARACTERISTICS

X_1	X_2	r
ordinal	ordinal	polychoric
dichotomous	dichotomous	tetrachoric
ordinal	continuous	polyserial
dichotomous	continuous	biserial

Most software provides options for analysis using WLS in an SEM context. You should be using this estimator if some of your variables are ordinal in nature. In SAS, as an example, you have to run PROC CORR in SAS to calculate the polychoric correlations and save them in a data set. This is done by asking for polychoric correlations for the ordinal variables and then saving the output as a correlation matrix, with means and standard deviations. Using the confirmatory factor analysis example, analyzing the measurement structure of seven measures of well-being, we use the following code as a first step:

```
proc corr data=temp outplc=ryffordinal polychoric nomiss;
var personal_sa--judge_aut;
run;
```

PROC CALIS then calls in these data and in a first run, asks for an output data set of the weights necessary for WLS, using an "outwgt=" option to name a weight data set. This is commented out in the second run. In this second run, you call in these weights using the "inwgt" option. Note that "method=wls" and you also specify "asycov=unbiased," which should be used with this kind of estimation. The "data=" option refers to the data set just created holding the polychoric correlations. The PROC CALIS command here would look like this:

```
proc calis data=ryffordinal (type=corr) inwgt=nsfhdata.ryffweight
/*outwgt=nsfhdata.ryffweight*/ asycov=unbiased pestim cov method=wls
mod simple;
```

The specification of this run is the same as the one shown in Chapter 7. We can compare results directly, using the graphic output of the measurement model in Figure 9.4. This should be noted: The initial example in Chapter 7 uses the standard ML approach to estimation, but it *is* formally inappropriate for ordinal variables.

FIGURE 9.4 ● THE RYFF MEASUREMENT MODEL USING WEIGHTED LEAST SQUARES

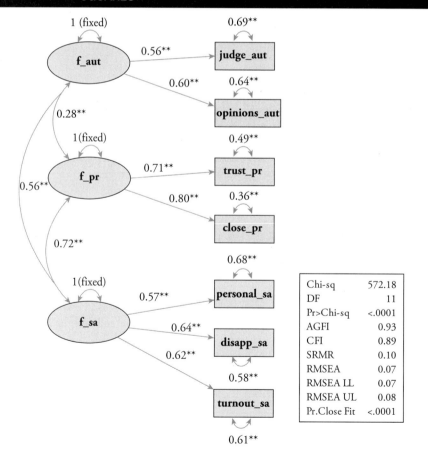

Chi-sq	572.18
DF	11
Pr>Chi-sq	<.0001
AGFI	0.93
CFI	0.89
SRMR	0.10
RMSEA	0.07
RMSEA LL	0.07
RMSEA UL	0.08
Pr.Close Fit	<.0001

Factor loadings are not remarkably different, but there are some notable differences: The loadings for positive relations are higher here; two of the loadings for self-acceptance are noticeably higher; and the correlation between autonomy and self-acceptance is quite a bit lower. Other parameters are similar. Overall, the results support the idea of three distinct underlying factors a little more clearly.

We advocate using the approach used here to estimate factor models when the measures are ordinal rather than pretending they are interval. It is our experience across numerous examples that the results usually improve and clarify the measurement model.

Of course, it is important to note that this is only one example of the difference resulting from two approaches to estimation. Results in complex structural models may be quite different.

9.3.3 A Structural Model: A Panel Model for Domestic Violence and Marital Quality

The measures of violence and marital quality in the National Survey of Families and Households are both basically ordinal. But because we want to consider the difference between using ML and WLS, we estimate a model for the reciprocal effect of marital quality and domestic violence over time both ways. Causal reciprocity is plausible here: It is reasonable to expect that violence will reduce assessments of marital quality, but low marital quality may also act as a basis for domestic violence.

At both Waves 1 and 2, six years apart, we have three indicators of domestic violence:

• HIT	= how often the couple ends up hitting or throwing things in arguments.
• YOUHIT	= how many fights in the past year have resulted in the respondent hitting their spouse
• HITYOU	= how many fights in the past year have resulted in the spouse hitting the respondent

And there are four indicators of marital quality:

• HAPPY	= rated marital happiness
• TIME	= how much time the couple spends together alone
• NOARGUE	= few or no disagreements about money
• STABLE	= the reverse coding of the respondents estimated chances of an eventual divorce

The standardized estimates from an initial model using ML are shown in Figure 9.5, using output from the classic SEM program LISREL (v. 8.72). The graphic looks different than the output from SAS, but basic conventions are the same: Latent variables are circles; measured variables are rectangles. We specify the effects of violence and marital quality as current because these effects are more likely to occur over short time lags (recently) than over a six-year period.

However, we recognize this is a choice that is necessary to identify the structural model, respecting the rules we discussed in the last chapter. Note however that the identifying assumptions here are reasonable: Both violence and marital quality have effects on their own state six years later (the stability), but each only has indirect effects on the other variable through this over time stability.

FIGURE 9.5 ● THE MARITAL VIOLENCE—MARITAL QUALITY PANEL MODEL ESTIMATED WITH ML ASSUMPTIONS

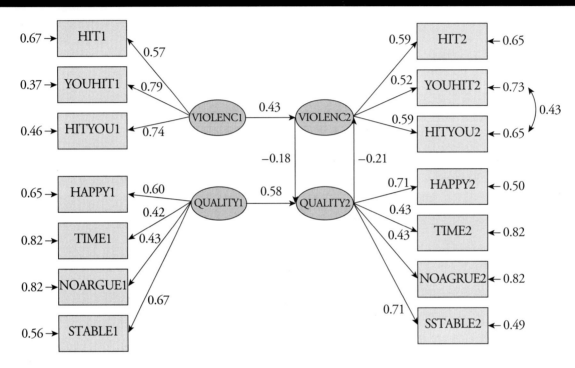

This model suggests a balanced reciprocity between violence and marital quality. Each affects the other, in the expected direction, with about the same level of influence. Domestic violence appears to be less stable than marital quality over time. There *are* some questions about the factor loadings: The loadings for violence are quite different at Waves 1 and 2, and some of the marital quality loadings are below .50. This is not a universal threshold, but it is a sign of potentially weakly related indicators.

The same model was estimated using WLS. The results are shown in Figure 9.6.

The results are different in key areas relative to the model using ML. The results suggest stronger effects of violence on marital quality than in the original model (although we do not test for this difference), thus changing the balance of the reciprocal effects. The conclusion following from this result would put more emphasis on the importance of violence as a basis for the decline in marital quality. Also, the factor loadings are generally quite a bit higher than in the ML model. First, loadings for domestic violence are more similar across waves, and they are very high. Second, no loadings for marital quality are below .5. Third, also notice that the estimated stability of domestic violence is higher in this model, suggesting, importantly, that domestic violence situations are more typically chronic than episodic.

FIGURE 9.6 ⬢ THE MARITAL VIOLENCE—MARITAL QUALITY PANEL MODEL ESTIMATED WITH WLS

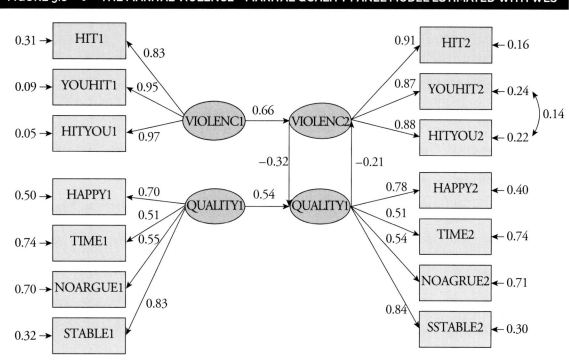

In addition, in results not shown, the fit of the model improves here relative to the ML solution, presumably because the estimator fits the situation better. In this case, there appear to be clear benefits to estimating the model based on the more appropriate assumptions of ordinality.

9.4 NONLINEAR EFFECTS IN SEM MODELS

How does one incorporate nonlinear effects among latent variables into SEM models? As noted earlier, there have been numerous recent developments attempting to answer this question. If there is a solution, the solution has to extend to the consideration of continuous by continuous interactions as well. However, in the interest of practicality, we encourage researchers to use the multiple-group approach discussed earlier in this chapter. When using a continuous variable as the modifier, one would have to divide up the variable into two or three categories and then run multiple models on those subgroups.

In this section, we concentrate on nonlinear effects, to make the point that this variation can be incorporated into these models. We discuss a recent approach using a marginal maximum likelihood approach that fares well in simulations (Harring et al., 2012) and also—unlike some other recent approaches—is a one-step method that provides information both on the measurement model and the structural effects.

9.4.1 Using Marginal Maximum Likelihood Estimation in a Nonlinear Mixed Model

As discussed in Codd (2011) and Harring et al. (2012), one can estimate a nonlinear SEM in one step by recognizing that the nonlinear model requires a different approach to estimation. Codd (2011) suggests using a nonlinear estimation procedure, not necessarily intended for

SEM models, such as PROC NLMIXED in SAS. This program is more flexible than standard approaches because, basically, you write your own model. Simulations conducted by Harring et al. (2012) also suggest that marginal maximum likelihood estimation (MML)—stated without explanation here—is one of the preferred approaches.

In this approach, one uses a nonlinear mixed model approach to write out the exact model you want to estimate, in equation form, and specify a marginal maximum likelihood approach to estimating the model. The code presented here is based on Codd (2011). The issue is that this approach basically estimates an "initial" model—there is no fitting process involved. However, one could fit the measurement model first and include those extra parameters in the program.

In this example, we investigate a non-linear effect of mastery on depression in a structural equation framework. The prediction is that it is possible to have "too much of a good thing", and that excessive levels of sense of mastery will often lead to higher depression, after reaching a low point in the upper mid-range of mastery (Wheaton, 1985). Thus, we want to estimate a quadratic model. We have a latent variable for mastery, with three indicators (named *solveprob, havecontrol, and lifeworkout* in the program), and a latent variable for depression, also with three indicators (*blues2, effort2,* and *depress2* in the program).

PROC NLMIXED can be used to write out the equations in a way that is not unlike PROC CALIS, but there are also crucial differences. We have simplified the measurement model in the following code so as not to entertain unnecessary complexity, given the issues in estimating a model that converges and produces a solution.

The code in SAS follows:

```
proc nlmixed data=sesmh technique=dbldog maxiter=500 maxfunc=1000;
        parms intcept=8 dep22=.85 dep24=.8 control1=.4 control3=.6
                int4=2 int5=2 int6=5 int9=1.2 int11=2.3 int12=3
                e4=1.5 e5=1.2 e6=1.8 e9=.3 e11=.5 e12=.7
                kappa=3 phi11=1 psi11=.8
                b2mast=-.25 b3sq=.08;
        random fmast err ~ normal([kappa,0],[phi11,0,psi11]) subject=mcaseid;
        dep = intcept+ b2mast*fmast + b3sq*(fmast**2) + err;

        eps4 = blues2 - int4 - dep22*dep;
        eps5 = depress2 - int5 - 1*dep;
        eps6 = effort2 - int6 - dep24*dep;
        eps9 = lifeworkout - int9 - control1*fmast;
        eps11 = solveprob - int11 - control3*fmast;
        eps12 = havecontrol - int12 - 1*fmast;

        det = e4*e5*e6*e9*e11*e12;
        sum = ((eps9**2/e9) + (eps11**2/e11) + (eps12**2 / e12) + (eps4**2/e4)
                (eps5**2/e5) + (eps6**2 / e6));
        LnL= log (1/sqrt(det))-(.5)*sum;
        dummy=1;
        model dummy~general(LnL);
        run;
```

On the line for PROC NLMIXED, we refer to the technique of estimation: This is *not* the method of estimation but the algorithm used to find a solution. We choose "dbldog," for purely practical reasons: It led to a solution while the default technique did not. There are a number of options to try here, and whatever works is fine. We increased the number of iterations and possible function calls as well, since our model exceeded the defaults. Again, experimentation is fine.

The PARMS statement gives starting values for all of the parameters to be estimated in the program. This is not necessary in PROC CALIS, but it *is* here. These are just educated guesses about the values of each parameter—as a starting point in the estimation process.

The RANDOM statement and the program code following specify the model. The RANDOM statement names the latent variable for mastery (*fmast*) and the name of the error term in the equation for depression below(*err*). This statement specifies the form of the distribution of these variables as normal, with means "kappa" and 0, in that order, and with variances specified by parameter names in the 2 x 2 covariance matrix following: [phi11,0,psi11]). Phi11 is the variance of *fmast*, Psi11 is the variance of *err,* and the matrix says that there is no covariance between these variables. The SUBJECT= specification names the subject case id variable.

After this statement, you simply write out the equations of the model, in a specific form. The equation for "dep" is the structural equation of interest; coefficients for the linear (*bmast*) and quadratic (*bmastsq*) components of the effects of mastery are given names here. Note that the independent variables and the dependent variable referred to here are both defined later as latent variables. The measurement part of the model is written in a series of equations, essentially the same as in PROC CALIS, but in this form: The error term is on the left, isolated, and the remaining terms are on the right of the equality. So, for example, `eps4 = blues2 - int4 - dep22*dep;` is the same as: `blues= int4 + dep22*dep +eps4;` —the more familiar form used in PROC CALIS.

The lines from DET to the end are standard. These statements together specify a marginal ML approach. Note that the DET statement contains parameters not referred to directly in the measurement equations, but the SUM statement does include both these parameters and the actual names for the error terms. The LnL statement states the likelihood function, and the model statement simply uses a "dummy" to refer to the approach to estimation for the model. The dummy variable here is just a placeholder because SAS requires something before the tilde in this statement.

Results from PROC NLMIXED simply list the estimates for the parameter as you name them. Table 9.4 shows the essential output.

Results are not standardized, but they could be, by first standardizing the variables involved before running the program. The measures of depression and control both produce satisfactory factor loadings relative to the scaling indicator set at 1. Most importantly, we see that the program produces the results for a nonlinear model for the effects of the mastery latent variable. As expected, this effect is quadratic and U-shaped, with increases in depression occurring at very high levels of mastery.

If a technique can be used to estimate a nonlinear relationship, it can be used to assess interactions among latent variables as well, simply by writing those interactions into the structural equations of the model.

TABLE 9.4 ● NLMIXED OUTPUT FOR THE SPECIFIED MODEL

Parameter Estimates								
Parameter	**Estimate**	**Standard Error**	**DF**	***t* Value**	**Pr > |t|**	**95% Confidence Limits**		**Gradient**
Intercept	6.5378	6.8637	9437	0.95	0.3409	−6.9166	19.9922	−162.208
dep22	0.8993	0.001892	9437	475.32	<.0001	0.8955	0.9030	−231.487
dep24	0.7892	0.01035	9437	76.25	<.0001	0.7689	0.8094	12.2327
control1	0.5082	0.02505	9437	20.29	<.0001	0.4591	0.5573	61.2078
control3	0.5047	0.06458	9437	7.81	<.0001	0.3781	0.6312	−95.7621
int4	2.3304	6.9718	9437	0.33	0.7382	−11.3358	15.9966	−53.3132
int5	2.7627	7.7450	9437	0.36	0.7213	−12.4192	17.9446	−108.492
int6	2.5362	6.1130	9437	0.41	0.6782	−9.4466	14.5189	−7.31741
int9	2.4924	0.09710	9437	25.67	<.0001	2.3021	2.6828	−260.452
int11	2.2608	0.04816	9437	46.95	<.0001	2.1664	2.3552	377.748
int12	1.2875	0.2566	9437	5.02	<.0001	0.7845	1.7905	−463.127
e4	0.8250	0.07316	9437	11.28	<.0001	0.6816	0.9684	673.451
e5	0.7066	0.07898	9437	8.95	<.0001	0.5518	0.8615	420.959
e6	2.2561	0.03763	9437	59.96	<.0001	2.1823	2.3298	44.2047
e9	0.8742	0.01509	9437	57.95	<.0001	0.8446	0.9037	245.536
e11	1.1032	0.03448	9437	32.00	<.0001	1.0356	1.1708	63.3596
e12	0.9052	0.01337	9437	67.70	<.0001	0.8790	0.9314	−780.097
kappa	2.2822	0.2592	9437	8.80	<.0001	1.7740	2.7903	459.255
phi11	0.6913	0.06106	9437	11.32	<.0001	0.5716	0.8110	429.505
psi11	2.089E-8	0.007657	9437	0.00	1.0000	−0.01501	0.01501	1582.68
b2mast	−6.5265	0.1347	9437	−48.46	<.0001	−6.7905	−6.2625	−83.4395
b3sq	1.1657	0.1204	9437	9.68	<.0001	0.9297	1.4017	−36.5872

Concluding Words

This chapter fills in some fundamentally important issues in using structural equation models. Three kinds of generalization of SEM were considered: applying models across groups and comparing results, using alternative estimators when there are ordinal or nonnormal measures in the model, and incorporating nonlinear and interactive structural equation models at the latent variable level. Again, flexibility is important in making the most of a technique—appropriately. Sticking to the basics may be common, but it can be misleading. Unstated assumptions accompany the application of these methods to single groups or assuming ordinal equals interval or by looking the other way about nonlinearities. Our last example proves we should go back and reconsider the role of mastery more broadly.

There are some fundamental messages discussed in this chapter about the use of SEM methods. They include the following: (a) Use these methods where they produce unique possibilities in analysis not covered in other methods—such as comparing both measurement and structural relations in the same model across groups; (b) pay attention to the appropriateness of the estimator used in the model; (c) factor analysis, a common technique used in a number of disciplines, will benefit from both a confirmatory approach and the use of estimators that are appropriate for less than interval variables; and (d) explicit representation of nonlinearities and interactions at the structural level is possible within the context of these methods, and there may be advantages to estimating these parameters this way—because the latent variables involved are formally free of measurement error problems.

Starting in the next chapter, we turn out attention to a very different set of methods, involving the effects of social contexts, nested social realities, on individual behavior, choices, attitudes, and functioning.

AN INTRODUCTION TO HIERARCHICAL LINEAR MODELS

In this chapter, we introduce the hierarchical linear model, an approach that is as much a distinct perspective on the social world as it is a set of statistical techniques. This dual function—statistical *and* conceptual—is important to understanding the point of using these models, usually known as "HLM" models for short reference. The HLM model applies to clustered data where individuals share membership in a larger social unit (neighborhoods, workplaces, schools, organizations, communities, nations), and there is a variety of social units sampled. Because subgroups of individuals live in the same neighborhood or go to the same school or work together in the same workplace, they are exposed to common rules, norms, policies—in general, social contexts. This model focuses on *separating* the influences at the social contextual level from the influences that result from individual-level differences.

Some researchers see the results of clustering a nuisance factor to be taken into account but otherwise ignored. The fundamental problem of clustering in units is that the observations within units are no longer "independent" because their error terms in regular regressions are in fact correlated, reflecting exposure to common influences at the contextual level. One approach is to see this problem as something to be adjusted for in the estimation procedure—thus removing the problematic effects of correlated errors across observations within units. But we advocate a fully explicit approach to the fact of social contexts. The essential contributions of the HLM model include the theoretical and conceptual perspectives it yields. At its core, this model encourages us to see that there are separate and nested layers of social reality. Once this conceptual point is accepted, we think differently about how layers of social reality combine and how they interact, and we have a method for clearly separating the role of context from individual differences within contexts.

Theoretically, these methods are particularly well-suited to address a classic problem for social science: how to represent and estimate the effects of larger social contexts on individuals, apart from the problematics in theoretical discourse about reductionism (because there is no reduction) or concerns about the ecological fallacy (because data is collected at multiple levels, not just one). From the perspective of theory in social science, the very idea of crossing levels of social reality is sometimes represented as an "unresolvable" issue, or it is seen as a non-issue. It *is* an issue, but HLM methods point to both a clarification and a resolution of this problem.

A fundamental hypothesis motivating the use of hierarchical linear models is that the social structures, policies, demographic composition, and social climates within which we are embedded *directly* affect individual behavior over and above psychological, biological, and social individual level factors.

There are many possible applications of modeling influences across levels of social reality. Here are a variety of examples of questions that could be asked in different types of studies:

1. Effects of schools on student performance
2. Effects of the workplace (organization) on worker productivity
3. Effects of neighborhood insecurity on individual well-being
4. Effects of family structure on child development
5. Effects of the political system on participation in political protests
6. Effects of ethnic culture on individual attitudes
7. Effects of community-level marriage markets on individual risk of divorce
8. Effects of community arts institutions on individual knowledge and tastes
9. Effects of hospitals on individual mortality risk and health status
10. Effects of government gender policy on women's income trajectories
11. Effects of penetration of wireless coverage on protest behavior
12. Effects of gun laws on individual risk of victimization
13. Effects of unemployment rates on risk of divorce in marriages
14. Effects of neighborhood crime rates on children's grades in school

10.1 INTRODUCTION TO THE MODEL

10.1.1 Distinguishing Individual from Contextual Level Effects

The distinction between individual and contextual effects is fundamental to the point of hierarchical linear models. These models incorporate this distinction and make possible a clearly separate role of both individual-level factors—as expressed in the usual regression model, for example—and ***context effects.*** The distinction between individual and contextual factors rests on one question: Does the variable vary across individuals *within* a given context, or is it the same for all individuals in that context? If the former, it is an individual-level factor; if the latter, it is a contextual factor.

Suppose we consider income as an example and a sample of people clustered by neighborhood. We sample a number of people per neighborhood, and a number of neighborhoods. In this situation, the individual's personal income is an individual factor, but the mean income of the neighborhood is a contextual factor. ***Both may be important,*** but it is important to understand that they are not the same thing. The average income of the neighborhood may have separate effects on individual-level behavior over and above the individual's income—that is why this is a *multilevel* model.

10.1.2 Partitioning of Variance and the Role of Contextual Differences

The question that arises in considering the effects across layers of social reality is how to decide when the contexts in which we are embedded are important in predicting our behavior, over and above the usual individual-level differences. How do we separate these two sources of influence?

A useful analogy is the concept of partitioning of variance in regression into portions "explained" and "unexplained" that together add up to the total variance. The basic idea of partitioning of total variance is to subdivide the total variance of Y into nonoverlapping portions from distinct sources.

Imagine a situation in which we are studying differences in the use of alcohol across neighborhoods, and we want to know whether *any* neighborhood factors make a difference in drinking at the individual level. We impose an important requirement for the relevance of social context in general as follows: *If there are no differences in the average level of* Y *across Level-2 units, then contextual factors cannot be relevant to* Y *at the individual level.*

Put in other terms, if the average level of drinking does not differ across neighborhoods, then there can be no effect of neighborhood-level differences on drinking. This is because the contextual factor can only impact the individual score by first shifting the mean level of Y for everyone in that neighborhood.

We can imagine the partitioning of the total variance in Y as having two components across levels: differences among people on Y ***within*** neighborhoods (the individual-level variance) and differences in the level of Y ***between*** neighborhoods (the context-level variance).

The individual's Y score in a neighborhood j can be written as having two components:

$$Y_{ij} = \overline{Y_j} + e_{ij}$$

This says that person i's Y score in group j is composed of the mean level of Y in that group plus the individual's deviation from the group mean (e_{ij}). If we take the variance of both sides of this equation, we get

$$V(Y_{ij}) = V(\overline{Y}_j) + V(e_{ij})$$

That is, the total variance in Y on the left side is made up of two components: the variance of the group means across neighborhoods plus the variance among individuals within neighborhoods.

If we can accept that what follows is an intuitive approximation and not exactly what is estimated in hierarchical models, we can write out versions of each variance as follows:

$$V(Y_{ij}) = \frac{\sum (Y_{ij} - \overline{Y})^2}{N-1} \rightarrow \text{The standard formula for the total variance in } Y \text{ in the sample.}$$

$$V(\bar{Y}_j) = \frac{\sum\limits_{j=1}^{J}(\bar{Y}_j - \bar{Y})^2}{J}$$

→ The variance of the J group level means around the grand mean.

$$V(e_{ij}) = \frac{\sum\limits_{j=1}^{J}\sum\limits_{i=1}^{k}(Y_{ij} - \bar{Y}_j)^2}{N - J - 1}$$

→ The total variance of the errors around group means added across groups, with n per group = k.

Putting this together, we can see how the total variance can be divided between individual-level variance and context-level variance:

$$\frac{\sum(Y_i - \bar{Y})^2}{N-1} = \frac{\sum\limits_{j=1}^{j}\sum\limits_{i=1}^{k}(Y_{ij} - \bar{Y}_j)^2}{N - J - 1} + \frac{\sum\limits_{j=1}^{J}(\bar{Y}_j - \bar{Y})^2}{J}$$

In other words: *Total variance = individual variance within groups + variance of means across groups.*

Looking at the preceding equation is helpful because we see that differences among individuals are added up across groups but is restricted to the variance among individuals *within* groups, and we also see that an explicit separate portion of the total variance in Y is made up of the differences among context-level means at the contextual level. The numerators of these formulas especially show the partitioning: The total deviation around the grand mean is divided into deviations of individuals from their group means and then deviations of these group means from the grand mean. We should note there are other approaches to partitioning the total variance into contextual and individual pieces. The approach used here is called *group-mean centering*.

A fundamental starting point of hierarchical linear models is whether there is significant context-level variance reflecting differences among group means on Y. When there is, you can see this as "permission" to discuss the possibility that there *are* contextual differences that may affect Y. Otherwise, if this variance is too small, we have information that in this case an individual-level model may be sufficient.

10.1.3 Developing a Model at Each Level

The idea that there is variance at both levels—individual and contextual—promotes the idea that you can have a separate model for each level, called the Level-1 model (at the individual level) and the Level-2 model (at the contextual level). Relying on an intuitive approach to this issue again, we have a model at the individual level that looks very familiar, except that there is a unique model for each group or, in our example, each neighborhood:

$$Y_{ij} = \beta_{0j} + \beta_{1j}X_{ij} + e_{ij}$$

denoting the fact that each person's Y score (i) occurs within a neighborhood j; β_{0j} is the intercept instead of the usual α (by HLM convention); there is a separate intercept for each neighborhood j; the effect of X on Y is estimated in the same way in J neighborhoods (resulting in J regressions for the effect of X on Y); and the error is random for person i in group j. We note here that β in the HLM notation is not the standardized regression coefficient but in fact the **unstandardized coefficient.** As noted earlier, we are subscribing to the common notation—and terms—used in each method so that our material connects more directly with topic-specific literatures.

At this point, it is fair to say that you should not expect notational or terminological consistency from method to method.

The process of estimating a two–level hierarchical model can be thought of as occurring in steps. At this first step, we have J groups and, in each group, a different number of i individuals. Imagine that this individual level model is first estimated in *each* Level-2 unit.

10.1.3.1 Estimating the Individual Level Regressions across Units

Using data from a recent Toronto neighborhood-based study (2011 Neighbourhood Effects on Health and Well-Being Study, O'Campo, et al., 2015), we document varying rates of daily alcohol use (in drinks per day) among 809 married women across 87 neighborhoods (census tracts). Our interest is in the effects of immigrant status at the individual level. In this subsample, we would then estimate 87 regressions for the effect of immigrant status on alcohol use, one in each neighborhood.

Notice that these within-group regressions will vary across neighborhoods. In Figure 10.1, we show examples of the estimated slopes in 12 neighborhoods.

What should be obvious from looking at these within-neighborhood regressions is that they are not the same—there is variability in the impact of immigrant status on alcohol use across neighborhoods. Also note that most of the slopes are negative—8 out of 12—while others are either flat or slightly positive. **Something** may be determining the variation in these slopes at the neighborhood level.

What may also be obvious from looking at these plots is not only that the effect of immigrant status varies by neighborhood but the average level of drinking in neighborhoods also varies. In fact, the mean number of drinks varies from a low of .66 to a high of 2.99 across neighborhoods. Thus, there are two issues that can be assessed here in understanding the role of the neighborhood: how this social context directly affects drinking propensity, potentially independent of and bypassing individual predictors, and how social context actually changes the effect of individual risk factors in drinking.

10.1.3.2 Building a Level-2 Model for the Role of Neighborhood

The results from the 87 sampled neighborhoods in Toronto can be seen as a **sample** of estimates. There are 87 estimates of the neighborhood mean alcohol use and 87 estimates of the effect of immigrant status. And because these estimates do vary across neighborhoods, we could develop a model to try to understand **how** these estimates vary. Put another way, we could specify the determinants of higher or lower average levels of drinking across neighborhoods, as well as factors that cause the slope for immigrant status to increase or decrease. In the latter case, we are seeing the possibility of a *cross-level* interaction between some neighborhood-level factor and immigrant status.

If we write out the model at the neighborhood level, it could initially look like this:

$$\beta_{0j} = \gamma_{00} + u_{0j}$$

$$\beta_{1j} = \gamma_{10} + u_{1j}$$

where the first model is a model for variation in the intercept β_{0j}—with an overall grand mean γ_{00} and an error for each neighborhood u_{0j}, expressing the variability in the mean level of Y

FIGURE 10.1 ● INDIVIDUAL REGRESSIONS OF ALCOHOL USE IN 12 NEIGHBORHOODS

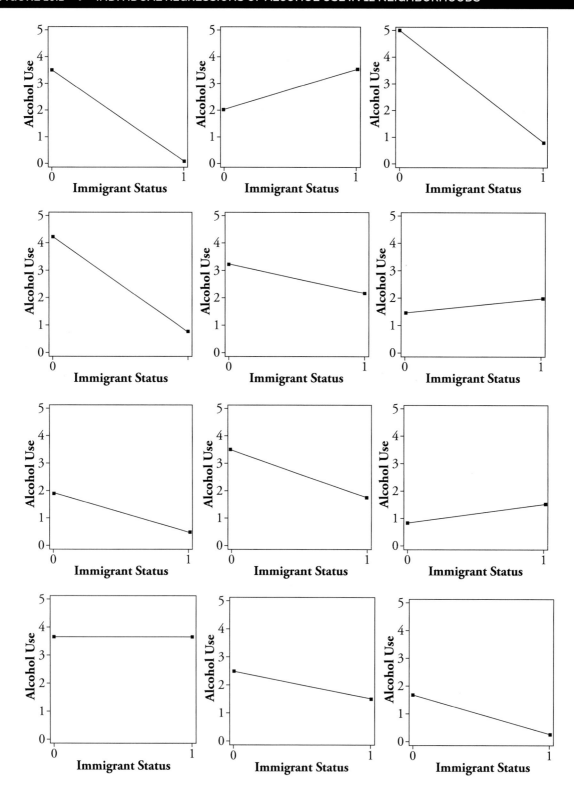

across neighborhoods and the second model is a model for variation in the slope of immigrant status β_{1j}—including an average impact denoted by γ_{10} and variation in the slope across neighborhoods, denoted by u_{1j}. In both models there is an average, plus unique variation in each neighborhood.

The idea in the hierarchical linear model is to propose specific "fixed effects"—that is, specific neighborhood variables, which account for the variation in the mean level of alcohol use across neighborhoods (the first model) and/or interact with immigrant status to determine differences in its impact across social contexts. For example, given that we have an N of 87 at Level 2, we could specify the percentage of immigrants in the neighborhood as a Level-2 factor in these models. Designating this fixed variable generally as W, then the models would look like this:

$$\beta_{0j} = \gamma_{00} + \gamma_{01}W_j + u_{0j}$$

$$\beta_{1j} = \gamma_{10} + \gamma_{11}W_j + u_{1j}$$

where γ are regression coefficients, W_j is a group-level variable, and u are random errors in these equations, standing for unspecified neighborhood factors that determine variation in the β coefficients across groups. The unusual feature here is that the dependent variables in these equations *are the intercepts and slopes from the regressions within-groups at the first level.*

What we hope to achieve is the explanation of differences across neighborhoods using W_j that either help account for differences in alcohol use across individuals or differences in the effects of immigrant status across social contexts or both. We return to this example in a later section, but first we turn to a more formal statement of the two-level HLM model.

10.2 A FORMAL STATEMENT OF A TWO-LEVEL HLM MODEL

We introduce the formal HLM model borrowing directly from a classic example of Raudenbush and Bryk (2002) because the example is so clear. In this example, Raudenbush and Bryk study the relationship between students' SES and their math performance across a number of schools.

Overall, if we were *ignoring* the hierarchical data structure, we would have

$$Y_i = \beta_0 + \beta_1 X_i + e_i$$

where Y = math performance and X = student SES. It will often be helpful in using these models to "center" the X variable in some way. Basically, this will help disentangle Level-1 and Level-2 effects in the model and gives a clear interpretation of intercepts as well. Using this approach, we have

$$Y_i = \beta_0 + \beta_1(X_i - \bar{X}) + e_i$$

Note this changes the definition of β_0: It is now the value of Y at $\bar{X}$. For some types of models, this will have advantages. We also point out, however, that there are multiple approaches to centering, an issue we discuss later.

The results in Figure 10.2 show the effects of SES on achievement in two types of schools, one Catholic, the other public.

It appears that Catholic schools are both more "effective" and "equitable" than public schools: effective because $\beta_{01} > \beta_{02}$, meaning that the mean level of math achievement is higher in Catholic schools, and equitable because $\beta_{11} < \beta_{12}$ meaning that the effect of SES is weaker in Catholic schools.

10.2.1 The Level-1 Model

In a population of schools, the model for the within-school effects (Level-1) is

$$Y_{ij} = \beta_{0j} + \beta_{1j}(X_{ij} - \bar{X}._{j}) + e_{ij}$$

where $\bar{X}._{j}$ is the mean of X within schools, and so values of X are centered on school-specific means. This is called *group-mean centering*. Interpretively, this means that β_{0j} is the *unadjusted* mean of Y in group j.

We introduce the following concepts:

- $E(\beta_{0j}) = \gamma_{0}$ The average school mean math achievement for the population of schools

- $E(\beta_{1j}) = \gamma_{1}$ The average slope for the effect of SES on achievement across schools (in the case of $X_{ij} - \bar{X}._{j}$)

- $Var(\beta_{0j}) = \tau_{00}$ Population variance among school means

- $Var(\beta_{1j}) = \tau_{11}$ Population variance among school slopes

- $Cov(\beta_{0j}, \beta_{1j}) = \tau_{01}$ Population covariance between slopes and intercepts

This last quantity is also important as a measure of collinearity in the model, and it *is* affected by how X is scaled. Reducing this covariance is one reason we center X variables at Level 1.

FIGURE 10.2 ● SES AND MATH ACHIEVEMENT IN SCHOOLS (ADAPTED FROM RAUDENBUSH & BRYK, 2002)

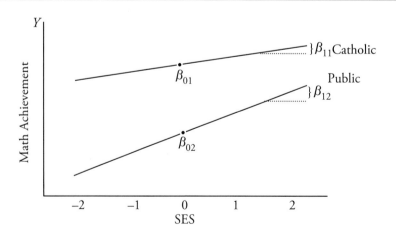

10.2.2 The Level-2 Model

Assume that both β_{0j} and β_{1j} vary in a way that depends on characteristics of the school, (e.g., level of funding, policies, organizational features, streaming, etc.). In this example, we assign $W_j = 1$ if a Catholic school, and 0 if a public school.

The Level-2 model here would be

$$\beta_{0j} = \gamma_{00} + \gamma_{01}W_j + u_{0j}$$

$$\beta_{1j} = \gamma_{10} + \gamma_{11}W_j + u_{1j}$$

Definitions of parameters in this case are:

γ_{00} = mean math achievement for public schools

γ_{01} = mean math achievement difference between public and Catholic schools

γ_{10} = average SES—achievement slope within public schools

γ_{11} = difference in average SES—achievement slopes between Catholic and public schools

u_{0j} = the unique effect of school j on mean achievement net of W_j (error)

u_{1j} = the unique effect of school j on the SES—achievement slope, net of W_j (error)

The error in predicting the β coefficients at the second level is extremely important: u_{0j} and u_{1j} represent random error at the second level in determining variation of both β_{0j} and β_{1j}. These errors basically allow for the fact that all of the differences among schools are not fully specified by the W_j variable or set of variables. In other words, they stand for unknown sources of variance in Y at Level 1 due to differences among schools at Level 2 and thus signify whether there are random contextual effects on Y that are not yet specified.

10.2.3 The Full "Mixed" Model

Substitute the Level-2 equations above for β_{0j} and β_{1j} into the original Level-1 equation for Y (repeated here):

$$Y_{ij} = \beta_{0j} + \beta_{1j}(X_{ij} - \bar{X}._j) + e_{ij}$$

to get

$$Y_{ij} = (\gamma_{00} + \gamma_{01}W_j + u_{0j}) + (\gamma_{10} + \gamma_{11}W_j + u_{1j})(X_{ij} - \bar{X}._j) + e_{ij}$$

To work this equation out, collect terms so that you have main effects from Level 2 and Level 1 first, then any interaction between them, followed by the different error components. This is done in two steps to produce the full combined model:

$$Y_{ij} = \gamma_{00} + \gamma_{01}W_j + u_{0j} + \gamma_{10}(X_{ij} - \bar{X}._j) + \gamma_{11}W_j(X_{ij} - \bar{X}._j) + u_{1j}(X_{ij} - \bar{X}._j) + e_{ij}$$

$$Y_{ij} = \gamma_{00} + \gamma_{01}W_j + \gamma_{10}(X_{ij} - \bar{X}._j) + \gamma_{11}(W_j \cdot (X_{ij} - \bar{X}._j)) + u_{0j} + u_{1j}(X_{ij} - \bar{X}._j) + e_{ij}$$

This is the basic equation to understand in hierarchical models. Note the following:

- Effects expressed as γ are the regression coefficients

- The structure of the model is essentially like a two-way interaction model with X entered as a centered variable

- Allowance is made both for the *main effects* of the context—where X is centered at Level 1 — and its effect on the impact of X at the individual level. This model thus includes a number of possibilities: (a) The effect of X may be spurious, due to W; (b) W can have direct effects that bypass X; (c) The effect of W may affect Y by shifting the level of X at Level 1 first (mediation); and (d) the impact of X can vary by context (W).

- Note the complexity of the error term in this model—there are three different components, reflecting different sources of variance in Y. This is a form of "variance components" model because the error comes from multiple sources.

10.2.4 The Estimation Issue

There is a problem due to the structure of the errors in this model. OLS estimation assumes that random errors in the model are independent across observations, are normally distributed, and have constant variances. But OLS assumes this by specifying e_{ij} as the only error component. There are actually *three* components to the error here.

The problems caused by the structure of the errors in this model include:

1. The errors *are* dependent within each school because the u_{0j} components are the same in each school and thus, overall, errors are correlated across observations.

2. The $u_{1j} \cdot (X_{ij} - \bar{X}._j)$ term suggests the direct possibility that X is correlated with part of the error term at the 2nd level.

3. Errors do not have a constant variance across levels of X or W because u_{0j} and u_{1j} vary across schools and because the error depends also on $(X_{ij} - \bar{X}._j)$, which varies across students.

The general conclusion is that standard OLS regression analysis is inappropriate. This is basically caused by the error structure at Level 2. If the Level-2 model is fixed rather than including random error at Level-2, OLS *is* appropriate.

The details of estimating these models is beyond this book, but we should discuss the basic logic. The standard default choice is called ***restricted maximum likelihood***. Full maximum likelihood has a problem here: The estimates of error variances and covariances in the model depend on the point estimates of the fixed effects, which themselves are estimated. Thus, ***restricted*** maximum likelihood is used because it adjusts for the uncertainty (degrees of freedom) used in estimating fixed effects.

Parameters are not estimated collectively but in a procedure that uses estimates at each level iteratively to help inform estimation of the variances and the fixed effects, in turn. Basically, the procedure uses preliminary estimates of the variance components—the random effects—to help inform estimation of the fixed effects, and then those estimates are used to inform estimation of the variances, until criteria for best estimates are reached.

Estimates of fixed effects in the model are "precision-weighted." This means that smaller samples in Level-2 units are downweighted due to a larger variance of estimation, and larger samples are upweighted. This results in a "weighted least squares" estimator, a modification of the usual OLS estimator.

Two sources of information are used to derive an "optimal shrinkage estimator" for the fixed effects at Level 1. Suppose you have two estimates of each β_{qj} at Level 1, with q effects at Level 1:

- The OLS estimate of β_{qj} within groups
- The "best" estimate of β_{qj} from the Level-2 model

Then the optimal shrinkage estimator is

$$\beta_{qj}^{*} = \lambda_j \hat{\beta}_j + (1 - \lambda_j)\hat{\hat{\beta}}_j$$

where $\hat{\beta}_j$ is the OLS estimator from level-1; $\hat{\hat{\beta}}_j$ is the "best" estimate from the group data; and λ_j is the estimate of the precision for group j. Note again that this approach de-emphasizes data in low precision groups relative to high precision groups and, at the same time, uses the best estimate from the Level-2 model relatively more in low precision groups.

10.3 SUB-MODELS OF THE FULL HLM MODEL

It is helpful to see that the full HLM model contains a sequence of sub-models that can be considered in a typical analysis. ***It is important to consider the results of simpler models before building more complex models.*** The purpose is to test basic hypotheses in simpler models in order to inform the specification of more complex models.

To show how models are interrelated, we continue with the example from Raudenbush and Bryk (2002) focusing on school effects on student math achievement. In this example, we assess the effects of SECTOR (type of school where 1 = Catholic and 0 = *P*ublic) and MEANSES of the school on student math achievement scores, in 160 schools with 7,185 students.

We start with the simplest model and move to the most elaborate.

10.3.1 One-Way ANOVA with Random Effects

A One-Way Analysis of Variance (ANOVA) tests whether there are overall group differences in Y, but in this case, these group differences are random (not specified) rather than fixed.

The model is

$$Y_{ij} = \beta_{0j} + e_{ij} \qquad \text{(Level 1)}$$

$$\beta_{0j} = \gamma_{00} + u_{0j} \qquad \text{(Level 2)}$$

where

β_{0j} is the mean for the jth group,

e_{ij} is the deviation on Y for person i in group j,

γ_{00} is the grand mean,

u_{0j} is the random effect of unit j (mean = 0, var = τ_{00}).

The combined model is

$$Y_{ij} = \gamma_{00} + u_{0j} + e_{ij}$$

This is a one-way ANOVA with an intercept equal to the grand mean, a group effect in u_{0j} and a person effect e_{ij}. This is called a *random effects* model because the group effects are construed as random only and thus are not measured. These "random effects" are in fact variances.

The purposes of this model are

- To provide a point estimate of the grand mean and a confidence interval
- To provide information about the total variability in the outcome at each of the two levels

Of interest here especially is the significance of the variance of u_{0j}. If this variance is *not* different from zero, then there is little variability in Y means between Level-2 units and thus little evidence of *any* Level-2 differences. If this is the case, the entire analytical problem can be reduced to an OLS model with fixed effects but only including individual-level factors.

10.3.1.1 Results: School Effects on Student Math Achievement

Results of this model show an overall average school mean (γ_{00}) of 12.64 on math achievement, with

$$Var(e_{ij}) = 39.15$$

$$\text{and } Var(u_{0j}) = 8.62$$

where $Var(u_{0j})$ is the variance among school mean levels of math achievement.

This partitioning of the variance shows that most of the variation in the outcome is at the student level, but some is still between schools. You can estimate the ***intra-class correlation***, which is the percentage of variance in math achievement between schools, as follows:

$$\hat{\rho} = \left. Var(u_{0j}) \middle/ (Var(e_{ij}) + Var(u_{0j})) \right. = \left. 8.62 \middle/ (8.62 + 39.15) \right. = .18$$

This means about 18% of the variance in math achievement is between schools.

We can test the significance of the variance across schools using a χ^2 with J - 1 *df*. Here $\chi^2 = 1,660$ with 159 *df* ($N = 160$), indicating significant variation among schools. This means we can and should proceed to model Level-2 effects here. If this test was not significant, *there would be no justification for discussion of contextual effects.*

10.3.2 Means-as-Outcomes Regression (the "Cross-Over Effect")

If we add a Level-2 variable to the previous model, then we are predicting differences in group means from a group characteristic at Level 2. Aneshensel and Sucoff (1996) call this a "cross-over" effect. It is an effect on individual variation but due to individual embeddedness in a social unit. Our intention in this model is to try to explain the variance across schools, using a measured characteristic of schools that maps to the unmeasured differences and thus reduces the remaining variance across schools to nonsignificance.

The model in this case is

$$Y_{ij} = \beta_{0j} + e_{ij}$$

$$\beta_{0j} = \gamma_{00} + \gamma_{01}W_j + u_{0j}$$

yielding the combined model

$$Y_{ij} = \gamma_{00} + \gamma_{01}W_j + u_{0j} + e_{ij}$$

The effect of W_j here is the ***cross-over effect***. It stands for the direct main effect of context on individual behavior.

Now u_{0j} is a residual variance at the second level after taking into account the effect of W_j. Thus, one can add W_j to the model to explain the random variance represented by u_{0j}. If the error becomes insignificant (eventually), then we have specified the Level-2 random variance in terms of fixed variables—a good thing. The point here would be to specify all of the random variance in terms of fixed variables at Level 2.

10.3.2.1 Results for the Cross-Over Effects Model

Returning to the empirical example, we consider the effect of the *MEANSES* of the school (where *MEANSES* is the average of the SES scores of students at the school). We add to the basic one-way ANOVA a specific model for the β_{0j}:

$$\beta_{0j} = \gamma_{00} + \gamma_{01}(MEANSES)_j + u_{0j}$$

So the combined model in this case is

$$Y_{ij} = \gamma_{00} + \gamma_{01}(MEANSES)_j + u_{0j} + e_{ij}$$

The results show $\gamma_{01} = 5.86$ with the standard error $= .36$, which is very significant. In this model, the error variance between schools is now lower $= 2.64$.

We can calculate the variance explained *between schools* using a comparison with the one-way ANOVA:

$$\frac{\tau_{00_{(1)}} - \tau_{00_{(2)}}}{\tau_{00_{(1)}}} = \frac{8.62 - 2.64}{8.62} = .69$$

Thus, *MEANSES* explains a substantial portion (69%) of the variance between schools.

Further, the net error variance between schools is now

$$= \frac{2.64}{2.64 + 39.16} = .06$$

where

$$Var(e_{ij}) = 39.16$$

This is small but still significant, with $\chi^2 = 633.5$ and 158 *df*.

10.3.3 Random Coefficients Model

Both of the previous models are appropriately called "random intercept" models: They focus on differences in the mean intercepts in Y across schools. If we conceive of *both* β_{0j} and β_{1j} as randomly varying over groups, in a model with X at Level 1, we have the ***random-coefficients*** model.

The model is

$$Y_{ij} = \beta_{0j} + \beta_{1j}(X_{ij} - \overline{X}._j) + e_{ij}$$

$$\beta_{0j} = \gamma_{00} + u_{0j}$$

$$\beta_{1j} = \gamma_{10} + u_{1j}$$

and the combined model is

$$Y_{ij} = \gamma_{00} + \gamma_{10}(X_{ij} - \overline{X}._j) + u_{0j} + u_{1j}(X_{ij} - \overline{X}._j) + e_{ij}$$

Here, Y_{ij} is a function of the grand mean, the average slope (i.e., effect) for X across groups, plus random error having three components. The variance of the u_{1j} component tests for differences in the effects of X across level-1 units. This is the variance of the individual level slopes in Level-1 units around the average slope. So this model tests for the presence of "any" Level-2 influence on the effect of X on Y at Level 1, thus signaling the possibility of a cross-level interaction. When this variance is significant, we have reason to assess interactions between specific Level-2 contextual W and Level-1 X variables. More broadly, these interactions are interpretable as the influence of context on changing the meaning and consequences of individual-level factors.

10.3.3.1 Results for the Random Coefficients Model

Table 10.1 shows the fixed effects and random effects part of the model.

This suggests that student SES is in fact related to math achievement differences. In results at the 2nd level, the random variance of u_{1j} is .65 and significant at the .003 level ($\chi^2 = 213$ with 159 *df*). This suggests that some Level-2 factor may be determining differences in the effect at Level 1, in other words, interacts with the Level-1 X.

We can calculate variance explained ***at Level 1*** by comparing σ^2 to the one-way ANOVA. Using σ^2 to represent $V(e_{ij})$:

$$R^2 = \frac{\sigma^2_{(\text{ANOVA})} - \sigma^2_{(\text{random coefficients})}}{\sigma^2_{(\text{ANOVA})}} = \text{in this case, } .062$$

This is the same as the usual R^2 calculated in an OLS regression.

TABLE 10.1 ⬤ FIXED EFFECTS IN THE RANDOM COEFFICIENTS MODEL		
	Coefficient	***t***
γ_{00} (mean achievement)	12.64	—
γ_{10} (SES)	2.19	17.26

10.3.4 The "Full" Model: Intercepts and Slopes as Outcomes

The next logical step is to model the β_j coefficients at Level 2. When we do this, we have the "full" multilevel model:

$$Y_{ij} = \beta_{0j} + \beta_{1j}(X_{ij} - \bar{X}_{\cdot j}) + e_{ij} \tag{1}$$

$$\beta_{0j} = \gamma_{00} + \gamma_{01}W_j + u_{0j} \tag{2}$$

$$\beta_{1j} = \gamma_{10} + \gamma_{11}W_j + u_{1j} \tag{3}$$

As before, by substituting Equations 2 and 3 into Equation 1, we get the combined Level-1 and Level-2 full model:

$$Y_{ij} = (\gamma_{00} + \gamma_{01}W_j + u_{0j}) + (\gamma_{10} + \gamma_{11}W_j + u_{1j})(X_{ij} - \bar{X}_{\cdot j}) + e_{ij}$$

$$= \gamma_{00} + \gamma_{01}W_j + \gamma_{10}(X_{ij} - \bar{X}_{\cdot j}) + \gamma_{11}(W_j(X_{ij} - \bar{X}_{\cdot j})) + u_{0j} + u_{1j}(X_{ij} - \bar{X}_{\cdot j}) + e_{ij}$$

Please note the varying approximations to the full model represented by simpler models.

Typically, modeling β_{1j} may be very important since it expresses the hypothesis that a Level-1 effect of X depends on (changes due to) a Level-2 factor. When modeling β_{1j} we want to test the variance of u_{1j} as we add variables at Level 2. If this error approaches zero, we can claim we have fully specified the impact of social context on the varying effect of X across schools. In other words, you are trying to express the random differences across schools using a measured ("fixed") variable or variables that account for these random differences. This happens when the fixed variable W varies in a way that overlaps with the differences in slopes.

10.3.4.1 Results for the Full Model

The result from the random coefficients model suggests a model for β_{1j} is called for. Also we know that MEANSES predicts β_{0j}. The full model adds two variables at Level 2: school MEANSES and SECTOR (Catholic vs. Protestant), with SES as X at Level 1:

$$Y_{ij} = \beta_{0j} + \beta_{1j}(SES)_{ij} + e_{ij}$$

$$\beta_{0j} = \gamma_{00} + \gamma_{01}(MEANSES)_j + \gamma_{02}(SECTOR)_j + u_{0j}$$

$$\beta_{1j} = \gamma_{10} + \gamma_{11}(MEANSES)_j + \gamma_{12}(SECTOR)_j + u_{1j}$$

In the combined model, the effects are

$$Y_{ij} = \gamma_{00} + \gamma_{01}(MEANSES)_j + \gamma_{02}(SECTOR)_j + \gamma_{10}(SES)_{ij} + \gamma_{11}(MEANSES)_j(SES)_{ij} +$$

$$\gamma_{12}(SECTOR)_j(SES)_{ij} + u_{0j} + u_{1j}(SES)_{ij} + e_{ij}$$

In this model, we see two 2-way interactions across levels, expressing the idea that the effect of the student's SES may depend on the average SES of the school as well as whether the school is Catholic versus public. Results are shown in Table 10.2.

TABLE 10.2 ● FIXED EFFECTS IN THE FULL TWO-LEVEL MODEL		
Results	**Coefficients**	**_T_-value**
School Means		
Intercept (γ_{00})	12.10	—
Mean SES (γ_{01})	5.33	14.45
Catholic sector (γ_{02})	1.23	4.00
SES—Achievement Slopes		
Intercept (γ_{10})	2.94	18.36
Mean SES (γ_{11})	1.03	3.35
Catholic sector (γ_{12})	−1.64	−6.64

This table presents results in a classic HLM —but unique—format: predictors of mean differences (the model for β_{0j}) separately from predictors of differences in slopes for X (the model for β_{1j}). In our examples, we will use a more traditional format, as expressed by the combined Level-1 / Level-2 model.

The results for the combined model in equation format are

$$Y_{ij} = 12.10 + 5.33(MEANSES)_j + 1.23(SECTOR)_j + 2.94(SES)_{ij} + 1.03(MEANSES)_j(SES)_{ij}$$

$$-1.64(\text{SECTOR})_j(SES)_{ij} + u_{0j} + u_{1j}(SES_{ij}) + e_{ij}$$

The results indicate a direct cross-over effect of school SES (γ_{01}) on student's math performance, as well as an effect of school sector (γ_{02}). In addition, there is a strong effect of student SES at the individual level (γ_{10}) and two interactions with student SES, indicating that the effect of student SES increases with school SES (γ_{11}), and the effect of student SES is weaker in Catholic schools (γ_{12}).

These two interactions account for *all* of the variance in the slopes, according to results. That is, the variance of u_{1j} is .21, which is not significantly different from 0.

This means that the random variation in the effect of student SES has been specified by the two interactions and that no *further* unspecified factors at Level 2 need to be considered. This kind of result is a clearly valuable feature of HLM models with random effects.

10.3.5 Testing a Series of Models

By testing a series of models, we learn what is necessary in fitting a better-specified model. Usually, you should start with a one-way ANOVA model. If there is no random variance in this model, you do not have an HLM issue—return to standard regression approaches, armed with this evidence. If there is random variance, you can test cross-over effects that may specify the sources of overall Level-2 variance. Ideally, one could specify all of the random variance through the inclusion of the "right" Level-2 factors.

The next step is to consider the random coefficients model. This tests for the presence of randomly varying effects of Level-1 Xs. In other words, we learn whether the effect of X at Level 1 may depend on *some* Level-2 factor yet to be specified. If the random part of the effect of X is not significant, this suggests general effects of X that do ***not*** depend on context.

At this point, you have a good idea of what random effects need to be included and which Level-2 factors may be essential. The "full" model includes both, as necessary, and given random slopes at Level 2, tests for specific cross-level interactions between Level-2 and Level-1 factors. Again, one can assess how much of the random effects of X are accounted for by these interactions.

10.3.5.1 Terminology

One of the confusing aspects of hierarchical models is the distinction between "fixed effects" and "random effects." This can be clarified as follows: Fixed effects refer to the estimated coefficients of variables in the model and the intercept. Random effects refer to ***variances*** for unmeasured components of the model, like the variance of Y means across groups.

10.4 THE THREE-LEVEL HIERARCHICAL LINEAR MODEL

Examples to this point have considered two-level models. Next, we turn to the extension of the basic two-level model to three levels. The three-level model introduces some notational and linguistic complexities. You have to be aware what each equation is for and the fact that there is now a cascade of effects across levels. In the end, however, despite the apparent complexity, interpretation follows the general rules that are involved in interpreting a three-way interaction.

Conceptually, the three-level model is a straightforward extension of the two-level model. Generally, you are interested in three-level models if your data have two levels of nesting of individual observations—that is, individuals are grouped in increasingly inclusive social units. Here are some examples:

- Students within classrooms within schools
- Children within families within neighborhoods
- Workers within workplaces within multinational corporations
- Patients within hospitals within health care systems.

In the classic application of these kinds of data structures, you are interested in separating Level-2 from Level-3 effects on individuals. For example, in the study of neighborhood effects, the literature suggests increasingly that some neighborhood effects are in fact proxies for unestimated family-level effects that vary across neighborhood and thus need to be taken into account. Or school effects could be masking the average difference in the quality of classroom (teacher) effects within classrooms and also hide the variation within schools due to classroom effects.

Sometimes both contextual levels will have impacts. For example, differences in quality of care given to patients may depend not only on hospital characteristics but also more general regional health care policies about the sharing of resources. Job satisfaction may depend on whether you work in the "marketing," "manufacturing," or "research" departments of a company, as well as on company-wide policies.

10.4.1 The Structure of the Model

We use the example of children within families within neighborhoods. To give some concreteness to the model, we assume that Y is the delinquency score of sampled children in each family.

10.4.1.1 Level-1 Model

The individual level model is now

$$Y_{ijk} = \beta_{0jk} + \beta_{1jk}X_{ijk} + e_{ijk}$$

where

Y_{ijk} is the delinquency of kid i in family j in neighborhood k.

β_{0jk} is the intercept for family j in neighborhood k (a family mean).

β_{1jk} is the effect of X (e.g., gender) in family j in neighborhood k.

e_{ijk} is the deviation of kid i's score from the predicted score in family j in neighborhood k.

10.4.1.2 Level-2 Model

The family level model is

$$\beta_{0jk} = \gamma_{00k} + \gamma_{01k}W_{jk} + u_{0jk}$$

$$\beta_{1jk} = \gamma_{10k} + \gamma_{11k}W_{jk} + u_{1jk}$$

where

γ_{00k} is the mean delinquency of families within neighborhood k.

γ_{01k} is the effect of W_{jk} (e.g., family structure) on family level differences in neighborhood k.

u_{0jk} is the random effect of family j in neighborhood k on delinquency.

γ_{10k} is the average effect of X within families in neighborhood k.

γ_{11k} is the effect of W_{jk} at the family level in neighborhood k on the effect of X at Level 1 (e.g., how family structure alters the impact of child gender).

u_{1jk} is the random effect of family j in neighborhood k on the impact of X on delinquency (i.e., the random effect of families on the impact of X in neighborhood k).

10.4.1.3 Level-3 Model

The neighborhood level model is

$$\gamma_{00k} = \delta_{000} + \delta_{001}Z_k + v_{00k}$$ (model for the variation in the average delinquency in families across neighborhoods)

$$\gamma_{01k} = \delta_{010} + \delta_{011}Z_k + v_{01k}$$ (model for the cross-over effects on families)

$$\gamma_{10k} = \delta_{100} + \delta_{101}Z_k + v_{10k}$$ (model for the average effects of X across neighborhoods)

$$\gamma_{11k} = \delta_{110} + \delta_{111}Z_k + v_{11k}$$ (model for neighborhood differences in the cross-level effect of families on the impact of X)

where, in general terms

δ_{000}, δ_{010}, δ_{100}, and δ_{110} are intercepts in the neighborhood-level model for the γ at the family-level.

δ_{001}, δ_{011}, δ_{101}, and δ_{111} reflect the effects of Z as a neighborhood characteristic on the model for family-level differences.

v_{00k}, v_{01k}, v_{10k}, and v_{11k} are random effects reflecting the deviation of neighborhood k from predicted family-level differences.

10.4.1.4 The Combined Model

If we now substitute for the γ at Level 2 using the Level-3 model, we end up with

$$\beta_{0jk} = (\delta_{000} + \delta_{001}Z_k + v_{00k}) + (\delta_{010} + \delta_{011}Z_k + v_{01k})W_{jk} + u_{0jk}$$

$$= \delta_{000} + \delta_{001}Z_k + \delta_{010}W_{jk} + \delta_{011}Z_kW_{jk} + v_{00k} + v_{01k}W_{jk} + u_{0jk}$$

$$\beta_{1jk} = (\delta_{100} + \delta_{101}Z_k + v_{10k}) + (\delta_{110} + \delta_{111}Z_k + v_{11k})W_{jk} + u_{1jk}$$

$$= \delta_{100} + \delta_{101}Z_k + \delta_{110}W_{jk} + \delta_{111}Z_kW_{jk} + v_{10k} + v_{11k}W_{jk} + u_{1jk}$$

Now we can substitute for the β in the Level-1 model to get the fully combined model across three levels:

$$Y_{ijk} = (\delta_{000} + \delta_{001}Z_k + \delta_{010}W_{jk} + \delta_{011}Z_kW_{jk} + v_{00k} + v_{01k}W_{jk} + u_{0jk})$$
$$+ (\delta_{100} + \delta_{101}Z_k + \delta_{110}W_{jk} + \delta_{111}Z_kW_{jk} + v_{10k} + v_{11k}W_{jk} + u_{1jk})X_{ijk} + e_{ijk}$$

$$Y_{ijk} = \delta_{000} + \delta_{001}Z_k + \delta_{010}W_{jk} + \delta_{011}Z_kW_{jk} + v_{00k} + v_{01k}W_{jk} + u_{0jk}$$
$$+ \delta_{100}X_{ijk} + \delta_{101}Z_kX_{ijk} + \delta_{110}W_{jk}X_{ijk} + \delta_{111}Z_kW_{jk}X_{ijk} + v_{10k}X_{ijk} + v_{11k}W_{jk}X_{ijk} + u_{1jk}X_{ijk} + e_{ijk}$$

Rearranging terms,

$$Y_{ijk} = \delta_{000} + \delta_{001}Z_k + \delta_{010}W_{jk} + \delta_{100}X_{ijk} + \delta_{011}Z_kW_{jk} + \delta_{101}Z_kX_{ijk} + \delta_{110}W_{jk}X_{ijk} + \delta_{111}Z_kW_{jk}X_{ijk}$$
$$+ v_{00k} + v_{01k}W_{jk} + v_{10k}X_{ijk} + v_{11k}W_{jk}X_{ijk} + u_{0jk} + u_{1jk}X_{ijk} + e_{ijk}$$

10.4.1.5 Interpretive Possibilities

Note that the full model contains a three-way interaction of Z at Level 3, W at Level 2, and X at Level 1. This stands for the possibility that the effect of X depends simultaneously on two layers of social context—family and neighborhood—but in a way that changes depending on categories of W and Z. In words, something about neighborhood (e.g., percentage single-parent families) changes the degree to which W changes the impact of X. If this three-way interaction fails, there are other possibilities in the model for two-way interactions of X with each layer of context separately. Also, the two layers of context may themselves interact in predicting Y.

There are also a number of sources of error in the three-level model. Each one stands for a difference source of random effect. For example, the variance of v_{00k} reflects neighborhood variance in delinquency, while the variance of u_{0jk} reflects family-level variance in delinquency. It is important to assess these random effects carefully at the beginning of an analysis because it may suggest important simplifications of the model.

It will be important in these models to look for opportunities to simplify the specification as the analysis progresses: Considering too many possibilities for random effects often causes major problems in estimation. Some of these simplifications may be a priori; some may follow from early results.

An example of a three-level model will be presented in a later section.

10.5 IMPLICATIONS OF CENTERING LEVEL-1 VARIABLES

There is widespread debate about best practices for centering variables at Level 1. Each of the two major approaches—grand-mean centering and group-mean centering—leads to a different interpretation of the Level-2 effects. Advice on the differences in results often resorts to an "it depends on the question" retreat to generalities. While this advice is fair, it is not helpful because it is not clear what it means in practice.

In this section, we briefly discuss the differences in centering methods and then describe the general differences in the interpretation of results caused by centering.

Discussions of this issue cite three ways of coding X at Level 1:

1. ***Raw scores (Natural Metric)***

   When X has no real zero value, problems result from using raw X scores. For example, if X is an achievement test that varies from 200 to 800, the intercept β_{0j} is the expected outcome for someone with a score of zero, which is absurd. Further, β_{0j} and β_{1j} will tend to be more collinear (correlated) in this instance.

   When X has a real zero value, interpretation is clearer, but collinearity problems may still be substantial.

2. **Grand mean centering**

   Another way to represent X is to use grand mean centering—that is, $(X_{ij} - \bar{X})$, where $\bar{X}$ is the grand mean. This results in β_{0j} as the *adjusted* mean in group j—that is, taking into account the effect of X. In other words, $\beta_{0j} = \mu_j - \beta_{1j}(\bar{X}_{\cdot j} - \bar{X})$.

3. **Group mean centering**

   Here $X = (X_{ij} - \bar{X}_{\cdot j})$, meaning that X is measured as a deviation score from the *mean of that group*. This is a common approach used in HLM models. Both of the last two centering approaches reduce the correlation between β_{0j} and β_{1j}.

   Interpretively, $\beta_{0j} = \mu_j$, the *unadjusted* mean in group j. This has an important effect on interpretation, since variation in β_{0j} maps to the group level variance directly.

10.5.0.1 Relationship Between Group Mean Centering and Raw Scores

Group-mean centered models have a known relationship to the raw score approach, but it should be noted that the underlying models are not the same. Suppose we designate the group-mean centered value of X as X_{dj}, for deviations from the *group* mean. Then

$$X_{dj} = X_{ij} - \bar{X}._j$$
$$X_{ij} = X_{dj} + \bar{X}._j$$

Substituting this value for X into a *raw score* model produces

$$Y_{ij} = \gamma_{00} + \gamma_{01}W_j + \gamma_{10}\left(X_{dj} + \bar{X}._j\right) + \gamma_{11}\left(X_{dj} + \bar{X}._j\right)W_j + u_{0j} + u_{1j}\left(X_{dj} + \bar{X}._j\right) + e_{ij}$$
$$= \gamma_{00} + \gamma_{01}W_j + \gamma_{10}X_{dj} + \gamma_{10}\bar{X}._j + \gamma_{11}X_{dj}W_j + \gamma_{11}\bar{X}._jW_j + error$$
$$= \left(\gamma_{00} + \gamma_{10}\bar{X}._j\right) + \left(\gamma_{01} + \gamma_{11}\bar{X}._j\right)W_j + \gamma_{10}X_{dj} + \gamma_{11}X_{dj}W_j + error$$

The equation shows that you can re-establish equivalence with the raw score model by adding $\bar{X}._j$ back into the model explicitly, the so-called "***compositional effect,***" such as the mean SES of a student sample in a school. An important fact is that unless the $\bar{X}._j$ is put in the model, then the effect of W_j is not corrected for average compositional differences. At times, this is what you want (as in growth curve models . . . to be discussed in a later section), but sometimes, it is not exactly what you intend. You can choose to control for the mean of X within groups as a variable at the second level—that is, in the model for β_{0j}:

$$\beta_{0j} = \gamma_{00} + \gamma_{01}W_j + \gamma_{02}\bar{X}._j + u_{0j}$$

In general

1. Raw score models are generally the most confounded across levels and suffer the most from collinearity.

2. A grand-mean centered model is more interpretable because it provides a useful interpretation of the outcomes at Level 2 (e.g., adjusted group means), and it helps in estimation relative to a raw score model because of the reduction in confounding across levels. But it also "privileges" Level-1 effects over Level-2 effects as a result.

3. Group-mean centering is best designed for separating within from between group effects and demonstrating those effects in the model. If you are using mean levels of X as the aggregate variable, it makes sense to use this model. If you are using *population* values at the aggregate level (e.g., census indicators, school statistics, organizational profits or losses), then one must consider whether this effect covaries with aggregate Level-1 variables, and if it does, how one should interpret effects of W_j.

4. Group-mean centering separates the effects of X at Level 1 from W at Level 2 most completely.

5. Group-mean centering works optimally if you expect cross-level interactions. Given the importance of this hypothesis, group-mean centering will often be used in the literature.

10.6 SAMPLE SIZE CONSIDERATIONS

Much is stated in the HLM literature about the issue of necessary sample sizes. The issue is complex and requires consideration of the goals of the study and which inferences are important. In general, you need to have a number of Level-2 units; the most often cited minimum is around 25 to 30 (Hox & Maas, 2004; Raudenbush & Sampson, 1999). If you have only 10 to 15 groups, then "controlling" for group-level differences overall may require inclusion of dummy variables for group differences. Between 15 and 25, it is difficult to know what to suggest. The minimum sample and the optimal sample size are two different things; a commonly used goal in designed HLM research is to have at least 50 to 70 Level-2 units.

An often repeated conclusion is that the number of Level-2 units has more impact on estimation than the average sample size per Level-1 unit. The simulations of Hox and Maas (2004) give some guidance about the effects on parameter estimation in HLM models of different combinations of sample size situations at Level 1 and Level-2. Their simulation has three variables: number of groups, group size, and the intraclass correlation (ICC), the percentage of variance between groups.

Table 10.3 shows the variations tested.

TABLE 10.3 ● SIMULATION PARAMETERS TO ASSESS THE EFFECTS OF SAMPLE SIZES AT LEVEL 1 AND LEVEL 2			
	Parameter Value		
Number of Groups	30	50	100
Group Size	5	30	50
ICC	.1	.2	.3

The importance of this simulation is that secondary analyses of existing data may depend on these kinds of results. This is because the level of clustering in large-scale surveys may be smaller than in studies explicitly designed for modeling hierarchical effects. Maas and Hox tested the effects of these 3 x 3 x 3 = 27 conditions on both fixed and random parameters and both point and interval estimates.

Results are summarized in these points:

- Both fixed and random parameter estimates show little bias across all conditions. Thus, point estimates are not greatly affected by the range of sample sizes considered.

- Results for impacts on the standard errors suggest *some* impact of both number of groups and group size.

- The number of groups has a small effect on the estimation of standard errors for fixed effects—in fact, the effect is described as "trivial."

- The number of groups has a larger impact on the standard errors of Level-2 random effects. With 30 Level-2 units, for example, the standard errors are "too short," implying overestimation of significance. The problem is still considered to be modest (15% too small). At an $N = 50$, the standard errors are still about 9% too small.

- The standard errors for Level-1 random error are affected less across conditions.

- Group sizes had little effect on the "correctness" of the standard errors of Level-2 random parameters. The degree to which estimated standard errors are off relative to the true standard error is actually slightly smaller than in the case of a number of groups = 30 and comparable to a number of groups = 50. In other words, detection of random effects is less sensitive overall to within-group sample sizes than the number of groups.

Overall, these results are encouraging for the plausibility of analysis of secondary data using HLM techniques—to a limit. In these cases, the average sample size per group will often equal between 3 and 10, but fortunately, the number of groups is typically large.

10.7 ESTIMATING MULTILEVEL MODELS IN SAS AND STATA

Singer and Willett (2003) have "translated" the HLM model into SAS, and the approach used in this section closely follows their approach. We first use PROC MIXED in SAS to model hierarchical data with continuous outcome variables. We use the series of models discussed in the introductory section to demonstrate the software implementation of the HLM model.

One of the data requirements of using these models is the proper merging of Level-1 observations with the appropriate Level-2 unit information—which often exists in separate data files. In a typical application, there are multiple Level-1 observations within each Level-2 unit. If the data exist in separate files, there *must* be a linking variable in the individual level data—that is, the ID variable in the Level-2 data set must also exist in the Level-1 data set.

10.7.1 Neighborhood Effects on Immigrant Women's Alcohol Consumption

We now return to our example from the first section focusing on immigrant women's alcohol consumption across neighborhoods in Toronto.

The issue here is how neighborhood context may condition the tendency to see alcohol as a accepted social behavior and/or a form of coping behavior. We imagine social contexts as often playing the role of passive interventions—or treatments—presenting possibilities, normative expectations, or differential access to essential resources. Theoretically, we pursue two main hypotheses: (1) that the *prevalence* of similar others in the neighborhood will act as a kind of implicit social support and a normative baseline for behavior, and thus the within-group norms about drinking unique to immigrant groups will prevail; and (2) the socioeconomic standing of the neighborhood will define drinking norms that encourage alcohol use among immigrants. These two predictions express opposite possibilities: One contextual influence increases the negative effect of immigrant status, due to stronger proscriptions against drinking, while the other weakens this effect, due to the possibility that these neighborhoods may especially represent norms about assimilation for immigrants.

Our two neighborhood-level indicators are the *percentage of immigrants in the neighborhood* and *the percentage of single detached homes in the neighborhood*. A higher percentage of single detached homes signals neighborhood stability or affluence, compared to neighborhoods predominantly populated by apartment buildings, row houses, or semi-detached homes. The prevalence of single detached homes reflects a greater likelihood of home ownership and potentially a commitment to neighborhood investment.

Our individual-level data from respondents are first merged with Statistics Canada census tract data (Statistics Canada, 2010) (Level-2 data). We merge these data sets together after sorting each by census tract number—here the variable is *"ctname"* (the common identifier across each dataset).

```
proc sort data=nehwdata.interviewswct2;
by ctname;
run;
proc sort data=census.census06;
by ctname;
run;
data hlmnehw;
merge census.census06 nehwdata.interviewswct2;
by ctname;
if participant_ID=. then delete;
run;
```

Note here that after merging, we get rid of unmatched cases by deleting all cases where the individual-level ID is missing. This happens because the census file covers all of Canada, while our sample is only a sample of tracts in Toronto.

10.7.2 General Background to Preparation of Data

Without replicating the entire SAS data step here—since it mostly codes variables like any other data step, we note some of the unique features that are necessary to run an HLM model.

Once data are merged, you can use the census-level variables in the data step to develop the necessary variables at Level 2 in the analysis. In this case, we are interested in the percentage of immigrants in the neighborhood because this factor reflects the influence of "person-environment" fit on the implications of the nativity status of women in this study, and we include the percentage of single detached homes in the neighborhood as a proxy for the effects of socioeconomic disadvantage.

In this example, we use group-mean centering. This is achieved in SAS by centering each X value taken as a deviation from the means within groups, so that the adjusted mean is zero in each group. This yields an interpretation of the intercept as the overall mean of Y in each group and so defines the interpretation of the Level-2 model for β_{oj}.

After completing the data step, the following run of PROC STANDARD achieves group-mean centering, by centering variables with a mean of 0 *by* neighborhood:

We proceed with testing our models in stages.

```
proc standard data=hlmnehw_complete_weight
out=hlmnehw_complete_weight_2 mean=0;
by ctname;
var reduc yrsincan immigrant age;
run;
```

10.7.3 One-Way ANOVA

Recall that this model is

$$Y_{ij} = \beta_{oj} + e_{ij}$$
$$\beta_{0j} = \gamma_{00} + u_{0j}$$

Before we can establish *any* role for neighborhood, we first need to run a one-way ANOVA to test whether there are overall differences in alcohol use across neighborhoods among these women.

The run of PROC MIXED for the one-way ANOVA is as follows:

```
/*One-way ANOVA with Random Effects*/
proc mixed data=temp noclprint covtest info update;
class ctname;
model alcoholuse =   / solution ;
random intercept  / sub=ctname ;
weight nehwweight;

title1 'A One-Way Random Effects ANOVA Model for Immigrant Women's Alcohol Use';
run;
```

In PROC MIXED, the MODEL statement is used to identify fixed effects and the RANDOM statement is used to specify random effects.

- In the PROC statement
  - NOCLPRINT prevents the printing of the *class*-level information giving the number of neighborhoods involved. The first time you run the program, leave out this command to ensure the Level-2 variable appears as expected.
  - COVTEST asks for variance and covariance components and tests.
  - INFO gives basic information about the number of Level-1 and Level-2 observations.
  - UPDATE prints iteration information to the LOG window in SAS, mainly useful in more complex models. You can also inspect the function values step-by-step in the estimation process, to ensure the model is not in trouble (as indicated by little change in the function across iterations or the function getting larger).

- The CLASS statement specifies the Level-2 group ID variable. Here it is *ctname*.

- In the MODEL statement
  - There are no explicit independent variables in this model besides the intercept (it is assumed).
  - The / SOLUTION option asks to print the estimates for fixed effects.

- The RANDOM statement
  - This statement is crucial to running various hierarchical models properly. By default, there is always one random effect (e_{ij}). Here, we specify that the intercept has random components at Level-2, using the special term *intercept*. This means that the intercept at Level 1 is not *only* a fixed effect (γ_{00}), but also has a random component, standing for variation across Level-2 units.
  - The SUB= option specifies the multilevel structure, by specifying *ctname* as the Level-2 unit. This ensures that the variance component (u_{0j}) at Level 2 is estimated using this variable as the identifier for Level-2 units..

- The WEIGHT statement specifies a weight at Level 1, here *nehwweight*.

The program uses restricted ML by default. You can add METHOD=REML in the PROC statement if you want to be explicit. You can also ask for ML by specifying METHOD=ML.

The results below indicate a significant τ_{00} (the variance of u_{0j}). The "intercept" random parameter is the variance of u_{0j}, and the "residual" parameter is the variance of e_{ij}.

TABLE 10.4 ● RESULTS FOR THE ONE-WAY ANOVA MODEL

Dimensions	
Covariance Parameters	2
Columns in X	1
Columns in Z per Subject	1
Subjects	87
Max Obs per Subject	16

Number of Observations	
Number of Observations Read	809
Number of Observations Used	649
Number of Observations Not Used	160

Covariance Parameter Estimates								
Cov Parm	Subject	Estimate	Standard Error	Z Value	Pr > Z	Alpha	Lower	Upper
Intercept	ctname	0.3134	0.09501	3.30	0.0005	0.05	0.1870	0.6307
Residual		1.6248	0.09659	16.82	<.0001	0.05	1.4510	1.8321

Solution for Fixed Effects								
Effect	Estimate	Standard Error	DF	t Value	Pr > |t|	Alpha	Lower	Upper
Intercept	1.4643	0.08491	85	17.25	<.0001	0.05	1.2955	1.6331

This result suggests that there is random variance in alcohol use at the neighborhood level, tested by the significance of the intercept variance—meaning that there is unspecified neighborhood variation in alcohol consumption. Thus, we proceed with a cross-over effect model.

The intra-class correlation, the percentage of total variance of alcohol use between neighborhoods, is

$$\hat{\rho} = \tau_{00} \Big/ (\tau_{00} + \hat{\sigma}^2) = .3134 \Big/ (.3134 + 1.6248) = .16$$

About 16% of the total variance in alcohol use among these women occurs due to overall neighborhood differences. This is *not* a trivial portion of the total variability in drinking, suggesting that norms, observation, prevalence of drinking institutions, social networks, social support, and possibly family structure at the neighborhood level—the average workings of each—together have a substantial impact.

10.7.4 The Cross-Over Effect Model

To specify the neighborhood variance, we consider both *the percentage of immigrants in the neighborhood* ("*immigrantcensus*") and the *percentage of single detached homes in the neighborhood* ("*persinglehome*").

Our prediction is actually that these factors may or may not directly affect the use of alcohol in the neighborhood in general, but if they do, the effect of each is likely to be negative. A higher presence of immigrants suggests stronger norms against drinking, and higher SES also suggests normative restrictions on the amount of drinking.

The model estimated here is

$$Y_{ij} = \beta_{0j} + e_{ij} \tag{1}$$

$$\beta_{0j} = \gamma_{00} + \gamma_{01}(immigrantcensus)_j + \gamma_{02}(persinglehome)_j + u_{0j} \tag{2}$$

This leads to the following combined model:

$$Y_{ij} = \gamma_{00} + \gamma_{01}(immigrantcensus)_j + \gamma_{02}(persinglehome)_j + u_{0j} + e_{ij}$$

Note in this model that there are two random effect components (u_{0j} and e_{ij}), as before, and two fixed effects at Level 2. The run of PROC MIXED in this case is similar, except we are adding the two fixed Level-2 variables to the model. Also, the DDFM=BW option in the MODEL statement uses the "between / within" method for computing degrees of freedom for fixed effects, which is appropriate in these kinds of models:

```
/*Cross-Over Effect of Percent Immigrants and Percent Single
Detached homes*/
proc mixed data=temp noclprint covtest info update ;
class ctname;
model alcoholuse = immigrantcensus persinglehome / solution ddfm=bw ;
random intercept   / sub=ctname ;
weight nehwweight;
title1 'A Cross-Over Effect Model for Immigrant Women's Alcohol Use';
run;
```

Output from SAS in Table 10.5 shows the results for the random and fixed effects part of the model.

The solution for the fixed effects shows that both neighborhood variables have an overall negative effect on alcohol use. The percentage of immigrants in the neighborhood reduces drinking, but the percentage of single detached homes does as well. By including both variables, we partial out the SES component from the effects of the prevalence of immigrants in the neighborhood.

TABLE 10.5 ● RESULTS FROM THE CROSS-OVER EFFECTS MODEL

				Covariance Parameter Estimates					
Cov Parm	Subject	Estimate	Standard Error	Z Value	Pr > Z	Alpha	Lower	Upper
Intercept	ctname	0.05386	0.05185	1.04	0.1494	0.05	0.01508	1.6885
Residual		1.6225	0.09595	16.91	<.0001	0.05	1.4497	1.8283

			Solution for Fixed Effects					
Effect	Estimate	Standard Error	DF	t Value	Pr > |t|	Alpha	Lower	Upper
Intercept	3.2808	0.2336	84	14.04	<.0001	0.05	2.8162	3.7454
immigrantcensus	−0.3425	0.04235	562	−8.09	<.0001	0.05	−0.4257	−0.2593
persinglehome	−0.09521	0.02566	562	−3.71	0.0002	0.05	−0.1456	−0.04482

We also see the tau parameter reduces in magnitude since we've captured some of the potential neighborhood-level variations in alcohol use. Now it is just .054, compared to .313 in the first model. To show how the explanation of variance at Level 2 can be calculated, we take the original between-neighborhood variance from the one-way ANOVA model and assess the percentage change represented by this model:

$$\frac{\tau_{00_{(1)}} - \tau_{00_{(2)}}}{\tau_{00_{(1)}}} = \frac{.3134 - .0539}{.3134} = .83$$

Thus these two Level 2 variables explain 83% of the variance across neighborhoods on their own, which is substantial. This basically means we have chosen two key factors that together explain the variation in drinking across neighborhoods, since the remaining intercept is not significant (p =.1494).

We now proceed to test whether the impact of nativity status at Level 1 varies across neighborhoods using the random coefficients model.

10.7.5 The Random Coefficients Model

In this model we consider the effects of nativity—foreign versus native-born—at the individual level and test whether there are random differences in its slope across neighborhoods. Here the variable for nativity status is called *immigrant*. For generality, we include a control for age in this model, but we only test the random effects of immigrant status, since that is the focus of our cross-level interactions.

The model we are estimating here, in HLM terms, is

$$Y_{ij} = \beta_{0j} + \beta_{1j}(immigrant)_{ij} + \beta_{2j}(age)_{ij} + e_{ij}$$

$$\beta_{0j} = \gamma_{00} + u_{0j}$$

$$\beta_{1j} = \gamma_{10} + u_{1j}$$

$$\beta_{2j} = \gamma_{20}$$

The combined model here is

$$Y_{ij} = \gamma_{00} + \gamma_{10}(immigrant)_{ij} + \gamma_{20}(age)_{ij} + u_{0j} + u_{1j}(immigrant)_{ij} + e_{ij}$$

Notice the Level-2 model here. There is a random component to the effect of immigrant status at Level 2, but the effect of age is considered "fixed" across neighborhoods, and so its equation at Level 2 has no random component.

The main change in PROC MIXED in this model involves adding individual-level X variables to the MODEL statement and specifying another random effect in the RANDOM statement for the possible varying effect of immigrant status across neighborhoods:

```
/*Random Coefficients Model*/
proc mixed data=temp noclprint covtest info update ;
class ctname;
model alcoholuse = immigrant age / solution ddfm=bw notest;
random intercept immigrant / sub=ctname type=un ;
weight nehwweight;

title1 'A Random Coefficients Model for Immigrant Women's Alcohol Use';
run;
```

The model requires covariance components for intercepts *and* slopes ($\tau_{00}, \tau_{01}, \tau_{11}$). This is because the random coefficients model includes the possibility of both random intercept and random slope parameters, giving rise to covariances between these parameters. PROC MIXED allows for many different variance/covariance structures. We choose the "unstructured" specification of the variance/covariance matrix by specifying in the RANDOM statement "TYPE=UN" after the slash, which allows for separate estimation of all components of the matrix. This choice requires the fewest assumptions, but in complex models, some constraints on this matrix may be necessary. Singer and Willett (2003) review a number of other choices here, but the issue often comes up more in growth curve models. If you can reach a solution using the unstructured (free) covariance matrix, you should use this option.

We allow for random effects of the ***effect*** of drinking across neighborhoods—that is, $V(\beta_{1j}) = V(u_{1j})$. Even though immigrant status is a dummy variable, it is important to center this variable: Otherwise, the Level-2 model will not be predicting the general mean within groups but the mean of the native-born, coded 0 on the dummy variable.

Relevant parts of the output from PROC MIXED are shown in Table 10.6.

Compared to their native born counterparts, immigrant women report less alcohol consumption, and older respondents drink more.

The output under "Covariance Parameters Estimates" needs to be interpreted in light of the order of the X variables in the model: UN(1,1) stands for the random intercept variance, as usual, and the UN(2,2) parameter stands for the random slope for immigrant status. The random variance denoted by UN(2,2) is significant, indicating that immigrant status does have significant varying effects across neighborhoods ($\mu_{1j} = .432, p = .0359$). This result allows us to conclude that there may be important cross-level interactions, specifically between the percentage of immigrants and/ or single detached homes in the neighborhood and individual nativity status. UN(2,1) is the

TABLE 10.6 ●	THE RANDOM COEFFICIENTS MODEL

Covariance Parameter Estimates					
Cov Parm	**Subject**	**Estimate**	**Standard Error**	**Z Value**	**Pr Z**
UN(1,1)	ctname	0.3021	0.09530	3.17	0.0008
UN(2,1)	ctname	0.008551	0.1043	0.08	0.9346
UN(2,2)	ctname	0.4316	0.2397	1.80	0.0359
Residual		1.4786	0.09256	15.97	<.0001

Null Model Likelihood Ratio Test		
DF	**Chi-Square**	**Pr > ChiSq**
3	35.24	<.0001

Solution for Fixed Effects					
Effect	**Estimate**	**Standard Error**	**DF**	**t Value**	**Pr > |t|**
Intercept	1.6089	0.08746	85	18.40	<.0001
immigrant	−0.6435	0.1441	561	−4.47	<.0001
AGE	0.01732	0.006179	561	2.80	0.0052

covariance between the random intercept and random slope across neighborhoods. You usually want this parameter to be small and nonsignificant.

10.7.6 The "Full" Model

When we put these results together into one model, we retain the cross-level effects of both the percentage of immigrants in the neighborhood and the percentage of single detached homes. These effects are still interpretable as "average" effects in this model: The effects of Level 2 variables are on average differences across neighborhoods, and the effects of Level-1 variables represent the average effect within neighborhoods.

In this model, we test the cross-level interactions between percentage immigrant and immigrant status and percentage single detached homes and immigrant status at Level 1.

The HLM specification of the full model are as follows:

$$Y_{ij} = \beta_{0j} + \beta_{1j}(immigrant)_{ij} + \beta_{2j}(age)_{ij} + e_{ij}$$

$$\beta_{0j} = \gamma_{00} + \gamma_{01}(immigrantcensus)_j + \gamma_{02}(persinglehome)_j + u_{0j}$$

$$\beta_{1j} = \gamma_{10} + \gamma_{11}(immigrantcensus)_j + \gamma_{12}(persinglehome)_j + u_{1j}$$

$$\beta_{2j} = \gamma_{20}$$

We create the interactions between immigrant status with both Level-2 variables when we replace β_{1j} in the Level-1 equation with its determinants in the Level-2 equation. The final combined equation here is

$$Y_{ij} = \gamma_{00} + \gamma_{01}(immigrantcensus)_j + \gamma_{02}(persinglehome)_j + \gamma_{10}(immigrant)_{ij} + \gamma_{20}(age)_{ij}$$
$$+ \gamma_{11}(immigrantcensus_j * immigrant_{ij}) + \gamma_{12}(persinglehome_j * immigrant_{ij}) + u_{0j}$$
$$+(immigrant)_{ij} u_{ij} + e_{ij}$$

The PROC MIXED for the full model is:

```
proc mixed data=temp noclprint covtest info update ;
class ctname;
model alcoholuse =  immigrant age immigrantcensus persinglehome immigrant*
                    immigrantcensus immigrant* persinglehome/ solution ddfm=
                    bw notest;
random intercept immigrant  / sub=ctname type=un ;
weight nehwweight;
title1 'A Full Model for Immigrant Women's Alcohol Use';
run;
```

The main differences compared to prior programs are the two cross-level interactions involving immigrant status and the percentage of immigrants and immigrant status and the percentage of single detached homes at the neighborhood level. You write out the interactions explicitly. Note that both Level-2 and Level-1 independent variables are specified on the same line, like a combined model.

We show the entire output from the final model in Table 10.7, so that you can see the various parts of what PROC MIXED prints.

TABLE 10.7 ● THE FULL COMBINED MODEL

Dimensions	
Covariance Parameters	4
Columns in X	7
Columns in Z per Subject	2
Subjects	87
Max Obs per Subject	16

Number of Observations	
Number of Observations Read	809
Number of Observations Used	649
Number of Observations Not Used	160

Iteration History			
Iteration	Evaluations	-2 Res Log Like	Criterion
0	1	2487.58495907	
1	2	2482.89889197	0.00000067
2	1	2482.89845539	0.00000000

(Continued)

TABLE 10.7 ● Continued

				Covariance Parameter Estimates				
Cov Parm	**Subject**	**Estimate**	**Standard Error**	**Z Value**	**Pr Z**	**Alpha**	**Lower**	**Upper**
UN(1,1)	ctname	0.02123	0.04905	0.43	0.3326	0.05	0.002734	2195634
UN(2,1)	ctname	0.004571	0.07069	0.06	0.9484	0.05	−0.1340	0.1431
UN(2,2)	ctname	0.3382	0.2207	1.53	0.0628	0.05	0.1288	2.2105
Residual		1.4838	0.09259	16.03	<.0001	0.05	1.3178	1.6834

Null Model Likelihood Ratio Test		
DF	**Chi-Square**	**Pr > ChiSq**
3	4.69	0.1962

			Solution for Fixed Effects					
Effect	**Estimate**	**Standard Error**	**DF**	**t Value**	**Pr > |t|**	**Alpha**	**Lower**	**Upper**
Intercept	3.4967	0.2290	84	15.27	<.0001	0.05	3.0413	3.9520
immigrant	−0.7308	0.5133	75	−1.42	0.1587	0.05	−1.7533	0.2918
AGE	0.02263	0.005955	483	3.80	0.0002	0.05	0.01093	0.03433
immigrantcensus	−0.3408	0.04134	483	−8.25	<.0001	0.05	−0.4220	−0.2596
persinglehome	−0.1143	0.02512	483	−4.55	<.0001	0.05	−0.1636	−0.06491
immigrant*immigrantc	−0.06309	0.09474	483	−0.67	0.5058	0.05	−0.2492	0.1231
immigrant*persingleh	0.1216	0.05492	483	2.21	0.0274	0.05	0.01364	0.2295

The SAS output for this model shows that there is no interaction between the prevalence of immigrants and the effect of immigrant status (p = .5058), but there is an interaction between the percentage of detached homes and immigrant status (p = .0274). This interaction suggests immigrants drink relatively more in higher SES neighborhoods. Thus, the "structure" effect here wins, relative to the "culture" effect expressed by the prevalence of immigrants.

The results also show that UN(2,2) is no longer significant, meaning that we are able to specify the source of the randomly varying slope for immigrant status in the random coefficients model using the cross-level interaction between the prevalence of single detached homes and individual immigrant status. The logic here is that this interaction specifies a basic reason for the randomly varying slope of immigrant status across neighborhoods.

10.7.7 Estimating the HLM Example in STATA

We present the final and full model in STATA for comparison (with cross-level interactions). This model is specified using the **xtmixed** command:

```
xtmixed alcoholuse c.immigrant##c.immigrantcensus c.immigrant##c.
persinglehome  age  || ctname: immigrant , var  cov(un)
[pweight=nehwweightnew]
```

We provide an overview of the other statements in the command line:

- **xtmixed** is the standard command for mixed models (i.e., models with more than one level of data). We then identify the dependent and independent variables followed by ‖ which separates the model from specification options. All independent variables listed prior to the double bars will have fixed effects estimated in predicting Y.

- **ctname** is the classifying measure or Level 2 designation. This model specifies a random effect for "immigrant" at Level 1.

- **var** specifies that we want to estimate the correspondent variances for each coefficient

- **cov** indicates that we want the covariances between the random components presented. We can then define the structure of the covariance matrix in parentheses. As discussed earlier, we want an unstructured matrix.

- **pweight** is the option to specify the person/case weight for the data.

Here, we are asking STATA to estimate the fixed effects for the interaction terms which can be generated in the model, rather than previously coded, using the ## option. Specifying these interactions implies the presence of the main effects for these variables as well. The prefacing 'c.' is used to tell STATA that these are continuous measures (remember, this is the case for the Level 1 immigrant variable, given that each respondent's value is centered by the group mean of the census tract in which they reside).

TABLE 10.8 ● RESULTS FROM THE "FULL MODEL" IN STATA

```
Mixed-effects regression              Number of obs      =        649
Group variable: ctname                Number of groups   =         86

                                      Obs per group: min =          2
                                                     avg =        7.5
                                                     max =         16

                                      Wald chi2(6)       =     173.84
Log pseudolikelihood = -894.35584     Prob > chi2        =     0.0000

                            (Std. Err. adjusted for 86 clusters in ctname)
```

		Robust				
alcoholuse	Coef.	Std. Err.	z	P>|z|	[95% Conf.	Interval]
immigrant	-.704682	.5204597	-1.35	0.176	-1.724764	.3154003
immigrantcensus	-.3428148	.0392632	-8.73	0.000	-.4197693	-.2658603
c.immigrant#c. immigrantcensus	-.0684462	.0851112	-0.80	0.421	-.2352611	.0983687
immigrant persinglehome	0	(omitted)				
	-.1172652	.0207377	-5.65	0.000	-.1579102	-.0766201
c.immigrant#c. persinglehome	.1236016	.0558448	2.21	0.027	.0141478	.2330554
age	.0226138	.0060173	3.76	0.000	.0108201	.0344075
_cons	3.520993	.2166841	16.25	0.000	3.0963	3.945686

(Continued)

TABLE 10.8 ◆ Continued

Random-effects Parameters	Estimate	Robust Std. Err.	[95% Conf.Interval]	
ctname: Unstructured				
var(immigr~t)	.0573899	.1552315	.0002861	11.51371
var(_cons)	.0001116	.0013048	1.25e-14	996780.6
cov(immigr~t,_cons)	.0025307	.0146418	-.0261667	.0312281
var(Residual)	1.961151	.1582251	1.674312	2.297131

All results in Table 10.8 are comparable to the PROC MIXED results, and can be interpreted similarly to the SAS output presented earlier. However, it must be noted that STATA uses a slightly different estimation method than SAS (maximum likelihood, rather than restricted maximum likelihood). For this reason, you will see slightly different coefficients, standard errors, and fit statistics in the STATA versus SAS output.

10.8 ESTIMATING A THREE-LEVEL MODEL

Running three-level models is a straightforward extension of the two-level case. This example predicts exposure to stress in childhood, composed mainly of parental deaths, divorce, and abuse, as a function of the mother's age at the birth of the child (Level 1, the person), the mother's education (Level 2, family-level differences), and neighborhood disadvantage (Level 3, the neighborhood), an index of seven socioeconomic indicators about the neighborhood derived from the U.S. Census, and focusing on issues such as percentage in poverty, percentage with less than a complete primary education, percentage of males unemployed, and percentage of families on public assistance.

There are two levels of hierarchy in this question: Children are nested in families, and families are nested in neighborhoods. We use the National Survey of Children (Zill, Furstenberg, Peterson, & Moore, 1992) data to estimate this model. In this study, for a subsample of the total sample, two children were interviewed from each household. That means that there could be correlated errors across children within households; thus, we **have** to consider family-level differences. In addition, we have information on each zip code in the United States from the 1970, 1980, and 1990 Censuses. We treat zip code area as a rough measure of neighborhood here. The National Survey of Children data records the zip code respondents lived in at each wave. That is all we need to link the individual data to neighborhoods. Also, the same case number was used for people in the same families, so we can group children by family as well.

It is typical in studying hierarchical models to have to merge the data on individuals with the data on higher-level social units. Here, we have some variables replicated for parents across the two children in families, so we use this source of information to specify family-level effects. **Mother's education** is common to both children, so it operates as a family-level variable. Many others could be specified here: quality of the marriage, employment status of the parents, family-level activities, parenting style as reported by the parent, and sibling structure are examples.

At the individual level, we take the ***age of the mother*** as an individual-level variable, since it varies by child. We predict that younger age will be a signal of higher risk for stress accumulation in children.

After merging data and coding the relevant variables (not shown), we run a one-way ANOVA program as follows:

```
options pageno=1;
proc mixed data=kidcen covtest noclprint info update;
class case newzip76;
model  stress1 = / solution ddfm=bw;
random intercept / sub=newzip76 type=un;
random intercept / sub=case(newzip76) type=un;
*weight wave2wt;
title1 '1-way ANOVA in 3-Level Model with stress exposure at time-1 as outcome';
run;
```

In this program, *newzip76* is the Level-2 identifier—the zip code. *Case* is the family case ID. There are two random statements in the program: The first has a "SUB=" option using the neighborhood variable, *newzip76*, and the second has a SUB= option using a variable for family, *case*, which is nested in neighborhoods (*newzip76*). The SUB= option in this statement says, in effect, that the variable *case* is nested in the variable *newzip76*. Note you should put the RANDOM statement for Level 3 in first and then the RANDOM statement for Level 2.

The results from the one-way ANOVA are shown in Table 10.9. The main result of importance here is the fact that there is random variation in stress exposure at both the family level and the neighborhood level. This suggests that both family and neighborhood factors may be affecting the risk of stress exposure among children as they grow up.

TABLE 10.9 ● ONE-WAY ANOVA FOR A THREE-LEVEL MODEL

Model Information	
Data Set	WORK.KIDCEN
Dependent Variable	stress1
Covariance Structure	Unstructured
Subject Effects	newzip76, case(newzip76)
Estimation Method	REML
Residual Variance Method	Profile
Fixed Effects SE Method	Model-Based
Degrees of Freedom Method	Between-Within

Number of Observations	
Number of Observations Read	514
Number of Observations Used	506
Number of Observations Not Used	8

(Continued)

TABLE 10.9 ⬤ Continued

Iteration History			
Iteration	Evaluations	-2 Res Log Like	Criterion
0	1	1066.08125401	
1	2	901.53361958	0.00195174
2	1	901.50677798	0.00000601
3	1	901.50669774	0.00000000

Covariance Parameter Estimates					
Cov Parm	Subject	Estimate	Standard Error	Z Value	Pr > Z
UN(1,1)	newzip76	0.06740	0.03730	1.81	0.0354
UN(1,1)	case(newzip76)	0.2654	0.03947	6.72	<.0001
Residual		0.1508	0.01343	11.23	<.0001

The next program estimates the effect of mother's age, mother's education, and neighborhood disadvantage on stress exposure in children. This is a three-level model with mother's age at the child's birth from Level 1, mother's education from Level 2, and neighborhood disadvantage from Level 3. No interactions are specified, and only the mother's education's slope was allowed to vary randomly at a higher level. This was done because, in an earlier run, the effect of mother's age on eventual stress for the child was found to have no random variation at either the family or the neighborhood level.

The program used here is:

```
proc mixed data=kidcenc covtest noclprint info update;
class case newzip76;
model stress1 = momage momeduc1 ndindex76 / solution ddfm=bw;
random intercept momeduc1 / sub=newzip76 type=un;
random intercept / sub=case(newzip76) type=un;
run;
```

The selected results below show that (a) the random effects of neighborhood are not explained in this model; (b) the random effect of mother's education is explained across neighborhoods, although it is not clear in the output, because very small values of a variance are set to zero; (c) there is still random family-level variance to explain; and (d) mother's education has a negative effect on the child's stress exposure, but the effect of mother's age and neighborhood disadvantage are both nonsignificant.

In fact, neighborhood disadvantage *did* have a significant impact in a model without mother's education. This could indicate that social selection into neighborhoods based on education may explain apparent neighborhood impacts on the rate of stress experience at the individual level, if we believe that the current education of individuals determines the neighborhood you live in more than neighborhood determines achieved education among adults. This is reasonable since education is typically completed at an earlier stage of transition from adolescence to adulthood. Neighborhoods still have a net independent impact on the distribution of stress in children's lives, after taking into account family-level effects, but these random effects are not specified in this model.

| TABLE 10.10 ● RESULTS FOR A SIMPLIFIED FINAL THREE-LEVEL MODEL |

Covariance Parameter Estimates					
Cov Parm	Subject	Estimate	Standard Error	Z Value	Pr Z
UN(1,1)	newzip76	0.2143	0.1154	1.86	0.0317
UN(2,1)	newzip76	−0.00784	0.003802	−2.06	0.0391
UN(2,2)	newzip76	0	—	—	—
UN(1,1)	case(newzip76)	0.2739	0.04036	6.79	<.0001
Residual		0.1474	0.01342	10.99	<.0001

Solution for Fixed Effects					
Effect	Estimate	Standard Error	DF	t Value	Pr > |t|
Intercept	1.2320	0.2823	101	4.36	<.0001
momage	−0.00945	0.007837	383	−1.21	0.2286
momeduc1	−0.06629	0.01510	383	−4.39	<.0001
ndindex76	0.007307	0.007989	101	0.91	0.3626

10.9 PUBLISHED EXAMPLES

Over the last twenty years, HLM models have been applied to a rich array of empirical problems. This is a literature that is still growing in scope, and, because of the embedded theoretical perspectives made possible using HLM models, the diversity and originality of the examples using HLM is noteworthy.

Here we consider three examples, on quite diverse issues, using diverse kinds of data.

10.9.1 Understanding Spatial Variations in Tolerance

This example was published in Social Forces in 2006 (Moore & Ovadia, 2006), but the importance of the issue today is, perhaps, even more acute than when this article was published. The issue of tolerance is generally important to social science, as a marker of "civil society", and a soft cornerstone of how democracies are supposed to work.

The opening paragraph of this article speaks loudly to current issues (2006, p. 2205).

> Civil liberties are a cornerstone of American ideology, but they have been denied to many Americans either through *de jure* or *de facto* means for much of the nation's history. While court decisions and legislation in the past 50 years have explicitly guaranteed these rights, there nevertheless remains public debate in the United States about such issues as free speech, privacy and assembly, especially for controversial groups. The passage of referenda that restrict the civil rights of illegal immigrants and the movement to ban same-sex marriages are just two recent examples that suggest that not all Americans are comfortable with putting the principle of universal rights into practice.

The authors argue that region and urbanicity affect tolerance. These are considered climates in which tolerance is either encouraged or discouraged, where norms and collective beliefs help determine the range of individual beliefs that are possible. The authors rely on a widely used distinction between "compositional" and "contextual" effects to examine their questions.

The "compositional" explanation here is that some areas produce higher or lower levels of tolerance purely because of the aggregated presence of more individual-level characteristics that affect tolerance, such as lower education, older age, or fundamentalist beliefs. The "contextual" explanation is that differences in norms, values, practices, culture, history, or structure at the group level produce differences in tolerance tendencies, over and above compositional effects. In this article, contextual effects are interpreted as basically cultural.

What is unusual in their approach but is shared in some of the literature on place in geography (Macintyre, Ellaway, & Cummins, 2002) is that it is possible to see the demographic profiles of places as the foundation of contextual effects—that is, they are not only compositional effects. In this interpretation, the average education of an area is more than simply the summation of the education of individuals: Implicitly, it operates also as a norm, an expectation, and as a reference point. Using this reasoning, the authors study the net effect of a number of demographic variables that could affect tolerance at the contextual level, which in this case are PSUs—metropolitan areas and rural counties. These include region (south/nonsouth), religious denomination, age, racial/ethnic identification, urbanicity, education, and mobility, which is associated with exposure to and acceptance of diversity.

Using GSS data merged with PSU data, the authors study a summed tolerance scale, consisting of 15 items measuring tolerant attitudes, asking about levels of acceptance of extreme groups, both on the left and the right. This is not a generalized measure of tolerance, but it is a familiar indicator, derived from work on "social distance" (Allport, 1954).

This paper is a good example of the use of HLM because it is a classic example of the basic point of HLM models, and it follows the sequence of issues we have followed in this chapter. Results begin by discussing the variability in tolerance scores across PSUs, making the point there is a wide range of tolerance at the PSU level. Figure 10.3 shows this variability and the accompanying text reports an intercept variance (τ_{00}) = 3.083, with χ^2 = 2123, p < .0001. The actual intra-class correlation here is 12.3%, meaning that about 12% of the total variance in tolerance at the individual level occurs across PSU units. These results are used as the basis for proceeding with an HLM model of tolerance.

Three HLM models are tested initially: one focusing on the effects of urbanicity and southern region, a second adding individual controls, and a third adding other contextual effects.

FIGURE 10.3 ● THE MEANS OF TOLERANCE SCORES ACROSS 179 PSU'S

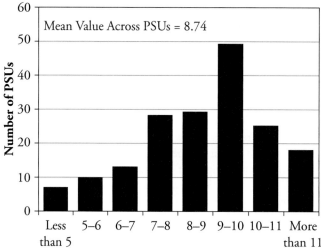

Source: Moore, L. M., & Ovadia, S. (2006, June). Accounting for spatial variation in tolerance: The effects of education and religion. *Social Forces, 84*(4), 2211.

TABLE 10.11 ● AN HLM MODEL FOR TOLERANCE

Individual–level	PSU–level	Model1	Model 2	Model 3
Intercept	Intercept2	8.542***	9.128***	9.317***
	South	−1.547***	−.688***	−.254
Percentage	Metropolitan area	1.526***	.760***	.118
	College Graduates			.053**
	Evangelical Protestant			−.016**
	Mainline Protestant			−.013
	Black Protestant			−.016
	Jewish			−.049
	Other Affiliation			−.001
	No Affiliation			.010
	More than 65 Years Old			−.013
	New Residents			.017
Racial Diversity Index				.003
Year			−.007	−.009
Male			.056	.059
Years of Education			.505***	.501***
Family Income (log)			.327***	.327***
Birth Year			.059***	.059***
Different MA/County than Age 16			.463***	.427***
Race/Ethnicity (White is reference)				
Black			−.499***	−.503*
Hispanic			−1.136***	−1.189***
Asian			−.836**	−.869**
Religious Attendance			−.233***	−.230***
Religion (Catholic is reference)				
Evangelical Protestant			−1.422***	−1.368***
Mainline Protestant			−.154	−.118

(Continued)

	Modell	Model 2	Model 3
TABLE 10.11 ● Continued			
Black Protestant		−.617**	−.560**
Jewish		.371*	.386*
Other affiliation		.147	.132
No affiliation		.853***	.850***
PSU Variance (tau)	1.898	.418	.268
χ^2	1163***	493***	364***

Source: AU: Moore, L. M., & Ovadia, S. (2006, June). Accounting for spatial variation in tolerance: The effects of education and religion. *Social Forces, 84*(4), 2212.

Results for Model 1 show cross-over effects for both urban areas and living in the South. These effects are in opposite directions: Urban areas promote tolerance while living in the South *per se* decreases tolerance. But this finding is before controlling for a standard range of predictors of tolerance at the individual level. Model 2 adds these controls, including year, age, gender, SES, race, mobility, and religion. The effects of the two contextual variables do change somewhat. This suggests that some part of these effects are "compositional," due to the configuration of individual demographic profiles more typical in the South or urban areas that also predict differences in tolerance.

This is still a cross-over effect model, with individual-level controls, and the article notes that the τ_{00} is now only .418. This suggests that a sizable portion of the starting random variance across PSUs is due to compositional factors. But, the remaining Level-2 variance is still very significant, as Table 10.11 shows. Model 3 adds further contextual information, focusing on Level-2 demographic differences. Most of these variables are the mean of the individual predictors at the PSU level. But, importantly, these effects are interpreted as contextual, with emergent causal properties of their own. A higher percentage of college graduates increases tolerance, while a higher percentage of Evangelical Protestants reduces tolerance. These two variables together explain the contextual effect of South/non-South and urban / rural. This article is unusual in its use of related contextual information to explain an observed contextual cross-over effect. Usually, the theorizing that follows from this kind of association is a translation of fallout at the individual level. In this case, the original associations are explained through an association with what can be thought of as norms established by average demographic profiles.

This article also follows the sequence of models we considered in this chapter by hypothesizing and finding cross-over interactions between contextual percentages or means of demographic predictors and individual status on these predicators. For example, is the effect of being an Evangelical Protestant enhanced in areas with more other Evangelical Protestants? If this is the case, this would argue for a normative interpretation of the contextual effect. The generalization of this hypothesis is very important in HLM applications: The effect of an individual status will be multiplied or suppressed depending on the implicit normativity, social similarity, and social support due to the varying prevalence of the same status at the contextual level (Young & Wheaton, 2013).

While the effect of individual educational status and the educational level at the PSU level operate independently, the effect of Evangelical Protestant changes depending on the prevalence of the same religious category in the area. Figure 10.4 plots this interaction.

The plot shows that in general, higher percentages of Evangelical Protestants are associated with less tolerance, but this effect is enhanced for individuals who are Evangelical Protestants

FIGURE 10.4 ● THE INTERACTION BETWEEN INDIVIDUAL AND CONTEXTUAL EVANGELICAL PROTESTANT STATUS

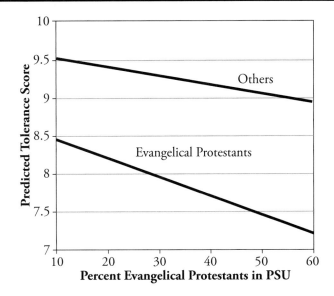

themselves. Notably, and importantly in understanding cross-level effects, there is still a negative effect on tolerance for individuals of other religions. This is one of the core issues in understanding the point of HLM analyses: The effects of context not only shape the meaning of individual statuses, they also have general meaning for everyone in that context.

10.9.2 Contextual Effects in the Darfur Genocide

Hagan and Rymond-Richmond (2008) present a very unusual application of HLM models—by using the collective dynamics of village attacks in Darfur as a contextual explanation for variations in the extent of genocide across places. Both the data they draw from and the nature of the explanation suggest a particularly creative application of an HLM approach. Using a theoretical perspective based on a collective framing process of racially targeted groups, they summarize their approach as follows:

> Our critical collective framing theory argues that this racial targeting was the socially constructed and critically contingent mechanism that mediated the influence of population–resource competition on genocidal victimization. We build on . . . account[s] of the role of cursing in the "righteous slaughters" of intimates and acquaintances. We hypothesize that racial epithets played a parallel role in transforming individual motivation and intent into collectively organized dehumanization and violence. More specifically, we hypothesize that the aggregation and concentration of racial epithets during attacks created a collective effect that intensified the severity of genocidal violence. (2008, p. 876)

This article is meticulous about how cross-level effects could occur in this situation. The first link establishes the importance of government-led "crisis framing," which intensifies conflict among groups and tends to target the most disadvantaged groups. In effect, the process of crisis framing leads to the "unmixing" of previously mixed groups. The second link focuses on the transformation and use of legitimate government authority by illegitimate (gang and militia) groups. In this process, government agents enlist groups, including unofficial militia groups as well as individual citizens, in collective action, trading the legitimacy of government authority for the effective implementation of nonlegitimate ends, in this case, targeted atrocities involving specific Darfuri groups. The third link focuses on essential collective dynamics, referred to as "genocidal priming." A key element at this stage is the use of racial epithets uttered during attacks on villages and the use of dehumanizing language, language that can help trigger collective action and (seemingly) justify it. The identification of a group as distinct ethnically, racially, and religiously supports this process, leading to the view that the targeted group is "subhuman."

As Hagan and Rymond-Richmond note, they are able to analyze the "historically unprecedented" U.S. State Department's Atrocities Documentation Survey collected during the Darfur genocide. These data are the results of interviews of survivors from 22 villages that had at least 15 or more identified survivors (total $N = 932$), thus allowing for a hierarchical approach to the data. The authors use standard health questions with coding of narrative interviews to derive outcome variables for the analysis. Respondents reported up to 20 instances of victimization in their interview, involving themselves, their families, and others they could observe, including issues such as bombings, rape, killing, abduction, assault, destruction of property, and theft. The victimization severity score was constructed based on the number but also legal seriousness rating of the type of victimization. As an example of what these data produce, Hagan and Rymond-Richmond can estimate the effects of both individual reports of racial epithets during attacks and the overall rate of epithets at the contextual level—a crucial contextual variable in their analysis.

We do not report in detail on the first set of results in this article because they use a logistic HLM framework to predict the reporting of racial epithets during attacks on villages. However, these results are essential in developing the bigger picture involved. Interestingly, there were fewer reported rebels in the villages where racial epithets were heard, thus contradicting apparent reasons for an attack. We note the following two preliminary findings: Racial epithets were heard most often when *both* government forces and unofficial militias were joined in the attack (Sudanese and Janjaweed in Table 10.12), and there was an interaction between the presence of governmental and militias forces together and the density of the village in predicting racial epithets.

TABLE 10.12 ◆ CONTEXTUAL EFFECTS IN THE DARFURI GENOCIDE

Model b(se)	Model 1 b(se)	Model 2 b(se)	Model 3 b(se)	Model 4 b(se)	Model 5 b(se)	Model 6 b(se)
Individual Level Respondent						
Age	−.005* (.002)	−.004* (.002)	−.004* (.002)	−.004* (.002)	−.004* (.002)	−.004* (.002)
Gender	−.057 (.056)	−.138** (.055)	−.140** (.056)	−.132* (.058)	−.130* (.059)	−.136** (.058)
Zaghawa		−.023 (.105)	−.023 (.104)			
Fur		.321** (.125)	.257 (.153)			
Masalit		.265** (.099)	.012 (.167)			
Jebal		.224*** (.050)	.256*** (.060)	.174*** (.031)	.261*** (.047)	.214*** (.056)

Model	Model 1	Model 2	Model 3	Model 4	Model 5	Model 6
b(se)	b(se)	b(se)	b(se)	b(se)	b(se)	b(se)
Attacking Groups						
Janjaweed	.157 (.178)	.162 (.183)	.144 (.184)	.145 (.194)	.143 (.189)	.137 (.191)
Sudanese	.375** (.156)	.386** (.150)	.372** (.151)	.375** (.151)	.365** (.151)	.374** (.152)
Sudanese and Janjaweed	.509*** (.110)	.432*** (.116)	.422*** (.117)	.428*** (.121)	.416*** (.123)	.425*** (.125)
Rebel Activity						
Rebels in Settlement	.138 (.239)	.228 (.209)	.229 (.211)	.215 (.212)	.204 (.217)	.210 (.218)
Missing Rebel Data	.330** (.111)	.306*** (.085)	.295*** (.085)	−.314*** (.094)	−.290** (.089)	−.286** (.088)
Particular Targets Women		.448*** (.086)	.442*** (.087)	.467*** (.093)	.462*** (.095)	.457*** (.094)
Attacks						
First Peak		.223** (.078)	.216** (.079)	.210** (.078)	.189** (.075)	.199** (.078)
Second Peak		.190* (.093)	.189* (.091)	.189* (.091)	.211** (.090)	.220** (.090)
Bombing		.061 (.045)	.067 (.045)	.054 (.043)	.051 (.037)	.058 (.041)
Racial Intent						
Individual Racial Intent		.387*** (.067)	.387*** (.087)	.397*** (.085)	.365*** (.083)	.367*** (.084)
Settlement Clusler Level						
Settlement Density				.686* (.316)	.449 (.299)	.243 (.405)
Bombing						−.137 (.288)
Rebel News						−.032 (.115)
Collective Racial Intent			1.225* (.565)		1.107* (.553)	1.066* (.518)
Cross–Level Interaction						
Bombing X Collective Racial Intent					.781** (.306)	.747* (.341)
Bombing, X Settlement Denttity					.131 (.156)	.133 (.166)
Intercept	−.023	−.011	−.077	−.013	−.012	−.014

Note: N=932 individuals (Level I) and 22 settlement areas (Level 2).

*p<.05; ** p<.01; *** p<.001

Source: Hagan, J., & Rymond-Richmond, W. (2008). The collective dynamics of racial dehumanization and genocidal victimization in Darfur. *American Sociological p values Review, 73*(6), 890. www.jstor.org/stable/25472566

This background leads to the assessment of victimization severity in Table 10.12, from the article. Model 1 shows again that the combination of governmental and militia forces increased the severity of victimization, but also, governmental forces alone also increased victimization to a lesser extent.

Models 2 and 3 show that both the presence of individually reported racial intent and collective racial intent increase the chances of more severe victimization in these attacks. Note that this is a classic HLM cross-over effect: The individual experience of the predictor is only part of the story. Importantly, collective intent—the widespread communication of racial epithets—increases the level of victimization independently and generally. Note also that the effect of joined government and militia forces is only partially explained by Model 3, by about 20%. Although settlement density is initially significant in Model 4, it is not significant in Model 5 while collective racial intent is significant. This suggests that settlement density may have helped activate collective racial intent—that is, collective intent mediates the effect of settlement density. Models 5 and 6 incorporate cross-level interactions because bombing is individually reported at the individual level. Clearly, bombing multiplies the victimization when occurring in a context of racial intent.

As an example of the application of HLM, this paper obviously has unusual features, both in terms of the data and the variables considered. This is not a standard neighborhood effects model, using census data. As a result, this paper especially helps to suggest the range of applications that are possible using the HLM framework. This is important because the predominant emphasis in HLM-based modeling is on census-based distinctions for the effects of context, and it will be important going forward to find and apply unusual sources of contextual data—as in this example.

10.9.3 The Effects of Classroom Context on First Grade Children

We continue our consideration of unusual contexts by focusing on an article by Melissa Milkie and Catharine Warner, entitled "Classroom Learning Environments and the Mental Health of First Grade Children," in the *Journal of Health and Social Behavior* in 2011. This paper is possible because of a unique survey of preschool children in the United States, called the ECLS-K, initially sampling over 20,000 children in kindergarten in about 1,200 schools. Interviews were completed in the spring of the first grade.

Although there is a large literature on school effects, as we have seen, this paper moves down one level of context to consider the effects of classroom differences, reported by the teacher. The teacher is an important authority figure at the beginning of the educational experience: Teachers have attitudes, are in professional social networks, have different skills, and different priorities, but they are clearly operating in very different resource and behavioral contexts. And the focus on first grade children is important, since many believe this is an origin point for expectations about later educational achievement.

Features of the classroom environment reported by the teacher include six types of variables: (1) the lack of material classroom resources; (2) lack of respect from colleagues; (3) low standards at the school level; (4) interference due to bureaucratic paperwork; (5) interference due to problem behavior in the class; and (6) the number of children in the class at below-grade reading level. Multiple outcome measures are considered, but here we focus on individual learning problems, rated on a scale indicating "difficulties with attentiveness, task persistence, and flexibility" (2011, p. 8).

Table 10.13 from the article reports results for learning problems. Many of the individual-level predictors are as expected—and many of the classic individual predictors are in fact included in this study. Putting aside the effects of teacher characteristics, which particularly could be confounded with school-level effects, we see that a number of features of classroom context independently contribute to the level of learning problems in first grade (Model 2), including the absence of standard classroom materials (therefore, indirectly, funding), a teacher who is not respected by colleagues, interference from problem behavior—which affects the learning chances of everyone in the class—and the contextual effect of the prevalence of children at below-grade reading level. This last finding is important since it suggests that segregation by ability or quality of schools has a multiplying effect on educational inequality.

The absence of an interaction between child SES and classroom conditions, reported in the text, is also important because it implies that classroom problems affect students from a wide array of backgrounds. However, there is an interaction between Black and low standards, indicating that the effects of low standards are worse among White students. This would be expected in a situation where White students are more typically privileged, and thus low standards make a difference.

This study identifies a set of cross-over effects that shift the chances of early learning problems for all children in the classroom. This is the logic of the cross-over effect: It is not just a signal that children who would have learning problems will experience worse problems in these classrooms. In fact, this is *not the finding here.* The finding is that all children are more likely to experience learning problems in certain classrooms.

TABLE 10.13 ● CLASSROOM EFFECTS ON LEARNING PROBLEMS IN FIRST GRADE

Variable	Model I		Model 2		Model 3	
	B	*SE*	*B*	*SE*	*B*	*SE*
Intercept	1.920***	.008	1.921***	.008	1.922***	.008
Child characteristics						
Boy	.294***	.012	.292***	.012	.292***	.012
Black	.151***	.023	.126***	.024	.129***	.024
Hispanic	.019	.022	.005	.023	.003	.023
Asian	−.130***	.034	−.124***	.034	−.127***	.034
Other	.072*	.031	.052	.031	.045	.031
SES	−.145***	.009	−.135***	.010	−.135***	.010
Foreign–born parent	−.041	.022	−.054*	.022	−.053*	.022
Two biological parents	−.148***	.016	−.146***	.016	−.146***	.016
Full–time maternal employment	.035**	.013	.036**	.013	.035**	.013
Hours of nonparental care	.002*	.001	.002*	.001	.002*	.001
Moves	.016	.013	.018	.013	.018	.013
Midwest	.045	.025	.044	.025	.043	.025
South	.007	.023	.009	.024	.010	.024

(Continued)

TABLE 10.13 ● Continued

Variable	Model I		Model 2		Model 3	
	B	*SE*	*B*	*SE*	*B*	*SE*
West	.027	.026	.007	.027	.009	.027
Urbanicity	−.016	.011	−.024*	.011	−.022	.011
Teacher and school characteristics						
Teacher Black			.070*	.034	.73*	.034
Teacher Hispanic			.071*	.035	.070*	.035
Teacher other			.057	.045	.055	.045
Teacher graduate degree			.027	.018	.027	.018
Teacher experience			−.001	.001	−.001	.001
Private school			.078**	.024	.078***	.024
Class size			−.001	.002	−.001	.002
Learning environment						
Lack of classroom resources			.044*	.019	.044*	.019
Teacher feels low respect from colleagues			.041***	.012	.041***	.012
Teacher feels school has low standards			.006	.010	.008	.010
Teacher feels interference from paperwork			.007	.008	.007	.008
Teacher feels interference from problem behavior			.018*	.008	.018*	.008
Number of peers below level in reading			.009**	.003	.009***	.003
Interaction effects						
Black x Low Standards					−.058*	.025
Conditional variance components						
Among classrooms	.064***	.005	.060***	.005	.058***	.005
Proportion explained	—		.065		.084	
Among Individuals	.362***	−.006				
Proportion explained	.110					
—log–likelihood	21,178.400		21.196.600		21,315.600	

Source: Milkie, M. H., & Warner, C. H. (2011). Classroom learning environments and the mental health of first grade children. *Journal of Health and Social Behavior*, 52, 12.

Concluding Words

We began this chapter with examples that typify the emphasis in the current literature on contextual effects, focusing on the effects of neighborhoods and of schools. All of the HLM literatures have relevance for each other, however, since often the focus is on contexts that compete in the end. In the Milkie and Warner paper, for example, the question is whether these effects reflect or stand apart from standard school effects. And there is a developing literature on the meeting point between school and neighborhood effects on children.

We chose examples from the literature to demonstrate how broadly HLM models could be applied. The contexts under discussion in these papers included cities and counties, villages, and school classrooms. There are a myriad of other possibilities: It is possible to ask important questions about variations across total institutions, such as prisons, about nations; varying in social policy, about First Nations reservations; varying in culture and history; about clearly bounded social networks, about the coaching of sports teams, about variations in building style in multiple-dwelling housing, about variations in family structure, and . . . fill in your own blanks. The issue is finding the appropriate data to promote the kinds of questions that are possible.

A common mistake in thinking about HLM models is that they are merely a statistical adjustment for respondent clustering and thus overlapping left-out causes and correlated error terms across individuals sharing space or common membership. This is a misunderstanding of the theoretical possibilities the HLM defines and makes possible. In the Hagan and Rymond-Richmond paper, they study *both* the effect of individually reported racial intent and the average-level of racial intent at the contextual level. Each can have an effect, and the HLM model allows us to see a separate role for each. Without the clear distinction made by considering nested levels of social reality, we may not ask these questions. In the HLM model, one of the most useful features is the ability to ask whether the effect of one's own education (an individual status) depends on the educational context in which you were raised (the prevalent status in the context), either at the family or the neighborhood level, or on the quality of the school contexts in which you were educated. These questions point to cross-level interactions that raise and speak to important policy questions we simply do not have the answer to, sufficiently, at this time.

In the next chapter, following the general logic of this book, we expand the HLM model to include other kinds of dependent variables, invoking the general linear model and focusing on cross-level logistic and Poisson models.

Practice Questions

1. Results are attached (Table 10.A) for an analysis of neighborhood effects on the body mass index, as a measure of obesity, using the 2011 Toronto Study of Neighbourhoods, Health and Well-Being (O'Campo et al., 2015). This is a study of adults from 25–65 in 87 Toronto neighbourhoods (census tracts), with 20–30 respondents per neighborhood, and a total *N* of 2,412.

The variables used in these results are

Level 1
- *cage:* Age in years, group-mean centered (this is the focal Level 1 variable considered in interactions across neighborhoods)
- *cfemale:* A dummy variable for female, also group-mean centered

Level 2

- ***poverty1:*** The percentage of households in the neighborhood below the poverty line
- ***perlone:*** The percentage of lone parent families in the neighborhood, as a percentage of all Census families
- ***physical_mn:*** This is the mean level of physical activity among neighborhood residents.

The purpose in this analysis is to estimate the effects of poverty, percentage lone parent families, and average levels of physical activity in the neighborhood on the body mass index and to assess interactions of the first two with age—interactions that tell us how these neighborhood factors change in impact as we get older.

Results from four models are shown: a one-way ANOVA, a cross-over effects model for all Level 2 variables, a random coefficients model for the effects of age and female, and a final model. The final model focuses on possible cross-level interactions with age; other possible interactions are not considered here.

Answer these questions:

a. Using the results of the one-way ANOVA, calculate and interpret in words (one sentence) the intraclass correlation. Do you conclude that there are neighborhood differences in obesity?

b. The cross-over effects model shows the effects of poverty, percentage lone parent families, and the average level of physical activity per resident in the neighborhood. What percentage of the variance in body mass index across neighborhoods is explained by these neighborhood-level variables?

c. Using the cross-over effects model, does the average level of physical activity in the neighborhood affect obesity and in what direction?

d. The random coefficients model includes the fixed and random effects of both Level 1 variables. The run of PROC MIXED used here is shown below:

```
proc mixed data=hlmnehw_complete_weight
noclprint covtest ;
class ctname;
model bmi = cage cfemale / solution covb ;
random intercept  cage cfemale / sub=ctname
type=un ;
weight nehwweightv2;
title 'random coefficients model'; run;
```

Use the estimates in the "Covariance Parameter Estimates" table in the output to decide whether each of the Level 1 variables have significant variation in their slopes across neighborhoods and cite the evidence used from this table in each case.

e. Using the results of the random coefficients model and earlier results, calculate the percentage of individual-level variance in obesity (BMI) explained by the Level 1 variables in this equation.

f. In a "final model," two interactions are added: between percentage below the poverty line and age and between percentage lone parent families and age. Evaluate the significance of each interaction (assuming borderline cases are significant) and where significant, interpret the interaction by calculating the effect of ***the neighborhood measure*** at two levels of age: -10 and +10 years below and above the mean of 0. Note here that the neighborhood measure is considered focal, and age is the modifier.

g. Using the "final model," write out the ***Level 1 and Level 2 equations*** for this model—but not the combined model.

TABLE 10.A ⬡ NEIGHBORHOOD EFFECTS ON THE BODY MASS INDEX

One-Way ANOVA

Dimensions	
Covariance Parameters	2
Columns in X	1
Columns in Z Per Subject	1
Subjects	87
Max Obs Per Subject	31

Covariance Parameter Estimates					
Cov Parm	Subject	Estimate	Standard Error	Z Value	Pr > Z
Intercept	ctname	15.9441	3.0541	5.22	<.0001
Residual		153.41	4.5410	33.78	<.0001

Solution for Fixed Effects					
Effect	Estimate	Standard Error	DF	t Value	Pr > |t|
Intercept	28.6179	0.5059	86	56.57	<.0001

The Cross-Over Effects Model

Dimensions	
Covariance Parameters	2
Columns in X	4
Columns in Z Per Subject	1
Subjects	87
Max Obs Per Subject	31

Covariance Parameter Estimates					
Cov Parm	Subject	Estimate	Standard Error	Z Value	Pr > Z
Intercept	ctname	12.9852	2.7008	4.81	<.0001
Residual		153.44	4.5431	33.77	<.0001

Solution for Fixed Effects					
Effect	Estimate	Standard Error	DF	t Value	Pr > |t|
Intercept	34.6514	3.1406	84	11.03	<.0001
poverty1	0.1957	0.06660	2265	2.94	0.0033
perlone	−0.2132	0.09061	2265	−2.35	0.0187
physical_mn	−2.2997	1.0145	2265	−2.27	0.0235

The Random Coefficients Model

Dimensions	
Covariance Parameters	7
Columns in X	3
Columns in Z Per Subject	3
Subjects	87
Max Obs Per Subject	31

(Continued)

TABLE 10.A ● **Continued**

Covariance Parameter Estimates					
Cov Parm	Subject	Estimate	Standard Error	Z Value	Pr Z
UN(1,1)	ctname	9.2622	2.0923	4.43	<.0001
UN(2,1)	ctname	−0.4426	0.1121	−3.95	<.0001
UN(2,2)	ctname	0.02890	0.01034	2.79	0.0026
UN(3,1)	ctname	−11.6981	2.6591	−4.40	<.0001
UN(3,2)	ctname	0.1978	0.1759	1.12	0.2607
UN(3,3)	ctname	19.3379	5.5480	3.49	0.0002
Residual		141.61	4.2993	32.94	<.0001

Solution for Fixed Effects					
Effect	Estimate	Standard Error	DF	t Value	Pr > |t|
Intercept	28.7425	0.4224	86	68.04	<.0001
cage	0.07955	0.03076	86	2.59	0.0114
cfemale	−2.5613	0.7037	86	−3.64	0.0005

The Full Model

Dimensions	
Covariance Parameters	7
Columns in X	8
Columns in Z Per Subject	3
Subjects	87
Max Obs Per Subject	31

Covariance Parameter Estimates					
Cov Parm	Subject	Estimate	Standard Error	Z Value	Pr Z
UN(1,1)	ctname	7.2952	1.8702	3.90	<.0001
UN(2,1)	ctname	−0.3783	0.1010	−3.75	0.0002
UN(2,2)	ctname	0.02028	0.009399	2.16	0.0155
UN(3,1)	ctname	−11.0825	2.5111	−4.41	<.0001
UN(3,2)	ctname	0.1369	0.1651	0.83	0.4068
UN(3,3)	ctname	19.4646	5.5477	3.51	0.0002
Residual		141.75	4.3061	32.92	<.0001

Solution for Fixed Effects					
Effect	Estimate	Standard Error	DF	t Value	Pr > |t|
Intercept	31.9053	2.2854	84	13.96	<.0001
poverty1	0.1351	0.05083	2091	2.66	0.0079
perlone	−0.09149	0.06716	2091	−1.36	0.1733
physical_mn	−1.6536	0.7531	2091	−2.20	0.0282
cage	−0.1280	0.08558	84	−1.50	0.1384
cfemale	−2.6215	0.7049	86	−3.72	0.0004
poverty1*cage	−0.00778	0.004075	2091	−1.91	0.0564
perlone*cage	0.01757	0.005408	2091	3.25	0.0012

2. Results are attached for (Table 10.B) an analysis of the same data as used in the previous question. In this case, physical activity is the dependent variable. The variables used in this analysis are

Level 1

- **physical:** An index of physical activity within the last week, measured by frequency of participation in three activities each day (bicycling, walking for 10 minutes or more, and fitness or sports)
- **age:** In years (this is the focal Level 1 variable considered in interactions across neighborhoods).
- **reduc:** Education in years
- **female:** A dummy variable for female

Level 2

- **SES:** This is a measure of neighborhood disadvantage using three commonly used items: (1) poverty rate, (2) the unemployment rate of males over the age of 15; and, (3) percentage of lone parents in the neighborhood. These measures are standardized and combined in this index. Higher scores stand for **disadvantage.**
- **totservices:** This is a total count of all community services available in the neighborhood, based on 2010 administrative data on community resources (including nonprofit childcare services, recreational facilities and community centers, social organizations, health resources, housing services, youth programs, and support groups).

Results from four models are shown: a one-way ANOVA, a cross-over effects model for SES and community services, a random coefficients model for the effects of age, education, and gender, and a final model. The final model focuses on possible cross-level interactions with age; other possible interactions are not considered here.

Answer these questions:

a. Using the results of the one-way ANOVA, calculate and interpret in words (one sentence) the intra-class correlation. Do you conclude that there are neighborhood differences in physical activity?

b. The cross-over effects model shows the effects of SES and community services. What percentage of the variance in activity across neighborhoods is explained by these two neighborhood-level variables?

c. The random coefficients model includes the fixed and random effects of all three Level 1 variables. The run of PROC MIXED used here is shown following:

```
proc mixed data=hlmnehw_complete_
weight  noclprint covtest ;
class ctname;
model physical = age reduc female / solution
covb ;
random intercept age reduc female /
sub=ctname type=un ;
weight nehwweight;
run;
```

Use the estimates in the "Covariance Parameter Estimates" table to decide whether each of the three Level 1 variables have significant variation in their slopes across neighborhoods and cite the evidence used from this table in each case.

d. Using the results of the random coefficients model and earlier results, calculate the percentage of individual-level variance in physical activity explained by the three Level 1 variables in this equation.

e. In a "final model," two interactions are added: between neighborhood SES disadvantage and age and between total community services and age. Evaluate the significance of each interaction, and where significant, interpret the interaction by describing (in words) how age alters the impact of the neighborhood measure. Note here that the neighborhood measure is focal and age is the modifier.

f. Using the results throughout, specify a simplified "best" model, by writing out the Level 1 and Level 2 equations that represent this model. Use these equations to specify a combined model.

TABLE 10.B ● NEIGHBORHOOD EFFECTS ON PHYSICAL ACTIVITY

One-Way ANOVA

Dimensions	
Covariance Parameters	2
Columns in X	1
Columns in Z Per Subject	1
Subjects	87
Max Obs Per Subject	31

Covariance Parameter Estimates					
Cov Parm	Subject	Estimate	Standard Error	Z Value	Pr > Z
Intercept	ctname	0.2167	0.04473	4.85	<.0001
Residual		1.9779	0.05801	34.10	<.0001

Solution for Fixed Effects					
Effect	Estimate	Standard Error	DF	t Value	Pr > |t|
Intercept	2.4470	0.05837	86	41.93	<.0001

The Cross-Over Effects Model

Dimensions	
	2
Columns in X	3
Columns in Z Per Subject	1
Subjects	87
Max Obs Per Subject	31

Covariance Parameter Estimates					
Cov Parm	Subject	Estimate	Standard Error	Z Value	Pr > Z
Intercept	ctname	0.1549	0.03590	4.31	<.0001
Residual		1.9781	0.05803	34.09	<.0001

Solution for Fixed Effects					
Effect	Estimate	Standard Error	DF	t Value	Pr > |t|
Intercept	2.3560	0.05845	85	40.31	<.0001
ses	−0.1701	0.06242	2322	−2.72	0.0065
totservices	0.03521	0.009542	2322	3.69	0.0002

The Random Coefficients Model

Dimensions	
Covariance Parameters	11
Columns in X	4
Columns in Z Per Subject	4
Subjects	87
Max Obs Per Subject	31

Covariance Parameter Estimates

Cov Parm	Subject	Estimate	Standard Error	Z Value	Pr Z
UN(1,1)	ctname	0.2088	0.05576	3.74	<.0001
UN(2,1)	ctname	−0.04947	0.02151	−2.30	0.0214
UN(2,2)	ctname	0.03836	0.01629	2.36	0.0093
UN(3,1)	ctname	−0.01804	0.02409	−0.75	0.4540
UN(3,2)	ctname	0.01421	0.01363	1.04	0.2971
UN(3,3)	ctname	0.06654	0.01956	3.40	0.0003
UN(4,1)	ctname	−0.08230	0.05211	−1.58	0.1142
UN(4,2)	ctname	0.01465	0.02489	0.59	0.5560
UN(4,3)	ctname	−0.00683	0.02867	−0.24	0.8116
UN(4,4)	ctname	0.2084	0.07916	2.63	0.0042
Residual		1.8208	0.05601	32.51	<.0001

Solution for Fixed Effects

Effect	Estimate	Standard Error	DF	t Value	Pr > |t|
Intercept	2.4039	0.06643	86	36.18	<.0001
AGE	−0.05344	0.03673	86	−1.45	0.1494
reduc	0.06947	0.04080	86	1.70	0.0922
FEMALE	0.00	0.07715	86	0.54	0.5930

The Full Model

Dimensions

Covariance Parameters	11
Columns in X	8
Columns in Z Per Subject	4
Subjects	87
Max Obs Per Subject	31

Number of Observations

Number of Observations Read	2412
Number of Observations Used	2404
Number of Observations Not Used	8

Covariance Parameter Estimates

Cov Parm	Subject	Estimate	Standard Error	Z Value	Pr Z
UN(1,1)	ctname	0.1736	0.04966	3.49	0.0002
UN(2,1)	ctname	−0.03825	0.01934	−1.98	0.0480
UN(2,2)	ctname	0.03039	0.01526	1.99	0.0232
UN(3,1)	ctname	−0.02119	0.02272	−0.93	0.3511
UN(3,2)	ctname	0.01533	0.01314	1.17	0.2432
UN(3,3)	ctname	0.06741	0.01959	3.44	0.0003
UN(4,1)	ctname	−0.08993	0.04990	−1.80	0.0715
UN(4,2)	ctname	0.01460	0.02378	0.61	0.5392
UN(4,3)	ctname	−0.00850	0.02862	−0.30	0.7664
UN(4,4)	ctname	0.2043	0.07828	2.61	0.0045
Residual		1.8214	0.05606	32.49	<.0001

(Continued)

TABLE 10.B ● **Continued**

		Solution for Fixed Effects			
Effect	**Estimate**	**Standard Error**	**DF**	**t Value**	**Pr > |t|**
Intercept	2.3485	0.06845	85	34.31	<.0001
ses	−0.1806	0.05984	2055	−3.02	0.0026
totservices	0.02547	0.009707	2055	2.62	0.0088
AGE	0.007750	0.04044	84	0.19	0.8485
reduc	0.07631	0.04092	86	1.86	0.0656
FEMALE	0.03161	0.07673	86	0.41	0.6814
totservices*AGE	−0.01906	0.007092	2055	−2.69	0.0073
ses*AGE	−0.03533	0.04099	2055	−0.86	0.3888

3. Results are attached (Table 10.C) for four hierarchical linear models estimated in PROC MIXED to assess individual and neighborhood effects on *internalizing problems* in children, using the Toronto Study of Intact Families.

At the neighborhood level, one variable is considered: *pcnohs,* the percentage of individuals in the neighborhood with less than a high school education.

At the individual level, the effects of two variables are considered: (1) *femalec,* a group-mean centered dummy variable for a female child and (2) *pareducc,* the maximum level of education of the two biological parents in years (also group-mean centered). These variables were considered in that order in the results.

Results of four models are shown: Model 1 is a one-way ANOVA model; Model 2 is a cross-over effects model, Model 3 is a random Coefficients model, and Model 4 is the "full" model incorporating results from the previous models.

Answer these questions:

a. Find the appropriate result in the appropriate model to calculate the percentage of the variance in internalizing problems that can be attributed to differences between neighborhoods.

b. How much of the variance between neighborhoods is explained by the percentage of individuals with less than a high school education?

c. In the random coefficients model and sticking to strict standards of significance ($p < .05$), which Level 1 variables have random slopes at the neighborhood level? What do these random slopes mean?

d. Assume there is an interaction between parental education and the percentage with less than a high school education in the final model (it is not quite significant at the two-tailed level, but is significant one-tailed). Given this interaction, who has more internalizing problems: a child in a neighborhood with a high percentage of adults with less than a high school education (at 11%, the 75th percentile) and whose parents have a university education or a child in a neighborhood with the *same* high percentage of adults with less than a high school education whose parents have a high school education?

e. Using the results of the final model, write out the implied specification of the "best" model, first as a two-level HLM model and then as a combined model. Explain how the previous results leads to this final model, in terms of which terms are included and excluded.

TABLE 10.C ● NEIGHBORHOOD EFFECTS ON INTERNALIZING PROBLEMS IN CHILDREN

1 Way ANOVA Model

The Mixed Procedure

Covariance Parameter Estimates

Cov Parm	Subject	Estimate	Standard Error	Z Value	Pr > Z
Intercept	cmact	0.1062	0.03466	3.06	0.0011
Residual		0.9199		18.63	<.0001

Fit Statistics

-2 Res Log Likelihood	2608.4
AIC (smaller is better)	2612.4
AICC (smaller is better)	2612.4
BIC (smaller is better)	2619.6

Solution for Fixed Effects

Effect	Estimate	Standard Error	DF	t Value	Pr > |t|
Intercept	0.006323	0.04133	280	0.15	0.8785

Cross-Over Effects Model

The Mixed Procedure

Covariance Parameter Estimates

Cov Parm	Subject	Estimate	Standard Error	Z Value	Pr > Z
Intercept	cmact	0.09723	0.03351	2.90	0.0019
Residual		0.9198	0.04926	18.67	<.0001

Fit Statistics

-2 Res Log Likelihood	2610.3
AIC (smaller is better)	2614.3
AICC (smaller is better)	2614.4
BIC (smaller is better)	2621.6

Solution for Fixed Effects

Effect	Estimate	Standard Error	DF	t Value	Pr > |t|
Intercept	−0.1449	0.07242	279	−2.00	0.0464
pcnohs	0.01588	0.006282	279	2.53	0.0120

Random Coefficients Model

The Mixed Procedure

Cov Parm	Subject	Estimate	Standard Error	Z Value	Pr Z
UN(1,1)	cmact	0.1211	0.03514	3.45	0.0003
UN(2,1)	cmact	0.01135	0.04878	0.23	0.8161
UN(2,2)	cmact	0.1318	0.1009	1.31	0.0956
UN(3,1)	cmact	−0.01688	0.009339	−1.81	0.0706
UN(3,2)	cmact	0.000309	0.01856	0.02	0.9867
UN(3,3)	cmact	0.01255	0.004948	2.54	0.0056
Residual		0.8032	0.04959	16.20	<.0001

(*Continued*)

TABLE 10.C ● **Continued**

Fit Statistics

-2 Res Log Likelihood	2569.1
AIC (smaller is better)	2583.1
AICC (smaller is better)	2583.3
BIC (smaller is better)	2608.6

Null Model Likelihood Ratio Test

DF	Chi-Square	Pr > ChiSq
6	40.33	<.0001

Solution for Fixed Effects

Effect	Estimate	Standard Error	DF	t Value	Pr > |t|
Intercept	0.004239	0.04066	280	0.10	0.9170
femalec	0.1721	0.08927	589	1.93	0.0544
pareducc	−0.04124	0.01783	589	−2.31	0.0210

Full Model

The Mixed Procedure

Covariance Parameter Estimates

Cov Parm	Subject	Estimate	Standard Error	Z Value	Pr Z
UN(1,1)	cmact	0.1078	0.03380	3.19	0.0007
UN(2,1)	cmact	−0.01187	0.008968	−1.32	0.1856
UN(2,2)	cmact	0.01117	0.004711	2.37	0.0089
Residual		0.8309	0.04819	17.24	<.0001

Fit Statistics

-2 Res Log Likelihood	2581.8
AIC (smaller is better)	2589.8
AICC (smaller is better)	2589.8
BIC (smaller is better)	2604.3

Null Model Likelihood Ratio Test

DF	Chi-Square	Pr > ChiSq
3	30.87	<.0001

Solution for Fixed Effects

Effect	Estimate	Standard Error	DF	t Value	Pr > |t|
Intercept	−0.1380	0.07162	279	−1.93	0.0550
pcnohs	0.01475	0.006190	279	2.38	0.0179
femalec	0.1779	0.07951	588	2.24	0.0256
pareducc	0.007603	0.03125	588	0.24	0.8079
pcnohs*pareducc	−0.00556	0.003122	588	−1.78	0.0753

THE GENERALIZED HIERARCHICAL LINEAR MODEL

In the first section of this book, we developed a more "flexible" approach to regression, finally arriving at the generalized linear model. This model collects a number of variants of regression into a single organizational framework, using the common concept of a *link function*. A link function linearizes an otherwise nonlinear model so that the actual regression model we see involves some transformed linear version of an underlying nonlinear model.

Here we invoke the same type of generalization, this time applied to the hierarchical linear model. The generalized HLM (GHLM) has a linear predictor component—that is, the structural model, as usual, as well as a specific *error structure*, depending on the type of nonlinear model estimated, and a *link function*, which states the way in which the nonlinear function is transformed.

The GHLM raises some new issues in estimation, but the model mainly departs from the usual HLM ***at Level 1 only***. That is because the structure of the errors at Level 1 are different in a nonlinear model and because the dependent variable being modeled is a transformation of *Y*. The model at Level 2 and beyond is essentially the same as the regular HLM because the basic fact that coefficients from Level 1 are being modeled at Level 2 across a set of level-2 units still holds. We consider first an example of HLM modified to estimate a logistic model at Level 1.

11.1 MULTILEVEL LOGISTIC REGRESSION

Recall that the link function in the case of logistic regression for a dichotomous outcome is

$$L(y_i) = \ln\left(\frac{P}{1-P}\right)$$

and the error distribution is binomial. The actual observed Y_{ij} in groups is dichotomous, typically coded 1 and 0. In a one-way ANOVA model estimated across groups, we can consider the observed *Y* as having the following structure:

$$Y_{ij} = P_j + e_{ij}$$

where P_j is the probability that $Y = 1$ in group j. The error in this model has a mean of 0, as usual, but it can only take on two values as a deviation from the $P_j : -P_j$, and $1 - P_j$. When $Y = 1$ the error is by definition $1 - P_j$, and when $Y = 0$, the error is $-P_j$. This error structure means that we do not have a normal distribution of errors and if there are Xs in the model, we also do not have constant error variance. The preceding model amounts to a ***linear probability model***, as discussed in the chapter on logistic regression.

Instead of modeling the actual Y_{ij}, we model the $Pr(Y)$, in other words, P_{ij}, using a logistic link function at Level 1. This transforms the Level-1 model using generalized linear model notation from Chapter 5 to η, which is in this case the log of the odds of Y. That is

$$L(y_{ij}) = \eta_{ij} = \ln\left(\frac{P_{ij}}{1 - P_{ij}}\right)$$

Now the ***combined*** one-way ANOVA model is

$$\eta_{ij} = \ln\left(\frac{P_{ij}}{1 - P_{ij}}\right) = \gamma_{00} + u_{0j}$$

Note that there is no Level-1 error in this model. This is because the error is a direct function of the estimated P_{ij} and is not a separate parameter. In fact, this Level-1 error variance is simply $P_{ij}(1 - P_{ij})$, and its distribution follows the binomial distribution, not the normal. When we consider Xs in the model, we have at Level 1

$$\eta_{ij} = \beta_{0j} + \beta_{1j}X_{ij} + u_{0j}$$

There is still random variance at Level 2, since the model at Level 2 is a model for the coefficients, with variance across groups.

11.1.1 Estimation

Estimation of GHLM models is even more fragile than in the linear HLM case. As such, there are many approaches to estimation. The best known approaches include (a) a "*penalized quasi-likelihood*" approach (PQL); (b) numerical integration approaches; and (c) Laplace approximation of ML. Comments on the relative merits of these approaches suggest that the latter two are often superior to the first. Recent software implements all three approaches. Laplace approximation is computer intensive but tends to be less biased, with smaller standard errors, than PQL.

Most of the available algorithms used to estimate these models are quite sensitive to model conditions—in fact, many model conditions. Sparse data, correlated variables, complex models, multiple random effects, and very large samples can all cause problems with convergence. When it comes to software choices, it is important to point out that these methods are in a state of ongoing development, and although we use a SAS-based example here, it may be a good idea with these methods to experiment with other programs that are dedicated to HLM models as well.

Some words of advice—do not ask too much of these models. Start simply and proceed step-by-step. Investigate the structure of the clustering in your data, looking for sparse Level-2 units. Balance the issues of sample size and the distribution of the dependent variable: Generally outcomes that are rare run into trouble more often in smaller samples, and so more evenly distributed outcomes will work better. Rare outcomes may require larger samples, but these have their own problems. In general, the more complex the model, the less likely it will converge.

11.1.2 Generalization to Other Logistic Models

The principles of applying the hierarchical model to logistic regression extend to the case of the ordinal (*cumulative logit*) and multinomial models as well. In each case, the same transformations of the basic logistic model to accommodate multiple outcome categories apply at Level 1. In the multinomial case, of course, there are multiple Level-1 models—in fact, M-1 models for an M category outcome. Accordingly, there would be M-1 *sets* of models for Level-2 coefficients in the multinomial model.

11.1.3 Why Use a Hierarchical Approach?

A paper by O'Campo, Xue, Wang, and Caughy (1997) discusses explicitly the implications of estimating the usual individual-level logistic regression when there are Level-2 effects on the Level-1 outcome and model. In 1997, using an individual-level logistic approach was more the norm than it may be now. What follows is from the pre-publication paper—*Economic, Physical, and Political Characteristics of Neighborhood of Residence and the Risk of Low Birth Weight*—that explicitly discussed the differences between a standard logistic regression approach and the HLM approach. In a later section, we will discuss the actual published paper.

The abstract of this paper is instructive about the problem and is reproduced following:

Abstract

Low birth weight remains an important public health problem in the U.S. Most research on low birth weight focuses on individual-level determinants of low birth weight such as health behaviors or use of prenatal care. We sought to determine how characteristics of residential neighborhood influenced low birth weight. We first present a theoretically based framework that describes the mechanisms by which neighborhoods can lead to adverse health outcomes. Our research question centered on whether neighborhood economic, physical and political characteristics directly and indirectly influenced the risk of low birth weight and whether neighborhood factors moderated the relation between individual-level risk factors and low birth weight. We used methods of multi-level statistical modeling to investigate our research question. Direct neighborhood level determinants of low birth weight included high crime (OR=2.49), low wealth (OR=5.50) and low level of political organization (OR=2.54). Interactions and confounding between individual- and neighborhood-level characteristics were observed. When multi-level models accounted for neighborhood levels of wealth, the two-fold gap between African-American and White births was no longer significant. Methods of multi-level modeling facilitated testing of a model emphasizing environmental and social factors in determining poor health outcome. The application of such models also resulted in a better explanatory model for low birth weight. (O'Campo et al., 1997)

This study posited a number of contextual factors that may directly or indirectly influence the risk of low birth weight in newborns and used data from 29 neighborhoods in Baltimore to study pregnancy outcomes. The paper directly compares results from using standard logistic regression versus a hierarchical logistic regression, which takes into account both the random and fixed effects of neighborhood characteristics (including SES characteristics, crime, crowding, unemployment, and neighborhood organizations).

The general form of the Level-2 model is

$$\text{Logodds(LBW)} = \beta_{0j} + \beta_{1j} \text{ Maternal Race}_{ij} + \beta_{2j} \text{ Married}_{ij}$$

$$\beta_{0j} = \gamma_{00} + \gamma_{01} \text{ Wealth}_j + u_{0j}$$

$$\beta_{1j} = \gamma_{10} + \gamma_{11} \text{ Wealth}_j + u_{1j}$$

$$\beta_{2j} = \gamma_{20} + \gamma_{21} \text{ Wealth}_j + u_{2j}$$

In fact, various Level-1 and Level-2 predictors are considered, including age and education. We describe some of the essential differences in findings in the individual-only versus hierarchical analysis in these points:

- Results in the individual-only results followed what has been reported widely in the literature. For example, being unmarried increased the risk of low birth weight by 1.87, and being African American increased the risk by 1.73. Both of these effects were significant.

- In the multilevel analysis, important confounding effects were observed for race and neighborhood wealth. Once average neighborhood wealth was entered into the models African American race was no longer a statistically significant determinant of low birth weight. This finding re-locates the risk of low birth weight to the neighborhood level and away from individual differences in race.

- On the other hand, the risk due to being unmarried increased more than two-fold from 1.87 to 4.37. Note that the overall profile of risk shifts in the multilevel model.

- The protective effect of increasing maternal education changed by 9% from an odds of .93 to .85.

- Average neighborhood wealth moderated the effect of marital status on the risk of low birth weight. With married women in a wealthy neighborhood as a reference group, results showed that being unmarried in a low wealth neighborhood increased the odds four-fold compared to the reference group. But being married in low-wealth neighborhoods yielded a similar risk of low birth weight as the reference group. Put another way, marital status counteracted the effects of low neighborhood wealth, but there was little effect of marital status in high wealth neighborhoods.

- The number of community groups was a moderator of the relation between maternal education and low birth weight. In general, women giving birth in very organized neighborhoods had lower overall risks of having a low birth weight infant (a main effect). But also, the effect of low education on increasing risk was weaker in more organized neighborhoods.

These results are important signals that multilevel models may be crucial in coming to the correct conclusions ***even at the individual level*** about risk or predictive factors. In addition, until multilevel models are estimated explicitly, we miss the direct and modifying roles of context in understanding outcomes.

11.2 RUNNING THE GENERALIZED HLM IN SAS

The Generalized version of HLM can be estimated in two SAS programs: PROC NLMIXED—implying nonlinear mixed models—and PROC GLIMMIX. GLIMMIX is a newer procedure in SAS for nonlinear mixed models; it also has the advantage that it is set up very much like PROC

MIXED. GLIMMIX is well-suited for a wide range of standard applications, including binomial logistic, cumulative ordinal logit, complementary log–log, multinomial logistic, probit, Poisson, negative binomial, and log-normal models.

We begin with an example of multilevel binomial logistic regression. We show code that executes this program as an example of what needs to be considered in estimating these models; the particular defaults and selectable options will change depending on the software, but decisions are required on each of the issues raised here.

11.2.1 A Multilevel Model for Employment Status

The following example uses data from the last wave of the National Survey of Children, showing the effects of neighborhood characteristics (defined by zip code) on employment status at the individual level (employed/not employed). Years of completed education and gender are the Level-1 predictors, and we focus on the parent respondent as the Level-1 unit of analysis. The neighborhood characteristic that we use in this model is the percentage of adults with less than primary school education in each zip code (%*PCADULTLTP81*). We are interested in whether women's opportunities for employment are more affected in low education neighbourhoods. Thus we are interested first in whether gender has random effects across neighborhoods.

The Level-1 model for the log odds of being employed is

$$Logit(EMP_{ij}) = \ln\left(\frac{P_{ij}}{1-P_{ij}}\right) = \beta_{0j} + \beta_{1j}(EDUCATION)_{ij} + \beta_{2j}(FEMALE)_{ij}$$

The Level-2 model is

$$\beta_{0j} = \gamma_{00} + \gamma_{01}(\%PCADULTLTP81)_j + u_{0j}$$

$$\beta_{1j} = \gamma_{10}$$

$$\beta_{2j} = \gamma_{20} + \gamma_{21}(\%PCADULTLTP81)_j + u_{2j}$$

Substituting for the Level-1 model yields the combined model

$$Logit(EMP_{ij}) = \gamma_{00} + \gamma_{01}(\%PCADULTLTP81)_j + \gamma_{10}(EDUCATION)_{ij} + \gamma_{20}(FEMALE)_{ij}$$
$$+ \gamma_{21}(\%PCADULTLTP81_j \cdot FEMALE_{ij}) + u_{0j} + u_{2j}(FEMALE_{ij})$$

As in the three-level example for PROC MIXED using these data, we start off by creating a data set that links individual records to neighborhood characteristics via zip codes. The SAS code used to run a series of logistic models for employment status is:

```
* Model 1 - One Way Analysis of Variance with Random intercepts

proc glimmix data=empcen OR asycov method=laplace;
class zip81;
model emp(event==1=)= /link=logit dist=binomial ddfm=bw solution chisq;
random intercept/subject=zip81 type=un;
covtest 'no random effect' zerog;
title1 'Random Intercept GLIMMIX Model';
```

```
title2 'with employed as outcome';
run;


* Model 2 - Cross-Over Effects

proc glimmix data=empcen asycov OR method=laplace;
class zip81;
model emp(event==1=)=pcadultltp81 /link=logit dist=binary ddfm=bw solution chisq;
random intercept/subject=zip81 type=un;
covtest 'no random effect' zerog;
title1 'Cross Over Effects GLIMMIX Model with %adults with less than primary
school education' ;
title2 'with employed as outcome';
run;


* Model 3 - Random Coefficients Model

proc glimmix data=empcen asycov OR method=laplace;
class zip81;
model emp(event==1=)=respeduc2 female /link=logit dist=binary ddfm=bw solution;
random intercept female /subject=zip81 type=un;
covtest 'no random effects' zerog;
covtest 'intercept only' 0 0 . / estimates;
covtest 'female only' . 0 0 ;
title1 'Random Coefficients GLIMMIX Model with gender and level of education,
gender random at level2' ;
title2 'with employed at time-2 as outcome';
run;


* Model 4 - Full Model with Level1 and Level2 predictors

proc glimmix data=empcen asycov OR method=laplace; /* using method=mspl makes
results equivalent to HLM */
class zip81;
model emp(event==1=)=pcadultltp81 female respeduc2 pcadultltp81*female/
link=logit dist=binary ddfm=bw solution;
random intercept female/ subject=zip81 type=un;
covtest 'no random intercept' zerog;
covtest 'intercept only' 0 0 . / estimates;
covtest 'female only' . 0 0 / estimates ;
title1 'Full GLIMMIX Model ' ;
run;
```

11.2.1.1 Model 1: One-Way ANOVA

You can see that this procedure is set up very similarly to PROC MIXED. The OR option in the PROC line asks for odds ratios, where appropriate; ASYCOV prints the asymptotic covariance matrix of the covariance parameter estimates. METHOD=LAPLACE asks for the Laplace approximation.

The MODEL statement names the dependent variable and specifies the event category in the parentheses following the dependent variable name. The link function is "logit," and the "dist" option is "binomial"; together this implies a binomial logistic model. The RANDOM statement is very much like PROC MIXED. Here we specify a random intercept, with the subject parameter equal to the 1981 zip code, and the type of covariance structure set to unrestricted. The COVTEST statement asks for a test of the random intercept using the keyword "zerog."

11.2.1.2 Model 2: Cross-Over Effect

The main addition here is the effect of *%PCADULTLTP81* in the model line, to test the cross-over effect on employment.

11.2.1.3 Model 3: Random Coefficients Model

Here the MODEL line includes the two Level-1 predictors, respondent's education and gender. There are other important changes here. "Female" is added to the random statement, to test for random effects. GLIMMIX has a unique method for testing random effects compared to PROC MIXED: You must use multiple COVTEST statements to test each random effect.

You have to imagine a covariance parameter matrix following the order of the random effects you specify. Here, UN (1,1) would refer to the variance of the intercept, UN (2,1) would be the covariance between the intercept and the gender variance, and UN (2,2) would refer to the variance of the gender slope across neighborhoods.

The first statement using the "nozerog" option is the most general test: Including the intercept, it tests for any random effects across all of the random effects included. The second COVTEST statement tests the significance of the random intercept variance by restricting it to zero in the covariance parameter matrix and testing the implied difference in fit. Note that you state which parameters need to be set to zero in this test, and the "." refers to free parameters to be estimated. You have to set the covariance to zero as well because if the intercept variance is zero, the covariance must also be zero. The third COVTEST statement tests the random effect of gender using the same method, taking into account the fact that this variance is the third element in the covariance matrix.

11.2.1.4 Model 4: Full Model

This model includes both Level-1 and Level-2 variables and the interaction between percentage of adults with less than primary education and gender.

The results for the one-way ANOVA model are shown in Table 11.1.

TABLE 11.1 ● RESULTS FOR A ONE-WAY ANOVA LOGISTIC MODEL

Model Information	
Data Set	WORK.EMPCEN
Response Variable	emp
Response Distribution	Binomial
Link Function	Logit
Variance Function	Default
Variance Matrix Blocked By	ZIP81
Estimation Technique	Maximum Likelihood
Likelihood Approximation	Laplace
Degrees of Freedom Method	Between-Within

(Continued)

TABLE 11.1 ● (Continued)

Iteration History					
Iteration	**Restarts**	**Evaluations**	**Objective Function**	**Change**	**Max Gradient**
0	0	4	1157.4207971	.	12.91447
1	0	3	1156.8844554	0.53634173	0.843486
2	0	3	1156.8756234	0.00883198	0.279357
3	0	2	1156.8744292	0.00119419	0.010031
4	0	2	1156.8744277	0.00000151	0.000125

Fit Statistics	
-2 Log Likelihood	1156.87
AIC (smaller is better)	1160.87
AICC (smaller is better)	1160.89
BIC (smaller is better)	1166.61
CAIC (smaller is better)	1168.61
HQIC (smaller is better)	1163.20

Covariance Parameter Estimates			
Cov Parm	**Subject**	**Estimate**	**Standard Error**
UN(1,1)	ZIP81	0.7779	0.2453

Solutions for Fixed Effects					
Effect	**Estimate**	**Standard Error**	**DF**	**t Value**	**Pr > |t|**
Intercept	−0.1191	0.1153	129	−1.03	0.3033

Tests of Covariance Parameters Based on the Likelihood					
Label	**DF**	**-2 Log Like**	**ChiSq**	**Pr > ChiSq**	**Note**
no random effect	1	1193.34	36.46	<.0001	MI

The results from this one-way ANOVA indicate that there is significant random variation in the log odds of being employed across neighborhoods (variance of $u_{0j} = .7779$, $p = < .0001$). The predicted probability of being employed for all respondents is .47 $[e^{-.1191}/1 + e^{-.1191}]$, but there is significant variability depending on the respondent's neighborhood.

A cross-over effects model is estimated in Model 2. The main results are shown in Table 11.2.

TABLE 11.2 ● RESULTS FOR A LOGISTIC CROSS-OVER EFFECTS MODEL

Response Profile		
Ordered Value	**emp**	**Total Frequency**
1	0	438
2	1	423
The GLIMMIX procedure is modeling the probability that emp='1'.		

Iteration History					
Iteration	Restarts	Evaluations	Objective Function	Change	Max Gradient
0	0	4	1154.0326182	.	293.4477
1	0	4	1153.5285812	0.50403706	91.97349
2	0	2	1153.4112566	0.11732458	0.881299
3	0	2	1153.401348	0.00990855	4.798223
4	0	2	1153.4008058	0.00054221	0.721923
5	0	2	1153.400802	0.00000376	0.040113

Covariance Parameter Estimates			
Cov Parm	Subject	Estimate	Standard Error
Intercept	ZIP81	0.7340	0.2383

Solutions for Fixed Effects					
Effect	Estimate	Standard Error	DF	t Value	Pr > |t|
Intercept	0.2737	0.2371	128	1.15	0.2505
pcadultltp81	−0.02018	0.01083	128	−1.86	0.0648

Results show that the percentage of adults with less than primary school at the neighborhood level decreases the log odds of being employed, although this effect is only significant one-tailed ($\gamma_{01} = -.02$, $p = .032$, one tailed). The estimate of u_{0j} for this model is .734, and when compared to the estimate of u_{0j} from the preceding one-way ANOVA model (.7779), we can say that 5.6% [(.7779 − .734)/.7779 = .056] of the variation in employment status across neighborhoods is explained by the contextual prevalence of adults with less than primary education.

A random coefficients model was also run (Model 3, shown in Table 11.3), with both education and gender predicting employment at Level 1 and random slopes at Level 2 for gender. The results indicate that the education of the respondent is positively related to the probability of employment ($\gamma_{10} = .1563$, $p < .0001$), and women have a much lower chance of employment ($\gamma_{20} = -5.52$, $p = .0002$). The covariance tests also show that the female slope varies significantly across neighborhoods, suggesting that some neighborhood conditions help determine employment chances for women.

TABLE 11.3 ● RESULTS FOR THE LOGISTIC RANDOM COEFFICIENTS MODEL

Covariance Parameter Estimates			
Cov Parm	Subject	Estimate	Standard Error
UN(1,1)	ZIP81	1.1620	0.3653
UN(2,1)	ZIP81	−3.8007	3.1149
UN(2,2)	ZIP81	54.0652	31.7024

(Continued)

TABLE 11.3 ● (Continued)

Solutions for Fixed Effects					
Effect	Estimate	Standard Error	DF	t Value	Pr > |t|
Intercept	−0.02979	0.1350	129	−0.22	0.8258
respeduc2	0.1563	0.03757	729	4.16	<.0001
female	−5.5217	1.4816	729	−3.73	0.0002

Tests of Covariance Parameters Based on the Likelihood							
					Estimates H0		
Label	DF	-2 Log Like	ChiSq	Pr > ChiSq	Est1	Est2	Est3	Note
no random effects	3	1160.95	55.44	<.0001	0	0	0	–
intercept only	2	1149.33	43.83	<.0001	0	0	26.9836	MI
female only	2	1119.27	13.76	0.0006	0.9264	0	0	MI

The final model (Model 4) includes both Level-2 and Level-1 fixed predictors, and the interaction between *pcadultltp81* and female, to test for the impact of living in a low education neighborhood on further reducing women's employment chances. The results are shown in Table 11.4.

TABLE 11.4 ● RESULTS FOR A FINAL LEVEL-2 LOGISTIC MODEL

Model Information	
Data Set	WORK.EMPCEN
Response Variable	emp
Response Distribution	Binary
Link Function	Logit
Variance Function	Default
Variance Matrix Blocked By	ZIP81
Estimation Technique	Maximum Likelihood
Likelihood Approximation	Laplace
Degrees of Freedom Method	Between-Within

Covariance Parameter Estimates			
Cov Parm	Subject	Estimate	Standard Error
UN(1,1)	ZIP81	1.0929	0.3518
UN(2,1)	ZIP81	−3.9178	3.0013
UN(2,2)	ZIP81	51.9182	31.9467

Solutions for Fixed Effects					
Effect	Estimate	Standard Error	DF	t Value	Pr > |t|
Intercept	0.4019	0.2748	128	1.46	0.1460
pcadultltp81	−0.02238	0.01261	128	−1.77	0.0785
female	−2.9411	2.6042	728	−1.13	0.2591
respeduc2	0.1586	0.03769	728	4.21	<.0001
pcadultltp81*female	−0.1400	0.1210	728	−1.16	0.2476

Tests of Covariance Parameters Based on the Likelihood					Estimates H0			
Label	DF	-2 Log Like	ChiSq	Pr > ChiSq	Est1	Est2	Est3	Note
no random intercept	3	1149.33	49.48	<.0001	0	0	0	–
intercept only	2	1139.18	39.33	<.0001	0	0	24.5620	MI
female only	2	1111.80	11.96	0.0015	0.8857	0	0	MI

Looking at the parameter estimates first, note that the interaction between the educational status of the neighborhood and gender is *not* significant. This interaction could be removed from the model. When we re-estimate the model by removing this interaction, we see the results in Table 11.5:

TABLE 11.5 ● RESULTS FOR A MODEL WITHOUT THE INTERACTION

Solutions for Fixed Effects					
Effect	Estimate	Standard Error	DF	t Value	Pr > |t|
Intercept	0.4615	0.2741	128	1.68	0.0947
pcadultltp81	−0.02514	0.01241	128	−2.03	0.0449
female	−5.6670	1.4911	729	−3.80	0.0002
respeduc2	0.1570	0.03765	729	4.17	<.0001

Note that the low educational status of the neighborhood has an independent negative effect on employment chances, for both genders, over and above the impact of differences in individual education at the individual level. This means that context has a net impact on employment chances. Both individual-level factors here also have an effect, but these effects do not depend on the educational status of the neighborhood.

11.3 MULTILEVEL POISSON REGRESSION

The generalized HLM can accommodate various nonlinear models in which *Y* is transformed using a link function. The Poisson model for count data may be useful because, in part, it does not depend on the normality of the errors as a starting assumption. *Y* is transformed by the log link function. With the standard assumption that we are measuring exposure to an event over a defined period of time, the dependent variable is then the log of the expected event rate.

11.3.1 A Multilevel Model for a Count of Recent Traumatic Life Events

We use data from the 1991 Toronto Mental Health and Stress Study (Turner & Wheaton, 1991) to demonstrate the Poisson mixed model. Our outcome variable is a count of traumatic life events occurring within the past two years as reported by the respondent. We model whether the number of recent traumatic life events depends on the percentage of low-income households in the respondent's neighborhood, the respondent's age in years, and whether he/she was born in Canada. The variable *bestfsa* in this example is a group-level neighborhood ID, at the FSA level (this is the three first letters of the postal code in Canada, a somewhat larger area than typically denoted by census tracts).

Our measure of recent exposure to trauma counts "yes" responses to 19 questions about traumatic events in the last two years. As can be seen in Table 11.6, the distribution of recent traumatic events (*rectraumr2*) shows that there is a marked positive skew, with the majority of respondents reporting no recent traumatic life events within the past two years.

TABLE 11.6 ● A COUNT OF RECENT TRAUMATIC EVENTS OVER THE LAST TWO YEARS

rectraumr2	Frequency	Percent	Cumulative Frequency	Cumulative Percent
0	872	62.60	872	62.60
1	357	25.63	1229	88.23
2	110	7.90	1339	96.12
3	37	2.66	1376	98.78
4	12	0.86	1388	99.64
5	2	0.14	1390	99.78
6	2	0.14	1392	99.93
7	1	0.07	1393	100.00

Our decision to use the Poisson mixed model seems reasonable given this distribution. Remember that the Poisson distribution assumes a natural relation between the mean and the variance, specifically that they are roughly equivalent. The mean for *rectraumr2* is .55 and the standard deviation is .88. Although slightly overdispersed, our choice of the Poisson distribution for this analysis is appropriate as a starting point—but we advocate the same sequence of considerations as we discussed in Chapter 5. Taking into account an observed "flattening" of the effect of age after 30 using a spline, the Level-1 model for the log of the expected count of recent traumatic life events is

$$\ln(RECTRAUMR2_{ij}) = \beta_{0j} + \beta_{1j}(AGE)_{ij} + \beta_{2j}(AGEKNOT30)_{ij}$$
$$+ \beta_{3j}(BORNCANADA)_{ij}$$

where *ageknot30* allows for a change in direction in the effect of age.

The Level-2 model, assuming no cross-level interactions, is

$$\beta_{0j} = \gamma_{00} + \gamma_{01}(LOINCPPER)_j + u_{0j}$$

$$\beta_{1j} = \gamma_{10}$$

$$\beta_{2j} = \gamma_{20}$$

$$\beta_{3j} = \gamma_{30}$$

Note here that fixed effects at Level 1 have no random components in the Level-2 model. Substituting for the Level-1 model yields the combined model

$$\ln(RECTRAUMR2_{ij}) = \gamma_{00} + \gamma_{01}(LOINCPPER)_j + \gamma_{10}(AGE)_{ij} + \gamma_{20}(AGEKNOT30)_{ij}$$
$$\gamma_{30}(BORNCANADA)_{ij} + u_{0j}$$

In estimating this model, we first developed a cut point for the effect of age using splines. In these data, the cut point was age 30. Our coding here followed the same logic as in Chapter 3 on nonlinear regression.

The runs of GLIMMIX used here are reproduced:

```
/* model 1*/
proc glimmix data=traumevts list maxopt=500;
class bestfsa;
model rectraumr2=/dist=poisson link=log ddfm=bw solution;
nloptions tech=dbldog upd=ddfp;
random intercept/subject=bestfsa type=un;
covtest 'no random effects' zerog;
title1'Traumatic Life Events, 2yrs';
run;

* model 2 ;
proc glimmix data=traumevts maxopt=500;
class bestfsa;
model rectraumr2=ageupto30 ageafter30 canborn loincpper/dist=poisson link=log
ddfm=bw solution;
random intercept /subject=bestfsa;
covtest 'no random effects' zerog;
title1 'Traumatic Life Events, 2yrs glimmix';
 title2 'Add age, Canadian born, neighbourhood effects (percent low income hh)';
run;
```

To specify a Poisson model in GLIMMIX, we specify "dist=poisson" and "link=log" in the options for the MODEL statement. There are some unique issues in estimating these models that are likely to come up whatever the software used. The default number of optimizations is increased to 500 in the one-way ANOVA model, but we also could have increased the number of iterations using an option in the NLOPTIONS statement. The NLOPTIONS statement includes a number of options for fine tuning the estimation process. Here we use a method of optimization called a "double dogleg" optimization rather than the default "quasi-Newton," with a specific update technique appropriate for that approach. At times, you will have to experiment with the choices here to get a model to converge. This was necessary in this model in this case. But, in this example, we had to *remove* these NLOPTIONS to estimate a model with fixed effect predictors.

The two models shown are an intercept only model (one-way ANOVA) and a model that includes individual-level effects for age and Canadian birth, and the neighborhood-level effect for the percentage of households with low income.

The one-way ANOVA results are shown in Table 11.7.

TABLE 11.7 ● ONE-WAY ANOVA FOR NEIGHBORHOOD VARIATION IN RECENT TRAUMATIC EVENTS

Model Information	
Data Set	WORK.TRAUMEVTS
Response Variable	rectraumr2
Response Distribution	Poisson
Link Function	Log
Variance Function	Default
Variance Matrix Blocked By	bestfsa
Estimation Technique	Residual PL
Degrees of Freedom Method	Between-Within

Dimensions	
G-side Cov. Parameters	1
Columns in X	1
Columns in Z per Subject	1
Subjects (Blocks in V)	74
Max Obs per Subject	76

Optimization Information	
Optimization Technique	Double Dogleg
Parameters in Optimization	1
Lower Boundaries	1
Upper Boundaries	0
Fixed Effects	Profiled
Starting From	Data

Covariance Parameter Estimates			
Cov Parm	Subject	Estimate	Standard Error
UN(1,1)	bestfsa	0.08280	0.03140

Solutions for Fixed Effects					
Effect	Estimate	Standard Error	DF	t Value	Pr > |t|
Intercept	−0.6209	0.05283	73	−11.75	<.0001

Tests of Covariance Parameters Based on the Residual Pseudo-Likelihood					
Label	DF	-2 Res Log P-Like	ChiSq	Pr > ChiSq	Note
no random effects	1	5301.87	19.68	<.0001	MI

Results from the intercept-only model indicate that the average expected count of recent traumatic life events is $\gamma_{00} = \exp(-0.6209) = .537$. The variance of the random intercept indicates that there is significant variation ($p = < .0001$) between neighborhoods. Given significant variation in recent traumatic life events between neighborhoods, we proceed to fit a model with Level-2 variables that might explain this variation.

The second model includes a neighborhood-level variable for the percentage of low-income households as well as age and nativity at Level 1. We would expect that as the percentage of poor households in a neighborhood increases that the expected count of recent traumatic life events will also increase. The results for this model are shown in Table 11.8.

TABLE 11.8 ● CROSS-OVER EFFECTS OF LOW-INCOME NEIGHBORHOOD WITH INDIVIDUAL PREDICTORS

Model Information	
Data Set	WORK.TRAUMEVTS
Response Variable	rectraumr2
Response Distribution	Poisson
Link Function	Log
Variance Function	Default
Variance Matrix Blocked By	bestfsa
Estimation Technique	Residual PL
Degrees of Freedom Method	Between-Within

Number of Observations Read	1393
Number of Observations Used	1371

Dimensions	
G-side Cov. Parameters	1
Columns in X	5
Columns in Z per Subject	1
Subjects (Blocks in V)	74
Max Obs per Subject	76

Covariance Parameter Estimates			
Cov Parm	Subject	Estimate	Standard Error
Intercept	bestfsa	0.06914	0.02915

Solutions for Fixed Effects					
Effect	Estimate	Standard Error	DF	t Value	Pr > |t|
Intercept	−0.9713	0.1448	72	−6.71	<.0001
ageupto30	−0.1041	0.01078	1294	−9.66	<.0001
ageafter30	−0.01143	0.006722	1294	−1.70	0.0892
canborn	0.1854	0.08345	1294	2.22	0.0265
loincpper	0.01402	0.007470	72	1.88	0.0646

Tests of Covariance Parameters Based on the Residual Pseudo-Likelihood					
Label	DF	-2 Res Log P-Like	ChiSq	Pr > ChiSq	Note
no random effects	1	5132.12	14.47	<.0001	MI

The results indicate that both age and being born in Canada are significantly associated with recent traumatic life events. Between the ages of 18 and 30, each additional year reduces the expected count of traumatic life events by approximately 10%, controlling for other effects in the model. After age 30, the adjusted slope for age is much flatter. The expected count of recent traumatic life events for respondents who are born in Canada is approximately 18% higher than the expected count for those born outside of Canada, controlling for other effects in the model. The coefficient for percentage of low-income households is significant if we consider this a one-tailed test ($p = .03$) but not for a two-tailed test. Each 10% increase in low-income households increases the rate of exposure to traumatic events by 14%. Of course, you can also interpret these effects by exponentiating the coefficients.

Even though percentage low income has a borderline effect here, there is still unexplained variation between neighborhoods that is not accounted for in this model, since the random effect for *bestfsa* is still significant.

11.4 PUBLISHED EXAMPLE

As an example of published work using GHLM, we consider a paper closely related to but also different than the draft paper discussed earlier on low birthweight in Baltimore. Compared to the earlier draft, the focus and analytical questions here are distinct, and the data source has been expanded. As in the earlier version, however, a fundamental motivation of this paper is that previous research emphasized individual-level factors almost exclusively. O'Campo et al. (1997) explain the advantages of using a multilevel approach in four points:

> "Analyses that include both individual level and macrolevel data—referred to as contextual or multilevel models -- have several advantages. First, multilevel analytic methods are more consistent with social theories than are traditional methods of analysis… in that they explicitly accommodate the multiple levels of data. Second, multilevel methods can contribute new knowledge to our current understanding of public health issues by allowing for the inclusion of macrolevel factors in our current explanatory models, thereby bridging the micro-macro gap by increasing our understanding of how contextual factors translate into differences in individual-level risk. Further, these methods may eliminate potential confounding of individual-level explanatory models due to the omission of macrolevel factors. Finally, by improving our understanding of how contextual factors influence individual health outcomes, we will be better equipped to design effective intervention strategies." (1997, p. 1113)

The second and final points here are important to the application of HLM methods. In this paper, the authors make explicit the possibility that macro-level factors have their effects through shifts in the state, or effects, of individual-level risk factors. This approach imagines that individual-level risk may be misunderstood unless it is anchored to its origins in social contexts. While some papers imply this connection, few propose an explicit model to test it. The final point is also worthy of note: HLM models are especially well-positioned to suggest points of intervention since they occur at a contextual rather than individual level. From a policy perspective, more lives are changed more efficiently if interventions occur at the contextual level rather than relying on individual programs. Such passive change interventions, for example, do not depend on the compliance of individuals for participation.

The individual-level predictors included here were maternal age, maternal education, prenatal care, and in an important evolution of this paper, health insurance. At the neighborhood level, the focus was on neighborhood wealth, the unemployment rate, and the crime rate. Table 2 from the paper (see Table 11.9) shows the final model. Note that nonsignificant effects are not shown in this table, though they are present in the underlying model.

Results at the individual level suggest some unusual findings, at least at first glance. Prenatal care and health insurance both predict a *higher* risk of low birthweight. But note that these are marginal effects in the presence of interactions in this model. While the finding of any positive risk due to these factors in any group may seem counter-intuitive, prenatal care is a measure of the trimester for the initiation of care, so later care implies higher risk as expected, and health insurance depends on Medicaid status, itself an indicator of socioeconomic need.

TABLE 11.9 ● A 2-LEVEL LOGISTIC MODEL OF LOW BIRTHWEIGHT IN BALTIMORE				
	β	SE(β)	Odds Ratio	95 % Confidence Interval
Direct effects				
Maternal age	.022	.004	1.02	1.01, 1.03
Maternal education	−.129	.018	.87	.85, .91
Prenatal care	.227	.025	1.25	1.19, 1.32
Health Insurance status	.401	.068	1.49	1.31, 1.70
Per capita income < $8000	.103	.049	1.11	1.02, 1.22
Interaction effects via maternal age[a]				
Unemployment	.002	.001	. . .	. . .
Interaction effects via maternal education				
Per capita crime rate	−.769	.329	. . .	. . .
Interaction effects via prenatal care[b]				
log(average wealth)	−.118	.054	. . .	. . .
Unemployment	−.017	.007	. . .	. . .
Interaction effects via health insurance status				
Per capita income < $8000	−.439	.090	. . .	. . .
Per capita income $8000–$11000	−.302	.092	. . .	. . .

Note: Parameter estimates are for individual-level, neighborhood-level, and interaction effects.

[a]The interaction effects via maternal age are adjusted for number of community groups.

[b]The interaction effects via prenatal care are adjusted for crime rate and rate of housing violations.

Source: O'Campo, P., Xue, X., Wang, M. C., & Caughy, M. (1997). Neighborhood risk factors for low birthweight in Baltimore: A multilevel analysis. *American Journal of Public Health, 87*, 1115, Table 2. doi: 10.2105/AJPH.87.7.1113.

What seems most significant about the results at Level 2 is the prevalence of cross-level interactions, suggesting that social contexts *do* act as passive interventions that shift the relevance of the usual Level-1 risk factors. It is true that low per capita income at the neighborhood level predicts higher risk overall, as would be expected, but also note that this effect is over and above the effect of insurance at Level 1.

Interactions help frame the relevance and consequences of both prenatal care and Medicaid insurance at the individual level. For health insurance, the positive effect on risk was greater in higher income neighborhoods and was substantially reduced in low-income neighborhoods. This is consistent with the idea that in low-income neighborhoods, other risk factors come into play and are definitive in that context. In higher income neighborhoods, Medicaid status becomes a more isolated and decisive reflection of family need. Late onset prenatal care has an effect on risk, but again two neighborhood characteristics matter in defining its relevance. Neighborhood wealth lowers the risk due to late onset prenatal care as one would expect. Interestingly, unemployment, as a negative neighborhood characteristic, works in the opposite manner: Increases in unemployment are associated with a reduced risk due to late onset prenatal care.

There are other cross-level interactions here: Maternal education is protective but is even more protective in high crime neighborhoods, and age is a risk factor that is activated by higher unemployment rates. In total, there are five cross-level interactions here.

These interactions have a number of important implications. First, they do represent program targets that can be manipulated by social policy. But second, these interactions sometimes have complex implications that require care in choosing targets for appropriate interventions. Third, the interactions suggest, strongly, that an overly generalized focus on individual risk to promote interventions may produce disappointing outcomes. If interventions designed around prenatal care apply to all equally, then findings here suggest some money will be spent inappropriately, and indirectly, funding where it counts most may be diluted. Interactions tell us there are places for intervention and that there are places where intervention may not help.

Concluding Words

In this chapter, we provide two examples of generalizations of the basic hierarchical linear model. There are many other possible, beyond the logistic and Poisson cases we consider. But the generic framework is the same for all cases, and we can refer back to earlier chapters to understand how to interpret results for specific cases. An important point about the GHLM is that it only operates differently at Level 1, while the Level-2 model is the same, regardless of how the Level-1 model is specified and estimated. This feature derives from the general fact in HLM models that the Level-2 model is a model for the coefficients at Level 1.

There is one more variation of HLM to consider: growth curve models. This is an approach that represents within-person change over time as Level 1 in a multilevel model, with the "person" as Level 2. The structure of this model is the same as other HLM models, but it is used for quite distinct purposes. Fundamentally, the growth curve model traces individual trajectories in some outcome over time and is usually used to look for general themes in those trajectories traceable to either fixed or varying person characteristics and experience. We turn to this elaboration of the HLM model in the next chapter.

GROWTH CURVE MODELS

The hierarchical linear model can be adapted to include the study of differences in the form and rates of individual change over time. Because this approach is rooted in developmental psychology, we refer to this change in terms of "growth curves." But any kind of change can be studied, including negative change.

This model has some unique and flexible features. First, it focuses on individual differences explicitly rather than averaging them out and seeing the individual difference as a "deviation." Second, this is an important method for life course, aging, and developmental approaches—in fact, anything that focuses on *trajectories* of change in an individual state or trait over time. Third, the most unusual feature of this model is that at Level 1, we consider *within-person* differences over time. Then Level 2 is the individual level. All layers of context are, in effect, bumped up one layer, with the first layer now taken by changes over time for individuals. Because of this feature, it is possible to estimate growth curve models in any longitudinal data set, even without further contextual information.

The implications of this structure are exemplified by this scenario: If we study 500 people in a panel study at three points in time, the N at Level 2 is 500, the N per Level–2 unit is 3, and the N at Level 1 is therefore 500 x 3 = 1500. In other words, we have what is called a "person-period" (or person-time) data set, just as in the case of the panel regression and discrete time hazard models discussed in later chapters.

12.1 DERIVING THE STRUCTURE OF GROWTH MODELS

To reflect the introduction of this "new" level (within person over time), we use new symbols for the Level 1 model.

The Level 1 model for Y_{ti}, the value of Y for person i at time t, is

$$Y_{ti} = \pi_{0i} + \pi_{1i}a_{ti} + \pi_{2i}a_{ti}^2 + \ldots + \pi_{pi}a_{ti}^p + v_{ti}$$

This conceptualizes each individual's change over time as (possibly) a curve of order P, where the π are the intercept and regression coefficients, and the a are *variables* representing time, such as the person's age. The within-individual over-time error is v_{ti}.

The Level 2 model we have, for $P+1$ growth parameters is

$$\pi_{pi} = \beta_{P0} + \beta_p X_i + e_{pi}$$

where

X_i are measured X predictors at the person level, and β_p are the effects of person-level variables on "growth" rates—that is, the effects of individual characteristics on change over time. In effect, the π are like the β in the previous applications of HLM, and the β are analogous to the γ.

One of the most important features of growth curve models is the allowance for nonlinear growth. This is specified by quadratic, cubic, quartic, or higher order functions for the effects of time at Level 1. But it can also be represented by splines or piecewise segments. In all cases, the idea is to map differential trajectories in people's lives over time—for example, mapping the growing health disparities in subgroups, the increasing inequalities in income rooted in childhood experience, or the short-term self-limiting effects that are proposed as life "turning points" but turn out in the long run to be a blip in the life course.

To allow for *any* nonlinear growth at Level 1, we can estimate a quadratic model for time, as follows:

$$Y_{ti} = \pi_{0i} + \pi_{1i}a_{ti} + \pi_{2i}a_{ti}^2 + v_{ti}$$
$$\pi_{0i} = \beta_{00} + \beta_{01}X_1 + e_{0i}$$
$$\pi_{1i} = \beta_{10} + \beta_{11}X_1 + e_{1i}$$
$$\pi_{2i} = \beta_{20} + \beta_{21}X_1 + e_{2i}$$

This model allows for individually different starting points (in π_{0i}), as well as individually different curves for change after that starting point. Substituting the Level-2 model into the Level-1 model, we get

$$Y_{ti} = \beta_{00} + \beta_{01}X_1 + \beta_{10}a_{ti} + \beta_{11}a_{ti}X_1 + \beta_{20}a_{ti}^2 + \beta_{21}a_{ti}^2 X_1 + e_{0i} + a_{ti}e_{1i} + a_{ti}^2 e_{2i} + v_{ti}$$

This model shows that X_1 may alter the whole trajectory—both the direction and rate of change, for each individual. In this model, it is important to note that the *number* of observations and spacing of observations *can* vary. That is, missing data are possible—an important point of flexibility. The a variables can also be coded as time-points for observation—if they are evenly spaced—or as age or as historical time, as long as they are a measure of time.

The nonlinear effects of time can be converted to splines, and there are some advantages to doing so. First, using a piecewise approach allows you to test for the random effects of different segments of time rather than all at once. It is possible that these random effects only occur over a specific period of life, and this is important information. Second, by using splines, you reduce the collinearity between different components of the random effect of time—the linear and squared component for example—and this makes the issue of specificity of random effects a question that can be addressed.

Of course, the focus here is the idea of cross-level interactions between the circumstances in individual lives—status, disadvantage, family structure, childhood poverty, race, gender, education—and the way in which time works—how time promotes, flattens, or dampens the level of important life outcomes.

12.1.1 Individual Trajectories

Often, you may only have two waves of observation to work with. For this case, the individual growth trajectories are automatically linear—with an important exception when individuals are at different ages at time one, as we will discuss later. However, starting with a "cohort-study" example, we see from the plot in Figure 12.1, the individual growth trajectories for sixteen individuals over two waves of data. In a growth curve model, we want to model this variability, using Level-2 individual characteristics.

This figure makes clear that for some, change is positive, but for some, it is moderated, flat, or even negative.

FIGURE 12.1 ● LINEAR GROWTH TRAJECTORIES OVER TWO POINTS IN TIME

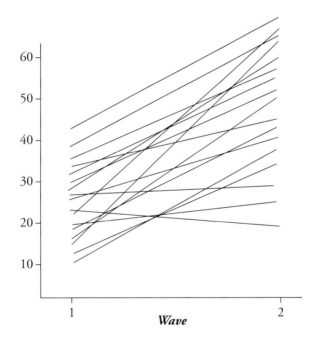

It takes *at least* 3 waves of observation in a cohort design to consider nonlinear growth curves, as shown in Figure 12.2.

The unique trajectories shown suggest that we should consider differential nonlinearity in growth over time. This figure makes obvious that some people increase in *Y* rapidly but then level off while others start slowly and then increase in *Y* more clearly after the second wave.

This situation is straightforwardly handled by the general model introduced earlier, since it tests for differential nonlinearity in general and also due to *X*. If β_{20} and β_{21} are both zero in the model at Level 2 for the nonlinear effect of time, the model reduces to a linear growth model.

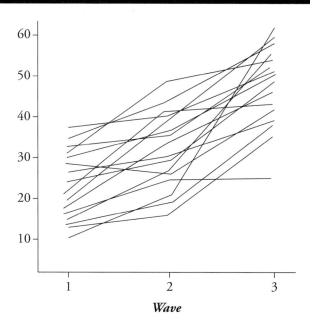

FIGURE 12.2 ● GROWTH TRAJECTORIES OVER THREE POINTS IN TIME

12.1.2 The Effect of Early Instruction on Cognitive Growth

This example is based on the famous Head Start study, with an N here of 143 children. Four measures of natural science knowledge were taken over a year, as a function of home language and amount of direct instruction. An important issue in growth curve models is the coding of time. Usually, one wants to have a "zero point" for time, so that the intercept is the initial status on the outcome at the beginning of the study. This is very different than in the previous HLM models, where the intercept was a mean within groups.

For simplicity and because of the short time frame, a linear growth model is assumed:

$$Y_{ti} = \pi_{0i} + \pi_{1i} a_{ti} + v_{ti}$$

We start with a ***random-coefficient*** model at Level 2, to assess individual variation in growth over time. In the context of growth models, this is also known as the "unconditional growth model." It is the usual starting model in growth curve analysis:

$$\pi_{0i} = \beta_{00} + e_{0i}$$
$$\pi_{1i} = \beta_{10} + e_{1i}$$

This Level-2 specification allows for "random" differences in growth coefficients. Results for this model are useful in deciding on the best specification for further Level-2 models (see Table 12.1).

Interpreting these results, β_{00} is the mean intercept of all individual growth rates at the beginning of the study (in a logit metric, due to the way the test was scored). Since the time point of zero represents the beginning of the study, $\beta_{00} = -.135$ is the average logit initial score. β_{10} is the mean growth rate in knowledge for all individuals, equal to .182 over the year.

Both e_{0i} and e_{1i} have very significant variability around the mean. This indicates first, that there is significant variability among children at the beginning of the study, and second, that

TABLE 12.1 ● RESULTS FOR A LINEAR GROWTH MODEL FOR THE IMPACT OF HEAD START

	Results	Estimate	t
Fixed Effects:	β_{00}	−.135	−27
	β_{10}	.182	727

		Variance	df	χ^2	P
Random Effects:	e_{0i}	1.69	139	356.9	<.001
	e_{1i}	.04	139	724.9	<.0001
	V_{ti}	.42			

there is significant variability in learning rates over time. Thus, there is variance to explain in both π_{0i} and π_{1i}.

If we add home language (1 = non-English, 0 = English) and total hours of instruction in that program year to the second level model we have:

$$\pi_{0i} = \beta_{00} + \beta_{01}(LANGUAGE)_i + \beta_{02}(HOURS)_i + e_{0i}$$
$$\pi_{1i} = \beta_{10} + \beta_{11}(LANGUAGE)_i + \beta_{12}(HOURS)_i + e_{1i}$$

As we did for HLM models, we can substitute the Level-2 model (the person level) into the Level-1 model (the time level) to get

$$Y_{ti} = \beta_{00} + \beta_{01}(LANGUAGE)_i + \beta_{02}(HOURS)_i + e_{0i}$$
$$+ (\beta_{10} + \beta_{11}(LANGUAGE)_i + \beta_{12}(HOURS)_i + e_{1i})a_{ti} + v_{ti}$$

$$Y_{ti} = \beta_{00} + \beta_{01}(LANGUAGE)_i + \beta_{02}(HOURS)_i$$
$$+ \beta_{10}a_{ti} + \beta_{11}(LANGUAGE_i)a_{ti} + \beta_{12}(HOURS_i)a_{ti} + e_{0i} + e_{1i}a_{ti} + v_{ti}$$

The full model shows that differences in language and hours of instruction may affect the growth rate, over and above the average growth rate. Table 12.2 shows the results.

TABLE 12.2 ● HEAD START RESULTS FOR A FULL TWO-LEVEL GROWTH MODEL

Model for π_{0i}		Coefficient	t
Baseline,	β_{00}	.895	3.35
Language,	β_{01}	−.463	−1.52
Hours,	β_{02}	.0015	1.79
Model for Growth Rate, π_{1i}			
Baseline,	β_{10}	.03	.74
Language,	β_{11}	.187	4.20
Hours,	β_{12}	.00047	3.78

The effects of language and hours on initial status were nonsignificant. This signifies that there were no initial differences in levels of science knowledge at the beginning of the study due to language or what would become differences in hours of instruction and thus, indirectly, whatever in the background caused differences in hours of instruction.

However, both language and hours of instruction affected the rate of learning: Non-English families progress *more* quickly, and hours of instruction also led to faster progress.

12.1.3 A Quadratic Growth Model

In this example, we consider the effects of time since marriage on marital happiness. Time is measured in years since the beginning of the marriage. Thus, the initial value for time is 0, for people married less than one year. We imagine in this example that a large sample of couples is followed over many years to track the changes in marital happiness. Thus, each marriage has its own growth trajectory for marital happiness.

The model at Level 1 is:

$$Y_{ti} = \pi_{0i} + \pi_{1i}a_{ti} + \pi_{2i}a_{ti}^2 + v_{ti}$$

$$MARHAP_{ti} = \pi_{0i} + \pi_{1i}YEARS_{ti} + \pi_{2i}YEARS_{ti}^2 + v_{ti}$$

where the intercept is the initial level of marital happiness and the effect of years is quadratic.

There is a Level 2 model here, allowing for both random intercept effects and random effects for the linear component of time. There are no person-level characteristics considered in this model – though they could be. Formally, this is an unconditional growth model which will tell us (a) whether there were initial differences in marital happiness at time of marriage and (b) whether the trajectories for marriages differed over time. Thus the model at Level 2 is

$$\pi_{0i} = \beta_{00} + e_{0i}$$
$$\pi_{1i} = \beta_{10} + e_{1i}$$
$$\pi_{2i} = \beta_{20}$$

You may note here that there is no random effect for the squared component of time. This is because testing this component of the random effect of time resulted in the model not converging. This does happen commonly in data situations with few waves and likely reflects the high level of collinearity. The full combined model is

$$MARHAP_{ti} = \beta_{00} + \beta_{10}YEARS_{ti} + \beta_{20}YEARS_{ti}^2 + e_{0i} + e_{1i} + v_{ti}$$

The results here suggest a significant quadratic effect overall:

$$MARHAP_{ti} = 6.1413 - .02792 \cdot YEARS_{ti} + .000643 \cdot YEARS_{ti}^2 + e_{0i} + e_{1i} + v_{ti}$$

This pattern stands for a decline in marital happiness in the early to mid years of marriage, followed by a rise in the later years. Results for the random components are not shown here, but there is a strong random intercept effect here, standing for individual differences in the initial marital happiness across marriages. There are also random differences in the effects of time, standing for different trajectories over time.

The graph on Figure 12.3 shows the growth trajectories of three marriages, reflecting differences in these trajectories over time. There are unique patterns of decline, the minimum point in happiness, and the rate of rise in happiness thereafter. In fact, it is these individual trajectories that are modeled at Level 2.

FIGURE 12.3 ● QUADRATIC GROWTH TRAJECTORIES OF MARITAL HAPPINESS IN THREE MARRIAGES

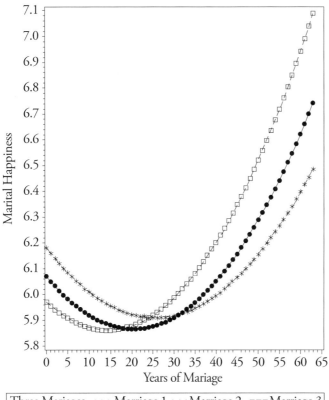

12.1.4 Piecewise Linear Growth Models

An alternative to the nonlinear function approach is to piece together changes in direction over time by using linear models between adjacent time points. This approach directly fits models for the kinds of three-wave trajectories shown earlier rather than "smoothing" the change in a quadratic, cubic, or higher-order function. This approach is attractive when we want to focus on the comparison of growth curves in different time periods or we want to know if the predictors of growth change over specific periods or when we want to turn a nonlinear function into a series of linear segments, as in a spline regression. There is an additional reason for considering this approach: By using distinct segments for an effect, we avoid the problem of collinearity that often occurs when using polynomials.

As an example, suppose we want to study the effect of age on changes in depression in the NSFH over Waves I and II. Even though there are only two waves here, there is a wide variety of ages available at each wave, and so we can treat age as the time variable at Level 1. This is called an *accelerated* longitudinal design. A prior spline regression suggests four distinct segments in the effects of age: from 17 to 22, from 23 to 38, from 39 to 68, and greater than 68.

The Level 1 model for time is thus divided up into four variables, one for each segment:

$$Y_{ti} = \pi_{0i} + \pi_{1i}a_{1ti} + \pi_{2i}a_{2ti} + \pi_{3i}a_{3ti} + \pi_{4i}a_{4ti} + v_{ti}$$

Where a_{1ti} = age 17 to 22, a_{2ti} = age 23 to 38, a_{3ti} = age 39 to 68, and a_{4ti} = age greater than 68.

To code the segments for a piecewise linear regression, use the approach shown in Table 12.3.

TABLE 12.3 ● CODING OF PIECEWISE LINEAR SEGMENTS

Age	17	18	19	...	22	23	24	...	38	39	...	68	69	70
a_{1ti}	0	1	2	...	5	5	5	5	5	5	5	5	5	5
a_{2ti}	0	0	0	0	0	1	2	...	16	16	16	16	16	16
a_{2ti}	0	0	0	0	0	0	0	0	0	1	...	30	30	30
a_{4ti}	0	0	0	0	0	0	0	0	0	0	0	1	1	2

The following SAS code creates these variables; we present this code mainly to reflect the logic of creating these variables, which will not vary across types of software. Note that each variable is centered so that it starts at 0. This allows the intercept in the growth curve model to be 0, at the initial age.

```
agegt17=age-17;
if 0<=agegt17<=5 then age17to22=agegt17;
if agegt17>5 then age17to22=5;
if agegt17=. then age17to22=.;

if 5<agegt17<=21 then age23to38=agegt17-5;
if agegt17<=5 then age23to38=0;
if agegt17>21 then age23to38=16;
if agegt17=. then age23to38=.;

if 21<agegt17<=51 then age39to68=agegt17-21;
if agegt17<=21 then age39to68=0;
if agegt17>51 then age39to68=30;
if agegt17=. then age39to68=.;
```

```
if agegt17>51 then agegt68=agegt17-51;
if agegt17<=51 then agegt68=0;
if agegt17=. then agegt68=.;
```

First, we note that *Agegt17* is centered so that it starts at 0 because the youngest age at Time 1 is 17. In the first segment, captured by *age17to22*, values increase from 0 at 17 to 5 at age 22 by just setting *age17to22* equal to *agegt17* in the range from 0 to 5. Typical of this coding, you do have to calculate the adjusted starting points and end points of each segment. When this variable reaches 5, the maximum value of the segment, it stays at 5 throughout later ages.

The second segment is coded by the variable *age23to38*. The trick here is to make sure it starts at 1 at age 23. This is done by noting that the range covered is equal to values greater than 5 and up to and including 21 on the centered age variable and then making *age23to38* equal to that variable minus 5. So when *agegt17* equals 6—the first value that qualifies in the If condition—the actual value of this variable is 6 – 5 = 1. Values outside of the range over which *age23to38* varies need to be set to constant values: Values 5 or less are set to 0, and values greater than 21 (the adjusted value for 38) are set to the top value of the range throughout (16). Later segments follow the same logic.

The results of this growth model in SAS PROC MIXED are shown in Table 12.4.

TABLE 12.4 ● RESULTS FOR A PIECEWISE LINEAR GROWTH MODEL OF DEPRESSION

Effect	Estimate	Standard Error	DF	t Value	Pr > |t|
Intercept	1.9979	0.08279	13E3	24.13	<.0001
age17to22	−0.1145	0.01791	9591	−6.39	<.0001
age23to38	−0.01698	0.002439	9591	−6.96	<.0001
age39to68	−0.00077	0.001243	9591	−0.62	0.5379
agegt68	0.01425	0.003624	9591	3.93	<.0001

Solution for Fixed Effects

Unlike a standard spline regression, here the coefficients are the actual slopes that apply to each age segment. Thus, we can see from the coefficients that depression declines rapidly from 17 to 22 but then flattens out considerably, exhibiting a shallower negative decline up to age 38, is essentially flat across midlife, from ages 39 to 68, and then increases after that.

The general trajectory by age is shown in the plot in Figure 12.4. This result is different from the earlier result for age and depression in Chapter 3 because this is a growth curve model—that is, it is not static. This model incorporates real changes in depression over time.

FIGURE 12.4 ● A PIECEWISE LINEAR GROWTH MODEL FOR DEPRESSION OVER THE ADULT LIFE COURSE

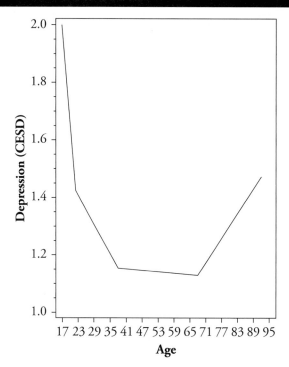

12.2 RUNNING GROWTH MODELS IN SAS

12.2.1 Data Structures for Growth Models

The Level-1 model is a "within-person" model, with multiple-time points. In essence, that means that you need a "person-period" data set for the Level-1 model: This is a data set that has multiple observations per person, equal to the number of repeated observations for that person. Each observation contains information for all variables but only at that point in time. It is not necessary for each person to be measured at each wave to be included in this approach. They can be represented by whatever waves are observed.

Time-varying variables that change at each observation must be programmed so that the data contains the relevant value at each time point. Methods for creating an appropriate person-period data set for this kind of model are discussed in the examples that follow.

We present first a simple and generic example of implementing growth curves in SAS, based on Singer (1998).

12.2.1.1 An Unconditional Growth Model

Start with a simple linear growth model with random effects only at the 2nd level:

$$Y_{ti} = \pi_{0i} + \pi_{1i}(\text{TIME}_{ti}) + v_{ti}$$
$$\pi_{0i} = \beta_{00} + e_{0i}$$
$$\pi_{1i} = \beta_{10} + e_{1i}$$

This is the unconditional growth model again: It tests for random variation in both initial status and change over time.

The combined model has two fixed effects and three random effects:

$$Y_{ti} = \underbrace{\beta_{00} + \beta_{10}(\text{TIME}_{ti})}_{\text{fixed}} + \underbrace{e_{0i} + \text{TIME}_{ti} \cdot e_{1i} + v_{it}}_{\text{random}}$$

The growth curve model requires you to create a person-period data set first. In this case, assuming you have a data set where each observation contains all of the multiple-wave information for each person and you call the time variables T1 to T4 (it could be ages or other time markers), and the outcome variables are ACH1 to ACH4, standing for achievement, then the SAS code that follows will create a person-period data set, from a "flat file" called *temp*:

```
data followup;
   Set temp;
array tvar(4) t1-t4;
array out(4) ACH1-ACH4;
do i=1-4;
   TIME = tvar(i);
   ACH = out (i);
   output;
end;
```

Notice here that a different value of ACH for each time point is written to the values for this variable *over* time. The OUTPUT statement looks innocuous, but it is the essential statement here: It writes a new observation to a new data set at each iteration of the DO loop.

If there are other time varying variables you need to handle them the same way in this DO loop. The code for the unconditional growth model in PROC MIXED is

```
proc mixed noclprint covtest;
Class id;
Model ach=time / solution ddfm=bw notest;
Random intercept time / subject=id type=un;
```

The main difference compared to previous HLM examples is the use of "ID" as the class variable and the "subject" identifier in the random statement. This is actually the case id of the respondent.

If you want β_{00} to equal initial status on Y, you must code TIME= 0 at the first time point.

12.2.1.2 Adding Person-Level Effects

The model now—using "COVAR" to stand for any individual-level variable—is

$$Y_{it} = \pi_{0i} + \pi_{1i}(\text{TIME}_{ti}) + v_{ti}$$
$$\pi_{0i} = \beta_{00} + \beta_{01}(\text{COVAR})_i + e_{0i}$$
$$\pi_{1i} = \beta_{10} + \beta_{11}(\text{COVAR})_i + e_{1i}$$

The combined model here is

$$Y_{it} = \beta_{00} + \beta_{10}(\text{TIME}_{ti}) + \beta_{01}(\text{COVAR})_i + \beta_{11}(\text{COVAR}_i \cdot \text{TIME}_{ti}) + v_{ti} + e_{0i} + \text{TIME}_{ti} \cdot e_{1i}$$

The SAS code in PROC MIXED is

```
proc mixed noclprint covtest;
Class id;
Model ach= time covar time*covar / solution ddfm=bw notest;
Random intercept time /type=un sub=id;
```

As before, TYPE=UN specifies an unconstrained error matrix. For models in which only π_{0i} is random, we would have "*compound symmetry*" as a structure, which means that TYPE=UN can be dropped. However, PROC MIXED allows you to assess the viability of different assumptions about error structures, using the REPEATED statement. Basically, you want to compare the likelihood ratio of different models, in which TYPE=CS (compound symmetry), or TYPE=UN, or TYPE=AR (ARIMA structure), and so forth.

To use the REPEATED statement *instead* of the RANDOM statement:

- Create a new class variable called TIME, for the measure of time.

- Specify both ID and TIME in the CLASS statement.

- Specify REPEATED as

```
Repeated time / type=ar(1) sub=id R;
```

There are many alternative error structures that can be used here: See Singer and Willett (2003) for a complete discussion of the different types and structures of error covariance matrices that are possible. The advantage of TYPE=UN is that it makes no assumptions about these relationships in the error covariance matrix and thus allows for the least restrictive approach to estimating the model.

12.3 MODELING THE TRAJECTORY OF NET WORTH FROM EARLY TO MID-ADULTHOOD

We turn to a more realistic example of a growth curve model, using the National Longitudinal Survey of Youth, 1979 (NLSY79) data to track changes in family net worth from the age of 21 to 49 among the youth originally sampled in 1979. The concept of net worth goes beyond family income, by adding in all assets currently owned (houses, values of investments) minus all of the debts currently owed (mortgages, loans, credit cards, business losses, etc.).

Our interest in this example is to test the long-term effect of childhood poverty on net worth trajectories in adulthood. This can be done by testing a two-way interaction between childhood poverty and the age trajectory over this period. Of course, our hypothesis is that childhood poverty will suppress the net worth trajectory at some point—but we do not know at what point in the life course: It could be at the starting point in adulthood; it could be over the 20s; or it could be more in midlife, when children are more likely to make demands on finances.

Childhood poverty is a fixed factor in this model: It does not change over the period of observation. In this analysis, it is coded into three groups: no poverty over the four-year period at the beginning of the study, poverty in one or two of those years ("unstable"), and poverty for three or more of those years ("stable").

We also demonstrate how to code and incorporate time-varying factors over the life course, by tracking changes in marital status over time. We do this in two ways: At each time point, we assess the two-year lagged effect of marital status on net worth while also assessing the effect of entries into and exits out of marriage over that period. There are many other possibilities in this analysis, but here we focus on (a) the shape of the trajectories for net worth over the early to middle stages of adulthood, (b) the role of childhood poverty and how its implications evolve over time, and (c) the main effects of marital status and transitions into and out of marriage during adulthood.

12.3.1 Setting Up the Data

We are following net worth from 1986 to 2006 in the NLSY: In 1986 the youngest age was 21, and in 2006 the oldest age was 49. We include 11 time points, in two-year increments.

We show the coding here in some detail because this is the first of a number of examples that use person-period data. This is a common data structure used by many methods, as we will see in the chapters ahead.

In the data step, you need to develop variables that stand for the value of time-varying variables at each wave over this period. The code fragment that follows shows the logic of doing this for three variables: marital status, age, and family net worth at each point in time:

```
/* code marital status starting in 1985 for lagged effect */

array marstat (11) r1890801 r2445301 r3074700 r3656800 r4418400 r5081400
                   r5166700 r6479300 r7007000 r7704300 r8496700;

array marryr (11) marrlag86 marrlag88 marrlag90 marrlag92 marrlag94 marrlag96
     marrlag98 marrlag00 marrlag02 marrlag04 marrlag06;

array nonmarryr (11) notmarrlag86 notmarrlag88 notmarrlag90 notmarrlag92
     notmarrlag94 notmarrlag96 notmarrlag98 notmarrlag00 notmarrlag02
     notmarrlag04 notmarrlag06;

do i=1 to 11;

if marstat(i)=1 then marryr(i)=1; else marryr(i)=0;
if marstat(i)>=2 then nonmarryr(i)=1; else nonmarryr(i)=0;
if marstat(i)<0 then marryr(i)=.;

end;

/*code age as main time variable */

array ages (11) r2258110 r2871300 r3401700 r4007600 r5081700 r5167000 r6479800
r7007500 r7704800 r8497200 t0989000;

array agebyyr (11) age86 age88 age90 age92 age94 age96 age98 age00 age02 age04
age06;

do i=1 to 11;

agebyyr(i)=ages(i);
if ages(i)<0 then agebyyr(i)=.;
end;
```

```
/* dependent variable net worth */

array net (11) r2153901 r2735401 r3293301 r3911001 r5046601 r5728001 r6426001
r6940101 networth2002 r8378701 networth2006;
array out (11) famnetworth86 famnetworth88 famnetworth90 famnetworth92
famnetworth94 famnetworth96 famnetworth98 famnetworth00 famnetworth02
famnetworth04 famnetworth06;

do i=1 to 11;
out(i) = net(i);
if net(i)<0 then out(i)=.;
end;
```

Creating these variables begins, in each case, by defining two arrays: one for the input variables in the appropriate years for each variable and one for the output variables, renamed and/or recoded. We use the last two years of the survey year as the suffix of the output variables. One can use lagged values of independent variables here: For example, the actual variables used for marital status are that status from 1 to 2 years before that wave.

Essentially, most of this coding focuses on renaming and recoding original variables as necessary. The time variable here is embodied by the individual ages from 1986 to 2006. After this data step, creating a data set called "merged," you begin another data step to create a person-period data set, as follows:

```
data growthnetworth;
      set merged;

array worth (11) famnetworth86 famnetworth88 famnetworth90 famnetworth92
famnetworth94 famnetworth96 famnetworth98 famnetworth00 famnetworth02
famnetworth04 famnetworth06;

array agexyr (11) age86 age88 age90 age92 age94 age96 age98 age00 age02 age04 age06;

array marrlag (11) marrlag86 marrlag88 marrlag90 marrlag92 marrlag94 marrlag96
marrlag98 marrlag00 marrlag02 marrlag04 marrlag06;

array notmarrlag (11) notmarrlag86 notmarrlag88 notmarrlag90 notmarrlag92
notmarrlag94 notmarrlag96 notmarrlag98 notmarrlag00 notmarrlag02 notmarrlag04
notmarrlag06;

array gain86to06 (11) marr86 marr88 marr90 marr92 marr94 marr96 marr98 marr00
marr02 marr04 marr06;

array loss86to06 (11) div86 div88 div90 div92 div94 div96 div98 div00 div02
div04 div06;

array unempinlf (11) unemp86 unemp88 unemp90 unemp92 unemp94 unemp96 unemp98
unemp00 unemp02 unemp04 unemp06;

do i=1 to 11;
famnetworth = worth(i);
age = agexyr(i);
marriedlag = marrlag(i);
notmarriedlag=notmarrlag(i);
entermarr = gain86to06(i);
exitmarr = loss86to06(i);
unemployed = unempinlf(i);
```

```
agecen=age-21;

age2=agecen**2;
age3=agecen**3;
age4=agecen**4;
wave=1984+(i*2);

output;
end;
```

This code uses arrays to bring in the time-varying variables from the prior data step. In the DO loop, new variables are named for each time-varying variable, using the values in turn from each time point. At the bottom of the DO loop, an ***output*** statement writes a new observation for each iteration.

We also center the values of age—our measure of time. This is done by subtracting the minimum value of age from raw age, so that it shifts the minimum value to 0. When this is done, the intercept becomes differences on the outcome at the initial wave—when respondents are 21. We also develop polynomial values of age here to test the nonlinearity of time, including quadratic, cubic, and quartic effects.

Finally, we make the variable "wave" equal to its actual year values using a mathematical "trick" to create it: Wave = 1984 + ($i*2$), so that in 1986, when $i = 1$, it is 1986, in 1988, when $i = 2$, it is 1988, in 1990, when $i = 3$, it is 1990, and so forth.

It is helpful to see the person-period data this data step produces. In Table 12.5, we reproduce the first 55 observations, showing the structure of the data and values for both time-specific and the newly written variables for age.

TABLE 12.5 ● A PERSON-PERIOD DATA SET SHOWING WRITTEN VALUES OF AGE

Obs	Rcaseid	wave	agecen	age	age86	age88	age90	age92	age94	age96	age98	age00	age02	age04	age06
1	3	1986	3	24	24	26	29	30	33	34	36	38	40	.	44
2	3	1988	5	26	24	26	29	30	33	34	36	38	40	.	44
3	3	1990	8	29	24	26	29	30	33	34	36	38	40	.	44
4	3	1992	9	30	24	26	29	30	33	34	36	38	40	.	44
5	3	1994	12	33	24	26	29	30	33	34	36	38	40	.	44
6	3	1996	13	34	24	26	29	30	33	34	36	38	40	.	44
7	3	1998	15	36	24	26	29	30	33	34	36	38	40	.	44
8	3	2000	17	38	24	26	29	30	33	34	36	38	40	.	44
9	3	2002	19	40	24	26	29	30	33	34	36	38	40	.	44
10	3	2004	.	.	24	26	29	30	33	34	36	38	40	.	44
11	3	2006	23	44	24	26	29	30	33	34	36	38	40	.	44
12	6	1986	4	25	25	27	29	31	33	35	.	39	41	45	45
13	6	1988	6	27	25	27	29	31	33	35	.	39	41	45	45
14	6	1990	8	29	25	27	29	31	33	35	.	39	41	45	45
15	6	1992	10	31	25	27	29	31	33	35	.	39	41	45	45
16	6	1994	12	33	25	27	29	31	33	35	.	39	41	45	45
17	6	1996	14	35	25	27	29	31	33	35	.	39	41	45	45
18	6	1998	.	.	25	27	29	31	33	35	.	39	41	45	45

(Continued)

TABLE 12.5 ● Continued

Obs	Rcaseid	wave	agecen	age	age86	age88	age90	age92	age94	age96	age98	age00	age02	age04	age06
19	6	2000	18	39	25	27	29	31	33	35	.	39	41	45	45
20	6	2002	20	41	25	27	29	31	33	35	.	39	41	45	45
21	6	2004	24	45	25	27	29	31	33	35	.	39	41	45	45
22	6	2006	24	45	25	27	29	31	33	35	.	39	41	45	45
23	7	1986	0	21	21	24	26	28	30	31	33	35	38	39	41
24	7	1988	3	24	21	24	26	28	30	31	33	35	38	39	41
25	7	1990	5	26	21	24	26	28	30	31	33	35	38	39	41
26	7	1992	7	28	21	24	26	28	30	31	33	35	38	39	41
27	7	1994	9	30	21	24	26	28	30	31	33	35	38	39	41
28	7	1996	10	31	21	24	26	28	30	31	33	35	38	39	41
29	7	1998	12	33	21	24	26	28	30	31	33	35	38	39	41
30	7	2000	14	35	21	24	26	28	30	31	33	35	38	39	41
31	7	2002	17	38	21	24	26	28	30	31	33	35	38	39	41
32	7	2004	18	39	21	24	26	28	30	31	33	35	38	39	41
33	7	2006	20	41	21	24	26	28	30	31	33	35	38	39	41
34	8	1986	6	27	27	30	32	33	36	37	39	42	43	45	47
35	8	1988	9	30	27	30	32	33	36	37	39	42	43	45	47
36	8	1990	11	32	27	30	32	33	36	37	39	42	43	45	47
37	8	1992	12	33	27	30	32	33	36	37	39	42	43	45	47
38	8	1994	15	36	27	30	32	33	36	37	39	42	43	45	47
39	8	1996	16	37	27	30	32	33	36	37	39	42	43	45	47
40	8	1998	18	39	27	30	32	33	36	37	39	42	43	45	47
41	8	2000	21	42	27	30	32	33	36	37	39	42	43	45	47
42	8	2002	22	43	27	30	32	33	36	37	39	42	43	45	47
43	8	2004	24	45	27	30	32	33	36	37	39	42	43	45	47
44	8	2006	26	47	27	30	32	33	36	37	39	42	43	45	47
45	13	1986	6	27	27	29	31	33	35	37	39	42	43	46	47
46	13	1988	8	29	27	29	31	33	35	37	39	42	43	46	47
47	13	1990	10	31	27	29	31	33	35	37	39	42	43	46	47
48	13	1992	12	33	27	29	31	33	35	37	39	42	43	46	47
49	13	1994	14	35	27	29	31	33	35	37	39	42	43	46	47
50	13	1996	16	37	27	29	31	33	35	37	39	42	43	46	47
51	13	1998	18	39	27	29	31	33	35	37	39	42	43	46	47
52	13	2000	21	42	27	29	31	33	35	37	39	42	43	46	47
53	13	2002	22	43	27	29	31	33	35	37	39	42	43	46	47
54	13	2004	25	46	27	29	31	33	35	37	39	42	43	46	47
55	13	2006	26	47	27	29	31	33	35	37	39	42	43	46	47

You can see that each person has 11 observations, so that the data set is structured by person and then waves within persons. You can also track how age at each wave is written to the person-period data. For example, for respondent with ID = 3, the age in 1986 is 24. That becomes 3 when centered by subtracting 21 (agecen). Moving forward to a later year, we see that age96 = 34, and the value of age in the wave for 1996 is 34. The centered value of age is then that value minus 21, which is 34 - 21 = 13 in 1996.

Values for the same observations on the married dummy variable are shown in Table 12.6.

TABLE 12.6 ● A PERSON-PERIOD DATA SET SHOWING WRITTEN VALUES OF MARITAL STATUS OVER TIME

Obs	R caseid	wave	Marrlag	marrlag 86	marrlag 88	marrlag 90	marrlag 92	marrlag 94	marrlag 96	marrlag 98	marrlag 00	marrlag 02	marrlag 04	marrlag 06
1	3	1986	1	1	1	1	1	1	1	1	1	1	1	.
2	3	1988	1	1	1	1	1	1	1	1	1	1	1	.

Obs	caseid R	wave	Marrlag	marrlag 86	marrlag 88	marrlag 90	marrlag 92	marrlag 94	marrlag 96	marrlag 98	marrlag 00	marrlag 02	marrlag 04	marrlag 06
3	3	1990	1	1	1	1	1	1	1	1	1	1	1	.
4	3	1992	1	1	1	1	1	1	1	1	1	1	1	.
5	3	1994	1	1	1	1	1	1	1	1	1	1	1	.
6	3	1996	1	1	1	1	1	1	1	1	1	1	1	.
7	3	1998	1	1	1	1	1	1	1	1	1	1	1	.
8	3	2000	1	1	1	1	1	1	1	1	1	1	1	.
9	3	2002	1	1	1	1	1	1	1	1	1	1	1	.
10	3	2004	1	1	1	1	1	1	1	1	1	1	1	.
11	3	2006	.	1	1	1	1	1	1	1	1	1	1	.
12	6	1986	0	0	0	0	1	1	1	1	.	1	1	1
13	6	1988	0	0	0	0	1	1	1	1	.	1	1	1
14	6	1990	0	0	0	0	1	1	1	1	.	1	1	1
15	6	1992	1	0	0	0	1	1	1	1	.	1	1	1
16	6	1994	1	0	0	0	1	1	1	1	.	1	1	1
17	6	1996	1	0	0	0	1	1	1	1	.	1	1	1
18	6	1998	1	0	0	0	1	1	1	1	.	1	1	1
19	6	2000	.	0	0	0	1	1	1	1	.	1	1	1
20	6	2002	1	0	0	0	1	1	1	1	.	1	1	1
21	6	2004	1	0	0	0	1	1	1	1	.	1	1	1
22	6	2006	1	0	0	0	1	1	1	1	.	1	1	1
23	7	1986	0	0	0	0	1	1	0	0	0	0	0	0
24	7	1988	0	0	0	0	1	1	0	0	0	0	0	0
25	7	1990	0	0	0	0	1	1	0	0	0	0	0	0
26	7	1992	1	0	0	0	1	1	0	0	0	0	0	0
27	7	1994	1	0	0	0	1	1	0	0	0	0	0	0
28	7	1996	0	0	0	0	1	1	0	0	0	0	0	0
29	7	1998	0	0	0	0	1	1	0	0	0	0	0	0
30	7	2000	0	0	0	0	1	1	0	0	0	0	0	0
31	7	2002	0	0	0	0	1	1	0	0	0	0	0	0
32	7	2004	0	0	0	0	1	1	0	0	0	0	0	0
33	7	2006	0	0	0	0	1	1	0	0	0	0	0	0
34	8	1986	1	1	1	0	0	0	0	0	0	0	0	0
35	8	1988	1	1	1	0	0	0	0	0	0	0	0	0
36	8	1990	0	1	1	0	0	0	0	0	0	0	0	0
37	8	1992	0	1	1	0	0	0	0	0	0	0	0	0
38	8	1994	0	1	1	0	0	0	0	0	0	0	0	0
39	8	1996	0	1	1	0	0	0	0	0	0	0	0	0
40	8	1998	0	1	1	0	0	0	0	0	0	0	0	0
41	8	2000	0	1	1	0	0	0	0	0	0	0	0	0
42	8	2002	0	1	1	0	0	0	0	0	0	0	0	0
43	8	2004	0	1	1	0	0	0	0	0	0	0	0	0
44	8	2006	0	1	1	0	0	0	0	0	0	0	0	0
45	13	1986	0	0	0	1	1	1	1	1	1	0	0	0
46	13	1988	0	0	0	1	1	1	1	1	1	0	0	0
47	13	1990	1	0	0	1	1	1	1	1	1	0	0	0
48	13	1992	1	0	0	1	1	1	1	1	1	0	0	0
49	13	1994	1	0	0	1	1	1	1	1	1	0	0	0
50	13	1996	1	0	0	1	1	1	1	1	1	0	0	0
51	13	1998	1	0	0	1	1	1	1	1	1	0	0	0
52	13	2000	1	0	0	1	1	1	1	1	1	0	0	0
53	13	2002	0	0	0	1	1	1	1	1	1	0	0	0
54	13	2004	0	0	0	1	1	1	1	1	1	0	0	0
55	13	2006	0	0	0	1	1	1	1	1	1	0	0	0

It is helpful to trace how the values for married in each year are written to the value for the married over time. ID = 7 was not married in 1986 or 1988 or 1990 but was married by 1992. However, by 1996, this person was unmarried again.

12.3.2 The Unconditional Growth Model

The initial model we considered tested for the nonlinear effects of age. Both the quartic and cubic components were not significant, but there was a quadratic effect. The signs of these effects suggest either a net loss in worth over early adulthood—suggesting greater debts— or a flat line while debts counteract assets. But after some point on this curve, the effect is positive.

PROC MIXED is used here similarly to the case for HLM. The code for this model is

```
proc mixed data=growthnetworth covtest noclprint info update;
class rcaseid;
model famnetworth = agecen age2 / solution ddfm=bw notest ;
random intercept age / sub=rcaseid type=un;

title 'Growth Curve Model for Family Net Worth';
    run;
```

In this case, the *subject=* option in the RANDOM statement refers to the case id of the respondent, and there are random effects for both the intercept and age. We did not test a separate random effect of age squared. We did not pursue a spline version in this example, but it would help to distinguish different components of random effects. Many results in the literature using growth curves stick to a "smooth function" version of time, to show differences in trajectories exactly, and we follow that practice here.

Results for this model are shown in Table 12.7.

| TABLE 12.7 ● RESULTS FOR AN UNCONDITIONAL GROWTH MODEL FOR NET WORTH | | | | | |

Covariance Parameter Estimates					
Cov Parm	Subject	Estimate	Standard Error	Z Value	Pr Z
UN(1,1)	Rcaseid	3.486E11	8.2193E9	42.41	<.0001
UN(2,1)	Rcaseid	−1.29E10	2.9046E8	−44.27	<.0001
UN(2,2)	Rcaseid	4.7891E8	10405819	46.02	<.0001
Residual		2.142E10	1.5364E8	139.42	<.0001

Solution for Fixed Effects					
Effect	Estimate	Standard Error	DF	*t* Value	Pr > |t|
Intercept	22001	3569.83	5314	6.16	<.0001
agecen	−1592.20	558.20	44E3	−2.85	0.0043
age2	470.77	16.5257	44E3	28.49	<.0001

Note that the quadratic effect of age suggests a low point in net worth around the age of 22.7, uncentered. This can be figured out from applying the calculation from the first derivative to the age coefficients here, remembering that the minimum = $(-b_1) / 2b_2$. This produces a value of 1.7; translated, it is 22.7, given that in the centered version of age 21 = 0.

Both the random effect of initial status and the random effect of age here are significant—in fact, very significant. This is more typical in growth curve models where it is easy to expect differences over time due to individual characteristics. This result does suggest that both initial status and the nature of trajectories of net worth vary across individuals.

12.3.3 Adding the Effect of Marital Status and Marital Transitions

Adding individual Level-2 variables to the model is straightforward, as shown in this code for PROC MIXED:

```
proc mixed data=growthnetworth covtest noclprint info update;
class rcaseid;
model famnetworth = agecen age2 marriedlag entermarr exitmarr
                            / solution ddfm=bw notest ;
random intercept age / sub=rcaseid type=un;
title 'Growth Curve Model for Family Net Worth';
run;
```

The only difference here is the added main effects for married, as a lagged dummy variable, and dummy variables for entering and exiting marriage over the last two years. Results are shown for the fixed effects only in Table 12.8.

TABLE 12.8 ● EFFECTS OF MARITAL STATUS AND MARITAL TRANSITIONS ON NET WORTH

Solution for Fixed Effects					
Effect	Estimate	Standard Error	DF	*t* Value	Pr > |t|
Intercept	14190	3610.90	5310	3.93	<.0001
agecen	−2239.68	559.72	43E3	−4.00	<.0001
age2	489.08	16.7193	43E3	29.25	<.0001
marriedlag	21233	2011.08	43E3	10.56	<.0001
entermarr	6909.31	7775.39	43E3	0.89	0.3742
exitmarr	−20171	7025.88	43E3	−2.87	0.0041

These results suggest that *being* married increases net worth over time, as expected, but a recent entry into marriage does not. However, also as expected, leaving a marriage reduces average net worth by over $20,000. The effects of age, net of marital status, appear to be slightly stronger, with a stronger decline in the initial phase and a stronger rate of increase after the minimum point in net worth.

12.3.4 The Effects of Childhood Poverty on Initial Status

Are there overall effects of childhood poverty on the *starting* differences in net worth we observe—that is, net worth at age 21? This is a straightforward cross-over effects model for the intercept at Level 1, which is the initial measured net worth. The run of PROC MIXED simply adds the poverty dummy variables to the MODEL statement:

```
proc mixed data=growthnetworth covtest noclprint info update;
class rcaseid;
model famnetworth = agecen age2 marriedlag entermarr exitmarr
                    stablepoverty unstablepoverty / solution ddfm=bw notest;
random intercept age / sub=rcaseid type=un;
title 'Growth Curve Model for Family Net Worth';
run;
```

We note that the reference group here are people not in poverty at all over the four years at the beginning of the NLSY. Results suggest powerful effects for these background variables, as shown in Table 12.9.

TABLE 12.9 ● THE EFFECT OF FAMILY POVERTY DURING ADOLESCENCE ON INITIAL DIFFERENCES IN NET WORTH

Covariance Parameter Estimates					
Cov Parm	Subject	Estimate	Standard Error	Z Value	Pr Z
UN(1,1)	Rcaseid	3.38E11	8.0376E9	42.05	<.0001
UN(2,1)	Rcaseid	−1.25E10	2.8358E8	−43.95	<.0001
UN(2,2)	Rcaseid	4.6386E8	10147143	45.71	<.0001
Residual		2.097E10	1.5239E8	137.60	<.0001

Solution for Fixed Effects					
Effect	Estimate	Standard Error	DF	t Value	Pr > |t|
Intercept	22747	3802.80	5308	5.98	<.0001
agecen	−2311.35	560.04	43E3	−4.13	<.0001
age2	492.09	16.7331	43E3	29.41	<.0001
marriedlag	19663	2020.73	43E3	9.73	<.0001
entermarr	6765.27	7774.35	43E3	0.87	0.3842
exitmarr	−20173	7025.03	43E3	−2.87	0.0041
stablepoverty	−30982	5090.12	5308	−6.09	<.0001
unstablepoverty	−16405	2914.56	5308	−5.63	<.0001

For those who experienced stable poverty, initial net worth is actually less than zero, if they are unmarried: This can be seen by adding the "stablepoverty" coefficient to the intercept. The average net worth in this group is $22,747 − $30,982 = -$8,235. Unstable poverty also has an effect, but it is moderated and almost halfway between the reference value of $22,747 and the stable poverty group. Their average net worth at 21 is in fact $22,747 − $16,405 = $6,342.

We also notice here a somewhat reduced random intercept variance, which was 3.49E11 in the original unconditional model, and is 3.38E11 here. Of course, finding *all* of the reasons for these initial differences would require many more variables than poverty alone, analogous to what we would expect when explaining individual differences in a standard regression.

12.3.5 The Impact of Poverty on Net Worth over Time

In the final model, we estimate the differential net worth trajectories due to differences in childhood poverty. This is a "cross-level" interaction between personal poverty history in adolescence and time. As in the case of HLM, we simply write out the interactions we want to estimate as part of the MODEL statement:

```
proc mixed data=growthnetworth covtest noclprint info update;
class rcaseid;
model famnetworth = agecen age2 marriedlag entermarr exitmarr
                    stablepoverty unstablepoverty stablepoverty*agecen stablepoverty*age2
                    unstablepoverty*agecen unstablepoverty*age2 / solution ddfm=bw
                    notest ;
random intercept age / sub=rcaseid type=un;
title 'Growth Curve Model for Family Net Worth';
run;
```

The interactions here involve both levels of poverty crossed with both components of the effects of time. Results shown on Table 12.10 clearly suggest the importance of early poverty for the development of net worth in middle adulthood.

TABLE 12.10 ● THE EFFECTS OF POVERTY ON THE DEVELOPMENT OF NET WORTH IN ADULTHOOD

Solution for Fixed Effects					
Effect	Estimate	Standard Error	DF	t Value	Pr > |t|
Intercept	19491	4553.53	5308	4.28	<.0001
agecen	−2282.16	702.44	43E3	−3.25	0.0012
age2	580.19	20.8010	43E3	27.89	<.0001
marriedlag	19878	2018.22	43E3	9.85	<.0001
entermarr	6558.60	7769.71	43E3	0.84	0.3986
exitmarr	−20216	7020.17	43E3	−2.88	0.0040
stablepoverty	−7345.00	13358	5308	−0.55	0.5825
unstablepoverty	−14227	7845.59	5308	−1.81	0.0698
agecen*stablepoverty	−1961.15	2167.29	43E3	−0.90	0.3655
age2*stablepoverty	−259.23	68.1405	43E3	−3.80	0.0001
agecen*unstablepover	1033.46	1232.51	43E3	0.84	0.4018
age2*unstablepoverty	−257.67	37.1100	43E3	−6.94	<.0001

Both interactions are significant: For both stable and unstable poverty, we see that there are no differences in the trajectories in early adulthood, but after that point, there is a depressed rate of growth in net worth, increasing inequalities in net worth through middle adulthood.

One can work out the unique curves of each group from the coefficients, but it is helpful to supplement these calculations by plotting the trajectories separately across the three poverty status groups. This can be done using code that produces predicted values for each group separately. We demonstrate this using a model that excludes the effect of marriage transitions—but that is only to simplify the coding here. The DO loops here create the predicted values:

```
data null;
group=0;
array pov (3) nopov unstable stable;
do povgrp=1 to 3;
nopov=0; unstable=0; stable=0;
pov(povgrp)=1;
```

```
group=group+1;
do age=0 to 28;

networth = 27381 - 1574.92*age + 558.59*age**2 - 9706.26*stable - 14763*unstable
    - 2333.08*age*stable - 245.89*(age**2)*stable + 649.43*age*unstable
    - 240.12*(age**2)*unstable;

output;
end;
end;
```

This produces a data set with predicted values of net worth, separately for the three groups. We plotted the differential trajectories using PROC GPLOT:

```
PROC GPLOT DATA = plotit;
   PLOT networth*age = group /
haxis=axis2 vaxis=axis1 legend=legend1 frame;
RUN;
```

The resulting plot in Figure 12.5 clearly shows the incremental disadvantage due to childhood poverty.

FIGURE 12.5 ⬡ PLOTTING THE EFFECT OF FAMILY POVERTY ON NET WORTH THROUGH MID-ADULTHOOD

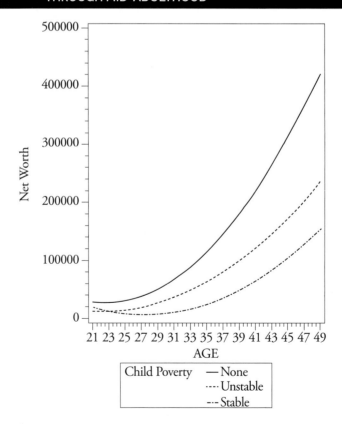

The reason this example is useful is that it clearly shows the nature of the growth in disparities in wealth over time, in other words, the multiplicative consequences of poverty in childhood that do take time to develop over adulthood. By the age of 50, there is almost a $300,000 difference in net worth for those from stable poverty backgrounds versus those with no poverty background.

12.4 MODELING THE TRAJECTORY OF INTERNALIZING PROBLEMS OVER ADOLESCENCE

This example uses the National Survey of Children data to estimate a growth curve model for internalizing problems, including primarily feelings of depression and anxiety. An important issue in growth curve models in general is the consistency of measures used over time in a study: Each measure at each wave must be the same for the model to make sense. In adults, this is usually not a problem, but with children, it can be a problem. For example, mothers may report variables for children up to a certain age, such as 12, and then children report their own values after that age. This creates a potential problem of comparability over time.

In this example, we consider the role of neighborhood disadvantage (an index of seven indicators at the neighborhood level) in a three-level growth curve model. In this model, the effects of time are at Level 1, person effects are at Level 2, and neighborhood effects are at Level 3. We model a cross-over effect of neighborhood disadvantage through time and also the dependence of the impact of time on neighborhood disadvantage, using interactions. The issue is *when* differences by neighborhood begin to appear and how growth trajectories in depression diverge beyond that point. To take into account nonlinear change, we model the trajectories as potentially cubic, to allow for complex changes over a formative and unstable period of life.

In this example, using the ***accelerated longitudinal design*** approach discussed earlier, we follow changes in internalizing problems from the age of 12 to age 24. Neighborhood disadvantage is measured during school-age childhood: from 6 to 11 years old, and thus appears as a fixed background variable in this analysis. We do not show the details of the program used to produce the results. Time is modeled using the variables *kidyrgt10* (which is the child's age minus 10, so that 10 equals the zero point of time), *kidyrsq* (the square of *kidyrgt10*), and *kidyrcu* (the cube of *kidyrgt10*).

A number of models were considered, leading to a "final" model with nonlinear effects of time and an interaction between background neighborhood disadvantage (*origndi*) and time. The results from this model show that the effect of age is cubic and that *all* of the components of the age effect interact with neighborhood disadvantage. The coefficients are difficult to interpret, but the plot following the results (Figure 12.6) shows the nature of the differential trajectory of depression resulting from contrasting past neighborhoods.

TABLE 12.11 ● RANDOM EFFECTS IN A THREE-LEVEL GROWTH MODEL

Covariance Parameter Estimates					
Cov Parm	Subject	Estimate	Standard Error	Z Value	Pr Z
UN(1,1)	zipcode	0.4334	0.1692	2.56	0.0052
UN(1,1)	casenum(zipcode)	10.9511	2.1801	5.02	<.0001
UN(2,1)	casenum(zipcode)	−0.7663	0.2354	−3.26	0.0011
UN(2,2)	casenum(zipcode)	0.08200	0.03100	2.65	0.0041
Residual		4.2742	0.7378	5.79	<.0001

TABLE 12.12 ● FIXED EFFECTS FROM THE FINAL THREE-LEVEL MODEL

Solution for Fixed Effects					
Effect	Estimate	Standard Error	DF	t Value	Pr > |t|
Intercept	13.8737	0.5090	496	27.26	<.0001
kidyrgt10	0.3862	0.2830	1220	1.36	0.1726
kidyrsq	−0.1155	0.04491	1220	−2.57	0.0102
kidyrcu	0.005813	0.002119	1220	2.74	0.0062
origndi	−1.3760	0.5456	1220	−2.52	0.0118
kidyrgt10*origndi	0.7083	0.3032	1220	2.34	0.0196
kidyrsq*origndi	−0.1055	0.04784	1220	−2.21	0.0276
kidyrcu*origndi	0.005192	0.002257	1220	2.30	0.0216

There are random effects both at the person and neighborhood level included in this model (Table 12.11). These random effects stand for overall neighborhood differences (expressed through the neighborhood identifier, *zipcode*), overall person differences at initial status (UN [1,1] for casenum nested in zipcode), and differences in the effect of time across individuals (UN [2,2] for casenum nested in zipcode). The actual coefficients from this model are shown in Table 12.12.

According to the plot in Figure 12.6, differences in depression appear around the age of 19, and especially in high disadvantage neighborhoods, it accelerates rapidly. Prior to that point, past neighborhood disadvantage has little effect. Note that the information this model yields is unique: The literature says nothing about the moment of onset of contextual impacts on mental health in the life course; this model speaks to that issue. It also shows us that inequality grows rapidly after that point.

FIGURE 12.6 ● THE EFFECTS OF CHILDHOOD NEIGHBORHOOD DISADVANTAGE ON DISTRESS DURING THE ADULT TRANSITION.

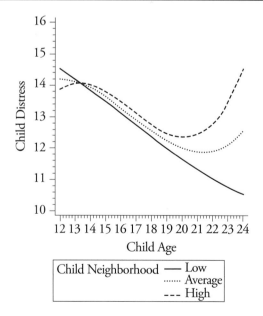

12.5 PUBLISHED EXAMPLES

12.5.1 Gender and Race Differences in Occupational Stratification over the Life Course

Tracking differential occupational trajectories over adulthood by race and gender is a natural fit for a growth curve approach. As with previous examples, the growth curve model allows us to see *when* trajectories diverge or converge. The timing of these changes has to be part of the explanation, whereas a static outcome approach—such as asking what explains occupational achievement at age 50—may miss essential differences in the pivotal moments in the life course when changes occur.

Miech, Eaton, and Liang (2003) applied the growth curve model to study race and gender differences in occupational standing over adulthood using the National Longitudinal Survey of Youth data from 1982 to 1998. Miech et al. review two broad and opposite arguments present in the literature: Inequalities should diminish over adulthood (market forces enhance the inefficiency of discrimination in hiring over time; government interventions may have reduced inequality after the civil rights movement); versus, inequalities should persist or grow over adulthood (due to a segmented labor market, with strong barriers for mobility from secondary to the primary "good" jobs, vague hiring criteria for upper management positions, tendencies for reproduction of authority through homophily in hiring). Thus, there is a need to track occupational trajectories to address the plausibility of these arguments.

This article measures occupational standing by disaggregating the usual overall socioeconomic index (SEI). The SEI is based on the aggregate predicted status of occupations from average incomes and educational levels within occupations, but in this paper, Miech et al. study the occupational earnings and occupational education levels of the occupations individuals report separately. This is done in part to uncover gender differences in the level of and rate of conversion of education into earnings.

The authors present the growth curve model using the same notation and structure as we have used in this chapter. Following, we show the equations from the article for their two-level model. Level 1 is a model for occupational standing, with time (year) specified as a quadratic effect. Level 2 shows person characteristics, such as race and gender, as a generic X variable, with effects on initial differences in the intercept model and differences in both components of the slopes for time.

$$\text{Occupational standing}_{ti} = \pi_{0i} + \pi_{1i}(\text{Year}_{ti}) + \pi_{2i}(\text{Year}_{ti})^2 + e_{ti} \qquad \text{(Level 1 Model)}$$

$$\pi_{0i} = B_{00} + B_{0a}X_a + r_{0i} \qquad \text{(Level 2 Model)}$$

$$\pi_{1i} = B_{10} + B_{1b}X_b + r_{1i} \qquad \text{(Level 2 Model)}$$

$$\pi_{2i} = B_{20} + B_{2c}X_c + r_{2i}, \qquad \text{(Level 2 Model)}$$

Source: Miech, R. A., Eaton, W. & Liang, K. Y. (2003). Occupational stratification over the life course: A comparison of occupational trajectories across race and gender during the 1980s and 1990s. *Work and Occupations, 30*(4), 449.

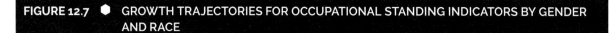

FIGURE 12.7 ● GROWTH TRAJECTORIES FOR OCCUPATIONAL STANDING INDICATORS BY GENDER AND RACE

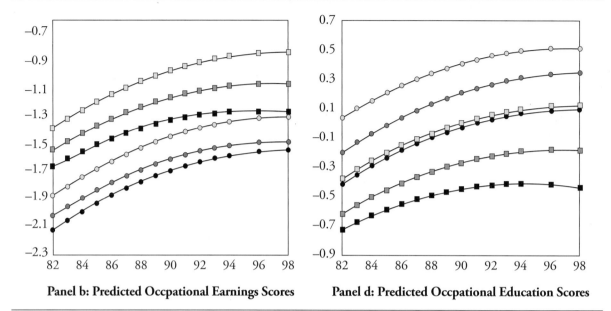

Panel b: Predicted Occpational Earnings Scores   **Panel d: Predicted Occpational Education Scores**

Source: Miech, R. A., Eaton, W. & Liang, K.-Y. (2003). Occupational stratification over the life course: A comparison of occupational trajectories across race and gender during the 1980s and 1990s. *Work and Occupations, 30*(4), 454, Figure 1, Panel b and Panel d.

Because *X* affects both the linear and squared parameter for time at Level 1, this model allows for differences in trajectories at both phases of the quadratic growth curve and thus, across both of the phases of adulthood included (early and mid).

Growth curve results are especially suitable for graphical presentation, as our examples have shown. Figure 1 from the article (Figure 12.7) shows trajectories for both predicted occupational earnings and education scores.

The note below the figure interprets the coding of the lines in the graph: Squares are men, circles are women; open is for Whites, gray for Hispanics, and Black for African Americans. The difference in the shape and ordering of the trajectories for earnings versus education is important to the results: These differences could have been hidden had the authors studied only the overall SEI.

This graph is based on results in Table 2 (Table 12.13) from the article, focusing on the earnings equation, including results for both the intercept and time slope components:

The table is organized into two panels: Effects on the intercept, which translates to initial differences in early adulthood, and effects on the slope components, both linear and quadratic. The outcome here is in a "started logit" format, which we do not define here, other than to note that this defines the range of the coefficients in the table. Interpretation of effects on initial differences is important in this kind of analysis since starting differences can insidiously multiply over time. Model 1 in the table shows that women start with lower occupational earnings, as do Hispanics and African Americans, and *there is no gender x race interaction.* Thus, gender differences apply across racial groups, and race differences apply across gender. This means, for example, that African American women are at a double, but additive, disadvantage—from the outset. Controlling for education and academic ability measured at Wave 1 (Models 2 and 3) reduces racial

TABLE 12.13 ● EFFECTS OF GENDER, RACE, AND ACADEMIC ABILITY ON OCCUPATIONAL EARNINGS IN THE NLS-Y: INTERCEPT AND SLOPE COMPONENTS						
	Model 1		Model 2		Model 3	
Variables:	**Beta**	***t*–value**	**Beta**	***t*–value**	**Beta**	***t*–value**
Intercept terms						
Reference intercept	−1.38****	−82.02	−1.52****	−83.96	−1.58****	−64.90
Age	.08****	18.84	.05****	9.76	.06****	10.32
White supplement	−.09****	−3.89	−.04**	−2.19	−.03	−1.30
White	reference group		reference group		reference group	
Hispanic	−.16****	−4.81	−.03	−0.94	.03	0.85
African American	−.28****	−9.72	−.17****	−6.56	−.08***	−2.74
Female	−.49****	−22.93	−.52****	−26.12	−.51****	−25.99
Female × Hispanic	.01	0.28	.01	0.19	.02	0.45
Female × African American	.03	0.75	4.04E-3	0.11	.01	0.28
< 12 years education			−.13****	−5.17	−.07***	−2.77
12 years of education			reference group		reference group	
13 to 15 years education			.06**	2.50	.01	0.56
16+ years education			.76****	24.02	.67****	19.12
(Age) × (< 12 years education)			−.02**	−2.29	−.02**	−2.39
(Age) × (13 to 15 years education)			.04****	3.74	.03****	3.60
(Age) × (16+ years education)			.03**	2.39	.02**	2.10
Academic ability: top quartile					.17****	5.50
Academic ability: 2nd quartile					.05*	1.73
Academic ability: 3rd quartile					reference group	
Academic ability: 4th quartile					−.09****	−3.21
Slope terms						
Reference slope	7.05E-2****	27.13	5.08E-2****	14.62	4.35E-2****	8.56
Age	−8.61E-3****	−8.33	−7.90E-3****	−7.12	−7.76E-3****	−6.98
White	reference group		reference group		reference group	
Hispanic	−5.20E-3*	−1.76	−2.90E-3	−0.98	−5.16E-4	−0.17
African American	−1.05E-2****	−4.06	−9.38E-3****	−3.63	−4.81E-3*	−1.75
Female	1.14E-3	0.54	1.85E-3	0.88	2.03E-3	0.97
Female × Hispanic	2.67E-3	0.62	9.71E-4	0.23	1.63E-3	0.39
Female × African American	8.78E-3**	2.38	6.63E-3*	1.81	6.79E-2**	1.86
< 12 years education			−2.94E-3	−0.47	5.51E-3	0.83
12 years education			reference group		reference group	
13 to 15 years education			447E-2****	7.17	3.81E-2***	5.97
16+ years education			3.40E-2****	4.68	2.04E-2**	2.54
(Age) × (< 12 years education)			1.95E-3**	1.96	2.04E-3**	2.05
(Age) × (13 to 15 years education)			−3.15E-3****	−3.34	−3.20E-3****	−3.40
(Age) × (16+ years education)			5.40E-6	0.01	−2.20E-4	−0.21
Academic ability: top quartile					2.50E-2****	3.48
Academic ability: 2nd quartile					1.50E-3***	2.35
Academic ability: 3rd quartile					reference group	
Academic ability: 4th quartile					−7.99E-3	−1.20
Slope² term						
Reference slope²	−2.23E-3****	−17.63	−1.28E-3****	−7.10	−9.83E-4***	−3.63
Age	2.60E-4****	461	2.58E-4****	4.48	2.59E-4****	4.49

(Continued)

TABLE 12.13 ◆ Continued					
	Model 1		**Model 2**		**Model 3**	
Variables:	**Beta**	**t–value**	**Beta**	**t–value**	**Beta**	**t–value**
< 12 years education			−1.96E-4	−0.56	−4.85E-4	−1.31
12 years education			reference group		reference group	
13 to 15 years education			−1.91E-3****	−5.64	−1.68E-3****	−4.84
16+ years education			−1.77E-3****	−4.61	−1.25E-3***	−2.92
Academic ability: top quartile					−1.02E-3***	−2.59
Academic ability: 2nd quartile					−6.65E-4*	−1.90
Academic ability: 3rd quartile					reference group	
Academic ability: 4th quartile					9.01E-5	0.25

Source: Miech, R. A., Eaton, W. & Liang, K.-Y. (2003). Occupational stratification over the life course: A comparison of occupational trajectories across race and gender during the 1980s and 1990s. *Work and Occupations, 30*(4), 455–456, Table 2.

differences somewhat, especially for Hispanics, but it has little effect on gender differences. This is clearly an important finding, signifying that women at the same level of education as men received significantly lower returns to earnings.

We quote directly from the article's discussion of results for the *slope* terms because it is a good example of dealing with the essentials in the results—and dealing with them efficiently (Table 12.13):

> Rates of increase in occupational earnings over the life course were not equal across all demographic groups: Black males experienced significantly lower increases in occupational earnings than did other study members. The lower rate of increase for Black men is indicated by the significant, negative value of the slope term African American (−.0105); this same term does not indicate a lower rate of increase for Black women, for whom the significantly positive, countervailing value of the Female × African American slope term (.00878) indicates a rate of increase similar to other demographic groups. The lower growth rate for African American men led to a widening gap in occupational earnings over the life course, as depicted in Panel B of Figure 1 by a widening distance between the occupational trajectory for Black as compared with White and Hispanic men. (Miech et al., 2003, pp. 455–457)

But the table also shows that the gap between males and females does not increase relatively with time, and much to most of the earnings difference occurs in this sample at initial entry into the labor market. Thus, this method locates when inequalities start and grow but also where groups converge or diverge. The figure shows the reduced rate of increase in earnings among African American men especially, flattening out over time, and at the same time, the gender and race difference means that White women catch up with African American men at later ages.

12.5.2 Social Dynamics of Health Inequalities

Our second example focuses on trajectories of change in physical health in the British Household Panel Survey (Sacker, Clarke, Wiggins, & Bartley, 2005). The BPHS is a nationally representative longitudinal survey of close to 9000 adults with waves available for this paper from 1991 to 2001. Respondents include a wide range of ages, from 20 to 60, thus allowing for an accelerated growth curve design.

The focus was on the effect of occupation on health status as an outcome. Occupational class was measured in five categories: (1) managerial and professional occupations; (2) intermediate occupations; (3) small employers and own account workers; (4) lower supervisory and technical occupations; (5) semi-routine and routine occupations. Occupation changes with time, so this analysis includes the effect of occupational mobility on health.

The authors find that a quadratic growth curve is sufficient to capture health trends in a two-level growth model. Results for the estimated trajectories by occupation are shown in Figure 12.8. Although model results are not presented, the curves in this figure suggest a cross-level interaction between occupation and age.

The curves speak clearly about the emergence of health inequalities. All occupational groups start at similar levels of health at age 20: It appears that routine occupations and/or small employers are an exception, but there are no *significant* differences at this point. However, over time the last two occupational categories (lower supervisory and technical, and routine) start to separate from others by mid-adulthood, especially after age 40. Both of these categories show a stronger decline in health from ages 40 to 60 than in other occupations. Health in the more advantaged occupations remains at the "good" level at age 60 (around 4), but in the disadvantaged occupations, average health is between "good" and "fair" (between 4 and 3).

FIGURE 12.8 ● HEALTH TRAJECTORIES BY OCCUPATION IN THE BPHS

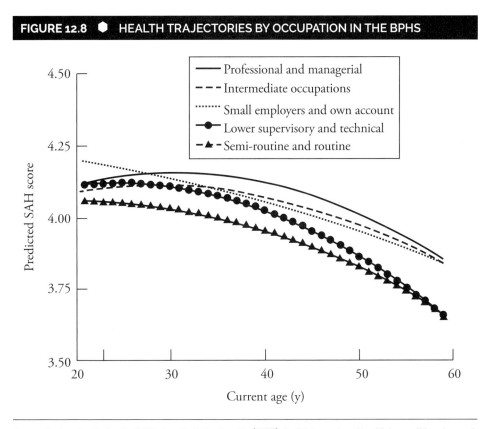

Source: Sacker, A., Clarke, P., & Wiggins, R., & Bartley, M.. (2005). Social dynamics of health inequalities: A growth curve analysis of aging and self assessed health in the British household panel survey 1991–2001. *Journal of Epidemiology and Community Health*, 59, 498, Figure 1.

The authors note that these findings are somewhat affected by occupational mobility over time, and this somewhat dilutes the observed health disparities here due to the sharing of risk exposures as people change occupations. When they analyze a subgroup of people with stable occupations, the differences due to occupation are in fact more pronounced.

Although use of a graphical representation of results is not necessary with growth curves, it is the representation that makes most sense and is the most efficient. The graphs can be produced by fairly complex models, with many coefficients. As a result, we encourage the use of plotted trajectories as a matter of course when using this method.

Concluding Words

Growth curves simply add another level to the structure of an HLM model. In this chapter, we have emphasized the correspondence between the model, the results, and the plotted trajectories that can be used for interpretation. Because this book is, in effect, a survey of techniques, we have not considered the specification of growth curves in an SEM framework and the advantages of doing so (Jung & Wickrama, 2005; Singer & Willett, 2003).

Recent developments in growth models include the study of *trajectory classes*, in which individual trajectories are grouped into an optimal set of trajectory types over time. In this approach, one can study the prediction of trajectory class membership and thus attempt to explain different types of change over time. Modules to do this exist in all of the major software packages.

In the next section, we turn to a different use of longitudinal data: the study of fixed and random effects in panel regression. This method introduces a very important class of models that attempt to "control" for even unmeasured confounders in a regression, as long as they are stable over time.

Practice Questions

1. A table is reproduced for this question, (Table 12.A) from an article on gender differences in math trajectories from elementary school through high school, using the National Educational Longitudinal Survey (NELS) (Leahey & Guo, 2001).

   The main outcome tracked over time is a "Math IRT" score, for Grades 8, 10, and 12. Thus, grade is the measure of time at Level 1. Note it has a quadratic effect in this model. The following description from the article explains the independent variables:

   We fit a curvilinear growth model to examine the extent and timing of gender differences in a multivariate context. We use grade [at Level 1] because all students were in the same grade when the survey and the accompanying cognitive tests were administered. . . . We center grade (with values of 8, 10, and 12) at eight, so that the intercept represents the average math score for a girl in the 8th grade. We have dichotomous variables indicating whether the mother has a bachelor's degree or more (mother's education high) or less than a high school degree (mother's education low) in the base year 1988, and whether the child's family annual income is greater than $50,000 (family income high) or less than $10,000 (family income low) in 1987. Family size is a measure counting all household members in 1988, and "live with both parents" is a dichotomous variable indicating whether the child lived with both parents in the base year. (Leahey & Guo, 2001, p. 725).

Note that the excluded groups on dummy variables are "middle" levels of education and income. "Covariate" effects in the table are person-level (Level–2) variables. *Also note that "male" (a dummy variable) is also a person-level factor at Level 2, although it is not included with the other person-level variables.*

Answer these questions:

a. Using only the first model for MATH IRT scores overall, derive the quadratic equations for the effects of grade that apply to girls and to boys (*to do this, ignore the other covariate effects in the model). Note the interactions between grade and grade-squared with male.*

b. Imagine you were re-estimating this model to exclude non-significant effects. Write out the Level-1 and Level-2 model you would estimate, taking into account the random effects at the bottom of the table.

c. Write out the SAS statements you would use for the MODEL and RANDOM statements to estimate this model in PROC MIXED. Make up variable names as necessary.

TABLE 12.A ⬡ BEST-FITTING CURVILINEAR GROWTH MODELS FOR MATH IRT SCORE, REASONING SCORE, AND GEOMETRY SCORE TRAJECTORIES, NELS DATA

Fixed Effects	Math IRT Model 3		Reasoning Model 4		Geometry Model 5	
	B	S.E.	B	S.E.	B	S.E.
Intercept	42.25**	.57	8.82**	.25	9.13**	.43
Male	−.01	.17	.02	.07	.01	.13
Grade (slope)	2.88**	.27	3.38**	.38	−.82	.66
Male* grade	−.17*	.08	−.18*	.11	−.32*	.09
Grade^2 (acceleration)	−.35**	.07	.56**	.09	1.05**	.15
Male * grade^2	.09**	.02	.09**	.02	.16**	.04
Covariate effect on intercept						
Mother's educ. low	−3.02**	.27	.30*	.11	−.15	.20
Mother's educ. high	4.25**	.20	−.31**	.09	.22	.15
Family income low	−2.68**	.38	.26	.16	−.14	.29
Family income high	3.04**	.19	−.26**	.08	.15	.14
Family size	−.24**	.07	.02	.03	−.01	.05
Live with both parents	3.06**	.51	−.28	.22	.16	.39
Covariate effect on slope (grade)						
Mother's educ. low	−.34**	.12	.13	.17	1.12**	.30
Mother's educ. high	.49**	.09	−.67**	.13	−1.83**	.26
Family income low	−.47**	.18	−.04	.25	1.00*	.44
Family income high	.20*	.09	−.23	.12	−1.22**	.21

(Continued)

TABLE 12.A ● Continued

Fixed Effects	Math IRT Model 3		Reasoning Model 4		Geometry Model 5	
	B	S.E.	B	S.E.	B	S.E.
Family size	−.00	.03	−.06	.04	.06	.08
Live with both parents	.29	.24	.24	.34	−1.28**	.60
Covariate effect on acceleration (grade^2)						
Mother's educ. low	.03	.03	−.34**	.04	−.61**	.07
Mother's educ. high	−.04	.02	.63**	.03	1.16**	.05
Family income low	.08	.04	−.24**	.06	−.49**	.10
Family income high	.01	.02	.36**	.03	.72**	.05
Family size	.01	.01	−.00	.01	−.03	.02
Live with both parents	.01	.06	.26**	.08	.68**	.14
Random effects						
Intercept	56.74**	.92	—	—	—	—
Grade	1.08**	.04	6.59**	.11	20.02**	.32
Residual	7.39**	.12	11.95**	.13	37.34**	.40
Observations	26,253		26,253		26,253	
Log-likelihood	−81707.1		−80424.5		−95262.2	

Note: All significance tests are two-tailed except for tests for the gender terms, which are one-tailed.

*p < .05 ** p < .01

Source: Leahey, E., & Guo, G. (2001, December). Gender differences in mathematical trajectories. Social Forces, 80(2), 713–732.

2. The results in the table that follows (Table 12.B) are from a study of high-risk infants for learning problems (Campbell et al. 2001). Half of the infants were randomly assigned to an early education program provided through a child-care center. This treatment involved an enriched curriculum of cognitive, language, motor, and social development skills. The main outcomes include test achievement scores in reading and math.

Table 12.B from the article shows the effect of the treatment on reading and math achievement, but differences are significant only for math achievement. The accompanying figure shows the growth curves trajectories in math for both the treatment and control groups.

Answer these questions:

a. The article reports no interaction between the treatment and time. Given the trajectories shown, what made more of a difference here: initial differences due to the treatment or the acquisition of math skills over time?

b. Given the results in the table, at what age do we expect the minimum math skills on the test used here?

c. Write out the equations for the final Level-2 model for the results in the table.

TABLE 12.B ● ACADEMIC ACHIEVEMENT OVER TIME AS A FUNCTION OF TREATMENT AND AGE

Factor	B	SE
Reading achievement		
Intercept		
Treatment group	93.44***	1.65
Control group	86.64***	1.70
Slope		
Linear trend	0.09	0.08
Math achievement		
Intercept		
Treatment group	93.25***	1.58
Control group	87.73**	1.62
Slope		
Linear trend	−0.70***	0.08
Quadratic trend	0.05**	0.02

**$p < 01$. *** $p < 001$.

Source: Campbell, F. A., Pungello, E. P., Miller-Johnson, S., Burchinal, M. & Ramey, C. T. (2001). Development of cognitive and academic abilities: Growth curves from an early childhood educational experiment. *Developmental Psychology, 37(2)*, 231–242.

FIGURE 12.A ● A MATHEMATICS ACHIEVEMENT GROWTH CURVES AS A FUNCTION OF PRESCHOOL TREATMENT

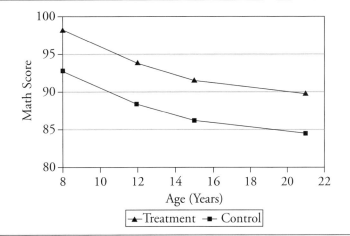

Source: Campbell, F. A., Pungello, E. P., Miller-Johnson, S., Burchinal, M. & Ramey, C. T. (2001). Development of cognitive and academic abilities: Growth curves from an early childhood educational experiment. *Developmental Psychology, 37(2)*, 231–242.

INTRODUCTION TO REGRESSION FOR PANEL DATA

In multiple chapters to this point, we have considered different approaches to analyzing longitudinal data, including structural equation models for panel data and growth curve models applied to person-period data. In Chapter 15, we continue this focus by discussing event history (aka survival) models. In each of these cases, we learn that analyzing change is useful and adds to our interpretive options.

From the previous chapter forward, we will focus on methods that make analytical use of person-period data. We introduced this rearrangement of the data in introducing growth curves. In this chapter, we use the same data structure but in a different way. As in the case of growth curves, a panel regression proceeds from a rearrangement of the data from **one** combined observation for multiple waves (T) to T observations for T waves. But in addition, this method takes further advantage of information across the observations on the same person to address basic problems of "unobserved heterogeneity," a term referring to the influence of all of the unmeasured variables in the error term of the over-time regression.

We can define the two "extremes" of how longitudinal data are usually structured. *Time series data*, in the classic econometric perspective, refer to many observations over time on one unit, such as a country, firm, or even a single individual. *Panel data* typically have observations on many cross-sectional units (individuals) but only over a few points in time. The "in-between" case is *pooled times series/cross-section data* where you have a number of observations for each unit and you have multiple units. The methods of this section are most useful for pooled cross-section/time series data but still can be used in normal panel data situations.

In recent years, there has been a tremendous growth in the availability of over-time panel studies. Some of these studies, like the National Longitudinal Survey (NLS) (Bureau of Labor Statistics, U.S. Department of Labor, 2019a) and Panel Study of Income Dynamics (PSID)

(Survey Research Center, n.d.) in the United States and the British Household Panel Survey (BHPS) (Institute for Social and Economic Research, 2018) have more than 10 follow-ups over time. Many of the ongoing panel studies in Canada, like the National Population Health Survey (NPHS) (Statistics Canada, 2013a) and the Survey of Labour and Income Dynamics (SLID) (Statistics Canada, 2013b) have eight or more time points. Typically, however, panel studies are restricted to 3 to 4 time points.

There are many uses of panel data beyond the goals of any one technique. A list of possibilities—only some of which we explore here—include the following:

1. To take into account selection processes due to other prior variables that both determine X and influence Y and thus lead to the general spuriousness of the effect of X on Y.

2. To isolate the effects of events, programs, policies, or social changes that occur between time points.

3. To make relatively stronger causal statements about the effect of X on Y, in models with lagged Ys. These models yield the interpretation that X affects change in Y since the previous wave.

4. To account for heterogeneity bias caused by unobserved and stable components of error that are both confounded with X and determine Y. This is one of the fundamental problems of the basic regression model, and in cross-sectional data, it is difficult to take this issue into account.

13.1 THE GENERALIZED PANEL REGRESSION MODEL

In the previous chapter, we gave examples of writing over-time values of variables that change to a single variable in a person-period data set. To generalize this discussion, when a cross-sectional regression is repeated on the same units over time or time series are pooled across units, we have a data set with up to T observations per person, where T = *2 to t* time points in the study.

13.1.1 Panel Data Sets

A distinction should be made between the way in which panel data sets are arranged for the methods in this chapter versus the way in which they are arranged for use in structural equation modeling. In the case of structural equation modeling, we analyzed the usual "flat file" data set, involving one observation per person but with information embedded in that observation across all waves. For methods using a person-period structure, panel data are *stacked* into a data set of $N \bullet T$ observations, with T observations per person, as shown in Table 13.1.

TABLE 13.1 ● THE STRUCTURE OF A PERSON-PERIOD DATA SET			
Person ID	Wave	Days depressed this week	Domestic hours worked this week
1	1	2	25
1	2	2	35
1	3	0	30
2	1	1	10
2	2	2	15
2	3	5	35

These are the observations of two individuals, each measured three times (Waves 1, 2, and 3). The same variables (depressed, hours worked) are measured at each wave and are assumed to be constructed the same way, so that their scores can be compared. The table shows how *person-period data sets* are organized. The total N here is 2 persons x 3 periods = 6. In this example, we assume that domestic hours worked might be an independent variable predicting days depressed in the last week.

13.1.2 The General Model

We begin with a statement of the most general regression model possible for data that includes variation across cross-sectional units (e.g., individuals) as well as over time. Given that we have N individuals observed over T time points, we can write the most general model possible this way (assuming for simplicity only one measured independent variable):

$$Y_{it} = \alpha_{it} + \beta_{it} X_{it} + u_{it}$$

Notice that we have added a subscript (t), representing time, to the usual regression model. Specifically, this model (theoretically) allows for a unique effect of X on Y for *each* individual at *each* point in time. Note also that both the intercept and the regression coefficient now may vary over time, *as well as over individuals*. Using the conventional notation for this method the *b's have become β as well.*

The problem is that this model cannot be estimated: There is in fact one observation available to estimate each regression coefficient, and of course, this is impossible. Thus, actual models for panel data involve simplifications of (that is, restrictions on) the general model.

13.1.3 The "Unrestricted" Model: The Variable Intercepts/Variable Slopes Model

We have to make some assumption to make the model workable, so the question is, which assumption is the most acceptable and still allows us to take into account important sources of confounding in the effect of X on Y? The first assumption usually applied is that effects do not change over time—that is, the effect of X on Y for individual i is constant over time. This could be a problematic assumption in especially long panel studies, and it may also hide interesting social changes.

This model can be written as follows:

$$Y_{it} = \alpha_i + \beta_i X_{it} + u_{it}$$

Notice that the t subscripts for the intercept and the β coefficients are gone. This signifies that the model specifies one effect of X on Y but uses changes through time to estimate this effect. The model retains the possibility of a unique effect per individual: Thus the i subscript persists. In this model, there is a separate regression for each individual, based on T observations.

This model is sometimes called the "unrestricted model" because it is the most general model that can be estimated. This is an unwieldy model to work with, specifically when using panel data with large N, although it does act as a baseline. Successive models make further restrictions on this model, and thus standard F-tests can be used to assess the viability of these restrictions.

13.1.4 The Variable Intercepts/Constant Slopes Model

This is a very important model in the literature on panel models. In this model, it is assumed that the effect of X is common across individuals, but as in the previous model, that the intercepts vary—that is, each individual has their own intercept. The model, in its most general form, can be written

$$Y_{it} = \alpha_i + \beta X_{it} + u_{it}$$

The only difference with the previous model is that here there is only one common effect of X (thus no i subscript). At the same time, allowing individuals to have unique intercepts has important implications. *The main implication is that **all stable individual differences** over time, even those not measured and included in the model, can be taken into account and adjusted for.* This is thought to be one of the fundamental contributions of the panel model. Each intercept is basically a dummy variable for each individual. These intercepts do not specify what the individual differences are, but differences among intercepts necessarily capture the sum total of all stable individual differences, including biology, genetic givens, ascribed social statuses, family background, ethnicity, place of origin, and so forth. Importantly, this is one of the few models that can claim to adjust for confounding of unmeasured variables with the measured Xs in the model.

The model above is what is usually called a "fixed effects model." It is called this because it specifies stable individual differences as fixed variables in the regression. There are actually two ways of estimating unique individual effects in these models, and they have different implications. Besides the ***fixed effects model,*** which itself can be represented in multiple forms (see section 13.1.4.1), there is also the ***random effects model.*** The latter model imagines the unique effect of the individual as an additional error term, but one that is not correlated with the X variables in the model. The fixed effects model, on the other hand, assumes there *is* confounding between the unmeasured variables and the independent variables in your model.

13.1.4.1 Fixed Effects Model

In the preceding model, there is a unique dummy variable intercept for each person in the data. These dummy variables represent the manifest surface of a complex reality that cannot be disaggregated but nonetheless theoretically stands for the sum total of all of the unique stable characteristics of the person. The key word there is "stable." One can speculate broadly about what is embedded in these dummy variable intercepts, but the factors included usually involve one of three types of person factors: past starting points in life (childhood poverty in a study of adults), fixed biological or genetic parameters (excluding those that do change), and ascribed statuses that (typically) do not change over the life course for most people. Although these person differences are not measured, they are *captured* by the dummy variables.

Of course, using dummy variables to stand for individual differences may pose practical problems in large data sets. This model is sometimes called the "*least squares dummy variable model.*" An equivalent model uses a transformation to remove the intercepts and therefore the dummy variables from the equation while taking their effects into account.

This is done by noting that, in general

$$\alpha_i = \bar{Y}_i - \beta \bar{X}_i$$

where $\bar{Y}_i$ and $\bar{X}_i$ are the means for each individual over time. This is how the intercept is estimated in general, as reviewed in the first chapter on regression. When we substitute for the intercept in the fixed effects dummy variable model on the previous page, we get

$$Y_{it} = (\bar{Y}_i - \beta \bar{X}_i) + \beta X_{it} + u_{it}$$ ⟨ Replacing the intercept

$$Y_{it} - \bar{Y}_i = +\beta X_{it} - \beta \bar{X}_i + u_{it}$$ ⟨ Subtract *Y* mean from both sides

$$Y_{it} - \bar{Y}_i = \beta(X_{it} - \bar{X}_i) + u_{it}$$ ⟨ Factor out β.

Note there is no intercept in this model, but it is equivalent to the least squares dummy variable model because the differences in individual means on Y (and X) are taken into account in the model. In fact, the derivation above proves that the β derived in this model is the same as in the original model. The X and Y variables in the model are centered on the over-time means for each individual. This model is often called the "*mean-corrected*" model. In this model, the "fixed effect" is the person-specific effect averaged over time, which is adjusted out of the model.

There is a price to pay in this model. Any X that is stable over time will go to zero and be removed from the model as well. Thus, we cannot "see" the effects of Xs we may want to know about, such as gender or race or ethnicity. This is just as true of the dummy variable model, since if you include any specific fixed X, it will be collinear with—a constituent part of—the dummy variables in the model, by definition.

13.1.4.2 Random Effects Model

The random effects model conceptualizes the missing variables as error (sometimes referred to as random but meaning "unmeasured") but separates these effects from truly random effects in the model. Thus, instead of explicit dummy variables for individual differences, we have the following model:

$$Y_{it} = \alpha + \beta X_{it} + u_{it} + v_i$$

where v_i is a unique stable component of error for individual i and thus captures unmeasured individual differences. The differences between this formulation and the fixed effects model are that the individual differences are still part of the error and so must be assumed to be uncorrelated with Xs in the model. Thus, we see a trade-off in the two models. The fixed effects model adjusts for ***confounded*** and stable unmeasured individual differences but also purges the model of stable measured Xs. The random-effects model allows us to see the effects of stable Xs but only adjusts for individual differences that are uncorrelated with X.

This seems to suggest that in many cases, the fixed effects model will be more relevant in social science data. But in fact, there is considerable debate about the appropriateness of the two models in different situations. Many observers simply do not make an overall recommendation. Hsiao (2003) ultimately recommends the random effects model when N is large because of greater efficiency of estimation (using generalized, not ordinary, least squares—see Section 13.1.4.4) but then adds that if the missing variables are correlated with X, the fixed effects model should be used. Allison (1994) points out that the possibility of confounding of missing Xs and measured Xs is sufficiently prevalent in the social sciences that a fixed effects model will often be safer.

13.1.4.3 The Hausman Specification Test

There is a widely used test that helps decide this issue. The Hausman specification test is a comparison of the variance/covariance matrix of estimates from the fixed effects model with the same matrix for the random effects model. If there is no statistically significant difference between the matrices of the two models, this implies that there is no correlation between unmeasured and measured Xs and that the random effects model could be used with greater confidence. If there is a difference (and therefore the test is significant), this implies that the unmeasured stable Xs are correlated with Xs in the model, and the fixed effects model is appropriate. This test is a Wald χ^2 test with k - 1 degrees of freedom where k is the number of regressors in the model. This test is available in most statistical packages.

13.1.4.4 Generalized Least Squares

The random effects model cannot be estimated using OLS because the resulting estimates are not efficient and the standard errors are biased. This problem is caused by the fact that the error terms for different observations on the same individual over time are correlated in this model. Generalized least squares (GLS) takes this problem into account.

It is useful to understand at least the logic of GLS estimation. In this case, we have serially correlated error for individuals because of the presence of similar components of the individual error terms over time. The situation is *similar* to general autocorrelation in the error terms over time, caused, for example, by the presence of unmeasured causes that tend to change with time and also affect Y.

In that case, the autocorrelation can be represented as a "first-order" autoregressive process:

$$u_{it} = \rho u_{i,\,t-1} + e_{it}$$

where e is the random part of the overall error, u refers to a systematic component, and ρ is the regression coefficient standing for continuity in the error over time. This is a regression model where the value of the error lagged one point in time predicts the value of the current error, plus the random component.

If ρ were known (and it is usually not), one can remove its effects from the model for the effect of X on Y as follows. Note that the model at any time t is

$$Y_{it} = \alpha_i + \beta X_{it} + u_{it} \tag{1}$$

And the lagged model at the previous time point is

$$Y_{i,\,t-1} = \alpha_i + \beta X_{i,\,t-1} + u_{i,\,t-1} \tag{2}$$

Multiplying the lagged model (2) by ρ produces

$$\rho Y_{i,\,t-1} = \rho \alpha_i + \rho \beta X_{i,\,t-1} + \rho u_{i,\,t-1} \tag{3}$$

If we now subtract this model from the model at time t (Model 1 – Model 3) we get

$$Y_{it} - \rho Y_{i, t-1} = (\alpha_i - \rho \alpha_i) + (\beta X_{it} - \rho \beta X_{i, t-1}) + (u_{it} - \rho u_{i, t-1})$$
$$Y_{it} - \rho Y_{i, t-1} = \alpha_i (1 - \rho) + \beta (X_{it} - \rho X_{i, t-1}) + e_{it}$$

Note that in this regression of Y on X, we get an estimate of both α and β from the original model, but the effect of ρ has been removed from Y, X, *and the error term*. In other words, the error term now satisfies the assumption of randomness. This is the logic of what GLS accomplishes.

"Feasible" generalized least squares in fact has to estimate ρ first to substitute for it in the model. This is done by analyzing the residuals at successive time points to first estimate an autoregressive model for ρ. Most computer software implementing the random effects model will by default use a GLS approach to estimating the model.

13.1.5 The Constant Intercept/Constant Slopes Model

The most restrictive model usually considered is one in which *both* the intercept and the slopes are assumed to be the same across individuals (i.e., cross-sectional units). This model is written as follows:

$$Y_{it} = \alpha + \beta X_{it} + u_{it}$$

Note that the i subscript is now gone from the intercept, signifying a common intercept for all individuals. This model assumes that individuals do not have stable overall differences on Y beyond those in the model, and so this model will *often* not be appropriate in analyses of individuals as the cross-sectional units. But it could be more relevant when data use other kinds of cross-sectional units.

One can see that these models—the "unrestricted" (variable intercepts/variable slopes) model, the variable intercept/constant slopes model, and the constant intercept and slopes model—are all nested, since each one imposes a further restriction on the previous model. You can use F-tests to assess the viability of these models, as for all nested regression models. In this case, the F-test utilizes the sum of squares error in each model.

The hypothesis of the first model is that both intercepts and slopes vary. The alternative hypothesis represented by the second model is that there is one common slope, but intercepts still vary. The alternative hypothesis of the third model is that both the intercept and slope can be safely assumed to be common across individuals. Most software for panel regression produce some form of these tests and there are multiple forms possible.

If you were to construct these tests manually using the sum of squares error from each model, the F-tests are constructed as follows:

1. Variable intercepts/constant slopes versus unrestricted (variable intercepts/variable slopes model):

$$F_{21} = \frac{(SSE_2 - SSE_1)/[(N-1)K]}{SSE_1/[NT - N(K+1)]}$$

2. Constant intercepts and slopes versus variable intercepts/constant slopes:

$$F_{32} = \frac{(SSE_3 - SSE_2)/(N-1)}{SSE_2/[N(T-1) - K]}$$

3. Constant intercepts and slopes versus unrestricted model:

$$F_{31} = \frac{(SSE_3 - SSE_1)/(N-1)(K+1)}{SSE_1/[NT - N(K+1)]}$$

Where

Model 1 = the unrestricted model (variable intercepts/variable slopes)

Model 2 = the variable intercepts/constant slopes model

Model 3 = the constant intercepts and slopes model

SSE   = sum of squares error (printed in the regression)

N = number of cross-sectional units

T = number of waves of observation

K = number of independent X variables in the equation

Actually, as we shall see, SAS prints out the test of the collective fixed effects for individuals in the variable intercept/constant slope model. This test amounts to a test of the difference between Model 2 and Model 3. It is usually very significant in these kind of data.

13.2 EXAMPLES OF PANEL REGRESSION

In this section, we present two examples of panel regression. In each case, we start with a "naïve" OLS regression of the person-period data, to show the differences in results when fixed effects are used. We also test for the relevance of a fixed effects versus a random effects specification. In this chapter, we are using examples that only require a few (3) waves in a panel. But in the next chapter, we will consider data that utilizes more waves.

13.2.1 The Effects of Marital Status on Depression: 1988–2002

This example uses all three waves of the National Survey of Families and Households to estimate the effects of marital status on depression. The Wave 3 data were collected in 2001–2003, resulting in a 13 to 15 year follow-up of Wave I. A caveat is important here: the NSFH wave III follow-up data targeted a subset of the original sample, due to budget constraints. The subsample studied in the Wave 3 panel involves people who were either at least 30 at the beginning of the study or, if under 30, already had children 5 or older at the time. This does change the nature of the sample substantially, since people in their twenties without children or with very young children are excluded.

The length of the NSFH study (1987–2003) allows us to look at the effect of marital status on depression across a period in which there were presumably significant changes in the meaning of and support for marriage as an institution. Still, one of the repeated findings in the literature on marriage and well-being is that it tends to reduce depression more than merely cohabiting (Simon, 2002; Amato, 2014). Here we consider marital statuses and depression across three waves, controlling for gender and age.

We do not need to show how these variables are constructed over time, except to say that they should be constructed ***exactly the same way at each wave***. You start by creating a separate variable for each measure at each point in time, except for fixed variables, which only require one variable. For variables that vary, you need to have a distinct measure for each wave. For depression, you would have a *cesd1,* a *cesd2,* and a *cesd3,* standing for depression at Waves 1, 2, and 3. The items used should be the same at each wave, and they have to be coded the same way. There are five marital statuses tracked over time at all three time points: married, cohabiting, divorced or separated, widowed, and never married.

13.2.1.1 Creating Person-Time Data

Once you have the variables created at each time point, you need to create a *person-period* data set. This is a data set in which each respondent's observation merged over time is turned into *separate* observations specific to each point in time. The SAS code to create the data set for this example is shown following, to demonstrate the logic of creating person-period data.

```
data panelreg;
  set temp;

array dep (3) cesd1 cesd2 cesd3;
array marr (3) married1 married2 married3;
array ds (3) divsep1 divsep2 divsep3;
array wid (3) widow1 widow2 widow3;
array coh (3) cohab1 cohab2 cohab3;
array taskhrs (3) rtaskhrs1 rtaskhrs2 rtaskhrs3;
array time (3) t1 t2 t3;
array marxtime (3) marxt1 marxt2 marxt3;
array cohxtime (3) cohxt1 cohxt2 cohxt3;
array dsxtime (3)  divxt1 divxt2 divxt3;
array widxtime (3) widxt1 widxt2 widxt3;

do i= 1 to 3;

depressed=dep(i);
married=marr(i);
divsep=ds(i);
widow=wid(i);
cohab=coh(i);
hometaskhrs=taskhrs(i);
wave=i;

depnmiss=nmiss(of cesd1 cesd2 cesd3);
if depnmiss>=2 then delete;
do j= 1 to 3;

if i=j then time(j)=1; else time(j)=0;

marxtime(j)= married*time(j);
```

```
cohxtime(j) = cohab*time(j);
dsxtime(j) = divsep*time(j);
widxtime(j) = widow*time(j);
end;
output;
end;
```

Note that you start a new DATA step after the original data step that created the unique measures of each variable at each point in time (that data step created a data set labeled "temp"). This is actually not necessary because you could embed the new data step here as extra code at the end of the first data step creating the wave-specific variables. But our advice here is to separate these tasks: check the integrity of the created variables first at each wave and then create the person-period data.

Here we create a second data set called "panelreg," based on temp. The first set of arrays contain variables that measure depression, marital status, and domestic task involvement over three waves. There are also arrays to create dummy variables to represent the effect of time and interactions between time and marital status. This is a way to introduce the possibility of a kind of "variable slopes" model, which allows for variation in the effects of X across time units. These interactions assess whether the net impact of marriage versus cohabitation is shifting over time or whether the effects of marital disruption are changing historically or as people age. Notice that given the kind of data we have here, time could stand for changes due to history *or* changes due to aging. We cannot separate the two in this design.

The "i" do loop creates a single variable for depression and marital status (and home task hours) from the separate measures at each point in time. Note the "output" command near the bottom of this loop. This command outputs a new observation for every value of i in the loop. This will result in three observations for each person in the study.

The *depnmiss* variable is a count of the number of missing values on depression across the three waves. The following command deletes observations in which at least 2 of the 3 depression measures are missing. SAS will only run the random effects model if there are at least two intact observations for each person.

The "j" do loop is executed for each value of i in the main loop. It is used to create separate time dummy variables for each observation and interactions of these dummy variables with marital status. The following statement

```
if i=j then time(j)=1; else time(j)=0;
```

makes the variable $t1 = 1$ when $i = 1$, $t2 = 1$ when $i = 2$, and $t3 = 1$ when $i = 3$, and 0 otherwise. Once these dummy variables are created, interactions with marital status can be created. Note that the arrays called "time," "marxtime," "cohxtime", "dsxtime", and "widxtime" are ***output*** arrays. This means they name variables to be created in the DO loop below them, instead of manipulating already existing variables as in the ***input*** arrays above them.

The first "end" statement closes the j loop, and the second "end" statement closes the i loop. The OUTPUT command must be between the two because only then are all of the relevant new variables created for each observation.

The first 48 observations of the "panelreg" data set, representing the data from 16 individual respondents, are shown in Table 13.2 for selected variables. You can see that *mcaseid,* the id for each person, is the same across each set of three observations while the variable "wave" indicates the wave of the study. Further, the time dummy variables are equal to 1 at the appropriate wave and 0 otherwise.

The print out of the data shows how the time-varying variables are created. "*Depressed*" is the current level of depression: At Wave 1, it is based on cesd1, at Wave 2 on cesd2, and at Wave3 on cesd3. As a specific example, look at observations 46 through 48, for person id 415. The specific scores for depression at each wave are written in turn to the variable "depressed" across the three waves, so that depressed at Wave 1 is taken from the *cesd1* value (1) , at Wave 2 is taken from the *cesd2* value (4) , and at Wave 3 is taken from the *cesd3* value (2.91667). The variables "married" and "cohab" are also shown: Each takes it current value from the time-specific dummy variable for that marital status. This person was not married at Waves 1 and 2 but was cohabiting at Wave 3.

In our analysis, we use the created variables for depression and marital status that vary over time.

TABLE 13.2 ● SELECTED OBSERVATIONS FROM THE "PANELREG" DATA SET

Obs	Mcaseid	wave	t1	t2	t3	depressed	cesd1	cesd2	cesd3	married	Married1	Married2	Married3	cohab	Cohab1	Cohab2	Cohab3
1	58	1	1	0	0	0.50000	0.50000	1.08333	0.50000	1	1	1	1	0	0	0	0
2	58	2	0	1	0	1.08333	0.50000	1.08333	0.50000	1	1	1	1	0	0	0	0
3	58	3	0	0	1	0.50000	0.50000	1.08333	0.50000	1	1	1	1	0	0	0	0
4	120	1	1	0	0	0.50000	0.50000	1.50000	0.45455	1	1	1	1	0	0	0	0
5	120	2	0	1	0	1.50000	0.50000	1.50000	0.45455	1	1	1	1	0	0	0	0
6	120	3	0	0	1	0.45455	0.50000	1.50000	0.45455	1	1	1	1	0	0	0	0
7	133	1	1	0	0	1.58333	1.58333	0.75000	0.50000	1	1	1	1	0	0	0	0
8	133	2	0	1	0	0.75000	1.58333	0.75000	0.50000	1	1	1	1	0	0	0	0
9	133	3	0	0	1	0.50000	1.58333	0.75000	0.50000	1	1	1	1	0	0	0	0
10	146	1	1	0	0	3.00000	3.00000	3.75000	4.00000	1	1	1	1	0	0	0	0
11	146	2	0	1	0	3.75000	3.00000	3.75000	4.00000	1	1	1	1	0	0	0	0
12	146	3	0	0	1	4.00000	3.00000	3.75000	4.00000	1	1	1	1	0	0	0	0
13	162	1	1	0	0	0.16667	0.16667	0.58333	0.41667	1	1	1	1	0	0	0	0
14	162	2	0	1	0	0.58333	0.16667	0.58333	0.41667	1	1	1	1	0	0	0	0
15	162	3	0	0	1	0.41667	0.16667	0.58333	0.41667	1	1	1	1	0	0	0	0
16	167	1	1	0	0	1.75000	1.75000	1.50000	0.83333	1	1	1	1	0	0	0	0
17	167	2	0	1	0	1.50000	1.75000	1.50000	0.83333	1	1	1	1	0	0	0	0
18	167	3	0	0	1	0.83333	1.75000	1.50000	0.83333	1	1	1	1	0	0	0	0
19	170	1	1	0	0	0.16667	0.16667	0.41667	0.08333	1	1	1	1	0	0	0	0

(Continued)

TABLE 13.2 ● (Continued)

Obs	Mcaseid	wave	t1	t2	t3	depressed	cesd1	cesd2	cesd3	married	Married1	Married2	Married3	cohab	Cohab1	Cohab2	Cohab3
20	170	2	0	1	0	0.41667	0.16667	0.41667	0.08333	1	1	1	1	0	0	0	0
21	170	3	0	0	1	0.08333	0.16667	0.41667	0.08333	1	1	1	1	0	0	0	0
22	213	1	1	0	0	0.00000	0.00000	0.16667	0.41667	1	1	1	1	0	0	0	0
23	213	2	0	1	0	0.16667	0.00000	0.16667	0.41667	1	1	1	1	0	0	0	0
24	213	3	0	0	1	0.41667	0.00000	0.16667	0.41667	1	1	1	1	0	0	0	0
25	250	1	1	0	0	1.36364	1.36364	0.91667	0.83333	1	1	0	1	0	0	0	0
26	250	2	0	1	0	0.91667	1.36364	0.91667	0.83333	0	1	0	1	0	0	0	0
27	250	3	0	0	1	0.83333	1.36364	0.91667	0.83333	1	1	0	1	0	0	0	0
28	268	1	1	0	0	6.25000	6.25000	1.08333	5.16667	0	0	1	0	0	0	0	0
29	268	2	0	1	0	1.08333	6.25000	1.08333	5.16667	1	0	1	0	0	0	0	0
30	268	3	0	0	1	5.16667	6.25000	1.08333	5.16667	0	0	1	0	0	0	0	0
31	319	1	1	0	0	0.16667	0.16667	0.41667	0.50000	1	1	0	0	0	0	0	1
32	319	2	0	1	0	0.41667	0.16667	0.41667	0.50000	0	1	0	0	0	0	0	1
33	319	3	0	0	1	0.50000	0.16667	0.41667	0.50000	0	1	0	0	1	0	0	1
34	330	1	1	0	0	0.33333	0.33333	0.00000	0.08333	0	0	0	0	0	0	0	0
35	330	2	0	1	0	0.00000	0.33333	0.00000	0.08333	0	0	0	0	0	0	0	0
36	330	3	0	0	1	0.08333	0.33333	0.00000	0.08333	0	0	0	0	0	0	0	0
37	380	1	1	0	0	0.83333	0.83333	1.50000	1.08333	0	0	0	0	0	0	0	0
38	380	2	0	1	0	1.50000	0.83333	1.50000	1.08333	0	0	0	0	0	0	0	0
39	380	3	0	0	1	1.08333	0.83333	1.50000	1.08333	0	0	0	0	0	0	0	0
40	393	1	1	0	0	0.00000	0.00000	0.00000	0.16667	1	1	1	1	0	0	0	0
41	393	2	0	1	0	0.00000	0.00000	0.00000	0.16667	1	1	1	1	0	0	0	0
42	393	3	0	0	1	0.16667	0.00000	0.00000	0.16667	1	1	1	1	0	0	0	0
43	407	1	1	0	0	0.33333	0.33333	0.00000	0.00000	1	1	1	1	0	0	0	0
44	407	2	0	1	0	0.00000	0.33333	0.00000	0.00000	1	1	1	1	0	0	0	0
45	407	3	0	0	1	0.00000	0.33333	0.00000	0.00000	1	1	1	1	0	0	0	0
46	415	1	1	0	0	1.00000	1.00000	4.00000	2.91667	0	0	0	0	0	0	0	1
47	415	2	0	1	0	4.00000	1.00000	4.00000	2.91667	0	0	0	0	0	0	0	1
48	415	3	0	0	1	2.91667	1.00000	4.00000	2.91667	0	0	0	0	1	0	0	1

13.2.1.2 Running PROC PANEL in SAS

The SAS commands that follow run three programs: a standard OLS regression of these data using PROC REG, PROC PANEL (specifically for panel regression), and PROC GLM (the standard general linear model program in SAS). We include controls for gender and age and age-squared in the standard regression to illustrate a point about the fixed effects model.

Note that you must sort the data by the respondent id variable and then the time variable before running PROC PANEL. In that PROC, you need to tell the program how the data is structured by cross-sectional unit and time by using the "id" statement: This statement lists the respondent id variable first (mcaseid) and then the variable for time (wave). In the MODEL statement of the first run of PROC PANEL, we only include time and marital status. In the second run of PROC PANEL, we include fixed controls for gender and age (these controls are removed in later runs). As we will see in the results, SAS deletes these variables from the estimates shown in PROC

PANEL—for good reason. They are part of the overall fixed effects represented by the dummy variables in the model and thus are perfectly collinear with those intercepts. As noted earlier, this could be seen as a disadvantage of this model.

The options in the MODEL statement specify the type of model—*fixone* for a fixed effects model for cross-sectional units only (*fixtwo* if time is to be included as a fixed effect)—and *noint* to suppress the intercept. This last command is necessary here because there will be a separate dummy variable for *each* person in this regression, not N - 1 dummy variables. Specifying "noint" allows the model to replace the usual intercept with the series of intercepts standing for the mean on Y over time for **each** person in the sample.

Finally, PROC GLM is run for comparison and to show that there is a way to run the fixed effects model in that program, using the ABSORB command for the individual fixed effects. In this case, you need to name the individual id variable, which here is *mcaseid*. The solution option actually prints out the coefficients.

```
proc reg data=panelreg simple;
model depressed=t2 t3 married divsep widow cohab female ageatwave1 ageatwave1sq;
test married-cohab=0;
run;

proc sort data=panelreg;
by mcaseid wave;
run;

proc panel data=panelreg;
id mcaseid wave;
model depressed=t2 t3 married divsep widow cohab / fixone noint;
test married-cohab=0;
run;

proc panel data=panelreg;
id mcaseid wave;
model depressed=t2 t3 married divsep widow cohab female ageatwave1 ageatwave1sq / fixone noint;
test married-cohab=0;
run;

proc glm data=panelreg;
absorb mcaseid;
model depressed=t2 t3 married divsep widow cohab/ noint solution;
run;
```

The output from the initial OLS model is shown in Table 13.3. The OLS regression results show that being married is related to the lowest levels of depression and that depression among the married is significantly lower than depression among the never married specifically. Cohabitors are also less depressed than the never married, but the effect appears to be weaker than among the married. The results of the post-hoc test assess this question, and suggest that there is a significantly lower level of depression among the married relative to cohabitors. There are weaker positive effects on depression of being divorced or separated and widowed, relative to the never married. Finally, we see the standard expected findings for female and age as well, with an inverse quadratic effect of age.

The time dummy variables here suggest that on the whole, depression in this sample is declining over time: This effect may simply reflect the shifting age structure of the sample.

TABLE 13.3 ● RESULTS FOR THE EFFECTS OF MARITAL STATUS ON DEPRESSION IN AN OLS REGRESSION

Analysis of Variance

Source	DF	Sum of Squares	Mean Square	F Value	Pr > F
Model	9	949.37496	105.48611	65.57	<.0001
Error	13379	21525	1.60884		
Corrected Total	13388	22474			

Root MSE	1.26840	R-Square	0.0422
Dependent Mean	1.11295	Adj R-Sq	0.0416
Coeff Var	113.96724		

Parameter Estimates

Variable	DF	Parameter Estimate	Standard Error	t Value	Pr > |t|
Intercept	1	2.09172	0.15642	13.37	<.0001
t2	1	−0.04294	0.02708	−1.59	0.1129
t3	1	−0.08831	0.02910	−3.04	0.0024
married	1	−0.36813	0.03526	−10.44	<.0001
divsep	1	0.06899	0.04118	1.68	0.0939
widow	1	0.11743	0.05458	2.15	0.0314
cohab	1	−0.18462	0.04350	−4.24	<.0001
female	1	0.25557	0.02346	10.89	<.0001
ageatwave1	1	−0.03318	0.00668	−4.97	<.0001
ageatwave1sq	1	0.00027114	0.00006961	3.89	<.0001

Test 1 Results for Dependent Variable depressed

Source	DF	Mean Square	F Value	Pr > F
Numerator	1	31.65203	19.67	<.0001
Denominator	13379	1.60884		

Results for the fixed effects model from PROC PANEL are shown in Table 13.4—with some observations for the individual fixed effects necessarily deleted since there are 4,591 fixed effects for the 4,591 individuals in the sample printed in the output!

TABLE 13.4 ● RESULTS FOR A FIXED EFFECTS MODEL FOR MARITAL STATUS

Model Description	
Estimation Method	FixOne
Number of Cross Sections	4591
Time Series Length	3

Fit Statistics			
SSE	8851.4103	DFE	8792
MSE	1.0068	Root MSE	1.0034
R-Square	0.6061		

F-Test for No Fixed Effects and No Intercept			
Num DF	Den DF	F Value	Pr > F
4591	8792	3.32	<.0001

Parameter Estimates						
Variable	DF	Estimate	Standard Error	t Value	Pr > |t|	Label
CS1	1	1.093451	0.5822	1.88	0.0604	Cross Sectional Effect 1
CS2	1	1.217188	0.5822	2.09	0.0366	Cross Sectional Effect 2
CS3	1	1.343451	0.5822	2.31	0.0210	Cross Sectional Effect 3
CS4	1	3.98234	0.5822	6.84	<.0001	Cross Sectional Effect 4
CS5	1	0.787896	0.5822	1.35	0.1760	Cross Sectional Effect 5
CS6	1	1.760118	0.5822	3.02	0.0025	Cross Sectional Effect 6
CS7	1	0.621229	0.5822	1.07	0.2859	Cross Sectional Effect 7
CS8	1	0.593451	0.5822	1.02	0.3080	Cross Sectional Effect 8
CS9	1	1.325984	0.5816	2.28	0.0226	Cross Sectional Effect 9
CS10	1	4.343871	0.5814	7.47	<.0001	Cross Sectional Effect 10
CS11	1	0.634255	0.5812	1.09	0.2751	Cross Sectional Effect 11
CS12	1	0.175408	0.5794	0.30	0.7621	Cross Sectional Effect 12
CS13	1	1.195264	0.5804	2.06	0.0395	Cross Sectional Effect 13
CS14	1	0.454562	0.5822	0.78	0.4349	Cross Sectional Effect 14
CS15	1	0.510118	0.5822	0.88	0.3809	Cross Sectional Effect 15
CS16	1	2.781276	0.5797	4.80	<.0001	Cross Sectional Effect 16
CS17	1	1.02597	0.7120	1.44	0.1496	Cross Sectional Effect 17
CS18	1	4.204562	0.5822	7.22	<.0001	Cross Sectional Effect 18
CS19	1	1.915144	0.5816	3.29	0.0010	Cross Sectional Effect 19
CS20	1	1.278177	0.5807	2.20	0.0278	Cross Sectional Effect 20
CS21	1	1.815673	0.5822	3.12	0.0018	Cross Sectional Effect 21
CS22	1	2.917624	0.7123	4.10	<.0001	Cross Sectional Effect 22
CS23	1	0.155426	0.5804	0.27	0.7889	Cross Sectional Effect 23
CS24	1	1.093661	0.5816	1.88	0.0601	Cross Sectional Effect 24
CS25	1	0.454562	0.5822	0.78	0.4349	Cross Sectional Effect 25
CS26	1	0.662242	0.5811	1.14	0.2544	Cross Sectional Effect 26
CS27	1	1.08181	0.5816	1.86	0.0629	Cross Sectional Effect 27
CS28	1	1.511707	0.7101	2.13	0.0333	Cross Sectional Effect 28
CS29	1	0.426784	0.5822	0.73	0.4635	Cross Sectional Effect 29
CS30	1	2.675408	0.5794	4.62	<.0001	Cross Sectional Effect 30
CS31	1	2.266746	0.5803	3.91	<.0001	Cross Sectional Effect 31
CS32	1	1.248254	0.5805	2.15	0.0316	Cross Sectional Effect 32
CS33	1	1.072092	0.5804	1.85	0.0648	Cross Sectional Effect 33
CS34	1	0.932963	0.7096	1.31	0.1886	Cross Sectional Effect 34
CS35	1	2.567636	0.7120	3.61	0.0003	Cross Sectional Effect 35
CS36	1	1.593451	0.5822	2.74	0.0062	Cross Sectional Effect 36
CS37	1	1.27597	0.7120	1.79	0.0731	Cross Sectional Effect 37
CS38	1	1.676784	0.5822	2.88	0.0040	Cross Sectional Effect 38
CS39	1	0.760118	0.5822	1.31	0.1917	Cross Sectional Effect 39

(Continued)

TABLE 13.4 ● Continued

Parameter Estimates						
Variable	DF	Estimate	Standard Error	t Value	Pr > |t|	Label
CS40	1	0.745156	0.5816	1.28	0.2002	Cross Sectional Effect 40
CS41	1	1.02597	0.7120	1.44	0.1496	Cross Sectional Effect 41
CS42	1	0.565673	0.5822	0.97	0.3312	Cross Sectional Effect 42
CS43	1	3.253842	0.7110	4.58	<.0001	Cross Sectional Effect 43
CS44	1	0.593871	0.5814	1.02	0.3070	Cross Sectional Effect 44
CS45	1	0.637366	0.5816	1.10	0.2732	Cross Sectional Effect 45
CS46	1	0.139708	0.5804	0.24	0.8098	Cross Sectional Effect 46
CS47	1	0.455149	0.7096	0.64	0.5213	Cross Sectional Effect 47
CS48	1	3.489638	0.7114	4.91	<.0001	Cross Sectional Effect 48
CS49	1	0.636707	0.7101	0.90	0.3700	Cross Sectional Effect 49
CS50	1	0.787896	0.5822	1.35	0.1760	Cross Sectional Effect 50
.						.
.						.
.						.
CS4561	1	0.6896	0.5816	1.19	0.2358	Cross Sectional Effect 4561
CS4562	1	0.676784	0.5822	1.16	0.2450	Cross Sectional Effect 4562
CS4563	1	0.717378	0.5816	1.23	0.2175	Cross Sectional Effect 4563
CS4564	1	1.704562	0.5822	2.93	0.0034	Cross Sectional Effect 4564
CS4565	1	3.500819	0.5804	6.03	<.0001	Cross Sectional Effect 4565
CS4566	1	0.550712	0.5816	0.95	0.3437	Cross Sectional Effect 4566
CS4567	1	1.73234	0.5822	2.98	0.0029	Cross Sectional Effect 4567
CS4568	1	0.953186	0.5794	1.64	0.1000	Cross Sectional Effect 4568
CS4569	1	0.73276	0.5814	1.26	0.2076	Cross Sectional Effect 4569
CS4570	1	0.399426	0.5814	0.69	0.4921	Cross Sectional Effect 4570
CS4571	1	0.843661	0.5816	1.45	0.1469	Cross Sectional Effect 4571
CS4572	1	1.649007	0.5822	2.83	0.0046	Cross Sectional Effect 4572
CS4573	1	0.621229	0.5822	1.07	0.2859	Cross Sectional Effect 4573
CS4574	1	1.147071	0.5812	1.97	0.0484	Cross Sectional Effect 4574
CS4575	1	1.010118	0.5822	1.74	0.0827	Cross Sectional Effect 4575
CS4576	1	1.003527	0.7114	1.41	0.1584	Cross Sectional Effect 4576
CS4577	1	0.393785	0.5808	0.68	0.4978	Cross Sectional Effect 4577
CS4578	1	1.151742	0.5816	1.98	0.0477	Cross Sectional Effect 4578
CS4579	1	0.484303	0.7120	0.68	0.4964	Cross Sectional Effect 4579
CS4580	1	0.884045	0.5816	1.52	0.1286	Cross Sectional Effect 4580
CS4581	1	2.621816	0.7096	3.69	0.0002	Cross Sectional Effect 4581
CS4582	1	2.204562	0.5822	3.79	0.0002	Cross Sectional Effect 4582
CS4583	1	1.176784	0.5822	2.02	0.0433	Cross Sectional Effect 4583
CS4584	1	0.720699	0.5816	1.24	0.2153	Cross Sectional Effect 4584
CS4585	1	2.881899	0.5818	4.95	<.0001	Cross Sectional Effect 4585
CS4586	1	0.470699	0.5816	0.81	0.4184	Cross Sectional Effect 4586
CS4587	1	0.71186	0.7114	1.00	0.3170	Cross Sectional Effect 4587
CS4588	1	1.73234	0.5822	2.98	0.0029	Cross Sectional Effect 4588
CS4589	1	1.384045	0.5816	2.38	0.0174	Cross Sectional Effect 4589
CS4590	1	0.40097	0.7120	0.56	0.5733	Cross Sectional Effect 4590
CS4591	1	0.926784	0.5822	1.59	0.1114	Cross Sectional Effect 4591
t2	1	−0.03259	0.0217	−1.50	0.1329	
t3	1	−0.07696	0.0250	−3.07	0.0021	
married	1	−0.36249	0.0531	−6.82	<.0001	
divsep	1	−0.02978	0.0456	−0.65	0.5136	
widow	1	0.005769	0.0567	0.10	0.9189	
cohab	1	−0.3176	0.0528	−6.01	<.0001	

Test Results				
Test	Type	Statistic	Pr > ChiSq	Label
Test0	Wald	0.90	0.3430	married - cohab = 0

Results shown include the fixed effects for the first 50 and last 30 individuals in the data (leaving out over 4500 other effects listed), just to give an idea of the total individual differences captured. The F-test shows there are significant (and strong) individual differences—as do the coefficients: Person 12 was depressed only .17 days in the past week on average over time while person 10 was depressed 4.3 days. These individual differences capture all of the various effects of stable unmeasured variables ***not*** in this model. Note that the R^2 in the standard regression model is .0422 and in the fixed effects model is .6061. This difference implies that there are important and essential sources of depression due to fundamental individual differences.

The results for marital status contrast interestingly with the previous results. Most notably, here the effect of cohabiting is stronger and closer to the effect of marital status. In fact, the post-hoc test of the difference between the married and cohabiting groups here is not significant. This finding is unique in the context of the literature on this issue. The "standard" finding is that cohabitation produces reduced benefits to well-being relative to marriage, but this finding suggests there is no difference. The fixed effects model suggests that it is not the institutional and legal benefits of marriage that matter to mental health but the simple presence of a partner who is there today and will most likely be there tomorrow.

The difference in findings across models is important because it implies that in a standard regression, some of the components of the error term are in fact confounded with marital status and notably with who is in the cohabiting group. Note finally that the effects of divorced or widowed status are not significant in this model—an unusual finding that would require further investigation as well.

If we include fixed *measured* variables as controls, we see the output illustrated in Table 13.5.

TABLE 13.5 ● WHAT HAPPENS IF YOU INCLUDE FIXED VARIABLES IN A FIXED EFFECTS MODEL

Variable	DF	Estimate	Standard Error	t Value	Pr > |t|	Label
t2	1	−0.03259	0.0217	−1.50	0.1329	
t3	1	−0.07696	0.0250	−3.07	0.0021	
married	1	−0.36249	0.0531	−6.82	<.0001	
divsep	1	−0.02978	0.0456	−0.65	0.5136	
widow	1	0.005769	0.0567	0.10	0.9189	
cohab	1	−0.3176	0.0528	−6.01	<.0001	
female	0	0	.	.	.	
ageatwave1	0	0	.	.	.	
ageatwave1sq	0	0	.	.	.	

As you can see, SAS deletes variables that are fixed. These variables are hidden in the mix of variables embedded in the individual fixed effects and thus cannot be estimated separately. This may be a disadvantage, but in the next chapter, we consider a hybrid method that does show the effects of this type of variable as well as implement a version of fixed effects. Other than the deleted variables, other estimates here are exactly the same.

Results in Table 13.6 show the same fixed effects model estimated in PROC GLM. Note that the results are exactly the same as in PROC PANEL. This is accomplished by using the ABSORB command. However, one needs to run PROC PANEL to estimate other kinds of panel models, including the random effects model.

TABLE 13.6 ● A FIXED EFFECTS MODEL FOR MARITAL STATUS IN GLM

Test Results				
Test	**Type**	**Statistic**	**Pr > ChiSq**	**Label**
Test0	Wald	0.90	0.3430	married - cohab = 0

Source	DF	Sum of Squares	Mean Square	F Value	Pr > F
Model	4596	13622.60677	2.96401	2.94	<.0001
Error	8792	8851.41027	1.00676		
Corrected Total	13388	22474.01704			

R-Square	Coeff Var	Root MSE	depressed Mean
0.606149	90.15427	1.003373	1.112951

Parameter	Estimate	Standard Error	t Value	Pr > |t|
t2	−.0325934122	0.02168558	−1.50	0.1329
t3	−.0769643430	0.02503216	−3.07	0.0021
married	−.3624873603	0.05311259	−6.82	<.0001
divsep	−.0297834875	0.04559400	−0.65	0.5136
widow	0.0057685614	0.05666284	0.10	0.9189
cohab	−.3176022724	0.05282834	−6.01	<.0001

13.2.1.3 Models to Test the Stability of Effects over Time

The time dummy variables in this model allow us to assess whether the effect of marital status is changing over time. For example, we might want to know whether the mental health benefits of marriage are declining while the mental health benefits of cohabiting are increasing. You can test such interactions in PROC PANEL as you normally would in any regression program. The SAS code that follows was used to test the general interaction between marital status and time:

```
proc panel data=panelreg;
id mcaseid wave;
model depressed=t2 t3 married divsep widow cohab
    marxt2 marxt3 cohxt2 cohxt3 divxt2 divxt3 widxt2 widxt3/ fixone noint;
```

This run produces the results shown in Table 13.7. Because this model and the previous fixed effects model are nested in the same way that all progressively inclusive regression models are, a standard *F*-test can be used to assess the overall interaction. Without applying this formal test, it is quite obvious that there is little evidence of any change in the effect of marital status overall, although there *may* be some decline in the effect of divorce over time. This interaction should be assessed further by taking into account age differences in the interaction as well.

TABLE 13.7 ● TESTING AN INTERACTION BETWEEN MARITAL STATUS AND TIME IN A FIXED EFFECTS MODEL

Parameter Estimates					
Variable	DF	Estimate	Standard Error	t Value	Pr > |t|
t2	1	−0.02162	0.0822	−0.26	0.7926
t3	1	−0.04495	0.0751	−0.60	0.5497
married	1	−0.34183	0.0810	−4.22	<.0001
divsep	1	0.051773	0.0811	0.64	0.5230
widow	1	0.075587	0.1057	0.72	0.4745
cohab	1	−0.37406	0.1007	−3.72	0.0002
marxt2	1	0.01004	0.0870	0.12	0.9081
marxt3	1	−0.00308	0.0820	−0.04	0.9701
cohxt2	1	−0.01635	0.1339	−0.12	0.9028
cohxt3	1	0.069035	0.1069	0.65	0.5186
divxt2	1	−0.02593	0.0947	−0.27	0.7842
divxt3	1	−0.25008	0.1124	−2.22	0.0261
widxt2	1	−0.12996	0.1163	−1.12	0.2638
widxt3	1	0.006624	0.1472	0.05	0.9641

Finally, we compare results from the random effects model to the fixed effects model, by running the following program in PROC PANEL. Note that this program designates "ranone" as the type of model, which specifies a one-way (cross-sectional) random effects model. The "noint" option is removed here because the missing effects are migrated to be part of the error rather than fixed effects, and so the intercept needs to be re-introduced.

```
proc panel data=panelreg;
id mcaseid wave;
model depressed=t2 t3 married divsep widow cohab / ranone;
test married-cohab=0;
run;
```

Output from the random effects model in Table 13.8 includes the Hausman specification test. If this test is significant, this is interpreted as indicative of confounding between the missing unmeasured variables and the Xs in the model. Since the test is significant here, we would conclude that the random effects model is potentially misspecified and that the fixed effects model is more appropriate.

Note as well that the random effects model implies again that there *is* a difference in the effect of married versus cohabiting. The results from the random effects model also point to a potential advantage of this model: If we can establish no confounding between unmeasured and measured predictors, then we can also see the effects of fixed variables in the model. As noted earlier, in the next chapter we discuss a hybrid method that allows for the estimation of fixed effects *and* the explicit inclusion of fixed variables in the model.

TABLE 13.8 ● A RANDOM EFFECTS MODEL FOR MARITAL STATUS

Model Description	
Estimation Method	RanOne
Number of Cross Sections	4591
Time Series Length	3

Fit Statistics			
SSE	13472.6203	DFE	13382
MSE	1.0068	Root MSE	1.0034
R-Square	0.0195		

Variance Component Estimates	
Variance Component for Cross Sections	0.631868
Variance Component for Error	1.006757

Hausman Test for Random Effects		
DF	m Value	Pr > m
6	37.98	<.0001

Parameter Estimates					
Variable	DF	Estimate	Standard Error	t Value	Pr >1.412122 |t|
Intercept	1		0.0375	37.66	<.0001
t2	1	−0.03548	0.0216	−1.65	0.1000
t3	1	−0.09269	0.0239	−3.88	0.0001
married	1	−0.41346	0.0373	−11.09	<.0001
divsep	1	0.017575	0.0388	0.45	0.6509
widow	1	0.016856	0.0494	0.34	0.7329
cohab	1	−0.25644	0.0422	−6.08	<.0001

13.2.2 Running Fixed Effects Models in STATA

We replicate two models from the previous example in STATA, first to show the comparable syntax but also to illustrate how the person-period data is created in STATA.

13.2.2.1 Creating a Person-Period Dataset in STATA

Compared to SAS, creating a person-period dataset in STATA is quite simple. First, as you do in SAS, code the variables across all relevant waves with a suffix identifying the designated wave (i.e., married1, married2, married3; divsep1 divsep2 divsep3, etc.). Then, use the *xtset* command to reset the data. In this case, we state that we want to create a person period dataset where individuals are nested within waves, denoted by the variables *mcaseid* and *wave*, respectively. Here is the suggested syntax to use when the coded data by wave are open in STATA.

```
xtset mcaseid wave
```

13.2.2.2 A Fixed-Effects Model of Marital Status Predicting Depression in STATA

STATA uses the *xtreg* command to estimate panel regression results. The *fe* option indicates that we are estimating a fixed effects model to account for unmeasured heterogeneity. The *fe* option automatically suppresses the intercept.

```
xtreg depressed t2 t3 married divsep widow cohab, fe
```

The results in Table 13.9 are comparable to the previous SAS output presented for the PROC PANEL model excluding time-variant effects.

TABLE 13.9 ● A FIXED EFFECTS MODEL FOR MARITAL STATUS PREDICTING DEPRESSION IN STATA

```
Fixed effects (within) regression          Number of obs    =   13389
Group variable: mcaseid                    Number of groups =    4591

R-sq: within   = 0.0107                     Obs per group: min =      2
      between  = 0.0341                                    avg =    2.9
      overall  = 0.0248                                    max =      3

                                            F(6,8792)        =   15.90
corr(u_i, Xb) = 0.0392                      Prob > F         =  0.0000
```

depressed	Coef.	Std. Err.	t	P>|t|	[95% Conf. Interval]	
t2	-.0325934	.0216856	-1.50	0.133	-.0751022	.0099154
t3	-.0769643	.0250322	-3.07	0.002	-.1260332	-.0278955
married	-.3624874	.0531126	-6.82	0.000	-.4666004	-.2583743
divsep	-.0297835	.045594	-0.65	0.514	-.1191584	.0595914
widow	.0057686	.0566628	0.10	0.919	-.1053039	.116841
cohab	-.3176023	.0528283	6.01	0.000	-.4211582	-.2140464
_cons	1.389993	.046151	30.12	0.000	1.299526	1.48046
sigma_u	.9936746					
sigma_e	1.003373					
rho	.49514376	(fraction of variance due to u_i)				

```
F-test that all u_i=0:      F(4590, 8792) =      2.81        Prob > F = 0.0000
```

Next, we test the interaction between time and marital status in predicting depression. As in Chapter 10, we use the ## option to generate these interaction terms within the model itself. Note that you do not have to include the lower order terms of the interactions separately; these are implied.

```
xtreg depressed i.t2##married i.t3##married i.t2##i.cohab i.t3##i.
cohab i.t2##i.divsep i.t3##i.divsep i.t2##i.widow i.t3##i.widow , fe
```

TABLE 13.10 ● TESTING AN INTERACTION BETWEEN MARTIAL STATUS AND TIME IN A FIXED EFFECTS MODEL IN STATA

```
Fixed effects (within) regression          Number of obs    =   13389
Group variable: mcaseid                     Number of groups =    4591

R-sq: within  = 0.0122                      Obs per group: min =      2
      between = 0.0295                                      avg =    2.9
      overall = 0.0228                                      max =      3

                                            F(14,8784)       =    7.77
corr(u_i, Xb) = 0.0283                      Prob > F         = 0.0000
```

depressed	Coef.	Std. Err.	t	P>|t|	[95% Conf. Interval]	
1.t2	-.0216236	.0822251	-0.26	0.793	-.1828042	.1395569
1.married	-.3418339	.08101	-4.22	0.000	-.5006324	-.1830354
t2#married						
1 1	.0100401	.0869728	0.12	0.908	-.1604469	.1805271
1.t3	-.0449471	.0751254	-0.60	0.550	-.1922105	.1023163
t3#married						
1 1	-.0030754	.0820202	-0.04	0.970	-.1638542	.1577034
1.cohab	-.3740569	.1006694	-3.72	0.000	-.5713924	-.1767214
t2#cohab						
1 1	-.0163482	.1338997	-0.12	0.903	-.278823	.2461266
t3#cohab						
1 1	.0690351	.106938	0.65	0.519	-.1405883	.2786586
1.divsep	.0517732	.0810564	0.64	0.523	-.1071164	.2106627
t2#divsep						
1 1	-.0259333	.0947053	-0.27	0.784	-.2115778	.1597112
t3#divsep						
1 1	-.2500835	.1124038	-2.22	0.026	-.4704212	-.0297457
1.widow	.0755873	.1056953	0.72	0.475	-.1316003	.2827749
t2#widow						
1 1	-.1299649	.1163056	-1.12	0.264	-.3579512	.0980214
t3#widow						
1 1	.0066241	.1471753	0.05	0.964	-.2818739	.2951221
_cons	1.356463	.0724862	18.71	0.000	1.214373	1.498553

```
sigma_u |  .99554151
sigma_e |  1.0030696
    rho |  .49623341   (fraction of variance due to u_i)

F-test that all u_i=0:     F(4590, 8784) =      2.82          Prob > F = 0.0000
```

The names of the variables in Table 13.10 are quite different in this output compared to the SAS results. This is because of STATA's unique approach to generating the interaction effects between marital status and time within the model. Regardless of these differences, the coefficients and their respective errors are the same as the previously reported in SAS: "`1.t2`" represents the lower-order term for Time 2 on depression (b = -.022, se = .082); and "`1.married`" is the lower order term for the variable married (b = .010, se = .087), for example.

The '1 1' following each interaction term notes the presence of both variable conditions. For example, "`t3#divsep, 1 1`" corresponds to the interaction coefficient impacting depression given responses at (a) Time 3 of (b) divorced or separated respondents, compared to otherwise. This is the statistically significant interaction shown previously; β = -.250, se = .112. While these results might be difficult to read at first, they do present an efficient way of testing interactions *within* the model rather than generating separate variables in the person-period data set prior to estimation.

13.2.3 Interpreting Effects in a Panel Regression

The results in the previous example describe differences in depression due to marital status. The results *look* very much like a cross-sectional regression, but there is an important difference. Recall the individual mean-corrected version of the fixed effects model, which was shown to be equivalent to the individual dummy variable fixed effects model:

$$Y_{it} - \overline{Y}_i = \beta(X_{it} - \overline{X}_i) + u_{it}$$

In this model, the means are the individual means *over time*, and thus both X and Y at each time point are measured as deviations from this person-specific mean. This form of the model shows that the effect of X depends on and derives from *change* in X over time. If, for example, someone is married throughout, then their average value on married is 1 and the value of the deviation score on married is therefore 0 (1 – 1) throughout. And if they are not married throughout, their average value is 0, and the value of the deviation score above is also 0 (0 – 0) throughout. For someone who was married at Time 1 but not at Times 2 and 3, their mean on married is .333. Then their score at $T1$ will be .666 and at later waves –.333. This is still a difference of 1 on married, but their overall tendency on X has been removed from the variable. Only individuals who change in marital status will have nonconstant values of X in this model and thus contribute to the estimated effect of X. ***Thus, the effect of* X *derives from the observed changes in marital status in the sample, and these are related to the observed changes in* Y.**

This discussion is intended to illustrate that the effects of marital status here are *not* like a cross-sectional regression where statuses are compared to each other in a static model. Here the effect of each marital status reflects the impact of change in that status directly.

13.2.4 The Effects of SES (Education and Income) on the Body Mass Index

This example is based on findings reported by David Kryszajtys and Yvonne Daoleuxay (2018) in a course assignment on fixed and random effects, with some changes in coding. The data are from the National Longitudinal Survey of Youth (NLSY97) (Bureau of Labor Statistics, U.S. Department of Labor, 2019b) on children of the original NLSY sample. The goal is to estimate the effects of both education and income on the body mass index (BMI), over three time periods:

2004, 2008, and 2013. The "children" were 19 to 24 in 2004, 23 to 28 in 2008, and 28 to 33 in 2013. In this example, we focus on women only.

In our approach to their analysis, we emphasize the relative importance of education versus family income in comparing results for OLS versus fixed effects models. In doing so, we raise the possibility of *differential* selection for educational and income achievement, based on stable personal characteristics. This kind of question is not usually addressed using fixed effects models, but it is possible to have multiple time-varying variables in the model, remembering, in this case, that income is in part a mediator of the effects of education.

Education is measured here as the highest degree attained and so appears as a series of dummy variables. High school graduation is the reference group, with less than high school (*noeduc*), GED high school equivalent (*ged*), two-year associate's degree after high school (*AA*), bachelor's degree (*bach*), and post-graduate degree (*grad*), as the groups compared to high school. Income is measured as family-level income, in units of 10,000 dollars. The body mass index is calculated based on height and weight values as follows:

$$BMI = 703 \times weight\ (lbs)\ /\ [height\ (in)]^2$$

We show results for a fixed control in the OLS case only. This control is self-identified racial category (Black, Hispanic, Native American, Asian, and Mixed-Other relatives to White). We also controlled in both models for marital status as a time-varying control, using four categories: never married—not cohabiting, never married—cohabiting *(nevmarrcoh)*, currently married *(married)*, and formerly married *(marloss)*. The reference group is never married—not cohabiting. We combined both cohabitation categories among the formerly married since there was no difference between them in BMI.

We again observe important differences between a regular OLS regression of the person-period data and a fixed effects regression. In the OLS results (Table 13.11), we see the effect of two controls: race and marital status. It is clear from the results that individuals in marital statuses that involve a partner have a significantly higher BMI. Both never married cohabiting and currently married have higher BMI scores relative to the never married not cohabiting. Formerly married individuals do not differ from the non-cohabiting never married. Both Blacks and Hispanics have higher BMI scores than Whites, and Asians have significantly lower scores.

TABLE 13.11 ● AN OLS MODEL FOR SES AND BMI

Parameter Estimates				
Variable	**DF**	**Parameter Estimate**	**Standard Error**	**t Value**	**Pr > |t|**
Intercept	1	25.39340	0.20952	121.20	<.0001
t2	1	2.00643	0.20350	9.86	<.0001
t3	1	3.42811	0.21537	15.92	<.0001
income	1	−0.06128	0.01297	−4.72	<.0001
noeduc	1	0.34967	0.27762	1.26	0.2079
ged	1	−0.23676	0.32696	−0.72	0.4690
AA	1	−0.46056	0.28508	−1.62	0.1062
bach	1	−2.12493	0.22179	−9.58	<.0001
grad	1	−2.97174	0.38149	−7.79	<.0001

Parameter Estimates					
Variable	DF	Parameter Estimate	Standard Error	*t* Value	Pr > |t|
Black	1	2.88434	0.20363	14.16	<.0001
Hispanic	1	1.23460	0.28230	4.37	<.0001
NativeAm	1	1.38404	0.84428	1.64	0.1012
Other_Mixed	1	0.22278	0.26113	0.85	0.3936
Asian	1	−2.10889	0.67815	−3.11	0.0019
nevmarrcoh	1	0.62332	0.23303	2.67	0.0075
married	1	0.75675	0.20065	3.77	0.0002
marloss	1	−0.25402	0.35366	−0.72	0.4726

Focusing on the two focal variables here, income has a negative effect on BMI: Each increase of $10,000 lowers BMI scores by .061 on average. This is not a large effect, given the mean is 27.51, and the standard deviation is 7.55. Given a standard deviation in income around $64,000, the difference in BMI between individuals who are −2 and +2 standard deviations on income using the measured units is 4 x 6.4 x .−.061 = −1.56 BMI points. The BMI range from −2 to +2 standard deviations is 4 x 7.55 = 30.2. Thus, we should be cautious about interpreting the effect of income here as "significantly significant."

The effect of education here appears to be a bit more substantial, where there is an effect. First, we see no differences among educational groups without a university education. But having a university degree, whether bachelor's or graduate, reduces BMI scores by over 2 points on average, and in the case of a graduate degree, by close to 3 points.

We tested both random effects and fixed effects models and found the Hausman test again suggested a fixed effects model was preferable. Results for the fixed effects model are shown on Table 13.12.

TABLE 13.12 ● A FIXED EFFECTS MODEL FOR SES AND BMI

Parameter Estimates						
Variable	DF	Estimate	Standard Error	*t* Value	Pr > |t|	Label
t2	1	1.424566	0.1120	12.72	<.0001	
t3	1	2.596655	0.1310	19.82	<.0001	
income	1	−0.02808	0.00893	−3.14	0.0017	
noeduc	1	−0.63819	0.3675	−1.74	0.0825	
ged	1	−0.33145	0.3618	−0.92	0.3597	
AA	1	0.021987	0.2274	0.10	0.9230	
bach	1	−0.20722	0.2043	−1.01	0.3106	
grad	1	−0.60917	0.3182	−1.91	0.0556	
nevmarrcoh	1	0.944069	0.1626	5.81	<.0001	
married	1	0.994792	0.1855	5.36	<.0001	
marloss	1	−0.09904	0.3096	−0.32	0.7491	

Estimates of the effects of all three time-varying variables show quite distinct patterns compared to the OLS analysis. First, we see that the impact of income is now only −.028 per $10,000. This effect is significant, but it is less than 50% of the size of the estimated effect in OLS. Second, the effects of education are also substantially reduced here, with only grad-level education approaching significance, with a *b* of -.61—much smaller than in the OLS model. What does this mean? The comparison of results here suggests that SES may be less causal than is often assumed. Instead, a significant portion of the effect seems to be based on person selection for SES *and* BMI. The question, of course, is what stable individual differences are at issue in explaining this selection. Given that there is range of possibilities, one source that should be kept in mind involves structurally based differences in exposures and opportunities. For example, people in poor areas of urban environments may have both reduced access to decent schooling and relatively plentiful access to unhealthy food sources—such as fast food chains. They may also have reduced opportunity for physical exercise outside of the home. Thinking this way, we see that "individual differences" can be patterned by structural location and that what we are observing is partially explained by the multi-generational transfer of status.

Finally, we also observe that the effects of having a partner are *stronger* in the fixed effects model relative to the OLS model. This happens when the unobserved variables not measured act as a suppressor on the observed relationship. Thus, people who show a strong health-prone profile may be more likely to have a partner and a lower BMI, but the net effect of having a partner may be to increase the BMI.

13.3 PUBLISHED EXAMPLES

13.3.1 The Effects of State Beer Taxes on Automobile Fatality Rates

There are many examples in many literatures illustrating the potential importance of taking fixed effects into account. Here we consider the effect of state beer taxes on the automobile fatality rates in the 48 contiguous states of the United States, using findings based an analysis in Ruhm (1996). The policy at issue is whether governmental increases in taxes on beer will lower motor vehicle fatalities.

A standard regression in 1988, however, shows something disturbing—that higher beer taxes are associated with higher fatality rates (Figure 13.1).

FIGURE 13.1 ● STATE BEER TAXES AND VEHICLE FATALITIES IN 48 STATES

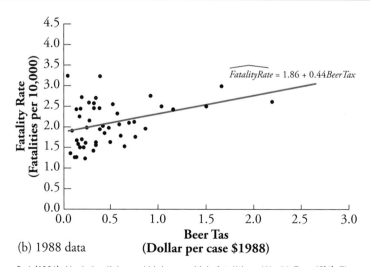

(b) 1988 data **Beer Tas (Dollar per case $1988)**

Source: Ruhm, C. J. (1996). Alcohol policies and highway vehicle fatalities. *J Health Econ 15*(4): Figure 8.1.

It is important to be suspicious of this finding. There are numerous opportunities for "omitted variable bias" here. For example, there are differences across states in traffic density due to differences in terrain and population. It turns out that the Western states have lower density, thus lower fatalities but also lower alcohol taxes in general. Another example is the culture of "drinking and driving," which may also vary by state, depending on average education, history, etc.

You can conduct a fixed effects analysis for two waves by using change scores for each variable. The same variables were measured in 1982, so you could construct $Y_{1988} - Y_{1982}$ as the dependent variable and $X_{1988} - X_{1982}$ as the independent variable. This first difference approach achieves the same thing as using the usual fixed effects specification (Allison, 1994) since stable state-level tendencies are differenced out.

This is how this works. If we estimate a cross-sectional equation for two points in time, 1982 and 1988, we have two estimates for the effect of beer taxes:

$$FatalityRate_{i1988} = \beta_0 + \beta_1 BeerTax_{i1988} + \beta_2 Z_i + u_{i1988}$$

$$FatalityRate_{i1982} = \beta_0 + \beta_1 BeerTax_{i1982} + \beta_2 Z_i + u_{i1982}$$

Here Z stands for the fixed effect at the state level. If we subtract these two equations, we get the following:

$$FatalityRate_{i1988} - FatalityRate_{i1982} = \beta_1(BeerTax_{i1988} - BeerTax_{i1982}) + (u_{i1988} - u_{i1982})$$

Here the effect of Z is subtracted out and the new error term is uncorrelated with the beer taxes. When the difference equation is used, it leads to the result shown in Figure 13.2.

FIGURE 13.2 ● FIXED EFFECTS MODEL FOR THE EFFECT OF BEER TAXES ON MOTOR VEHICLE FATALITIES

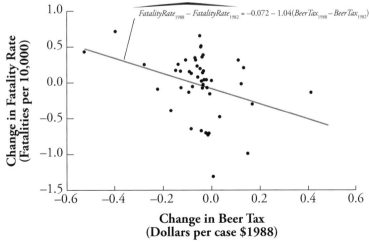

Source: Ruhm, C. J. (1996). Alcohol policies and highway vehicle fatalities. *J Health Econ* 15(4): Figure 8.2.

Obviously, there was something very important left out of the standard OLS regression. Now the effect is negative, as expected. This happens because there are hidden confounders with both beer taxes and fatalities at the state level.

Although this finding is controversial, a review of all studies on this issue by Wagenaar, Tobler, & Komro (2010) concludes the alcohol taxes do reduce motor vehicle deaths.

13.3.2 Explaining Occupational Sex Segregation and Wages

Another example of fixed effects in the literature comes from Paula England's and colleagues' *American Sociological Review* article on occupational sex segregation (England, Farkas, Kilbourne, & Dou, 1988). The authors test two competing perspectives on the causes of occupational sex segregation and women's overrepresentation in low paying jobs: *classic economic* versus *sociological views*. From an economic perspective, women "choose" occupations with higher starting wages but with lower appreciation of human capital (leading to lower wage accumulation) to accommodate child-related interruptions in their employment trajectory. A sociological view, alternatively, underscores that women are essentially tracked into lower paid and less prestigious occupations because of discriminatory hiring practices where women are assumed to be more committed to family than work.

The authors use panel data from the *National Longitudinal Survey*, which started with cohorts of men and women between 14 and 24. The survey started in 1966 and 1968 for men and women, respectively (see England et al., 1988, for additional information on the follow-up studies). The authors main outcome of interest is wages (using a log transformed version to better estimate a linear association). Their two main predictors include (a) sex segregation and (b) human capital. The authors measure segregation using a census based measure of "occupational percent female." They specify "human capital" by weeks of employment experience since one year prior to the first wave of the survey. Given the longitudinal nature of the data, the authors estimate fixed effects across all models and outline the significant benefits of such an approach:

> *Removing fixed effects is particularly important for our test of occupational percent female on pay because it assures us that all stable pay-relevant but unmeasured individual differences between individuals in predominantly female and male occupations have been controlled.*

> The method also permits more accurate estimates of effects of experience than is possible in the cross-sectional analyses comprising much of the literature. The effects of experience on earning are not computed by comparing individuals with more and less experience, as in cross-sectional studies. *Rather, the longitudinal features of the data are used to assess returns to experience as individuals accumulate it.* (emphasis added; England et al., 1988, p. 549).

The last point is important. It underscores the advantage of a longitudinal approach using fixed effects to truly capture respondents' *accumulated* experience "as it happens."

England et al.'s study has been seen as an important contribution to research attempting to understand gender differences in wages in general but also the phenomenon of occupational sex segregation. Not only did the authors tackle a major (and controversial) interdisciplinary debate in the literature by testing whether women are discriminated against because of their expected domestic roles, they also employ several unique approaches to testing their hypotheses. For example, the authors test the economic view of women's tendency to select into occupations with lower human capital appreciation by predicting wages with a constructed interaction term

Take-Away Point

The results, combined, provide evidence for a sociological view over an economic view of occupational sex segregation. Discrimination may be to blame for women's overrepresentation in lower paying jobs – a breakthrough finding at the time.

Finding #1

The significant interaction effect provides partial evidence for the economic view: Human capital has lower appreciation in female dominated occupations.

Finding #2

However, Finding #1 is undermined by the negative effect of "% female in occupation" on wages, suggesting that women don't "opt" for occupations with average higher salaries (i.e., this is the effect of PF when experience =0.

Finding #3

In subsequent analyses, the authors find that for every 1 percent female in one's occupation, wages decrease: White women's wages decrease .08 percent; Black women's decrease .11 percent (based on the logged coefficient x 100).

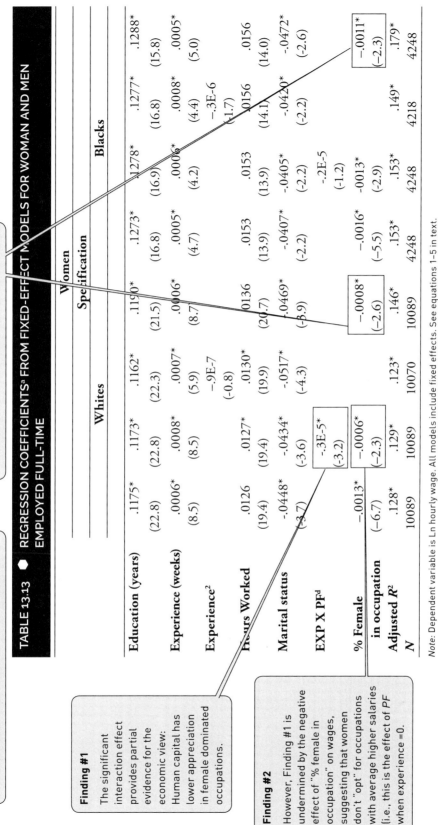

TABLE 13.13 ● REGRESSION COEFFICIENTS[a] FROM FIXED-EFFECT MODELS FOR WOMAN AND MEN EMPLOYED FULL-TIME

Women — Specification

	Whites				Blacks			
Education (years)	.1175* (22.8)	.1173* (22.8)	.1162* (22.3)	.1190* (21.5)	.1273* (16.8)	.1278* (16.9)	.1277* (16.8)	.1288* (15.8)
Experience (weeks)	.0006* (8.5)	.0008* (8.5)	.0007* (5.9)	.0006* (8.7)	.0005* (4.7)	.0006* (4.2)	.0008* (4.4)	.0005* (5.0)
Experience²			-9E-7 (-0.8)			-2E-5 (-1.2)	-3E-6 (-1.7)	
Hours Worked	.0126 (19.4)	.0127* (19.4)	.0130* (19.9)	.0136 (20.7)	.0153 (13.9)	.0153 (13.9)	.0156 (14.1)	.0156 (14.0)
Marital status	-.0448* (-3.7)	-.0434* (-3.6)	-.0517* (-4.3)	-.0469* (-3.9)	-.0407* (-2.2)	-.0405* (-2.2)	-.0420* (-2.2)	-.0472* (-2.6)
EXP X PF[d]	-.3E-5* (-3.2)							
% Female in occupation	-.0013* (-6.7)	-.0006* (-2.3)		-.0008* (-2.6)	-.0016* (-5.5)	-.0013* (-2.9)		-.0011* (-2.3)
Adjusted R²	.128*	.129*	.123*	.146*	.153*	.153*	.149*	.179*
N	10089	10089	10070	10089	4248	4248	4218	4248

Note: Dependent variable is Ln hourly wage. All models include fixed effects. See equations 1–5 in text.

[a] The *t*-statistic is in parentheses under coefficient.

[b] Female regressions include the instrumental variable from the equation predicting full-time employment. See text.

[c] Specification 4 includs all DOT variables listed in Table 2.

[d] Interaction term of Experience times % Female in Occupation.

*$p<.05$, 2-tailed test.

*Adapted from p. 553 of the original article

Source: England, P., Farkas, G., Kilbourne, B., & Dou, T. (1988). Explaining occupational sex segregation and wages: Findings from a model with fixed effects. *American Sociological Review,* 53(4), 544–558 Table 4, page 553.

between experience and whether the respondent is employed in a female dominated occupation. This interaction tests whether experience has as much impact in female-dominated occupations. If it does not, this implies that there is less appreciation due to human capital in certain occupations women select into—that is, they "choose" these occupations because of the attendant characteristics of these occupations—for example, there may be less relative *depreciation* of human capital due to interruptions.

The authors do in fact find evidence to support this expectation among White women only (compared to all men and Black women), lending support to neoclassical economic views. However, they claim that for the theory to be fully supported, they would also have to find evidence that women receive relatively high starting wages in their selected occupations, which is not the case. Instead, the findings suggest that regardless of gender or race, as the percentage of females in the occupation increases, starting wages decrease overall. This evidence is therefore more consistent with a sociological argument: Women are tracked into lower paying jobs, and the financial returns to their experience in these occupations are also lower.

The results and annotated findings are presented in Table 13.13. We focus on key coefficients from the sample of women to best signify the authors' evidence for sociological versus economic views of occupational sex segregation and wage differences. The fixed effects are in the background—but they represent an important set of alternative hypotheses that are implicitly controlled.

13.3.3 The Effects of Class Size on Public University Student Grades

A final example of a study effectively using a fixed effects approach resonates closely with most of us, whether currently a student or remembering one's own educational experience. Think about the size of your current or last statistics class. Does that have any impact on your grades? Are there fewer instructor-student interactions in larger classes compared to smaller sized ones? How does the quality of performance feedback differ across the two? Kokkelenberg and his colleagues (2006) address these questions, based on a previous literature underscoring the importance of size in affecting performance. The authors argue, however, that "no such agreement exists in the literature concerning the effect of class size in higher education." (Kokkelenberg et al, 2006:223). This is largely due to (1) limited data (i.e., cross-sectional) and (2) limited methods. Kokkelenberg and his colleagues address these limitations by using longitudinal data from students enrolled at U.S. public universities. The sample includes "one observation per student per course" measured from "Fall 1992 through Spring 2004," resulting in 998,898 observations. Students were taking courses in five faculties: Arts and Sciences, Education and Human Development, Engineering, Nursing, and Management.

The article uses multiple methodological approaches to demonstrate the robustness of their findings, including panel regression with fixed effects. For our purposes, we concentrate on these results only. We should note their outcome measure is ordinal in nature—grades scored from A to F, so they are using a fixed effects model for an ordinal logistic model, as discussed in the *next* chapter. To simplify the final results, the authors use a series of binary measures to compare grades (e.g., "C or lower vs. C+ or better; A- or lower vs. A, etc.).

The article uses a two-way fixed effects model: one for the students, and one for the semester (time)

$$W_{itj} = \beta_0 + \beta_i + \beta_t + \beta_1 E_{it} + \beta_2 A_{it} + \beta_3 CS_j + \beta_4 \tilde{W}_{DJ}$$

Here β_i is the student fixed effect and β_t the semester fixed effect. These two variables allow the authors to control for individual attributes not explicitly contained in the experience (*E*) and relative ability (*A*) variables (which may evolve over time) and time fixed effects, which control for grade inflation, if present.

This statement underscores the importance of a fixed effects model in estimating the impact of class size on university students' grades. The number of time-invariant unaccounted factors that may otherwise distort this association should be considered, and the analytical design used here allows a wide assessment of the impact of alternative inputs to grades. Based on the fixed effects analyses, the authors find statistically significant evidence that size does matter: the greater the class size, the lower the probability of receiving a higher level grade. We present the authors' results in Table 13.14.

TABLE 13.14 ● FIXED EFFECTS REGRESSION RESULTS FROM KOKKELENBERG ET AL. (2006)							
Variable/ statistic	C or lower versus C+ or better	C+ or lower Versus B— or better	B— or lower Versus B or better	B or lower Versus B+ or better	B+ or lower Versus A-or better	A-or lower Versus A	Ordinal non-fixed effects
Ability	0.176	0.184	0.149	0.169	0.153	0.142	0.620
	(6.50)	(7.14)	(6.13)	(6.89)	(5.91)	(4.68)	(219.75)
Experience	NS	0.027	0.57	0.069	0.076	0.063	0.067
		(1.29)	(3.09)	(4.08)	(4.48)	(3.33)	(32.25)
Log class size	−0.445	−0.450	−0.401	−0.426	−0.441	−0.504	−.338
	(−9.38)	(−10.62)	(−10.79)	(−12.38)	(−12.85)	(−13.11)	(−68.6)
Department	3.060	3.257	2.843	2.762	2.370	1.958	2.174
	(17.59)	(20.22)	(20.09)	(21.08)	(18.63)	(14.12)	(127.84)
N	10,000	10,000	10,000	10,000	10,000	10,000	10,000
Persent β significant at							
0.01	42	71	80	88	89	81	
0.05	48	71	80	88	89	81	
0.10	51	71	80	88	89	81	

(t-statistics in parentheses).

NS = not statistically significantly different from zero.

Note: Identified coefficients are all statistically significant. NS denotes non-significant results.

Source: Kokkelenberg, E., & Dillon, M., & Christy, S. (2006). The effects of class size on student grades at a public university. *Economics of Education Review*, 27, 230. 10.1016/j.econedurev.2006.09.011.

The results suggest that class size has a general effect on the likelihood of higher versus lower grades—note the negative coefficients across all models. In other words, the larger the class size, the worse the grades among students enrolled in public universities. Further, the authors underscore that class size—according to these fixed effects results—has a substantial impact controlling also for measured ability and year. These results should influence how universities make decisions around resources and class sizes, and for those currently enrolled, could make you reconsider the size of classes in which you enroll.

Concluding Words

This chapter has presented an overview of the classic approach to panel regression using fixed and random effects. The social science literature using these methods is diverse: Depending on the type of data (typically), some use fixed effects and some use random effects to control for stable unobserved differences that are not explicitly measured in the data. We have presented the standard test used to decide which model is more appropriate, but in our experience and from a quick survey of the literature using social, political, or psychological data, the necessity of fixed effects predominates.

The theme throughout this chapter is the potential for differences in results between OLS and a fixed effects model. Whether assessing the effect of marital statuses on depression, the effect of SES on obesity, or the effect of state beer taxes on motor vehicle fatalities, we observed essential differences in findings comparing OLS to the fixed effects findings. We consider these examples a caution about the potential for misleading findings when taking a standard OLS approach. As a specific example, consider the differences in the interpretation of the effects of marriage on mental health comparing OLS to fixed effects. In the OLS model, traditional marriage clearly has the most beneficial effect—a finding consistent with the literature on this question. But in the fixed effects model, cohabitation has roughly the same beneficial effect as marriage—a finding that would contradict much of the existing literature and lead to a different theoretical interpretation of the features of relationships that matter for mental health. If the positive effects generalize to cohabiting, the implication is that the presence of a partner is the essential ingredient and not necessarily the social status or legal advantages of the more traditional form of marriage.

While this chapter sticks to the basics of these methods, the next focuses on important elaborations and applications of these methods that go beyond the standard approach. We focus on the use of these methods to assess the effects of events, transitions, or natural treatments that occur between waves in selected samples at risk for these changes. So, for example, instead of studying all marital transitions symmetrically, where entries and exits have mirrored effects, we study the specific effect of divorce in a sample of married persons.

We consider the dynamic panel model, which includes the lagged effect of the dependent variable and thus accounts for reverse causation more explicitly. We also elaborate these methods to consider important hybrid versions, including fixed effects for logistic regression and using SEM for fixed effects, thus allowing both for the estimation of fixed effects and explicit representation of the effects of fixed variables that *are* measured in the data, such as gender, race, ethnicity, or age.

Practice Questions

1. The results for this question involve an analysis of the effects of a female spouse/partner's earnings and her egalitarian gender ideology on her male partner's egalitarian gender ideology, reported across three waves of the National Survey of Families and Households (NSFH). The sample is restricted to men who are either married or cohabiting across all three waves. Results here consider an interaction between the female partner's earnings and her gender ideology in predicting the male partner's gender ideology.

   The variables in this analysis are

   - *rgenid*: The dependent variable—the male partner's gender role egalitarianism score, with higher scores indicating more liberal attitudes. Range is 0 to 4.
   - *spgenid*: The same scale, but measured for the female spouse/partner. Range is 0 to 4.
   - *searninc*: The earned income of the female spouse/partner.

- **sgenxsearn**: An interaction between **spgenid** and **searninc**.
- **married**: A dummy variable for married (= 1) versus cohabiting (= 0).
- **t2, t3**: Dummy variables for Waves 2 and 3 of the NSFH respectively.

Results for three models are shown: an OLS model using panel data (Table 13.A), a fixed effects model (Table 13.B), and a random effects model (Table 13.C). Answer these questions:

a. Use the appropriate models and results to decide whether a random effects model or a fixed effects model applies in this case.

b. Using your preferred model, interpret the interaction between spousal earnings and her gender role egalitarianism in predicting her male partner's gender egalitarianism. *To do this, note that the spgenid scale starts at 0 for the most conservative attitudes and goes up to 4 for the most liberal attitudes.* Use these values to derive the effect of spousal earnings among conservative versus liberal female partners.

c. According to the results from the preferred model, is gender egalitarianism among males increasing, decreasing, or staying the same over time? Cite evidence from the results to support your conclusion.

TABLE 13.A ◆ THE OLS MODEL

Number of Observations Read	2508
Number of Observations Used	2449
Number of Observations with Missing Values	59

Analysis of Variance

Source	DF	Sum of Squares	Mean Square	F Value	Pr > F
Model	6	886.26668	147.71111	253.80	<.0001
Error	2442	1421.26170	0.58201		
Corrected Total	2448	2307.52838			

Root MSE	0.76289	R-Square	0.3841
Dependent Mean	1.65843	Adj R-Sq	0.3826
Coeff Var	46.00092		

Parameter Estimates

Variable	DF	Parameter Estimate	Standard Error	t Value	Pr > F
Intercept	1	0.73324	0.09771	7.50	<.0001
t2	1	0.08157	0.03827	2.13	0.0331
t3	1	0.25565	0.03806	6.72	<.0001
married	1	−0.23729	0.09212	−2.58	0.0101
searninc	1	−0.00256	0.00090713	−2.82	0.0049
spgenid	1	0.56122	0.01612	34.82	<.0001
sgenxsearn	1	0.00158	0.00038929	4.05	<.0001

TABLE 13.B ● THE FIXED EFFECTS MODEL

Model Description

Estimation Method	FixOne
Number of Cross Sections	836
Time Series Length	3

Fit Statistics

SSE	548.9708	DFE	1607
MSE	0.3416	Root MSE	0.5845
R-Square	0.7621		

F-Test for No Fixed Effects and No Intercept

Num DF	Den DF	F Value	Pr > F
836	1607	3.17	<.0001

Parameter Estimates

Variable	DF	Estimate	Standard Error	t Value	Pr > |t|	Label
t2	1	0.088158	0.0298	2.96	0.0031	
t3	1	0.246089	0.0295	8.35	<.0001	
married	1	−0.2753	0.1103	−2.50	0.0127	
searninc	1	−0.00235	0.000857	−2.74	0.0062	
spgenid	1	0.266949	0.0200	13.38	<.0001	
sgenxsearn	1	0.001212	0.000367	3.31	0.0010	

TABLE 13.C ● THE RANDOM EFFECTS MODEL

Model Description

Estimation Method	RanOne
Number of Cross Sections	836
Time Series Length	3

Fit Statistics

SSE	805.0628	DFE	2442
MSE	0.3297	Root MSE	0.5742
R-Square	0.2537		

Variance Component Estimates

Variance Component for Cross Sections	0.332215
Variance Component for Error	0.341612

Hausman Test for Random Effects

Coefficients	DF	m Value	Pr > m
6	6	174.58	<.0001

Parameter Estimates

Variable	DF	Estimate	Standard Error	t Value	Pr > |t|
Intercept	1	1.043064	0.0973	10.72	<.0001
t2	1	0.085741	0.0291	2.95	0.0032
t3	1	0.249826	0.0288	8.66	<.0001
married	1	−0.27111	0.0919	−2.95	0.0032
searninc	1	−0.00218	0.000789	−2.77	0.0057
spgenid	1	0.411757	0.0164	25.10	<.0001
sgenxsearn	1	0.001295	0.000338	3.83	0.0001

2. Results for this question are derived from an analysis of the effects of an egalitarian gender ideology on marital arguments, reported across three waves of the NSFH. The sample is restricted to married women married to the same husband across all three waves. **For this question, consider all tests of significance as one tailed**—that is, assume you have predicted that greater egalitarianism would produce fewer arguments in marriages.

Four models are presented: an initial OLS model, a fixed effects model, a fixed effects model with interactions, and a random effects model (Tables 13.D through 13.G).

The variables in this analysis are

- **argue**: A scale measuring frequency of marital disagreements (the dependent variable).
- **rgenideology**: The respondent's gender egalitarianism, a two-item scale. Higher scores represent beliefs in gender equality.
- **sgenideology**: The spouse's (husband's) gender egalitarianism, a two-item scale. Again, higher scores represent beliefs in gender equality.
- **domestictasks**: The number of domestic hours per week reported by the respondent.

- **t2, t3**: Dummy variables for Waves 2 and 3 of the NSFH respectively.
- **sgenxt2**: sgenideology x t2.
- **sgenxt3**: sgenideology x t3.

Answer these questions:

a. Use the appropriate models and results to decide whether a random effects model or a fixed effects model applies in this case.

b. Given your decision in (a), interpret the effect of both respondent and spouse egalitarianism on marital arguments.

c. According to the results from the "best model," what matters more to reducing marital arguments: reductions in the respondent's gender egalitarianism or increases in the spouse's gender egalitarianism?

d. Are there changes in the impact of spousal egalitarianism on arguments over time?

e. Assume you are a hired consultant. Comparing the results of the OLS model to the fixed effects model, what would your recommendation be to a group of husbands about their gender attitudes? In giving this advice, you are choosing one model, so what is misleading in the results of the other model?

TABLE 13.D ● THE OLS MODEL

Number of Observations Read	1785
Number of Observations Used	1758
Number of Observations with Missing Values	27

(*Continued*)

TABLE 13.D ● Continued

Analysis of Variance					
Source	DF	Sum of Squares	Mean Square	*F* Value	Pr > F
Model	5	4575.60613	915.12123	7.05	<.0001
Error	1752	227261	129.71500		
Corrected Total	1757	231836			

Root MSE	11.38925	R-Square	0.0197
Dependent Mean	5.62924	Adj R-Sq	0.0169
Coeff Var	202.32312		

Parameter Estimates					
Variable	DF	Parameter Estimate	Standard Error	*t* Value	Pr > |t|
Intercept	1	3.17441	1.15049	2.76	0.0059
t2	1	1.08226	0.66864	1.62	0.1057
t3	1	−2.03839	0.67193	−3.03	0.0025
sgenideology	1	0.50424	0.31497	1.60	0.1096
rgenideology	1	0.06044	0.29775	0.20	0.8392
domestictasks	1	0.28483	0.08747	3.26	0.0012

TABLE 13.E ● THE FIXED EFFECTS MODEL

Model Description	
Estimation Method	FixOne
Number of Cross Sections	595
Time Series Length	3

Fit Statistics			
SSE	108169.1955	DFE	1158
MSE	93.4104	Root MSE	9.6649
R-Square	0.5334		

F-Test for No Fixed Effects and No Intercept			
Num DF	Den DF	*F* Value	Pr > F
595	1158	2.16	<.0001

Parameter Estimates						
Variable	DF	Estimate	Standard Error	*t* Value	Pr > |t|	Label
t2	1	0.954289	0.5724	1.67	0.0958	
t3	1	−2.25094	0.5894	−3.82	0.0001	
sgenideology	1	−0.88816	0.4791	−1.85	0.0640	
rgenideology	1	1.35736	0.4499	3.02	0.0026	
domestictasks	1	0.246556	0.1139	2.17	0.0306	

TABLE 13.F ● THE FIXED EFFECTS MODEL PLUS INTERACTIONS WITH TIME

Model Description

Estimation Method	FixOne
Number of Cross Sections	595
Time Series Length	3

Fit Statistics

SSE	107671.0667	DFE	1156
MSE	93.1411	Root MSE	9.6510
R-Square	0.5356		

F-Test for No Fixed Effects and No Intercept

Num DF	Den DF	F Value	Pr > F
595	1156	2.16	<.0001

Parameter Estimates

Variable	DF	Estimate	Standard Error	t Value	Pr > |t|	Label
t2	1	−1.26082	1.7377	−0.73	0.4683	
t3	1	−0.57884	1.7869	−0.32	0.7461	
sgenideology	1	−0.91965	0.5916	−1.55	0.1203	
rgenideology	1	1.341111	0.4494	2.98	0.0029	
domestictasks	1	0.24713	0.1138	2.17	0.0301	
sgenxt2	1	0.8455	0.6279	1.35	0.1784	
sgenxt3	1	−0.60134	0.6286	−0.96	0.3390	

TABLE 13.G ● THE RANDOM EFFECTS MODEL

Model Description

Estimation Method	RanOne
Number of Cross Sections	595
Time Series Length	3

Fit Statistics

SSE	163272.0190	DFE	1752
MSE	93.1918	Root MSE	9.6536
R-Square	0.0240		

Variance Component Estimates

Variance Component for Cross Sections	37.88432
Variance Component for Error	93.41036

(Continued)

TABLE 13.G ⬢ Continued

Hausman Test for Random Effects			
Coefficients	DF	m Value	Pr > m
5	5	16.68	0.0051

Parameter Estimates					
Variable	DF	Estimate	Standard Error	t Value	Pr > |t|
Intercept	1	3.267158	1.2332	2.65	0.0081
t2	1	1.033934	0.5686	1.82	0.0692
t3	1	−2.11578	0.5740	−3.69	0.0002
sgenideology	1	0.035699	0.3340	0.11	0.9149
rgenideology	1	0.493055	0.3151	1.56	0.1179
domestictasks	1	0.269666	0.0893	3.02	0.0026

3. This question focuses on the impact of divorce on depression using panel regression methods. The effects of divorce and death of a spouse were estimated in the **last two waves** (1992–1994 and 2001–2002) of the National Survey of Families and Households. There are two dummy variables for divorce: divorce within the last two years (**div_12**) and divorce three or more years earlier (**div3_up**). **Widow** is a general dummy variable for death of a spouse. There is also a dummy variable for Time 3, labeled **t3.**

Three models were estimated: (1) a pooled OLS model which assumes constant intercepts and slopes (Table 13.H); (2) a fixed effects model with constant slopes and variable intercepts (Table 13.I); (3) a random effects model (Table 13.J).

Answer these questions:

a. Use the results from the appropriate model to determine whether a fixed effects or a random effects model is more appropriate.

b. Given your decision in (a), decide whether there are significant effects of divorce within the last two years, and divorce three or more years in the past.

c. Comparing the OLS results to the results in your chosen model, cite two misleading findings in the OLS results.

TABLE 13.H ⬢ THE OLS MODEL

Model Description	
Estimation Method	Pooled
Number of Cross Sections	2659
Time Series Length	2

Fit Statistics			
SSE	9594.4405	DFE	5314
MSE	1.8055	Root MSE	1.3437
R-Square	0.2494		

(Continued)

TABLE 13.G ● Continued

Parameter Estimates

Variable	DF	Estimate	Standard Error	t Value	Pr > |t|	Label
div_12	1	1.716688	0.1503	11.42	<.0001	
div_3up	1	0.649183	0.0660	9.83	<.0001	
widow	1	0.873572	0.0717	12.18	<.0001	
t3	1	0.807659	0.0282	28.64	<.0001	

TABLE 13.I ● THE FIXED EFFECTS MODEL

Model Description

Estimation Method	FixOne
Number of Cross Sections	2659
Time Series Length	2

Fit Statistics

SSE	2197.5100	DFE	2655
MSE	0.8277	Root MSE	0.9098
R-Square	0.7085		

F-Test for No Fixed Effects and No Intercept

Num DF	Den DF	F Value	Pr > F
2659	2655	3.36	<.0001

Parameter Estimates

Variable	DF	Estimate	Standard Error	t Value	Pr > |t|	Label
div_12	1	0.730614	0.1850	3.95	<.0001	
div_3up	1	−0.04316	0.1482	−0.29	0.7709	
widow	1	0.394185	0.1022	3.86	0.0001	
t3	1	−0.03742	0.0265	−1.41	0.1584	

TABLE 13.J ● THE RANDOM EFFECTS MODEL

Model Description

Estimation Method	RanOne
Number of Cross Sections	2659
Time Series Length	2

Fit Statistics

SSE	4399.0159	DFE	5313
MSE	0.8280	Root MSE	0.9099
R-Square	0.0220		

(Continued)

TABLE 13.J ● Continued

Variance Component Estimates	
Variance Component for Cross Sections	0.555932
Variance Component for Error	0.827687

Hausman Test for Random Effects			
Coefficients	DF	m Value	Pr > m
4	4	6.30	0.1779

Parameter Estimates					
Variable	DF	Estimate	Standard Error	t Value	Pr > |t|
Intercept	1	0.950109	0.0236	40.24	<.0001
div_12	1	0.937683	0.1236	7.58	<.0001
div_3up	1	0.226048	0.0643	3.52	0.0004
widow	1	0.515362	0.0655	7.87	<.0001
t3	1	−0.05459	0.0256	−2.13	0.0329

VARIATIONS AND EXTENSIONS OF PANEL REGRESSION

In this chapter we consider some important variations of panel regression, with special attention given to the generalizability of fixed-effects methods.

We consider three elaborations here: (1) evaluations of the effects of events between waves; (2) dynamic panel models including the lagged effect of the dependent variable; and (3) generalizations of the application of fixed effects to other methods discussed in this book, including logistic regression and structural equation models.

14.1 MODELS FOR THE EFFECTS OF EVENTS BETWEEN WAVES

Allison (1994, 2005) discusses models designed to detect the effects of changes, events, policies, interventions, life transitions, or role losses, which occur between waves.

The distinction between this application of panel regression and the approach of the previous chapter is the use of a sample specifically at risk for the event in question. If we want to study divorce, as opposed to general changes in marital status, we begin with a sample of married individuals. If we want to study the effects of losing a job, we start with a sample of employed workers. Of course, some events imply universal risk, such as a residential move or the death of a loved one. In all of these examples, it may be important to think about life history as a context for the event, including prior marriages, jobs, deaths, or moves, and to also consider "counteracting" events, such as a marriage after a divorce or getting a new job.

We discuss a general approach to coding and analyzing the effect of events that occur between waves, incorporating a fixed effects approach. We do not distinguish between two-wave versus multi-wave examples, as is sometimes done (Allison, 1994), because the approach we discuss here applies to both cases.

14.1.1 Modeling the Effects of Marital Disruption on Depression

We use the NSFH data—which uses retrospective reports of timing between waves—to illustrate the coding and analysis of the effects of two kinds of marital disruption: divorce and widowhood. We note this example relies on the very detailed recording of the timing of events in this study, and so we will present a second example relying more on "real-time" change data, such as in the NLSY.

To estimate the effect of an event, it is important that you create the "event" variables appropriately. To study the effects of marital disruption—and in contrast to the approach in the previous chapter—you begin by selecting on individuals who are married at time one. There are various ways of doing this in different statistical packages, but in SAS, after merging data from different waves, you could add an IF statement like this:

```
if marcohab=1 or marcohab=2;
```

This statement reads in data only if the person had Codes 1 or 2 on *marcohab*, the variable for Wave 1 marital status. These codes cover the two variations of currently married in the data. You then create separate measures of divorce and widowhood for each wave after that. To do this, at Wave 1, you set everyone to 0 on both dummy variables created to represent divorce or widowhood over time:

```
/* Marital disruption dummy variables set to zero at T1 */

div1=0;
wid1=0;
```

At Waves 2 and 3, you "update" these variables with information about divorces and deaths between waves gathered at each time point. We use the variable "mut1utra" at Wave 2 to do this because it is the status of the Wave 1 union. Everyone in this sample will either have a 3 or 4, for separation or divorce, a 5 for widowhood, or 7 for "still intact."

```
/* Marital disruption dummies at T2 reflect who got divorced or widowed since T1 */

if mut1utra=3 or mut1utra=4 then div2=1; else div2=0;
if mut1utra=5 then wid2=1; else wid2=0;
```

The excluded group here are those still married. At Wave 3, you update again. You should treat everyone who was disrupted by Wave 2 as having the same status at Wave 3—because a divorce did occur. You add to the sub-sample of divorced and widowed progressively across waves. A variable called "divtime" was developed at Wave 3 (code not shown) to measure the first divorce occurring after Wave 2, and the same approach was used to develop a variable called "widtime," for the death of a spouse. Then these statements were used to create dummy variables for divorce and widowhood at Wave 3:

```
/* dummy variables for (further) marital disruption by wave III */

if mut1utra=7 and divtime>0 then div3=1; else div3=0;
if 3<=mut1utra<=4 then div3=1;
if mut1utra=7 and widtime>0 then wid3=1; else wid3=0;
    if mut1utra=5 then wid3=1;
```

Of course, the approach will depend on what the data presents as options. Note that there are two ways you get a "1" on these variables by Wave 3: if you had already been disrupted by Wave 2 or if there is positive evidence that you were married at Wave 2 but experienced a divorce or spousal death since then. Table 14.1 shows the overall coding at each wave.

TABLE 14.1 ● CODING OF DIVORCE OVER TIME IN AS SAMPLE OF MARRIED PEOPLE

Dummy Variables:	Div 1	Div 2	Div 3
Divorced at			
T1 T2 T3			
No No No	0	0	0
No Yes Yes	0	1	1
No No Yes	0	0	1

You create the person-time data as discussed in the previous chapter. After creating these data, you can proceed to estimate the effects of marital disruption, taking into account stable fixed effects. But first it may help to see what a PROC REG *without fixed effects* would produce as estimates in this situation (Table 14.2).

TABLE 14.2 ● OLS ESTIMATION OF THE EFFECTS OF DIVORCE AND WIDOWHOOD ON DEPRESSION

Number of Observations Read	7908
Number of Observations Used	7908

Analysis of Variance

Source	DF	Sum of Squares	Mean Square	F Value	Pr > |t|
Model	5	194.16811	38.83362	28.09	<.0001
Error	7902	10924	1.38240		
Corrected Total	7907	11118			

Root MSE	1.17575	R-Square	0.0175
Dependent Mean	0.98647	Adj R-Sq	0.0168
Coeff Var	119.18857		

Parameter Estimates

Variable	DF	Parameter Estimate	Standard Error	t Value	Pr > |t|
Intercept	1	0.86959	0.03045	28.56	<.0001
t2	1	−0.02124	0.03286	−0.65	0.5180
t3	1	−0.09837	0.03377	−2.91	0.0036
divsep	1	0.37315	0.05469	6.82	<.0001
widow	1	0.54887	0.06359	8.63	<.0001
nkids	1	0.04386	0.00865	5.07	<.0001

The results here suggest that both divorce and widowhood have significant effects on depression. You can also estimate this model using PROC PANEL using this code to implement a fixed effects model:

```
proc sort data=panelreg;
by mcaseid wave;
run;

proc panel data=panelreg;
id mcaseid wave;
model depressed=t2 t3 divsep widow nkids/ fixone noint;
run;
```

The results are shown on Table 14.3.

TABLE 14.3 ⬥ ESTIMATING THE EFFECTS OF DIVORCE AND WIDOWHOOD IN PANEL

Model Description	
Estimation Method	FixOne
Number of Cross Sections	2636
Time Series Length	3

Fit Statistics			
SSE	4633.9339	DFE	5267
MSE	0.8798	Root MSE	0.9380
R-Square	0.5832		

F-Test for No Fixed Effects and No Intercept			
Num DF	Den DF	F Value	Pr > F
2636	5267	3.20	<.0001

Parameter Estimates					
Variable	DF	Estimate	Standard Error	t Value	Pr > |t|
t2	1	0.024875	0.0277	0.90	0.3695
t3	1	−0.02772	0.0293	−0.95	0.3444
divsep	1	0.044237	0.0697	0.63	0.5260
widow	1	0.325786	0.0728	4.48	<.0001
nkids	1	−0.0254	0.0500	−0.51	0.6113

Looking at the results for "divsep" and "widow" in Table 14.3, we can see that the results here are different in some essential respects. According to the fixed effects model, divorce has no net significant effect overall on depression, but widowhood—the death of spouse— still does.

An important feature of this example is that it demonstrates the potential importance of fixed effects. Although divorce had a strong impact in the OLS regression, results which adjust for fixed effects show no significant impact on depression. What does this mean? One possibility is that the fixed effects are capturing strong selection factors into divorce, which are accounting for its effects in these data. This interpretation is made more plausible by the fact that the effect of widowhood is much closer to the original regression estimate, although there are age selection factors here as well that likely explain part of the effect.

14.1.1.1 Evaluating the Time-Dependent Effects of Change

A major issue with the preceding results is that *time since the event* was not taken into account. So if the effects of divorce dissipate with time, then we are only seeing the effect of divorce *averaged over time.*

It is possible to divide the divorce or widowhood events into time frames relative to the current wave in the data. For example, to detect differences in the effect of divorce within the last two years, from two to four years, from greater than four years, you could subdivide the divorce event as follows (using divorces between Waves 1 and 2 as an example):

```
if 0<=cmint2-cmmarend<=24 and div12=1 then div12last2=1; else div12last2=0;
if 24<cmint2-cmmarend<=48 and div12=1 then div122to4=1; else div122to4=0;
if 48<cmint2-cmmarend<=100 and div12=1 then div124up=1; else div124up=0;
```

These statements use two measures of time: *cmint2,* the century month of the Wave 2 interview, and *cmmarend,* the century month of the separation or divorce. When the divorce or separation happened within the last 24 months, a dummy variable *div12last2* is set to 1, otherwise it is 0. If the marital separation or divorce happened between 24 and 48 months ago, then *div122to4* is 1 and 0 otherwise. If the marital separation happened more than 4 years ago, then *div124up* is 1 and 0 otherwise. The reference group is still those who remain married over time. The same subdivision of cases is applied to events between Waves 2 and 3. The person-period data set created to estimate the effects of time then uses a single variable for each of the time frames.

Of course one can experiment with functions of time to better specify the effect of the event. It is possible to use finer gradations of dummy variables first to better pinpoint the decay function for the effect of the event. This was done for divorce using one-year increments, resulting in the estimated effects on four different outcomes shown in Figure 14.1.

The graphs show the effect coefficient on the *Y*-axis and time since the event on the *X*-axis. Effect on depression lasts at least two years. This is not mirrored by effects on happiness: An initial negative effect quickly returns to no effect within two years. There are no gender differences in these effects, in a fixed effects context. However, there *are* gender differences in the effects of divorce on drinking: Males show larger and more lasting effects on drinking frequency and a major effect on the frequency of binge drinking up to four years later.

This approach was used to guide the construction of the dummy variables into efficient but sensitive time frames. It would also have been possible to specify time as a nonlinear function and then create splines based on the best fitting function.

Figure 14.1 also makes clear that part of the problem in detecting an effect of divorce in the first example is that the effect was diluted by time and therefore misleading. However, we see here that the effect of divorce and separation in the first year is very strong and persists through the second year.

14.1.1.2 The Effects of Time on the Consequences of Divorce and Widowhood

The same approach to specifying the role of time can be applied to widowhood and compared to the profile for divorce. Results in Table 14.4 use dummy variables for both divorce and

FIGURE 14.1 ● THE LAGGED EFFECTS OF DIVORCE ON FOUR OUTCOMES

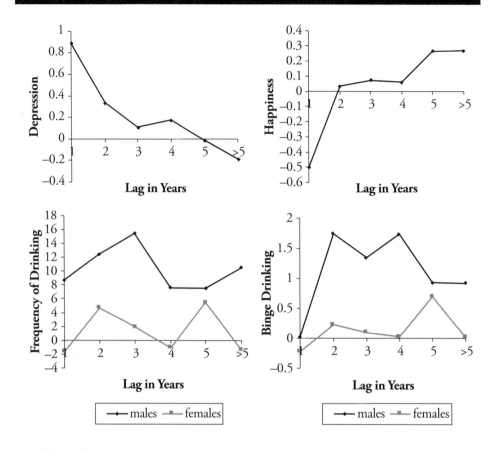

TABLE 14.4 ● COMPARING THE TIME-DEPENDENT EFFECTS OF DIVORCE VERSUS WIDOWHOOD

Parameter	Estimate	Standard Error	t Value	Pr > |t|
divrecent	0.6385419008	0.18816106	3.39	0.0007
divmid	0.1558190685	0.17311772	0.90	0.3682
divlong	−.1760653019	0.15593800	−1.13	0.2590
widrecent	0.5035193066	0.14822304	3.40	0.0007
widmid	0.6148593057	0.15583219	3.95	<.0001
widlong	0.1787262384	0.12149442	1.47	0.1414
t3	−.0136675912	0.02713026	−0.50	0.6145

widowhood divided into three segments: within two years ("recent"), two to four years ("mid"), and beyond four years ("long").

Results are shown for a fixed effects model. The effects of divorce last for two years but are nonsignificant after that. Of course, this effect is not contextualized at all by prior history or contingencies in the divorce process—which almost certainly would further diversify these estimates. Widowhood has more lasting effects on depression, for up to four years. Based on these results, we would conclude that widowhood has more lasting effects and therefore stronger effects overall on changes in mental health over time,

14.1.1.3 The Effect of Counteracting Events

Looking only at the effect of an event representing an exit from a role could be misleading if we do not take into account later entries into the same role. To assess the effects of remarriage here, we can code later marriages after these marital losses. The approach we take here codes remarriage as a conditionally coded dummy variable *only among those who have previously experienced a disruption event,* in other words, among those at risk for this secondary event. This approach allows us to see how much remarriage cancels the effect of divorce or widowhood.

Coding the effects of remarriage involves some special considerations. First, obviously, timing is important: The marriage must occur after the marital loss, and it should be the first marriage after the marital loss. Second, the conditional coding for remarriage implies the following: differences between 1 and 0 on this variable only occur *among those previously divorced or who lost a spouse,* and all those who are continuously married are 0 on this variable, and thus a constant.

An important point here is that the time-dependent effects of the original event should be taken into account. Here is an example of why it matters. The first result in Table 14.5 shows the effect of remarriage after a divorce, where divorce is only specified as occurring *sometime* between the waves of the study.

TABLE 14.5 ● THE EFFECTS OF REMARRIAGE AFTER DIVORCE

Parameter	Estimate	Standard Error	t Value	Pr > |t|
divsep	0.1937911180	0.14885679	1.30	0.1931
widow	0.4110303996	0.10256791	4.01	<.0001
t3	−.0542656937	0.02640715	−2.05	0.0400
marafterdiv	−.4723631261	0.23957519	−1.97	0.0488

In this model, it looks like remarriage has a (barely) significant effect on reducing depression after a divorce. When we distinguish the effects of divorce by time, the effect of remarriage after divorce looks quite different (Table 14.6).

TABLE 14.6 ● THE EFFECTS OF REMARRIAGE AFTER DIVORCE, WITH TIME SINCE DIVORCE SPECIFIED

Parameter Estimates				
Parameter	Estimate	Standard Error	t Value	Pr > |t|
divrecent	0.6574749017	0.18930865	3.47	0.0005
divmid	0.1804789945	0.17530104	1.03	0.3033
divlong	−.1248419592	0.16349193	−0.76	0.4452
widow	0.3838141808	0.10220500	3.76	0.0002
t3	−.0270494750	0.02686719	−1.01	0.3141
marafterdiv	−.1601890621	0.24598787	−0.65	0.5150

Here remarriage has no significant effect. Importantly, almost all of the remarriages here occur after the effect of divorce has already dissipated. Because we underestimated the effects of recent divorce in the first case, this distorted the effects of remarriage. In this model, remarriage has little effect on reducing depression, in a fixed effects context. As a reminder, this is not an estimate of the effect of the first marriage. In most cases, this is the second.

We can estimate the effects of remarriage after both divorce and widowhood in the same model, taking into account the time decay in the effects of the original events (Table 14.7).

TABLE 14.7 ⬤ THE EFFECTS OF REMARRIAGE AFTER DIVORCE AND WIDOWHOOD				
Parameter	**Estimate**	**Standard Error**	***t* Value**	**Pr > |t|**
divrecent	0.6499835650	0.18894828	3.44	0.0006
divmid	0.1725559077	0.17497097	0.99	0.3241
divlong	−.1444787065	0.16327221	−0.88	0.3763
widrecent	0.4923055996	0.14836467	3.32	0.0009
widmid	0.6259130419	0.15597174	4.01	<.0001
widlong	0.2220276518	0.12464219	1.78	0.0750
t3	−.0130383048	0.02713044	−0.48	0.6309
marafterdiv	−.1623449586	0.24550367	−0.66	0.5085
marafterwidow	−.5787527213	0.36966422	−1.57	0.1176

Again we see no effect of remarriage after divorce. Although the effect of remarriage after widowhood is not significant, we should contextualize the result by pointing out the few number of cases here, thus lowering the power to detect this effect. The coefficient is roughly the same size in opposite sign as the effect of the original event. We might conclude—with more cases—that remarriage after the death of a spouse is beneficial.

14.1.2 The Effects of Marriage on BMI among Women

This example uses a more common feature of longitudinal data: changes measured by differences in status across waves of the study coupled with less precise measures of timing. Following through with the Kryszatys and Daoloeuxay example from the previous chapter focusing on changes in the body mass index over time, we present results here using the NLSY, where the data are (mostly) gathered annually. The sample here is from the National Longitudinal Survey of Youth starting in 1997, including youth born between 1980 and 1984.

The coding considerations in this example may be both instructive in implementing the method as well as more generalizable to more applied cases, so we will review the coding in more detail. Kryszatys and Daoloeuxay (2018) assessed the impact of marriage as an event on changes in BMI from 2004 to 2013. The BMI was only measured three times over those waves—2004, 2008, and 2013, and so the focus in the analysis is on those waves, approximately five years apart. However, marital transitions were reported in the usual year-by-year interviews (except for 2012).

Coding marriage as an event and time since the marriage works a bit differently compared to the first example. We first list the steps involved:

- Select an at risk sample of never married women in 2003.

- Code all of the marital status variables from 2003 to 2013. Each is a dummy variable for marital status in that year. Note the skip of 2012, where there was no interview.

```
/************* Label marital status and code as binary *************/
mar03=S2022000;
mar04=S3822900;
```

```
mar05=S5423000;
mar06=S7525100;
mar07=T0025400;
mar08=T2020300;
mar09=T3611000;
mar10=T5211400;
mar11=T6662800;
mar13=T8134000;

array mar (10) mar03₋mar13;
do i=1 to 10;
if mar(i)=3 or mar(i)=4 then mar(i)=1;else mar(i)=0;
end;
```

- Code the event wave by wave, looking for the first evidence of a transition from "never married" to "married." If and when that occurs, note the year, and develop measures of time since marriage by the next wave. For example, to code marriages up to 2008, the second wave in which BMI is measured, we could use the code that follows, which finds the first evidence of a marriage from 2004 to 2008 (marwave2), notes the year in a variable called "yearmar2," calculates time since the marriage in "timesincemarwave2," develops time since marriage dummy variables (short, long), and then, importantly, uses an IF/THEN LEAVE statement to leave the array given that marwave2=1. This last statement is essential: It stops the DO loop from proceeding and overwriting the evidence of the marriage with later marital statuses, and it allows measuring the year of the marriage.

```
array marw2(5) mar04 mar05 mar06 mar07 mar08;
do i=1 to 5;
if marw2(i)=1 then marwave2=1; else marwave2=0;

if marwave2=1 then yearmar2=i+2003;
timesincemarwave2=2008-yearmar2;

if marwave2=1 and 0<=timesincemarwave2<=2 then marwave2_short=1;
else marwave2_short=0;

if marwave2=1 and 3<=timesincemarwave2<=4 then marwave2_long=1;
else marwave2_long=0;

if marwave2=1 then leave;
end;
```

- Do the same for marriages between Waves 2 and 3 and code marriage = 1 at Wave 3 if marriage = 1 at Wave 2. Because some people got married before Wave 2, it is necessary to develop longer time frame dummy variables for time since marriage, so those values may now exceed four years, and be five (2008) to nine years in total (2004). This dummy variable has the suffix "longest" in the output that follows.

- Create a person-period data for the fixed effects analysis. This is done basically the same way as for examples in the previous chapter, except that here we include only the last two waves:

```
data panelevent;
set temp;

array marb (2) marwave2 marwave3;
array div (2) divaftermarr2 divaftermarr3;
array marshort (2) marwave2_short marwave3_short;
array marlong (2) marwave2_long marwave3_long;
array marlongmax (2) marwave2_longest marwave3_longest;
array time (2) t2 t3;
array inc (2) faminc2 faminc3;
array bmia (2) bmi2 bmi3;

do i=1 to 2;

waveevent=i+1;
married= marb(i);
divaftermarr=div(i);
marrecent=marshort(i);
marmid =marlong(i);
marlongest= marlongmax(i);

bmi=bmia(i);
income = inc(i);

do n=1 to 2;
if i=n then time(n)=1; else time(n)=0;
end;

incmiss=nmiss(of faminc2 faminc3);
if incmiss>=1 then delete;
bmimiss=nmiss (of bmi2 bmi3);
if bmimiss>=1 then delete;

if marlongest=. then marlongest=0;
if marmid=. then marmid=0;
if marrecent=. then marrecent=0;

output;
end;
run;
```

The initial estimates of the effect of marriage are surprising, and instructive. The results using OLS actually suggest a *negative* effect of marriage on BMI (Table 14.8).

But the fixed effects results suggest, if anything, the opposite: a barely nonsignificant *positive* effect. (see Table 14.9).

TABLE 14.8 ● OLS ESTIMATION OF THE EFFECT OF GETTING MARRIED ON THE BMI

		Parameter Estimates			
Variable	DF	Parameter Estimate	Standard Error	t Value	Pr > |t|
Intercept	1	27.92240	0.18397	151.78	<.0001
t3	1	1.33176	0.24675	5.40	<.0001
married	1	−0.87128	0.25670	-3.39	0.0007

TABLE 14.9 ● FIXED EFFECTS ESTIMATION OF THE EFFECT OF GETTING MARRIED ON THE BMI

			Parameter Estimates			
Variable	DF	Estimate	Standard Error	t Value	Pr > |t|	Label
t3	1	1.074215	0.1131	9.50	<.0001	
married	1	0.458807	0.2570	1.79	0.0744	

It is unusual to see this much of a change in the estimated effects of an event, but it is possible if the stable selection factors into marriage are strong. One possibility is that a genetic or biologically based propensity for greater weight also leads to a lower probability of getting married. This would induce a negative component in the association between getting married and BMI, which is manifest in the OLS model as a negative effect of getting married. When fixed effects are used, this component is taken out of the estimate of the effect of getting married and included as a component of the fixed effects. As a result, getting married has almost a net positive effect on the BMI, instead of a negative effect.

The reversal of sign here generalizes to the analysis taking into account time since the event. Those results (not shown) suggest that in an OLS context, the effect of marriage on BMI gets increasingly negative (beneficial) over time while, in the fixed effects model, the effect is never quite significant, though in the positive direction.

14.2 DYNAMIC PANEL MODELS

You may notice that models to this point do not include the dynamic impact of X on Y—that is, the effect of X on Y in the presence of a lagged value of Y at the previous wave. The inclusion of a lagged Y has attractive interpretive features because it explicitly takes into account the issue of reverse causation—as we saw for structural equation modeling—but the inclusion of this type of variable in the model can be problematic in data that have too few waves. There is no strong "border" qualifying data for using a dynamic panel model approach because the suggested minimum number of waves varies depending on the type of data and the sample size. Examples in the literature typically use at least 10 time points, but one can find suggestions for using these methods when the number of time points (T) is 5, especially if the number of cross-sections is large. However, it should be obvious that these methods cannot be applied easily when T is as low as 3.

There are other issues to consider in applying the dynamic panel model we consider here. First, because of the presence of lagged Y, we are estimating only the short-term impact of X rather than its cumulative impact over time. Controlling for Y_{t-1} means that we are absorbing part of the lagged effect of X on Y as well. Second, Allison et al. (2018) point out that the estimation procedure we discuss here (generalized method of moments—GMM) can be both biased and inefficient under some conditions and that using an SEM approach often improves estimates. We discuss this SEM approach later, but we include the GMM approach here because it is widely used. We do not review the main features of GMM here, except to say that it does not require complete knowledge of the distribution of the data as in ML.

The model under consideration is

$$Y_{it} = \alpha_i + \lambda_t + \beta X_{it} + \eta Y_{i,t-1} + u_{it}$$

Where: α_i refers to fixed effects dummy variables for cross-sections, λ_t refers to a fixed effect set of dummy variables for time, and we introduce a distinction between coefficients for X and lagged Y, leading to the use of η for the effect of lagged Y. The GMM estimator can be used to estimate this model with *less* bias and greater efficiency than the traditional panel model estimators we have used to this point.

What is the problem that arises uniquely in this type of model? When you introduce Y on the right-hand side of the equation, you clearly face the likely probability that this new independent variable will be correlated with the error term for Y at time t, since this variable is the same Y lagged one time point. The analytical advantage of introducing lagged Y is that you can now interpret the effects of X variables as effects on *change* in Y, over and above its previous state. This means you can account for the direction in Y over time and also make a stronger causal statement than without a lagged Y in the model.

We draw on an example here from Sebastien St. Arnaud (St. Arnaud, 2005). In his paper, St. Arnaud explores how policy-relevant groups and the ideological preferences of policymakers affect the minimum wage rate. This is done with time-series cross-sectional analyses on the determinants of provincial minimum wages in ten Canadian provinces for the period of 1976 to 2003. Note that this means that $T = 28$ and $N = 10$, a very different data situation than in the examples to this point. St. Arnaud proposes that change in the minimum wage is the result of political pressures from policy-relevant groups (labor movements) and decisions of policymakers in accordance with the ideological preference of their party membership. In addition, because market conditions (i.e., the unemployment rate, economic growth) influence governmental decisions, he includes controls for these effects. Table 14.10 (from the paper) presents summary statistics and theoretical expectations of the variables (in terms of hypothesized direction of the impact of each X on Y).

TABLE 14.10 ● SUMMARY STATISTICS AND THEORETICAL EXPECTATIONS OF THE VARIABLES							
Variables:	**Variation**	**Mean**	**Std. Dev.**	**Min.**	**Max.**	**Observations**	**Theoretical Expectations**
Adjusted Minimum Wage	overall	6.85	0.90	5.43	9.6	N = 280	Dependent variable
	between		0.47	6.10	7.47	n = 10	
	within		0.78	5.08	9.54	T = 28	

Variables:	Variation	Mean	Std. Dev.	Min.	Max.	Observations	Theoretical Expectations
Union Density (%)	overall	34.12	6.92	21.1	57.6	N = 280	Positive
	between		6.36	24.81	47.90	n = 10	
	within		3.36	23.92	43.82	T = 28	
Conservative Government	overall	0.54	0.50	0	1	N = 280	Negative
	between		0.26	0.00	1.00	n = 10	
	within		0.43	−0.21	1.22	T = 28	
Unemployment rate lagged one year	overall	10.16	3.83	2.7	20.8	N = 280	Negative
	between		3.49	6.17	17.25	n = 10	
	within		1.92	4.82	15.42	T = 28	
Real GDP per capita (in thousands)	overall	28.10	7.65	14.5	54	N = 280	Positive
	between		7.02	20.51	43.12	n = 10	
	within		3.74	21.18	42.37	T = 28	

Note: Between refers to the variation between the units (provinces) while *within* refers to the variation over time. Data sources are reported in the Appendix 1.

Source: St-Arnaud, S. (2005). *The rise and fall of provincial minimum wages: Labor movements, business interests and partisan theory.* Paper prepared for the 2005 Annual Meetings of the American Sociological Association, August 13–16, Philadelphia, Pennsylvania.

The expected effect of union density on wages is positive while the effect of conservative governments is predicted to be negative. The variable names in the analysis are:

```
identifi   =   Provinces identification (cross-section)
year       =   Year (wave)

Dependent Variable
adjminw    =   Log of the real minimum wage (adjusted to 2003
               dollars)

Independent Variables

unionden   =   Union density
right      =   Dummy for conservative government (1 = Conservative
               government; 0 = liberal and left governments)
lagunemr   =   Unemployment rate lagged one year
gdpcapun   =   Real GDP per capita
minlag     =   Real minimum wage lagged one time point
```

The first model estimated takes the following form:

$$ADJMINW_{it} = \alpha + \beta X_{it} + \mu_{it}$$

where $ADJMINW_{it}$ is the minimum wage measure described above, α is a common intercept, βX_{it} is a vector of covariates (union density, conservative government, unemployment rate and real GDP per capita (in thousands) for the ith province in tth year. This model is estimated with OLS and does not include fixed effects or random effects and is used for comparison. The code (following), as an example, employs the "pooled" option in the MODEL statement in PROC PANEL to specify OLS:

```
/* This procedure sorts the input data*/
proc sort data=temp;
     by identifi year;
     run;

/* This syntax specifies the pooled (OLS) model*/
Proc panel data=temp;
     id identifi year;
     model adjmin=unionden right lagunemr gdpcapun / pooled;
     run;
```

The OLS model suggests, rather suspiciously, that neither union density nor government policy have significant effects on the minimum wage.

Subsequent analyses (not shown here) were conducted to assess the plausibility of fixed effects versus random effects. The Hausman test suggests that the fixed effects model is more appropriate. Furthermore, significant F-tests reveal that both province and year fixed effects

TABLE 14.11 ● OLS ESTIMATION OF THE DYNAMIC PANEL MODEL

The PANEL Procedure

Pooled (OLS) Estimates

Dependent Variable: adjmin

Model Description

Estimation Method	Pooled
Number of Cross Sections	10
Time Series Length	28

Fit Statistics

SSE	147.7747	DFE	275
MSE	0.5374	Root MSE	0.7331
R-Square	0.3525		

Parameter Estimates

Variable	DF	Estimate	Standard Error	t Value	Pr > |t|	Label
Intercept	1	9.406016	0.4029	23.34	<.0001	Intercept
unionden	1	004784	0.00811	0.59	0.5559	unionden
right	1	−0.16471	0.0905	1.82	0.0699	right
lagunemr	1	0.17013	0.0156	10.94	.0001	lagunemr
gdpcapun	1	0.03205	0.00719	4.46	<.0001	gdpcapun

should be included in the model. The inclusion of province fixed effects means that unobserved province-specific factors that are not captured by the independent variables included in the model will be captured by the province-specific intercept. Similarly, the inclusion of year fixed effects controls for global shocks or policies that might affect the minimum wage in all the provinces over time.

The second model estimated takes the following form:

$$ADJMINW_{it} = \beta X_{it} + v_i + e_t + \varepsilon_{it}$$

This model is the two-way fixed effect model. The model is similar to Equation 1 but includes province (v_i) and year (e_t) fixed effects and the error term (ε_{it}).

The following syntax runs this model, using a default estimator for panel models:

```
/* This syntax specifies the two-way fixed effects model*/
Proc panel data=temp;
     id identifi year;
     model adjmin=unionden right lagunemr gdpcapun / noint fixtwo ;
     run;
```

The results are shown in Table 14.12.

TABLE 14.12 ● A TWO-WAY FIXED EFFECTS MODEL

The PANEL Procedure
Fixed Two Way Estimates: MODEL1
Dependent Variable: adjmin adjmin

Model Description

Estimation Method	FixTwo
Number of Cross Sections	10
TS Length	28

Fit Statistics

SSE	0.1892	DFE	239
MSE	0.1892	Root MSE	0.4349
R-Square	0.8019		

F-Test for No Fixed Effects and No Intercept

Num DF	Den DF	F Value	Pr > F
37	239	56.49	< .0001

Parameter Estimates

Variable	DF	Estimate	Standard Error	t Value	Pr > |t|	Label
unionden	1	−0.02583	0.0112	−2.31	0.0218	unionden
right	1	−0.1975	0.0684	−2.89	0.0043	right
lagunemr	1	−0.04726	0.0245	−1.93	0.0544	lagunemr
gdpcapun	1	0.002613	0.0144	0.18	0.8558	gdpcapun

These results incorporate fixed effects (not shown) and suggest that *both* union density and right government policy affect minimum wages, although the effect of union density is in the opposite direction to what one would predict.

In the next model, the effect of minimum wages lagged one year is included in the equation, but we still use the default estimator. The equation now is

$$ADJMINW_{it} = \eta\,ADJMINW_{it-1} + \beta X_{it} + v_i + e_t + \varepsilon_{it}$$

The syntax here is similar to the last model, except that the variable *minlag* (the variable name for the lagged minimum wage) is added to the equation. The results are shown in Table 14.13.

TABLE 14.13 ● TWO-WAY FIXED EFFECTS WITH LAGGED Y, DEFAULT PANEL MODEL ESTIMATOR

The PANEL Procedure

Fixed Two Way Estimates: MODEL1
Dependent Variable: adjmin adjmin

Model Description

Estimation Method	FixTwo
Number of Cross Sections	10
TS Length	28

Fit Statistics

SSE	19.2463	DFE	237
MSE	0.0812	Root MSE	0.2850
R-Square	0.9153		

F-Test for No Fixed Effects and No Intercept

Num DF	Den DF	F Value	Pr > F
37	237	21.04	< .0001

Parameter Estimates

Variable	DF	Estimate	Standard Error	t Value	Pr > |t|	Label
minlag	1	0.745507	0.0417	17.87	<.0001	
unionden	1	−.00819	0.00755	−1.08	0.2791	unionden
right	1	−0.10253	0.0453	−2.27	0.0244	right
lagunemr	1	−0.01291	0.0163	−0.79	0.4292	lagunemr
gdpcapun	1	−0.00119	0.00943	−0.13	0.8995	gdpcapun

The results here are quite different compared to the previous model: Now union density fails to have a significant effect, but a conservative government continues to have a significant impact. Note that the conclusions possible based on the sequence of results to this point are crucially different model to model.

Finally, we estimate the GMM model, using this syntax:

```
/* This syntax specifies the GMM model*/

Proc panel data=temp;
id identifi year;
instruments exogenous=(unionden right lagunemr gdpcapun) constant depvar;
model adjmin=unionden right lagunemr gdpcapun/ noint gmm time ;
run;
```

A new feature in this run is the use of the INSTRUMENTS statement. The choice of instruments depends on which variables you believe are truly exogenous. In the case of this model, all of the original Xs are chosen, but one could experiment here. The CONSTANT and DEPVAR options are typical for this situation. In addition, the options "gmm" and "time" are added to the model line to get PROC PANEL to estimate the model with GMM and ask that the time fixed effects be included with the cross-section fixed effects. The cross-section fixed effects are treated implicitly here, thus there is no explicit reference to them in the code. The results of this run are shown in Table 14.14.

TABLE 14.14 ● TWO-WAY FIXED EFFECTS WITH GMM ESTIMATOR

The PANEL Procedure

Dependent Variable: adjmin adjmin
The PANEL Procedure
GMM: First Differences Transformation
Dependent Variable: adjmin adjmin

Model Description

Estimation Method	GMM
Number of Cross Sections	10
TS Length	28
Estimate Stage	1

Fit Statistics

SSE	59.6894	DFE	248
MSE	0.2407	Root MSE	0.4906
Sargan Test			

Prob

DF	Statistic	ChiSq
238	88.68	<.0001

Parameter Estimates

Variable	DF	Estimate	Standard Error	t Value	Pr > |t|
unionden	1	0.010437	0.00539	1.94	0.0538
right	1	−0.31194	0.0596	−5.23	<.0001
lagunemr	1	−0.08151	0.0121	−6.73	<.0001
gdpcapun	1	0.017565	0.00579	3.03	0.0027

Now we see clearly significant effects for government policy, and borderline significant effects for union density as well, *in the predicted direction.* In fact, all variables are significant in this model. Overall, the use of a lagged *Y* here may clarify the effects of the *X*s considerably, as long as the GMM method is used. Note that the test for further autocorrelation of the errors (not shown), after the adjustments used in this model, is nonsignificant, which is desirable.

14.3 FIXED EFFECT METHODS FOR LOGISTIC REGRESSION

Allison (2005) discusses a numbers of generalizations of fixed effects methods in the book *Fixed Effects Regression Methods for Longitudinal Data.* Here we discuss his implementation of the generalization to logistic regression.

Following the logic that the estimation of change over time requires change in *Y*, the estimation of logistic models in a panel takes advantage of the information among individuals who change states on the outcome over time. Our example focuses on changes in full-time work status among women over time, using three waves of the NSFH. This means we are studying women who either entered into fulltime work or exited fulltime work or both over this period.

The odds in this case would be the probability of entering fulltime work versus the probability of leaving fulltime work. That is,

$$\ln\left(\frac{\Pr(y_1 = 0, y_2 = 1)}{\Pr(y_1 = 1, y_2 = 0)}\right)$$

This is called *conditional logistic regression*, indicating that the values studied are conditional on baseline status.

You need to create a person-wave data set for all waves, following the logic of the earlier examples. The logistic model we consider specifies depression, marital status, and wave of the study as determinants of work status, in a sample restricted to women only. So the person-wave data will use wave-specific measures of depression, marital status, and working to write values for these variables across waves of the study. Wave of the study is a class variable in the analysis to follow.

```
proc sort data=panelreg;
by mcaseid;
run;

proc logistic data=panelreg descending;
    class wave / param=ref;
    model working = wave depressed married divsep widow cohab;
    strata mcaseid;
run;
```

The STRATA statement has the effect of absorbing the effect due to *mcaseid*, much like the approach used by GLM. Thus, each woman in the sample is a fixed effect to be adjusted out of the results. The CLASS statement treats wave of the study as a set of dummy variables in the analysis, using the PARAM=REF specification.

The results are shown in Table 14.15.

TABLE 14.15 ● FIXED EFFECTS FOR A BINARY LOGISTIC REGRESSION FOR WORK STATUS

Class Level Information

Class	Value	Design Variables	
wave	1	1	0
	2	0	1
	3	0	0

Strata Summary

Response Pattern	working 1	working 0	Number of Strata	Frequency
1	0	1	2	2
2	0	2	78	156
3	1	1	89	178
4	2	0	51	102
5	0	3	871	2613
6	1	2	547	1641
7	2	1	640	1920
8	3	0	660	1980

Model Fit Statistics

Criterion	Without Covariates	With Covariates
AIC	2731.486	2616.649
SC	2731.486	2666.059
−2 Log L	2731.486	2602.649

Testing Global Null Hypothesis: BETA=0

Test	Chi-Square	DF	Pr > ChiSq
Likelihood Ratio	128.8367	7	<.0001
Score	125.8356	7	<.0001
Wald	119.7509	7	<.0001

Type 3 Analysis of Effects

Effect	DF	Wald Chi-Square	Pr > ChiSq
wave	2	74.8603	<.0001
depressed	1	13.5013	0.0002
married	1	0.3700	0.5430
divsep	1	3.7138	0.0540
widow	1	2.6355	0.1045
cohab	1	3.6583	0.0558

(Continued)

TABLE 14.15 ●   (Continued)

Analysis of Maximum Likelihood Estimates						
Variable		DF	Estimate	Standard Error	Wald Chi-Square	Pr > ChiSq
wave	1	1	0.6087	0.0730	69.6097	<.0001
wave	2	1	0.4519	0.0729	38.4256	<.0001
depressed		1	-0.1180	0.0321	13.5013	0.0002
married		1	-0.1625	0.2671	0.3700	0.5430
divsep		1	0.4952	0.2570	3.7138	0.0540
widow		1	-0.5108	0.3146	2.6355	0.1045
cohab		1	0.4449	0.2326	3.6583	0.0558

The STRATA summary shows the frequencies of patterns of work status over the three waves. For example, there were 660 women working at all three waves (response pattern 8), and 871 women not working at all three waves (response pattern 5). These observations are not considered in the logistic regression. The conditional logistic model only considers women who changed statuses over the course of the study.

Results suggest that depression reduces the chances of working, net of the influence of any fixed effects that may also feed into depression. Divorced status increases the chance of working, as does cohabitation, but the effect of marriage, relative to being single, is nonsignificant.

14.3.1 Multinomial and Ordinal Logistic Regression

The extension of fixed effects methods to multinomial and ordinal logistic regression is quite straightforward. Allison implements a mean-corrected model, introduced in the previous chapter, by using overtime person means to create variables expressed as deviations from the person-specific means. These data are then input to PROC SURVEYLOGISTIC, a program closely related to PROC LOGISTIC, but with the additional ability to take into account clustering adjustments to the standard errors. PROC LOGISTIC can recognize repeated observations, using the STRATA statement, but cannot adjust for dependence within repeated observations. This suggests that PROC SURVEYLOGISTIC may be quite generally useful for these kinds of models.

The example we consider looks at sense of control as an outcome—a five category ordinal outcome, as a function of current depression, marital status, and wave of the study. These variables are the same as those used in the previous example.

First you create the mean-adjusted variables as follows:

```
proc means data=panelreg NWAY NOPRINT;
   by mcaseid;
   var depressed hhincome married divsep widow cohab;
   output out=means mean= mdep minc mmarr mdiv mwid  mcohab;
run;

data paneldev;
   merge panelreg means;
   by mcaseid;

   depdev=depressed-mdep;
   hhincdev=hhincome-minc;
```

```
    marrdev=married-mmarr;
    divdev=divsep-mdiv;
    widdev=widow-mwid;
    cohabdev=cohab-mcohab;
```

run;

PROC MEANS here is used to create a unique mean value of all independent variables for each individual, using a BY statement, which computes separate means for each distinct value of *mcaseid* (the person-level id). These data are output as a data set, which is then merged with the original panel data by *mcaseid*) to create a new data set called "paneldev." The deviation variables are created in this DATA step.

These data are then input to PROC SURVEYLOGISTIC, using the deviation variables as the independent variables:

```
proc surveylogistic data=paneldev;
    class wave (param=ref);
    model control(REF='1')=  depdev hhincdev marrdev divdev widdev cohabdev wave
/ LINK=LOGIT;
    cluster mcaseid;
```

run;

Wave is again a class variable. The cluster statement specifies the grouping factor here, which is the individual. After the slash in the MODEL statement, we specify LINK=LOGIT, which works for an ordinal (as well as binomial) logistic model. We would use GLOGIT here if this was a multinomial model

The results here are shown in Table 14.16.

In general, we see that depression lowers the sense of control, and income increases the sense of control, over and above fixed effects. Marital status has little to do with it, perhaps due to selection factors into marriage.

TABLE 14.16 ● A FIXED EFFECTS MODEL FOR ORDINAL LOGISTIC REGRESSION

Score Test for the Proportional Odds Assumption		
Chi-Square	DF	Pr > ChiSq
558.1157	24	<.0001

Model Fit Statistics		
Criterion	Intercept Only	Intercept and Covariates
AIC	21455.297	21394.628
SC	21483.250	21478.485
−2 Log L	21447.297	21370.628

(Continued)

TABLE 14.16 ● (Continued)

Testing Global Null Hypothesis: BETA=0			
Test	Chi-Square	DF	Pr > ChiSq
Likelihood Ratio	76.6693	8	<.0001
Score	75.7810	8	<.0001
Wald	103.7484	8	<.0001

Type 3 Analysis of Effects			
Effect	DF	Wald Chi-Square	Pr > ChiSq
depdev	1	42.0944	<.0001
hhincdev	1	6.5780	0.0103
marrdev	1	0.1617	0.6876
divdev	1	1.6961	0.1928
widdev	1	0.8610	0.3535
cohabdev	1	0.5245	0.4689
wave	2	26.7782	<.0001

Analysis of Maximum Likelihood Estimates						
Parameter		DF	Estimate	Standard Error	Wald Chi-Square	Pr > ChiSq
Intercept	1	1	−1.7009	0.0413	1695.1130	<.0001
Intercept	2	1	0.5400	0.0370	212.8866	<.0001
Intercept	3	1	1.5606	0.0442	1243.8507	<.0001
Intercept	4	1	3.8508	0.0854	2035.3943	<.0001
depdev		1	−0.1423	0.0219	42.0944	<.0001
hhincdev		1	0.00114	0.000445	6.5780	0.0103
marrdev		1	0.0694	0.1726	0.1617	0.6876
divdev		1	−0.2227	0.1710	1.6961	0.1928
widdev		1	−0.1825	0.1967	0.8610	0.3535
cohabdev		1	−0.1185	0.1637	0.5245	0.4689
wave	1	1	−0.2048	0.0447	20.9720	<.0001
wave	2	1	0.000632	0.0397	0.0003	0.9873

Odds Ratio Estimates			
Effect	Point Estimate	95% Wald Confidence Limits	
depdev	0.867	0.831	0.905
hhincdev	1.001	1.000	1.002
marrdev	1.072	0.764	1.504
divdev	0.800	0.572	1.119
widdev	0.833	0.567	1.225
cohabdev	0.888	0.644	1.224
wave 1 vs 3	0.815	0.746	0.889
wave 2 vs 3	1.001	0.926	1.082

14.4 FIXED-EFFECTS METHODS FOR STRUCTURAL EQUATION MODELS

Allison (2005) has implemented a *version* of fixed effects methods using structural equation modeling. Actually, it would be more accurate to call this implementation a *fixed-effects equivalent model* because it fulfills the terms of a fixed effects model but uses a different method for specifying the fixed effects.

While it is true that the implementation of the concept of fixed effects in the SEM framework takes a very different approach, there are in fact some essential advantages of using this framework, as discussed in the following examples.

14.4.1 A Basic Model

We begin this section with a simple example, in order to show how the SEM specification of fixed effects works. Mechanically and technically, this is *not* a standard fixed effects model. In effect, Allison specifies the fixed effects case as an important modification of the random effects case.

Recall that in the random effects model case, the model is

$$Y_{it} = \alpha + \beta X_{it} + u_{it} + v_i$$

Where v_i is a unique component of error for individual *i,* thus capturing unmeasured stable individual differences.

The implementation of this model is unlike any of our previous examples. First, we do not use a person-period data set. Instead, we use the traditional "flat-file" data set, which has one observation per person with all of the variables across waves included in that one observation. Second, we specify a separate equation for the effect of X on Y at each point in time (three equations in

FIGURE 14.2 ● A RANDOM EFFECTS MODEL IN SEM

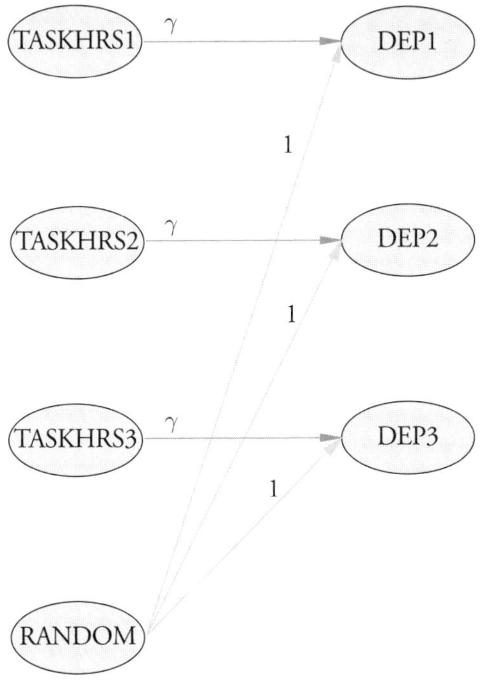

a three-wave model) and constrain the effect of X to be equal across waves. Third, the random effect v_i is specified as an unobserved variable in this model, *even in the fixed effects specification*. The model in Figure 14.2 shows the basic specification, focusing on the effects of domestic task burden on depression across three waves of the NSFH:

Not shown are the errors for depression over time and the correlations among the exogenous domestic task variables. The "RANDOM" unobserved factor is shown as causing depression at all points in time, with unstandardized coefficients set to 1. This specification is a standard treatment of how error terms are represented in unstandardized equations—there is nothing new here. Note that the random individual-level component of error is *not* correlated with the time-varying independent variables (*taskhrs*, representing the number of hours per week spent in domestic tasks). This fact makes this equivalent to a random effects model. When we estimate this model, we get the standardized results shown in Figure 14.3.

FIGURE 14.3 ● STANDARDIZED ESTIMATES IN THE RANDOM EFFECTS MODEL FOR DOMESTIC TASK BURDEN

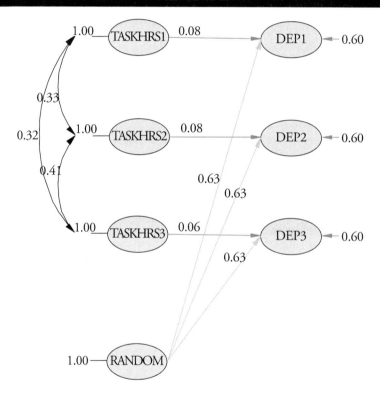

The results in the output verify that the variance of the random unobserved variable is very significant (not shown). The coefficients for the effect of task burden are equal in the unstandardized results but do not need to be in the standardized results. The effect here is .03 in the unstandardized model, with a t-value of 8.24.

The ***fixed effects equivalent*** model can be estimated by making one modification of this model: simply remove the assumption of zero correlation between the random unobserved variable and each of the task hours variables—however the software you use allows you do this. In effect, this correlation becomes a parameter to be estimated in the model.

Because these correlations are between a stable, unobserved variable that affects the outcome and the exogenous time-varying variable, this model implements the terms of a fixed effects model, without having to specify fixed effects per se. When this model is estimated, you get quite different results, as shown in Figure 14.4.

FIGURE 14.4 ◆ A STANDARDIZED FIXED EFFECTS MODEL FOR THE EFFECT OF DOMESTIC TASK BURDEN

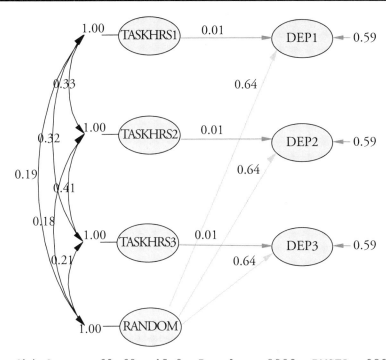

```
Chi-Square=60.60, df=9, P-value=.0000, RMSEA=.038
```

The effect of task hours here is now not significant. The correlations between task hours and the random unobserved variable are between .18 and .21 and are all significant. In effect, taking into account the confounding between the unmeasured random variable and task hours proved the effect of task hours to be spurious.

The difference in the fit of these two models is a measure of the necessity of the fixed effects model, equivalent to the Hausman specification test. You can conduct this test here by calculating the χ^2 difference between the two models, with df equal to the differences in degrees of freedom. In this case, the test is $\chi^2_R - \chi^2_F = 187.84 - 60.60 = 127.24$ with $12 - 9 = 3$ degrees of freedom. This is significant at less than the .00001 level. In other words, we can use this test to decide whether to use a random effects or a fixed effects approach.

14.4.2 A General Model for Causal Inference in Panel Data

Allison outlines the specification of fixed effects in panel data using a structural equations model approach, in a paper entitled *Causal Inference with Panel Data* (Statistical Horizons, https://statisticalhorizons.com/wp-content/uploads/2012/01/Causal-Inference.pdf).

Suppose we observe N individuals at T points in time, and we are concerned about the reciprocal effects of x and y. We also want to control for a set of time-varying control variables w_{it} and another set of fixed control variables z_i. This makes the case as general as possible. Note that fixed controls are considered and admissible using Allison's approach (an immediate advantage over the standard fixed effects approach).

The panel model that represents these relationships is as follows, taken directly from the article:

$$
\begin{aligned}
y_{it} &= \mu_t + \beta_1 x_{i(t-1)} + \beta_2 y_{i(t-1)} + \delta_1 w_{it} + \gamma_1 z_i + \alpha_i + \varepsilon_{it} \\
x_{it} &= \tau_t + \beta_3 x_{i(t-1)} + \beta_4 y_{i(t-1)} + \delta_2 w_{it} + \gamma_2 z_i + \eta_i + \upsilon_{it}
\end{aligned}
\quad , t = 1, \ldots, T
$$

Where μ_t and τ_t, are intercepts that vary with time, β_1, β_2, β_3, and β_4 are scalar coefficients, δ_1, δ_2, γ_1, and γ_2 are row vectors of coefficients, and ε_{it} and υ_{it} are random disturbances.

These equations are written out using standard SEM notation: The β are the effects of endogenous variables on each other, the γ and δ are the effects of exogenous variables. There are also unique symbols used for each set of intercepts and each equation's error term. What is important is that the α_i and the η_i terms stand for fixed effects in this model. The model allows for assessment of reciprocal causality in the usual way that a cross-lagged panel model does but with an additional feature—the presence of fixed effects that control for other unmeasured stable causes of each outcome.

This model also assumes that the w_{it} are also strictly exogenous to x and y. The fixed controls are automatically exogenous. By assigning time-varying controls to exogeneity, we emphasize the strictness of controls in assessing the reciprocal effect of x and y.

Allison presents an example based on the work of Paula England et al. (1988), with a focus on the effect of proportion female in an occupation. The data come from the demographic portion of the Current Population Survey of the U.S. in the years 1983, 1989, 1995, and 2001. The main variables of interest are the proportion female in an occupation and the median wage of females in that occupation. The sample is based on 178 occupations. Variables are labeled across the four waves MDWGF1 through MDWGF4 for median wages and PF1 through PF4 for proportion female. The main argument assessed is whether the proportion female has a net negative effect on wages, but we also have to consider the possibility that lower wages may *result* in a higher proportion female in the occupation—consistent with the argument that lower wage jobs may be less time demanding, and that men leave occupations with declining wages.

To simplify the example, Allison excludes the usual controls. The fixed effects are modeled as unobserved variables in the equation—following Teachman, Ducan, Yeung, and Levy (2001) and Allison (2005)—and they are allowed to be correlated with all time-varying predictors in the equation. To allow for the "sequential exogeneity" of x and y, error terms are allowed to be correlated with *future* values of the time-varying predictors in the model as well. With these assumptions, the model is still identified.

Allison used PROC CALIS in SAS to estimate this model. The run is as follows:

```
proc calis data=my.occ UCOV AUG;

lineqs
mdwgf4= t4 INTERCEPT + b1 pf3 + b2 mdwgf3 + falpha + e4,
mdwgf3= t3 INTERCEPT + b1 pf2 + b2 mdwgf2 + falpha + e3,
mdwgf2= t2 INTERCEPT + b1 pf1 + b2 mdwgf1 + falpha + e2;
```

```
STD
falpha=s1, e2-e4=sa:;

COV
falpha*mdwgf1 pf1 pf2 pf3=c0 c1 c2 c3:,
e2*pf3 =c4;
run;
```

The UCOV and AUG options here are unnecessary to the example—they are used to input covariance or cross-product matrices into the program, but it *can* use raw data input. The LINEQS statement is one long statement that specifies the model to be estimated, using multiple equations. This is the same statement used in the examples in Chapters 7. Allison splits the analysis of the two dependent variables into two parts, here including the model for wages only. This does allow more flexibility in the specification.

There is a separate equation for wages at each time point from Time 2 forward—there cannot be an equation for Time 1 because lagged effects are not possible then. On the right hand side of each equation, there is a coefficient and a variable for each component in the equation: Here "t" and "b" are coefficients, and "INTERCEPT", "pf$n$", and "mdwgf$n$" are variables. The lagged effect of wages controls for previous levels and thus means the effect of proportion female is net of previous wage levels. The error term is written as a series of "e" variables—though you could use any letter or name here. The fixed effects component is labeled "falpha." Note it is common to each equation. Crucial in this approach is the fact that the coefficients for the effects of proportion female and the lagged effect of wages are the *same* across the three equations. This imposes a fixed effects specification and makes identification of the fixed effects component possible.

The STD statement specifies the variances to be estimated in the model. There are two types here: The variance of the fixed effects, named "s1," and given parameter names for the variances of the error terms (the colon tells SAS to use sequential numbers as suffixes for the parameter names).

The COV statement describes the covariance parameters to be estimated. The fixed effect FALPHA is allowed to be correlated with wages at Time 1 only (where it is exogenous) and with values of proportion female—importantly. This could not be explicitly estimated in the standard fixed effects approach. Again, you make up parameter names for these estimates—whatever you choose. The final statement in the COV statement allows for a correlation between the error term at Time 2 and proportion female at Time 3, fulfilling the terms of "sequential exogeneity."

The equation for proportion female is constructed in mirror fashion, as follows:

```
PROC CALIS DATA=my.occ UCOV AUG;
LINEQS
pf4= t4 INTERCEPT + b1 mdwgf3 + b2 pf3 + feta + e4,
pf3= t3 INTERCEPT + b1 mdwgf2 + b2 pf2 + feta + e3,
pf2= t2 INTERCEPT + b1 mdwgf1 + b2 pf1 + feta + e2;
STD
feta=s1, e2 e3 e4=sa:;
COV
feta*pf1 mdwgf1 mdwgf2 mdwgf3=ca:,
e2*mdwgf3=cb;
RUN;
```

Note that the fixed effects component of the model here is labeled "feta"—pronounced F eta, not the cheese. Results for both equations are shown in Table 14.17.

TABLE 14.17 ●	RESULTS FOR A FIXED EFFECTS ANALYSIS OF THE CROSS-LAGGED EFFECTS OF PROPORTION FEMALE AND MEDIAN WAGES, 178 OCCUPATIONS

```
mdwgf2 =   -0.0836 * pf1 + 0.3434 * mdwgf1  +  7.9837 * Intercept + 1.0000 falpha + 1.0000 e2

Std Err    2.4323    b1    0.0640    b2        1.2411   t2

t Value    -0.0344          5.3680             6.4329


pf2    =    0.2994 * pf1 + -0.00054 * mdwgf1 + 0.3353 * Intercept + 1.0000 falpha + 1.0000 e2

Std Err    0.0820    b2    0.00151   b1        0.0384   t2

t Value    3.6534           -0.3572            8.7220
```

These results actually suggest *no* causal effect in either direction, at least in the presence of fixed effects. The fixed effects here stand for occupation specific characteristics that are unique to each occupation and stable over time. The most often cited finding from the literature is in fact that proportion female reduces the wages in an occupation. This result would argue with that conclusion.

14.4.3 Fixed Effects in Estimating Effects in Women's Work Careers

The example used here is based on a paper by Sarah Reid (and Wheaton) (2011), focusing on the effects of job exits vs. employment interruptions on women's status achievement. The specific purpose of the paper was to compare the influence of the *duration* of job interruptions—the primary concern of much of the gender and work literature on achievement differences—with the influence of the context of leaving jobs—that is, the reasons cited for leaving. The point here is to compare human capital explanations of relative losses in status over time with status characteristics explanations—that is, using worker ideals derived from the hegemonic role of the male worker.

It is quite common to study the impact of maternal leaves specifically, but in this case, Reid and Wheaton study a complete census of reasons for leaving jobs over the entire job history, using a sample of 888 married women in Toronto. Over 230 reasons were offered for leaving past jobs, and these were coded into a set of six types of reasons. Women were asked about every job since leaving school, including how long they had the job, why they left the job, and how long it was until the next job. Every occupation for each of a possible nine jobs was coded into an occupational status score. The measures used were

- *momlfseix:* The SEI of each job, from 1 to 9, where x is the number of the job.

- *timeoutx*: The time in years between the end of the last job and the beginning of the next job.

- *reasons for leaving jobs (for x = 1 to 9), a set of dummy variables:*
  - *involx*: layoffs, getting fired, end of contracts, health problems.
  - *familyx*: leaving to take care of kids or a new child, including maternal leaves.
  - *volperotherx*: leaving for personal reasons, but not family.
  - *negx*: leaving due to negative job conditions, such as no opportunities, low pay, bad physical conditions, undesirable work hours, problems with a boss, and so forth.
  - *posx*: Leaving due to positive job opportunities elsewhere.
  - *ILMx*: This is the reference group of reasons, standing for internal job change in the same organization.

The analysis was set up as a person-job model. Following Allison, Reid and Wheaton created equations predicting the SEI of the next job, using the time out of work since the last job, the reason for leaving the last job, and the previous job SEI as predictors. Thus, this model tests the net impact of reasons versus interruptions in predicting the mobility trajectory of women.

The run in PROC CALIS in SAS is set up as follows:

```
proc calis maxiter=1000 data=jobhist6to9 omethod=nrr /*ucov aug*/ pshort /*mod*/ /*stderr*/ simple
nobs=301;
title 'Reasons and timeout effects on women_s work status';

lineqs
momlfsei2 =t22 INTERCEPT + b12e invol1 + b32e volperother1
+ b42e family1 + b52e neg1 + b62 momlfsei1 + b72e pos1 + b82e timeout1 + falpha + e22,
momlfsei3 =t33 INTERCEPT + b12e invol2 + b32e volperother2
+ b42e family2 + b52e neg2 + b62 momlfsei2 + b72e pos2 + b82e timeout2 + falpha + e33,
momlfsei4 =t4 INTERCEPT + b12l invol3 + b32l volperother3
+ b42l family3 + b52l neg3 + b62 momlfsei3 + b72l pos3 + b82l timeout3 + falpha + e4,
momlfsei5 =t5 INTERCEPT + b12l invol4 + b32l volperother4
+ b42l family4 + b52l neg4 + b62 momlfsei4 + b72l pos4 + b82l timeout4 + falpha + e5,
momlfsei6 =t6 INTERCEPT + b12l invol5 + b32l volperother5
+ b42l family5 + b52l neg5 + b62 momlfsei5 + b72l pos5 + b82l timeout5 + falpha + e6;

std
   falpha=g2_sfix,
   e22 e33 e4 e5 e6=g2_s2 g2_s3 g2_s4 g2_s5 g2_s6;

cov
   falpha*invol1 volperother1 family1 neg1 pos1 timeout1 momlfsei1
   invol2 volperother2 family2 neg2 pos2 timeout2
   invol3 volperother3 family3 neg3 pos3 timeout3
   invol4 volperother4 family4 neg4 pos4 timeout4
   invol5 volperother5 family5 neg5 pos5 timeout5
= g2_phi__,
e22 invol3=cinvol3, e22 volperother3=cper3, e22 family3=cfam3, e22 neg3=cneg3, e22 pos3=cpos3,
```

```
e33 invol4=cinvol4, e33 volperother4=cper4, e33 family4=cfam4, e33 neg4=cneg4, e33 pos4=cpos4,
e4 invol5=cinvol5, e4 volperother5=cper5, e4 family5=cfam5, e4 neg5=cneg5, e4 pos5=cpos5,
    e22 timeout3=ctime3, e33 timeout4 = ctime4, e4 timeout5 = ctime5;

*pathdiagram diagram=all emphstruct;

run;
quit;
```

As before, the LINEQS statement here includes the equations to be estimated; the STD statement states the variances in the program to estimate and gives them parameter names; and the COV statement is used to state the covariances that have to be estimated. These include (1) covariances between the random unobserved factor (*falpha*) and the independent variables and (2) covariances between the errors for each job equation and the independent predictors of the next job.

14.4.3.1 LINEQS Statement

The LINEQS equations are set up starting at job 2, which is necessary because we include the lagged effects of the previous job in the model, and continuing up to job 6. This defines a sample large enough to estimate these equations—we cannot include all jobs (up to 9) because so few people have that many jobs. Each equation for each job predicts the SEI of that job using the reason for leaving the *prior* job, the SEI of the prior job, and the time in-between jobs. The special term INTERCEPT can be used in each equation.

Parameter names to be estimated—the coefficients—are specified using a unique name you make up. To implement the fixed effects model, you must set equal at least two equivalent effects over time. Here, for example, "b12e" is the effect of *invol* up to job 3, and "b12l" is the effect of *invol* for jobs 4 through 6. Using this approach, we used this model to assess differences in effects over time, like an interaction between the focal variable and time. Thus, the effect of each reason is given a different name early versus later in career, with the suffix "e" for early and "l" for later. The random unobserved factor *falpha* is stated the same way in every equation, and there is an error term, also named arbitrarily.

14.4.3.2 STD and COV Statements

The STD (standard deviations) statement gives names to the parameters for the variances to be estimated. This includes *falpha* and all of the error terms.

The COV statement is usually more involved but basically serves to give names to the covariances that have to be estimated. Each covariance is stated as a pair equal to a name, such as "e22 invol3 = cinvol3." Note that you can state the covariances for one variable with many others by using "*", where the first variable is paired with ALL of the variables after the asterisk. When you do this, you have to name the parameters using a reference like g2_phi__. The last underscore tells SAS to fill in consecutive numbers for the parameters. We note that the random effect denoted by "faplha" is allowed to covary with all Time 1 variables as well as the job exit and interruption variables at later waves. Also, error terms are allowed to covary with all later job exit and interruption variables.

In all of these statements, individual equations or parameter sets are separated by commas. If you wanted to test this model against a random effects model, you just delete the covariances with "falpha," rerun the model, and evaluate the change in fit.

The results (Table 14.18) show that distinguishing between early and later career is important. We tested the difference in fit between two models to test the interaction with stage of career, by comparing a model with the effects of reasons for leaving jobs stable and equal across *all* jobs with one specified as above, allowing for unique effects on jobs 2 and 3 versus 4 through 6.

Results show important differences in the effects of many of the reasons over time, but they also reveal less specificity to the "mommy penalty" than is often reported in the literature. There is no comparison to men here, but it would enhance our understanding of the uniqueness of these effects among women.

In the table, variables, errors, and the intercept are highlighted. Surprisingly, none of the reasons for leaving jobs early in career have significant effects on the status of the next job (ns means "not significant"). This could be due to a small N here per reason, but differences with the effects of reasons later in career are quite clear. And it is also the case that job interruptions early in career *do* have significant effects on reducing the status of the next job. This is the length of the interruption, not the reason, suggesting it is the length per se and not the particular context of leaving a job that matters early in career. In other words, early career may be a grace period in terms of activating the negative effects of leaving a job for family reasons or due to getting laid off.

Later in career, however, the effects of a wide array of reasons for leaving jobs begin to be important. Leaving for family reasons does not specifically have more negative effects than other reasons, such as involuntary job terminations or other personal reasons, but all three of those reasons have stronger negative effects than leaving due to negative job conditions. Leaving due to job opportunities seems to have a stronger positive effect early in career, but it is not quite significant then. Later in career, leaving for a better job does little in terms of conversion to a higher status job.

The pattern for job interruptions is the opposite of the pattern for reasons: Later in career, the length of interruptions has little effect whereas it has an important effect early in career, lowering status by 2.1375 points *per year out of work*.

Note two things about the interpretation of these results. First, these effects are over and above whatever is captured by the fixed effects. Second, they are also net of the status of the last job, so we cannot interpret these effects as the effect of prior status on either reasons or interruptions. Thus, this is an example of a dynamic panel model, and Allison et al. (2018) show that this approach to estimation has efficiency advantages over the more widely used GMM approach.

This model contains a number of advantages over the standard fixed effects model. Anything one can do in SEM can be layered with the fixed effects approach taken here. Perhaps the most important advantage is not highlighted in this example: the ability to include fixed variables in the analysis. We demonstrate that this is a straightforward addition to the model by including the effects of parental education on the woman's own occupational status.

The only difference in the program involves adding the effect of "*mmaxpareduc*" to each equation and setting these effects equal over time. This variable is the maximum level of either parent's education.

TABLE 14.18 ● ESSENTIAL RESULTS FROM A FIXED EFFECTS ANALYSIS OF REASONS FOR LEAVING JOBS ON STATUS ACCUMULATION AMONG WOMEN

Linear Equations

```
momlfsei2 = 44.7929 (**) INTERCEPT + −4.0374 (ns) invol1 + −4.0464 (ns) volperother1 + −5.1394 (ns) family1 + −1.7390 (ns) neg1 + 0.1855 (**) momlfsei1 + 0.9148 (ns) pos1 + −2.1375 (**) timeout1 + 1.0000 falpha + 1.0000 e22
momlfsei3 = 44.7519 (**) INTERCEPT + −4.0374 (ns) invol2 + −4.0464 (ns) volperother2 + −5.1394 (ns) family2 + −1.7390 (ns) neg2 + 0.1855 (**) momlfsei2 + 0.9148 (ns) pos2 + −2.1375 (**) timeout2 + 1.0000 falpha + 1.0000 e33
momlfsei4 = 48.3204 (**) INTERCEPT + −6.0977 (**) invol3 + −8.1109 (**) volperother3 + −6.2257 (**) family3 + −2.6556 (ns) neg3 + 0.1855 (**) momlfsei3 + 0.3672 (ns) pos3 + −0.4162 (ns) timeout3 + 1.0000 falpha + 1.0000 e4
momlfsei5 = 46.9783 (**) INTERCEPT + −6.0977 (**) invol4 + −8.1109 (**) volperother4 + −6.2257 (**) family4 + −2.6556 (ns) neg4 + 0.1855 (**) momlfsei4 + 0.3672 (ns) pos4 + −0.4162 (ns) timeout4 + 1.0000 falpha + 1.0000 e5
momlfsei6 = 50.3694 (**) INTERCEPT + −6.0977 (**) invol5 + −8.1109 (**) volperother5 + −6.2257 (**) family5 + −2.6556 (ns) neg5 + 0.1855 (**) momlfsei5 + 0.3672 (ns) pos5 + −0.4162 (ns) timeout5 + 1.0000 falpha + 1.0000 e6
```

TABLE 14.19 ● THE FIXED EFFECTS MODEL WITH THE FIXED EFFECTS OF PARENTAL EDUCATION

Linear Equations

```
momlfsei2 = 37.4606 (**) INTERCEPT + −4.6141 (**) invol1 + −4.1385 (**) volperother1 + −5.8395 (ns) family1 + −2.2126 (ns) neg1 + 0.1802 (**) momlfsei1 + 0.0912 (ns) pos1 + −2.1720 (**) timeout1 + 0.7566 (**) mmaxpareduc + 1. falpha + 1. e22
momlfsei3 = 37.1720 (**) INTERCEPT + −4.6141 (**) invol2 + −4.1385 (**) volperother2 + −5.8395 (ns) family2 + −2.2126 (ns) neg2 + 0.1802 (**) momlfsei2 + 0.0912 (ns) pos2 + −2.1720 (**) timeout2 + 0.7566 (**) mmaxpareduc + 1. falpha + 1. e33
momlfsei4 = 40.1191 (**) INTERCEPT + −5.9873 (**) invol3 + −8.7277 (**) volperother3 + −6.9289 (**) family3 + −2.4697 (ns) neg3 + 0.1802 (**) momlfsei3 + 0.1390 (ns) pos3 + −0.3953 (ns) timeout3 + 0.7566 (**) mmaxpareduc + 1. falpha + 1. e4
momlfsei5 = 39.1824 (**) INTERCEPT + −5.9873 (**) invol4 + −8.7277 (**) volperother4 + −6.9289 (**) family4 + −2.4697 (ns) neg4 + 0.1802 (**) momlfsei4 + 0.1390 (ns) pos4 + −0.3953 (ns) timeout4 + 0.7566 (**) mmaxpareduc + 1. falpha + 1. e5
momlfsei6 = 42.1130 (**) INTERCEPT + −5.9873 (**) invol5 + −8.7277 (**) volperother5 + −6.9289 (**) family5 + −2.4697 (ns) neg5 + 0.1802 (**) momlfsei5 + 0.1390 (ns) pos5 + −0.3953 (ns) timeout5 + 0.7566 (**) mmaxpareduc + 1. falpha + 1. e6
```

```
lineqs
momlfsei2 =t22 INTERCEPT + b12e invol1 + b32e volperother1
+ b42e family1 + b52e neg1 + b62 momlfsei1 + b72e pos1 + b82e timeout1 + b92 mmaxpareduc + falpha + e22,
momlfsei3 =t33 INTERCEPT + b12e invol2 + b32e volperother2
+ b42e family2 + b52e neg2 + b62 momlfsei2 + b72e pos2 + b82e timeout2 + b92 mmaxpareduc + falpha + e33,
momlfsei4 =t4 INTERCEPT + b121 invol3 + b321 volperother3
+ b421 family3 + b521 neg3 + b62 momlfsei3 + b721 pos3 + b821 timeout3 + b92 mmaxpareduc + falpha + e4,
momlfsei5 =t5 INTERCEPT + b121 invol4 + b321 volperother4
+ b421 family4 + b521 neg4 + b62 momlfsei4 + b721 pos4 + b821 timeout4 + b92 mmaxpareduc + falpha + e5,
momlfsei6 =t6 INTERCEPT + b121 invol5 + b321 volperother5

    + b421 family5 + b521 neg5 + b62 momlfsei5 + b721 pos5 + b821 timeout5 + b92 mmaxpareduc +
falpha + e6;
```

Importantly, *falpha* cannot be correlated with the fixed variables you do include. In effect, you are pulling them out of the random error component and specifying their effect in the equation as fixed variables. Thus, this method actually "corrects" one of the core disadvantages of the usual fixed effects approach.

The results show that indeed parent's education has the expected effect. But it also does not essentially change the effects of the time-varying variables—as it shouldn't (see Table 14.19).

There are still other applications of fixed effects to methods discussed in Allison (2005), including Poisson and negative binomial regression, continuous and discrete time event history models (considered next), and mixed models like HLM models and growth curve models. We refer the reader to Allison (2005) for detailed discussions of fixed effects applied to these models.

14.5 PUBLISHED EXAMPLE

14.5.1 Amato and Anthony (2014): The Effects of Parental Divorce and Death

In this chapter, we provided some examples of studying the effects of events between waves on outcomes in a fixed effects context. Amato and Anthony (2014) provide an excellent example, focusing on the impact of parental divorce or death on children's developmental health and well-being. As they explain, "[i]n the absence of true experiments, child fixed effects regression models provide reasonably strong evidence to decide whether divorce has causal effects on children" (p. 370). In other words, the ability to make definitive statements about the impact of divorce on children is enhanced by using fixed effects models, given that these models have two advantages: First, they account for unmeasured heterogeneity surrounding children's personality dispositions, genetic criteria, the quality of parental and marital relationships, and other constant social and demographic factors; and second, they better specify causation by analytically incorporating *time* into the models. As Amato and Anthony point out, this is particularly important with the study of divorce because family problems may precede divorce over a period of years, and it is difficult to separate the effects of the prior family context from the effect of divorce per se.

Amato and Anthony use two nationally representative datasets, including the Early Childhood Longitudinal Study, Kindergarten Cohort, and the National Education Longitudinal Study—comprising a different age group of children (younger children and adolescents respectively).

This is how the authors can assess the impact of divorce at different life stages. Further, this is one of only a handful of studies that is analytically able to address "in real time" the important association between parental divorce and child well-being while also taking into account a range of potential background causes also confounded with well-being that are usually not measured.

The authors compare the effects of divorce to the effects of death, specifically because of the debate about the common versus unique elements in these events. On the one hand, parental divorce often includes a volitional element on the part of at least one parent. In the case of death, however, the loss does not have an element of choice. The differences in meaning changes the potential consequences. On the other hand, Amato and Anthony argue that both divorce and death reflect in common a fundamental fact: parental loss and thus a foundational transition in a child's life.

So what do the authors find using a fixed effects approach? Overall, divorce results in significantly worse outcomes for children, overall. This pattern is particularly interesting when examining internalizing problems among children of divorce (i.e., anxiety and depression symptoms). Figure 14.5 displays changes in internalizing problems between children whose parents were divorced (Black dashed line) compared to those whose parents had not divorced (grey solid line).

FIGURE 14.5 ● CHANGE IN INTERNALIZING PROBLEMS DUE TO PARENTAL DIVORCE

Note the gap between the lines on the right side of the figure: Children of divorce are more likely to report internalizing problems over time.

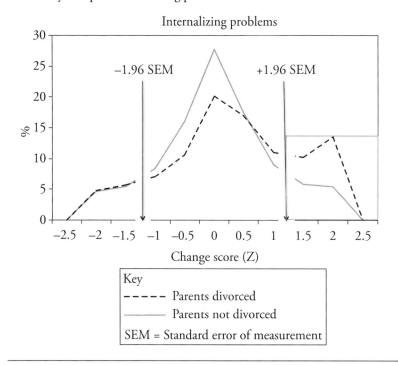

Source: Amato, P. R., & Anthony, C. J. (2014). Estimating the effects of parental divorce and death with fixed effects models. *Journal of Marriage and the Family*, 76(2), 380, Figure 1. doi:10.1111/jomf.12100.

FIGURE 14.6 ● EFFECT OF DIVORCE PROPENSITY ON MATH AND READING ACHIEVEMENT OVER TIME

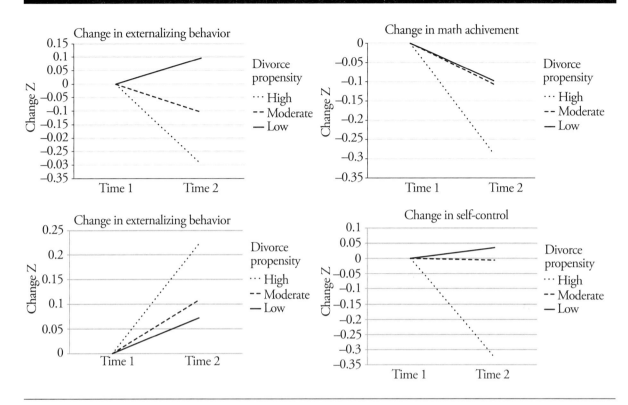

Source: Amato, P. R., & Anthony, C. J. (2014). Estimating the effects of parental divorce and death with fixed effects models. *Journal of Marriage and Family, 76*(2), 381, Figure 2. doi:10.1111/jomf.12100.

We highlight the noteworthy difference between those on the higher end of the scale: *the percentage of children with changes in their standardized internalizing scores between 1.5–2.5 is far greater among children of divorce compared to children with married parents* (using the Early Childhood Longitudinal Kindergarten Study).

The authors also plot change scores in other outcomes, such as reading and math achievement. The charts in Figure 14.6 show that those children whose parents had a high predicted divorce probability across waves also reported reduced achievement scores over time (using the Early Childhood Longitudinal Kindergarten Study).

These results provide important evidence of the consequences of divorce using panel data with fixed effects. The authors explicate the contribution of their approach in the following passage:

> One might argue that our results *underestimate* the effect of divorce because they did not account for the "early effects" of divorce, that is, declines in children's well-being due to marital conflict or other disturbed family relationships that precede (and may be causes of) marital disruption. Because the predivorce measures of outcomes absorbed the effects of these early family problems, they were implicitly controlled in our analysis. (Amato, & Anthony, 2014, p. 382)

Concluding Words

This chapter discusses techniques that reflect the power of combining the features of different analytical methods. We began with an important application of fixed effects: studying the effects of events, transitions, and in general, all natural interventions and treatments. Our approach extended the usual discussion of these methods to include two important additional issues: time since the event and the effects of counteracting events.

The rest of the chapter relied heavily on Paul Allison's innovative work on fixed effects. In that work, he has generalized the use of fixed effects to almost all of the techniques we discuss in this book. If there is a single chapter in this book that comes close to "having it all," this is it. The general panel model with fixed effects has some very general features, combining the structure of SEM with the interpretive logic of fixed effects. As a result of these generalizations, the use of fixed effects becomes accessible in a range of analytical situations.

There is just one remaining topic to consider: event history analysis, sometimes known as survival analysis, sometimes known as proportional hazard models. This technique is part of a family of techniques that incorporate time into the study of events—a family that includes techniques used in biology, medicine, engineering, and business. The essential question we address is this: When it is not enough to study the occurrence of an event because *when it happens* is meaningful; how do we conduct an analysis that fundamentally takes into account time and thus gives meaning to the length of time it takes for an event to happen? For many events we might study in logistic regression, the time component is crucial. It is not whether we are married but also why we got married early or late. It is not whether we return to taking drugs but how long after a drug intervention program. It is not whether we got promoted but how long it took to get promoted. Event history models are designed to explicitly include the effect of time and take into account the possibility that the effect of important causes of the event change with time at risk for the event as well.

EVENT HISTORY ANALYSIS IN DISCRETE TIME

Event history analysis is a technique for the analysis of the probability of occurrence of an event *at a given point in time*. Examples of events that would be studied this way are death, divorce, arrest, graduation, first promotion on a job, having a child, getting married, moving, organizational failure, revolution—any event that can be dated and related to other events or circumstances and has a defined "risk" period.

The risk period is defined by the onset of risk for the event under study due to a prior event. The nature of the prior event varies depending on the target event under study—for example, birth if studying death, marriage if studying divorce, age of fertility if studying having a baby, founding an organization if studying time to failure.

15.1 OVERVIEW OF CONCEPTS AND MODELS

It is important to distinguish this method from what is achieved by a standard logistic regression. Event history models incorporate the time it takes for an event to occur as essential information, so that we are not just predicting whether or not someone will experience an event but whether and **when**. The reason this is important is highlighted by this example, taken from Allison (2014): If you study recidivism over a 12-month period for a sample of released offenders, a logistic regression could only study whether they repeated an offence up to 12 months later, while an event history model would include what month the offence occurred in. This is important since those who commit offenses earlier are also likely to be at higher risk on the explanatory variables.

In many situations where we see logistic regression as the method of choice, an event history model may be more appropriate. To be explicit about this claim: This is not just a matter of "asking different questions." Looking back at the chapter on logistic regression, the examples studied included examples where timing was not an issue (voting) but also outcomes where timing may be important (risk of divorce, given different premarital cohabitation histories). The question is whether the event studied in a logistic regression framework *should* include the issue of timing, not whether it is possible to ignore timing simply by asking whether someone experienced the event at any time over an observation period.

15.1.1 Problems with Traditional Approaches

We review three classic problems with using approaches to studying event occurrence that do not incorporate the timing of the event (Allison, 2014):

1. Traditional regression approaches—for example, using prediction of the occurrence of an event in logistic regression—do not distinguish among times of event occurrence. Using the previous example, if a prisoner is released from jail and the dependent variable is the probability of arrest in the next 12 months, it clearly means something if the prisoner is arrested 1 month versus 11 months later.

2. "Length of time to event occurrence" has sometimes been used in a standard OLS regression. If the former prisoner is not arrested after 12 months, their value is 12, but in fact this group is "censored," meaning some may still be arrested later, and OLS *cannot* take this into account. OLS thinks the event happened at month 12.

3. If explanatory variables change in value over the observation period and the date of occurrence of the event in the dependent variables is not determined, then there is ambiguity as to which comes first—change in the explanatory variable or change in the dependent variable—and to make matters worse, this may only occur for part of a sample.

15.1.2 What Is an Event History and What Does It Do?

These kinds of methods go by many different names: survival models, proportional hazard models, event history models, and failure time models, to name a few. These terms are closely related, but they are not always the same model. The most general terms are "survival models" and "event history models."

An ***event history*** is a dated record showing (a) the onset, duration, and termination of a risk period for a defined event in a sample of n observations where the termination of risk could be the event happening or the end of the observation period, and (b) the time-specific states of relevant explanatory variables that control the occurrence versus non-occurrence of the event over the defined period of risk.

Note that explanatory variables come in two forms: (1) *fixed*: things that do not *typically* or cannot change over time—for example, nativity, race, parents' education, if studying a period in later life—and (2) *time-varying*: variables that change over the risk period for the event. This distinction between types of explanatory variables is very important in event history analysis.

15.1.3 The Risk Period

An essential issue in these models is defining the onset of risk for the event. Every event history starts at the beginning of this risk period.

For many issues, "birth" may be the onset of risk, if the event can occur at any time in life. But many types of events have a "precipitating event" that defines the beginning of a period of risk (see Table 15.1).

TABLE 15.1 ● DEFINING THE ONSET OF RISK FOR SELECTED EVENTS	
To Study	**Define a Risk Period Starting with**
Divorce	Marriage
Having a child	Earliest childbearing age
Entering first full-time job	Minimum age of employment
Dropping out of school	Minimum age of required schooling
Getting laid off	Date of starting the job
Getting a promotion	Start of job, or last promotion
Change in political leadership	Last change in leadership
Finishing PhD	Entry into the PhD program
Victim of partner abuse	Onset of relationship

You may be able to see from some of these examples that the beginning of risk is sometimes difficult to define. There is an additional issue in considering these examples: Some are *repeatable events*. To study these events properly, you would want to conduct separate analyses of each risk period, with the ability to compare the model across risk periods. This issue is addressed by what are called "multiple-spell" models.

15.1.4 Two Models: Discrete versus Continuous Time

Event history models come in two forms: ***continuous-time*** models and ***discrete-time*** models. The distinction between these two types of models is *fundamental* to the whole way you approach event history analysis.

Continuous-time models assume that an event could occur at any time while discrete-time models assume that events can occur only at certain times. For example, getting a job may occur at any time, but promotions may be scheduled due to a once-a-year review. Or dropping out of school tends to occur at the end of a school year while criminal victimization may occur at any time.

In fact, however, most data we collect only measure time at discrete points, and the size of the discrete intervals may make the application of a continuous-time model problematic. On the other hand, sometimes the level of detail in the measurement of time is sufficient to make the difference between using a discrete-time approach versus a continuous-time approach trivial. The issue of *choice* of which model to use can be quite complicated and requires consideration of a number of factors. In this book, we emphasize the discrete-time approach because it is flexible, it preserves information about the empirical distribution of risk over time, and it is still applicable when the measurement of time allows for sufficient detail that the results of the discrete-time model converge to the continuous-time model (Singer & Willett, 2003).

15.2 THE DISCRETE-TIME EVENT HISTORY MODEL

15.2.1 Introduction

Assume you have data with observations of an event in some discrete unit of time, such as months or years. In this case and when the event occurs only at discrete points, then we define the **hazard rate** for the event as a conditional probability in **each** time period:

$$P_{it} = \Pr\left[T_i = t \,/\, T_i \geq t\right]$$

This reads as follows: The probability that an event occurs in an interval t for individual i, given that it has not already occurred by the beginning of the interval t, and where T_i is the time of event occurrence.

Since this is in fact a probability, we can model its occurrence using a logistic model *once* we have data in a person-period data set form (i.e., in the same general form discussed in the sections on growth curves and panel regression).

$$P_{it} = \frac{1}{1 + e^{-(a_t + bX)}}$$

That is,

$$\ln \frac{P_{it}}{1 - P_{it}} = a_t + bX$$

Note that the probability studied here has two subscripts—i and t—signifying that the model studies the individual probability of the event *at a point in time* and thus changes with time. The subscript "t" for the intercept "a" is very important: It represents the fact that at each time interval there may be a different baseline probability of the event (or in the language of these models, a different *hazard* of the event).

This *is* a standard logistic model with two important differences:

1. There are multiple intercepts for time: one per risk period in the sample. These intercepts will show the pattern of the hazard for the event over time, given that each intercept stands for the log odds of the event at each point in time. Using this approach, there is no need to make assumptions about the overall shape of the hazard curve over time.

2. The model is applied to a "person-period" data set of observations, not the original data set. This new data set has multiple observations for each person, equaling *the number of risk periods that a person experienced up to the occurrence of the event **or** up to the end of observation if the event did not occur (called a censored observation).* Unlike previous examples of person-period data in earlier chapters, in this case, the number of observations per person *varies*.

15.3 BASIC CONCEPTS

15.3.1 The Survival Function

The survival function describes the percentage of people remaining from the original sample at risk who have not yet experienced the target event over time. For example, we see in Figure 15.1 a plot of the percentage of women *not* going to work after the birth of their first child over time (in years), in the National Survey of Families and Households data over the two decades 1960 through1980.

FIGURE 15.1 ⬢ A SURVIVAL FUNCTION FOR WOMEN NOT GOING TO WORK AFTER THEIR FIRST CHILD: 1960–1980.

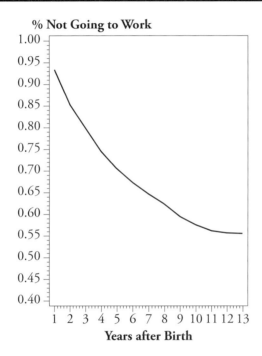

Note that after three years about 80% have not entered the labor force, and after five years, about 70% still have not sought work. The early decline in this curve flattens out, and after 13 years, just under 55% of the sample have *not* returned to work.

15.3.2 The Hazard Function

The hazard function describes the conditional probability of a target event—and thus the distribution of risk—over time. In the current example, the hazard is the conditional probability that a woman enters the work force in a particular period after having a first child. Figure 15.2 shows the hazard function year by year.

FIGURE 15.2 ⬡   A HAZARD FUNCTION FOR WOMEN GOING TO WORK AFTER THEIR FIRST CHILD: 1960–1980.

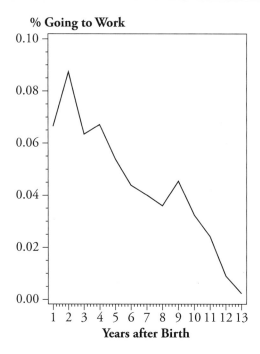

Note that in each period, some women started working, and this reduces the available population at risk in the next period. The available population in each period is the denominator of the hazard in that period, with the number of women who go to work as the numerator of the hazard.

The survival and hazard functions can be derived from defining the population at risk, those who experienced the event, and those who are censored (did not experience the event but their observation period is over) in each period.

To examine the basis of survival and hazard probabilities, consider the example in Table 15.2, showing how the survival and hazard values above are derived from an event history (for the first nine periods in Figures 15.1 and 15.2).

Note the following in this table:

1. (Column 2 - Column 3 - Column 4) gives Column 2 in the next year, defining the available "population" at risk for going to work in that year.

2. Censored observations occur because some women's observation time ended before they returned to work. For example, the 26 censored observations in Year 1 stand for 26 women in the sample who had a baby the year of the study and did not go to work in Year 1; the 313 in Year 2 had a baby the year before the study and had not yet gone to work.

3. Column 6 is Column 3/Column 2 in a year; this is the **hazard probability** each year.

4. Column 5 is $(1 - \text{hazard in year } t) \times$ the survival rate at $t - 1$—that is, the proportion of the original at-risk population remaining after taking into account those who experience the event in each risk period. These are the **survival probabilities**.

TABLE 15.2 ●	AN EVENT HISTORY OVER NINE PERIODS, WITH SURVIVAL AND HAZARD PROBABILITIES				
	Numbers			Proportions	
Period (Year) (1)	"At home" (2)	"Went to work" (3)	"Censored" (4)	"Still at home at the end of the year" Survival (5)	"Went to work during the year" Hazard (6)
1	2,160	143	26	.933	.066
2	1,991	173	313	.852	.087
3	1,505	95	390	.798	.063
4	1,020	69	278	.744	.067
5	673	37	155	.703	.055
6	481	21	83	.672	.044
7	377	15	54	.645	.040
8	308	11	32	.622	.036
9	265	12	22	.594	.045

Note, in general that

$$S_t = (1 - h_t) \cdot S_{t-1}$$

That is, the survival rate at time t is $= (1 - $ the hazard at time $t) \times$ the survival at time $t - 1$. This is the formula for finding successive survival rates in a discrete time model.

The hazard function here shows only the overall effect of time. We elaborate the model by asking this question: How do other variables affect this probability?

15.3.3 Differences in Hazard Functions

One can visualize the effect of independent variables on the hazard by plotting separate hazard profiles and survivor functions by groups.

For example, in Figure 15.3, we plot two hazard functions for women going to work after a first child: one for women having this child in the 1960s and one for women having the child in the 1970s. The plot shows the effect of decade as a displacement on the hazard upward. It is constant in terms of the odds and proportional in terms of the probabilities. This means that the differences will look smaller the smaller the baseline probability.

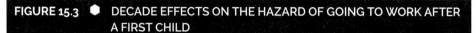

FIGURE 15.3 ● DECADE EFFECTS ON THE HAZARD OF GOING TO WORK AFTER A FIRST CHILD

Hazard

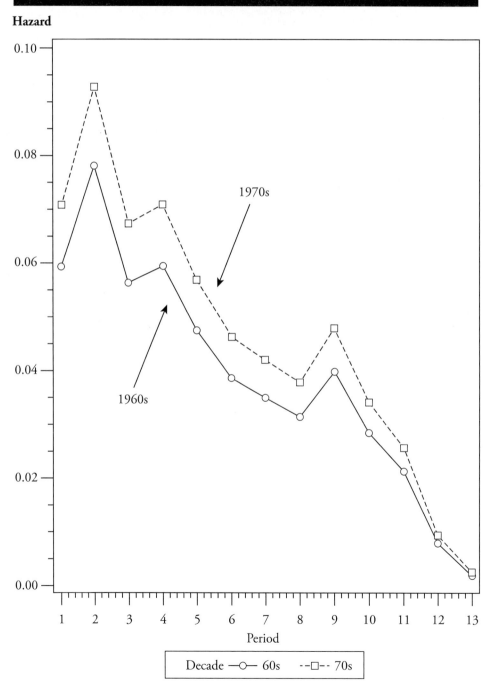

The plot in Figure 15.4 shows the corresponding survival functions. We see that a higher proportion of mothers in the 1960s chose to remain full time "homemakers" than in the 1970s.

FIGURE 15.4 ● DECADE DIFFERENCES IN PROPORTION NOT GOING TO WORK AFTER A FIRST CHILD

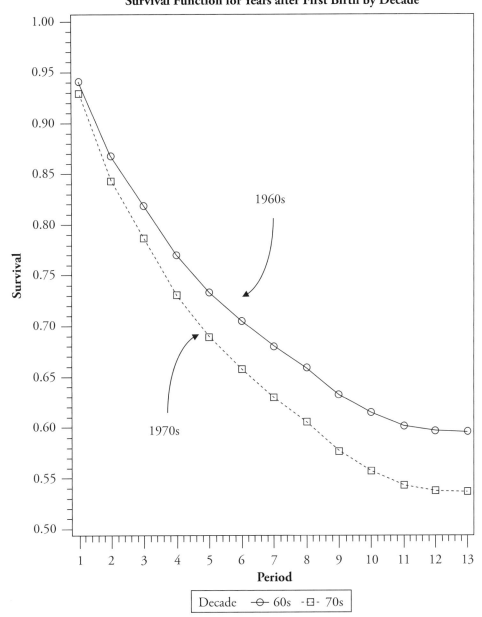

Survival Function for Years after First Birth by Decade

Writing out the model used here would look like this, given DECADE is a dummy variable = 1 if the 1970s, and = 0 if the 1960s:

$\widetilde{Logodds}$ (going to work) $= \alpha + \alpha_2 t_2 + \alpha_3 t_3 + ... + \alpha_{13} t_{13} + \beta$ (DECADE).

Note that in this case t_1 is omitted, so α is the log odds in Year 1 for the 1960s. In this model, β is the effect of "risk" factors on the log odds of event occurrence, in this case a dummy variable for decade, and α_t are the baseline levels of the log odds in each time interval, expressed here as a difference from α.

As in any logistic model, you can interpret (1) effects on the odds (e^b), (2) effects on the hazard (the probability), or (3) % increases/decreases in the odds (due to a one-unit increase in x): $100(e^b - 1)$.

15.4 CREATING AND ANALYZING A PERSON-PERIOD DATA SET

The discrete-time approach requires you apply logistic regression to a transformed person-period data set. This data set is constructed in two stages:

1. The first stage creates and keeps the variables necessary for the analysis.

2. The second stage creates a person-period data set based on these variables.

In the first stage, you need to create these variables:

1. The **duration** either until occurrence of the event in time periods or the total number of periods of observation if the event does not occur.

2. A **censoring** dummy variable, which is 1 if the observation is censored (no event) and 0 if the observation is *not* censored (the event occurs within the observation period).

3. Predictors of the event, either (a) **fixed**: anything that does not change over the observation period, or (b) **time-varying**: things that do change over the observation period and allow for a possibly different value in each observation period.

In the second stage, creating the person-period data set means that you have to allow for multiple observations per person, each one including all values of all variables in each time period. Unlike previous versions of person-period data, here the number of observations per person varies, depending on the period of observation or the timing of the event.

The *number* of observations in the person-period data set can be figured out from the frequencies for the duration variable. In Table 15.3, we show the frequencies for a censoring variable constructed from the previous example involving women going to work after having a first child. "Censor" shows that 607 of the 2,160 women selected go to work—that is, experienced the target event, and 1,553 are censored.

TABLE 15.3 ● FREQUENCY OF CENSORED AND UNCENSORED OBSERVATIONS

censor	Frequency	Percent	Cumulative Frequency	Cumulative Percent
0	607	28.10	607	28.10
1	1553	71.90	2160	100.00

In Table 15.4, we show the frequencies of the duration variable, labeled "*riskper.*" This variable gives the number of people in the sample at each observed risk period, up to 29 maximum.

Note that multiplying the frequency by the risk period number and adding will yield the sample size of the person-period data set. The total N of the person-period data is calculated as follows:

$$\sum_{i=1}^{j} (value \ x \ frequency) = (169 \times 1) +$$

$$(486 \times 2) +$$

$$(485 \times 3) +$$

$$\ldots\ldots$$

$$(1 \times 29)$$

$$= 10,264 \text{ observations.}$$

TABLE 15.4 ● **THE DISTRIBUTION OF RISK PERIODS FOR GOING TO WORK AFTER A FIRST CHILD**

riskper	Frequency	Percent	Cumulative Frequency	Cumulative Percent
1	169	7.82	169	7.82
2	486	22.50	655	30.32
3	485	22.45	1140	52.78
4	347	16.06	1487	68.84
5	192	8.89	1679	77.73
6	104	4.81	1783	82.55
7	69	3.19	1852	85.74
8	43	1.99	1895	87.73
9	34	1.57	1929	89.31
10	42	1.94	1971	91.25
11	27	1.25	1998	92.50
12	25	1.16	2023	93.66
13	18	0.83	2041	94.49
14	12	0.56	2053	95.05
15	13	0.60	2066	95.65
16	12	0.56	2078	96.20
17	13	0.60	2091	96.81
18	8	0.37	2099	97.18
19	10	0.46	2109	97.64
20	8	0.37	2117	98.01
21	9	0.42	2126	98.43
22	6	0.28	2132	98.70
23	2	0.09	2134	98.80
24	6	0.28	2140	99.07
25	4	0.19	2144	99.26
26	6	0.28	2150	99.54
27	6	0.28	2156	99.81
28	3	0.14	2159	99.95
29	1	0.05	2160	100.00

In the prior graphs, there are only 13 periods, but there are actually 29 in total. Sparseness in later periods led to the necessity of collapsing periods at the high end. This is often necessary in these models.

15.4.1 Form of the Data

The example that follows shows how the original data is written out in person-period form (Table 15.5). First, we show four observations from the original data set (panel A), with values for variables "*censor*," "*riskper*," "*yearmom*" (the year the first child was born), "*yearmom2*" (the year the second child was born), "*yrwkmom*" (the year the mother goes to work), and "*marr1-marr29*" (29 dummy variables showing marital status in each time period). This is the "time-varying" variable in the analysis. Second, we show the corresponding person-period data for these four observations (panel B).

TABLE 15.5 ● TRANSFORMING ORIGINAL OBSERVATIONS INTO PERSON-PERIOD OBSERVATIONS

A. Original Data

Obs	MCASEID	censor	riskper	yearmom	yearmom2	yrwkmom	marr1	marr2	marr3	marr4	marr5	marr6	marr7	marr8	marr9	marr10	marr11	marr12	marr13	marr14	marr15	marr16	marr17	marr18	marr19	marr20	marr21	marr22	marr23	marr24	marr25	marr26	marr27	marr28	marr29
1	16	1	3	78	80	.	1	1	1	1	1	1	1	1	1	0	0	0	0	0	0	0	0	0	0	0	0	0	0	0	0	0	0	0	0
9	159	0	3	71	75	73	0	0	0	0	0	1	1	1	1	1	1	1	1	1	1	1	1	1	1	1	1	1	1	1	1	1	1	1	1
12	239	1	7	75	81	.	0	0	0	0	1	0	1	1	1	1	1	1	1	1	1	1	1	1	1	1	1	1	1	1	1	1	1	1	1
33	1186	0	5	63	67	67	1	1	1	1	0	0	0	0	0	0	0	0	0	0	0	0	0	0	0	0	0	0	0	0	0	0	0	0	0

B. Person-Period Data

Obs	MCASEID	censor	riskper	working	partner	t1	t2	t3	t4	t5	t6	t7	t8	t9	t10_11	t12_13	t14_15	t16_19
1	16	1	3	2	1	1	0	0	0	0	0	0	0	0	0	0	0	0
2	16	1	3	2	1	0	1	0	0	0	0	0	0	0	0	0	0	0
3	16	1	3	2	1	0	0	1	0	0	0	0	0	0	0	0	0	0
33	159	0	3	2	0	1	0	0	0	0	0	0	0	0	0	0	0	0
34	159	0	3	2	0	0	1	0	0	0	0	0	0	0	0	0	0	0
35	159	0	3	1	0	0	0	1	0	0	0	0	0	0	0	0	0	0
45	239	1	7	2	0	1	0	0	0	0	0	0	0	0	0	0	0	0
46	239	1	7	2	0	0	1	0	0	0	0	0	0	0	0	0	0	0
47	239	1	7	2	0	0	0	1	0	0	0	0	0	0	0	0	0	0
48	239	1	7	2	0	0	0	0	1	0	0	0	0	0	0	0	0	0
49	239	1	7	2	1	0	0	0	0	1	0	0	0	0	0	0	0	0
50	239	1	7	2	0	0	0	0	0	0	1	0	0	0	0	0	0	0
51	239	1	7	2	1	0	0	0	0	0	0	1	0	0	0	0	0	0
174	1186	0	5	2	1	1	0	0	0	0	0	0	0	0	0	0	0	0
175	1186	0	5	2	1	0	1	0	0	0	0	0	0	0	0	0	0	0

Obs	MCCASE	rciser	workspin	pnoener	Dr	1	2	3	4	5	6	7	8	9	t1	t1	t1	t1	t1	t1

	MCCASE	rciser	workspin	pnoener	Dr	t1	t2	t3	t4	t5	t6	t7	t8	t9	t10	t11	t12	t13	t14	t16
176	1186	5	2	0	0	1	0	0	0	0	0	0	0	0	0	1	1	1	1	1
177	1186	5	2	0	0	0	1	0	0	0	0	0	0	0	2	1	1	2	4	6
178	1186	5	1	0	0	0	0	1	0	0	0	0	0	0	1	1	1	1	2	9

It is important to understand the transformation of the original "flat-file" data into person-period form. For example, look at case number 159. This woman had a child in 1971 (Period 1) and went to work in 1973. Thus, she contributes three observations to the person-period data set. Her data is *not* censored since she went to work, so "working" in the person-period data set converts from 2 to 1 in the final period (where 2 = not working, and 1 = working in the logistic regression). She also has no partner over this period, as shown by *Marr* 1-3.

Case number 239 *is* censored because she had a second child before she went to work. In general, there are often multiple forms of and reasons for censoring to take into account. Having a second child before going to work removes her from the risk set, since the birth of a second child starts a second risk period. Thus, working is coded as 2 throughout, indicating "not working." Her censor value is 1. Note that she was partnered in periods 5 and 7, and this is reflected in the person-period data by the values of the variable "partner" across periods.

15.4.2 Results for a Model with Four Main Effects

Results in Table 15.6 show an event history model with 13 time periods (some collapsed), and four main effects:

- *later:* Becoming a mother in the 70s relative to the 60s
- *nonwhite:* A dummy variable = 1 if nonwhite and 0 if White
- *agemom:* Age of the mother at first birth
- *partner:* The presence of a partner in each period (time-varying)

Looking at the time dummy variables, we know from the coefficient for $t_2(-1.1591)$ that the hazard of going to work in the second year after a birth for a White woman in the 1960s without a partner and *who is zero years old* at the time of the birth would be

$$b_2 = \frac{1}{1 + e^{-(-1.1591)}} = .239$$

Case number 239 *is* censored because she had a second child before she went to work. In general, there are often multiple forms of and reasons for censoring to take into account. Of course this is an absurd number. If we adjust the age at birth to a realistic age, like 22, then we get

$$b_2 = \frac{1}{1 + e^{-(-1.1591 + (-.0527 \times 22))}} = .09$$

The effect of each variable on the odds of going to work is

later: $\qquad e^{.2176} = 1.243$

$$\text{nonwhite:} \qquad e^{-.1094} = .90$$

$$\text{agemom:} \qquad e^{-.0527} = .95$$

$$\text{partner:} \qquad e^{-.2357} = .79$$

This means, for example, that having a child in the 1970s increased the odds of going to work 1.24 times compared to the 1960s. And having a partner reduces the odds by just over 20%.

TABLE 15.6 ● RESULTS FOR A FOUR VARIABLE DISCRETE TIME EVENT HISTORY MODEL

The LOGISTIC Procedure

Response Profile

Ordered Value	working	Total Frequency
1	1	606
2	2	9629

NOTE: 29 observations were deleted due to missing values for the response or explanatory variables.

Model Fit Statistics

Testing Global Null Hypothesis: BETA=0

Test	Chi-Square	DF	Pr > ChiSq
Likelihood Ratio	9730.2058	17	<.0001
Score	7981.5635	17	<.0001
Wald	4069.2316	17	<.0001

The LOGISTIC Procedure

Analysis of Maximum Likelihood Estimates

Parameter	DF	Estimate	Standard Error	Chi-Square	Pr > ChiSq
t1	1	−1.4687	0.2488	34.8600	<.0001
t2	1	−1.1591	0.2472	21.9775	<.0001
t3	1	−1.5097	0.2576	34.3369	<.0001
t4	1	−1.4403	0.2670	29.0905	<.0001
t5	1	−1.6476	0.2929	31.6513	<.0001
t6	1	−1.8971	0.3277	33.5035	<.0001
t7	1	−1.9894	0.3590	30.7109	<.0001
t8	1	−2.0747	0.3939	27.7458	<.0001
t9	1	−1.8151	0.3863	22.0765	<.0001
t10_11	1	−2.1020	0.3709	32.1196	<.0001
t12_13	1	−2.1831	0.4227	26.6750	<.0001
t14_15	1	−2.9829	0.6344	22.1074	<.0001
t16_29	1	−3.2439	0.5153	39.6342	<.0001
later	1	0.2176	0.0914	5.6627	0.0173
nonwhite	1	−0.1094	0.0949	1.3303	0.2488
agemom	1	−0.0527	0.0107	24.2797	<.0001
partner	1	−0.2357	0.0984	5.7346	0.0166

Note the following issues in this model:

1. There is no intercept. Why? Because the effects of all time periods are represented explicitly. This is a choice. You can do this by asking for the "/noint" option in the model statement of PROC LOGISTIC.

2. The later time periods are collapsed because the number of events in these periods begins to be very small. This becomes all the more important if one wants to estimate an interaction of any variable with time . . . which is a very important possibility.

3. One *could* model the hazard profile as an explicit linear or nonlinear function of time by replacing the time dummy variables with a more efficient specification of the effect of time. You could, for example, model the effect of time as a quadratic function or a spline function. Note that the dummy variable approach makes no *a priori* assumptions about the shape of the hazard function, unlike fully parametric approaches that specify a form to the hazard function.

15.4.3 Other Issues

15.4.3.1 Interactions with Time and Nonproportional Hazards

In typical applications of continuous time models, one of the fundamental assumptions is that hazards are proportional (as shown earlier). In effect, this means that the effects of all independent variables do not change with time. This assumption *can* be tested and modified in the continuous-time model, to take into account interactions with functions of time. However, either an assumption about the *nature* of the time-dependent process is necessary and/or or the entire process is more opaque than in the discrete-time model.

The ability to consider interactions with time is a built-in and flexible feature of the discrete-time model. In this model, any time-dependent process works equally well (time here refers to time since the onset of risk). Suppose we think that "decade" will have an effect on going to work, in part by specifically increasing *early* going to work in years one and two and *later* going to work after a child reaches school age. This suggests that we need to test this interaction. This can be done straightforwardly in this model.

There are many possibilities for studying interactions that model specific ways in which the probability of an event varies with time. Suppose you believe that a social movement, such as feminism, historically may have reduced the time to first promotion in jobs for women. This can be tested as a two-way interaction between the "onset" of feminism (a year) by gender. But further, you may want to assess the differential time distribution of promotion chances, allowing for gender-specific effects early or later in a job career in particular. If this is the case, you need to test the interaction with time as well.

To test for an interaction between decade (*later*) and time in predicting going to work after having a first child, you can assess a model with two-way interactions, such as

$$\widehat{\text{LogOdds}} \text{ (going to work)} = \alpha_1 t_1 + \alpha_2 t_2 + \ldots + \alpha_{13} t_{13} + \beta_1 (nonwhite) + \beta_2 (agemom)$$

$$+ \beta_3 (partner) + \beta_4 (later \times t_1) + \beta_5 (later \times t_2) + \ldots + \beta_{16} (later \times t_{13})$$

This model is unusual in two respects. First, following the specification used in the previous additive model, we choose to use no intercept and show the effects of all time dummy variables covering all periods. This is fine, as long as "no intercept" is specified. Second, as a result, there is no main effect for "later" in this model. That is directly caused by not using an intercept. So the effect of "later" at the baseline time period (t_1) has to be represented explicitly as an interaction term.

If there is an interaction, the hazard profiles will no longer be proportional, and the hazards for "later" will converge or diverge at specific points.

15.4.3.2 Modeling Time

It is obvious that there are many time dummy variables here. If you choose to be more efficient, you can fit nonlinear or spline models for time, as referenced above. It is helpful in this case to also test for the **_sufficiency_** of fit by comparing the the baseline dummy variable model with the "time as a continuous function" model or the spline model. One approach to this involves the a χ^2 difference test, with $df = df_1 - df_2$, as discussed earlier for logistic regression. However, we also noted in Chapter 4 that comparing models with different sets of variables may be problematic in a logistic regression. In that chapter, we suggested either using a linear probability model, and thus comparing the fit statistics available in that context, or using the BIC (Raftery, 1995).

15.4.3.3 Competing Risks

It is possible to estimate models for outcomes with multiple categories. For example, instead of studying just "going to work" as an event, one could study "going to work full-time" versus "going to work part-time" versus "not going to work." Note that this is exactly like a multinomial logistic regression.

15.4.3.4 Repeated Events

Discussion to this point poses the problem as if the event can only happen once. But many types of events are inherently repeatable—for example, having a child, losing a job, getting married, as examples.

How does this affect our results for a single event? "It depends," but often we assume each event is unique—that is, having a first child is very different from having a second child. Though this may often be a safe assumption, we don't know whether or how they are different unless they are both considered in one analysis. Do we expect the effects of predictors of entering the labor force after bearing a child to be the same for a first child as for a second? There is good reason to think not: The experience of having a prior child may change the salience of certain predictors when a second child is born.

To study this, we would conduct a "multiple-spell" event history analysis. This is an analysis done in a single data set with data for each spell concatenated one after the other. Note that this allows for tests of hypotheses across spells—for example, to assess the stability of the model across repeated events.

In the next section, we present an extended example of the various programming issues and sequence of results typical of a discrete-time event history analysis.

15.5 STUDYING WOMEN'S ENTRY INTO THE WORK ROLE AFTER HAVING A FIRST CHILD

We focus on the logic of an event history analysis in this example, with just enough syntax to communicate the range of issues that have to be considered. Our example is not a simple one: We find that existing examples are often so simple that the real issues the analyst faces, the actual decisions, never arise. In this example, we try to build in most of the complexities that should arise in a discrete-time analysis. But this is just one example, and we acknowledge that other examples may present other unique issues. For example, our example uses retrospective life history data with time measured in months, but in some panel data, event occurrence may be measured in real time across waves, and the spacing between waves may result in time periods that are considerably longer than what is optimal for these kinds of models.

We include portions of the syntax here less to communicate the specifics—in SAS or any other language—than to make the point that the complexities in the coding, the issues that arise, have to be faced somehow.

The National Survey of Families and Households (NSFH) contains extensive information on life histories involving employment, marriage, childrearing, and so forth. Optimally, the data used should contain dating information for each event and each transition of interest. In these data, dates are coded in century months, relative to 1900.

This example looks at the timing of women's return to work after having a first child in the decades from 1950 to 1990. The beginning of risk for re-entry into the labor force is the birth of the first child. The question is, What predicts a woman returning to work sooner rather than later? In the program that follows, we focus on the impact of decade—that is, historical period.

The analysis considers the following independent variables in predicting going to work:

- Decade

- Having a partner

- Age of mother at time of birth of child

- The respondent's mother's education

- Whether the respondent worked full-time in the two years before the birth

- Time period (year) after birth of the child—that is, age of child

The general outline of this analysis is to address the following issues in turn: (a) estimate the effect of time period (age of child), (b) look at social change via the effect of decade on the propensity of women to work after birth of a first child, and (c) estimate the interaction between decade and period, to see if social change applied differentially to certain years after birth of the child. For example, did women specifically go back to work more in Years 1 to 3 in the 1980s relative to the 1960s?

The general point of this analysis is to assess the effect of historical change on women's labor force behavior after having their first child. In the example in this section, we study whether and when women returned to *either* full-time or part-time work—that is, any paid work. Later, we consider the importance of that distinction.

All event histories begin with an at-risk population. We restrict that population further to women who have already worked before the birth of their first child. This excludes women who start work for the first time after their first child. This is done to help control for the general trend of women entering into the labor force over the period studied.

The syntax we use is derived from the very useful templates provided in the work of Judith Singer and John Willett (2003). We will refer to sections of the program we run to distinguish the purposes of each section and to make clear the importance of the order in which programming issues are considered.

Note that this example uses data from Waves 1 and 2 of the NSFH only, although one would normally use all waves available. Thus, even what we present here is simplified.

The program itself occurs in three main phases: (1) developing the variables from the original data necessary to write a person-period data set; (2) writing the person-period data set; and (3) running a series of logistic regressions on the person-period data to test various hypotheses.

15.5.1 Defining the At-Risk Population

Usually you begin by merging data across waves. The important thing to remember when beginning an event history analysis is to include all variables that reflect the timing of events.

You must select an at-risk sample in the syntax using variables from the original data that define risk for the target event. In SAS, you would use an IF statement like this:

```
/*DEFINING AT-RISK POPULATION -- women whose first child was born 1950-1989 and who had already
  had at least one job*/

if (m2dp01=2) and (((601<=m205p01m<=cmint) and (0<m529t01m<m205p01m)) or ((m205p01m<0 or
  m205p01m>=9996) and (cmint<=mj5p01m<=1080) and ((0<m529t01m<mj5p01m) or (m529t01m>=9996 and
  0<mo10t1m<mj5p01m))));
```

Translating this statement, we select all women who had a first child between 1950 through 1989 (four decades), using information from both Waves 1 and 2 of the NSFH, who also had a job before the birth of this child. Note that you have to take into account women who had a first child by Wave 1 and women who did not yet have a child by Wave 1 but did by Wave 2. This aspect of developing a proper data set for analysis is crucial. Time here is defined by the onset of risk for all sample members, not calendar time. For reference, the century months referred to in this statement (in variables labeled *cmint* or ending in "m") are restricted to a maximum of 1080—the last month of 1989. This is because we are studying the propensity to go to work up until the end of the 1980's only.

Take note of the "and /or" logic and the parentheses in the IF statement: It expresses the logic of selecting the sample appropriately. The IF statement reads roughly like this: If the respondent is a woman and had a first child before Wave 1 and a job before that child or did not have a child by Wave 1 but had a first child by Wave 2 and had a job in the job history before that child.

15.5.2 Preliminary Variables Needed to Define Onset of Risk

```
/* DETERMINING CENTURY-MONTH OF WAVE 2 INTERVIEW (cmint2) */
cmint2=(mr35*12)+mr33;
/* CREATING VARIABLE IDENTIFYING THOSE INTERVIEWED ONLY AT TIME 1 (respt1) */
if mr35=. then respt1=1; else respt1=0;
/* CREATING SINGLE VARIABLE FOR MONTH IN WHICH FIRST CHILD WAS BORN (cmntkd1) FROM TWO SOURCES*/

if 601<=m205p01m<=cmint then cmntkd1=m205p01m;
if m205p01m<0 or m205p01m>=9996 and cmint<=mj5p01m<=1080 then cmntkd1=mj5p01m;

/* CONVERTING TO YEAR OF BIRTH OF FIRST CHILD*/

yearmom=floor((cmntkd1-1)/12);
```

Often you will start by defining certain variables that are needed later in the program. This usually includes variables that represent the timing of the interviews and of the events of interest. Here we create these variables: the century month of the Wave 2 interview (*cmint2*), a dummy variable representing whether the respondent participated only in Wave 1 of the study (*respt1*), = 1 if only a Wave 1 respondent, and 0 if both waves, and the century month for the birth of the first child (*cmntkd1*). The last variable is absolutely crucial here. It defines the starting point of risk for going to work for that woman. Note that you have to use Wave 1 information if the child was born by the first interview and Wave 2 information if the child was born between the first and second interview. Also note that if a respondent does not make it to Wave 2, this does *not* mean they are deleted from the data: In fact, their information up to Wave 1 is useful.

We also convert the century month of the birth of the first child to a year, in the variable *yearmom*. The floor function takes the lowest integer of the century month minus 1, divided by 12. One century month is subtracted to ensure that Decembers (multiples of 12) do not turn into the following year. We could have retained the time metric using months, but for expository purposes, reducing the metric to years makes the entire example easier to follow.

15.5.3 Focal Variable in Analysis

```
/* CREATING MATERNITY DECADE VARIABLE (50s is reference) -- MAIN FOCUS OF ANALYSIS */

if 601<=cmntkd1<=720 then decade50=1; else decade50=0;

if 721<=cmntkd1<=840 then decade60=1; else decade60=0;

if 841<=cmntkd1<=960 then decade70=1; else decade70=0;

if 961<=cmntkd1<=1080 then decade80=1; else decade80=0;
```

This section creates the dummy variables for the main variable in our analysis—decade of the birth. Decade50 is the reference group. The first month of 1950 is century month 601; the last month of 1989 is 1080.

The hypothesis here is that social change resulted in a reduced delay in going to work in later decades. Because we have coded these decades separately, we will be able to detect roughly when the social change first occurred and whether it was progressive over time. But in fact, if we wanted to detect the exact historical moment changes in the hazard occurred, we would rely on a more continuous specification of historical year.

15.5.4 Developing Measures of Work History to Detect the Timing of the First Job after the Birth of the First Child

```
/* This section creates a work history from start and end times of jobs, and then creates
 a variable which gives the year in which the mother goes to work after the birth of her
child. This is necessary for the dependent variable in the event history model. */

array startwrk(14) m529t01m m531t02m m531t03m m531t04m m531t05m m531t06m m531t07m
        m531t08m m531t09m m531t10m begwrk2t1m begwrk2t2m begwrk2t3m begwrk2t4m;

array endwrk(14) m530t01m m532t02m m532t03m m532t04m m532t05m m532t06m m532t07m
        m532t08m m532t09m m532t10m endwrk2t1m endwrk2t2m endwrk2t3m endwrk2t4m;
```

```
array wrkatall (14) m534t01 m534t02 m534t03 m534t04 m534t05 m534t06 m534t07 m534t08
        m534t09 m534t10 some1-some4;
array workyr(14) workyr1-workyr14;
/* DETERMINING YEAR OF ENTRY INTO FULL-TIME EMPLOYMENT AFTER BIRTH OF FIRST CHILD (yrwkmom) */
do i=1 to 14;
    if 0<startwrk(i)<9990 and 1<=wrkatall(i)<=2 then workyr(i)=floor((startwrk(i)-1)/12); else
workyr(i)=.;
    if 0<startwrk(i)<cmntkd1 and (cmntkd1+3)<=endwrk(i)<=9995 then delete;
    if startwrk(i)>=cmntkd1 and 0<startwrk(i)<9990 and 1<=wrkatall(i)<=2 then yrwkmom=workyr(i);
else yrwkmom=.;
    if yrwkmom~=. then leave;
end;
```

The code fragment shown here (some details are omitted) is the basis of correctly measuring the timing of the first job after the first birth. This is the basis of the dependent variable in the event history model.

The required information is a complete work history, with dating of the start and stop times for each job (values held in variables *m529t01m* to *begwrk2t4m* for start months and *m530t01m* to *endwrk2t4m* for stop months). Often this will involve tracking an ongoing job at one wave and using the following wave or waves to designate when the job ended. The goal is to build a complete history *across waves*.

The fragment shown is one of the crucial sections of the program. It takes a set of work period start and stop times from both waves and does the following: (1) converts each work century month start time and end time to a year (using the floor function); (2) deletes individuals who worked through the birth and did not stop work for at least two months. (These women are deleted because their prior work period did not stop, and thus there was no decision to return to work. This group is sufficiently distinct from the target group here—suggesting different causation—to set aside in this analysis.); (3) finds the first starting work period at or after the birth of the child and uses that period to create a variable standing for the year the mother went to work (*yrwkmom*); (4) stops the DO loop as soon as a valid value for *yrwkmom* occurs so that it is not overwritten with later jobs, using a conditional "leave" statement to do this.

15.5.5 Information Used to Define Censoring

```
/* Information needed to designate censoring */
/* CREATING BIRTH OF SECOND CHILD VARIABLE (for censoring) (yearmom2) */

if 601<=m205p01m<=cmint and 0<m205p02m<=cmint then cmntkd2=m205p02m;
if 601<=m205p01m<=cmint and (m205p02m<0 or m205p02m>=9996) and
        cmint<=mj5p01m<=cmint2 then cmntkd2=mj5p01m;
if (m205p01m<0 or m205p01m>=9996) and cmint<=mj5p01m<=cmint2 and
        cmint<=mj5p02m<=cmint2 then cmntkd2=mj5p02m;
```

```
yearmom2=floor((cmntkd2-1)/12);

if cmntkd2>=9990 then yearmom2=.;

/* CREATING VARIABLES FOR YEAR OF RETIREMENT, and YEAR OF LAST INTERVIEW (yrbirth, yratret,
intyear) to be used for censoring indicator  */

yrbirth=floor((m485m-1)/12);

yratret=yrbirth+65;

if mr35~=. then intyear=mr35;

if mr35=. then intyear=myear;
```

There are various sources of censoring that need to be taken into account. First, women may have a second child before any observed work period after the first birth. Because we conceptualize the birth of a second child as the basis of a second risk interval (spell), we will censor observations so that the number of risk periods equals the number of years from Child 1 to Child 2. To do this, we find the century month of the second birth and convert it into years (*yearmom2*). Second, women may have reached the age of retirement before the end of the study. We should not count age beyond 65 as implying risk of going to work. To designate this, we created a variable for year at retirement age. Third, some respondents were not followed up at Wave 2, so we have to know whether the last date of interview was 1987–1988 or 1992–1994, so that we can assign the correct number of years of observation before censoring observations that represented never going to work, never having a second child, and not reaching retirement before the last interview. To do this, we need a variable called *intyear*, which is the last year of interview.

15.5.6 Developing Indicators of Censoring and Duration of Risk

```
/* CREATING CENSOR VARIABLE (censor) */

if (yrwkmom>=0 and 0<=yearmom2<=yrwkmom) or (yrwkmom>=0 and 0<yratret<yrwkmom) or yrwkmom=.
then censor=1; else censor=0;

/* CREATING DURATION VARIABLE (riskper) */
/* need to account for distinct reasons for censoring...
        including 2nd child, retiring, and dropping out of study */

if censor=0 then riskper=yrwkmom-yearmom+1;

else if censor=1 and yrwkmom>0 and 0<=yearmom2<=yrwkmom then riskper=yearmom2-yearmom+1;

else if riskper=. and censor=1 and yrwkmom>0 and 0<=yratret<=yrwkmom then riskper=yratret-
yearmom+1;

else if censor=1 and yrwkmom=. and 0<yearmom2<9990 then riskper=yearmom2-yearmom+1;

else if censor=1 and yrwkmom=. and yearmom2=. and 0<yratret<=intyear then riskper=yratret-
yearmom+1;

else if censor=1 and yrwkmom=. and yearmom2=. and yratret>intyear then riskper=intyear-
yearmom+1;
```

This section is fundamental to the whole program. It develops two variables—a measure of whether the observation is censored (1 = yes, 0 = no) and the total duration of observed risk (*riskper*), either up to the event (going to work) or until censoring. You need to know the values of both variables to figure out whether someone went back to work before censoring.

The variable censor tells us whether the observation is censored, for any reason. You have to account for any of the reasons for censoring in setting this variable to 1. There are generally two types of cases: cases where the woman did go back to work—but after the occurrence of a censoring event—and cases where she never went back to work during the period of observation (*yrwkmom*=.). This is why it is very important that you catch all cases of going to work in *yrwkmom*, so that when it is missing, it maps exactly to never returning to work.

The variable *riskper* counts the number of years of observed risk for that respondent. *Riskper* is coded so that it counts the periods of risk for everyone, including those who never went to work. Thus, we specify when people went back to work from two sources of information: by the fact that *censor* = 0, and by the years of risk coded by *riskper*. Note the hierarchical logic in assigning values to *riskper*, starting with people who work, then taking into account the reasons for censoring, in a defined order, starting with a second birth, then retirement, then observation up to the final interview year without going to work.

The maximum number of risk periods in these data is 45, meaning everyone experiences a differing number of risk periods, and the maximum number experienced by anyone was 45. This was actually found from a frequency for *censor* and *riskper* (see Table 15.7).

15.5.7 Fixed Control Variables

You can group together all of the fixed variables you create for the program into one section of the syntax. There are no special issues here—you could be coding these variables for a standard logistic regression since their value does not change across risk periods.

In our example, we created controls for the age of the mother at the first child's birth (*agemom*), race (*Black, Hispanic vs. White*), the education of the mother of the mother (*momed*), and a count of the number of months in the two years before the birth the mother worked full-time, reduced to a dummy variable measuring working at least 12 of the 24 months prior to the birth (*fwrkb4*).

15.5.8 Time-Varying Variables

```
/*A) Time varying variable for married partner status in each period after the birth.
    This will be a 1/0 dummy variable for each period. */
/* (1) Collect info on all start and end times, transform into years, then into periods.*/

array startmarr (11) m96m m103t02m m103t03m m103t04m m103t05m startmarrcm21-startmarrcm26;

array endmarr (11) endmarrcm11--endmarrcm15 endmarrcm21--endmarrcm26;

array startyear (11) startmarryr1-startmarryr11;

array endyear (11) endmarryr1-endmarryr11;

array startper (11) startmarrper1-startmarrper11;

array endper (11) endmarrper1-endmarrper11;
```

```
do i=1 to 11;

if 0<startmarr(i)<9990 then startyear(i)=floor((startmarr(i)-1)/12);

if 0<endmarr(i)<9990 then endyear(i)=floor((endmarr(i)-1)/12);

startper(i)=startyear(i)-yearmom + 1;

endper(i) = endyear(i)-yearmom + 1;

end;


/* (2) Create the dummy variables for the presence of a marital partner in all 45 risk
periods    */

array marr (45) marr1-marr45;

do i=1 to 45;

do j= 1 to 11;

if i>=startper(j) and startper(j)~=. and i<endper(j) and 0<endper(j)<9990 then marr(i)=1; else
marr(i)=0;

if marr(i)=1 then leave;

end;

end;
```

One of the trickiest parts of these programs involves the creation of time-varying variables. The example here focuses on developing a measure of the presence of a married partner in each of the potentially 45 risk periods. Each is a dummy variable specific to each period.

Generally, you need to have the start month and end months of all marriages that occur up to Wave 2. That information can be used to convert to the risk periods in which a partner was present. As in the case of jobs, many marriages will span waves, and you need to follow the status of current marriages at each wave to specify if and when they ended. Often, there is some detective work here—to ensure that the marriage ending by the next wave is in fact the same marriage that was ongoing at the last. This depends on the level of detail in the data.

Subsection 1 in the code fragment is crucial. Here we collect the start time and end time variables for all marriages from Wave 1 (up to 5) and Wave 2 (up to 6) and first convert them to year variables and then to risk periods relative to *yearmom*, which is risk period 1 in the event history. The timing of the marriages must be considered in risk periods in order to work in the event history.

In Subsection 2, we write 45 dummy variables for partner status, one for each risk period. This is done using nested DO loops in "*i*" and "*j*." These work as follows: *i* is set to 1 first, and then values of *j* are inspected over the 11 marriage variables. We are looking for start times that are less than the value of *i* —the current risk period—and end times that are greater than the value of *i*. In these cases, we know a partner was present in that risk period, and a "1" is written to the dummy variable. When and if that dummy variable becomes 1, the *j* loop is stopped with a leave statement, and i is set to the next value. If there are no marriages that span the value of i, the dummy variable stays at 0, meaning no partner was present in that period.

When this section is done, you need to save all of the censoring, duration, and independent variables, including time-varying variables and timing variables you have created in a new data set, ready for passing to the next stage. Any variables that are useful in checking your coding should be saved as well.

15.5.9 Checking Coding

It is always useful to check the coding of your variables before continuing. You need to be sure that the logic of your variables does not unintentionally exclude cases and that the coding does what you intend.

Note in the frequencies in Table 15.7 that there are 1,534 censored observations and 652 noncensored observations (those who went to work before a second child or before retirement), totaling 2186 observations. Note also that everyone has a value for *riskper* and that there are a total of 45 possible risk periods. There can be no missing data on *riskper*. This is necessary for the rest of the program to work. If you do see some missing data here, it means you have to go back and figure out which cases you missed in the coding. As noted earlier, you can figure out the size of the person-period data set from the frequencies for *riskper*.

TABLE 15.7 ● FREQUENCIES FOR THE CENSORING AND DURATION VARIABLE

censor	Frequency	Percent	Cumulative Frequency	Cumulative Percent
0	652	29.83	652	29.83
1	1534	70.17	2186	100.00

riskper	Frequency	Percent	Cumulative Frequency	Cumulative Percent
1	184	8.42	184	8.42
2	536	24.52	720	32.94
3	508	23.24	1228	56.18
4	311	14.23	1539	70.40
5	193	8.83	1732	79.23
6	107	4.89	1839	84.13
7	63	2.88	1902	87.01
8	52	2.38	1954	89.39
9	37	1.69	1991	91.08
10	22	1.01	2013	92.09
11	19	0.87	2032	92.96
12	16	0.73	2048	93.69
13	13	0.59	2061	94.28
14	11	0.50	2072	94.78
15	11	0.50	2083	95.29
16	11	0.50	2094	95.79
17	5	0.23	2099	96.02
18	6	0.27	2105	96.29
19	4	0.18	2109	96.48
20	8	0.37	2117	96.84
21	4	0.18	2121	97.03
22	8	0.37	2129	97.39

riskper	Frequency	Percent	Cumulative Frequency	Cumulative Percent
23	6	0.27	2135	97.67
24	8	0.37	2143	98.03
25	4	0.18	2147	98.22
26	1	0.05	2148	98.26
27	9	0.41	2157	98.67
28	2	0.09	2159	98.76
29	4	0.18	2163	98.95
30	3	0.14	2166	99.09
31	4	0.18	2170	99.27
32	2	0.09	2172	99.36
33	1	0.05	2173	99.41
35	2	0.09	2175	99.50
36	1	0.05	2176	99.54
37	3	0.14	2179	99.68
38	2	0.09	2181	99.77
39	1	0.05	2182	99.82
41	1	0.05	2183	99.86
42	2	0.09	2185	99.95
45	1	0.05	2186	100.00

The first 50 observations from the original flat-file data are shown in Table 15.8. First we assess whether the censoring and duration information was written properly, using the five highlighted observations in Table 15.8. Specifically, you can check that the duration variable *riskper* and the censor variable are both correct based on the values of *yearmom* (first child), *yrwkmom* (went to work), *yearmom2* (second child), *yratret* (retirement year), and *intyear* (last interview year).

Observation 7 had a child in 1950. She is censored and had 27 years of observation before she was censored. Over that time, she did not go to work (*yrwkmom=.*), and she did not have a second child (*yearmom2=.*). But she was censored because she reached retirement age before the end of the study (in 1976), not because her last interview was in 1987. Thus her 27 risk periods include the 27 years, including the starting and ending risk year, from 1950 to 1976. Observation 19 is also a case who never went to work or had a second child. Her child was born in 1983, but she is censored by the year of her last interview, 1993. Looking at observation 34, she had a child in 1973 and went back to work in 1976. However, she had a second child in 1975, so this observation is censored. The value of censor is 1, and the value of *riskper* is 3, including three risk periods from 1973, 1974, and 1975. In the case of observation 41, she had a child in 1978 and went to work in 1981. She did not have a second child. The observation is not censored, and *riskper* is 4, which is appropriate.

TABLE 15.8 ● CHECKING THAT THE CENSORING AND DURATION VARIABLES ARE CORRECT

Obs	MCASEID	censor	riskper	yearmom	yrwkmom	yearmom2	yratret	intyear
1	53	1	3	82	85	84	122	92
2	90	0	1	67	67	69	109	87
3	104	0	2	76	77	79	118	87
4	175	1	2	86	.	87	128	92

(Continued)

TABLE 15.8 ⬥ Continued

Obs	MCASEID	censor	riskper	yearmom	yrwkmom	yearmom2	yratret	intyear
5	188	1	2	84	.	85	130	87
6	196	1	1	89	90	89	133	94
7	221	1	27	50	.	.	76	87
8	292	1	8	86	.	.	124	93
9	314	1	7	86	.	92	129	94
10	348	1	3	86	91	88	129	94
11	356	1	6	85	.	90	126	93
12	410	0	3	73	75	79	118	93
13	452	1	5	84	.	88	127	93
14	457	0	2	86	87	90	127	92
15	460	0	2	81	82	84	115	92
16	511	1	2	83	.	84	121	93
17	590	1	3	75	78	77	117	93
18	604	1	2	58	65	59	105	93
19	612	1	11	83	.	.	124	93
20	641	0	6	80	85	.	125	87
21	659	0	2	83	84	86	121	93
22	688	1	4	77	.	80	120	93
23	696	1	4	82	.	85	125	92
24	721	1	2	86	.	.	131	87
25	755	1	3	86	.	88	124	93
26	763	1	3	62	75	64	104	87
27	789	0	3	81	83	84	126	87
28	814	1	9	75	.	83	121	92
29	827	1	19	69	.	.	111	87
30	843	1	12	82	.	.	121	93
31	880	1	4	56	83	59	92	93
32	952	0	2	85	86	89	125	93
33	957	0	1	82	82	84	121	94
34	973	1	3	73	76	75	119	93
35	1006	0	3	64	66	71	107	93
36	1048	0	2	79	80	84	116	93
37	1077	0	1	84	84	87	128	92
38	1093	1	14	79	.	.	116	92
39	1102	1	4	88	.	91	124	93
40	4	1	5	63	67	67	106	92
41	1216	0	4	78	81	.	115	93
42	1224	1	4	85	.	88	116	93
43	1240	1	5	86	.	90	129	93
44	1274	1	5	81	.	85	122	94
45	1282	1	4	72	.	75	114	92
46	1309	0	7	75	81	83	116	93
47	1375	1	5	89	.	.	121	93
48	1396	0	2	69	70	.	109	93
49	1418	0	4	80	83	90	118	93
50	1439	0	2	57	58	60	100	94

Checking on the values of the time-varying variable involves checking that values for Marr1 to Marr45 based on the starting and ending years of all marriages—and then converted to periods—have been written properly.

TABLE 15.9 ⬡ CHECKING THE VALUES OF THE TIME-VARYING VARIABLE

Obs	MCASEID	censor	riskper	yearmom
34	973	1	3	73
41	1216	0	4	78

Obs	MCASEID	startmarryr1	startmarryr2	startmarryr3	startmarryr4	startmarryr5	startmarryr6	startmarryr7
34	973	72	82	.	.	.	.	90
41	1216	75	77	83	.	.	.	.

Obs	MCASEID	endmarryr1	endmarryr2	endmarryr3	endmarryr4	endmarryr5	endmarryr6	endmarryr7
34	973	77	83	.	.	.	.	93
41	1216	76	82	91	.	.	.	.

Obs	MCASEID	startmarrper1	startmarrper2	startmarrper3	startmarrper4	startmarrper5	startmarrper6	startmarrper7
34	973	0	10	.	.	.	.	18
41	1216	-2	0	6	.	.	.	.

Obs	MCASEID	endmarrper1	endmarrper2	endmarrper3	endmarrper4	endmarrper5	endmarrper6	endmarrper7
34	973	5	11	.	.	.	.	21
41	1216	-1	5	14	.	.	.	.

MCASEID / Obs	1	2	3	4	5	6	7	8	9	10	11	12	13	14	15	16	17	18	19	20	21	22	23	24	25	26	27	28	29	30	31	32	33	34	35
married	m	m	m	m	m	m	m	m	m	m	m	m	m	m	m	m	m	m	m	m	m	m	m	m	m	m	m	m	m	m	m	m	m	m	m
	a	a	a	a	a	a	a	a	a	a	a	a	a	a	a	a	a	a	a	a	a	a	a	a	a	a	a	a	a	a	a	a	a	a	a
	r	r	r	r	r	r	r	r	r	r	r	r	r	r	r	r	r	r	r	r	r	r	r	r	r	r	r	r	r	r	r	r	r	r	r
34 973	1	1	1	1	0	0	0	0	0	0	1	0	0	0	0	0	0	1	1	1	0	0	0	0	0	0	0	0	0	0	0	0	0	0	0
41 1216	1	1	1	1	0	1	1	1	1	1	1	1	0	1	0	0	0	0	0	0	0	0	0	0	0	0	0	0	0	0	0	0	0	0	0

In Table 15.9, we focus on two observations from the data and only print the necessary marriages to cover those two cases. To check the values of the time-varying variables, we follow through on the coding of the start times and end times of each marriage and the conversion of these values into periods. Observation 34 was married three times. She was married first in 1972 but ended that marriage in 1977. She married again in 1982, and that marriage ended in 1983. Her third marriage began in 1990 and is listed as "ending" in 1993; however, that is probably the current interview year at Wave 2, and the marriage may be ongoing. All of these values are translated into period values. Her first marriage started in period 0, one period before the beginning of the risk period in 1973, when she had her first child. This marriage ends in period 5, so marr1 to marr4 = 1 and marr5 = 0. The next marriage begins in period 10, for one year, so only marr10 = 1. This is after the actual observed risk period, so later values don't matter.

Observation 41 was also married three times: from 1975 to 1976, from 1977 to 1982, and from 1983 to 1991. The first marriage doesn't matter because it occurred before the beginning of the risk period (1978). However, the second marriage was the basis of the first child: It starts in risk period 0 and ends in risk period 5. Thus marr1 to marr4 = 1, and marr5 = 0 again. The next marriage begins in risk period 6 and ends in 14, so marr6 to marr13 = 1, and marr14 = 0, as expected.

15.5.10 Creating the Person-Period Data Set and Collapsing Time Periods

Because this section of the program is fundamental to the entire analysis to follow, we present the syntax in more detail. This syntax reflects what has been presented before about person-period data.

```
/* CREATING PERSON-PERIOD DATA SET */
/* creating new variables ('working', 'partner', smooth functions of time, and
   interaction terms for decade by time period) */

data hazwork;
  set part1;
array tper(45) t1-t45;
array marry(45) marr1-marr45;
array dec60(45) dec60x1-dec60x45;
array dec70(45) dec70x1-dec70x45;
array dec80(45) dec80x1-dec80x45;

array timecat(4)  t10_13 t14_17 t18_22 t23_45;
array newint60(4) dec60x10 dec60x14 dec60x18 dec60x23;
array newint70(4) dec70x10 dec70x14 dec70x18 dec70x23;
array newint80(4) dec80x10 dec80x14 dec80x18 dec80x23;

do i=1 to min(riskper, 45);
  if i=riskper and censor=0 then working=1; else working=2;
  partner=marry(i);
 time=i;
  timesq=i**2;
  timecu=i**3;
  time4o=i**4;
```

```
do j=1 to 45;
  if j=i then tper(j)=1; else tper(j)=0;
  dec60(j)=decade60*tper(j);
  dec70(j)=decade70*tper(j);
  dec80(j)=decade80*tper(j);
end;

/* collapsing time variables */

if i>=10 and i<=13 then t10_13=1; else t10_13=0;
if i>=14 and i<=17 then t14_17=1; else t14_17=0;
if i>=18 and i<=22 then t18_22=1; else t18_22=0;
if i>=23 then t23_45=1; else t23_45=0;

/* creating new interaction terms from collapsed time variables */

do k=1 to 4;
   newint60(k)=decade60*timecat(k);
   newint70(k)=decade70*timecat(k);
   newint80(k)=decade80*timecat(k);
end;

output;
end;

/* check for empty cells for dependent variable by time periods */

proc freq data=hazwork;
  tables working*(t1-t45)/ missprint;
run;
```

The first sections create the person-period data—named "hazwork"—from the flat-file data—named "part1." This complete code fragment is all one DO loop, with DO loops within it. The second last line—output;—is the line that tells SAS to write an observation of all of the new variables created in the DO loop.

The arrays "tper," "dec60," "dec70," and "dec80" are all output arrays, naming variables to be created in the DO loop. "Marry" is an input array holding the 45 variables from the previous data step for marriage, *marr1* to *marr45*.

Each person has multiple observations in the person-period data set, equal to the number of their risk periods. The main "DO loop" goes from period 1 to the minimum of the number of risk periods or 45. So this loop will stop when the number of risk periods is reached. This ensures that the correct number of observations are written to the *hazwork* data.

Note how the dependent variable—working—is created. When censor = 0 and *i* = riskper, that is the risk period the woman went to work, so the binary outcome is written to working = 1 in that observation and 2 otherwise. This coding is the default for SAS, but you could use 1 and 0 in other software.

Partner stands for whether there is a marital partner in each of the risk periods. A different value is assigned to *partner* for each period based on values of *marr1-marr45*.

Other variables are created in these DO loops. The primary loop (*i*) also creates a series of continuous functions of time. These can be used as an alternative to fitting dummy variables for time, given that they are more efficient. A set of time dummy variables and interactions of time with decade are created in the secondary loop (*j*). For each observation (*i*), for example, there will be 45 time dummy variables and 45 interactions with each of the decade variables. These variables will be used to test an interaction between decade and time after the birth.

The section that collapses variables is usually necessary and was added later. This section collapses the time variables in periods where there are few cases where a woman went to work. This is found from the PROC FREQ cross-tabulation of working by time periods. Basically, the point is to group later risk periods that are sparse in such a way to avoid increasing the prevalence in later categories while still having some observations that went to work. After looking at those tables, we collapsed *t10* to *t13*, *t14* to *t17*, *t18* to *t22*, and *t23* and up. The collapsing itself is done in a do loop more efficiently, using ranges of i to write new collapsed time period dummies. Then, using a different counter value (*k*), we add the updated interactions that are necessary in their own sub-loop.

The crucial issue in the later time periods is how many women went to work in that period. Table 15.10 is based on the frequencies for each time period.

TABLE 15.10 ● THE NUMBER OF WOMEN WHO WENT TO WORK IN EACH RISK PERIOD

Risk Period	N
1	143
2	252
3	99
4	46
5	28
6	26
7	14
8	8
9	10
10	3
11	1
12	2

Risk Period	N
13	3
14	1
15	1
16	4
17	1
18	1
19	0
20	2
21	1
22	2
23	1
24	1
25	0
26	0
27	1
28	1
29	0
30	0
31 to 45	1

After $t9$, where 10 people went to work, the frequencies drop. Collapsing 10–13 leads to nine observations, 14–17 produces seven, and 18–22 produces five. After that, there are only five, all the way to 45.

15.5.11 Checking the Person-Period Data

You can check that the person-period data was written properly by reviewing a printout of selected cases, as with the flat-file data. Table 15.11 shows this printout for four observations from the original data. Together they produce 16 observations in the person-period data. Only the necessary values for marital status and the dummy variables for risk period over time are shown.

TABLE 15.11 ● CHECKING WRITTEN VALUES IN THE PERSON-PERIOD DATA

MCASEID	riskper	censor	working	partner	marr1	marr2	marr3	marr4	marr5	marr6	marr7	t1	t2	t3	t4	t5	t6	t7
641	6	0	2	0	0	0	0	0	0	0	0	1	0	0	0	0	0	0
641	6	0	2	0	0	0	0	0	0	0	0	0	1	0	0	0	0	0
641	6	0	2	0	0	0	0	0	0	0	0	0	0	1	0	0	0	0
641	6	0	2	0	0	0	0	0	0	0	0	0	0	0	1	0	0	0
641	6	0	2	0	0	0	0	0	0	0	0	0	0	0	0	1	0	0
641	6	0	1	0	0	0	0	0	0	0	0	0	0	0	0	0	1	0
659	2	0	2	1	1	1	1	1	1	1	1	1	0	0	0	0	0	0
659	2	0	1	1	1	1	1	1	1	1	1	0	1	0	0	0	0	0
688	4	1	2	0	0	1	1	1	1	0	1	1	0	0	0	0	0	0
688	4	1	2	1	0	1	1	1	1	0	1	0	1	0	0	0	0	0
688	4	1	2	1	0	1	1	1	1	0	1	0	0	1	0	0	0	0
688	4	1	2	1	0	1	1	1	1	1	1	0	0	0	1	0	0	0
696	4	1	2	1	1	0	0	1	1	1	1	1	0	0	0	0	0	0
696	4	1	2	0	1	0	0	1	1	1	1	0	1	0	0	0	0	0
696	4	1	2	0	1	0	0	1	1	1	1	0	0	1	0	0	0	0
696	4	1	2	1	1	0	0	1	1	1	1	0	0	0	1	0	0	0

Mcaseid 641 produces six observations, corresponding to a *riskper* value of six. This woman did not have a partner throughout the risk period, so partner remains at 0 in each risk period. She did go to work in the sixth risk period—that is, when the child was five, and so the value of *working* converts from 2 to 1 in that period, consistent with the fact that *censor* = 0 for this observation. Whenever an observation is not censored, the last person-period observation should convert to the target event.

Mcaseid 659 is also not censored, and the number of risk periods is two. Thus working equals 2 in the first period, but changes to 1 in the second period, denoting the period this respondent went to work. They had a partner in both periods, so partner is equal to 1 in both time periods.

Both *Mcaseid* 688 and 696 are censored. There are four risk periods in each case. For 688, there is no partner in risk period 1 (marr1=0), but there is partner for the rest of the risk periods (marr2 through marr 4=1). For 696, there is a partner present in periods 1 and 4 only, resulting in a pattern of 1 0 0 1 across the risk periods, corresponding to the values of marr1 through marr4.

15.5.12 Analyzing the Person-Period Data

In this section, we present results of the event history analysis, in four parts: (1) a model showing the effects of time only; (2) a model showing the effects of decade; (3) a model showing the effects of decade with controls; and (4) a test of the interaction between decade and risk period, to test the hypothesis that the primary social change over time was specific to certain ages of the child.

We also show pieces of the syntax used for two of these models, in order to show how the models were estimated and then how we produced estimates of the hazard and survival values from the data and plotted these curves. We do this for the initial and last model.

15.5.12.1 The Time-Only Model

The syntax that follows starts with a logistic regression for time period only, using the "noint" option to signal including *all* of the time dummy variables in the model. This changes the interpretation of these variables in a crucial way: Instead of a difference between that time period and the first time period (the normal intercept), the coefficients are now the mean log odds of going to work in each time period.

The run of PROC LOGISTIC also outputs a data set of the estimates from the model, using the "out=estimate" option in the PROC line. This produces a specialized data set of parameter estimates from the model that can be passed on to other programming used to calculate the hazard and survival values in each time period.

```
/* MODEL 1 -- FITTING GENERAL MODEL WITH TIME EFFECTS ONLY

proc logistic data=hazwork out=estimate;
model working=t1-t9 t10_13 t14_17 t18_22 t23_45 / noint;
title1 'Model 1 -- Time Effects Only';
run;
```

Essential results from this model are shown in the Table 15.12.

TABLE 15.12 ● RESULTS FROM A TIME-ONLY MODEL

Model Information

Data Set	WORK.HAZWORK
Response Variable	working
Number of Response Levels	2
Model	binary logit
Optimization Technique	Fisher's scoring

Number of Observations Read	10479
Number of Observations Used	10479

Response Profile

Ordered Value	working	Total Frequency
1	1	652
2	2	9827

Analysis of Maximum Likelihood Estimates

Parameter	DF	Estimate	Standard Error	Wald Chi-Square	Pr > ChiSq
t1	1	−2.6593	0.0865	945.1456	<.0001
t2	1	−1.9379	0.0674	827.2867	<.0001
t3	1	−2.6253	0.1041	636.2274	<.0001
t4	1	−3.0101	0.1527	388.5724	<.0001
t5	1	−3.0959	0.1932	256.7547	<.0001
t6	1	−2.8010	0.2020	192.3073	<.0001
t7	1	−3.1691	0.2728	134.9307	<.0001
t8	1	−3.5410	0.3586	97.4816	<.0001
t9	1	−3.1001	0.3233	91.9632	<.0001
t10_13	1	−4.2813	0.3356	162.7173	<.0001
t14_17	1	−4.1109	0.3810	116.3874	<.0001
t18_22	1	−4.3148	0.4502	91.8618	<.0001
t23_45	1	−4.2580	0.4111	107.2654	<.0001

The parameter estimates are basically uninterpretable in this form, but they can be used to calculate the survival and hazard values for each time period, using the "estimate" data set. We note that the person-period data here contains 10,479 observations.

The second block of commands that follow starts a new data step using the "estimate" data in order to create a data set holding the survival and hazard values. The "estimate" data set passed from the logistic regression treats the variables in the model as the columns and their coefficients as values in one row.

The array lists the variables from the model, but SAS will interpret these references as the *coefficients for these variables*. Survival is set to 1 outside the "DO" loop, so that the calculations in the DO loop begin with the right value. The do loop then refers to the variable names held in the array "*per*"— in fact, the parameters for those variables—to calculate hazard values from the equation results, using the equation "x = per(i)" first to get the predicted log odds from the equation. For example, when $i = 6$, this refers to *t*6, which is –2.8010 in the model. This value will convert to a hazard of .05727, using the logistic formula for the hazard (hazard=1/(1+(exp(-x)));) in the next line. This value is passed to the formula for the survival, which uses the current value of survival and multiplies that value by 1 minus the hazard probability—that is, the proportion that survived in that period. At this point, the do loop outputs a new observation, returns to the beginning of the loop, and increments *i*.

```
/* deriving hazard and survival functions */

data estimate (replace=yes);
   set estimate;
array per (13) t1-t9 t10_13 t14_17 t18_22 t23_45;
survival=1;
do i=1 to 13;
  x=per(i);
  hazard=1/(1+(exp(-x)));
  survival=(1-hazard)*survival;
  output;
end;

keep i survival hazard;
```

After these data are produced, they can be printed using a PRINT function (Table 15.13).

TABLE 15.13 ● SURVIVAL AND HAZARD VALUES FROM THE TIME-ONLY MODEL

i	survival	hazard
1	0.93458	0.06542
2	0.81694	0.12587
3	0.76178	0.06753
4	0.72599	0.04697
5	0.69457	0.04328
6	0.65480	0.05727
7	0.62838	0.04035
8	0.61068	0.02817
9	0.58436	0.04310
10	0.57639	0.01364
11	0.56709	0.01613
12	0.55961	0.01319
13	0.55180	0.01395

These values can be plotted using the syntax that follows. We use the more traditional GPLOT here, but the more recent SGPLOT procedure could also be used. "Goptions" resets defaults, and then there are a series of statements setting up the lines and axes used in the plot. Axis1 becomes the horizontal axis for time period later, and Axes 2 and 3 become the *Y*-axis for survival and hazard values respectively. The SYMBOL line defines the color and special points used in the lines to be plotted: Here this is a continuous line (*L* = 1), in Black, and the points are joined directly (I = join).

PROC GPLOT is used to plot the values. The PLOT command is stated in an *Y * X* order. The count index *i* corresponds to each observation in the "estimate" data—reflecting the period number, but the *X* axis values are labeled using the Axis1 definition, the *Y* axis is labeled using the Axis2 definition for plotting survival values, and the Axis3 definition is used for plotting hazard values.

```
goptions RESET=GLOBAL targetdevice=activex vsize=7 in hsize=5 in norotate;

SYMBOL1 C=black I=join V=POINT L=1 W=1;

AXIS1 width=2 major=(w=1) label=(f=swissl 'Time Period After Birth')
order=(1 to 13 by 1) value=('1' '2' '3' '4' '5' '6' '7' '8' '9' '10' '14' '18' '23') length=5.5 in
ORIGIN=(,1.9 in);
AXIS2 width=2 major=(w=1) label=(f=swissl 'Survival') order=.4 to 1 by .1;
AXIS3 width=2 major=(w=1) label=(f=swissl 'Hazard');

proc gplot  data = estimate;
   plot  survival*i=1/ haxis=axis1 vaxis=axis2;
   TITLE1    J=C H=.2 IN f=ZAPF C=black
         'Figure 1. Survival Function Plot of Effects of Time After Birth';
run;

proc gplot data=estimate;
   plot hazard*i=1 / haxis=axis1 vaxis=axis3;
   TITLE1    J=C H=.2 IN f=ZAPF C=black
         'Figure 2. Hazard Function Plot of Effects of Time After Birth';
RUN;
```

The survival and hazard plots are shown in Figures 15.5 and 15.6.

FIGURE 15.5 ● **THE SURVIVAL PLOT FOR THE TIME-ONLY MODEL**

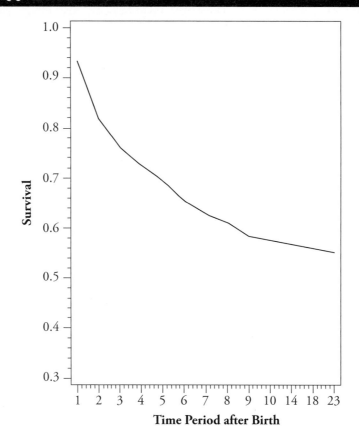

FIGURE 15.6 ◆ THE HAZARD PLOT FROM THE TIME-ONLY MODEL

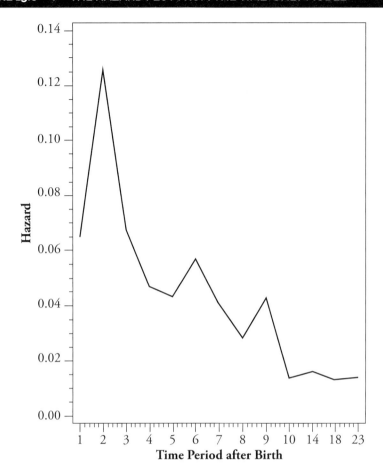

The survival plot shows a sharp decline in the early years, followed by a shallower decline in later periods. This means that most mothers went back to work in the early years. The plot shows that about 55% of the mothers have not returned to work after the observed risk periods. The flattening of the curve at $t = 9$ suggests there is an age beyond which it is unlikely the mother will return to work, given that they have not to that point.

The hazard function shows a spike in the hazard in the second period (when the child is 1), with a bumpy decline after that. There are spikes in periods 6 and 9, reflecting mothers' willingness to go back to work in anticipation of the child starting school or once a few years of school are completed. These functions are only averages since there are no variables included in this model. Obviously, the visual results are easier to interpret than the coefficients we started with.

15.5.12.2 The Effect of Decade of Birth

We added the effects of decade to the time-only model to assess the additive effects of decade, before adding controls. The parameter estimates are in Table 15.14, and the plots are in Figures 15.7 and 15.8. Adjustments were made to the calculation of the survival and hazard values to distinguish the plots by decade.

TABLE 15.14 ● PARAMETER ESTIMATES FOR THE EFFECT OF DECADE

		Analysis of Maximum Likelihood Estimates			
Parameter	DF	Estimate	Standard Error	Wald Chi-Square	Pr > ChiSq
t1	1	−3.0305	0.1410	462.0873	<.0001
t2	1	−2.3069	0.1294	317.7427	<.0001
t3	1	−2.9983	0.1526	386.0219	<.0001
t4	1	−3.3885	0.1899	318.2356	<.0001
t5	1	−3.4747	0.2239	240.7993	<.0001
t6	1	−3.1720	0.2307	189.1328	<.0001
t7	1	−3.5423	0.2948	144.3478	<.0001
t8	1	−3.9134	0.3757	108.5104	<.0001
t9	1	−3.4653	0.3415	102.9897	<.0001
t10_13	1	−4.6351	0.3522	173.1873	<.0001
t14_17	1	−4.4434	0.3948	126.6528	<.0001
t18_22	1	−4.6155	0.4607	100.3760	<.0001
t23_45	1	−4.4208	0.4165	112.6694	<.0001
decade60	1	0.3893	0.1510	6.6495	0.0099
decade70	1	0.4683	0.1369	11.7048	0.0006
decade80	1	0.4151	0.1377	9.0898	0.0026

FIGURE 15.7 ● SURVIVAL PLOT FOR THE DECADE MODEL

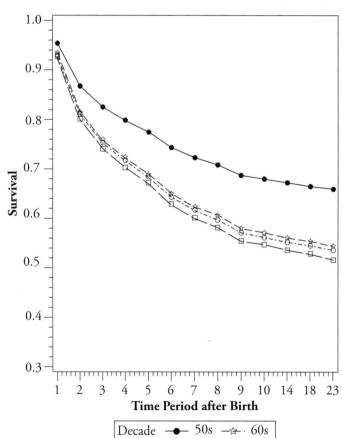

FIGURE 15.8 ⬣ HAZARD PLOT FOR THE DECADE MODEL

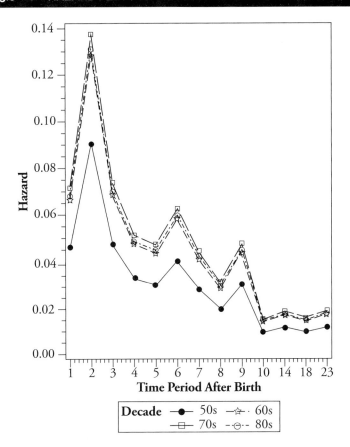

Note in these results the differences by decade are not incremental and linear. Basically, every decade after the 50's shows an increased propensity for women to go to work after a first child. But the plots suggest that the main shift occurred by the 1960s, and after that, further changes were small. In fact, while there is an additional small increase in the hazard in the 1970s, there is a slight drop-off in the 1980s. One can speculate as to a number of historical influences here: economic changes in the 1960s, feminism as a social movement in the late 1960s and 1970s, and the rise of conservative right governments and a backlash to feminism in the 1980s.

The plots show how a variable shifts the survival and hazard functions, here by a constant amount, because there is no interaction between time and decade.

15.5.12.3 Adding Control Variables

We added the four control variables to the decade model and re-estimated. All of the controls had the expected effect, except for the mother's mother's education (results not shown): The age of the mother had a negative effect on the probability of going to work, working full-time before had a positive effect, and having a partner had a negative effect.

The most straightforward way to compare these results to the previous model is to compare the hazard plots. Figure 15.9 shows the hazard plot for the decade model with controls. There *is* a

FIGURE 15.9 ● THE HAZARD PLOT FROM THE DECADE MODEL WITH CONTROLS

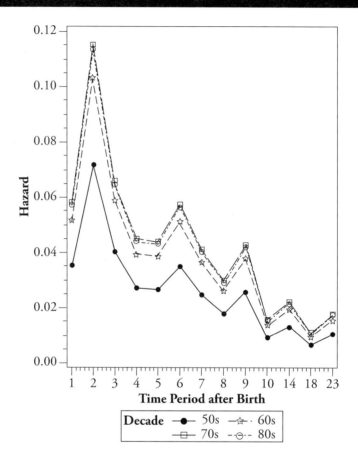

slight change in the results: The effects of decade70 and decade80 are each a little more distinct in this model compared to the model with no controls. In fact, there is evidence of a suppression effect, with a somewhat larger effect here than in the previous model. In addition, there is no evidence of a drop-off in the 1980s; instead, the hazards in the 1980s almost exactly equal the hazards in the 1970s.

15.5.12.4 Testing the Interaction Between Time Period and Decade

Given the impact of decade is still clear with controls, we tested the potential interaction between decade and time period, in other words, the age of the child. This interaction tests whether the shape of the hazard by time periods varied by decades. This could happen a number of ways—for example, if more women specifically went back to work in the pre-school years after 1970 but not during the school years or went back to work more in the teenage years specifically. Given that we are mapping social change in this model, it is important to be aware of the very real possibility that the shifts in hazards of going to work did *not* generalize across stages of the child's life.

The syntax used to estimate this model has developed in a number of ways compared to the time-only model. We review these changes briefly, mainly to point out the additional issues that must be considered. The syntax that follows shows the PROC LOGISTIC used, followed by the data step used to calculate survival and hazard values and the plots. We estimated the interaction both with and without controls: Here we show results for the model with controls.

```
  /* running logistic regression with controls*/

proc logistic data=hazwork simple out=estimate;
  model working=t1-t9 t10_13 t14_17 t18_22 t23_45 agemom momed fwrkb4 partner
                      dec60x1--dec60x9 dec60x10 dec60x14 dec60x18 dec60x23
                      dec70x1--dec70x9 dec70x10 dec70x14 dec70x18 dec70x23
                      dec80x1--dec80x9 dec80x10 dec80x14 dec80x18 dec80x23 / noint;
  title1 'Model 4 -- Interaction Effects of Time by Decade, with Controls';
run;

  /* deriving survival and hazard functions */

data estimate (replace=yes);
set estimate;

array per (13) t1-t9 t10_13 t14_17 t18_22 t23_45;
array d60xt(13) dec60x1--dec60x9 dec60x10 dec60x14 dec60x18 dec60x23;
array d70xt(13) dec70x1--dec70x9 dec70x10 dec70x14 dec70x18 dec70x23;
array d80xt(13) dec80x1--dec80x9 dec80x10 dec80x14 dec80x18 dec80x23;
array decxx (4) dec50 dec60 dec70 dec80;

do decn=1 to 4;
dec50=0; dec60=0; dec70=0; dec80=0;
decxx(decn)=1;
decade=(decn+4)*10;
survival=1;

do i=1 to 13;
  x=per(i) + dec60*d60xt(i) + dec70*d70xt(i) + dec80*d80xt(i)
  + agemom*24.67 + momed*10.74 + fwrkb4*.306 + partner*.675;
  hazard=1/(1+(exp(-x)));
  survival=(1-hazard)*survival;
 output;
end;
end;

keep i survival hazard decade;


 /*plotting hazard and survival functions */

SYMBOL1 C=black I=join V=DOT L=1 W=1;
SYMBOL2 C=red I=join V=dot L=1 W=1;
SYMBOL3 C=green I=join V=dot L=1 W=1;
SYMBOL4 C=blue I=join V=dot L=1 W=1;
LEGEND1 across=2 frame label=('Decade') value=('50s' '60s' '70s' '80s');

PROC GPLOT  DATA = estimate;
   PLOT  survival*i = decade /
haxis=axis1 vaxis=axis2 legend=legend1;
   TITLE1    J=C H=.2 IN f=ZAPF C=black
         'Figure 1. Survival Function Plot of Time x Decade Interaction';

PROC GPLOT  DATA = estimate;
   PLOT  hazard*i = decade /
haxis=axis1 vaxis=axis3 legend=legend1;
   TITLE1    J=C H=.2 IN f=ZAPF C=black
         'Figure 2. Hazard Function Plot of Time x Decade Interaction';
RUN;
```

Here are the main modifications of the programming necessary to run the interaction model:

- Note that the model here does not contain main effects for decade. This is because they are contained in the interactions, a consequence of the fact that all time periods are included. In this scheme, the time period variables are the effect of time in the 1950s, in other words, the reference group decade.

- The DO loops governing the production of the survival and hazard values have a number of additional features, including the following: (a) Special variables are set up to represent the decade variables (dec50 to dec 80), and the first do loop assigns a 1 to each of these in turn while the others are set at 0; (b) Dec50 never occurs in the equation itself, thus leaving the other decades at 0, which in fact stands for decade 50; (c) the equation for the log odds writes out the coefficients for the model multiplied by the values of the dummy variables for decade (either 1 or 0 depending on the decade); (d) controls are given a mean value.

- The plots use a syntax designating a distinct plot for each value of the variable "decade." This variable is in fact given a value in the highest level do loop, equal to 50, 60, 70, and 80 in turn.

The additive model for decade with controls is nested in this model. We did a traditional test of the Likelihood Ratio difference across the two models, which is 8983.977 - 8927.2012 = 56.78, with 54 - 20 = 34 *df*. This is significant at the .008 level. Taking our own earlier advice, we could have used a difference of differences in averaged marginal effects here as well. We proceed on the assumption that the interaction is significant.

Again, it is difficult to "see" the results from the estimated coefficients. We advocate plotting of results as a matter of course. We reproduce the hazard plot in Figure 15.10, and in this case, even the plot gets quite complex.

FIGURE 15.10 ⬢ THE HAZARD PLOT FROM THE INTERACTION MODEL

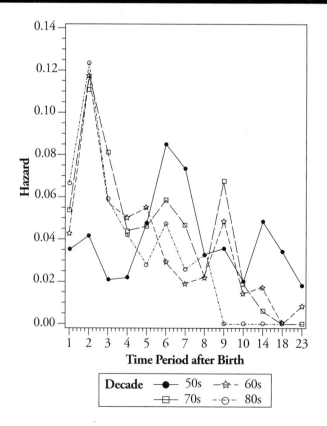

The plot does make clear that the effect of decade varied considerably across risk periods. Basically, in the 1950s, there was a very low hazard for going to work before the child started school, but this increased to a higher hazard after the child started school compared to all other decades. However, the pattern reverses again when the child is about 10 and then again during the teenage years, when the hazard is again highest in the 1950s. Note that these hazards pertain to a first return to work, so more of the women in later decades are already working earlier in the child's life. But the patterns in the hazard profiles by decade do suggest shifting norms that are quite specific to four stages of the child's life: preschool, early school, preteen, and teen.

There are anomalies in these results. While the 1980s did show the highest hazard in the early years (barely), the hazard of going to work during early school is noticeably lower than the 1970s. It is also apparent that the number of risk periods in the 1980s is limited by the time frame of the second wave: No one gets beyond period 9, and so the hazards from that point on appear to be 0.

15.6 THE COMPETING RISKS MODEL

The results to this point could be wrong if there is a shift across decades in the tendency to go back to part-time versus full-time work. This could, for example, explain the results for the 1980s compared to earlier decades.

The previous example uses a classic binary outcome, in part because this is the predominant application of discrete-time models but also to simplify and clarify the considerations in estimating these models. However, it is possible to generalize the approach used to this point to the case of competing risks—that is, where there is a multinomial outcome. The competing risks model

FIGURE 15.11 ● HAZARDS FOR RETURNING TO FULL-TIME VERSUS PART-TIME AFTER THE BIRTH OF A FIRST CHILD.

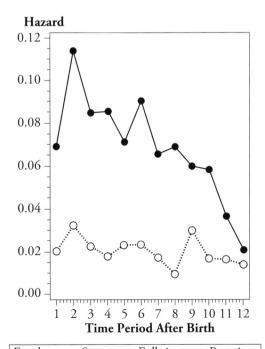

applies in general to any multi-category outcome where entering one category automatically excludes others—they are mutually exclusive.

Suppose we distinguish between going to work full time versus going to work part time versus not working after having a first child. Now we have a three category outcome. We know we can treat this issue straightforwardly by running PROC LOGISTIC with the multinomial option. We also have to distinguish every job in the job history by whether it was full-time or part-time.

The other main changes here are that we have to calculate distinct survival and hazard values for each level of the outcome—that is, for full-time and part-time separately. We also have to overlay the plots for the two outcomes so that we can show two distinct plots in the same graph.

Putting aside the parameter estimates, we show a hazard plot for a time-only model distinguishing full-time versus part-time work in Figure 15.11. The plot shows in general that the predominant work outcome was starting a full-time job after the first birth. The hazard plots differ notably: The full-time hazard plot shows higher hazards in the early years than in the later years, as before, but the part-time plot shows a relative constant hazard over time—with some minor ups and downs.

When we estimate the effect of decade distinguished by full-time versus part-time, we begin to see results that inform the results from the binary model (Figure 15.12).

FIGURE 15.12 ● THE EFFECTS OF DECADE IN THE COMPETING RISKS MODEL

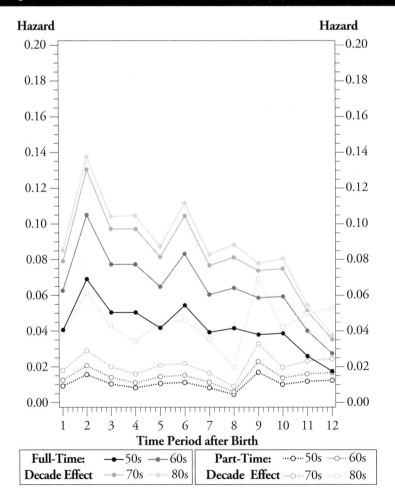

Decades are plotted in different shades of grey in this plot, and the line type varies also to signify full-time (line) versus part-time (dashes). The results here are quite different than in the previous analysis, especially with regard to the 1980s. First, it is clear there is a large increase in the hazard of going back to part-time work in the 1980s. Second, the increase in the hazard of going back to full-time work in the 1970s and 1980s reflects a larger increase relative to the 1960s than in the binary model. Third, the highest hazard overall is in the 1980s, although it is essentially the same as the 1970s for full-time work. Results here are more consistent with a continuing social change across decades but also with a shift from full-time to part-time work by the 1980s.

15.7 REPEATED EVENTS: THE MULTIPLE SPELL MODEL

To this point, our whole discussion has assumed we are predicting unique, one-time events—for example, returning to work after a *first* child. The model is implicitly assumed to be unique to the birth of the first child. A generalization of the event history model allows for the study of **repeated events**, either the same recurring event in successive risk periods (working after later births) or events related by a series of prior qualifications (like sequences of employment and nonemployment), in one model.

Here we discuss only the general modifications necessary to run a multiple-spell model, basically signaling that it can be done with straightforward modifications of the approach used to this point.

The generalization involves taking the one-spell event history model and extending it to include multiple spells. Why would we do this? There are many good reasons. Perhaps the clearest reason is that we simply don't know whether or how the model determining going to work in later spells compares to the first spell. It seems plausible that the existence of the first child would change considerations about going to work after a second child and having two children would modify the issues further after having a third child.

To conduct a multiple-spell analysis, you need to create a spell-person-period data set. This means you concatenate successive spells into one data set, using the same variables, but adding a variable called "spell" to each data set, equal to 1 in the first spell, 2 in the second spell, and so forth. This data set offers many analytical possibilities:

- You can study the effects of spell overall, net of the other inputs to risk.

- You can test the changes in the model across spells by estimating interactions between the spell and focal variables. For example, you could test whether the effect of decade changes for later children and thus whether the main social change in women going to work occurred for later children.

- You can also test complex interactions involving spell, period, and focal variables. You would do this to detect a shift in the effect of a focal variable by risk periods further depending on spell.

In fact, one of the fundamental reasons for developing a multiple-spell model is to test the three-way interaction between a focal variable and spell and risk period. In our previous example, we would expect a three-way interaction between decade, period, and spell if women specifically went to work in higher numbers after a first birth when the child was preschool in later decades, but the impact of preschool children was lower for later children in later decades. This approach pinpoints where and when the historical change occurs—but there are many possibilities to be considered.

One cannot access these possibilities by running separate event history models for each spell. This is akin to studying groups separately but without evidence of an actual interaction: There is no way to assess whether effects change across spells, only whether they are significant or non-significant within spells.

15.8 PUBLISHED EXAMPLE

Consider the possibility of combining discrete-time hazard analysis with other advanced methods discussed throughout this book. Barber, Murphy, Axinn, & Maples (2000) offer one intriguing example. This article uses event history analysis in conjunction with multilevel modelling to examine contraceptive use in Nepal. The authors argue that individual-level survival models are insufficient in answering their research questions. First, individual-level models neglect the possibility that individuals are differentially impacted by their local context. This variation is confounded in regression coefficients when researchers ignore place of residence. Second, decisions around permanent contraception depend upon individual-level characteristics and likely unfold over time. An individual-level hazard model estimating these effects might result in *duration bias*. The authors unpack this bias succinctly in the following statements:

> If a single-level hazard model is applied to multilevel data, duration bias results. …Suppose that the event is the initiation of permanent contraception and suppose that the macro context is the neighborhood and neighborhoods are heterogeneous—e.g. some neighborhoods are special in that their characteristics lead to delayed permanent contraceptive use. As time proceeds most of the women who have yet to experience the event will be from the neighborhoods that delay the event time. The estimator of the baseline hazard will not reflect the hazard for any one type of individual; rather it reflects an average hazard, calculated over the variety of macro-level contexts. At later times this average will be primarily over individuals from the special contexts. The unobserved heterogeneity of the contexts results in an underestimation of the baseline hazard. (Barber et al., 2000, p. 203)

> Suppose that the association of an individual level covariate, such as a woman's educational level, with the event, contraceptive timing, varies across contexts. The unobserved heterogeneity of the contexts then results in a second form of duration bias, a biased regression coefficient. At earlier times the regression coefficient of a woman's education level reflects a comparison of groups of women wherein each group is composed of subjects from the full variety of neighborhoods. But at later times, the regression coefficient for women's education reflects a comparison of groups of women wherein the groups are primarily composed of women from the special neighborhoods. To prevent this bias, we propose a multilevel model including random coefficients. The crux is that multilevel models of social behavior demand not only multilevel data but also multilevel statistical procedures (Barber et al., 2000, p. 203–204).

Following from this, the authors use longitudinal multilevel data from the Chiwan Valley Family Study to document how changing neighborhood conditions influence individuals' decisions to employ contraceptives in Nepal. Barber et al. hypothesize the following: (a) *individual level*: more educated women will have a higher hazard of contraceptive use; (b) *neighborhood level*: women living in neighborhoods with access to nearby schools will increase the hazard of contraceptive use; and (c) *cross-level*: the association between women's education and permanent contraceptive use is stronger in neighborhoods with a school nearby. The last hypothesis proposes a cross-level interaction, as discussed in Chapter 11 on hierarchical linear modeling.

Here is the model at Level 1:

$$\widehat{\text{LogOdds}}(p_{tjk}) = \beta_{0k} + \beta_{1k}\text{Educ}_j + \beta_{2k}\text{Chldrn}_{tj} + \beta_3\text{Time}_{tj}$$
$$+ B_4 Time^2_{tj.} \qquad\qquad (\text{CM 1a})$$

Source: Barber, J. S, Murphy S. A., Axinn W. G, & Maples J. (2000, August 1). Discrete-time multilevel hazard analysis. *Sociological Methodology, 30*, 201–235.

Where *Educ* is a binary indicator of whether the woman attended school before the birth of her first child, *Chldrn* is the total number of children the woman has had by time *t*, and *Time* is in years since the first birth. Note the baseline hazard profile is expressed as a quadratic effect of time.

Here is the model at Level 2:

$$\beta_{0k} = \gamma_{00} + \gamma_{01}Dis_k + \gamma_{02}\text{School}_{tk} + \in_{0k} \qquad (\text{CM 1b})$$
$$\beta_{1k} = \gamma_{10} + \gamma_{11}\text{School}_{tk} + \in_{1k}$$
$$\beta_{2k} = \gamma_{20} + \in_{2k}$$
$$\beta_3 = \gamma_{30}$$
$$\beta_4 = \gamma_{40}$$

Source: Barber, J. S, Murphy S. A., Axinn W. G, & Maples J. (2000, August 1). Discrete-time multilevel hazard analysis. *Sociological Methodology, 30*, 201–235.

Where *Dis* is the distance from the neighborhood to the nearest town, and *School* is whether there is a school within a five-minute walk from the neighborhood.

The results are presented in Table 15.15. The authors show findings from two software packages; HLM and MLN. The results are comparable across both packages (although the authors note that the variances associated with the random components should be interpreted with caution, Barber et al., 2000, p. 226).

TABLE 15.15 ⬡ RESULTS FOR A MULTILEVEL HAZARD MODEL OF CONTRACEPTIVE USE					
	Model 1		**Model 2**		**Parameter in CM**
	HLM	**MLN**	**HLM**	**MLN**	
Intercept	−4.50*** (.18)	−4.01*** (.14)	−4.48*** (.17)	−4.01*** (.15)	γ_{00}
Neighborhood Characteristics					
Distance to nearest town (time-invariant)	−.04** (.01)	−.04*** (.01)	−.04** (.01)	−.04*** (.01)	γ_{01}
School within 5 minute walk (time-varying)	.36*** (.11)	.26*** (.09)	.30*** (.10)	.29*** (.09)	γ_{02}
Individual Characteristics					
Ever went to school before first birth (time-invariant)	.66*** (.12)	.66*** (.10)	.58*** (.09)	.58*** (.09)	γ_{10}
Total number of children (time-varying)	.40*** (.04)	.34*** (.03)	.40*** (.04)	.41*** (.04)	γ_{20}
Cross-Level Effect					
School within 5 minute walk * Ever went to school	−.19 (.17)	−.16 (.16)			γ_{11}

Analyses highlight that education does influences women's contraceptive use: "Having attended school is associated with a .58 higher log-odds of permanent contraceptive use" (Barber et al, 2000, p. 223). But neighborhood context also matters: "Having a school within a 5-minute walk is associated with a .29 higher log-odds of permanent contraceptive use" (Barber et al., 2000, p. 223). These two findings are highlighted in Model 2, focusing on the results from MLN only.

The authors do not find support for a cross-level interaction—meaning that women's education and proximity to schools in one's neighborhood *do not* combine to influence permanent contraceptive use over and above the cumulative but separate additive effects (noted by the non-significant interaction term in Model 1). Instead, individual and neighborhood characteristics matter independent of one another, adding an additional layer of influence to the usual individual-level effect.

Concluding Words

This chapter considered the discrete-time event history model in some detail, primarily to provide guidance navigating a complex series of issues. Leaving out links in this chain would be fatal to understanding the thinking behind this model and especially the way in which time is conceived in this model. Time "zero" is unique to each individual; calendar time is not the issue. Risk periods measure the march of time beyond the onset of risk unique to each individual. This complicates the programming necessary to run an event history considerably.

What results is important, however, because the model makes time a central issue in considering the occurrence of an event. There are articles in major journals, recently, that use logistic regression in situations where an event history would have been more appropriate and could yield different results.

Our approach was not to present a simple example—on purpose. Every example will have its own peculiarities, but *any* one extended example will make the point that essential specific issues arise that require careful decisions along the way. Of course, this also means that one should also change assumptions to assess the sensitivity of the results to assumptions built into the programming along the way.

In the next—and final—chapter, we review the continuous-time event history model, with three issues in mind: (1) the continuous-time model is important because it is the dominant approach used in some disciplines; (2) it is important to understand the differences between the continuous and discrete time model in order to understand the choices available in estimating these models; and (3) we illustrate the point that in many applications, results from the two models will converge in any case.

Practice Questions

1. Results (and appropriate graphs) are attached for this question, showing the results of a discrete-time event history analysis of divorce from a first marriage, using the National Longitudinal Survey of Youth (NLSY) data. The focus in this analysis is on the effect of living with both biological parents at the age of 14 on the hazard of divorce.

    There were a total of 33 risk periods in this sample from the NLSY, starting in 1980. There are two forms of censoring in this model: death of the spouse and the final date of the interview if the marriage is still intact.

    The focal variable in this analysis is **bothpar14**, a dummy variable = 1 if the respondent was living with both biological parents at age 14, and = 0 otherwise.

    Other variables are

    -   *t1 to t33*: Time dummy variables representing from one to the thirty-third year of marriage

    -   *Ageatmarr*: The age of first marriage

    -   *Poverty*: A dummy variable = 1 if family was in poverty during adolescence, and 0 otherwise

    -   Interactions between living with both parents and year of marriage, noted by *parxt1* to *parxt33*

    Results from three models are shown: Model 1 includes the effects of time only—in this model, years of marriage, Model 2 adds the effect of *bothpar14* but also controls for *ageatmarr* and *poverty,* and Model 3 considers the interaction between *bothpar14* and year of marriage. The purpose of the last model is to see if the impact of living with both parents affects the timing of divorce as well as the overall hazard.

    These results are followed by tables showing the frequencies of *censor,* coded 1 if a censored observation and 0 if not, and a PROC PRINT of selected variables from the data used to define censoring and the number of risk periods (*riskper*).

Answer these questions:

a. Using Model 2 (Table 15.C), calculate the hazard of divorce in the third year of marriage for a person who lived with both parents at age 14, was **not** in poverty at the time, and got married at age 25.

b. Using Model 2 again, calculate the effect of living in poverty on the odds of divorce in each period.

c. Using Model 1 "time only" results (Table 15.B), calculate hazard and survival values to figure out the percentage of the sample that is still married after four years of marriage.

d. Using the hazard plot (Figure 15.A) for the interaction model (Model 3), approximately how many years into the marriage does the hazard of divorce *first* converge for those who with lived with both parents versus those who did not?

e. Looking at the results for the interaction model (Table 15.D), explain in a one or two sentences why the variable **bothpar14** does not appear as a main effect in this model.

f. Looking at the frequencies for **censor** (Table 15.E), what percentage of this sample got a divorce over the observation period in this study?

g. The PROC PRINT following the results (Table 15.F) shows the case id (**Rcaseid**) the values of censor (**censor**), the total risk periods (**riskper**), the year the marriage started (**marryear**), the year of a spousal death (**widowyear**), the year of a divorce (**divyear**), and the year of the last observed interview (**intyear**).

Focus on Rcaseids 5, 14, and 24.

Fill in a table structured like the one in Table 15.A showing the person-period observations for these three cases, using these variables: **Rcaseid, Censor, Riskper, Period,** and **Divorces Status. Period** is the number of the observation period for each observation. **Divorce Status** is the current status of being married (= 2) versus getting a divorce (= 1) in that period.

TABLE 15.A ● VALUES OF ESSENTIAL VARIABLES FOR THREE CASES

Rcaseid	*Period*	*Censor*	*Riskper*	*Divorce*

TABLE 15.B ● MODEL 1—TIME EFFECTS ONLY

Analysis of Maximum Likelihood Estimates					
Parameter	**DF**	**Estimate**	**Standard Error**	**Wald Chi-Square**	**Pr > ChiSq**
t1	1	−18.2029	98.2208	0.0343	0.8530
t2	1	−2.8215	0.0477	3501.4582	<.0001
t3	1	−2.5942	0.0449	3337.8086	<.0001
t4	1	−2.9356	0.0551	2839.5858	<..0001
t5	1	−2.7551	0.0530	2704.8423	<..0001
t6	1	−3.0940	0.0649	2271.0889	<.0001
t7	1	−2.9156	0.0623	2193.3496	<.0001

Analysis of Maximum Likelihood Estimates					
Parameter	DF	Estimate	Standard Error	Wald Chi-Square	Pr > ChiSq
t8	1	−3.3681	0.0799	1776.5855	<.0001
t9	1	−3.2394	0.0773	1756.9991	<.0001
t10	1	−3.4061	0.0868	1538.3334	<.0001
t11	1	−3.4993	0.0934	1402.5632	<.0001
t12	1	−3.6905	0.1061	1209.2375	<.0001
t13	1	−3.4933	0.0991	1243.5474	<.0001
t14	1	−3.6831	0.1118	1085.0461	<.0001
t15	1	−3.5858	0.1087	1088.4452	<.0001
t16	1	−3.7791	0.1236	935.4912	<.0001
t17	1	−3.7584	0.1245	911.0297	<.0001
t18	1	−3.8494	0.1350	812.4956	<.0001
t19	1	−3.8926	0.1401	772.1770	<.0001
t20	1	−3.7267	0.1340	773.0459	<.0001
t21	1	−3.6014	0.1308	757.5411	<.0001
t22	1	−3.9586	0.1616	599.7059	<.0001
t23	1	−4.2668	0.1938	484.7617	<.0001
t24	1	−4.5315	0.2306	385.9945	<.0001
t25	1	−3.7643	0.1663	512.4195	<.0001
t26	1	−3.8764	0.1909	412.1975	<.0001
t27	1	−3.6969	0.1913	373.4135	<.0001
t28	1	−3.8276	0.2260	286.7626	<.0001
t29	1	−3.7530	0.2454	233.9540	<.0001
t30	1	−4.3838	0.3803	132.8667	<.0001
t31	1	−3.8528	0.3573	116.2852	<.0001
t32	1	−3.5715	0.3832	86.8499	<..0001
t33	1	−4.6728	1.0047	21.6332	<..0001

TABLE 15.C ● MODEL 2—EFFECTS OF TIME AND LIVING WITH BOTH PARENTS AT 14 WITH CONTROLS

Analysis of Maximum Likelihood Estimates					
Parameter	DF	Estimate	Standard Error	Wald Chi-Square	Pr > ChiSq
t1	1	−16.9849	97.4747	0.0304	0.8617
t2	1	−1.6148	0.1036	243.0917	<.0001
t3	1	−1.3773	0.1027	179.9504	<.0001
t4	1	−1.7182	0.1074	256.1790	<.0001
t5	1	−1.5299	0.1066	205.7764	<.0001
t6	1	−1.8684	0.1130	273.5378	<.0001
t7	1	−1.6778	0.1121	224.0578	<.0001
t8	1	−2.1318	0.1225	302.9500	<.0001
t9	1	−1.9938	0.1211	271.2103	<.0001
t10	1	−2.1602	0.1272	288.4541	<.0001
t11	1	−2.2439	0.1321	288.6889	<.0001
t12	1	−2.4362	0.1412	297.8762	<.0001
t13	1	−2.2333	0.1362	268.9534	<.0001
t14	1	−2.4308	0.1453	279.8976	<.0001

(*Continued*)

TABLE 15.C ● Continued

Analysis of Maximum Likelihood Estimates					
Parameter	**DF**	**Estimate**	**Standard Error**	**Wald Chi-Square**	**Pr > ChiSq**
t15	1	−2.3312	0.1429	265.9833	<.0001
t16	1	−2.5344	0.1540	270.6749	<.0001
t17	1	−2.5116	0.1549	262.9255	<.0001
t18	1	−2.6124	0.1630	256.8832	<.0001
t19	1	−2.6544	0.1672	251.9889	<.0001
t20	1	−2.4959	0.1618	237.9927	<.0001
t21	1	−2.3770	0.1588	223.9306	<.0001
t22	1	−2.7446	0.1848	220.6361	<.0001
t23	1	−3.0596	0.2133	205.7963	<.0001
t24	1	−3.3373	0.2470	182.6048	<.0001
t25	1	−2.5801	0.1880	188.2982	<.0001
t26	1	−2.7092	0.2096	167.0293	<.0001
t27	1	−2.5421	0.2096	147.1494	<.0001
t28	1	−2.6920	0.2413	124.4726	<.0001
t29	1	−2.6367	0.2592	103.5026	<.0001
t30	1	−3.2820	0.3892	71.1145	<.0001
t31	1	−2.7603	0.3665	56.7100	<.0001
t32	1	−2.4761	0.3917	39.9523	<.0001
t33	1	−3.6062	1.0080	12.8002	0.0003
bothpar14	1	−0.3738	0.0358	108.8921	<.0001
ageatmarr	1	−0.0439	0.00359	150.1415	<.0001
poverty	1	0.3091	0.0347	79.2334	<.0001

TABLE 15.D ● MODEL 3—INTERACTION BETWEEN TIME AND LIVING WITH BOTH PARENTS AT 14

Analysis of Maximum Likelihood Estimates					
Parameter	**DF**	**Estimate**	**Standard Error**	**Wald Chi-Square**	**Pr > ChiSq**
t1	1	−17.2734	177.9	0.0094	0.9226
t2	1	−1.6712	0.1191	196.7810	<.0001
t3	1	−1.2809	0.1142	125.8772	<.0001
t4	1	−1.8922	0.1322	204.9561	<.0001
t5	1	−1.4679	0.1238	140.5157	<.0001
t6	1	−1.9469	0.1432	184.9069	<.0001
t7	1	−1.6582	0.1379	144.6779	<.0001
t8	1	−2.2228	0.1668	177.5007	<.0001
t9	1	−2.0485	0.1624	159.0383	<.0001
t10	1	−1.9776	0.1645	144.5734	<.0001
t11	1	−2.0287	0.1726	138.1904	<.0001
t12	1	−2.4465	0.2067	140.1538	<.0001
t13	1	−2.1288	0.1894	126.3376	<.0001
t14	1	−2.4066	0.2156	124.5456	<.0001
t15	1	−2.1877	0.2020	117.3319	<.0001
t16	1	−2.3576	0.2223	112.4394	<.0001
t17	1	−2.5452	0.2440	108.8457	<.0001
t18	1	−2.7574	0.2759	99.8961	<.0001
t19	1	−3.1369	0.3309	89.8725	<.0001

Analysis of Maximum Likelihood Estimates					
Parameter	DF	Estimate	Standard Error	Wald Chi-Square	Pr > ChiSq
t20	1	−2.7323	0.2844	92.2978	<.0001
t21	1	−2.3955	0.2551	88.1828	<.0001
t22	1	−2.5820	0.2847	82.2522	<.0001
t23	1	−3.3764	0.4199	64.6491	<.0001
t24	1	−2.8853	0.3477	68.8609	<.0001
t25	1	−2.5855	0.3176	66.2566	<.0001
t26	1	−2.8939	0.3913	54.6852	<.0001
t27	1	−2.5715	0.3687	48.6486	<.0001
t28	1	−2.6792	0.4223	40.2410	<.0001
t29	1	−2.3377	0.3944	35.1278	<.0001
t30	1	−4.0762	1.0071	16.3827	<.0001
t31	1	−2.5423	0.5932	18.3669	<.0001
t32	1	−3.1919	1.0126	9.9363	0.0016
t33	1	−17.4466	1691.6	0.0001	0.9918
ageatmarr	1	−0.0441	0.00359	150.7843	<.0001
poverty	1	0.3088	0.0347	79.0322	<.0001
parxt1	1	0.0667	212.9	0.0000	0.9998
parxt2	1	−0.2785	0.0995	7.8432	0.0051
parxt3	1	−0.5284	0.0921	32.9106	<.0001
parxt4	1	−0.1030	0.1185	0.7549	0.3849
parxt5	1	−0.4690	0.1094	18.3827	<.0001
parxt6	1	−0.2484	0.1377	3.2550	0.0712
parxt7	1	−0.3999	0.1303	9.4136	0.0022
parxt8	1	−0.2317	0.1712	1.8332	0.1757
parxt9	1	−0.2868	0.1649	3.0243	0.0820
parxt10	1	−0.6595	0.1779	13.7398	0.0002
parxt11	1	−0.7117	0.1909	13.8941	0.0002
parxt12	1	−0.3541	0.2267	2.4408	0.1182
parxt13	1	−0.5280	0.2074	6.4815	0.0109
parxt14	1	−0.4053	0.2390	2.8762	0.0899
parxt15	1	−0.5871	0.2267	6.7068	0.0096
parxt16	1	−0.6374	0.2568	6.1634	0.0130
parxt17	1	−0.3214	0.2719	1.3969	0.2372
parxt18	1	−0.1667	0.3057	0.2973	0.5856
parxt19	1	0.2706	0.3553	0.5799	0.4463
parxt20	1	−0.0438	0.3119	0.0197	0.8884
parxt21	1	−0.3435	0.2867	1.4351	0.2309
parxt22	1	−0.6124	0.3384	3.2756	0.0703
parxt23	1	0.0587	0.4664	0.0159	0.8998
parxt24	1	−1.1037	0.4633	5.6735	0.0172
parxt25	1	−0.3622	0.3652	0.9839	0.3212
parxt26	1	−0.1161	0.4418	0.0691	0.7926
parxt27	1	−0.3289	0.4251	0.5987	0.4391
parxt28	1	−0.3885	0.4950	0.6160	0.4325
parxt29	1	−0.8334	0.5014	2.7634	0.0964
parxt30	1	0.6481	1.0850	0.3568	0.5503
parxt31	1	−0.6983	0.7414	0.8873	0.3462
parxt32	1	0.5339	1.0917	0.2392	0.6248
parxt33	1	13.9111	1691.6	0.0001	0.9934

FIGURE 15.A ⬡ HAZARD PLOT FROM MODEL 3

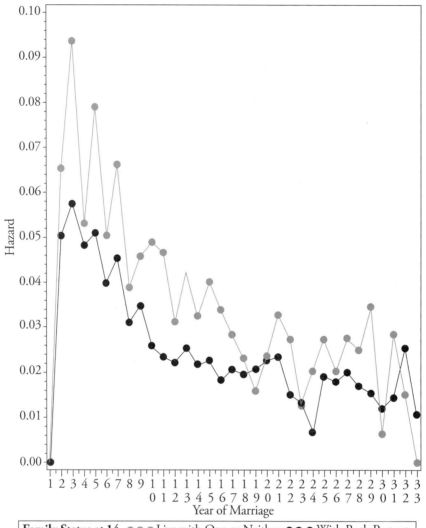

Family Status at 14 ●●● Live with One or Neither ●●● With Both Partents

TABLE 15.E ⬡ FREQUENCIES OF CENSOR

censor	Frequency	Percent	Cumulative Frequency	Cumulative Percent
0	3797	45.54	3797	45.54
1	4540	54.46	8337	100.00

TABLE 15.F ● PROC PRINT OF 25 CASES

Rcaseid	censor	riskper	marryear	widowyear	divyear	intyear
2	1	21	1982	.	.	2012
3	1	31	1982	.	.	2012
4	0	3	1981	.	1983	2000
5	1	5	1986	.	.	1990
6	1	23	1990	.	.	2012
7	0	5	1990	.	1994	2012
9	1	25	1988	.	.	2012
10	1	4	1983	.	.	1986
12	1	4	1983	.	.	1986
13	0	12	1989	.	2000	2008
14	0	8	1991	.	1998	2012
15	1	20	1993	.	.	2012
16	0	21	1988	.	2008	2012
17	0	11	2002	.	2012	2012
18	0	13	1980	.	1992	2012
20	1	25	1988	.	.	2012
21	1	21	1992	.	.	2012
22	0	25	1988	.	2012	2012
24	0	9	1986	.	1994	2000
25	1	25	1988	.	.	2012
26	1	7	1988	.	.	1994
27	1	28	1985	.	.	2012
28	0	4	1986	.	1989	2002
29	1	17	1996	.	.	2012
30	1	31	1982	.	.	2012

2. Results (and appropriate graphs) are attached for this question showing the results of another discrete-time event history analysis of divorce from a first marriage, this time in the NSFH data. There were a total of 44 risk periods in this sample from the NSFH. There are two forms of censoring in this model: death of the spouse, and reaching the final interview with the marriage still intact.

The focal variable in this analysis is *parlive,* a dummy variable =1 if the respondent grew up with both biological parents, and =0 otherwise.

Other variables are:

- *Decadexx*: Dummy variables for the decade of the beginning of the marriage, including the 1950s, 1960s, 1970s, and 1980s. The 1950s is the reference group here.

- *Black, Hisp*: Dummy variables for Black and Hispanic respondents, respectively.

- *Jobbing*: The woman's work status over the marriage, measured for each time period separately = 1 if working, 0 if not.

Interactions are also formed from these variables to represent the differential effect of growing up with both biological parents by decade. Please note, *this is not an interaction with time period*. These variables are

- *dec60xpar*:   decade60 x parlive
- *dec70xpar*:   decade60 x parlive
- *dec80xpar*:   decade80 x parlive

Only certain models are shown in the results. Model 1 includes the effects of time only—in this model, years of marriage; Model 3 considers the effect of decade plus the effect of growing up with biological parents; and Model 5 adds the interaction between decade and growing up with bio parents. The purpose of the last model is to see if the impact of "intact background" has changed over decades.

Answer these questions:

a. Using Model 3 (Table 15.H), calculate the hazard of divorce for women in the third year of marriage (Period 3) in the 1970s **and** in the 1950s, given they grew up with both parents. What is the effect of growing up with bio parents on the probability of divorce in the 1970s versus 1950s at this point of the marriage?

b. Using Model 1 "time only" results (Table 15.G), calculate survival values to figure out the percentage of the sample that is still married after five years of marriage. (i.e., completes five years of marriage without divorce).

c. Using the hazard plot for the interaction model or the results (Figure 15.B and Table 15.I), in which decade does intact family background have the largest effect on reducing the risk of divorce? In this plot, note that each difference by family background is coded by line type in two ways, using the legend definitions below. The plot does not look like an interaction because the X axis is years married. In this case, the interaction is shown by *the differences between the lines due for intact versus not intact background by decade.*

Legend for the lines in this plot: All dashed lines are intact; all solid lines are non-intact. "×" is for the 1950s, "∆" is the 1960s, "·" is the 1970s , and "▢" is the 1980s.

d. Forty observations from the data are also reproduced in Table 15.J.

The PROC PRINT shows for each case, the values of *censor*, *riskper* (total risk periods), *yearstartmar* (the year the marriage started), *yearendmar* (the year the marriage ended, if it ended by divorce), *yeardead* (year of death of spouse), the final interview year (*intyear2*), and values of work status for the selected risk periods.

Focus on Mcaseids 53, 117, and 196. In each case, account for their values of *censor* and *riskper* using the values of the other variables printed here—that is, *yearstartmar*, *yearendmar*, *yeardead*, and *intyear2*.

e. Using Model 5 (Table 15.I), whether the interaction is significant or not, calculate the impact of growing up with both biological parents on the *odds* of divorce in the 1980s.

TABLE 15.G ⬢ MODEL 1—TIME EFFECTS ONLY

Model Fit Statistics		
Criterion	**Without Covariates**	**With Covariates**
AIC	82704.935	17353.441
SC	82704.935	17524.373
-2 Log L	82704.935	17315.441

Testing Global Null Hypothesis: BETA=0			
Test	**Chi-Square**	**DF**	**Pr > ChiSq**
Likelihood Ratio	65389.4942	19	<.0001
Score	51861.9564	19	<.0001
Wald	20888.8746	19	<.0001

Analysis of Maximum Likelihood Estimates					
Parameter	**DF**	**Estimate**	**Standard Error**	**Wald Chi-Square**	**Pr > ChiSq**
t1	1	−3.9947	0.1150	1206.5464	<.0001
t2	1	−2.9757	0.0721	1701.8920	<.0001
t3	1	−2.8394	0.0698	1652.9040	<.0001

Analysis of Maximum Likelihood Estimates					
Parameter	DF	Estimate	Standard Error	Wald Chi-Square	Pr > ChiSq
t4	1	−2.9742	0.0768	1497.9812	<.0001
t5	1	−2.9159	0.0774	1419.5861	<.0001
t6	1	−2.9749	0.0823	1305.0975	<.0001
t7	1	−3.2965	0.0989	1110.8053	<.0001
t8	1	−3.1585	0.0956	1090.9196	<.0001
t9	1	−3.2057	0.1015	997.5121	<.0001
t10	1	−3.3374	0.1124	882.0086	<.0001
t11	1	−3.3622	0.1182	808.4810	<.0001
t12	1	−3.3522	0.1225	749.1396	<.0001
t13	1	−3.2373	0.1210	715.9703	<.0001
t14	1	−3.4435	0.1382	620.4890	<.0001
t15_17	1	−3.5700	0.0911	1537.0777	<.0001
t18_20	1	−3.6941	0.1067	1198.3999	<.0001
t21_23	1	−3.7660	0.1236	928.7738	<.0001
t24_26	1	−4.0509	0.1636	612.8938	<.0001
t27_44	1	−4.9524	0.1696	852.3969	<.0001

TABLE 15.H ● MODEL 3—TIME EFFECTS WITH DECADE EFFECTS AND INTACT BACKGROUND

Response Profile		
Ordered Value	divsep	Total Frequency
1	1	2030
2	2	57629

Model Fit Statistics		
Criterion	Without Covariates	With Covariates
AIC	82704.935	17171.634
SC	82704.935	17378.552
-2 Log L	82704.935	17125.634

Testing Global Null Hypothesis: BETA=0			
Test	Chi-Square	DF	Pr > ChiSq
Likelihood Ratio	65579.3009	23	<.0001
Score	51887.7427	23	<.0001
Wald	20441.4619	23	<.0001

(Continued)

TABLE 15.H ◆ Continued

				Analysis of Maximum Likelihood Estimates	
Parameter	**DF**	**Estimate**	**Standard Error**	**Wald Chi-Square**	**Pr > ChiSq**
t1	1	−4.1324	0.1299	1011.3522	<.0001
t2	1	−3.1100	0.0942	1089.2160	<.0001
t3	1	−2.9703	0.0927	1027.0365	<.0001
t4	1	−3.1041	0.0984	995.7100	<.0001
t5	1	−3.0427	0.0991	943.1497	<.0001
t6	1	−3.0965	0.1029	905.3907	<.0001
t7	1	−3.4125	0.1165	858.1101	<.0001
t8	1	−3.2689	0.1135	828.9352	<.0001
t9	1	−3.3099	0.1183	782.3638	<.0001
t10	1	−3.4349	0.1276	725.0021	<.0001
t11	1	−3.4523	0.1325	678.3996	<.0001
t12	1	−3.4354	0.1361	636.6949	<.0001
t13	1	−3.3149	0.1347	605.9916	<.0001
t14	1	−3.5162	0.1502	547.7291	<.0001
t15_17	1	−3.6268	0.1078	1131.9255	<.0001
t18_20	1	−3.7140	0.1204	951.0395	<.0001
t21_23	1	−3.7323	0.1347	767.5677	<.0001
t24_26	1	−3.9284	0.1715	524.3737	<.0001
t27_44	1	−4.7085	0.1735	736.3121	<.0001
decade60	1	0.3596	0.0714	25.3780	<.0001
decade70	1	0.6472	0.0685	89.1584	<.0001
decade80	1	0.4484	0.0795	31.8391	<.0001
parlive	1	−0.4676	0.0467	100.4227	<.0001

TABLE 15.I ◆ MODEL 5—TIME EFFECTS WITH DECADE BY INTACT BACKGROUND INTERACTION

	Response Profile	
Ordered Value	**divsep**	**Total Frequency**
1	1	2006
2	2	56817

	Model Fit Statistics	
Criterion	**Without Covariates**	**With Covariates**
AIC	81545.993	16899.732
SC	81545.993	17160.218
-2 Log L	81545.993	16841.732

Analysis of Maximum Likelihood Estimates					
Parameter	DF	Estimate	Standard Error	Wald Chi-Square	Pr > ChiSq
t1	1	−4.3403	0.1482	857.5057	<.0001
t2	1	−3.3117	0.1178	790.0323	<.0001
t3	1	−3.1848	0.1166	745.6718	<.0001
t4	1	−3.2934	0.1207	744.7711	<.0001
t5	1	−3.2134	0.1207	708.7283	<.0001
t6	1	−3.2530	0.1235	693.5681	<.0001
t7	1	−3.6019	0.1363	698.8628	<.0001
t8	1	−3.4234	0.1325	668.0287	<.0001
t9	1	−3.4686	0.1368	642.9282	<.0001
t10	1	−3.5817	0.1445	614.1998	<.0001
t11	1	−3.5850	0.1483	584.0890	<.0001
t12	1	−3.5966	0.1530	552.7176	<.0001
t13	1	−3.4446	0.1503	525.1785	<.0001
t14	1	−3.6475	0.1644	492.2663	<.0001
t15_17	1	−3.7643	0.1269	879.7918	<.0001
t18_20	1	−3.8462	0.1377	780.0057	<.0001
t21_23	1	−3.8954	0.1521	656.0270	<.0001
t24_26	1	−4.0555	0.1843	484.1430	<.0001
t27_44	1	−4.8499	0.1890	658.2121	<.0001
decade60	1	0.3493	0.1150	9.2287	0.0024
decade70	1	0.5710	0.1094	27.2397	<.0001
decade80	1	0.6730	0.1178	32.6349	<.0001
black	1	0.2804	0.0607	21.3415	<.0001
hisp	1	−0.0687	0.0895	0.5891	0.4428
parlive	1	−0.4260	0.1133	14.1314	0.0002
jobbing	1	0.2583	0.0478	29.1430	<.0001
dec60xpar	1	0.0242	0.1460	0.0274	0.8685
dec70xpar	1	0.1500	0.1377	1.1865	0.2760
dec80xpar	1	−0.3514	0.1542	5.1943	0.0227

FIGURE 15.B ● HAZARD PLOT FROM MODEL 5

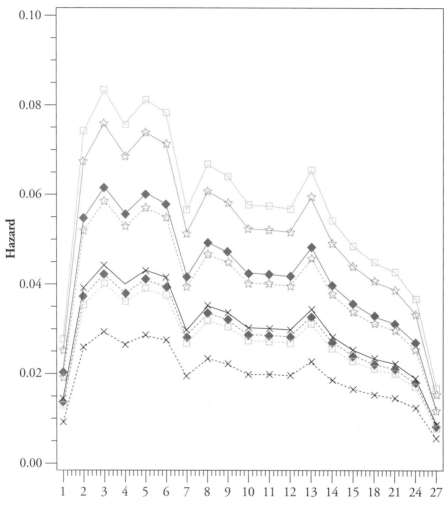

TABLE 15.J ● FORTY SELECTED OBSERVATIONS FROM THE DATA

Obs	MCASEID	riskper	censor	yearstartmar	yearendmar	yeardead	intyear2	work1	work2	work3	work4	work5	work6	work7	work8	work9	work10	work11	work12
1	29	27	0	64	90	.	93	0	0	0	0	0	0	0	0	0	0	0	0
2	53	12	1	81	64	.	92	1	1	0	1	1	1	0	0	0	0	0	0
3	58	5	0	60	.	.	92	0	0	0	1	1	1	1	1	1	1	1	1
4	109	18	1	76	.	.	93	0	0	1	0	0	1	0	0	0	0	0	0
5	117	5	0	54	58	91	94	0	0	0	0	0	0	0	0	0	0	0	0
6	120	20	1	74	.	.	93	0	0	0	0	0	0	0	0	0	0	0	0
7	133	24	1	70	.	.	93	0	0	0	0	0	1	1	1	0	0	0	0
8	146	23	1	70	.	.	92	1	0	0	1	1	0	1	1	1	1	1	0
9	159	18	1	76	.	.	93	0	1	1	1	1	1	1	1	1	1	1	1
10	162	16	1	78	.	.	93	1	0	0	0	0	0	0	0	1	1	0	1
11	167	30	1	64	.	.	93	0	0	0	0	0	0	0	0	0	0	0	0
12	175	8	0	85	93	.	92	1	1	1	1	1	1	1	1	0	0	0	0
13	196	8	0	86	80	.	94	0	0	0	0	0	0	0	0	0	0	1	0
14	239	2	0	79	76	.	94	1	0	0	0	0	0	0	0	0	0	0	1
15	247	3	0	74	.	.	94	0	0	0	0	0	0	0	0	0	0	1	0
16	250	5	0	86	90	.	93	0	0	0	0	0	0	0	0	0	0	0	0
17	284	4	0	52	55	.	92	0	0	0	0	0	0	0	0	0	0	0	1
18	292	10	1	84	.	.	93	0	0	0	0	0	0	0	0	0	0	0	0
19	306	13	0	82	88	.	94	1	1	1	1	1	1	1	1	0	0	0	1
20	314	4	0	85	77	.	94	1	0	1	0	1	1	0	0	0	1	1	0
21	327	11	0	67	.	.	92	0	0	0	0	0	0	0	0	0	0	1	1
22	348	11	1	84	87	.	94	1	0	0	0	1	0	0	0	0	0	0	0
23	351	14	0	74	81	.	93	0	0	0	0	0	0	0	0	0	0	0	0
24	364	3	0	79	70	.	94	0	0	0	0	0	0	0	0	0	0	1	0
25	380	15	0	56	89	.	92	1	1	1	1	1	1	1	1	0	0	1	1
26	410	18	0	72	.	.	93	1	1	1	1	1	1	1	1	1	0	0	1
27	444	19	1	75	.	.	93	1	0	0	0	0	0	0	0	0	0	0	0
28	452	12	1	82	84	.	92	1	1	1	1	1	1	1	1	1	1	0	1
29	457	9	1	84	.	.	92	1	0	0	0	0	0	0	0	0	0	0	0
30	460	10	0	75	.	.	92	1	1	1	1	1	1	1	1	0	0	0	0
31	486	23	1	71	.	.	93	1	1	1	1	1	1	1	1	1	1	0	0
32	508	5	1	89	.	.	93	0	0	0	0	0	0	0	0	0	0	0	0
33	511	13	1	81	.	.	93	0	0	0	0	0	0	0	0	1	1	1	0
34	566	10	0	84	86	.	93	1	1	1	1	1	1	1	1	0	0	0	0
35	590	15	0	72	.	.	93	0	0	0	0	0	0	0	0	0	0	0	0
36	604	37	0	57	83	.	93	1	0	0	0	0	0	0	0	0	0	0	0
37	612	3	0	81	81	.	93	0	0	0	0	0	0	0	0	0	0	0	0
38	638	4	0	78	82	.	94	1	1	0	0	0	0	0	0	0	0	0	0
39	646	4	0	79	.	.	93	1	1	1	1	1	1	1	0	0	1	1	1
40	659	16	1	78	.	.	93	1	1	1	1	1	1	1	1	0	1	1	1

THE CONTINUOUS TIME EVENT HISTORY MODEL

The continuous-time model for event history analysis is fundamentally different from the discrete-time model and yet in many situations will produce similar results.

A fundamental distinction between the two models is the underlying view of when an event can occur. In the discrete-time model, we assume that the event can only occur at certain times, like going back to school, or the timing of release from jail beyond a minimum term. In the continuous-time model, the event theoretically can happen at any time, like getting married or quitting a job or having a heart attack or moving to a new city.

This distinction means that in studying "any time" events, we are necessarily making discrete intervals out of a true continuous process. This is alright as long as the observation interval is *not too long* relative to the rate of occurrence of the event.

16.0.1 Hazard and Survival Concepts in Continuous Time

The hazard rate in the discrete-time model is a probability of the occurrence of an event in a discrete time interval.

In the continuous time model, the hazard rate is not *defined* in discrete intervals. The basic definition of the hazard rate here is in terms of an "instantaneous" probability at time t that an event will occur in the next "very short" interval.

That is, the hazard rate $= h(t) = \lim_{\Delta t \to 0} \dfrac{\Pr((t \leq T < (t + \Delta t)) \,/\, T \geq t)}{\Delta t}$

In words, this says that the hazard rate is the limiting value of the probability that an event occurs at T, which is greater than or equal to t and less than $t + \Delta t$, where the value of Δt is very small and given that the event does not occur before t.

The numerator of the hazard is actually a conditional probability, which can be seen if it is written this way:

$$h(t) = \lim_{\Delta t \to 0} \frac{\dfrac{\Pr(t \leq T < (t + \Delta t))}{\Pr(T \geq t)}}{\Delta t}$$

The survival probability is just

$$S(t) = \Pr(T \geq t) = 1 - F(t)$$

where $F(t)$ is the cumulative probability of the event up to t.

The cumulative distribution of t can be used to substitute in the formula for $h(t)$. The numerator of $h(t)$ is a conditional probability of the event over a (small) time interval. This numerator can be seen as

$$\frac{F(t + \Delta t) - F(t)}{S(t)}$$

that is, the function value (the cumulative probability) at $t + \Delta$ minus the function value (cumulative probability) at t, which just equals the probability of the event during a (very small) period, divided by the survival to point t. Plugging this value into the definition of the hazard and rearranging the denominator results in

$$h(t) = \lim_{\Delta t \to 0} \left\{ \frac{F(t + \Delta t) - F(t)}{\Delta t} \right\} \cdot \frac{1}{S(t)}$$

The first term in braces is the definition of the derivative of $F(t)$ with respect to t—that is, how the hazard changes as a function of t, which we call $f(t)$.

As a result, we write $h(t) = \dfrac{f(t)}{S(t)}$

That is, the hazard at t is equal to the probability density at t in the distribution of event times, divided by survival at t, which is the population still available for the event.

16.0.1.1 Hazards and Probabilities in Continuous Time

The concept of the hazard in the continuous-time model is fundamentally different than in the discrete-time model, due to the fact that in the continuous-time model you model the "instantaneous probability" over a small time interval while in the discrete-time model, you get an actual probability over an observable time period.

When an event is only observed in fact over larger grouped intervals, the hazard rate can exceed 1, because it is a rate of occurrence of an event defined in small continuous-time units but then applied to coarser, discrete time units. This is analogous to the problem with taking the derivative of a discrete variable. The notion of "instantaneous probability" is strained by larger time units of observation.

An important characteristic of the continuous-time model is that it produces the same hazard *rates*, regardless of the length of the interval chosen. The discrete-time rate comes down to a conditional probability in a time interval, so the size of the interval changes the rate.

16.1 THE PROPORTIONAL HAZARDS MODEL

The standard approach to studying the hazard rate in continuous time is to use Cox's proportional hazards model. This model is most appropriate when time is measured in finely distinguished units.

Using the classic language for this model, we can think of the effect of x as a treatment for a disease, with death as the outcome. In this context, X is a dummy variable for treatment, = 1 for those get a treatment and 0 for those who don't.

Let $h_0(t)$ be the hazard of death at time t for individuals with no treatment and $h_1(t)$ be the hazard of death at time t for individuals with the treatment. According to the assumptions of proportional hazards,

$$h_1(t) = \gamma \cdot h_0(t)$$

where γ is the *ratio* of the hazards of death for individuals with the treatment relative to individuals without the treatment. In this statement, γ is called the *constant of proportionality*.

Since γ expresses an overall ratio of the hazards, as follows:

$$\frac{h_1(t)}{h_0(t)} = \gamma$$

we can interpret γ as the exponential of the effect of X on the $\ln\left(\frac{h_1(t)}{h_0(t)}\right)$, because

$$\gamma = \left(\frac{h_1(t)}{h_0(t)}\right) = e^{\beta X}$$

where $e^{\beta x}$ expresses the effect of X as a constant multiplier of the left-hand ratio of two hazards. Note that this equation leads to $h_i(t) = h_0(t) \cdot e^{\beta X}$. That is, the hazard rate for person i at time t equals the baseline hazard for a reference group defined by $x = 0$, times the exponential of βx (the equation).

The hazard ratio in this model is formally called the **relative risk**. This concept is closely related to the odds ratio, as introduced in Chapter 5.

Taking the log of the above equation results in

$$\ln\left(\frac{h_1(t)}{h_0(t)}\right) = \beta X$$

Note that the baseline hazard, $h_0(t)$, which normally would be the intercept, is absorbed on the left side of the equation. This is done to estimate the equation using partial rather than maximum likelihood methods and allows the researcher to avoid making any assumption about the shape of the overall hazard function. As a result, the right side above has no intercept.

16.1.1 The Relative Risk versus the Odds Ratio

In Chapter 5 on the generalized linear model, we demonstrated how the concept of relative risk was related to the odds ratio. This connection becomes important in considering the continuous time model.

As a quick reminder, we note that the relative risk is the ratio of the probability of an event occurring for people higher on a risk factor versus those lower on a risk factor.

That is, $RR = \dfrac{P_{high}}{P_{low}}$,

whereas the odds ratio is

$$\text{or } \dfrac{\dfrac{P_{high}}{1 - P_{high}}}{\dfrac{P_{low}}{1 - P_{low}}}$$

In fact, in most cases of event history analysis, the two are very closely related because *per time period*, the probability of events is typically low. As shown earlier, this means the risk ratio approximates the odds ratio closely.

In the proportional odds model, we study the relative risk (RR) of two hazards, which are theoretically probabilities. This is the basic difference in interpretation compared to the discrete-time model. In many cases, if the measure of time is sufficiently detailed, results will be similar for the two approaches. This is especially the case because hazards are often small in discrete-time models if the time unit considered is small enough.

The only problem with the proportional hazards model is that information about the shape of the hazard profile is lost because the intercept is absorbed by the model in order to study the relative risk.

16.1.2 An Example Applying the Proportional Hazards Model

The output shown in Table 16.1 uses PROC PHREG, a program in SAS designed for estimating survival models, to run a proportional hazards model version of the example used in the discrete-time chapter, focusing on the effects of decade on the chances of returning to work after having a first child. The SAS code to run this model is

```
proc phreg data=part1 simple;
model riskper*censor(1)=decade60 decade70 decade80 agemom momed fwrkb4
partner/ ties=efron;

partner=0;
array marrtime {*} marr1-marr45;
 do i=1 to 45;
 if riskper=i then partner=marrtime[i];
 end;

run;
```

Note we use the Part1 data to run this model, not the person-period data. The MODEL statement specifies the variables that define the survival time (*riskper*), the censoring variable (*censor*), with the value that indicates censoring in parentheses (1), and the explanatory variables.

The "ties=efron" option tells SAS to use the "Efron" approximation to handle tied event times in the data (where two events occur at the same time, something which is really not supposed to happen in real continuous-time measurement). This approximation attempts to resolve ties by assuming different sequencing of the event times and recalculating the partial likelihood in each case.

You can use certain SAS programming statements after the model statement to create values for time-varying variables. The programming statements following the model statement use the array of partner status variables by risk period to inform SAS about the value of partner at each risk period. Here, we set partner = 0 initially. Otherwise, within the DO loop, partner is set to the value of the relevant variable from the marrtime array when riskper = i. Thus, if marr2 = 1, then partner = 1 when riskper = 2, but if marr2 = 0 then partner = 0 when i = 2.

The output is listed in the following table.

TABLE 16.1 ● A PROPORTIONAL HAZARDS MODEL FOR DECADE WITH CONTROLS

Model Information	
Data Set	WORK.PART1
Dependent Variable	riskper
Censoring Variable	censor
Censoring Value(s)	1
Ties Handling	EFRON

Number of Observations Read	2186
Number of Observations Used	1991

Summary of the Number of Event and Censored Values			
Total	Event	Censored	Percent Censored
1991	604	1387	69.66

Model Fit Statistics		
Criterion	Without Covariates	With Covariates
−2 LOG L	8547.933	8355.946
AIC	8547.933	8369.946
SBC	8547.933	8400.771

Testing Global Null Hypothesis: BETA=0			
Test	Chi-Square	DF	Pr > ChiSq
Likelihood Ratio	191.9872	7	<.0001
Score	193.9244	7	<.0001
Wald	184.1463	7	<.0001

Analysis of Maximum Likelihood Estimates						
Parameter	DF	Parameter Estimate	Standard Error	Chi-Square	Pr > ChiSq	Hazard Ratio
decade60	1	0.39618	0.16078	6.0715	0.0137	1.486
decade70	1	0.51253	0.14822	11.9566	0.0005	1.670
decade80	1	0.50082	0.15233	10.8095	0.0010	1.650
agemom	1	−0.05122	0.01041	24.1939	<.0001	0.950
momed	1	0.01766	0.01413	1.5627	0.2113	1.018
fwrkb4	1	1.01100	0.08446	143.2898	<.0001	2.748
partner	1	−0.31244	0.09352	11.1601	0.0008	0.732

16.1.2.1 Interpreting the Results

The coefficients in the proportional hazards model are in fact very similar to those obtained in the comparable discrete time model. Remember that the proportional hazards model is predicting log of the relative risk, not the log odds.

Thus, we interpret the coefficients in the continuous time model as affecting the log of *the relative risk* of returning to work. We can exponentiate the coefficients to interpret effects on the relative risk. For example, working full-time before the child was born increases the relative risk of returning to work in any period by $e^{1.011}$ or 2.75 times. The corresponding effect on the odds in the discrete-time model is $e^{1.0661} = 2.90$.

Note also that we have no information about the overall time profile for the event from the PHREG output—something that seems basically important in understanding the nature of the event. The discrete time model automatically includes this profile and allows us to see how time affects the probability of the event.

16.2 THE COMPLEMENTARY LOG-LOG MODEL

An alternative formulation of the continuous-time model uses the complementary log-log model, introduced earlier as a variant of the generalized linear model. The complementary log-log model is appropriate for data from a continuous-time process that have been grouped into larger discrete intervals, as is often the case. Because of this, this model may often be an effective way to estimate continuous-time processes.

This model in its linear form, is

$$\ln\left(-\ln\left(1 - P_t\right)\right) = \alpha_t + \beta_1 X_{1t} + \ldots \beta_k X_{kt}$$

where P_t is the cumulative probability of an event up to time t, and $S_t = 1 - P_t$.

Here the intercepts are time periods, as in the discrete-time model. From Chapter 5, recall that the form of the probability model (leading to the linear model above) is

$$P(Y) = 1 - e^{-e^{\beta X}}$$

which can be used to derive probabilities in this model.

This model is also interpretable in terms of the relative risk, although e^{bX} in this model is in fact an approximation to the relative risk.

Thus, the complementary log-log model

1. Studies the relative risk of hazard rates, just like the proportional odds model

2. Uses grouped data from discrete intervals to approximate the underlying ungrouped continuous-time model

3. Recovers the hazard profile because of Number 2.

So, there are advantages to this model in terms of flexibility.

16.2.1 Choosing a Model

A sometimes difficult question is, should I use the discrete-time or the continuous-time model? This is somewhat controversial and depends on the types of concepts typically under study in different disciplines (e.g., illness can occur at any time, but returning to school cannot).

No one states an overall preference, but a common position taken in the social sciences is that if the underlying process occurs in continuous-time, you should model it that way. Others take the position that the discrete-time model has advantages in terms of flexibility and information—such as an explicit rendering of the hazard profile—*and* converges to the continuous-time model anyway when

either   1. $p < .2$

or   2. the observed time intervals are short.

In general, one can use both approaches and compare results. Often they will be similar. Otherwise, these are some guidelines:

- If the event is rare, differences between models may not matter.

- If the data measures time of occurrence precisely and the event can happen at any time and is fairly prevalent, the continuous time model may be preferable. However, note that the two models converge when time is measured precisely in the discrete-time model.

- If the data measures event occurrence in grouped time intervals (e.g., per year) and the event can only occur at certain times, the discrete-time model is appropriate.

- If the data measures event occurrence in grouped time intervals but the underlying event can occur at any time, the complementary log-log continuous-time model is appropriate.

16.2.2 An Example of the Complementary Log-Log Model

Output in Table 16.2 uses PROC LOGISTIC to run a complementary log-log model with the event history data from the previous example. The SAS code to run this model with the person-period data set is

```
proc logistic data=hazwork out=estimate simple;

  model working=t1-t9 t10_13 t14_17 t18_22 t23_45 decade60 decade70 decade80
agemom momed fwrkb4 partner / noint link=cloglog;
  title1 'Model 3 -- Time Effects With Decade Effects and Controls';
  title2 'Using the C-LogLog Model';

run;
```

PROC LOGISTIC will run the complementary log-log model when you specify "link=cloglog" in the model options.

TABLE 16.2 ● RESULTS FROM A COMPLEMENTARY LOG-LOG MODEL

Model Information	
Data Set	WORK.HAZWORK
Response Variable	working
Number of Response Levels	2
Model	binary cloglog
Optimization Technique	Fisher's scoring

Number of Observations Read	10479
Number of Observations Used	9373

Response Profile		
Ordered Value	working	Total Frequency
1	1	604
2	2	8769

Analysis of Maximum Likelihood Estimates					
Parameter	DF	Estimate	Standard Error	Wald Chi-Square	Pr > ChiSq
t1	1	−2.3490	0.3023	60.3674	<.0001
t2	1	−1.6418	0.2969	30.5755	<.0001
t3	1	−2.2211	0.3077	52.1161	<.0001
t4	1	−2.6086	0.3304	62.3418	<.0001
t5	1	−2.6399	0.3510	56.5788	<.0001
t6	1	−2.3550	0.3572	43.4707	<.0001
t7	1	−2.7017	0.4107	43.2802	<.0001
t8	1	−3.0393	0.4797	40.1411	<.0001
t9	1	−2.6705	0.4612	33.5289	<.0001
t10_13	1	−3.6759	0.4608	63.6405	<.0001
t14_17	1	−3.3402	0.4812	48.1796	<.0001
t18_22	1	−4.0288	0.6474	38.7290	<.0001
t23_45	1	−3.5652	0.5728	38.7441	<.0001
decade60	1	0.3898	0.1608	5.8777	0.0153
decade70	1	0.5099	0.1485	11.7985	0.0006
decade80	1	0.4959	0.1525	10.5758	0.0011
agemom	1	−0.0514	0.0104	24.5490	<.0001
momed	1	0.0177	0.0142	1.5538	0.2126
fwrkb4	1	1.0128	0.0844	143.9490	<.0001
partner	1	−0.3118	0.0935	11.1202	0.0009

Association of Predicted Probabilities and Observed Responses			
Percent Concordant	72.9	Somers' D	0.469
Percent Discordant	26.1	Gamma	0.473
Percent Tied	1.0	Tau-a	0.057
Pairs	5296476	c	0.734

You can compare results here to the results for the same model from PROC LOGISTIC in discrete-time from the previous chapter. The estimates are again quite close. Note that in this model, as in the proportional hazards model, the interpretation of the exponentiated coefficients focuses on the relative risk, not the odds.

Note also that the hazards calculated in the SAS program have to be altered in this model to take into account the nature of the complementary log-log function. So the appropriate SAS code in the do loops used to calculate the hazard and survival values for this model is

```
hazard=1-exp(-exp(x));
survival=(1-hazard)*survival;
```

where "x" is, as before, the predicted value of the equation. The survival is calculated the same way, once the hazard is calculated.

In this case, the choice of model should be dictated by the definition of the underlying process. In general, one should remember that the complementary log-log model is more appropriate if the data are derived from an underlying continuous time process.

Concluding Words

This short chapter is meant to complement our emphasis on the discrete-time model, by reviewing the conceptual differences between the two models and the basis of choice for one versus the other. Continuous-time models are used widely and usually in the form of the proportional hazards model.

Our treatment of the options suggests that the proportional hazards model is often not the optimal choice. The first question is whether the underlying process occurs in continuous or discrete-time. But the second question must also be considered: the size of the actual time intervals measured in the data. When the time intervals are small, various demonstrations in the literature suggest the results from a discrete-time analysis will converge to results from a continuous-time analysis. When the time intervals are larger chunks, we suggest that the complementary log-log model may be preferable because it is designed for those kinds of data. That model also produces very similar results to the discrete-time model, especially for rare events.

In the end, in many data situations, it is possible to invoke either the discrete-time model or the complementary log-log model. Both are easy to implement once the data are coded properly, and both are flexible with regards to the shape of the hazard profile.

REFERENCES

Allison, P. (1994). Using panel data to estimate the effects of events. *Sociological Methods & Research*, *23*, 174–199. doi: 10.1177/0049124194023002002

Allison, P. (1999). Comparing logit and probit coefficients across Groups. *Sociological Methods & Research, 28*, 186–208.

Allison, P. (2005). *Fixed effects regression methods in SAS.* Cary, NC: SAS Institute.

Allison, P. (2012). Causal inference with panel data. *Statistical Horizons*. https://statisticalhorizons.com/wp-content/uploads/2012/01/Causal-Inference.pdf

Allison, P. (2014). *Event history and survival analysis* (2nd ed.). Thousand Oaks, CA: Sage.

Allison, P. D., Williams, R., & Moral-Benito, E. (2018). Maximum likelihood for cross-lagged panel models with fixed effects. *Socius: Sociological Research for a Dynamic World, 3*, 1–17.

Allport, G. (1979).*The nature of prejudice*. Reading, MA: Addison-Wesley Pub.

Amato, P. R. (2014). Marriage, cohabitation and mental health. *Family Matters, 96*, 5–13.

Amato, P. R., & Anthony, C. J. (2014). Estimating the effects of parental divorce and death with fixed effects models. *Journal of Marriage and the Family, 76*(2), 370–386. doi:10.1111/jomf.12100

Amato, P. R., & Booth, A. (1995). Changes in gender role attitudes and perceived marital quality. *American Sociological Review, 60*, (1), 58–66. www.jstor.org/stable/2096345

American National Election Studies (ANES). (2016). *ANES 2012 Time Series Study*. Ann Arbor, MI: Inter-university Consortium for Political and Social Research [distributor], 2016-05-17. https://doi.org/10.3886/ICPSR35157.v1

Aneshensel, C. S., & Sucoff, C. (1996). The neighborhood context of adolescent mental health. *Journal of Health and Social Behavior*, *37*(4), 293–310.

Asher, H. B. (1983). Causal modeling (2nd ed). *Quantitative Applications in the Social Sciences series*. Thousand Oaks, CA: Sage.

Atkinson, T., Blishen, B. R., Ornstein, M. D., & Stevenson, H. M. (1981). *Quality of Canadian Life: Social Change in Canada, 1977–1981*. Toronto: Institute for Social Research, York University.

Bagnardi, V., Zambon, A, Quatto, P. & Corrao, G. (2004). Flexible meta-regression functions for modeling aggregate dose-response data, with an application to alcohol and mortality. *American Journal of Epidemiology. 159*, 1077–1086.

Bandura, A. (1977). Self-efficacy: Toward a unifying theory of behavioral change. *Psychological Review, 84*, 191–215.

Barber JS, Murphy SA, Axinn WG, Maples J. 2000. Discrete-Time Multilevel Hazard Analysis. Sociological Methodology. 2000;30(1):201-235. doi:10.1111/0081-1750.00079

Bentler, P. & Bonett, D. (1980). Significance tests and goodness-of-fit in analysis of covariance structures. *Psychological Bulletin, 88*, 588–606. 10.1037/0033-2909.88.3.588

Bollen, K. A. (1989). *Structural equations with latent variables*. New York, NY: John Wiley and Sons.

Bollen, K. A., & Pearl, J. (2013). Eight myths about causality and structural equation models. In S. L. Morgan (Ed.), *Handbook of causal analysis for social research* (pp. 301–328). New York, NY: Springer.

Browne, M. W. (1984). Asymptotically distribution-free methods for the analysis of covariance structures. *British Journal of Mathematical and Statistical Psychology, 37*, 62–83.

Browne, M. W., & Cudeck, R. (1993). Alternative ways of assessing model fit. In K. A. Bollen and J. S. Long (Eds.), *Testing structural equation models* (pp. 136–162). Newbury Park, CA: Sage.

Bunge, M. (1959). *Causality: The place of the causal principle in modern science*. Cambridge, MA: Harvard University Press.

Bureau of Labor Statistics, U.S. Department of Labor. (2019a). *National longitudinal survey of youth 1979 cohort, 1979-2016* (rounds 1–27). Produced and distributed by the Center for Human Resource Research (CHRR), The Ohio State University. Columbus, OH: 2019.

Bureau of Labor Statistics, U.S. Department of Labor. (2019b). *National longitudinal survey of youth 1997 cohort, 1997–2017* (rounds 1–18). Produced and distributed by the Center for Human Resource Research (CHRR), The Ohio State University. Columbus, OH: 2019.

Campbell, D. T., & Stanley, J. C. (1964). *Experimental and non-experimental designs for research.* Boston, MA: Houghton Mifflin.

Campbell, F. A., Pungello, E. P., Miller-Johnson, S., Burchinal, M., & Ramey, C. T. (2001). The development of cognitive and academic abilities: Growth curves from an early childhood educational experiment. *Developmental Psychology, 37*(2), 231–242. https://doi.org/10.1037/0012-1649.37.2.231

Codd, C. (2011). *Nonlinear structural equation models: Estimation and applications* (Master's thesis). Ohio State University.

Davis, W. R. (1993). The FC1 rule of identification for confirmatory factor analysis: A general sufficient condition. *Sociological Methods and Research 21*, 403–437.

Demaris, A. (1992). *Quantitative applications in the social sciences: Logit modeling.* Thousand Oaks, CA: Sage. doi: 10.4135/9781412984836

Duncan, O. D. (1975). *Introduction to structural equation models.* New York, NY: Academic Press.

Durkheim, E. (1951). *Suicide, a study in sociology.* J. A. Spaulding & G. Simpson (Trans.). London: Routledge. (Original work published 1897)

England, P., Farkas, G., Kilbourne, B., & Dou, T. (1988). Explaining occupational sex segregation and wages: Findings from a model with fixed effects. *American Sociological Review, 53*(4), 544–558.

Gerber, T. P. (2000). Market, state, or don't know? Education, economic ideology, and voting in contemporary Russia. *Social Forces, 79*(2), 477–521. doi:10.2307/2675507.

Gerbing, D. W. & Anderson, J. C. (1992, November). Monte Carlo evaluations of goodness of fit indices for structural equation models, *Sociological Methods & Research, 21*(2), 132–160.

Gibbs, J. P., & Martin, W. T. (1964). *Status integration and suicide.* Eugene, OR: University of Oregon Books.

Glavin, P., Young, M., & Schieman, S. (2020). Labour market influences on women's fertility decisions: Longitudinal evidence from Canada. *Social Science Research*, 88–89.

Goldberger, A. S. (1964). *Econometric theory.* New York, NY: John Wiley.

Goodman, L. (1976). The relationship between the modified and more usual multiple regression approaches to the analysis of dichotomous variables. In D. Heise (Ed.), Sociological Methodology, 1976 pp. 83–110. San Francisco: Jossey-Bass.

Hagan, J., & Rymond-Richmond, W. (2008). The collective dynamics of racial dehumanization and genocidal victimization in Darfur. *American Sociological Review, 73*(6), 875–902. www.jstor.org/stable/25472566.

Hall, K. A. (1999), *Gender, marital status, and psychiatric disorder: An examination of social causation versus social selection explanations for the gender specific benefits of marriage for mental health* (Doctoral thesis, Department of Sociology, University of Toronto).

Harring, J. R., Weiss, B. A., & Hsu, J. C. (2012). A comparison of methods for estimating quadratic effects in nonlinear structural equation models. *Psychological methods, 17*(2), 193–214. doi:10.1037/a0027539

Hill, A. B. (1965). The environment and disease: Association or causation? *Proceedings of the Royal Society of Medicine, 58*, 295–300.

Hox, J., & Maas, C. J. M. (2004). Sufficient sample sizes for multilevel modeling. *Methodology.* 1. doi: 10.1027/1614-2241.1.3.85

Hsiao, C. (2003). *Analysis of panel data (econometric society monographs).* Cambridge, MA: Cambridge University Press. doi:10.1017/CBO9780511754203

Hu, L.-t., & Bentler, P. M. (1999). Cutoff criteria for fit indexes in covariance structure analysis: Conventional criteria versus new alternatives. Structural Equation Modeling, 6(1), 1–55. https://doi.org/10.1080/10705519909540118

Huang, F. L., & Cornell, D. G. (2012). Pick your poisson: A tutorial on analyzing counts of student victimization data. *Journal of School Violence, 11*(3), 187–206. doi: 10.1080/15388220.2012.682010

Institute for Social and Economic Research. (2018). *British household panel survey:* Waves 1–18, 1991–2009. [data collection]. *8th Edition.* UK Data Service. SN:5151. University of Essex. http://doi.org/10.5255/UKDA-SN-5151-2

Johnson, B. D. (1965). Durkheim's one cause of suicide. *American Sociological Review 30*(6), 875–886. Retrieved from www.jstor.org/stable/2090966

Jung, T., & Wickrama, K. (2008). An introduction to latent class growth analysis and growth mixture modeling. *Social and Personality Psychology Compass, 2*, 302–317. doi: 10.1111/j.1751-9004.2007.00054.x

Klein, J., & Cornell, D. (2010). Is the link between large high schools and student victimization an illusion? *Journal of Educational Psychology, 102*(4), 933–946. Retrieved from https://doi.org/10.1037/a0019896

Kokkelenberg, E., & Dillon, M., & Christy, S. (2006). The effects of class size on student grades at a public university. *Economics of Education Review, 27*, 221–233. doi: 10.1016/j.econedurev.2006.09.011.

Koltai, J. & Schieman, S. (2015). Job pressure and SES-contingent buffering: Resource reinforcement, substitution, or the stress of higher status? *Journal of Health and Social Behavior, 56*(2), 180–198.

Kryszajty, D., & Daoleuxay, Y. (2018). *Fixed effects analysis of the effect of SES on body mass index.* Paper submitted in Intermediate Data Analysis, Department of Sociology, University of Toronto.

Leahey, E., & Guo, G. (2001). Gender differences in mathematical trajectories. *Social Forces, 80*(2), 713–732.

Lerner, D. (1965). *Cause and effect.* New York, NY: Free Press.

Levinger, G. (1976). A social psychological perspective on marital dissolution. *Journal of Social Issues, 32*(1), 21–47.

Lewis-Beck, M. S., Tien, C. &, Nadea, R. (2010). Obama's missed landslide: A racial cost? *PS: Political Science and Politics, 43*(1), 69–76. Retrieved from www.jstor.org/stable/25699295

Long, J. S. (1983). *Confirmatory factor analysis. Quantitative applications in the social sciences.* Thousand Oaks, CA: Sage. doi: 10.4135/9781412983778

Long, J. S. (1997). *Regression models for categorical and limited dependent variables.* Advanced Quantitative Techniques in the Social Sciences Series (Vol. 7). Thousand Oaks, CA: Sage.

Long, J. S., & Mustillo, S. A. (2018). Using predictions and marginal effects to compare groups in regression models for binary outcomes. *Sociological Methods & Research,* 1–37.

Louie, P., & Wheaton, B. (2019). The Black-White paradox revisited: Understanding the role of counterbalancing mechanisms during adolescence. *Journal of Health and Social Behavior, 60* (2), 169–187

Macintyre, S., Ellaway, A., & Cummins, S. (2002). Place effects on health: How can we conceptualise, operationalise and measure them? *Social Science & Medicine, 55*(1), 125–139.

Mardia, K. V. (1970). Measures of multivariate skewness and kurtosis with applications. *Biometrika, 57*, 519–530.

Mardia, K. V. (1980): Tests of univariate and multivariate normality. In P.R. Krishnaiah (ed.), *Handbook of statistics* (Vol. 1, pp. 279–320). Amsterdam: North Holland: Elsevier.

Marini, M. M., & Singer, B. (1988). Causality in the social sciences. *Sociological Methodology, 18*, 347–409. doi: 10.2307/271053

Marsh, L. C., & Cormier, D. R. (2002). *Spline regression models. Quantitative applications in the social sciences.* Thousand Oaks, CA: Sage. doi: 10.4135/9781412985901

McCullagh, P., & Nelder, J. A. (1989). *Generalized linear models* (2nd ed.). London: Chapman and Hall.

McDonald, R. P., & Marsh, H. W. (1990). Choosing a multivariate model: Noncentrality and goodness of fit. *Psychological Bulletin, 107*(2), 247–255. Retrieved from https://doi.org/10.1037/0033-2909.107.2.247

Miech, R. A., Eaton, W. & Liang, K.-Y. (2003). Occupational stratification over the life course: A comparison of occupational trajectories across race and gender during the 1980s and 1990s. *Work and Occupations, 30*(4), 440–473. Retrieved from https://doi.org/10.1177/0730888403256459

Milkie, M. H., & Warner, C. H. (2011). Classroom learning environments and the mental health of first grade children. *Journal of Health and Social Behavior, 52*, 4–22.

Mirowsky, J. (1987). The psycho-economics of feeling underpaid: Distributive justice and the earnings of husbands and wives. *American Journal of Sociology, 92*(6),1404–1434.

Mirowsky, J. (2013). Analyzing associations between mental health and social circumstances. In C. S. Aneshensel, J. C. Phelan, & A. Bierman (Eds.), *Handbooks of sociology and social research. Handbook of the sociology of mental health* (p. 143–165). New York: Springer Science + Business Media.

Mirowsky, J., & Ross, C. E. (1992). Age and depression. *Journal of Health and Social Behavior, 33*(3), 187–205. Retrieved from www.jstor.org/stable/2137349

Mirowsky, J. & Ross, C. E. (2003). *Education, social status, and health.* New York, NY: Aldine de Gruyter.

Mize, T. D. (2019). Best practices for estimating, interpreting, and presenting nonlinear interaction effects. *Sociological Science 6*, 81–117.

Montazer, S., & Wheaton, B. (2011). The impact of generation and country of origin on the mental health of children of immigrants. *Journal of Health and Social Behavior, 52*(1), 23–42.

Mood, C. (2010). Logistic regression: Why we cannot do what we think we can do, and what we can do about it. *European Sociological Review, 26*(1), 67–82.

Moore, L. M., & Ovadia, S. (2006). Accounting for spatial variation in tolerance: The effects of education and religion. *Social Forces, 84*(4), 2205–2222.

Morgan, S.L., & Winship, C. (2015). *Counterfactuals and causal Inference: Methods and principles for social research* (2nd ed.). Cambridge, MA: Cambridge University Press.

Muthén, B. (1984). A general structural equation model with dichotomous, ordered categorical, and continuous latent variable indicators. *Psychometrika, 49*, 115–132.

O'Campo, P., Wheaton, B., Nisenbaum, R., Glazier, R. H., Dunn, J. R., & Chambers, C. (2015). The neighbourhood effects on health and well-being (NEHW) study. *Health & Place, 31*, 65–74.

O'Campo, P., Xue, X., Wang, M. C., & Caughy, M. (1997). Neighborhood risk factors for low birthweight in Baltimore: A multilevel analysis. *American Journal of Public Health, 87*, 1113–1118. doi: 10.2105/AJPH.87.7.1113

Pearl, J. (2005). Direct and indirect effects. *Proceedings of the American Statistical Association Joint Statistical Meetings 1572-1581*, Technical report R-273.

Pearl, J. (2009a). Causal inference in statistics: An overview. *Statist. Surv. 3*, 96–146. doi:10.1214/09-SS057

Pearl, J. (2009b). *Causality: Models, reasoning, and inference* (2nd ed., p. 464). Cambridge, MA: Cambridge University Press.

Pearlin, L. I., Menaghan, E. G., Lieberman, M. A., & Mullan, J. T. (1981). The stress process. *Journal of Health and Social Behavior, 22*(4), 337–356. Retrieved from www.jstor.org/stable/2136676

Pepe, M. S., Kerr, K. F., Longton, G. & Wang, Z. (2013). Testing for improvement in prediction model performance. *Statistics in Medicine, 32*, 1467–1482.

Radelet, M. L. (1981). Racial characteristics and the imposition of the death penalty. *American Sociological Review, 46*(6), 918–927.

Raftery, A. E. (1995). Bayesian model selection in social research. *Sociological Methodology, 25*, 111–163.

Raudenbush, S. W., & Bryk, A. S. (2002). *Hierarchical linear models: Applications and data analysis methods* (2nd ed.). Thousand Oaks, CA: Sage.

Raudenbush, S. W., & Sampson, R. J. (1999). Ecometrics: Toward a science of assessing ecological settings, with application to the systematic social observation of neighborhoods. *Sociological Methodology, 29*, 1–41.

Reid, S., & Wheaton, B. (2011). *Estimating the effects of women's job exits and career interruptions on their status achievement: A person-job fixed effects model.* Presented at the American Sociological Association meetings in Las Vegas, Nevada.

Ross, C. E., Mirowsky, J., & Pribesh, S. (2001). Powerlessness and the amplification of threat: Neighborhood disadvantage, disorder, and mistrust. *American Sociological Review, 66*, 568–591.

Rotter, J. B. (1966). Generalized expectancies for internal versus external control of reinforcement. *Psychological Monographs: General and Applied, 80*, 1–28. doi:10.1037/h0092976.

Ruhm, C. J. (1996). Alcohol policies and highway vehicle fatalities. *J Health Econ 15*(4), 435–454.

Ryff, C. (1989). Happiness is everything, or is it? Explorations on the meaning of psychological well-being. *Journal of Personality and Social Psychology, 57*, 1069–1081.

Sacker, A., Clarke, P., & Wiggins, R., & Bartley, M. (2005). Social dynamics of health inequalities: A growth curve analysis of aging and self assessed health in the British household panel survey 1991–2001. *Journal of Epidemiology and Community Health, 59*, 495–501.

Simon, R. (2002). Revisiting the relationships among gender, marital status, and mental health. *American Journal of Sociology, 107*(4), 1065–1096. doi:10.1086/339225

Singer, J. D. (1998). Using SAS PROC MIXED to fit multilevel models, hierarchical models, and individual growth models. *Journal of Educational and Behavioral Statistics, 23*(4), 323–55. Retrieved from www.jstor.org/stable/1165280

Singer, J. D., & Willett, J. B. (2003). *Applied longitudinal data analysis: Modeling change and event occurrence.* New York: Oxford University Press.

Sorbom, D. (1989). Model modification. *Psychometrika, 54*, 371–384.

South, S. J., & Lloyd, K. M. (1995). Spousal alternatives and marital dissolution. *American Sociological Review, 60*(1), 21–35. Retrieved from https://doi.org/10.2307/2096343

St. Arnaud, S. (2005). *The rise and fall of provincial minimum wages: Labor movements, business interests and partisan theory*. Paper prepared for the 2005 Annual Meetings of the American Sociological Association, August 13–16, Philadelphia, Pennsylvania.

Statistics Canada. (2010). *2006 census dictionary*. Ministry of Industry.

Statistics Canada (2013a). *National population health survey (NPHS) household component cycles 1 to 9* (1994/1995 to 2010/2011). Minister of Industry.

Statistics Canada. (2013b). *Survey of labour and income dynamics*. Minister of Industry.

Survey Research Center. (n.d.). *Panel study of income dynamics, public use dataset*. Ann Arbor, MI: Survey Research Center, Institute for Social Research, University of Michigan.

Sweet, J. A., & Bumpass, L. L. (1996). *The national survey of families and households—Waves 1 and 2*. Data Description and Documentation. Center for Demography and Ecology, University of Wisconsin-Madison. http://www.ssc.wisc.edu/nsfh/home.htm

Sweet, J. A. & Bumpass, L. L. (2003). *The national survey of families and households—Waves 1, 2, and 3*. Data Description and Documentation. Center for Demography and Ecology, University of Wisconsin-Madison. http://www.ssc.wisc.edu/nsfh/home.htm

Sweet, J. A., Bumpass, L., & Call, V. (1988). *The design and content of the national survey of families and households* (NSFH Working Paper #1). Madison, WI: Center for Demography and Ecology.

Teachman, Jay, Ducan, G. J., Yeung, W. J., & Levy, D. (2001). Covariance Structure Models for Fixed and Random Effects. *Sociological Methods and Research 30*, 242–270.

Thompson, M. P., Swartout, K. M., & Koss, M. P. (2013). Trajectories and predictors of sexually aggressive behaviors during emerging adulthood. *Psychology of violence*, 3(3), 247–259. doi:10.1037/a0030624

Turner, H. A., Shattuck, A., Hamby, S., Finkelhor, D. (2013). Community disorder, victimization exposure, and mental health in a national sample of youth. *Journal of Health and Social Behavior*, 54(2), 258–75.

Turner, R. J., & Wheaton, B. (1991). *The mental health and stress study*. University of Toronto. National Health Research Development Program, Health and Welfare Canada.

Umberson, D., Williams, K., Thomas, P. A., Liu, H., & Thomeer, M. B. (2014). Race, gender, and chains of disadvantage: Childhood adversity, social relationships, and health. *Journal of Health and Social Behavior*, 55(1), 20–38. doi:10.1177/0022146514521426

U.S. Department of Health and Human Services. (2000). *Head Start Program performance standards and other regulations*. Washington, DC: U.S. Dept. of Health and Human Services, Administration for Children and Families, Head Start Bureau.

Valenzuela, S. (2013). Unpacking the use of social media for protest behavior. *American Behavioral Scientist*, 57, 920–942. doi: 10.1177/0002764213479375

Vanderweele, T. J. (2015). *Explanation in causal inference: Methods for mediation and interaction*. New York, NY: Oxford University Press.

Wagenaar, A. C., Tobler, A. L., & Komro, K. A. (2010). Effects of alcohol tax and price policies on morbidity and mortality: A systematic review. *American Journal of Public Health*, *100*, 2270–2278. Retrieved from https://doi.org/10.2105/AJPH.2009.186007

Welsh, S., Dawson, M., & Nierobisz, A. (2002). Legal factors, extra-legal factors, or changes in the law? Using criminal justice research to understand the resolution of sexual harassment complaints. *Social Problems*, *49*(4), 605–623,

Wheaton, B. (1980). The sociogenesis of psychological disorder: An attributional theory. *Journal of Health and Social Behavior*, *21*(2),100–124. Retrieved from www.jstor.org/stable/2136730

Wheaton, B. (1985). Personal resources and mental health: Can there be too much of a good thing? In J. R. Greenley (Ed.), *Research in community and mental health* (pp 139–184). Greenwich, CT: JAI.

Wheaton, B. (2003). When methods make a difference. *Current Sociology*, *51*(5), 543–571.

Wheeler, S., Weisburd, D., & Bode, N. (1982). Sentencing the white-collar offender: Rhetoric and reality. *American Sociological Review*, *47*(5), 641–659. Retrieved from www.jstor.org/stable/2095164

Williams, R. (2015). *Interaction effects and group comparisons*. University of Notre Dame. Retrieved from https://www3.nd.edu/~rwilliam/

Williams, R. (2019). *Scalar measures of fit: Pseudo R² and information measures* (AIC & BIC). Retrieved from https://www3.nd.edu/~rwilliam/

Wonnacott, R. J., & Wonnacott, T. H. (1979). *Econometrics.* New York, NY: Wiley.

Wooldridge, J. M. (2002). *Econometric analysis of cross section and panel data.* Cambridge, MA: MIT Press.

Young, M., & Wheaton, B. (2013). The impact of neighborhood composition on work-family conflict and distress. *Journal of Health and Social Behavior, 54*(4), 481–497.

Young, M., Schieman, S., & Milkie, M. (2013). Spouse's work-to-family conflict, family stressors, and mental health among dual-earner mothers and fathers. *Society and Mental Health 4*, 1–20. Retrieved from https://doi.org/10.1177/2156869313504931

Zill, N., Furstenberg, F. F., Peterson, J., & Moore, K. (1992). *National survey of children: Wave I, 1976, Wave II, 1981, and Wave III, 1987.* Inter-university Consortium for Political and Social Research [distributor], 1992-02-16. https://doi.org/10.3886/ICPSR08670.v3

INDEX